The United Nations
and
Economic and Social
Co-operation

By

ROBERT E. ASHER, WALTER M. KOTSCHNIG,
WILLIAM ADAMS BROWN, JR., AND ASSOCIATES

Preface

IN THE SUMMER of 1951, the Brookings Institution began a series of studies on the United Nations. The series was initiated by the late Dr. Leo Pasvolsky who, until his death in 1953, was Director of the International Studies Group at the Institution. The general plan for the research was formulated in the winter of 1949–50 when many proposals for changes in the United Nations system were being widely discussed in the United States. Much of the public discussion indicated the need for a systematic analysis of the issues arising from the experience with the United Nations system and for a careful evaluation of the immediate and ultimate implications of the various courses of action being proposed. To assist in meeting this need became, therefore, the central purpose of the Brookings studies.

While this research has been under way, new developments have further affected the attitude of many Americans toward the United Nations, and some American pressures for changes in the United Nations system have been increasing. Now that the General Assembly and the Security Council have agreed in principle that a General Conference should be called at "an appropriate time" for the purpose of reviewing the Charter, it is hoped that the Brookings studies will be of special value in contributing to better public understanding of the problems that will be involved.

The studies are being published in seven volumes, of which some have already appeared. Although these volumes form a related series, each of them constitutes a separate study of a major feature of the United Nations system. The order given below is not the actual order of publication, but it represents the logical arrangement of the series.

One volume is entitled *A History of the United Nations Charter*. It will present, from the American point of view, the evolution and negotiation of the Charter as part of the developing United Nations system during the period from 1940 to 1945. A major purpose of the volume will be to show the principal ideas and proposals considered by the United States Government in reaching its final position on the specific provisions of the Charter.

Three volumes will analyze and appraise the principal activities and organizational problems of the United Nations and its related agencies since January 1946 when the Organization came into being.

One of these, entitled *The Organization and Procedures of the United Nations*, will cover the general organizational development of the United Nations. It will be concerned both with particular organizational problems in each of the principal organs—the General Assembly, the Security Council, the Economic and Social Council, the Trusteeship Council, the International Court of Justice, and the Secretariat—and with some of the general problems encountered, such as the interpretation of the Charter, the definition of domestic jurisdiction, and the admission of new Members.

The second of these, which has already been published, is entitled *The United Nations and the Maintenance of International Peace and Security*. It deals with methods and processes for maintaining peace and security through the United Nations. It covers the procedures that have been developed under the Charter for the peaceful settlement or adjustment of disputes and situations, the use of collective measures in threats to or breaches of the peace, and the regulation of armaments, and seeks to evaluate these methods and processes in light of the conditions in which the United Nations has had to function.

The third, entitled *The United Nations and Promotion of the General Welfare*, will cover the major activities undertaken by the United Nations in response to the insistent pressures that, during the postwar period, have brought to the fore issues in the field of general welfare. The work of the Organization and its related agencies in dealing with problems of international co-operation in economic and social affairs, in the promotion of human rights, and in the advancement of dependent peoples will be analyzed, and the efforts made to harmonize conflicting national views in solving these problems will be appraised. The chapters dealing with human rights, which will comprise Part Three of this volume, and with dependent peoples, which will comprise Part Four, have already been published as separate monographs under the titles of *The United Nations and Human Rights* and *The United Nations and Dependent Peoples*, respectively.

Another volume in the series will deal with *Regional Security and the United Nations*. It will analyze and appraise the history and activities of the principal regional security, collective defense, and similar arrangements that have developed within the framework of the United Nations Charter. The volume will describe how and why the arrangements came into existence and the manner in which they have functioned, and will analyze some of the problems raised by their establishment and operation, both within the scope of the individual groupings and in relation to the broader United Nations system.

A sixth volume, which has already been published, is entitled *Proposals for Changes in the United Nations*. It presents a description and analysis of the principal proposals advanced by governments and by private groups and individuals for changes in the United Nations system. The analysis includes a review of the major arguments advanced both for and against particular proposals, the impact of the proposals on the United Nations, and their implications for United States policy.

The final volume, entitled *The United States and the Future of the United Nations*, will attempt an over-all appraisal of the United Nations system from the American point of view. This volume, which will be based primarily on the studies in the other six volumes, will present general conclusions and recommendations regarding such changes as may appear to be desirable in the United Nations Charter or in the organization and functioning of the system.

The present publication includes the chapters that will comprise Part Two of the volume on *The United Nations and Promotion of the General Welfare*. Separate publication of these chapters in advance of the full volume has been undertaken because of current interest in the subjects they cover. An appropriate index for these materials will be provided in the full volume when it appears later this year.

The preparation of the manuscript for this monograph was a co-operative undertaking. Robert E. Asher was responsible for the preparation of the Introduction and Chapters II, IV, V, X, and XI, and undertook the task of co-ordinating the manuscripts for the other chapters. William Adams Brown, Jr. prepared Chapters I and III, and collaborated with Wilfred Owen and the late Priscilla St. Denis in the preparation of Chapter VI. Walter M. Kotschnig prepared Chapters VII, VIII, and IX. Louis Lazaroff provided materials on which portions of Chapters II and X are based, and Edward G. Posniak provided certain materials for Chapters V and X. A. Evelyn Breck, with the aid of Medora Richardson, edited the final manuscript.

It should be noted that although Mr. Kotschnig was Director of the Office of International Economic and Social Affairs, Department of State, when he wrote the chapters for which he is responsible, he wrote them in his personal capacity. His comments and conclusions do not, therefore, necessarily reflect the official views of the Department of State.

The conclusions in the present study are those of the individual authors. The general conclusions and recommendations that will be made in the final volume on *The United States and the Future of the United Nations* will take into account the conclusions reached in this and the other studies in the series, but they will be formulated from the point of view of the United Nations system as a whole and of United States policy with respect to it.

The authors and the Institution acknowledge with gratitude the many thoughtful comments and constructive suggestions made by a number of present and former officials in both government and international organizations who responded to inquiries or read drafts of the manuscript. Their courtesy and willingness in making their expert knowledge and experience available have aided in clarifying many difficult points and issues. The individual assistance of each of them is greatly appreciated.

After Dr. Pasvolsky's death, Robert W. Hartley was given the responsibility for bringing to completion this series of studies on the United Nations, and the manuscript for the present publication has been prepared under his direction. The Institution has had the benefit of continuing consultation with Ernest A. Gross, James N. Hyde, Joseph E. Johnson, C. Easton Rothwell, and Willard L. Thorp, who comprise an informal group, organized during the summer of 1953, to advise on the direction of the project, and to whom the Institution is heavily indebted for many helpful suggestions.

Finally, on behalf of the Institution, I wish to express grateful appreciation to the A. W. Mellon Educational and Charitable Trust of Pittsburgh for the generous grants that have made possible this series of studies on the United Nations system. The conclusions and recommendations of these studies have been reached, however, wholly independently of the Mellon Trust, which is not to be understood as approving or disapproving the views expressed in this and the other volumes in the series.

Robert D. Calkins
President

February 15, 1957

Contents

CONTENTS

PAGE

CHAPTER XI

APPENDIXES

THE UNITED NATIONS AND
ECONOMIC AND SOCIAL CO-OPERATION

Introduction*

FOR more than ten years, the United Nations and a group of related specialized agencies have been engaged in a momentous effort to promote orderly economic and social progress in a disorderly world. The fostering of economic growth, social change, and essential cultural adjustment—without sacrificing valued cultural assets or jeopardizing such economic and political stability as may have been achieved—is inherently difficult. The intrinsic complexity of this task has been increased by the political tensions and cleavages that have exacerbated international relations since the close of the Second World War.

When the General Assembly and the Economic and Social Council of the United Nations met for their respective first sessions in January 1946, the world economy was in a critical state and cracks had begun to appear in the wartime alliance. The dominant mood was nevertheless one of hope and confidence. The most devastating war of all time had at long last been brought to an end, and people could again devote their energies to productive undertakings. "Seldom before in human history," said the representative of the United States at the first meeting of the Council, "has an organization been created with greater opportunity to save mankind than has been given to the Economic and Social Council under the Charter of the United Nations."[1]

Bread, milk, meat, sugar, and fats and oils were being rationed in many countries. There were also severe shortages of other essential foodstuffs. The demand for coal, steel, timber, and electric power far exceeded the available supply. Countless homes in Europe and Asia had been destroyed or made uninhabitable, and the remaining dwellings—inadequate before the war—had become dangerously overcrowded in most of the larger cities. Vast numbers of refugees were unable to return to their homelands. Railways, highways, bridges, ports, and factories awaited repair and reconstruction. The prewar network of international trade and payments was disrupted. A welter of problems, long-term and short-term, needed attention.

* By Robert E. Asher.
[1] U.N. Economic and Social Council, First Session, *Official Records*, First Meeting (Jan. 23, 1946), p. 14.

3

It was recognized that many formidable obstacles would have to be surmounted before international co-operation could contribute significantly to the solution of the outstanding economic and social problems of the day. Some well-informed persons were frankly skeptical and quick to caution against exaggerating the potentialities of the new agencies. In the mood of the time, however, the obstacles to effective collaboration were for the most part viewed through a golden haze, and few appeared insuperable. The United Nations and the specialized agencies, it was assumed by the general public, would play a major role in repairing the ravages of war, in preventing depressions, and in promoting the "conditions of stability and well-being which are necessary for peaceful and friendly relations among nations."[2]

Ten years later the golden haze had been dissipated, and the barriers to international co-operation through global associations of sovereign states had become all too evident. At the same time, underlying conditions had improved tremendously. Both industrial and agricultural production at the end of the first postwar decade were at record levels. So, too, was international trade. Widespread depression had been avoided. Illiteracy had been reduced drastically. Life expectancy had been increased.

How much, if any, of this remarkable improvement in economic and social conditions should be attributed to the efforts of the United Nations and its affiliated agencies? What have been the major accomplishments of the United Nations system in each of the principal fields of activity? Have the organizational and constitutional arrangements impeded or facilitated the various endeavors? Have peaceful and friendly relations among nations been strengthened or strained? Answers to these questions could provide a basis for more realistic expectations regarding the second decade of the United Nations than those of the immediate postwar period.

The close relationship between the maintenance of international peace and security and the promotion of economic and social progress was clearly seen by the United States Secretary of State at a time when plans for the United Nations were still in an embryonic stage. Speaking in the late summer of 1943, he pointed out that:

The success of an organized system of international cooperation with the maintenance of peace as its paramount objective depends, to an important degree, upon what happens within as well as among nations. We know that political controversies and economic strife among nations are fruitful causes

[2] Charter of the United Nations, Art. 55. For the text of the Charter, see Appendix A.

of hostility and conflict. But we also know that economic stagnation and distress, cultural backwardness, and social unrest within nations, wherever they exist, may undermine all efforts for stable peace.

The primary responsibility for dealing with these conditions rests on each and every nation concerned. But each nation will be greatly helped in this task by the establishment of sound trade and other economic relations with other nations, based on a comprehensive system of mutually beneficial international cooperation, not alone in these respects, but also in furthering educational advancement and in promoting observance of basic human rights.[3]

Thus, from the beginning, the broad purposes of the United Nations have been twofold. There have, however, been important differences in the ways in which these purposes have been fulfilled. The Charter provided in some detail for the methods and processes to be used in the maintenance of international peace and security.[4] But in the solution of problems of an economic, social, cultural, and humanitarian character, the Charter specified only the general objectives to be achieved and authorized the use of a variety of methods and processes to attain those objectives. Much time since 1946, therefore, has been devoted to clarifying concepts, defining functions, and establishing machinery. Because of the very nature of the problems confronting the United Nations in the economic and social field, the Organization and the specialized agencies affiliated with it have become involved in a wide range of complex and controversial undertakings.

Emergency responsibilities of great magnitude have been assumed in connection with relief and rehabilitation in war-devastated areas, and with the care and resettlement of refugees. Noteworthy steps have been taken to deal with such long-range problems as the re-establishment of a functioning network of international trade and financial relationships, the maintenance of full employment, the improvement of social welfare services, and the economic and social development of underdeveloped countries. Serious differences of view have arisen regarding proposals for the promotion and protection of private foreign investment, for mitigating fluctuations in the prices of internationally traded primary commodities, and for supplementing loans to underdeveloped countries with grants-in-aid from an international fund. On the other hand, campaigns against communicable diseases, regulation of the traffic in

[3] "Our Foreign Policy in the Framework of Our National Interests," Radio Address of Sept. 12, 1943, U.S. Department of State *Bulletin*, Vol. 9 (Sept. 18, 1943), p. 177.

[4] See the volume in this Brookings series, *The United Nations and the Maintenance of International Peace and Security*.

STRUCTURE OF THE ECONOMIC AND SOCIAL COUNCIL

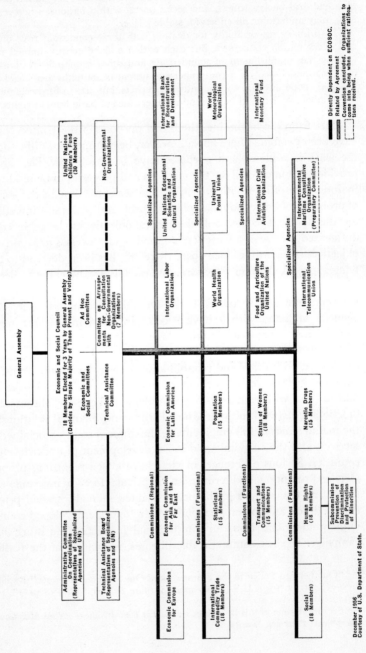

General Assembly

Administrative Committee on Coordination (Representatives of Specialized Agencies and UN)

Technical Assistance Board (Representatives of Specialized Agencies and UN)

Economic and Social Council — 18 Members Elected for 3 Years by General Assembly (Decides by Simple Majority of Those Present and Voting)

- Economic and Social Committees
- Technical Assistance Committee
- Ad Hoc Committees
- Committee on Arrangements for Consultation with Non-Governmental Organizations (7 Members)

United Nations Children's Fund (30 Members)

Non-Governmental Organizations

Commissions (Regional)
- Economic Commission for Europe
- Economic Commission for Asia and the Far East
- Economic Commission for Latin America

Commissions (Functional)
- International Commodity Trade (18 Members)
- Statistical (15 Members)
- Population (15 Members)

Commissions (Functional)
- Transport and Communications (15 Members)
- Status of Women (18 Members)

Commissions (Functional)
- Social (18 Members)
- Human Rights (18 Members)
- Narcotic Drugs (15 Members)
  - Subcommission on Prevention of Discrimination and Protection of Minorities

Specialized Agencies
- International Labor Organization
- United Nations Educational Scientific and Cultural Organization
- International Bank for Reconstruction and Development

Specialized Agencies
- World Health Organization
- Universal Postal Union
- World Meteorological Organization

Specialized Agencies
- Food and Agriculture Organization of the United Nations
- International Civil Aviation Organization
- International Monetary Fund

Specialized Agencies
- International Telecommunication Union
- Intergovernmental Maritime Consultative Organization (Preparatory Committee)

Legend:
- ▬ Directly Dependent on ECOSOC.
- ▨ Related by Agreement
- ⬚ Convention concluded. Organizations to come into being when sufficient ratifications received.

December 1956
Courtesy of U.S. Department of State.

6

narcotic drugs, and diffusion of agricultural technology have proved relatively noncontroversial.

The Economic and Social Council has been involved to some extent in all of these activities, in ways that have changed significantly over time. Designated by the Charter as a principal organ of the United Nations, it was, by a further provision of the same instrument, placed under the authority of another principal organ—the General Assembly. Moreover, the Council originally consisted of more than one third of the membership of the United Nations. Now that the membership of the Organization has increased to eighty while the membership of the Council remains fixed by the Charter at eighteen, the Council provides a place for fewer than one fourth of the members. This change has also had an effect on relations between the Council and the Assembly.

Under the Council, commissions have been established to deal with regional economic problems, demographic matters, transportation and communication, statistics, narcotic drugs, and other matters. The organizational network also includes—as the accompanying chart shows —ten specialized agencies dealing with labor, health, education, food and agriculture, civil aviation, telecommunications, postal services, meteorology, international investment, and monetary policy.[5]

Some contend that the United Nations has assumed responsibilities for matters that are beyond its proper scope and should be left to the domestic jurisdiction of its Member states. Others argue that, despite the wide range of its activities, the United Nations has not yet really begun to cope with the problems with which it should deal if it is to achieve the broad purposes set forth in its Charter. More co-ordination and consolidation of the organs and agencies have been claimed by some to be a vital need, whereas others have urged continuation of the present arrangements or the granting of even greater autonomy to the component parts of the system.

To aid in a better understanding of these and similar issues, this study seeks to analyze and appraise the major attempts to promote international economic, social, and cultural co-operation through the United Nations system, i.e., through the United Nations Organization and the cluster of specialized agencies that have been brought into relationship with it. The study reviews the more fruitful approaches to international co-operation, indicates where obstacles have been encountered that

[5] For summary information on specialized agencies, see Appendix B; for membership of the United Nations and the specialized agencies, see Appendix C; for membership of the regional economic commissions, see Appendix D.

set limits on such co-operation, and explores the nature of the existing limitations. It deals primarily with work undertaken during the ten years beginning on January 10, 1946, when the first session of the General Assembly was called to order. Where appropriate, however, important developments that occurred during the year 1956 have also been taken into account.

To provide perspective and background, the legacy of relevant experience inherited by the United Nations is described first. The provision of short-term aid in a variety of emergency situations is then discussed. The successes and failures of the United Nations system in dealing with some of the longer-range economic problems are analyzed next, specifically those problems connected with the expansion of international trade and the improvement of payments arrangements, the stimulation of production and investment, the maintenance of full employment and economic stability, and the development of transportation and communication. Reviewed thereafter are diverse programs in the social and cultural fields, including various types of social action to improve levels of living, measures in the interests of welfare and social defense, and international co-operation in educational, scientific, and cultural matters.

The pressing problems of the vast areas no longer resigned to grinding poverty and subordinate status—which are alluded to throughout the volume—are recapitulated and analyzed from a somewhat different point of view in a discussion devoted exclusively to the problems of underdeveloped countries. The endeavors of the United Nations system to cope with these problems are illustrative of a growing fusion of the international economic, social, and cultural programs designed to encourage more rapid growth in the least privileged areas of the world.

The study closes with a summary and appraisal of the record made. Some of the criteria for making this appraisal grow out of the Charter— the objectives it initially stated, the lines of action it laid down. Others derive from the conditions in which the United Nations has had to operate and the unanticipated situations with which it has had to deal. Still others result from the expectations of the peoples in its Member states—their demands, their illusions and disillusions, their fears, and their hopes.

CHAPTER I

The Inheritance of the United Nations*

THE depression of the 1930's, the Second World War, and the major lines of cleavage between developed countries, underdeveloped countries, and Communist-controlled countries that had become apparent even before the Charter entered into force left a lasting imprint on the economic and social work of the United Nations. In addition, there was in each of the major fields a legacy of specific experience and achievement. In some areas, the new organization was in a position to continue and expand prewar forms of co-operation that had met with general, if not universal, approval. In others, it had to decide whether it should or could supplement or expand emergency measures designed to ease the transition from war to peace. In still others, it had to adjust itself to new forms of long-range international co-operation devised during the war and still untested. Some account of the specific inheritance of the United Nations from the interwar and war years is therefore an essential preliminary to a survey of its economic and social activities.

League of Nations and the Interwar Years

International co-operation on economic and social problems was both intensive and experimental during the interwar period. There was a rich experience, particularly through the League of Nations, in the application of many of the methods and procedures now utilized by the United Nations system.[1] The League, however, did not during these years attempt to bring within its own orbit as wide a range of international activity as the United Nations has done. A history of its economic and social work from 1919 to 1939 would not contain chapters on "Full Employment and Economic Stability" and on "The Problems of the Underdeveloped Countries." The pressures that made these matters a central preoccupation of the United Nations were to a large

---

* By William Adams Brown, Jr.
[1] See the volume in this Brookings series, *The United Nations and Promotion of the General Welfare*, Part One.

extent the product of events during the depression of the 1930's and the Second World War, and it was only after 1939 that the League became intensively concerned with them.

As has been true in the postwar years, the initiative for certain major efforts of international co-operation during the interwar years came from sources outside the framework of any international organization. The onset of the depression of the 1930's, for example, called forth the greatest mobilization of financial resources to achieve an international objective that had ever been seen up to that time.[2] The League of Nations, not being endowed with vast and readily mobilized resources, was not able to play an important role in this remarkable, if unsuccessful, demonstration of international solidarity at a time of major crisis. Similarly, with the beginnings of recovery, when an effort was made to restore some measure of international collaboration in trade and payments, it was made in large part outside the League of Nations.

Co-operation through international organizations between the wars, nevertheless, deeply influenced the United Nations. Its failures led directly to a wartime search for new methods of organizing international action that would be more effective. Its successes, especially in social co-operation in which the work of the League underwent something of a renaissance after the onset of the depression, led to a search for methods of reviving and expanding types of collaboration that had proved effective.

The major fields of economic and social collaboration during the interwar years were international trade and payments, production and investment, transport and communications, and social and intellectual co-operation. In addition, an attempt was made to improve international co-operation in meeting the needs of individual countries requiring emergency assistance. The first step in tracing the evolution of the concrete problems confronting the United Nations when the Charter entered into force is to indicate the successes and failures recorded in each of these fields.

Co-operation to Meet
Disaster Situations

In the special field of emergency aid, the League sponsored an international organization that had the objective of giving first aid and co-

[2] Roger Auboin, *The Bank for International Settlements, 1930–1955*, Essays in International Finance, International Finance Section, Department of Economics and Sociology, Princeton University (1955), p. 10.

ordinating international action in the event of a "major disaster due to *force majeure*."[3] The convention and statutes of this organization, the International Relief Union, were drawn up by a conference convened by the Council of the League in 1927 and came into effect in December 1932. Eventually thirty governments ratified or acceded to the convention, but the United States was not among them.

Between 1932 and the beginning of the Second World War, when its activities were interrupted, the General Council of the Union met only twice. It contributed £1,000 to assist earthquake victims in two Indian districts in 1934, and sent some relief to earthquake victims in Baluchistan a year later. The bulk of its work was devoted to research on preventive measures that could be taken against disaster.

This effort, though well intended, could not be regarded as successful, and the International Relief Union was eventually liquidated by the United Nations.[4]

International Trade and Payments

Between the end of the First World War and the onset of the depression, no less than five important international conferences were called in an effort to reach agreement on general principles of conduct in the field of trade and payments. In these conferences, a large measure of agreement was reached on the desirability of incorporating, in commercial agreements, a most-favored-nation clause under which all supplying countries would be given equal treatment in the application of tariff rates to a given product. There was also general agreement on the necessity of checking competitive increases in tariffs, eliminating exchange controls and other nontariff barriers to trade, and returning to stable exchange rates. In an effort to give effect to these agreed principles, many methods were used, including protocols, conventions, and internationally agreed standards and models. Among these were a draft Convention on Prohibitions, a treaty for the Protection of Foreign Nationals and Enterprises, a draft treaty on the Protection of Industrial Property, a Model Convention for the Simplification of Customs Formalities, and a standard classification of customs nomenclature.

A great part of the work of drawing up these instruments was done

[3] U.N. Economic and Social Council, Tenth Session, *Relations with Inter-Governmental Organizations: Report by the Secretary-General*, Annex III, Doc. E/1574/Add. 1 (Jan. 23, 1950), p. 2
[4] See below, Chap. II.

by experts of the League of Nations. Much of it was enduring, for it was later drawn upon heavily in all the technical aspects of postwar co-operation in this field. With one exception, however, this work did not go to the heart of the central problems raised by the high-sounding resolutions of the major conferences. The exception was the draft Convention on Prohibitions, which contained definite commitments against the use of quantitative restrictions on trade and exchange controls except under certain specified conditions. The draft Convention on Prohibitions, which would have come into force if only one additional country had adhered to it, was the high-water mark in the effort to translate agreed principles into action prior to the depression. The next stage was a series of desperate actions in 1930 to stem a world-wide upward trend of tariffs. Among these were an International Conference for a Tariff Truce called by the League of Nations, the drafting of a Commercial Convention and a protocol for future negotiations, and the calling of an international conference to put the protocol into effect.

A final effort to check these trends was made at the London Economic Conference of 1933. Until then, most of the actions described above were either wholly or mainly European. It became clear, however, that regional collaboration could not cope with world-wide economic forces in a time of major crisis. It was also made clear that, once a chain reaction of economic defense and counterdefense is set in motion, the battle for international collaboration to uphold agreed principles by conventions, protocols, and conferences is already three quarters lost. The failure of the London Conference proved that this battle is wholly lost if great trading powers all give priority to domestic considerations or operate on different sets of priorities when domestic and international policies come into conflict.

The stated objectives of the London Economic Conference were in consonance with the principles laid down by the earlier conferences, but no agreement was reached on how domestic and international measures should be combined to give effect to these principles. The conference broke down because countries imposing direct trade and exchange controls would not relax them until currency stabilization was assured; countries on the gold standard (with bitter experience in inflation) would not adopt price-raising policies for fear of inflation; Great Britain would not adopt price-raising policies and a large public works program at the risk of unbalancing its budget; and the United States would not allow a domestic price-raising program to be interfered with by currency stabilization.

After the failure of the London Conference, the retreat from liberal trading principles became a rout. A large part of the trade in Central Europe and almost all of the trade of Europe with Latin America became bilateral. New philosophies of trade were developed that were hostile to multilateralism and to the most-favored-nation treatment, and these led to the growth of government-controlled trade, the planning of international trade, and the acceptance of autarchy as an objective of economic policy. Under German leadership and example, trade in a large part of Europe was made an instrument for increasing war potential and a weapon to achieve political aims. New administrative techniques of trade, both for offense and defense, were perfected, including clearing payments and compensation agreements, the control of trade and capital movements by exchange regulations, and the use of multiple exchange rates.

Although the League of Nations was opposed to these divisive tendencies, it made no further attempt to convene general conferences on international trade and exchange problems. Instead, meetings were organized "limited to certain groups of states which had the same kind of problems to face, either because of geographical propinquity or some other common feature, or attended by officials, groups or individuals interested in trade in particular commodities."[5] The League of Nations also drew up model conventions on double taxation, which became the basis of some two hundred agreements, and made a number of major economic reports.

These activities of the League kept the banner of liberal trading principles flying, but the two major attempts to revive them in practice, after the failure of the London Conference, were initiated by the United States. The first was the Trade Agreements Act of 1934, which, by giving the President authority—for a limited period of time—to enter into trade agreements without obtaining congressional approval for each agreement, made the reciprocal lowering of barriers a more feasible undertaking. Agreements negotiated under this program incorporated the unconditional most-favored-nation principle and also contained general clauses relating to nontariff barriers to trade that were in harmony with the recommendations of these conferences and of the experts of the League of Nations.

The second attempt was the Tripartite Declaration of 1936 dealing with foreign exchange policy. This declaration, signed by France, the United States, and the United Kingdom, contained a pledge that the

[5] F. P. Walters, *A History of the League of Nations*, Vol. 2 (1952), pp. 749-52.

adhering governments would maintain the greatest possible equilibrium
in the system of international exchanges and would support a general
policy of relaxing progressively the existing system of quotas and exchange controls with a view to their abolition. This fresh affirmation of
principles previously accepted was accompanied by a statement that
the signatories would pursue a policy that would tend to promote prosperity in the world and improve the standard of living. The new emphasis on the standard of living, which had been lacking in earlier declarations and agreements, was from this time carried forward into all future
negotiations and debates on the general problems of trade and payments.

This new approach was due in large measure to the acceleration
during the depression of four basic trends in the formulation of commercial policy—trends that have widened the area of international
conflict on many issues. They are: (1) special treatment of agricultural
products in international trade; (2) the growth of international cartels;
(3) the growth of regional and preferential arrangements; and (4) the
subordination of commercial policy to employment and development
policy. Even during the interwar period the first three of these trends
posed the twin problems that have hampered postwar efforts to achieve
a harmony of national views both within the United Nations and outside it: namely, conflicting approaches by a single country to different
trade problems, and conflicting approaches of different countries to a
single such problem.

The earlier failures of the League of Nations to obtain observance
by its members of general principles governing international trade and
monetary policies also demonstrated the inherent weakness of international action that goes no further than resolutions and recommendations. The alternative was to induce countries to undertake specific
commitments—for example, by becoming members of new international agencies of a more specialized type. Firmly held attitudes, however, toward currency stabilization, the maintenance of employment in
domestic industry and agriculture, and other matters affecting international trade and payments, were largely responsible for the insistence
of many countries that these new agencies should not be given authority
to interfere with the domestic policies of their members. Yet the same
experience that increased the sensitiveness of countries to any outside
interference in their domestic policies also increased their awareness of
the basic need for harmonizing domestic and foreign policies with respect to trade and payments if a workable world trading system were

to be reconstituted. This experience also proved that the problem of operating such a system effectively cannot be separated from that of preventing the international spread of depressions.

Production and Investment

During the interwar period, the concern of international agencies with production and investment problems took three principal forms. The first was encouragement of co-operation between labor and management for increased production and productivity, with a view to improved labor standards. This was an integral part of the work of the International Labour Organisation (ILO). The second was the assembly of information relating to world production and the analysis of influences affecting its fluctuations. This was an important part of the work of the Secretariat of the League of Nations, which regularly collected and published production statistics and, in its annual *World Economic Survey* and in special studies, analyzed the factors currently affecting production.[6] Third, there was the mobilization of credits and loans to meet the emergency problems of individual countries. This last was the major concern of the Financial Committee of the League.

The activities of the Financial Committee passed through four distinct phases, the first of which involved an attempt to put into effect an International Credits Scheme, the essence of which was the creation of a new type of security to be placed in the private financial market. Although this scheme was a failure, it laid the groundwork for the next phase. The second phase involved the development of reconstruction schemes for particular countries obtaining loans with the help of the League of Nations. It required no basic change in the principles of the International Credits Scheme, but considerable modification in its techniques as applied to individual countries. In particular, it involved the appointment of commissioners of the League with extensive powers. The two great successes of this phase were the reconstruction of Austria and Hungary in 1921 and 1924, but loans were also granted by the League to Esthonia and Danzig, and similar plans were considered for Albania, Portugal, and Rumania. The granting of extensive control over internal domestic economic and financial policies to an international agency in return for financial assistance was a feature of all these operations.

[6] See League of Nations, *Memorandum on Production and Trade, 1925 to 1929/30* (1931), and *World Production and Prices, 1938/39* (1939).

The third phase involved the application of the same principles and techniques to assist Greece and Bulgaria in connection with their serious refugee problems. The purpose of the League of Nations was to aid in absorbing these refugees into the economies of the receiving countries, and to do this, it had to be concerned with the whole range of their economic and financial problems. The fourth phase, which disclosed some of the basic weaknesses of the techniques employed by the League, was characterized by a second appeal for help from Austria, Hungary, Greece, and Bulgaria in the early stages of the depression of the 1930's. For many reasons, it proved impossible for the League to provide financial resources and to do more than offer advice and make general recommendations.

The work of the Financial Committee was a pioneering effort to meet problems that reappeared under another guise after the war and later had to be dealt with by different methods. The International Credits Scheme, for example, was the first serious attempt to develop the idea of mobilizing private financial resources with the aid of a guarantee by an international agency. The reconstruction loans of the League represented a harsh solution of an issue that arises whenever an international agency extends financial assistance to a sovereign country—namely the terms and conditions on which such assistance shall be granted. In the United Nations, this issue has been debated in the context not of reconstruction but of economic development, and the solutions that have been proposed are a far cry from the sterner ones adopted by the League.[7] The experience of the Financial Committee in dealing with refugee problems demonstrated that an international organization dealing with a major problem of resettlement must concern itself with many aspects of the internal affairs of the countries of resettlement. Finally, the failure of the Financial Committee to bring effective help to individual countries at the onset of depression, like the failures of the League in the trade and payments field after 1930, demonstrated that the real solution to problems of this kind lies in reducing the severity of the depression itself.

Transport and Communications

The beginning of the interwar period found a number of nineteenth century forms of international co-operation in the field of transport and communications still being actively carried on. Among these were the

[7] See below, Chap. IV.

Universal Postal Union, an International Meteorological Organization, international conventions regulating traffic on the Danube and Rhine, the Berne Convention regulating railway freight traffic in Europe, and rate conferences of private shipping companies.[8] Before the turn of the century, a nongovernmental International Maritime Committee was organized to establish rules and practices to govern international ocean commerce.

There were also co-operative organizations in the field of communications. An International Telegraphic Conference was held in Paris as early as 1865, and a treaty signed at that time established the International Telegraph Union. It was amended in 1885 to include provisions concerning international telephone service. In 1903, the first International Radio Conference was held in Berlin establishing the International Radio Telegraph Union. The resultant protocol embodies principles that are still the basic law of international radio regulations.[9] In 1927, the first International Table of Radio Frequency Allocation was adopted, and in 1932, the consolidation of principles and regulations governing radio, telephone, and telegraph operations was accomplished by a Madrid Telecommunications Convention. At that time, the International Telegraph Union and the International Radio Telegraph Union were merged into the International Telecommunication Union. It was commissioned to revise and keep up-to-date the regulations governing international telegraph, telephone, and radio communications. But the functions of the Union, although widened, did not undergo any radical change until after the Second World War.

A major step in filling the obvious gaps in this system of international collaboration was taken by the Aeronautical Commission of the Paris Peace Conference, which initiated, in 1919, an International Air Convention Relating to the Regulation of Aerial Navigation, which in turn established an International Commission for Air Navigation (ICAN). A further step was taken by the Assembly of the League of Nations, which in 1921 convoked an International Conference on Communications.

This conference drafted a Convention on Freedom of Transit and a Convention on the Regime of International Waterways, both of which were ratified by a large number of countries and were in effect until 1939. It also prepared for two other conventions: one on the Interna-

---

[8] These are discussed later in this study. See below, Chap. VI.
[9] Richard T. Black, "Telecommunications Policy and the Department of State," U.S. Department of State *Bulletin*, Vol. 30 (Jan. 8, 1954), pp. 83–87.

tional Regime of Maritime Ports, which provided that every contracting
state would grant to the vessels of every other contracting state equal
treatment with its own vessels in its various maritime ports, and one on
the International Regime of Railways, both of which were completed
in 1923 by a conference called by the Communications and Transit
Organization of the League.[10]

These four conventions dealt with long-familiar problems, mostly
technical in nature. Neither the United States nor the Soviet Union was
a signatory, and much of the co-operation achieved under them proved
to be the working out of orderly arrangements governing internal transport in Europe.[11]

In contrast, the International Commission for Air Navigation, whose
membership included all the major powers except the United States,
was confronted with problems that could be solved effectively only on a
nearly world-wide basis. During the period of its operations, which began in 1922 and continued until 1939, the main function of ICAN was
to ensure the application of the air convention, but its activities were in
practice limited largely to technical matters—due to the early incorpo-
ration into national and international law of the principle that every
state has the sole and exclusive sovereignty over its own air space.

This principle meant that although all states had the right to fly over
the high seas, every state had the full right, except as it might limit
itself by treaty or other international agreements, to determine the
methods by which it would allow the entry of foreign aircraft into its
territory. International co-operation on civil aviation, aside from technical matters, therefore meant co-operation on such major questions as
transit rights, routes, frequency of landings, and the pickup and discharge of cargo within the territory of a country by foreign planes. In
the interwar period, these problems were further complicated by
questions concerning the relation of civil aviation to disarmament.
During the Second World War, the activities of ICAN were much reduced, but the institution did not disappear, and after the liberation of
Paris, plans were made for the revival of its work.

None of the great economic and political problems in civil aviation
were dealt with by ICAN nor could much be accomplished about them
by the Communications and Transit Organization of the League, because Germany, the United States, and the Soviet Union were not
ready to join in international agreements on such matters. This was

[10] Walters, *op. cit.*, Vol. 1 (1952), pp. 143, 178–79.
[11] See below, Chap. VI.

also true of emerging problems in the field of radio communication, and only a small advance was made in the rest of the telecommunications field.[12]

Although the Communications and Transit Organization was frustrated in dealing with basic economic and political issues in civil aviation, it carried on one of the most fruitful operations of the League. Its activity was concentrated primarily on technical problems related to railway transport, inland navigation, ports and maritime navigation, road traffic, and power transmission in Europe. In these fields, it accomplished much useful work.[13] The failure of the great powers to employ it for consultation and co-operation on the emerging issues of aviation and radio communication as well as on technical problems illustrated, however, the fact that international organization as such could be no substitute for the willingness on the part of the major powers to use it.

Although the Communications and Transit Organization of the League met for the last time in 1939, its work was, as far as possible, carried forward thereafter by the Secretariat of the League. Consequently, the Economic and Social Council of the United Nations did not have to make a fresh start in the collection of data and the analysis of problems in the field of transport and communications.

Social and Cultural Co-operation

International co-operation during the interwar years on trade and payments and transport and communications was concerned mainly with the relations of governments in their day-to-day economic intercourse. In the field of investment, the emphasis was heavily on the special problems of individual countries in time of emergency. In the field of social co-operation, however, the emphasis was primarily on "the cares and anxieties of the individual and his family."[14] But these distinctions cannot be made too sharply. The objective of raising the standard of living was implicit in many forms of interwar "economic" co-operation, and the development of "social" co-operation, especially in the fields of health and labor, showed that the cares and anxieties of the individual cannot be separated from the problems of more effective utilization of resources, expansion of trade, and other economic problems.

[12] Walters, *op. cit.*, Vol. 1, p. 180.
[13] *Ibid.*
[14] *Ibid.*, Vol. 2, p. 750.

The interests of the ILO in conditions of labor were continually broadened. They were dealt with by international conventions and recommendations, studies, and co-operation with individual countries. The first interests of the ILO included the shortening of hours of work, the setting up of employment services, the improvement of conditions of work of children, young women, and prospective mothers. The reduction of industrial injuries and occupational diseases, and vocational training and placement of the handicapped, also became fruitful areas of work. To these were soon added leadership in the promotion of social security, in particular, social insurance, the improvement of techniques of discussion and negotiation between employers and workers, and more generally, the promotion of a fair share in the fruits of progress for workers and employers. The concern of the ILO with the problem of effective uses of resources in production and distribution was implicit between the wars, and its concern in general economic problems was destined during the war to become more explicit. This was also true of the work of the Health Committee of the League of Nations.

The first job of the Health Committee—an undertaking in which it was highly successful—was the control of epidemics immediately after the First World War. The second was to ensure in so far as possible that public health services would be guided by the principles of preventive medicine. These activities were supplemented by the conclusion of two sanitary conventions—the International Sanitary Convention of 1925 (Maritime) and the International Sanitary Convention on Aerial Navigation (1933).

It was a third phase of the work of the Health Committee that took it directly into the arena of economic policy and raised problems of co-ordination with the activities of other organs and agencies. This was the promotion of national action in combating some of the general social and economic conditions adversely affecting health, such as bad housing and malnutrition. The impetus to this broadening of the whole field of social co-operation was derived from studies of nutrition by the League of Nations begun in 1935 under Australian leadership. These studies culminated in the publication by the League in 1937 of a *Report on New Technical Efforts towards a Better Nutrition*. The ILO, the International Institute for Agriculture (not a League of Nations organization), and the committees of the League on Intellectual Cooperation and on Child Welfare were associated with these studies. The nutrition study emphasized the need for expansion of consumption so as to improve the health and physique of populations, and this emphasis led to a basic analysis

important factors in the creation of a new international agency—
Food and Agriculture Organization of the United Nations. More-
r, because the most acute problems in this area were in Africa, Asia,
l Latin America, the nutrition work of the League of Nations was a
erunner of the preoccupation of the United Nations system with the
ecial problems of the underdeveloped countries.

Although the failures of the League in the field of trade and payments
eemed to call for the creation of new agencies, the successes of the
League in focusing attention on neglected areas of international social
co-operation gave impetus to the creation of such agencies in these
fields. These successes depended in large measure on the willingness of
states to take action either under international auspices or in accordance with international recommendations on many matters falling within their domestic jurisdiction, and on their willingness to join in making
studies and recommendations on such matters.

Studies and Recommendations
of the League (1939–45)

Both the Economic, Financial and Transit Department of the League
of Nations Secretariat, after its removal to Princeton, New Jersey, and
the Delegation on Economic Depressions of the League undertook extensive analyses of the problems involved in easing the transition from
war to peace. These problems were also dealt with in studies and
recommendations by the International Labour Office, especially at the
ILO conferences of 1941 and 1944.

The work of the Secretariat took the form of a series of special studies
on the handling of relief and reconstruction problems after the First
World War; and that of the delegation took the form of a report on
postwar economic policy, the first volume of which was published in
1943.[18]

The general theme of the report of the delegation was that no government would be able to overcome its transitional problems by acting
alone. The most notable feature of the report was its insistence that the
solution of transitional problems involving international co-operation
should be directly correlated with measures for long-range collaboration. It placed great emphasis on employment, improved standards of

[18] The report was entitled *The Transition from War to Peace Economy*. For full references on this and other publications of the League that are mentioned below, see
Hans Aufricht, *Guide to League of Nations Publications*, 1951.

of the relation of nutrition not only to health bu
economic policy. Other studies carried on by the I
the League on housing, slum clearance, and town
ning, were regarded by the committee as of an impo.
even greater than that of the nutrition studies. Here
operation with the ILO was developed, and a Housin
the League was created.

The League also made pioneering and invaluable co
social co-operation in less controversial fields, such as narc
and the suppression of traffic in women and children. T
moreover, was active in the field of intellectual co-operation
it established a Committee on Intellectual Cooperation, and
an International Institute of Intellectual Cooperation. The co.
had three major aims—to improve the material conditions of i
tual workers; to build up international relations and contacts be
teachers, artists, scientists, and actors, and members of the intelle
professions; and to strengthen the influence of the League for pea
National committees on intellectual co-operation were also establish
under the auspices of the League. The effectiveness of this work w
modest, but one enterprise, the *Index Translationum*, survived the war.

One major line of cleavage cut across the whole field of social co-
operation. It has been described by the historian of the League as follows:

> None of the authoritarian States would participate, although it was always
> open to them to do so. Germany, Italy, and Japan were hostile to every form
> of international institution. The Russian attitude was different. They were par-
> ticularly well disposed toward the Health Committee [of the League] . . . but
> they took no part in any of the studies or meetings concerned with the general
> raising of the standards of living. In many aspects, these activities were based on
> ideas which found no place in a Communist economy. And, above all, the
> Russians desired to discourage any suggestion that all this could be placed on
> a level with the essential duties of the League.[17]

In one form or another, most of the activities of the League in international social co-operation survived the war. Many of them became
part of the inheritance of the United Nations in the form of well-organ-
ized work that needed only to be carried forward along established
lines. The energy and enthusiasm that went into the work of the League
on nutrition and related problems carried over into the war period, and

[15] *Ibid.*, Vol. 1, pp. 190–91.
[16] See below, Chap. IX.
[17] Walters, *op. cit.*, Vol. 2, p. 757.

living, and other objectives with strong social and humanitarian content, and recommended action during the transition, both by governments and international agencies, on a wide range of interrelated problems. To meet these needs, the delegation suggested the creation of several new international agencies, some of which were already being planned, although not entirely on the lines it recommended. Among them were an agency to deal with questions of commercial policy, an advisory agency for co-ordinating policies on full employment, an international reconstruction and development corporation, and a clearing or equalization fund along the lines finally agreed upon in establishing the International Monetary Fund. The delegation also emphasized the responsibility of creditor nations for taking radical and unilateral action for the reduction of trade barriers, a recommendation that was to be repeated in the debates of the United Nations organs and in the reports of United Nations experts.

The League also made general studies bearing on long-range problems, including the continuation of basic demographic studies, work on double taxation, and statistical work of several kinds. The main emphasis, however, was on trade and payments, economic stability, and the conditions of private investment.[19]

The mechanism by which a major economic depression may spread from one country to another and finally throughout the world had been laid bare in a famous report to the League of Nations Assembly in 1931, *The Course and Phases of the World Economic Depression*, and this had been followed in 1941 by a theoretical analysis of *Prosperity and Depression*. During the war, these themes recurred and, in addition, the special aspects of economic stability of particular interest to underdeveloped countries were analyzed.[20] Late in 1945, a special Joint Committee on Private Investment, which met in Princeton, was appointed and published its findings and recommendations early in 1946.

This body of work gave intellectual expression to currents of thought and concepts of national interest that influenced the practical work of

[19] In the field of trade and payments, the major publications were: *Commerical Policy in the Interwar Period: International Proposals and National Policies* (1942); *International Currency Experience: Lessons of the Interwar Period* (1944); *Europe's Trade: A Study of the Trade of European Countries with Each Other and with the Rest of the World* (1941); *The Network of World Trade* (1942); *Quantitative Trade Controls: Their Causes and Nature* (1943); *Trade Relations between Free Market and Controlled Economies* (1943); *Customs Unions* (1947); *International Cartels* (1948); *Industrialization and Foreign Trade* (1945); and *Commercial Policy in the Postwar World* (1945).

[20] See *The Course and Control of Inflation* (1946); *Economic Stability in the Postwar World* (1945); and *Raw Material Problems and Policies* (1946).

preparing postwar programs of international economic co-operation. This is shown first by the range of topics considered to be parts of "commercial policy"; second, by the emphasis placed on the idea that national import policies are fundamentally dependent on the state of domestic economic activity, particularly employment, and that no stable and liberal system of trade relationships can be attained in conditions of economic insecurity; third, by the firm conclusion that no liberal trading system is likely to survive a major world economic depression; fourth, by the recognition given to new currents stirring in the underdeveloped countries; and fifth, by a fresh stress on the interdependence of developed and underdeveloped countries.

The generally high quality of the analytical studies of the League of Nations provides an invaluable guide to an understanding of the substantive differences that divided the nations in their approach to the emergency problems of the transition and the long-range problems of co-operation in major economic and social fields after the Second World War. It was unfortunate, however, that what should have been among the first tasks of the new organization that was being born was in fact the last task of the dying organization that preceded it.

Emergency Action to Ease the Transition from War to Peace

In contrast to the situation prevailing during the First World War, many active steps were taken during the Second World War to prepare for the transition from war to peace. The major forms of emergency action planned during the war to meet transitional problems were the relief and rehabilitation of liberated and occupied territories, the handling of the refugee problem, attempts to meet an impending shortage of materials, especially food, and European co-operation to meet urgent transitional problems through regional co-operation.

Relief and Rehabilitation

The two major programs set in motion toward the end of the Second World War to meet the most urgent transitional problems of liberated and occupied territories were the civilian supply programs of the American and British military authorities and the program of the United Nations Relief and Rehabilitation Administration (UNRRA). Neither of these was concerned with long-range reconstruction, and at the time when the United Nations Preparatory Commission met in London in the winter of 1945–46, UNRRA—under a decision of its Council of the preceding August—was already making plans for its own liquidation.

Although UNRRA bore the name of the United Nations and carried on its major operations after the United Nations Charter was signed, it never became a part of the United Nations system. But its influence on the economic and social work of the new world organization was greater than that of any other predecessor organization except the League of Nations.

As an incident to its efforts to provide the greatest possible amount of relief and rehabilitation, UNRRA became involved in attempts to alleviate a world food shortage, in the problem of refugees, in the special needs of children, nursing mothers, and pregnant women, and in the broader fields of public health and education. Many of its workers in central, southern, and eastern Europe found themselves dealing with situations both in rural and urban areas that were characteristic of some of the long-range problems of underdeveloped countries. In most of its activities, moreover, it was found that there was need for technical assistance, including training programs, which the agency provided.

The experience of UNRRA in its main work of relief and rehabilitation also provided precedents that were important for the United Nations. Among the most useful were some of the principles developed by the UNRRA Council governing the granting of assistance and its use by those countries lacking the foreign exchange to pay for essential supplies. Foremost among these was the principle that the UNRRA program be designed to help people help themselves. Two other major principles were that in the distribution of relief no distinction should be made among recipients on the basis of race, creed, or political belief; and that receiving governments should be responsible for seeing that supplies were distributed in accordance with UNRRA principles. Both of these were later applied in all United Nations emergency operations, as was the requirement that such supplies should be exempt from export and import taxes. Still another principle was that the proceeds of sales of UNRRA goods, after payment of administrative expenses, should be used for further relief. This was a direct forerunner of the use of counterpart funds in United States assistance programs and such United Nations programs as that of the Korean Reconstruction Agency.

Another principle governing the use of UNRRA funds was that they should not be used for "reconstruction." The estimates of reconstruction needs far exceeded any sums that the agency could be reasonably expected to provide, and the use of such funds for this purpose ran counter to the American conviction that the main reliance for reconstruction after the war should be placed on private investment. However justifiable in the prevailing circumstances, this restriction on UNRRA activities had some unfortunate consequences. The difficulty of making a precise distinction between reconstruction and rehabilitation was demonstrated throughout its entire history, and the attempt to preserve it limited the scope, the variety, and the depth of the program that was followed.

The methods by which UNRRA acquired its very substantial resources not only set precedents for the United Nations but also provided some warnings. The agency was financed by voluntary and periodical contributions from national governments, and all subsequent United Nations emergency programs, with some variations, inherited this method of financing the bulk, if not all, of their operations. In the case of UNRRA, however, governments contributing to the program were not left free to contribute as much or as little as they chose. Administrative expenses were allotted by the UNRRA Council, and a formula was adopted for dividing, among contributing countries, the total burden of furnishing supplies and services on an equitable basis. It proved impractical to develop any formula that would adequately reflect the capacity to pay of the various contributing countries, and a rough-and-ready solution was found by obtaining from countries whose territory had not been occupied by the enemy a commitment to contribute 1 per cent of their national incomes as computed by them for this purpose. At the request of the council, two such contributions were solicited. UNRRA was, nevertheless, always in financial difficulties, and at one time had drastically to curtail its operations because of delays by the United States Congress in appropriating funds for the second American contribution.

There were other aspects of the experience of UNRRA that raised warning signals of trouble ahead for the United Nations. The United States provided about 70 per cent of the resources of the agency, each of its directors-general was an American, and Americans tended to expect it to behave as if it were a United States governmental agency. UNRRA therefore exemplified, in high degree, a problem that is bound to arise when an international agency carries out multilateral operations and a single country provides most of the funds.

Finally, the experience of UNRRA demonstrated once again the reluctance of the Soviet Union to allow important powers to be exercised by an international agency. This was manifest in the insistence of the Soviet Union on some form of veto power over decisions that might otherwise be taken by the policy-making organs of UNRRA, by its attitude on the details of agreements between the agency and recipient countries, and by the reluctance of Byelorussia and the Ukraine to furnish information required of all UNRRA "clients." Although these Soviet attitudes did not prove to be insuperable impediments to the work of the agency, and the intransigence of Eastern European countries on the matter of information has often been exaggerated, they were indicative of a problem that has been carried over into the United Nations. The first serious breach between the Soviet Union and other members of the UNRRA Council was on another issue, which also had important repercussions on the early work of the United Nations—the treatment of displaced persons and refugees.

Refugees and Displaced Persons

At the close of the Second World War, various voluntary organizations, the military authorities, and three international organizations were concerned with the problem of refugees and displaced persons. Although thirty governments contributed to the work of one of the international organizations—the Intergovernmental Committee on Refugees—its operational expenses were jointly underwritten by the United Kingdom and the United States. It accomplished some useful work, but the care of millions of displaced persons was wholly beyond its resources. Only a minor contribution to the refugee problem could be made by the Office of the High Commissioner of Refugees under the League of Nations, which was still caring for refugees from the First World War. The major responsibilities therefore devolved on UNRRA and the military authorities, who encountered considerable difficulty in defining their respective functions and responsibilities.

The number of displaced persons and refugees found by the Allied armies in their zones of occupation at the time of the German surrender, in May 1945, was about 8 millions.[21] In the months immediately preceding and following the surrender, approximately 5 to 6 millions were returned to their countries of nationality—a prodigious achievement on the part of the military authorities—but a new stream of refugees from Eastern Europe soon began to pour into the occupied zones,

[21] U.S. Displaced Persons Commission, *The Displaced Persons Commission: First Semi-Annual Report to the President and the Congress, Feb. 1, 1949* (1949), p. 2.

especially Western Germany and Austria. The role of UNRRA, unlike that of the Intergovernmental Committee on Refugees, was originally conceived in terms of providing temporary relief to displaced persons while assisting them in the process of repatriation. More than 750,000 were repatriated under its auspices, most of them before November 1945. There were many, however, who refused repatriation. When it became clear that the numbers of such persons would be substantial, the United States, British, and French governments agreed that, with the exception of traitors and war criminals, individuals who did not want to return to their country of origin should not be forced to do so and should be eligible for UNRRA assistance. The Soviet Government, however, insisted that all displaced persons and refugees should be repatriated, and interpreted the refusal of any such person to return voluntarily to his country of origin as clear evidence of guilt by reason of collaboration with the enemy. Such persons, it held, were subject to extradition.

On this issue, UNRRA was forced to take a stand, and it did so in a resolution passed by its council in August 1945. In the face of strenuous Soviet objection, the council decided that the agency would care for displaced persons without the agreement of their countries of origin, but, as a concession to the Soviet Union, required the administration to make every effort to encourage repatriation and to consult with the governments concerned. Until then all major decisions of the council, in spite of disagreements, had been made unanimously. This decision was the first open breach between East and West within UNRRA.

As early as 1944, it had become clear to UNRRA that there would still be a problem of dealing with displaced persons and refugees after its own work had come to an end. It therefore worked vigorously for the establishment of an effective United Nations refugee organization and made a considerable effort to have the organization ready in time. In its efforts to establish such an organization, the United Nations fell heir to all the bitterness that had arisen in UNRRA over the question of involuntary repatriation. It also fell heir to a serious problem of resettlement with which neither UNRRA nor the Intergovernmental Committee on Refugees had been able to cope.[22]

Shortages of Materials

One of the most difficult problems for UNRRA at the beginning of its operations was to obtain the supplies needed for its program in

[22] See below, Chap. II.

competition with the pressing demands arising from the conduct of the war. UNRRA frequently had difficulty in making out its case before the combined boards through which the United Kingdom and the United States handled the general problem of wartime allocations in behalf of the Allied powers.[23] As the war came to a close, this system of allocation suffered two kinds of pressure. One was from private interests anxious to be relieved of the check on their activities imposed by governmentally controlled allocations. The other was from countries in the United Nations alliance that were anxious to have a greater voice in the allocation process. The justice of this claim was recognized by Prime Minister Churchill and President Roosevelt when, in late 1944, they directed the combined boards to collaborate increasingly with the representatives of other members of the wartime coalition. Considerable progress was made before the end of the war in carrying out this directive.

Just before the end of the war, an American policy statement was developed dealing with the termination of the combined boards and the setting up of various international commodity committees additional to those already in being. This statement recognized that the continuation of some wartime controls was essential to an orderly transition from war to peace, and it strongly emphasized the need for a distribution of supplies during that transition that would be equitable in terms of the reconversion and rehabilitation of the world economy.

The recognition by the United Kingdom and the United States of the need for an equitable international distribution of supplies during the transition was in harmony with the recommendations of the Report of the League of Nations Delegation on Economic Depressions. The concept of equitable distribution in times of shortage later found frequent echoes in debates of the United Nations. The combined boards, however, did not really set a lasting precedent for the new world organization, although their international commodity committees did provide for continuity of policy and were utilized by the United Nations in efforts to combat the world food shortage.

Regional Co-operation in Europe

One other form of wartime emergency action that had important consequences for the United Nations was the attempt made in Europe

[23] S. McKee Rosen, *The Combined Boards of the Second World War—An Experiment in International Organization* (1951), *passim*. Canada alone among the other Allied powers was a member of one of the boards—the Combined Food Board.

to solve some of its most urgent transitional problems on a regional basis.

From 1940 to 1944, many suggestions had been put forward for postwar regional co-operation in Europe on a more or less permanent basis.[24] The general trend of thought, however, was toward a global approach, and the United Nations Charter made no specific provision for, although it did not rule out, regional organizations in the economic field. Nevertheless, there was a strong impulse to meet certain European problems on a regional basis. This expressed itself within the framework of UNRRA in the tendency of its Committee of the Council for Europe and the UNRRA European Regional Office (ERO), to act as if they were autonomous bodies; and in the establishment of three technical regional organizations known as the E organizations.

When the war ended, the intricate transport network on which the entire European economy depended was virtually paralyzed. To overcome this situation, a large measure of regional co-operation was needed, and to provide this, the European Central Inland Transport Organization (ECITO) was created. It was designed to serve as a co-ordinating and consultative organ to study the technical and economic conditions of international traffic in Europe and to give advice and make recommendations to the member governments on means of restoring and co-ordinating the transport capacity of the European system. These functions were divided into two categories: the first concerned with the problems of the transitional emergency period; and the second with long-range problems of European transport.

Another urgent economic problem was the restoration of coal production. In July 1945, the combined production of Belgium, Czechoslovakia, France, Germany, the Netherlands, Poland, and the United Kingdom was only 57 per cent of the aggregate prewar production of these countries.[25] The second of the E organizations, the European Coal Organization (ECO), was consequently established to promote the supply and equitable distribution of coal and scarce items of coal-mining supplies and equipment, and to safeguard as far as possible the interests of both producers and consumers.

The third E organization, the Emergency Economic Committee for

[24] See U.S. Department of State, *Postwar Foreign Policy Preparations, 1939–1946*, Publication 3580 (February 1950), pp. 25, 127, 138, 146, 148, 197–98, 228, 372, 394, 472, 482, 656.
[25] U.N. General Assembly, First Session, Second Part, *Official Records*, Supplement No. 3, "Preliminary Report of the Temporary Sub-Commission on Economic Reconstruction of Devastated Areas" (1947), p. 19.

Europe (EECE), was designed to consider a broad range of problems. It was an advisory body on economic questions relating to production, supply, and distribution during the final stages of the European war and the immediate transitional period, and on questions of reconstruction policy.

The E organizations were essentially emergency bodies. When, however, the United Nations took its first step toward the creation of a regional economic commission for Europe by appointing a Temporary Subcommission on the Economic Reconstruction of Devastated Areas, a possibility was opened up for the continuation of some of their activities under United Nations auspices.

The E organizations were an experiment in the selection of those areas of international co-operation that are suitable for a regional approach. The greater effectiveness of ECITO and ECO as compared with EECE showed that the more concrete and localized are the problems selected for regional treatment, the greater is the likelihood that they will be solved successfully on a regional basis. The experience of the E organizations also demonstrated once again the difficulties of obtaining Soviet membership in international economic organs of a specialized character, and in obtaining cordial co-operation from the Soviet Union once it had agreed to participate.[26]

Continuity and Innovation in Social and Cultural Co-operation

The inheritance of the United Nations from the emergency measures taken or planned during the latter part of the war was in part a demonstration of new methods of collaboration to meet a situation of economic and social crisis, in part an object lesson in some of the potentialities and limitations of regional economic collaboration, and in part the preservation and enrichment of international social collaboration, especially in the field of health.

Through its activities in education, in the introduction of social and child welfare activities, and in the revival and introduction of health programs, UNRRA became a link between the pioneer international collaborative efforts in these fields that existed before the war and those that followed after. As part of its public health program, UNRRA

[26] The Soviet Union joined neither ECO nor EECE. Efforts to obtain Soviet participation in the Provisional Organization for European Inland Transport formed in April 1945 were unavailing, and it was not until this organization was reorganized as ECITO in September 1945 that the Soviet Union accepted membership.

assumed responsibilities for administering certain international sanitary conventions that were revised by the UNRRA Council to meet wartime needs. It also assumed the duty of collecting and disseminating information on the appearance and movement of all communicable diseases that, in its opinion, constituted a menace to other countries. It became responsible for delineating yellow-fever areas of the world and establishing standards of yellow-fever vaccine. Its medical and sanitation supply programs as a whole were planned to fulfill four main functions: rehabilitation of hospitals, clinics, and laboratories; prevention of epidemic diseases; restoration of the drug industry; and provision of specialized supplies for war victims.

On such matters, the Health Committee of the League of Nations co-operated closely with it. This committee endeavored to maintain as far as possible its work on such subjects as epidemiological intelligence, malaria, nutrition, and biological standardization, and added to this the task of encouraging effective use of the international nomenclature on blood groups that had been worked out earlier.

Continuity of effort was also preserved in the field of narcotics control by measures to safeguard this control during the war, to adapt it to special wartime conditions, and to prepare for the early resumption in full of the prewar system. In contrast, aside from the collection of data and the publication of one important study, most of the work of the League for the protection of women and children lapsed during the war.[27]

Prior to the first meetings of the General Assembly and the Economic and Social Council of the United Nations, steps were taken to ensure that this work would be continued and expanded. The establishment of a World Health Organization had been proposed by several nations at the San Francisco Conference, and a draft constitution was developed by the United States Department of State and the United States Public Health Service in 1945 and early 1946 for this purpose. An advisory group of national health and civic leaders had urged the creation of such an organization in October 1945, and in December 1945, Congress formally requested the President to convoke a conference to establish it.

A great deal of thought was given to postwar educational co-operation by the Allied Ministers of Education, by the governments of the United States and the United Kingdom, and by many nongovern-

[27] See League of Nations, *Report on the Work of the League During the War, Submitted to the Assembly by the Acting Secretary-General* (October 1945), pp. 80–109, where all this work is described in detail.

mental organizations. A conference of Allied Ministers of Education was convened in 1944 to make plans for educational and cultural reconstruction and for a United Nations organization for educational co-operation. This suggestion was backed by the United States and other nations at the San Francisco Conference, and as a result, the commitments under Article 55 concerning educational and cultural co-operation were included in the Charter. Some of the major issues for a proposed international organization were settled in the earlier wartime discussions—for example, whether the organization should be temporary for educational reconstruction or a permanent body, and whether the emphasis should be shifted from the League of Nations idea of concentrating on contacts between intellectuals to a broader movement affecting all people. It was therefore possible to reach formal agreement on a constitution for the United Nations Educational, Scientific and Cultural Organization in two weeks in November 1945.

In 1944 also, a major step was taken by the International Labour Organisation, which had been moved temporarily to Montreal during the war, in preparation for its future work. The twenty-sixth session of the International Labour Conference, held in Philadelphia in the spring of 1944, laid down major objectives and actions suitable for various countries for progress toward social security and made important recommendations on employment policies during the transition from war to peace. Its most significant action, however, was the adoption of a Declaration of Aims and Purposes (the Philadelphia Charter), which was incorporated in the ILO constitution as an amendment. This declaration marked a definite rejection of a narrow conception of the functions of this organization and was, in fact, a bid on the part of the ILO for responsibilities of the type later assigned to the Economic and Social Council. It affirmed that "all human beings, irrespective of race, creed or sex, have the right to pursue both their material well-being and their spiritual development in conditions of freedom and dignity, of economic security and equal opportunity," and that the "attainment of the conditions in which this shall be possible must constitute the central aim of national and international policy."[28] The declaration further maintained that it was the responsibility of the ILO to examine all economic and financial policies and measures in the light of this fundamental objective, thus illustrating once again the tendency of international agencies concerned with any one major aspect of human

[28] "The Twenty-sixth Session of the International Labour Conference, Philadelphia, April–May 1944," *International Labour Review*, Vol. L (July 1944), p. 38.

relations to recognize the interdependence of all social and economic problems, and to stake out a claim to be heard in connection with all such problems.

Atlantic Charter and Article VII as Guidelines

The main lines of Anglo-American agreement on the course that should be followed in reconstructing international economic relations after the war were first laid down in the Atlantic Charter and in Article VII of the Mutual Aid Agreement between the United States and the United Kingdom of February 1942.[29] Both were in complete harmony with many conference resolutions and other international pronouncements of the interwar period.

The Atlantic Charter declared that the United States and the United Kingdom would endeavor, with due regard to their existing obligations, to further the enjoyment by all states of access on equal terms to the trade and raw materials of the world; that they desired to bring about the fullest collaboration among nations in obtaining for all improved labor standards, economic advancement, and social security; and that they hoped to establish a peace that would enable all men to live out their lives in freedom from fear and want.[30] These principles and objectives were incorporated in the Declaration by United Nations, which before the end of the war was adhered to by forty-seven countries;[31] and also in the famous Article VII of the Mutual Aid Agreement.

This article began by stating that in determining the benefits to be provided to the United States in return for lend-lease, the terms and conditions should "be such as not to burden commerce between the two countries, but to promote mutually advantageous economic relations between them and the betterment of world-wide economic relations." This most general aim was to be achieved by "agreed action . . . open to participation by all other countries of like mind, directed to the expansion, by appropriate international and domestic measures, of production, employment, and the exchange and consumption of goods . . . to the elimination of all forms of discriminatory treatment in

[29] Hereinafter referred to also as the Mutual Aid Agreement. For text of this agreement see U.S. Department of State *Bulletin*, Vol. 6 (Feb. 28, 1942), pp. 190–92.

[30] For text of the Atlantic Charter see U.S. Department of State *Bulletin*, Vol. 5 (Aug. 16, 1941), pp. 125–26.

[31] U.S. Department of State, *Toward the Peace, Documents*, Publication 2298 (1945), p. 2.

international commerce, and to the reduction of tariffs and other trade barriers." The principles of this article were, in one way or another, formally accepted by sixteen other governments before the end of the war, including the Soviet Union, China, and all the British Dominions except India.

The emphasis on employment and better standards of living in Article VII, and on improved labor standards, economic advancement, social security, and freedom from want in the Atlantic Charter, struck a note that was responsive to new currents of political and economic thought and feeling that had grown strong during the depression and war years. In simple language, it was carried forward in Article 55 of the United Nations Charter. But the word "development," which appears in Article 55 and which had so many implications for the work of the United Nations, is not to be found either in the Atlantic Charter or in Article VII. This is understandable, for both documents were the product of Anglo-American agreement and incorporated essentially the long-range economic objectives of the most highly developed of all nations, the United States.

These long-range objectives were stated most clearly in the references to nondiscrimination and reduction of trade barriers in Article VII and in the reference to "equal access" (a term never defined and impossible of precise definition) in the Atlantic Charter. But even here the interpretation to be put on the principle was obscured by the phrase "with due respect to existing obligations" in the Atlantic Charter (a phrase intended to safeguard imperial preference), and by the insistence of Great Britain that Article VII did not imply unilateral abandonment of the preference system. The failure of India to sign a mutual aid agreement containing Article VII was a warning that underdeveloped countries would not accept a policy of trade-barrier reduction that might interfere with their development programs. The acceptance of the article by the Soviet Union, whose economic system and policy were quite unsuited to any meaningful application of it, showed that the larger the number of nations, the more difficult it is to reach meaningful agreement on objectives in the field of trade and payments policy.

Because the establishment of a general world organization was completely speculative at the time Article VII was negotiated, the article did not look toward action by such an organization but toward agreed action by all countries "of like mind." The methods chosen were first, agreement between the United States and the United Kingdom and a few other major countries on principles and objectives; and second, agreement among a much larger number of countries at international conferences convened to draw up the basic instruments of new international organizations.

With the maturing of plans for the United Nations, a means was provided for shifting the sponsorship of such conferences from a small group of leading powers to a general international organization. But even before the United Nations was ready to assume this responsibility, a series of such conferences held under the aegis of Article VII demonstrated that the concept of agreed action by "like-minded countries" (another term extremely difficult to define) is quite different from the concept of agreed action by a world conference or, for that matter, by a regional conference. For in global and regional conferences the differences that have to be harmonized are not only differences on matters of secondary importance arising within a framework of common agreement on the general road to be traveled, but are the deep-seated cleavages on fundamental issues that arise among countries differently organized and in different stages of economic development.

Creation of New Agencies Under Article VII

Two months after the signature of the Mutual Aid Agreement between the United States and the United Kingdom in February 1942, a comprehensive proposal for postwar action in the fields of currency stabilization, international investment, food and agriculture, and all the various aspects of commercial policy was developed in the United States Treasury Department. This "single-package" approach emphasized the close interrelationships and mutual dependence of successful co-operation in all these fields. It did not prove practical, however, to include all of them in a single series of international negotiations. This would have required the solution of serious conflicts of jurisdiction between the various departments and agencies of the United States Government. These were not resolved, and the United States did not propose a "single-package" negotiation. Had it done so, there is little reason to suppose that similar conflicts of jurisdiction within other governments would not have arisen to complicate, if not to frustrate, negotiations of such an all-embracing character.

As a result, negotiations on commercial policy under Article VII on the one hand, and currency stabilization and international investment on the other, were carried on separately, and neither was closely related to negotiations in the field of food and agriculture. Although the principles of Article VII were also taken as a point of departure for negotiations in the fields of civil aviation and telecommunications, it was not until the autumn of 1945 that the United States sought to include these subjects in conversations that would parallel those on commercial policy. It was an oddity of Anglo-American leadership on postwar economic problems that this initiative was taken after, rather than before, an international conference on civil aviation. The actual approach to agreed action under Article VII was in fact not well coordinated in leadership, timing, or procedures. This was well illustrated at the outset by the selection of food and agriculture as the subject of the first major conference to be called under the aegis of this article.

Hot Springs Conference

During the Second World War, a group of men closely associated with the activities on nutrition of the League of Nations was actively preparing for an early revival of international co-operation in this field. Their plans and hopes made a strong appeal to President Roosevelt, who saw in them an opportunity to launch postwar economic and social co-operation among the United Nations in an area in which conflicts of view, at least as far as aims were concerned, would be less sharp than in the presumably more difficult fields of trade and finance. It was on his initiative that an international conference on food and agriculture, which led to the establishment of the Food and Agriculture Organization of the United Nations, was convened at Hot Springs, Virginia, in May 1943. This conference, therefore, became a sort of trial run in co-operation among the United Nations, and the selection of the subject of this trial run came as a surprise to most participants.[32]

The Hot Springs Conference was confronted both with a prospective short-run emergency food problem after the war and with the long-range problem of international co-operation to improve prewar standards of nutrition and food distribution throughout the world. The purport of its resolutions on the short-term problem was that governments should act in co-operation to increase production, to allocate supplies, and to prevent violent fluctuations in the prices of food, of instruments of production, and of other necessities including industrial goods, that might arise from unrestrained competition for inadequate supplies. On long-range policy, it made a comprehensive series of recommendations dealing not only with production policy as such, but with agricultural credit, co-operative movements, land tenure and farm labor, education and research, conservation of land and water resources, land settle-

---

[32] See the volume in this Brookings series, *A History of the United Nations Charter.*

ments for food production, occupational adjustments in rural population, and international commodity arrangements. It also made recommendations on the international distribution of food and on the organization of marketing.[33]

A fundamental question was raised in connection with proposed
resolutions on special international measures for wider food distribution.
In debating these resolutions the conference was in fact exploring not
only some of the practical limits of international collaboration between
sovereign states, but the moral and ethical basis of such collaboration
as well. Evidence showed that considerable numbers of people in certain
areas of the world were far from being able to meet minimum energy
needs and that the physical development of some of these people appeared to be retarded by insufficient food, while at the same time some
of the large food-exporting countries were unable to dispose of their
exportable supplies and were taking restrictive measures to reduce these
"surpluses." The continuation of such a situation was felt by some participants to be not only inconsistent with mutually advantageous international relations but also intolerable from a humanitarian and moral
point of view. Although the conference did not take decisive action on
this issue, it called upon the future Food and Agriculture Organization
to study the whole problem.

The resolutions and recommendations of the Hot Springs Conference
read very much like a check-list of the problems that later confronted
not only the Food and Agriculture Organization but also the other
economic and social organs of the United Nations. Frequent references
will be made to them at later points in this study, and it will be shown
that two of the most fundamental problems have not yet found any
generally acceptable solution. The stability of raw-material prices was
an issue that had become acute during the depression and continues to
raise extremely difficult technical as well as political issues. The international distribution of food supplies involved a question that was as
much ethical as it was economic: whether the existence of gross inequalities in available food supplies imposes a moral obligation on the more
favored nations to come to the aid of the less favored.

Bretton Woods Conference

The calling of the Hot Springs Conference was considered by important British officials to be a diversion from the main stream of ne-

[33] Ernest F. Penrose, *Economic Planning for the Peace* (1953), p. 125.

gotiation under Article VII of the Mutual Aid Agreement, which was concerned with commercial and foreign exchange policy and international investment. But even the main stream of these negotiations had been diverted into two channels: the Article VII conversations on commercial policy; and the negotiations for new agencies in the field of foreign exchange and investment, which were both started and concluded earlier than the commercial policy conversations.

Before the entry of the United States into the war, plans were being made for an inter-American stabilization fund, and plans for an inter-American bank had reached the stage at which a convention for such a bank had been submitted to the Congress for ratification. When the global postwar foreign economic objectives of the United States were formulated in Article VII, these two inter-American projects were dropped in favor of plans for a fund and a bank whose operations would be world-wide. These plans were the subject of intensive negotiations, lasting more than two years, before the convening of a conference at Bretton Woods to draw up articles of agreement for the two institutions. The negotiations were largely taken up by attempts to reconcile an American plan for a fund and a British proposal for an international clearing union. During these negotiations and at the conference itself, a large number of important issues, particularly between the United States and the United Kingdom, were compromised, and the compromises were incorporated in the Articles of Agreement of the International Monetary Fund.

For example, a preliminary issue that had to be decided before substantial progress could be made in drawing up the Articles of Agreement was whether the resources of the International Monetary Fund should be used to assist in solving the economic problems of the transition, or be reserved to assist member countries in stabilizing their exchange rates after reconstruction problems were solved. The United Kingdom took the position that they should be used for both purposes, whereas the United States wished them to be used for the second only, because it assumed that the transition would be short and that, except in times of seasonal and cyclical disturbance, resources to maintain exchange stability would soon be available from other sources. On this issue, the view of the United States prevailed, and one consequence of this was that the International Monetary Fund (IMF) was actually designed to meet a set of conditions that have not, up to the time of writing, been characteristic of international economic relations.

Another important issue settled at Bretton Woods had to do with foreign exchange rates. Although several of the smaller countries argued in favor of flexibility in exchange rates, there was general agreement that the promotion of exchange stability in a free market should be a major objective of the IMF. At Bretton Woods, there was, however, a serious Anglo-American disagreement regarding the concept of stability that should be applied, even though both countries agreed that it should not be identified with rigidly fixed rates. The United States position was that exchange rates should be altered only if there was a fundamental disequilibrium and only by a four-fifths vote of the Fund. This would, under weighted voting, have given a veto power over most proposed exchange-rate changes to the United States. To many British critics, this seemed too much like a return to the gold standard, even though prior international agreement on exchange rates was a radical departure from gold-standard principles. The United Kingdom wished to avoid any commitments that seemed to bind it in advance to fixed rates, and it was unwilling to give any international organization veto powers on such a vital matter as the sterling-dollar rate. A compromise was worked out that preserved the principle of international agreement on proposed changes, yet left the initiative and considerable freedom of action to vary rates within wide limits to the members of the Fund.

In its proposal for a clearing union and indeed throughout the negotiations, the British, with support from other countries, laid great stress on the responsibilities of creditor countries, the United States in particular, to correct their international creditor position by appropriate commercial and investment policy, and on their obligations pending such correction to supply the world markets with their own currency in sufficient amounts to relieve the heavy pressures on debtor countries. The United States resented the implication that the principal creditor country was to be held primarily—even solely—responsible for the balance-of-payments difficulties of all the other members of the Fund, and successfully insisted on safeguards that restricted access to the resources of the Fund and limited the obligations of the United States.

Closely related to the issue of creditor as well as debtor responsibilities for correcting balance-of-payments difficulties was the question how far the Fund should be allowed to go in making recommendations with respect to the internal policies of its members affecting their balances of payments. Although the original British plan had made some provision for such recommendations when the resources of the proposed clearing union had been heavily drawn upon, the British, Australian, and many other delegations were not willing to accept any commitments under the Fund that would require them to change their domestic economic and social policies in order to put their balances of payments in order. They held that if the principal creditor, the United States, did not take the necessary steps to correct its own imbalance on the credit side, the debtor countries were fully justified in maintaining or resorting to exchange controls or in altering their exchange rates if this were necessary to avoid deflationary measures that might lead to unemployment.

The vigor with which this point of view was pressed is to be explained largely in terms of the basic national attitudes developed as a result of the experience of the depression years. Although the United States was reluctant to accept this view, at least in the extreme form in which it was sometimes presented, it was agreed at Bretton Woods that the Fund should not refuse a request from a member for a change in its exchange rates if such a change were necessitated by the social and economic policies of that member.

The issue of domestic jurisdiction was one of several major problems that complicated negotiations with the Soviet Union, both for the Fund and the International Bank for Reconstruction and Development (IBRD). Soviet experts doubted whether the Soviet Union, in view of its totally different economic organization, could be fitted into the proposed agencies, and they sought exemptions from many of the suggested commitments. They also pressed for numerous exceptions in their favor on the ground that special treatment should be accorded to countries that had been invaded by the enemy. They strongly resisted any commitment to supply information of the kind usually regarded as appropriate and indeed essential before the resources of lending agencies, international or otherwise, are made available to borrowers.

Aside from these special difficulties with the Soviet Union, the negotiators of the Bank at Bretton Woods had to reconcile several other cleavages in national viewpoints. The British viewed the operations of the Bank as almost entirely in the form of guarantees, with only a limited role for direct loans from paid-in subscriptions. As a result, paid-in subscriptions were restricted to 20 per cent of total subscriptions, of which 18 per cent was to be in local currency, which could not be utilized for loans except with the consent of the member whose currency was involved. The remaining 2 per cent was to be paid in gold or dollars.

At the Bretton Woods Conference, the Latin American participants attempted to have half of the resources of the IBRD earmarked for development, and although they failed in this, they succeeded in having development added to the name of the Bank and having equal emphasis put on reconstruction and development in its Articles of Agreement. Another cleavage of opinion arose from the desire of the United States to confine the lending operations of the Bank to specific projects that directly increase the productivity of the borrowing country. The wish of many other delegations to have the Bank given authority to make restocking and stabilization loans was, however, met to the extent of allowing the Bank to make loans other than project loans "in special circumstances."[34] Moreover, the loans of the Bank, in accordance with the statement of purpose of the Bank in Article I of its Articles of Agreement, were to be made only when private capital was unavailable on reasonable terms; also, under Article V, Section 8, the Bank was to co-operate with any general international organization and with public international organizations having responsibility in related fields, and to give consideration to the views and recommendations of such organizations in making loans and guarantees relating to matters falling directly within their competence. These two provisions were a potential source of conflict with organs and agencies of the United Nations in which the underdeveloped countries were numerous and united in purpose.

Both the Hot Springs and Bretton Woods conferences recognized that their work was incomplete without international agreement on principles of commercial policy. Both passed resolutions urging governments to seek early agreement on ways and means to reduce obstacles to international trade, and in the resolutions adopted at Bretton Woods stress was also laid on co-operation to maintain high levels of employment and to bring about the orderly marketing of staple commodities at prices fair to the producer and consumer alike.

These resolutions pointed up a problem of co-ordination that had been rendered doubly acute by the very conferences that passed them. By bringing the Food and Agriculture Organization, the Fund, and the Bank into existence before the charter of an international trade organization had been drawn up, they foreclosed any possibility of a truly integrated approach to closely related problems. Commodity policy, with which the Food and Agriculture Organization was much concerned, was an integral part of the Article VII conversations on commercial policy, and in many ways commercial policy and foreign

[34] Art. III, Sec. 4 (vii), U.S. Department of State, *United Nations Monetary and Financial Conference, Bretton Woods, N.H., July 1 to July 22, 1944: Final Act and Related Documents*, Publication 2187 (1944), p. 73.

exchange policy are more intimately related to each other than investment policy is to either. Exchange controls and direct trade controls, for example, are often alternative means of achieving the same objectives, and there is a close relationship between the inconvertibility of currencies and discrimination in trade. It is doubtful, however, whether —as a practical matter—this problem could have been solved when the new agencies were being created, by entrusting responsibility for international co-operation in both fields to a single international body, inasmuch as co-operation in the field of currency stabilization required contributions of large resources that would not have been forthcoming without a system of weighted voting such as that provided for in the Fund.

Conversations on Commercial Policy

When the Bretton Woods Conference passed a resolution urging governments to agree on principles of commercial policy, the conversations on commercial policy under Article VII had just begun. For a period of eighteen months after the signature of the Anglo-American Mutual Aid Agreement, the United States and United Kingdom had been engaged in an effort to resolve conflicts of opinion within their respective countries sufficiently to justify the opening of these conversations. The first of them took place in October 1943 between American and British experts, and in the early months of 1944, between American and Canadian experts. Although contact was maintained among the experts of the three governments, these conversations were not formally renewed until the summer of 1945.

In the interval, the United States Government prepared a draft of a multilateral convention, including a draft charter for an international trade organization, which incorporated a code of conduct on the main subjects dealt with in the conversations—commercial policy, cartel policy, commodity policy, and employment. This code was modified in the second part of the conversations in the summer of 1945, and the whole negotiation was concluded in the autumn of 1945 when the British agreed in principle to the main points of the "Proposals for Consideration by an International Conference on Trade and Employment."[35]

---

[35] U.S. Department of State, *Proposals for Expansion of World Trade and Employment*, Publication 2411 (November 1945), pp. 8–28.

The history of these conversations provides an excellent illustration of the point made elsewhere in this study that there cannot be a co-ordinated approach to economic co-operation through international agencies unless there is a co-ordinated approach within the governmental structure of major countries. Of the total period of three and one-half years from the signature of the Mutual Aid Agreement to an accord in principle on the proposals, about three years were spent mainly in efforts to compromise domestic differences of opinion on the issues involved.

The proposals provided for a separate undertaking on the part of governments to seek full employment, under which each of the signatory nations would agree to take action "designed to achieve and maintain full employment within its own jurisdiction." They would also agree to refrain from seeking to "maintain employment through measures which are likely to create unemployment in other countries or which are incompatible with international undertakings designed to promote an expanding volume of international trade and investment in accordance with the comparative efficiencies of production." They further specified that nations signatory to the full-employment undertaking should make "arrangements," both individually and collectively, under the general sponsorship of the Economic and Social Council of the United Nations Organization, "for the collection, analysis, and exchange of information on employment problems, trends, and policies," and that they should "under the general sponsorship of the Economic and Social Council, consult regularly on employment problems and hold special conferences in case of a threat of widespread unemployment."[36]

A separate agency in the field of commodity policy was strongly supported by both British and American spokesmen for agriculture, and it was not until late in the negotiations that commodity policy was included in the scope of the proposed international trade organization. In the Article VII conversations, there was concurrence from the start that the prewar experience with commodity agreements largely dominated by producer interests should not be repeated, and that there was need for entrusting the responsibilities in this field to some international agency. It was much more difficult, however, to reach a basic solution on one important substantive question that cut across national lines. This question was whether the regulation of production and exports should be regarded as a normal, permanent feature of commodity agreements or an exceptional and temporary expedient to tide over special difficulties and be discarded as soon as possible. The latter conception was finally incorporated in the statement of principles governing commodity agreements that appeared in the proposals. In its essentials, this was carried over into the Havana Charter. The United Nations, therefore, was able to take Chapter VI of the Havana Charter as a point of reference in its discussions of commodity agreements.

A similar point of reference for United Nations discussions was provided in Chapter V of the Havana Charter, which dealt with restrictive business practices. The basic content of this chapter was also determined in the Article VII conversations, but it did not represent any real meeting of minds between the United States and the United Kingdom, whose views in this respect were shared by most European governments. The feasible limits of international co-operation in dealing with restrictive business practices affecting international trade were found to be not the acceptance of detailed commitments, as in commercial policy, nor agreement to act on a formal set of principles as in commodity policy, but merely agreement to follow certain procedures. What was really agreed to was the idea that the proposed international trade organization should in this area receive complaints, make recommendations, and request information on measures taken to carry out these recommendations. These were all procedures capable of being applied and later frequently applied (as in the Trusteeship Council) by some of the principal organs of the United Nations.

The proposals affirmed the principle of unconditional most-favored-nation treatment—a principle that the Economic Intelligence Service of the League of Nations had previously upheld. They laid down rules of conduct in technical matters, and they linked together much more closely than had the interwar conferences the related problems of tariff reduction and the elimination of preferences. Like the League of Nations Prohibitions and Restrictions Convention of 1927, they contained a general prohibition on quantitative restrictions, but with exceptions not contained in that convention, the two most important of which were the balance-of-payments exception, a major concern of the United Kingdom, and an agricultural exception directly related to the commitments made by the United States Government to American agricultural producers.

Agreement was also reached in the conversations on one major question of procedure in tariff matters. This was the question whether tariff reductions should be sought by some type of horizontal percentage cut agreed to in a single multilateral negotiation, or whether they should be sought through negotiations between pairs of countries. The former position was strongly maintained by the United Kingdom representatives, whereas the latter was the traditional method under the Trade Agreements Program of the United States and probably the only method acceptable to the United States Congress. Mainly for this reason, the horizontal reduction method was not accepted, but certain multilateral features were introduced through proposed negotiations for mutual concessions by groups of countries acting simultaneously.

It was the intention of the United States and the United Kingdom to hold the door open for eventual participation by the Soviet Union in the proposed trade organization. For this purpose, a state-trading formula was devised, which required state-trading countries to carry out their international trade on commercial principles, and to observe special rules, appropriate to their form of economic organization, which would have an effect equivalent to that of the commitments undertaken by other countries on the reduction of trade barriers and the elimination of discrimination.

Although the Soviet Union had accepted Article VII in its Mutual Aid Agreement with the United States, its representatives abroad made no secret of their suspicion of its basic aims. Even while the conversations were in progress, they left no doubt that, in their view, the real object of the advanced industrialized countries in advocating freer trade was to hold the market for manufactured goods in less developed countries and to check the industrialization of these countries.[37]

In the Article VII conversations, the interests of countries dependent mainly on raw material production were taken seriously into account in the exploration of buffer stocks and other devices to damp down fluctuations in the prices of primary commodities. The exclusion of this subject from the proposals was due more to the inherent difficulties that surround the practical operation of all such devices than to a lack of understanding of the importance attached to it by such countries. The viewpoint of the underdeveloped countries was also considered in another way, but with equally negative results. These countries were then, and have since remained, strong advocates of the traditional argument for high protection for infant industries. It was therefore suggested that this point of view might be met halfway by proposing fresh

[37] Penrose, *op. cit.*, p. 112.

exceptions, in the interest of economic development, to the ban on quantitative restrictions; but it was finally decided to postpone this issue until the Conference on Trade and Employment.

Civil Aviation and Telecommunications

The drive for the creation of new agencies under the general principles laid down in Article VII of the various mutual aid agreements was also a feature of wartime preparations for postwar co-operation in the field of transportation and communication. The major initiative was taken by the United States, which convened an international conference on civil aviation in Chicago in November 1944. This cut short efforts then being made to revive the work of the International Commission on Air Navigation.

At the conference in Chicago four basic documents were drawn up: an Interim Agreement on International Civil Aviation establishing a Provisional International Civil Aviation Organization; a permanent Convention on International Civil Aviation establishing a permanent International Civil Aviation Organization to which were attached twelve technical annexes; and two agreements relating to what came to be known as the Five Air Freedoms, which were to be administered in accordance with the principles of the interim agreement and the convention.

The first two of these freedoms were nontraffic freedoms. They provided for the privileges of flying across the territory of another nation and of landing for nontraffic purposes only. The third and fourth freedoms provided for the privileges of discharging and loading passengers, mail, and cargo coming from or destined for the home nation of an aircraft. The fifth freedom permitted the loading and discharging of passengers and cargo destined for and coming from any other nation. Thus, for example, an airline of country A would be permitted to load and discharge traffic between countries B and C in both of these countries.

Canada proposed an agreement on the first four freedoms, but the United Kingdom was unwilling to accept the third and the fourth, and the United States, whose aviation industry was certain to be in a strong competitive position after the war, insisted on the fifth freedom. The fifth freedom was also opposed even more strongly by the United Kingdom and by many other countries. This difference among nations was responsible for the drafting of the two air agreements for submission to prospective members of the international organization, one of which included only the first two freedoms, the International Air Services Transit Agreement, and one which included all five, the International Air Transport Agreement.[38]

The participants in the conference were also sharply divided on the question whether an international agency should be given authority to fix rates, capacities, and frequencies. The United Kingdom and some other countries favored such an agency, and Canada went even further by proposing that it should be given authority also to fix routes. To all this, the United States was strongly opposed. No agreement could be reached on these issues, and the convention consequently concerned itself mainly with technical matters, although it gave the new organization the function of studying and making recommendations on unsettled issues and provided a recourse to advisory and recommendatory powers assigned to the new international organization in regard, for example, to such matters as disputes over charges imposed for the use of airports and other disputes concerning these two agreements.

The period immediately following the Chicago conference was one in which a great number of very complex international civil aviation problems were under constant negotiation. Among these were the revival of air transport in Europe, the rights of passage over and entry into countries of Eastern Europe under Soviet influence, rights of entry of foreign aircraft into the Soviet Union itself, the disposition of the vast system of air bases and air arrangements of a military kind that had been built up by the United States during the war, and other similar problems. Many countries, including Britain, were reluctant to assume long-range international commitments on civil aviation until solutions of these problems had been worked out.

At the same time, countries, particularly in Europe where a chaotic condition prevailed, were being confronted with very urgent problems concerning radio frequencies. A conference on civil radio frequencies of liberated countries was held in London in September 1945, while at the same time an Inter-American telecommunication conference was being held in Rio de Janeiro. Suggestions were made for dealing with the frequency problem in Europe through a single agency on an interim basis, pending a permanent solution of the problem of international priority at a conference of the International Telecommunication Union or otherwise.[39]

---

[38] On the fate of these two agreements, see below, Chap. VI.
[39] On these conferences, see below, Chap. VI.

Inter-American Conference at
Mexico City

At various points in the foregoing survey of wartime preparations for postwar collaboration, it has been necessary to stress the special viewpoint of the underdeveloped countries. The general attitude of these countries on commercial policy and other economic questions was brought to sharp focus in the Inter-American Conference on Problems of War and Peace held in Mexico City in February–March 1945.

Although this conference was concerned mainly with political and security questions, there were two important economic items on its agenda: economic co-operation during the war and transition period, and consideration of methods to develop such co-operation for the improvement of the economic and social conditions of the people of the Americas.

The most urgent economic concerns of the Latin American countries at the time were that: (1) a sudden termination of huge wartime procurement contracts from the United States would precipitate social and economic disturbances; (2) the resumption of trade after the war on prewar patterns would compel the Latin American countries to relinquish much that had been gained in the field of industrialization since 1940; (3) the dollar balances accumulated during the war by Latin American nations would lose part of their purchasing power or be spent for imports not essential for economic development; (4) the Latin American countries would not receive an "equitable" share of available capital goods after the end of the war as compared to other areas; and (5) a decline in raw material prices would menace the stability of their economies.

The first of these fears was the product of the special economic relations between Latin America and the United States during the war, and did not have general significance for the United Nations. This was not true of the others. Although not all underdeveloped countries had made the same progress toward industrialization as had some Latin American countries, many of them attached primary importance to industrialization as the key to economic development and stability. They therefore shared the Latin American concern regarding the possible effects on their development plans of a resumption of prewar patterns of trade, and this point of view was repeatedly expounded in United Nations debates. The idea that underdeveloped countries had a right in times of scarcity to an "equitable" share of capital goods, and in times of inflation to safeguards against any fall in the purchasing power of their foreign exchange holdings—and that the advanced countries had an obligation to do something about this—also recurred regularly in United Nations debates in times of strain or crisis. The importance attached to measures for stabilizing primary commodities was, as has been already noted, a recurrent theme in other wartime negotiations and continued to be so under the United Nations.

Although the United States met these viewpoints halfway at the Inter-American Conference on Problems of War and Peace, there was no real harmony of views on certain basic long-run policies. The United States attempted at the conference to incorporate in the Economic Charter of the Americas the principle of free enterprise and the general commercial policy principles that were under discussion in the Article VII conversations. It was not successful, however, in including in this charter a declaration against the establishment of state enterprises for the conduct of trade, or a declaration that the reduction of trade barriers was an unequivocal aim of policy. The Latin American countries were not even willing to include in the charter a paragraph condemning the evils of economic nationalism, but only the evils of "excessive nationalism."[40] On trade policy, the lines of cleavage were very clearly drawn.

On the other hand, there was agreement on many forms of economic and social co-operation. The United States, for example, declared its intention to propose and support measures for closer co-operation among the American countries in public health, nutrition and food supply, labor, education, science, freedom of information, transportation, and economic development, including industrialization and the modernization of agriculture. These were all areas of co-operation that were soon to gain prominence in the efforts of the United Nations system to promote the welfare of underdeveloped countries.

The Legacy in Brief

Had the United Nations been content merely to continue or expand prewar forms of collaboration and new forms that emerged during the war, its task would have been definite and its objectives clear. The United Nations, however, was from the outset confronted with national

[40] U.S. Department of State, *Report of the Delegation of the United States of America to the Inter-American Conference on Problems of War and Peace, Mexico City, February 21–March 8, 1945,* Publication 2497 (1946), p. 123.

attitudes and aspirations that had never before occupied the center of the stage under traditional forms of international collaboration, in particular the preoccupation of its Members with full employment, economic development, and economic stability.

The preparations made during the war for new approaches to international co-operation on long-range economic and social problems were in striking contrast to the almost complete neglect of postwar economic problems during the First World War. They were significant for the United Nations in two principal ways. In the first place, they demonstrated that the lines of cleavage among the industrialized countries and between them and underdeveloped countries that had been intensified by the depression of the 1930's were not transitory. In the second place, they posed important organizational problems for the United Nations by creating new agencies that were already in being before the United Nations itself was organized. The United Nations was consequently, at the outset, confronted with the difficult problem of determining how meaningful the relations between its own organs and these agencies could be made. Were they to be purely formal? Were the organs of the United Nations to be confined to the fringes of the problems that were the special province of these new agencies; or were they to become an active force in harmonizing views and solving problems in the areas of their concern?

In recommending policies and selecting methods for promoting the economic and social objectives specified in the Charter, the members of the United Nations were confronted with a situation of almost infinite complexity. They had in the first place to provide the specialization necessary for effective action. Second, they had to consolidate the component parts into an over-all effort to achieve common objectives, and as a result to embark on an almost constant search for means of achieving co-ordination. Third, they had to harmonize, as far as possible, national viewpoints within each of the specialized fields in such a way that they would contribute to the pursuit of over-all objectives. The new organization therefore had to analyze economic and social problems and their interrelationships, to increase mutual understanding of national aims and aspirations, and to promote forms of political accommodation that would make it possible to deal with acutely controversial economic and social issues.

This formidable task was begun at a time when the true dimensions of the postwar reconstruction problem had not yet been disclosed. The time and resources needed to solve this problem were generally underestimated, and wartime preparations for an orderly transition to peace-time conditions were generally thought to be adequate. The extent to which the fledgling United Nations system would be called upon to deal with emergency problems for which it was not prepared was not fore-seen. This led to unexpected difficulties in harmonizing national atti-tudes toward some forms of long-range co-operation, because countries preoccupied with urgent short-run problems would not, and often could not, commit themselves in advance to follow policies that were de-sirable and appropriate in normal times. This would not in all prob-ability have been a major obstacle to the advancement of the economic objectives of the Charter if there had been a sufficient measure of inter-national agreement on what was desirable and appropriate in the long run. Unfortunately, despite the compromises reached at the Hot Springs, Bretton Woods, and Chicago conferences, and during the Anglo-American discussions on commercial policy under Article VII of the Mutual Aid Agreement, the prospective members of the United Nations remained divided on many important economic and social issues.

Economic Issues

One of the most important of these issues was the extent to which liberal commercial and foreign exchange policies should be subordi-nated to full-employment policies. Absolute priority for full employ-ment was being insisted on by Australia, and the position of the United Kingdom on this question was almost, if not quite, as strong. The United States was taking the more traditional and more long-range view that employment policy should not stand in the way of desirable economic adjustments brought about by the reduction of trade barriers and the elimination of trade discrimination, which would make a solid contribution to higher standards of living. The United States was not without supporters, but the countries inclined toward the British and Australian views were in the majority.

This conflict was closely related to, and in part responsible for, the raising of another issue on which there was an equally sharp clash of national viewpoints. During the negotiations leading up to the Bretton Woods Conference, Great Britain had fought for the principle of making creditor countries assume heavy international responsibilities for cor-recting their favorable balances of payments so that debtor countries would not have to carry the whole burden of making the economic adjustments required to restore or maintain international equilibrium. The United States, on the other hand, insisted that, as in the past, countries in balance-of-payments difficulties were responsible for putting their balances of payments in order.

Although shortly after the end of the war a large measure of agreement on commercial policy had been reached in principle by the United States and the United Kingdom, the issues that divided the various nations in this field were still numerous. The underdeveloped countries had made it clear that they did not accept the reduction of trade barriers as an unequivocal aim of policy, because they believed that the protection of new industries was indispensable for the carrying out of their development plans. Many of these countries saw positive advantages in the use of quantitative import restrictions in the interests of development, while the United States and Great Britain had agreed that such restrictions should be condemned in principle, even though this principle was diluted by major exceptions.

The attention of the underdeveloped countries was concentrated on the removal of all possible obstacles to the early fulfillment of their development plans. Among these were the possible loss of purchasing power of their foreign exchange reserves in times of inflation, and the instability of the prices of the primary commodities that were their principal exports. It was already clear that on questions of commodity policy, the underdeveloped countries would probably not see eye-to-eye with the major industrialized countries.

Another issue on which there was no common international approach at the end of the war was that of cartels. Most countries were agreed that cartels should not be allowed to have harmful effects on international trade, but the question whether cartels were contributing to orderly trade and to general economic stability, or had harmful effects was a bone of contention between the United States and many European countries. In addition, there was no real agreement on the principles that should govern international aviation and shipping. At the end of the war, the United States, because of the strong competitive position of its aviation industry, took a free-trade attitude (a stand it later reversed) toward international aviation, and on this, it was opposed by nearly all other countries. In the field of shipping, however, in which the American competitive position was not strong, both the American position and that of the principal maritime powers were exactly the opposite of the positions taken with respect to aviation.

In many cases in which the United States found itself ranged against other countries on specific issues of commercial, monetary, commodity, and transport policy, the main reason was its greater commitment to and belief in the virtues of free competitive enterprise. Confronted with immense problems of reconstruction and deeply committed to the principles of a welfare state, countries such as the United Kingdom felt compelled to rely heavily on economic planning and on a system of economic controls. Most underdeveloped countries believed that the allocation of resources to carry out development programs, including the resources derived from foreign investment, had to be guided by the state. Very few countries therefore shared the American conviction that reconstruction and development should be financed mainly by private capital investment.

Social and Political Issues

At the end of the war, opinion seemed much more united on proposals for collaboration to promote humanitarian, cultural, and social objectives than they were on basic economic issues. American initiative played a major role in the establishment of the Food and Agriculture Organization, partly because the prospects of expanding the work of the League of Nations for better nutrition and improved standards of living for masses of people living on near-subsistence levels had stirred the imagination of the President. American support for the far-reaching economic measures required to make this program effective, however, was much more reserved. Humanitarian considerations widely shared by all nontotalitarian countries also played a role in the establishment of the International Refugee Organization, the World Health Organization, and the United Nations Educational, Scientific and Cultural Organization, and in the adoption of the Declaration of Philadelphia by the International Labour Organisation. Even in these areas, however, there were some major differences in national attitude. These differences were well illustrated by the debates on the functions of UNESCO.[41]

At the time the United Nations Charter was signed, there were already many indications that fruitful co-operation with the Soviet Union on economic and social questions might be extremely difficult. The Soviet Union had made no secret of its suspicion that the liberal trade objectives of Article VII of the mutual aid agreements cloaked a design on the part of industrialized countries to preserve their export markets for manufactured goods at the expense of the development of

[41] See below, Chap. IX.

underdeveloped countries. Patient efforts to adjust the Articles of Agreement of the Fund and those of the Bank so as to meet the special requirements of the Soviet Union had not led that government to accept membership in these institutions. The Soviet Union refused to participate in the Chicago Aviation Conference of 1944, and at the end of the war, it was clear that the aircraft of other countries for some time to come would not be allowed to fly over Soviet territory. On the question of repatriation of refugees, which was to be a major concern of the IRO, there was an irreconcilable breach between the Soviet Union and the members of the UNRRA Council. Many important problems that were being actively canvassed by other countries were of no interest to the Soviet Union—for example, the relationships that should prevail between foreign trade and employment policies and the measures that might be taken to prevent the spread of depressions internationally. The Soviet Union was hostile to the ILO and considered its tripartite representation of government, employers, and workers as a major impediment to Soviet participation.

Despite the wide range of international disagreement on fundamental economic and social problems that existed at the time the Charter of the United Nations was signed, the general atmosphere that surrounded the drafters of the Charter was one of hope, even of enthusiasm, for a new era of international economic and social collaboration. There was a determination not to fall back into the economic anarchy of the depression years and to make new advances toward ameliorating the lot of masses of people through international collaboration on problems of health, education, and social welfare. In such an atmosphere, the lions in the path did not look excessively fierce or dangerous, and the path to be traveled seemed smoother and straighter than it really was.

CHAPTER II

Action in Emergency Situations*

ALTHOUGH it was recognized at the end of the Second World War that a welter of relief and reconstruction problems required the immediate attention of the United Nations, it was assumed that the new international organization would soon be able to concentrate exclusively on other matters. There was little realization of the extent to which the United Nations would continue during its first decade to be concerned with programs for meeting emergencies.

For the most part, the programs considered below were designed to provide short-term aid in connection with special problems arising in the wake of wars, floods, droughts, earthquakes, epidemics, and similar disasters not directly attributable to the functioning of the economic system. Some of these programs were intended to carry on activities initiated by the United Nations Relief and Rehabilitation Administration (UNRRA) after the liquidation of that agency, and all profited from the experience gained by it.[1] Of the four major United Nations programs to provide relief in the wake of war, two—the program of emergency assistance to needy children, and the program for the care and resettlement of the remaining refugees of the Second World War—are lineal descendants of UNRRA programs.

While the United Nations was still wrestling with the problem of refugees of the Second World War, it was compelled to assume a measure of responsibility for the refugees of two later wars. A new agency was created within the United Nations for the purpose of aiding the Arab refugees displaced from Palestine by the Arab-Israeli conflict. Refugee assistance required by the homeless as a result of the Korean war, however, was administered as part of the general relief and reconstruction program for the area rather than through a special refugee organization.

Concurrently with the operation of its emergency relief and rehabilitation programs, the United Nations system engaged in various actions

---

* By Robert E. Asher. Portions of this chapter are based on materials prepared by Louis Lazaroff.

[1] For information on the legacy bequeathed by UNRRA, see above, Chap. I, and the volume in this Brookings series, *The United Nations and Promotion of the General Welfare*, Part One.

to relieve the acute food shortage that characterized the immedi
postwar period and to develop machinery for handling future famin
The allocation functions of the wartime Combined Food Board wei
continued by successor agencies until 1949; *ad hoc* assistance was or
ganized in a few disaster situations; and much thought was given to
proposals, first for a World Food Board, later, for an International Commodity Clearing House, and still later, for a Famine Reserve. These
proposals, developed primarily in the Food and Agriculture Organization (FAO), would have required the assumption by international
agencies of more comprehensive responsibilities than key governments
were prepared to vest in them. By 1952, measures for mobilizing famine
relief had been divorced from other more controversial aspects of agricultural policy. No new international machinery was established to
provide foodstuffs in future famine emergencies, but agreement was
reached on arrangements for spotting potential famines and co-ordinating the voluntary efforts of nations to relieve them. Relatively little attention was devoted to the related problems involved in meeting potential emergency requirements for clothing, shelter, and other non-
food items.

During 1951 and 1952, another arm of the United Nations—the Collective Measures Committee of the General Assembly—undertook a
study of the measures that might be invoked in the gravest emergency
with which an international agency can be confronted—a threat to or a
breach of the peace. The committee considered not only the political
and military measures but also the economic and financial measures
that might be invoked to deter or weaken an aggressor nation, to aid
the victims of aggression, and to permit an equitable sharing of the cost
of collective action among co-operating countries. Although the entire
range of United Nations preparations to meet aggression is analyzed
and appraised elsewhere in this series,[2] the economic and financial
measures are reviewed here, in the context of emergency actions of an
economic and social character.

Relief and Rehabilitation
in the Wake of War

UNRRA financed a broad range of relief and rehabilitation services
to war-devastated areas in two continents. After the termination of

[2] See the volume in this Brookings series, *The United Nations and the Maintenance
of International Peace and Security.*

e program the United States financed a bilateral Post-UNRRA Relief
rogram and an Interim Aid Program to provide further grant assist-
ince to Austria, China, Greece, Italy, and certain other countries. These
were followed in 1948 by the European Recovery Program, which was
also initiated by the United States and was also operated outside the
United Nations framework.

The United Nations inherited from UNRRA, however, certain residual relief problems of the Second World War. It met these and the
new relief problems of two later wars by establishing four temporary
operating agencies: the United Nations International Children's Emergency Fund to help meet the needs of children; the International
Refugee Organization to care for and help resettle the remaining refugees of the Second World War; the United Nations Relief and Works
Agency for Palestine Refugees in the Near East, to aid Arab refugees
of the Arab-Israeli War; and the United Nations Korean Reconstruction Agency to bring succor to the victims of aggression in Korea.

Aid to Needy Children

The United Nations International Children's Emergency Fund
(UNICEF) was established by the General Assembly in December 1946
to utilize some of the residual funds of UNRRA for work that, with the
anticipated termination of the agency, threatened to come to a stop.[3] In
countries devastated by war, UNICEF was to aid needy children, nursing mothers, and pregnant women. It was to provide food, clothing, and
medical supplies, which were to be distributed, in accordance with
UNRRA principles, on the basis of need and without regard to race,
creed, nationality status, or political belief. Work was to be carried out
in co-operation with permanent international agencies such as the
World Health Organization, and only with the consent of the governments of the countries aided.

Total pledges and contributions to UNICEF from all sources during
its first three and one half years, from 1947 to mid-1950, amounted to
nearly $150 million, exclusive of the "internal matching" contributions
made by countries receiving UNICEF aid to meet locally incurred expenses and to make the program a properly co-operative undertaking.
Of the $150 million, approximately $32 million came from the residual
assets of UNRRA. Government contributions, mostly from the United

[3] Res. 57(I), Dec. 11, 1946.

States, accounted for $105 million. The balance of nearly $13 million came from voluntary private contributions and included the share of UNICEF of the funds raised by the world-wide United Nations Appeals for Children.

The aid was used to furnish: (1) dried skim milk, fats, fishliver oils, and some meat, for supplementing the diets of 4 to 8 million children per year; (2) cotton, wool, and leather for processing in the receiving countries into clothing, blankets, layettes, and shoes for 6 million children; (3) transport, medical equipment and supplies—and salaries for some professional personnel—for one of the largest mass immunization programs ever undertaken: the testing of 17 million children for tuberculosis and the giving of BCG vaccinations to 9 million; (4) imported equipment for milk-drying and milk-pasteurizing plants; (5) aid in building national child health and welfare services; and (6) insecticides, penicillin, and vaccines for the control of communicable children's diseases.[4]

Initially, the work of the Children's Fund was confined overwhelmingly to Europe, but as war-created needs began to be met and as impediments to freedom of operations in Eastern Europe increased, the focus shifted from Europe to the underdeveloped countries. By mid-1950, UNICEF had become a world-wide operation functioning in Asia, Latin America, the Middle East, and North Africa as well as in Europe. The General Assembly late in 1950 recognized that the initial emergency assignment of UNICEF had been substantially completed and, in effect, placed it on a trial basis as a permanent agency. On December 1, it extended the life of the organization for another three years, and officially ratified the shift in emphasis from meeting short-range requirements in Europe to meeting long-range child health and welfare needs in the underdeveloped countries.[5]

The action of the General Assembly was a defeat for the United States delegation, which had tried in the Social Commission, the Economic and Social Council, and the General Assembly to obtain support for reducing drastically the scope and operations of the agency. Member states from Asia and the Middle East argued vigorously and effectively against curtailment merely because "the emergency was over in

---

[4] U.N. General Assembly, Fifth Session, *Official Records*, Supplement No. 3, "Report of the Economic and Social Council Covering the Period from 16 August 1949 to 16 August 1950" (1950), pp. 89–90.

[5] Res. 417(V), Dec. 1, 1950.

Europe." Children in other regions, they said, had been for centuries, and still were, in a "state of emergency."[6]

For the next three years UNICEF concentrated on a long-range program, primarily in the underdeveloped countries, involving the strengthening of maternal and child welfare services, mass health campaigns, and child-feeding programs. During this period also, however, it provided emergency aid to children, pregnant women, and nursing mothers when they were victims of floods, earthquakes, and similar disasters; and supplies to such emergency programs as the United Nations Relief and Works Agency for Palestine Refugees and the United Nations Korean Reconstruction Agency. By the end of 1953, its three-year trial period over, UNICEF was established by the General Assembly as a permanent agency with no change in function. It continues to be financed, however, by voluntary annual contributions from governments, nongovernmental organizations, and private individuals.

UNICEF represented the first sizable operational responsibility to be assumed directly by the United Nations. In a comparatively brief period of time, it was transformed from a short-range emergency activity into a permanent vehicle of United Nations social policy. It illustrates the shift of United Nations focus from the restoration of prewar standards in Europe to raising the level of living in the underdeveloped countries. Many of the activities that UNICEF has helped to finance since 1950 could have been fully paid for by recipient governments without severely taxing their resources, had they attached sufficient importance to child welfare services. UNICEF helped demonstrate the permanent value of such services and, by making its aid conditional, offered governments an incentive for allocating local resources to programs benefiting needy children.

UNICEF was promptly and widely acclaimed one of the most successful undertakings of the United Nations, both in terms of services rendered and public support obtained.[7] Its popularity may be attributed partly to sentimental enthusiasm for such obviously humani-

[6] U.S. Department of State, *United States Participation in the United Nations: Report by the President to the Congress for the Year 1950*, Publication 4178 (1951), pp. 177–78. See also U.N. General Assembly, Fifth Session, Third Committee, *Official Records*, 278th–87th Meetings (Oct. 6–18, 1950), pp. 46–105. The statement that a "permanent state of emergency persisted in the underdeveloped countries" was made by the representative of France and subsequently echoed by spokesmen for the Philippines, Iraq, and other governments.

[7] See, for example, the discussions in U.N. Economic and Social Council, Thirteenth Session, *Official Records*, 481st–564th Meetings (July 30–Sept. 21, 1951).

tarian work as aiding needy, helpless children, and partly to the invidious role in which critics would inevitably be placed. More important is the fact that the problems tackled by UNICEF have been clearly defined; the remedies are known and accepted; and dramatic results are obtainable at modest cost.[8]

Refugees and Displaced Persons

As noted earlier in this study, it was clear in 1946 that there would still be a large problem of refugee care after the termination of UNRRA. The agency consequently urged the United Nations to establish a successor organization equipped to carry on a program of relief, repatriation, and resettlement.[9] In February 1946, the General Assembly took the first steps toward setting up such an agency, and in December of that year—six months before the proposed ending of UNRRA operations in Europe—the Assembly approved the constitution of a new, temporary specialized agency, the International Refugee Organization (IRO).[10]

The IRO was given a broader mandate than UNRRA. In addition to the displaced persons in Austria, Germany, and Italy inherited from UNRRA (including unaccompanied children outside their countries of origin), the IRO was made responsible for Jewish refugees who had fled the Nazis before the war, who had survived concentration camps, or who had been in hiding; for non-Germans in Germany and Austria expelled by the Nazis but who had returned and were unable to reestablish themselves; for Spanish Republicans and other refugees of the Spanish regime; and for racial, religious, national, or political refugees from the interwar period. The IRO was thus given responsibility for refugees formerly under the protection of the League of Nations High Commissioner for Refugees and the Intergovernmental Committee for Refugees as well as those inherited from UNRRA.

At the General Assembly, the debates over the status of children were particularly bitter. The Soviet Union demanded that children be returned immediately to their countries of origin. In reply, it was pointed out that this might be contrary to the interests of the child and that it was often impossible to determine the country of origin. It was decided

[8] For a review of UNICEF as a continuing program of the United Nations, after completion of its "emergency" phase, see below, Chap. VIII.
[9] See above, Chap. I.
[10] Res. 62(I), Dec. 14, 1946.

that, if possible, children and parents should be reunited, wherever the latter might be. Orphans or unaccompanied children about whose nationality there was no doubt whatsoever were to be returned to their country, provided, however, that the best interests of the individual child would be served thereby. In the final analysis, therefore, it was left to the discretion of IRO to decide the future of such orphans or unaccompanied children as well as the future of those whose nationality was in doubt.

Differences of view concerning the treatment of political dissidents were equally sharp. The Soviet bloc sought to deny them assistance from the international community, to force refugees from Communist regimes to return to their countries of origin, to limit resettlement to those persons who had left their homes before the end of the war, and to prohibit resettlement in other lands if the country of origin—for example, the Soviet Union—refused its consent. Led by the United States, the United Kingdom, and France, the majority supported the position that refugees who were not war criminals, ordinary criminals, or traitors, yet had valid reasons for refusing repatriation, were entitled to the protection of IRO. However, to meet the objections of Arab nations fearful of possible mass Jewish resettlement in Palestine, the IRO was obliged to avoid sponsoring any scheme that would create political difficulties in the countries of resettlement or in neighboring countries, to avoid imposing resettlement of refugees on sovereign nations, and to avoid policies of resettlement that might run counter to the desires of the majority of the indigenous populations of non-self-governing regions or territories.

Although the IRO was financed by voluntary contributions, strenuous efforts were made by the United States and the United Kingdom to secure widespread participation. The majority agreed that "to the extent practicable," expenditures for persons displaced as a result of action by Germany and Japan should be charged to those countries, but the Soviet proposal that no provision for such refugees be made in the budget of the IRO was defeated. Similarly, the majority defeated Soviet proposals to the effect that all countries receiving refugees should pay the costs involved; that the paying capacity of the countries devastated by war should be taken into account in assessing member governments for support of the International Refugee Organization; and that the assessment of ability to pay should be left to the individual governments.

The scale of contributions adopted by the IRO was based initially on the assumption that all or most of the Members of the United Nations would participate in the work of the organization. As it turned out, however, only sixteen Members and two nations not Members—Italy and Switzerland—did so, and contributions constantly fell short of real requirements. No nation in the Soviet bloc became a party to the constitution of the International Refugee Organization.

The Preparatory Commission for an International Refugee Organization began to function on July 1, 1947, when more than 700,000 persons became dependent on that agency for food and shelter. By the end of 1948, the IRO itself came into being. It operated until February 1952. During its life, over 1,619,000 persons registered with the IRO and came under its mandate. Unlike UNRRA, the IRO had responsibility for arranging both the repatriation and the resettlement of refugees. Approximately 73,000 persons were repatriated; over 1 million were resettled in forty-eight countries, most of them in the United States, Australia, Israel, and Canada. Both UNRRA and the IRO had early identified the so-called "hard-core" group of refugees consisting mainly of the aged, the infirm, and the sick, for whom resettlement was especially difficult. Despite the obvious obstacles, the IRO made arrangements for settling almost 32,000 such individuals.

Engaged as it was in helping people re-establish their lives, the IRO was obliged to carry on a broad and complex program of social welfare in the international sphere. The work of assisting refugees in returning to their former homes or going to new ones involved the identification, registration, and classification of persons; reuniting scattered families or what remained of them; the provision of food, clothing, housing; health services; vocational training, including special training for the handicapped; unearthing opportunities for resettlement and employment; arranging for the institutional care of persons who would require it for most or possibly all of their lives; the operation of a transport fleet for moving refugees under its mandate; and the provision of political protection for refugees. Gradually refugees dispersed throughout the world were registered with the Organization. Although the greatest number were concentrated in Germany, applicants for assistance appeared in more than twenty countries in Africa, the Americas, and Asia, as well as in Europe.

The IRO did not solve the refugee problem, but it did succeed, in the face of continued Soviet intransigence at the General Assembly and the Economic and Social Council, in arranging for the repatriation or resettlement of the bulk of the refugees under its mandate. It rapidly recruited an able international staff. In general, the member governments, although preoccupied during the latter part of the existence of the IRO with arrangements for successor agencies, assumed the necessary financial obligations, provided stable delegations to sessions of the IRO Council, co-operated in attempting to resolve problems of policy and administration, and accepted a share of the "hard-core" refugees expected to be permanent public charges. Of its over-all budget of nearly $400 million, the United States contributed more than half. The next largest contributions were made by the United Kingdom, France, and Canada in that order.

The IRO was assisted by more than one hundred voluntary agencies that could, through case work, help reach the individuals whose special problems would otherwise receive scant attention in a mass program. The voluntary agencies were especially valuable in helping to solve the problems of "hard-core" refugees, in helping refugees become established in the countries of resettlement, and in formulating programs for aid to refugees after the termination of the International Refugee Organization.

The IRO stressed the problems that would remain after its liquidation in February 1952. No provision had been made for the future care of thousands of persons in tragic circumstances. These included "hard-core" refugees and others inside and outside institutions in Germany and Austria; refugees in the Middle East, Greece, and Trieste; and Europeans who had been transferred from Shanghai to the Philippines by the IRO. More and more persons were slipping secretly into Western Europe from behind the Iron Curtain. For refugees who had been settled locally, there remained—especially in Germany—the complex question of their integration into the national community, with some assurance of material security and legal and political protection. Finally, as the IRO reminded the United Nations, there were over nine million homeless and uprooted people outside the IRO mandate whose problems had never been assumed as a responsibility of the United Nations: among them, Germans who had been transferred to Germany from other countries or who had fled the Allied armies; Chinese refugees in Asia and the Far East; and refugees on the Indian subcontinent.

With the liquidation of the IRO, United Nations policy on refugees shifted from emphasis on relief, repatriation, and resettlement to problems connected with the assimilation of refugees in the countries of settlement, and the legal and political protection due them. In establishing the new Office of United Nations High Commissioner for Refugees, the United Nations completed a circle and returned to the more limited role played by the League of Nations.[11]

Refugees of the Arab-Israeli Conflict

The relief program for Palestine refugees that the United Nations began late in 1948 with the hope of terminating in mid-1949 is still in operation. After eight difficult years, more refugees were in need of relief than at the beginning, and no early reduction in requirements was expected.

More than half of the 922,000 refugees under care in June 1956 were concentrated in Jordan, a small country, poor in resources, where they represented one third of the total population of the nation. The remaining refugees were to be found in the Egyptian-controlled Gaza Strip, and in Lebanon and Syria. Through June 30, 1956, the equivalent of $266 million had been contributed for their care, employment, and resettlement. Of this total, voluntary agencies had contributed the equivalent of approximately $16 million. About half the total number of refugees registered on June 30, 1956, were children fifteen years of age or under.

The international approach to the Palestine refugee problem has not been characterized by rigidity or reluctance to experiment. The program has passed through at least three major phases. For the first year, it was a straight relief operation. There was then a year during which the emphasis was on public works rather than direct relief. After mid-1951, the theme became "reintegration," *i.e.*, re-establishment of refugees, without prejudice to their claims to eventual repatriation or compensation, where they could be self-supporting rather than dependent on public works projects for employment. Each of these phases is described briefly below.

For some days before the proclamation of the State of Israel on May 15, 1948, Palestinian Arabs had been leaving Palestine, either in fear of the future or in the hope of returning to the area as conquerors. On the day after the proclamation, the Arab League—Egypt, Iraq, Jordan, Lebanon, Saudi Arabia, Syria, and Yemen—instituted armed action.

---

[11] For information concerning the work of the Office of the High Commissioner for Refugees, see below, Chap. VIII. For a comprehensive history of IRO, see Louise W. Holborn, *The International Refugee Organization* (1956).

Additional tens of thousands of Palestinian Arabs who lived on the Israeli side of the present armistice lines then fled, leaving behind them their houses, fields, shops, and careers. By November 1948, there were estimated to be three quarters of a million Arab refugees. Professional men as well as those who had been farmers or shopkeepers were reduced, almost without exception, to starvation levels. In the countries of refuge, they depressed even further the existing low level of wages, they increased the vulnerability of their havens to epidemics, and they became charges on economies that could not support them.

On November 19, 1948, the General Assembly identified aid to Palestine refugees as "one of the minimum conditions for the success of the efforts of the United Nations to bring peace to that land," and requested the Secretary-General to appoint a Director of United Nations Relief for Palestine Refugees, with appropriate responsibility for planning and implementing a relief program. Member and nonmember nations were urged to contribute approximately $32 million for relief from December 1, 1948 to August 31, 1949.[12] A month later, on December 11, 1948, the General Assembly resolved that:

. . . refugees wishing to return to their homes and live at peace with their neighbours should be permitted to do so at the earliest practicable date, and that compensation should be paid for the property of those choosing not to return and for loss of or damage to property which, under principles of international law or in equity, should be made good by the Governments or authorities responsible.[13]

The relief program was to have ended in August 1949. There being no improvement of the situation in Palestine by then, the Secretary-General extended the program pending a decision by the General Assembly.

When the General Assembly met, it had before it the report of a distinguished Economic Survey Mission, endorsed by the Director of Relief, recommending a drastic reduction in direct relief with emphasis instead on helping the Arab governments initiate and support public works programs in the countries where refugees were located. In December 1949, one year after the General Assembly had created the United Nations Relief for Palestine Refugees, it created a successor agency—the United Nations Relief and Works Agency for Palestine Refugees in the Near East (UNRWA)—to carry out the relief and works programs recommended by the Economic Survey Mission.[14]

[12] Res. 212(III), Nov. 19, 1948.
[13] Res. 194(III), Dec. 11, 1948.
[14] Res. 302(IV), Dec. 8, 1949.

The efforts of the new agency to set in motion a program of public works were impeded by delays in collecting contributions, sharp increases in prices following the outbreak of the Korean war, unexpected opposition from the refugees themselves, and limited co-operation from the governments in the area. A few road-building and afforestation projects were undertaken in Lebanon, Syria, and Jordan, but they proved five times as costly to finance as direct relief. Moreover, when the roadways were built or the forestry jobs done, the refugees found themselves with no alternative but to return to the relief rolls. Consequently, although direct relief was to have ended by December 1950, the General Assembly authorized UNRWA to continue such relief on a diminishing scale to June 30, 1952, and meanwhile to concentrate on projects that would lead to "reintegration" of the refugees.

By "reintegration projects," the General Assembly meant projects developed in collaboration with Middle Eastern governments to make the refugees permanently self-supporting, without prejudice to their right to return to their homes or to secure compensation. Reintegration was to be accomplished through assisting refugees in finding employment; training them for occupations in which there was a shortage of workers; making loans and grants to refugees for small enterprises; building homes in areas where jobs were available; developing agricultural opportunities through well-drilling, irrigation, and construction of access roads; and financing general economic development. It was recognized that the funds provided for this purpose would not be sufficient to solve the refugee problem, but it was hoped that the host countries would inaugurate parallel schemes for economic development.[15]

From July 1951 on, UNRWA sought to negotiate projects with the host governments. When the eighth session of the General Assembly convened in September 1953, the high hopes for the reintegration program had suffered the same fate as those for the earlier program of public works. There had been practically no change in the number of refugees requiring United Nations aid.[16] Despite denials by UNRWA

[15] U.N. General Assembly, Seventh Session, *Official Records*, Supplement No. 13, "Annual Report of the Director of the United Nations Relief and Works Agency for Palestine Refugees in the Near East, Covering the Period 1 July 1951 to 30 June 1952" (1952), pp. 7–8.

[16] Indeed the number of refugees on relief would have been greater than the 872,000 that it was, the Director stated, had not Israel in July 1952 assumed responsibility for some 19,000 Arab refugees within its borders. Moreover, the refugee movement at the outbreak of hostilities was a two-way flow, and Israel had promptly assumed responsibility for the 17,000 Jewish refugees who fled from Arab lands into Israel. It has since then taken in very many more Jewish refugees from Arab lands,

and the United Nations itself, the refugees continued to suspect that reintegration was designed to wean them from their goal of repatriation, and they remained reluctant to participate in the program. The members of the Arab League charged that the reintegration program meant in effect that the possibility of repatriation had been abandoned and that the refugees were being condemned to permanent exile. On the other hand, it should have been fairly obvious that the prospects for repatriation were growing dimmer as the years went by without any reduction in Arab-Israeli tensions.

Only a few reintegration projects were agreed on between UNRWA and the Middle Eastern governments. During 1953, at the request of UNRWA, a plan was drafted by an American firm, employed under the direction of the Tennessee Valley Authority, for using the Jordan Valley water resources for irrigation and hydroelectric power. The President of the United States appointed a personal representative with the rank of ambassador to explore the possibilities of the project with the governments of the region. Although progress has been made, no consensus has been reached. If and when large numbers of jobs are created through economic development projects, the refugees will inevitably have to compete for them with the almost equally destitute general population. In this competition, they are more than likely to be by-passed in favor of the indigenous population.

Meanwhile, the contributing governments have grown increasingly reluctant to continue supplying funds, and the host countries remain about as ill-equipped as ever to bear the burden unaided. In these circumstances, the eighth session of the General Assembly in late 1953—with the Soviet bloc abstaining, as it had throughout the controversy, but with no negative votes—decided to continue UNRWA until June 30, 1955, hopeful that it could negotiate a transfer of its continued heavy responsibility for direct relief to the Arab governments. No progress in this direction having been made, the ninth session of the General Assembly in December 1954 extended the life of the agency to June 30, 1960.[17]

The great accomplishment of the United Nations is that, because of the perseverance and unquenchable optimism of the free world, it has at least kept the refugees alive. It has supplied nearly a million persons with food rations of 1,500 to 1,600 calories per day. It has sheltered

---

repatriated a substantial number of Arab refugees, and released some of the funds held in blocked accounts of refugees in Lebanon.

[17] Res. 818(IX), Dec. 4, 1954.

about a third of this number in camps. It has prevented serious epidemics and has provided some schooling for children and some training for adults.

The political friction that has blocked and interfered with the operations of UNRWA at almost every stage in its history has manifested itself in a number of ways. Israel has contended that the Arab refugees are the responsibility of the Arab states, not of the United Nations; that the condition of the refugees is the direct result of the attack by the Arab states on Israel; that their return in large numbers would threaten Israeli internal security; and that the best solution is to settle the bulk of the refugees in the Arab states. In an attempt to make a package deal on the entire matter, Israel at one time offered to repatriate 100,000 Arab refugees provided this agreement were made part of a general political settlement. The offer was rejected by the Arab states, which contended that the policy of the United Nations was repatriation for all refugees who desired it. Nevertheless, a number of refugees have infiltrated back into Israel and have been accepted as citizens. The Arab states have charged that the condition of the refugees was worse than pictured by the director of the agency in his reports to the United Nations (although these reports have been notably frank); that the relief assistance given was desperately inadequate; that there was much sickness and few doctors; that the salaries of the international staff were too high; and that refugees should replace the many foreign nontechnical employees of UNRWA.

As the director stated, now that the "period of acute emergency is past, when the efforts of the international community were gladly accepted . . . the Agency is becoming something of an embarrassment to the host governments."[18] Despite some bans on their employment, refugees continue to glut the markets of their hosts with cheaper labor. In Jordan, every third person is on the ration list. In the Gaza Strip, where refugees constitute two thirds of the population, the Egyptian Government has been required to extend relief to its citizens as well. Host governments have ignored the international status of the agency and have interfered seriously with its operations. They have refused entry to some personnel of the agency and forced others to leave without explanation. They have attempted to impose income taxes on per-

---

[18] U.N. General Assembly, Eighth Session, *Official Records*, Supplement No. 12, "Annual Report of the Director of the United Nations Relief and Works Agency for Palestine Refugees in the Near East, Covering the Period 1 July 1952 to 30 June 1953" (1953), p. 3.

sonnel of the agency; landing charges on United Nations planes; excise taxes on supplies required by the agency; and taxes on interest earned by its bank deposits.

The United Nations for too long saw the Palestine refugee problem as a source of friction between the hostile states, which, if removed, would make peaceful settlement possible. It misgauged the bitterness of the conflict and underestimated vastly the difficulty of solving it through economic measures. In the present unhappy situation, there is much to be said for a United Nations policy that would place heavier responsibilities on the Arab governments to accept the bulk of the refugees, on the refugees to re-establish their lives in Arab lands, and on Israel to accept a small proportion and compensate the remainder.[19] The United Nations could then concentrate on assisting in the settlement of claims for compensation, removing the restrictions on mobility, which severely limit the ability of qualified refugees to take advantage of economic opportunities in different Middle Eastern countries, providing technical assistance and financial aid for projects that would raise the level of economic life generally in the region, and maintaining international peace in the area.[20]

Victims of Aggression in Korea

Within a few days of the outbreak of war in Korea on June 25, 1950, the United Nations appealed to Member governments for relief assistance as well as military aid for the victims of aggression. On July 31, the Security Council followed up its earlier broadside appeal with a resolution requesting the Unified Command to assume responsibility for the relief and support of the civilian population in Korea, and to establish, in the field, procedures for distributing emergency aid. The resolution went on to request the Secretary-General, the Economic and Social Council and other United Nations organs, and the specialized agencies to provide relief assistance to the Unified Command.[21] The

[19] The U.S. Secretary of State reported to the Senate Committee on Foreign Relations on February 24, 1956, that the United States stood ready to join with others in putting up the funds that would enable Israel to reimburse such refugees for their losses.
[20] See James Baster, "Economic Aspects of the Settlement of Palestine Refugees," *The Middle East Journal* (Winter 1954), pp. 58–68.
[21] Res. S/1657, July 31, 1950. The appeal to the Economic and Social Council, which elicited a prompt, favorable response, was made in accordance with Article 65 of the Charter, requiring the Economic and Social Council to assist the Security Council on the request of the latter.

United States Department of the Army assumed responsibility for estimating requirements on behalf of the Unified Command.

By October, when the General Assembly considered Korean relief, it was also confronted with the question of post-hostilities aid. The Assembly gave the Economic and Social Council two jobs. First, the Council was asked to develop plans in consultation with the specialized agencies for the relief and rehabilitation of Korea on termination of hostilities and—indicative of the hopes held by the Assembly for an early end to the war—to report on this problem within three weeks. Second—indicative of the desire that Korea should endure as a monument to the collective effort of the United Nations—the Council was asked to expedite a study of long-term measures for promoting economic development and social progress in Korea.[22]

The Economic and Social Council estimated that at least $250 million would be required between January 1, 1951, and early 1952, and made some organizational recommendations that were approved by the Assembly in December 1950. By a vote of 51 to 0, the General Assembly established the United Nations Korean Reconstruction Agency (UNKRA), to operate under the general guidance of the United Nations Commission for the Unification and Rehabilitation of Korea (UNCURK), and to be headed by an Agent-General appointed by the United Nations Secretary-General after consultation with UNCURK.[23]

A two-pronged policy thus emerged: the provision of emergency relief under the direction of the Unified Command (United States) during hostilities, and the provision of longer-term, post-hostilities aid through UNKRA. The purpose of the emergency program was to prevent disease and unrest behind the lines. Relief for the million or more homeless refugees, many of whom had moved south in order to get into the area controlled by the Unified Command, was but one aspect of the general problem of caring for the civilian victims of the war. As of the close of 1954, the Unified Command had received or had been promised for its emergency relief program the equivalent of more than $471 million from twenty-seven Member states and four states not members of the United Nations, from nongovernmental organizations, specialized agencies, the League of Red Cross Societies, and individuals. More than 95 per cent of this total, however, came from American sources. Nearly

---

[22] Res. 376(V), Oct. 7, 1950.
[23] U.N. General Assembly, Fifth Session, Plenary, *Official Records*, 314th Meeting (Dec. 1, 1950), p. 525. Res. 410(V), Dec. 1, 1950.

$420 million was contributed by the United States Government and $28 million by American private agencies.

Through the UNKRA program, the United Nations wished not only to provide subsistence but, in addition, to lay the groundwork for a model democratic economy that would adequately reflect the highest principles of the United Nations. Much of the policy set forth in the General Assembly resolution establishing UNKRA was a restatement of UNRRA policy, but there were also differences. The United Nations now stated that a program of relief and rehabilitation was necessary to provide the economic basis for a "unified, independent, and democratic government in Korea" and should be consistent with "the pattern of long-term economic development in Korea."[24]

Relief supplies were to be sold only in justified cases, and local currency proceeds so derived, or amounts equal to the value of the items supplied, were to be paid into an account under the control of the Agent-General. The funds were then to be used for additional relief and rehabilitation activity, to meet local currency expenses of the agency, or to combat inflation. Supplies were to be distributed equitably without discrimination as to race, creed, or political belief, and made available as appropriate through public and co-operative organizations, voluntary agencies, and "normal channels of private trade."[25]

The Korean Government was to take economic and financial action to ensure the effective use of United Nations and Korean resources, particularly action to combat inflation. It was to exempt supplies received under the program from import taxes, permit personnel of the United Nations to supervise distribution, and accord them the necessary privileges, immunities, and facilities.

The Agent-General of UNKRA was required to consult with and be guided generally by the United Nations Commission for the Unification and Rehabilitation of Korea on questions of policy concerning program and activities, and was to begin the relief and rehabilitation program after he, the Unified Command, and UNCURK had agreed the time was propitious.

On February 7, 1951, UNKRA was "activated." Until the negotiation of the cease-fire on July 27, 1953, however, the activities of the military in administering the United Nations emergency relief and short-term aid program dwarfed other efforts. UNKRA was confined to negotiating agreements with the Unified Command covering areas of responsibility; to organizational activities and planning schedules;

[24] *Ibid.*, Pt. B.
[25] *Ibid.*

and to carrying on a few minor projects complementing and supplementing the relief programs administered by the United Nations Civil Assistance Command, Korea (UNCACK). In January 1952, the Agent-General of UNKRA became responsible for recruiting a large share of the specialized civilian personnel needed in Korea. Personnel provided by the specialized agencies, nongovernmental organizations, and voluntary agencies were transferred to the United Nations Korean Reconstruction Agency, which in turn seconded them to the United Nations Civil Assistance Command. By 1953, more than half of the civilian personnel of the latter agency had been so provided.

The most important UNKRA activity during this period, however, was its development, together with the Unified Command and the Republic of Korea, of the first comprehensive long-range rehabilitation program. This program was designed to go into effect even before hostilities had come to an end. It envisaged the spending of $70 million for the period ending June 30, 1953, in the hope of helping the Korean Government halt the rapid economic deterioration in the country. The program, however, was late getting started and was not completed by its original target date.

With the cease-fire in July 1953, UNKRA entered a new and larger phase of activity. A $130 million reconstruction program for the year ending June 30, 1954, to supplement the earlier $70 million program, was approved a month after the cease-fire. Additional commitments authorized by the eighth session of the General Assembly would have brought the total program commitments by UNKRA, as of June 30, 1955, to $266 million. The necessary contributions were not forthcoming, however, and the program again fell considerably short of the goals set by the General Assembly.

Meanwhile the United States Government, having given aid to South Korea through the Economic Cooperation Administration before the outbreak of the war, having carried the main burden of Korean defense and relief during the war, and having been willing to pay a financial price for a truce,[26] made available an additional $200 million as the

---

[26] As Congressman Walter H. Judd said during the hearings on the Mutal Security Act of 1954, "A further fact is that the President of the United States promised them if they would agree to the truce we would give them up to one billion dollars of assistance in rehabilitating the country. We didn't say we would give it to the United Nations. This was one of the prices we paid for getting our boys out of the war there." The Minnesota Congressman's explanation was confirmed by a representative of the Department of State. *Mutual Security Act of 1954*, Hearings before the House Committee on Foreign Affairs, 83 Cong. 2 sess. (1954), pp. 450, 455–56.

first installment on a bilateral post-armistice program of economic re-habilitation in Korea. This further deflated UNKRA and gave the Government of Korea, whose leaders were expert in the politics of maneuver, additional opportunities for playing off one program against another.

The Korean Government had long been distrustful of the United Nations and at odds with UNKRA on basic issues. It wanted to decide what contracts would be let and to whom, whereas UNKRA was pre-pared to consult with the Korean Government on specifications but in-sisted that the Agent-General award contracts in accordance with a competitive bidding procedure. The Korean Government wanted ex-clusive control of the local currency proceeds derived from the sale of UNKRA supplies, although the General Assembly resolution that es-tablished the agency clearly gave the Agent-General control of the coun-terpart account. And like the governments of other underdeveloped countries, the Korean Government favored a program heavily weighted on the side of investment in capital facilities, including the inevitable steel mill. Fearful of the inflationary impact of a program that would put wages in the hands of workers without simultaneously increasing the available supply of consumer goods, UNKRA and the Unified Command urged less emphasis on investment and more on consumer goods. Thus, differences of opinion on program content were added to differences regarding financial and administrative procedures.

While these issues, as well as others, were postponing the signature of any over-all agreement between UNKRA and the Government of the Republic of Korea, the relations of the agency with the military com-mand were also far from smooth. The military authorities were not averse to an agency that would provide funds and personnel for use under military direction but, even in this relationship, difficulties arose in connection with security clearances for civilian personnel and the provision of facilities enabling them to eat, work, travel, and obtain information necessary to the discharge of their duties. UNKRA, how-ever, was intended to be more than an incidental aid to the achievement of military objectives, and the agency inevitably had views on economic and social objectives—and methods of attaining them—that were at variance with those of the military command.

Various arrangements were made to facilitate joint programing, co-ordinated operations, and orderly transfers of responsibility from one program to another, but the effect of the arrangements was to keep UNKRA in a subordinate role. An American civilian Economic Coordinator of Relief and Rehabilitation Operations, not an UNKRA official, became responsible for the establishment of over-all economic and financial policies, and the agency became responsible primarily for a series of long-range rehabilitation projects.

By the time a reasonably clear-cut role had been negotiated for UNKRA, and relationships with the military had grown more harmonious—as was the case after agreement early in 1953 on the $70 million UNKRA program—the enthusiasm of the governments that launched the agency had largely evaporated. The unexpected length of the Korean War and the retention of primary responsibility for relief operations by the military authorities during this period meant mounting administrative expenses, declining morale within the administrative staff, and extreme difficulty collecting pledges and contributions from Member governments. Although UNKRA had hoped that—with the termination of hostilities and the beginning, in 1953, of larger-scale, longer-range programing for relief and reconstruction—the promised contributions would be forthcoming more promptly, the reverse was the case.

The UNKRA program included projects to help rehabilitate agriculture, manufacturing, electric-power production, transportation, mining, housing, education, and health, sanitation, and welfare. Considerable quantities of various types of supplies were imported, including seeds, hatching eggs, fertilizer, irrigation equipment, spindles for the textile industry, dies for wire manufacture, briquetting presses to reduce the requirements for bituminous imports, railroad ties and trucks for the transportation system, rock-drilling equipment for mining, machines for fabricating earth blocks for the housing industry, educational materials ranging from books to supplies for vocational training, and medical supplies. In addition, UNKRA established a Small Industries Loan Fund with dollars and *hwan* resources to make loans to small, privately owned enterprises. By the end of 1954, these and related activities were beginning to bear fruit. Larger stocks of Korean-made goods, increased harvests, and greater fish catches by a more modern fishing fleet improved the prospects for eventual economic stability. Relations of the agency with the Government of Korea became more harmonious after the replacement of the first Agent-General in mid-1953, but at the cost of concessions to the views of the Government of Korea on program priorities.

The experience of this agency is proof that the specialized agencies, despite their autonomy, can be mobilized in response to resolutions of the

Security Council, the General Assembly, and the Economic and Social Council. The World Health Organization, Food and Agriculture Organization, International Refugee Organization, and United Nations Educational, Scientific and Cultural Organization all supplied teams of specialized personnel to help survey Korean requirements, to make recommendations within their own special fields of competence, and to provide technical services.

The experience of the agency illustrates also the fruitfulness of the relationships that the United Nations fosters with nongovernmental national and international voluntary agencies. Over and above the $28 million in supplies that these nongovernmental organizations contributed to the emergency program in response to the resolution of the Economic and Social Council, the voluntary agencies contributed approximately $8 million in relief supplies in support of their own programs in Korea. The United Nations agency, UNKRA, was able to systematize the efforts of private groups to provide material assistance to the Korean people, to encourage the establishment or continuation of specific programs in health, welfare, and other fields, and to support the voluntary agencies through the provision of ocean freight and direct program grants. Joint planning and programing in the social field between UNKRA and these voluntary agencies was achieved through the Korean Association of Voluntary Agencies.

In the first flush of enthusiasm, there had been hopes that Korea could be helped by UNKRA to rise from its ashes to heights it had never before attained. Despite the very substantial volume of economic aid obtained through multilateral and bilateral programs, however, it has become clear that South Korea will not emerge within the foreseeable future as a model of creative international relief efforts. The inadequate per-capita consumption levels of the prewar period had not been restored by the end of 1955, and interest in the area was clearly waning.

Emergency Action to Meet World Food Shortages

During the past ten years, the concern of the United Nations with world food problems has been focused on four main objectives: raising low levels of food production and consumption, and fighting chronic malnutrition; counteracting excessive fluctuations in the prices of agricultural products; promoting the rational disposal of intermittent agricultural surpluses; and relieving famine and other emergency situations.[27] The promotion of each of these objectives has presented special problems and called for special types of United Nations activity. The first three are treated later in this volume[28] and only the last is considered here, even though all four problems are closely interrelated.

Proposals for a World Food Board

In February 1946, during the first part of its first session, the General Assembly adopted a resolution, submitted by the major powers, that urged all governments and peoples to take prompt and drastic action separately and jointly through the new Food and Agriculture Organization to conserve supplies and to bring about the maximum production of grains.[29] This resolution also requested both the governments and the FAO to provide as much information as possible on the current world food situation and future outlook. At this time, it was generally expected that the period of postwar stringency would be brief and that it would soon be succeeded by one of agricultural surpluses. But when the General Assembly reconvened for the second part of its first session in October 1946, the situation had already taken a turn for the worse. The severe winter of 1946–47 in Europe, followed by an unprecedented drought in central and southeastern Europe, helped to convert a situation of temporary stringency into a world food crisis.[30]

While the first session of the General Assembly was in recess, the FAO responded to the resolution of February 1946 by calling a "Special Meeting on Urgent Food Problems," which was attended by the representatives of six international organizations and of twenty-one countries. After analyzing current food problems, this special meeting concluded that the existing machinery for meeting emergency food needs was inadequate.

Within a month after the special meeting, and in accordance with its recommendations, a new emergency agency was established—the International Emergency Food Council. This was in effect a successor to the Combined Food Board,[31] and like that board, it functioned through

[27] Food and Agriculture Organization, *Functions of a World Food Reserve—Scope and Limitations*, FAO Commodity Policy Studies No. 10 (1956), p. 3. (Hereinafter cited as *Functions of a World Food Reserve.*)
[28] See below, Chaps. III, IV, V, and VII.
[29] Res. 27(I), Feb. 14, 1946.
[30] For a vivid account of the serious view of the situation taken by the United States, see Harry S. Truman, *Memoirs: Year of Decisions* (1955), pp. 464–80.
[31] See above, Chap. I.

commodity committees and allocated food supplies to UNRRA and other claimants. Nineteen governments were represented on it; the Director-General of the FAO was a member of its Central Committee; and the FAO itself acted as secretariat.

At the same time, the Director-General of the FAO was, at the request of the special meeting, preparing suggestions for dealing with long-term problems of production, distribution, and consumption of agricultural products for submission to the September 1946 conference of the FAO. These took the form of proposals for a World Food Board acting through commodity committees and performing the following functions:

1. To stabilize prices of agricultural commodities on the world markets, including provision of the necessary funds for stabilizing operations.

2. To establish a world food reserve adequate for any emergency that might arise through failure of crops in any part of the world.

3. To provide funds for financing the disposal of surplus agricultural products on special terms to countries where the need for them is most urgent.

4. To co-operate with organizations concerned with international credits for industrial and agricultural development, and with trade and commodity policy, in order that their common ends might be more quickly and effectively achieved.[32]

For the purpose of stabilizing prices, the World Food Board, operating through its commodity committees, was to be given powers to hold stocks of each of the most important commodities, and to release or add to these stocks with a view to counteracting excessive market fluctuations.[33]

The proposed World Food Board, in brief, would be occupied with all the major problems relating to food and other agricultural products that have continued to concern the United Nations up to the present time. In September 1946, the FAO Conference accepted the general objectives of the proposed World Food Board, but did not agree to recommend its establishment. The conference decided instead to convene a Preparatory Commission for further study of the proposals. In addition, the FAO endorsed a resolution of the UNRRA Council on the need for special action to finance future imports of food for nations receiving UNRRA aid.

In October 1946, the Economic and Social Council, with the report of the Special Meeting on Urgent Food Problems in hand, requested the Secretary-General of the United Nations to assist the FAO in preparing proposals for long-term international machinery to deal with

---

[32] *Functions of a World Food Reserve*, p. 46.
[33] *Ibid.*

these problems, and directed the President of the Economic and Social Council or his alternate to participate in the meetings of the Preparatory Commission.

When the General Assembly reconvened, it had all this as background. It also had a *World Food Appraisal for 1946–47* issued by the FAO in September 1946 and the reports of the Secretary-General on the measures taken by United Nations organs and specialized agencies in response to the General Assembly resolution of the preceding February. In addition, it heard from the Secretary-General of the International Emergency Food Council. The Second (Economic and Financial) Committee of the General Assembly, to which these matters were referred, was less concerned with long-range problems than with the methods of meeting the more immediate relief problems, which would remain after UNRRA ceased activities on December 31, 1946.

On relief matters, the delegations were sharply divided in their conceptions of the scope and gravity of the problem, in their views on the need for international action, and in their ideas of methods to be employed. On the one hand there were nations, such as Denmark, that felt that drastic international action was required. On the other hand, there were those nations that followed the lead of the United States in questioning the need for new international relief machinery. Various compromises were suggested in an attempt to bring these two groups together. These compromises were rejected and the resolution that was finally adopted by the General Assembly, in December 1946, was confined largely to urging continued efforts by governments and international agencies to overcome the expected food deficit in 1947.[34] Having disposed in this hortative fashion of the immediate problem, the General Assembly was willing to look to the FAO and the Preparatory Commission on World Food Proposals to make concrete plans for long-range attacks on the food supply problem.

The Preparatory Commission met in 1946–47 and brought forward a series of recommendations for sales of foodstuffs, at special prices, for the improvement of nutrition and for a network of commodity stabilization methods of different kinds. Among the latter was the accumulation of three different kinds of reserves—working stocks, famine reserves, and price stabilization reserves—to be administered partly by international agreement. It was proposed that the famine reserves be held nationally by exporting and importing countries for use nationally and internationally under agreed conditions, and that the amount to be carried by

[34] Res. 45(I), Dec. 11, 1946.

each country should be decided for each commodity by international agreement.

In linking its famine-reserve proposal with a general stabilization program, the Preparatory Commission of government representatives was in agreement with the suggestions of the Director-General of the FAO, but it did not accept his proposal for a World Food Board.

Partly because of United States opposition, which reflected, among other things, awareness of congressional objections to international control of American food reserves, fear of compromising domestic freedom of action on price supports and other matters, dissatisfaction with the financial implications of the proposal, and the growing American interest in the contemplated International Trade Organization, the commission discarded the plan for a World Food Board in favor of a proposed World Food Council. The council was not to be a separate operating agency, but an integral part of the FAO with responsibility for consultation, review, and some types of action between the annual sessions of the FAO Conference. It was to examine current developments in intergovernmental commodity arrangements, particularly as they affected adequacy of the food supply, the use of food reserves, famine relief, and special food programs for the undernourished; to promote consistency and co-ordination of national and international agricultural commodity policies; to initiate study and investigation of critical agricultural commodity situations; and to advise on such emergency measures as would affect the export and import of supplies required under national programs of agricultural production.[35]

A World Food Council along these lines, although a come-down from the World Food Board, still seemed to the United States and some other countries too great a threat to their freedom of action in the politically sensitive area of agricultural policy. The third session of the FAO Conference in 1947 therefore established instead the FAO Council to act as the main FAO organ on world food questions in the intervals between sessions of the conference and assigned the following emergency functions to the new council:

1. Continuation of the allocation activities of the International Emergency Food Council through its commodity committees although the council itself was dissolved and incorporated into the new FAO Council as the International Emergency Food Committee.

2. Supervision and promotion of studies of continual commodity shortages.

[35] Food and Agriculture Organization, *Report of the FAO Preparatory Commission on World Food Proposals* (February 1947), pp. iii–vii, 11–14, 21–30, 52–55.

3. Advice on emergency measures to be taken regarding the import and export of agricultural products.

The functions and responsibilities of the new International Emergency Food Committee were similar to those of the Central Committee of the predecessor council. Eleven countries were elected to membership on the International Emergency Food Committee, and the ten commodity committees of the council on beans and peas, cereals, cocoa, fats and oils, feeds, fertilizers, meat and meat products, rice, seeds, and sugar were retained. During the eighteen months of its life, the International Emergency Food Council had been responsible for equitable international distribution of a massive volume of foodstuffs, and had stimulated the convening of a special cereals conference in Paris to consider the serious world grain situation.

During the months immediately following the establishment of the International Emergency Food Committee within the FAO Council, world conditions in food and agriculture continued to deteriorate. Reports of poor crops, a predicted serious world shortage of bread grains, and existing shortages of pesticides, farm machinery, and draft animals all pointed toward imminent famine in many countries. In 1948, however, the situation began to improve, and the need for allocating commodities became less urgent. In June 1949, the FAO Council terminated its International Emergency Food Committee. The world food situation was by that time characterized by surpluses of certain commodities, particularly in the dollar area, although supplies in other parts of the world were insufficient or barely sufficient. This situation prompted the FAO to convene a group of experts to propose measures for promoting the balanced expansion of world trade in agricultural products.

Proposals for an International Commodity Clearing House

The report of the experts recommended the establishment of a new international agency, the International Commodity Clearing House, to operate with a capital fund equivalent to $5 billion to carry on, with the consent of the countries concerned, a wide variety of commodity transactions.[36] In the short run—i.e., during the period of trade disequilib-

[36] Food and Agriculture Organization, Fifth Session of FAO Conference, *Report on World Commodity Problems*, Doc. C 49/10 (Nov. 21, 1949). The experts were: John B. Condliffe (United States), Colin Clark (Australia), J. K. Galbraith (United States), D. Ghosh (India), Gustavo Polit (Chile), and A. Radomysler (United Kingdom).

ım and currency inconvertibility—the purpose of these transactions would be generally to keep commodity trade moving and, in particular, to forestall the accumulation of surpluses in hard-currency countries in the face of need in soft-currency countries. In the long run, their purpose would be to moderate the effects on prices of short-run changes in commodity demand and supply.[37]

The capital fund was to be provided initially by national quotas, based on national incomes of member countries and payable in their own currencies. Of the quota of each nation, 20 per cent would be due when the country joined the organization and would become part of the general fund of the Clearing House. The other 80 per cent was to be available on call for use in the purchase of surplus commodities in the country in question.

Two main types of short-term transactions were envisaged. The first involved use of the 80 per cent for the acquisition of surpluses, presumably in hard-currency areas, at commercial prices. These were to be resold, for soft currencies, to countries that could not otherwise buy them. Pending convertibility, the Clearing House would hold the soft currencies of receiving countries, which would be guaranteed by those countries against losses from currency depreciation, in accounts for the supplying countries. The second type of short-run trading operation was to be financed by the Clearing House, using its own general fund (the 20 per cent of the national quotas) as a revolving fund, to purchase surpluses at less than commercial prices for resale outside the general channels of commerce, e.g., for relief purposes.

The proposals for an International Commodity Clearing House were not accepted by the FAO Conference. Had they been accepted, the bulk of the resources of the Clearing House probably would soon have been frozen in inconvertible currencies, for convertibility has not yet been achieved. Having rejected two well-intended but over-ambitious plans for the stabilization and better distribution of world food supplies under international auspices, the FAO Conference in 1949 contented itself with appointing a purely advisory Committee on Commodity Problems to analyze and interpret the international commodity situation and advise the council on suitable action.

Proposals for an Emergency Famine Reserve

The next effort of the United Nations to address itself to the problem of emergency rather than chronic food shortages began in August 1951

[37] *Functions of a World Food Reserve*, p. 51.

with the introduction jointly by Chile and the United States of a draft resolution at the thirteenth session of the Economic and Social Council. This resolution, which was subsequently adopted, in effect supported the existing pattern of bilateral assistance in times of emergency, and called on the FAO to keep "existing or emerging food shortages in individual countries under continuous surveillance," to continue its periodic studies of the problem, and—in case of pending shortages—to make emergency reports to the FAO Council, the FAO Conference, and the United Nations Secretary-General for transmission to the Economic and Social Council.[38]

At the next conference of the FAO, in November–December 1951, two important follow-up resolutions were passed. One of these directed the Director-General to initiate investigations of existing or potential food shortages or famine once he had learned of them, and to report the extent of need to the United Nations and appropriate specialized agencies; also to convene a special meeting of the FAO Council and interested governments for the purpose of working out a program of action if relief were deemed necessary. This resolution proved to embody the main approach of FAO to the problem of emergency food shortage from then on, and was reaffirmed in November 1953 after sustained effort to develop proposals for an emergency famine reserve had proved fruitless. These latter efforts were authorized in another resolution of the 1951 conference, which asked the FAO Council to study and explore suitable ways and means whereby an emergency food reserve could be established and made available promptly to member states threatened or affected by serious food shortage or famine.[39]

With this background of prior action by the Economic and Social Council and by the Conference of the Food and Agriculture Organization, the General Assembly, in January 1952, for the first time expressed a formal interest in setting up procedures for dealing with future famine emergencies resulting from natural causes.[40] The resolution of the Assembly was passed after extensive debate in which the United States, emphasizing the potentialities of private organizations, took the position that bilateral or voluntary action continued to be the best means of meeting famine emergencies, but that such voluntary efforts should be facilitated and co-ordinated through the United Nations. In contrast, India sought to have the General Assembly take a more favorable

[38] Res. 405(XIII), Aug. 31, 1951.
[39] For the text of these resolutions (Nos. 15 and 16), see Food and Agriculture Organization, *Report of the Sixth Session of the Conference, 19 November–6 December 1951* (March 1952), pp. 47–48.
[40] Res. 525(VI), Jan. 26, 1952.

stand on the question of establishing a famine reserve, and the Soviet Union proposed that world resources then being employed in the manufacture of armaments be used instead to increase food production. The resolution as passed endorsed the recommendation of the Economic and Social Council for reports by FAO in cases of emergency, and requested the Secretary-General, in consultation with the heads of FAO, WHO, and other agencies, to prepare recommendations for the fourteenth session of the Economic and Social Council on ways of bringing about concerted action by governments, intergovernmental organizations, and voluntary agencies in time of famine resulting from crop failure.

In the report to the Economic and Social Council called for by this resolution, the Secretary-General recommended a set of procedures to be followed by governments, intergovernmental organizations, and voluntary agencies in the event of a famine emergency. He stressed the importance of prior standing arrangements to facilitate the immediate provision of funds and supplies in the event of an emergency. In dealing with questions of finance, he referred to the studies the FAO was making on the possibility of setting up a famine reserve, and suggested that such a reserve would probably not meet all needs. Additional funds might be required to meet "the initial impact of a disaster, when suffering is likely to be most severe and when the danger of panic, hoarding, and inflation is most threatening."[41] Inasmuch as neither the specialized agencies nor the voluntary organizations could be expected to have on hand the funds required, the report suggested four other possible sources: advance voluntary pledges or contributions by governments to a special fund; budgeted contributions by governments to such a fund; use of the Secretary-General's authority to make special disbursements from the United Nations Working Capital Fund; and advances by United Nations agencies to be reimbursed from the responses to an appeal by the Secretary-General.

At its fourteenth session in mid-1952, the Economic and Social Council endorsed the Secretary-General's concept of the roles of the Food and Agriculture Organization, the United Nations, and the voluntary agencies. But, except for a reference to the pending studies by the FAO of ways and means of establishing an emergency famine reserve, the Council remained discreetly silent on the subject of financing famine relief.[42]

[41] U.N. Economic and Social Council, Fourteenth Session, *Food and Famine, Procedures for International Action in the Event of Emergency Famines Arising from Natural Causes*, Doc. E/2220 (May 14, 1952), p. 11.

[42] Res. 425(XIV), June 30, 1952.

The FAO famine-reserve studies were carried on by working parties of experts who elaborated a series of plans, of which the most practicable appeared to them to be the establishment of an internationally owned emergency relief fund equipped with the necessary organization and finance for drawing on nationally owned stocks as needed. As a working tool for the purpose of their calculations, the experts developed a kind of yardstick unit, the Emergency Food Reserve Unit, which was defined as the quantity of food required for supplementing the diet of one million people at the rate of 1,200 calories per person per day for one month. The total calorie intake assumed by the FAO for an emergency subsistence period was 1,900, but some 700 calories would presumably be available locally.[43] As a minimum, the experts advocated a reserve of twenty units, which would cost approximately $32 million and would be sufficient to maintain 5 million people for four months.

Upon receiving the report of the experts, the FAO Council decided that all the facts were available and that it was time for the governments to determine what they would do. At the FAO Conference of 1953, the governments declined to adopt the recommendations of the expert group. It was clear that, despite all preparatory work, the political decision to provide either funds or pledges under any of the alternate plans submitted would not be forthcoming. The President of the United States had just announced that $100 million in surplus American farm products were to be made available on a bilateral basis when needed to meet emergency famines abroad. Most of the surplus-producing nations, particularly those whose financial resources would be called on to maintain any form of international reserve, refused to support the suggestions of the FAO. On the other hand, with the exception of Pakistan, which had just benefited from American famine aid, the majority of the nations likely to be subject to famine urged adoption of an international reserve plan.

The discussion was vigorous. In general, the United States, Canada, and the countries favoring the unorganized, *ad hoc* approach called for under Resolution 15 of 1951, claimed that this approach had worked well in practice, and that the FAO experts had failed to demonstrate that it would not continue to work well. They asserted that governments would respond voluntarily and promptly in time of need, that it was questionable whether international action as contemplated under a reserve plan would be sufficiently speedy, and that it was also questionable whether famine needs were sufficiently great to warrant setting up new machinery. Those in favor of some form of reserve argued

[43] *Functions of a World Food Reserve*, p. 55.

variously that a reserve was necessary from the humanitarian point of view; that it would not be a substitute for national action, but a supplement to it; that purely *ad hoc* assistance would not allay the fears of the people subject to famine nor provide them with the necessary security; that, on the contrary, *ad hoc* assistance would always be uncertain and never assured or speedy.

The resolution of the conference as finally adopted stated that, although there was a difference of opinion regarding whether a reserve was necessary, in a sense this was academic, because Member nations evidently would not support it either by funds or stocks.[44] The 1953 resolution reaffirmed Resolution 15 of 1951, and supported *ad hoc* measures to relieve famine conditions as "useful and necessary." It warmly approved the $100 million aid proffered by the United States, urged other nations to aid also, and recommended that the FAO be prepared to co-ordinate such action. Finally, the resolution suggested that countries belonging to the International Monetary Fund should apply to it for additional foreign exchange to finance food imports during emergencies.

With the passage of this resolution, the whole structure of the FAO preparatory work for the establishment of an international reserve to meet emergency food shortages collapsed. Yet something remained as a result of all the effort. The FAO has assumed definite responsibilities for keeping under review situations in which there is danger of famine, for ascertaining the type and scope and for estimating the possible duration of imminent crises, and for mobilizing voluntary support in time of need. This has been made possible by separating the problem of famine relief from the problem of price stability for agricultural commodities. Until 1952, the two problems had often been considered together and had become confused in the process.

Emergency Aid for Other Purposes

International emergency relief requirements most frequently take the form of sharply increased needs for food (principally grains) from abroad. However, floods, fires, earthquakes, epidemics, and other disasters may require pumping equipment, tents and temporary shelters, clothing, blankets, and medical supplies in greater volume than a hardhit country can supply. During the course of its life, the United Nations has on several occasions assisted nations having emergency require-

---

[44] Food and Agriculture Organization, *Report of the Seventh Session of the Conference, 23 November–11 December* 1953 (1954), Res. 21.

ments of this type. When such situations have been brought to the attention of Member governments, the response has been voluntary, prompt, and generous, but no regular procedures have been established for meeting these emergencies.

Except for its interest in providing famine aid, the United Nations has never looked with favor on the establishment of such procedures. From the League of Nations, it inherited the International Relief Union, which had been brought into being by convention in 1932 for the purpose of giving aid and co-ordinating international action in the event of a "major disaster due to *force majeure*."[45] After the formation of the United Nations, the Union urged its member governments to support a plan to bring it into some kind of relationship with the new organization. Attempts to obtain funds from the United Nations Educational, Scientific, and Cultural Organization to continue its research activities were unsuccessful, as was its approach to the Economic and Social Council for a permanent relationship with the United Nations. With the support of the President of the International Red Cross Committee and some of its member governments, the International Relief Union sought to have its convention revised so as to enable it to co-ordinate the work of various temporary United Nations relief organizations and to "provide a centre for regular meetings of the representatives of the States interested in the establishment of an international relief programme."[46] Other member governments favored its termination, and the Economic and Social Council recommended in 1950 that United Nations Members belonging to the International Relief Union take steps to terminate it.[47]

Under the United Nations, the pattern of action in cases other than those involving serious shortages of food has included notification to United Nations organs and agencies concerned with social welfare, particularly the Children's Fund and the World Health Organization, and the transmittal of official appeals to Member nations for assistance. The Children's Fund has definite responsibilities for helping to meet the relief needs of women and children, and the World Health Organization has an obligation to assist in times of epidemic. None of the other agencies has been set up or financed to meet emergency relief requirements wherever they happen to arise.

There is no regular channel in the United Nations through which

[45] See above, Chap. I.

[46] U.N. Economic and Social Council, Tenth Session, *Relations with Inter-Governmental Organizations,* Doc. E/1574/Add. 2 (Jan. 30, 1950), p. 4.

[47] U.N. Economic and Social Council, Fourteenth Session, *Food and Famine, Procedures for International Action in the Event of Emergency Famines . . . ,* p. 3, note 2.

appeals for aid are initiated. The General Assembly was in session when northern Italy was inundated by severe floods late in 1951, and its Third (Social, Humanitarian, and Cultural) Committee adopted a resolution proposed by Uruguay requesting the President of the General Assembly and the Secretary-General to advise all United Nations organizations having social welfare responsibilities of Italian needs, and urging these agencies to provide immediate assistance. On other occasions, the initiative has been taken by the Economic and Social Council, by the FAO, or by UNICEF.

In a report to the Economic and Social Council on procedures for dealing with famine emergencies, the Secretary-General suggested that the procedures for meeting emergencies arising from crop failures could be applied to other disaster situations.[48] The resolution of the Economic and Social Council, which followed consideration of the Secretary-General's report, however, confined itself to United Nations action in times of famine emergency. Nevertheless, it is conceivable that in the future, the Secretary-General will, with the acquiescence of the General Assembly and the Economic and Social Council, invoke the procedures applicable to famine situations when other emergency situations are brought to his attention. The pattern may in this manner become accepted practice long before it is embodied in a formal resolution.

Collective Measures Against Future Aggression

Of a quite different order and character than the efforts of the United Nations to prepare for crises due to natural disasters were the efforts to prepare collective measures to meet the man-made disaster of aggression.

Only fortuitous circumstances had enabled the United Nations to take swift action against the North Korean aggression: there was a United Nations Commission on Korea present to report the facts of the attack, the Soviet delegate had boycotted the Security Council and therefore was not able to veto its action recommendations, and American forces were available in Japan to rush to Korea with desperately needed assistance to help check the initial onslaught. The United Nations, taking advantage of these circumstances, created and organized a cooperative military enterprise which was unique in history and which offered considerable promise for the future.

The Korean experience revealed the need for further planning to realize the potentialities of collective action through the United Nations and to

---

[48] *Ibid.*, p. 3.

strengthen the United Nations as an instrument of collective security in the future.[49]

The "Uniting for Peace" resolution adopted by the General Assembly, in November 1950, represented an important step in this direction. The resolution provided, among other things, for the establishment of a Collective Measures Committee of fourteen members to study and report on methods that might be used to strengthen international peace and security under the Charter.[50]

During 1951 and 1952, the committee considered political, military, and economic measures and embodied its conclusions in two major reports to the General Assembly.[51] The present discussion deals only with what the committee called "measures of an economic and financial character," a field which it analyzed with outstanding skill.[52]

Although the analysis of the committee was notably lucid and well-reasoned, it appears to have had little effect on the actions of Member governments. The elaboration of measures to be used at some unknown future date against a hypothetical aggressor that might have at its disposal resources as vast as those of the Soviet bloc, or as modest as those of Jordan, was inevitably a somewhat theoretical exercise. Enthusiasm for the project was generated primarily by the United States. It was carrying the brunt of the Korean burden, was alert to the possibilities of similar attacks on other vulnerable areas, and was determined that the United Nations should be better prepared to resist future aggression than it had been in Korea. At the same time, however, the United States was carrying on delicate negotiations with its North Atlantic Treaty partners regarding methods of sharing the cost of rearmament. The United States was eager to have Members of the world organization committed to effective resistance to aggression,

[49] U.S. Department of State, *United States Participation in the United Nations: Report by the President to the Congress for the Year 1951*, Publication 4583 (July 1952), p. 49.

[50] The fourteen members were: Australia, Belgium, Brazil, Burma, Canada, Egypt, France, Mexico, Philippines, Turkey, the United Kingdom, the United States, Venezuela, and Yugoslavia.

[51] U.N. General Assembly, Sixth Session, *Official Records*, Supplement No. 13, "Report of the Collective Measures Committee," (hereinafter cited as "First Report of the Collective Measures Committee"); U.N. General Assembly, Seventh Session, *Official Records*, Supplement No. 17, "Report of the Collective Measures Committee," (hereinafter cited as "Second Report of the Collective Measures Committee.")

[52] For a comprehensive discussion of United Nations activities in the preparation of collective measures against future aggression, see the volume in this Brookings series, *The United Nations and the Maintenance of International Peace and Security*, Chaps. XVI–XIX, particularly Chaps. XVI and XVIII.

but it was not at all eager for the United Nations to develop formulae for burden-sharing that might complicate the concurrent discussions of the subject in the North Atlantic Treaty Organization.

The underdeveloped countries were reluctant to undertake any commitments that might interfere with the realization of their development plans. It is worth noting, for example, that the "Uniting for Peace" resolution ends not with a recommendation that governments increase their readiness to take collective action against military aggression, but that they "intensify individual and collective efforts to achieve conditions of economic stability and social progress, *particularly through the development of under-developed countries and areas.*"[53] The underdeveloped countries were eager for the United Nations to develop detailed blueprints for a World Food Board or for utilizing a hypothetical fund to make grants-in-aid for economic development—projects that the United States considered academic—but they were hesitant to blueprint measures for repelling future aggression—an undertaking that the United States considered urgent. The closer the Korean situation moved toward an armistice, the more vocal became the fears of other nations that the studies of the Collective Measures Committee reflected a bellicose, and hence wrong, philosophy on the part of the United Nations.

The Soviet bloc, of course, was fundamentally opposed to the work of the Collective Measures Committee. Its representatives argued repeatedly that the committee was illegal, that its activities reflected the aggressive aims of imperialist powers, and that it should be abolished.

Weakening the Aggressor

Among the recent practical experiences on which the Collective Measures Committee could draw were the panoply of economic warfare measures employed in conjunction with military measures against the Axis Powers during the Second World War; the arms embargo invoked by the United Nations as part of the Palestine truce; the hastily-improvised machinery for repelling the attack on South Korea; and the ban on shipments of items of strategic importance to Communist China following its intervention in Korea. In addition, the United States, from 1948 on, had been negotiating with friendly nations, outside the United Nations framework, for withholding items of strategic importance from countries of the Soviet bloc. There were

[53] Res. 377 A (V), Nov. 3, 1950, para. 15. (Italics supplied.)

many lessons to be drawn from these experiences. Plans must be ready in advance or disastrous delays would occur at the crucial moment. The application of agreed measures should be prompt, thorough, and universal. Nevertheless, relatively few countries could be brought to terms by economic measures alone. The cost of applying sanctions, unless pro-rated in some manner, would fall very unevenly on co-operating countries. The employment of sanctions against nations breaching or threatening the peace was but one side of the coin, and the more questionable side at that; mobilizing assistance for the victim was the other side. In this field of emergency relief, there was likewise a legacy of practical experience on which to draw.

The Collective Measures Committee therefore considered both measures to weaken the economy of an aggressor and to strengthen the economy of the victim. It reminded Member governments that political, economic and financial, and military measures could be applied singly or in combination, according to the circumstances giving rise to the threat to, or breach of, the peace, the geographical location of the offending state, its economic self-sufficiency, and its sensitivity to moral pressure.[54] Some countries remain virtually immune to the effects of economic measures. Moreover, the efficiency of sanctions against states capable of economic endurance would diminish over time, both because of defections among the states participating in the sanctions and because of the ability of the states subjected to sanctions to adapt their economies to the changed situation. The countries most vulnerable to economic measures would be those that are highly developed and, at the same time, significantly dependent on international trade, particularly on imports of foodstuffs.[55]

Collective measures are not without cost to those employing them, ... The damage which is done to the economy of an aggressor by such measures is matched, in the aggregate, by a corresponding loss distributed over the economies of the countries applying the measures. The economic basis for the action lies in the assumption that each of the cooperating countries will suffer a small and bearable loss, while the counterpart effect will be concentrated on the single economy of the aggressor and will be much more damaging.[56]

In practice, the costs will fall unevenly on co-operating nations and tend to be greatest for those having special supply or market relationships with the transgressor. In the view of the committee, the central importance of measures to equalize the burden had not in the past been

[54] "First Report of the Collective Measures Committee," para. 22.
[55] *Ibid.*, paras. 44 and 50.
[56] *Ibid.*, para. 52.

sufficiently appreciated. The committee made a few general suggestions concerning such measures, including the provision of alternative markets, raw materials, loans, and grants, but concluded rather lamely that no rules for sharing the cost of economic measures could be laid down in advance.[57]

The committee discussed in turn each of the economic and financial measures available for use against a potential aggressor: a total or a selective embargo on its commodity trade, the banning of some or all financial transactions with the government or nationals of the aggressor, the severing of physical communications, and the blocking or vesting of funds or property abroad. The total embargo was recommended as the basic and most effective sanction; the arms embargo as the most obvious form of selective embargo. To guard against loss of time in debating which armaments to ban, the Collective Measures Committee in 1952 compiled a list of arms, ammunition, and implements of war designed for application *in toto* the moment an arms embargo was declared. Two additional lists were prepared. The first, designed as a logical supplement to an arms embargo, comprised items virtually as vital as armaments themselves, namely, items of primary strategic importance such as transport materials and equipment, petroleum and petroleum products, communications and electronic equipment, and air-field or road construction equipment. The second was a reference list of strategic items such as power-generating equipment that might be of major importance in particular instances of aggression.[58]

Strengthening the Victim of Aggression

The selection and continuation of measures to deter aggression depend, unfortunately, on imperfect knowledge of the requirements, inventories, and ability of the aggressor to find substitutes for anything that is being withheld. In theory, at least, rendering effective assistance to the victim is simpler because the needs of the victim can be ascertained directly. When hostilities occur, relief and refugee assistance must be regarded as essential features of the program, along with loans, grants, supplies, and the more traditional forms of aid.[59]

With the Korean experience fresh in mind, the committee concluded that during the period of hostilities, relief assistance must be the responsibility of the armed forces. Only after hostilities have ceased

[57] *Ibid.*, paras. 52–56.
[58] "Second Report of the Collective Measures Committee," App. H and I.
[59] "First Report of the Collective Measures Committee," paras. 57–59.

in the area to be assisted can the job be undertaken by civilian agencies.[60] Several extremely pertinent questions concerning this conclusion have been raised:

> ... Does it also follow that during a period of prolonged armistice negotiations, when hostilities still technically exist but when the military line is stabilized, that responsibility for relief and rehabilitation should rest with the armed forces? What is meant by the term "in the area"—the area immediately adjacent to the fighting, or the whole country in the case of Korea? Even though the military command must assume immediate responsibility for relief and rehabilitation, is it not possible to bring the military command under some overall international civilian direction that will give better assurance that nonmilitary considerations will receive due attention?[61]

An investigation of the readiness of the specialized agencies to co-operate, within the limits of their constitutions, in the application of collective measures brought forth expressions of willingness to do so. It became clear, however, that these agencies could commit themselves in advance to make only marginal contributions.

Although national governments could be expected to operate the basic economic and financial controls, international machinery would be needed to co-ordinate the undertaking. The Collective Measures Committee, therefore, recommended that a co-ordinating committee, whose membership should depend on the circumstances of the case, be established by the Security Council or the General Assembly immediately on the finding of a threat to or breach of the peace.[62]

Since 1952, the United Nations has done little to extend or refine its earlier studies of collective economic measures. This very fact jeopardizes the value of the work that has already been done, for in an era of rapid technical progress, sanction procedures and embargo lists tend to become useless unless they are continuously revised in the light of the most recent information. In the age of the hydrogen bomb, the framework developed by the Collective Measures Committee in the shadow of the Korean aggression can quickly become irrelevant.

As matters stand, the United Nations has compiled some useful source material for reference in the event of further threats to the peace. The suggested framework is itself incomplete and lacks the formal approval of the General Assembly. Despite the efforts of the United States and certain other countries to have the Assembly at its

---

[60] *Ibid.*, para. 144.

[61] See the volume in this Brookings series, *The United Nations and the Maintenance of International Peace and Security*, pp. 488–89.

[62] The major functions of this co-ordinating committee are described in the "First Report of the Collective Measures Committee," para. 114.

sixth session go on record as "approving" the first report of the Collective Measures Committee, the Assembly in the end "noted" rather than "approved" it. At the seventh session, China called for prompt negotiations among Member states to secure ratified agreements relating to their participation in collective measures, but its initiative evoked little favorable response.

Pattern Established by Practice

The efforts of the United Nations to solve economic and social problems that, initially at least, seemed to be of an emergency character, have met with only limited success. Each of the organs and agencies established to meet such situations was given complex assignments. Some had their terms of reference changed repeatedly during the course of their activity and were confronted with almost insuperable operational difficulties.

The operating programs have been dependent on periodic voluntary contributions. Because some of the programs have required substantial sums, and because all have required broad participation and a continued high level of sympathy, they have been seriously handicapped by inadequate financing and declining interest. Advance planning for more than a few months ahead has been impossible; pledges have not met requirements, and actual contributions have fallen short of pledges; contributions in inconvertible currencies and in kind have further complicated the problem. Most of the burden has tended to fall on a few of the richer, hard-currency nations, principally the United States, and these in turn have become restive under their burden.

To difficulties inherent in the system of financing must be added the difficulties resulting from major political differences among Member states. Thus far the United Nations has not succeeded in solving the problem of Palestine refugees and is still confronted with a tragic situation that seems destined to continue until there is greater Arab-Israeli agreement in the area.

The persistent attacks by the Soviet bloc on the work of the International Refugee Organization doubtless hampered its work. Nevertheless, the IRO was probably second only to UNICEF as the most successful of the major United Nations efforts in the emergency field, namely UNICEF, IRO, UNRWA, and UNKRA. Re-establishment of the Palestine refugees on a self-sufficient basis and the reconstruction of Korea are essentially long-range undertakings requiring substantially more resources than are likely to be contributed voluntarily to international emergency agencies. The relative success of UNICEF has been due not so much to the management or character of the machinery as to the fact that the objectives of UNICEF are universally supported, the concept is simple, and the cost is low.

In planning or carrying out relief programs, it has become the established practice of the United Nations to lean on private voluntary agencies for important specialized services.

None of the attempts of the United Nations to establish stand-by machinery to meet future disasters can be regarded as successful. Only a few remnants of the elaborate proposals for famine reserves have been adopted, and no formal arrangements have been made for meeting disaster requirements for non-food items.

The lack of adequate stand-by arrangements is unquestionably a deficiency but should not obscure the fact that, when face to face with an emergency, the international community has invariably accepted a share of the responsibility for relieving the emergency, either through *ad hoc* co-operation among established agencies, or through newly-created temporary bodies. The willingness of the international community to provide help in the event of sudden need, most dramatically illustrated in 1944–46 by UNRRA, is therefore firmly rooted in practice, although not clearly proclaimed in principle.

The absence of approved machinery for co-ordinating the application of collective economic and financial measures against an aggressor, and of arrangements for sharing equitably the cost of applying them, is also a deficiency. It is easy, however, to overestimate the potential value of economic sanctions because decisions concerning their employment are inevitably made without adequate knowledge of the aggressor's requirements, inventories, intentions, or willingness to suffer deprivation. It is open to question, therefore, whether the war-making capacity of the aggressor will be damaged severely enough to justify the superstructure engaged in administering the sanctions and the strains among governments applying them. On the other hand, supplies, loans, grants, and refugee aid for the victim are indubitably helpful. For this more traditional form of action in an emergency situation, the United Nations has ample precedents.

CHAPTER III

International Trade and Payments[*]

DURING the ten years since the first meetings of the principal organs of the United Nations, all efforts to harmonize national viewpoints and to solve long-range problems of international trade and payments, whether through the United Nations system or outside it, have been strongly influenced by the basic differences of national attitude described earlier in this study. As previously shown, however, the lines of cleavage that came to the surface in the international negotiations prior to the entry into force of the United Nations Charter were, except in the case of the Soviet Union, not such as to preclude fruitful and friendly negotiation. They were often the product, not of deep-seated differences in social organization or political philosophy, but of judgment regarding the policies that would best promote objectives that, although held in common, appeared to come into conflict in particular situations.

Questions of timing, priorities, and methods have been the staple of international discussion between the major trading countries, particularly between the United States and the countries of Western Europe and of the British Commonwealth. To some extent, this has also been true of the differences between the industrialized and the underdeveloped countries, although the tendency of the latter to make common cause in the United Nations against the industrialized countries on issues affecting trade and payments has frequently underscored the more fundamental character of these differences.

The case has been different with the Soviet Union and its Eastern European satellites. The relatively small fraction of international trade carried on by these countries and the basic differences between their forms of economic organization and those of other members of the United Nations have made it difficult for them to participate constructively in international co-operation in the field of trade and payments.[1]

[*] By William Adams Brown, Jr.

[1] In 1948 this group of countries accounted for about 7 per cent of total world trade, and in 1953 for about 9 per cent. This slight increase in their share of an expanding volume of world trade was due almost entirely to an expansion of trade among themselves and with mainland China. *Cf.* U.N. Economic Commission for Europe, *Economic Survey of Europe in 1954* (1955), pp. 112–13.

In the debates of the General Assembly and the Economic and Social Council, the Soviet bloc has actively sought to exploit the differences existing between the underdeveloped and the industrialized countries, but in the main, the impact of the Soviet Union on the trade and payments activities of the United Nations has been indirect. The tensions created by its political and military policies, which have divided the world into contending blocs, have had a pervasive effect on all forms of postwar international economic co-operation both within and outside the United Nations. It is these policies, rather than differences in economic organization, that have excluded the Soviet bloc from sustained and constructive participation in international negotiations and debates on the central problems of international trade and payments.

The work of the United Nations system in the field of international trade and payments has been influenced in an extremely complex way by the national attitudes of Member governments, by the actual progress made in improving the situation in world trade and payments, and by the international co-operation achieved outside the system. Until recently, the work has had to be carried on in circumstances that were not propitious for the achievement of common objectives through international agencies with nearly world-wide membership. It has been complicated further by the failure to develop an integrated approach to international trade and related problems through the proposed International Trade Organization, and by the multiplicity of agencies, both within and outside the United Nations system, concerned with one or another aspect of these problems.

During the period preceding the invasion of South Korea in June 1950, the work of the United Nations and related agencies was gradually taking form. The International Monetary Fund (IMF) had to make basic decisions concerning its functions and principles of operation in a period of fundamental international disequilibrium in world trade. The Economic and Social Council was called upon to sponsor negotiations for an International Trade Organization (ITO) and to wrestle with the problem of which functions to allocate to that organization. Hopes that the ITO would come into existence were finally extinguished about the time of the invasion of South Korea, but a related trade agreement—the General Agreement on Tariffs and Trade (GATT)—had in the meantime come into being and, under it, the first steps toward a reduction of trade barriers had been taken.

These activities were greatly influenced by the launching of the

European Recovery Program outside the framework of the United Nations. The need arose for reconciling a regional approach to trade and payments in Europe with the global principles to which the Fund and the GATT were committed. At this time also, the work of the regional economic commissions of the United Nations was beginning to take form and some consideration was given in their meetings to trade problems from the regional point of view. During this period, moreover, the interest of the Food and Agriculture Organization (FAO) in trade problems was developing. Meanwhile the Economic and Social Council was largely concerned to emphasize the interests of underdeveloped countries in trade policies and to discuss the general trade problem largely in terms of employment.

The influence of the Korean War in promoting rearmament and two years of extreme fluctuation in world prices had very significant repercussions on the whole approach of the international community to trade and payments problems. The period following the invasion of South Korea may therefore be considered separately. When progress toward international equilibrium was resumed in 1953–54, the IMF developed a new lending policy, which might be available as conditions favorable to convertibility emerged. At the same time, the GATT was confronted with difficult problems connected with regional activities in Europe, with its own relationships to underdeveloped countries, and with questions regarding its methods of negotiation.

From the End of the War to the Invasion of South Korea

The outstanding economic characteristics of the period preceding the invasion of South Korea were the gradual disclosure of the true dimensions of the recovery and reconstruction problem, the general readjustment of foreign exchange rates, and the progress made during the first two years of the European Recovery Program toward international equilibrium.

Emergency Action and the Fundamental Disequilibrium in Trade

At the end of the Second World War, it was widely assumed, especially in the United States, that after a short period of transition the International Bank for Reconstruction and Development (IBRD) would become the principal source of intergovernmental lending, that the operations of the International Monetary Fund would assure the orderly functioning of a system of multilateral payments, and that the proposed International Trade Organization would be able to play an important role in providing the international economic environment necessary for the maintenance of high levels of world trade. These hopes with regard to the Bank and the Fund, which formally became specialized agencies of the United Nations when agreements were reached on November 15, 1947, were not fulfilled because of the fundamental disequilibrium in trade. The disequilibrium in trade also greatly influenced the commitments that countries in balance-of-payments difficulties were willing to assume in the ITO negotiations.

The sponsorship of these negotiations raised several important problems for the Economic and Social Council with which it was not ready to deal effectively because it was still engaged in developing its own organization and in dealing with emergency economic problems such as the arrangements for the allocation of materials in short supply, the continuation of certain activities of the United Nations Relief and Rehabilitation Administration (UNRRA), and the economic reconstruction of devastated areas.[2] Although the Articles of Agreement of the Fund stated specifically that the Fund was "not intended to provide facilities for relief or reconstruction or to deal with international indebtedness arising out of the war," they did provide for transactions with members even during the postwar transitional period.[3] In judging requests for such assistance, the Fund was obligated to give its members "the benefit of any reasonable doubt,"[4] and it did so by selling to members $606 million in dollar exchange between March 1947 and April 1948. Of these sales $526 million were to European members.

The executive directors of the Fund acknowledged that in making these advances, the Fund was running the risk that its resources would be used for purposes other than temporary assistance, but stated that they were anxious to have the Fund "make a contribution to the maintenance of national economies and of exchange stability during

[2] United Nations, *Report of the Secretary-General on the Work of the Organization*, Doc. A/65 (June 30, 1946), p. 14. For a discussion of these activities, see Chaps. II and IV of this volume.

[3] United Nations Monetary and Financial Conference, Bretton Woods, N.H., July 1 to 22, 1944, *Articles of Agreement, International Monetary Fund and International Bank for Reconstruction and Development* (1945), Art. XIV, Sec. 1, p. 29. (Hereinafter cited as *Articles of Agreement*.)

[4] *Ibid.*, Sec. 5, p. 30.

the transitional period."[5] This was clearly an understatement inasmuch as the Fund was operating in a crisis situation in which France was living from hand to mouth as far as dollar reserves were concerned, and Britain was struggling with an exchange crisis, with no reasonable expectation that either country would soon be able to restore balance-of-payments equilibrium.[6] In 1947, the Bank made its contribution by extending four general-purpose loans to European members, amounting in all to nearly $500 million.[7] Of the combined total of $1,099 million made available, $979 million went to the Benelux countries, France, and Great Britain.

The main co-operative efforts to help countries in balance-of-payments difficulties to meet their essential import requirements, however, were made outside the United Nations system. They included very large grants and credits by the United States to individual countries; substantial credits within the British Commonwealth; the accumulation of European currencies by other countries, including Latin American countries; the extension of large credits in bilateral trade and payments agreements, particularly in Europe but also with Latin American countries; the major operations of the UNRRA program and the civilian supply programs of the American and British military authorities in occupied and liberated areas; and, in addition, substantial private grants mainly from the United States.[8]

This vast mobilization of resources financed a flow of essential imports into countries that had suffered extensive war damage or whose economies had been seriously weakened by the war. Although these imports were on a scale sufficient to maintain minimum standards of living during the first critical stages of reconversion and reconstruction, they were far from sufficient to meet the potential demands of many of the importing countries. These demands were restrained by numerous forms of government action. Aside from the brief period of sterling convertibility in 1947, almost every country in the world except the

[5] International Monetary Fund, *Annual Report of the Executive Directors for the Fiscal Year Ended April 30, 1948* (1948), p. 46.

[6] Of the British drawings on the Fund, $250 million was in September, October, and November 1947, immediately following the suspension of convertibility, and the remaining $60 million was drawn in March 1948. *The Economist* (Dec. 6, 1947), p. 933, and (Apr. 3, 1948), p. 563.

[7] See below, Chap. IV.

[8] International Monetary Fund, *Annual Report of the Executive Directors for the Fiscal Year Ending June 30, 1947* (1947), pp. 10–13. For a review of American loans and grants during this period, amounting to $14.5 billion, see also William Adams Brown, Jr. and Redvers Opie, *American Foreign Assistance* (1953), Chap. III, *passim*.

United States was carrying on its trade under severe exchange and direct trade controls or other forms of government regulation.

The period as a whole was marked by an impressive improvement in production, especially in war-devastated countries.[9] For a time, this improvement tended to obscure the true gravity of the prevailing economic dislocations. Unlike the First World War, the Second World War had seriously impaired the capacity of many countries producing raw materials. At the same time, almost all such countries were intent on diversifying their economies and reducing their dependence on the production of primary commodities. The situation was further complicated by the political obstacles that hindered an expansion of trade between Eastern and Western Europe, and by the virtual elimination of Germany and Japan from world markets. In the case of the Netherlands, France, and the United Kingdom, the balance-of-payments problem was further aggravated by the loss of very large sources of invisible income, which increased their dependence on exports of goods and services to meet their import requirements.

Although the volume of imports in 1946 of most countries outside the dollar area failed by substantial margins to reach prewar levels, largely because of difficulties in obtaining supplies from customary sources, most of these countries were in serious balance-of-payments difficulties. Their import demand was heavily concentrated on the Western Hemisphere, and especially on the United States. In 1946, exports from the United States exceeded those of 1938 by 90 per cent in volume, and exports from Canada surpassed the Canadian level of 1938 by 45 per cent. In both countries imports were about 40 per cent above prewar. The export surplus of the United States was no less than $7.7 billion, of which $4.9 billion was financed by United States government grants and credits, and $1.9 billion by the liquidation of gold and short-term dollar assets of other nations.[10]

These figures, of course, do not fully describe the disorganized pattern of world trade and payments that prevailed when the Fund and the Bank were completing their organizational work and were preparing to begin operations. This pattern was influenced by the availability of reserves of individual countries and the extent to which they could obtain loans and credits, as well as by supply factors. It was also influenced by restrictions imposed on trade and payments, by

[9] International Monetary Fund, *Annual Report . . . April 30, 1948*, pp. 2–3.
[10] For detailed comparisons between the situation in 1946 and that in 1938, see International Monetary Fund, *Annual Report . . . June 30, 1947*, pp. 4–10.

major changes in shipping, and by many other factors. The figures do, however, disclose the general characteristics of the "fundamental disequilibrium" that existed at that time and the dimensions of the problem still to be solved. Because the United States had an export surplus on current account with almost every other geographical area of the world, this problem was universally described as the dollar problem.

In order to meet their current account deficits with the United States in 1947, other countries had to liquidate $4.4 billion in gold and short-term dollar assets. The dollar deficit of Europe with the United States was by far the largest of any major geographical area, and in 1947, European gold and short-term dollar assets declined by $2 billion. The weakness of the British position was fully disclosed in the sterling convertibility crisis of 1947, while in the three major continental countries of Europe—France, Italy, and Germany—a state of economic and political crisis prevailed. The situation in the Eastern European countries, where Soviet influence was a major political factor, was economically and financially even more precarious.[11]

At this critical juncture, plans were formulated for a new large-scale program of international co-operation—the four-year European Recovery Program—which it was hoped would solve the main problems of European recovery. During the first half of this program, there was substantial progress toward general balance-of-payments equilibrium although this encouraging trend was temporarily reversed during the mild recession in the United States in the first half of 1949. The position of the United Kingdom in particular was adversely affected. The severe drain on British gold and dollar reserves was not due primarily to British trade relations with the United States but was the result mainly of increased gold and dollar payments to nondollar countries and to certain capital movements and other financial transactions motivated by rumors of impending sterling devaluation.[12] This outflow of capital was reversed when, on September 21, 1949, the sterling-dollar rate was lowered from $4.03 to $2.80 per pound. Two months before the devaluation of sterling, which was followed by a world-wide readjustment of exchange rates, United Kingdom import quotas had been reduced sufficiently to cut dollar imports by 25 per cent, and

[11] Brown and Opie, *op. cit.*, pp. 119–23.
[12] U.S. Department of Commerce, *Balance of Payments of the United States, 1949–1951*, A Supplement to the *Survey of Current Business* (1952), p. 6.

similar restrictions had been imposed by other Commonwealth countries.

Before the effects of sterling devaluation and the increased quantitative restrictions of the Commonwealth could be reflected in the figures of international trade, the trend of economic activity in the United States had again turned sharply upward and American imports from almost all major geographical areas began to increase. By the end of the third quarter of 1950, the United States export surplus on current account with the rest of the world almost disappeared. This was also true of the export surpluses of Canada with nondollar areas.

In most European countries, inflation was being brought under control, although there was still no assurance that its basic causes had been eliminated. European industrial production, Germany excepted, was above prewar levels by a considerable margin, and even agricultural production was slightly above prewar. Intra-European trade was steadily expanding. Merchandise imports from the United States were substantially reduced, and exports to the United States slightly increased. European exports to the rest of the world were rapidly expanded. The dollar deficit of the members of the Organization for European Economic Cooperation (OEEC), which in 1947 had been $7.5 billion, had been reduced in the first half of 1950 to an annual rate of $2 billion, and American aid was beginning to contribute to reserves.

There was also some improvement in Latin American and Far Eastern countries, but this was not comparable to that of Europe. The balance-of-payments position of many of these countries had been weakened by the decline in the prices of raw materials in the first half of 1949. This decline continued at irregular intervals immediately after the September devaluation, the fall of prices of metals and petroleum being especially serious for some Latin American countries. However, late in 1949 and in the first half of 1950, the prices of raw materials began to rise again, and this was the most general cause of such improvement as took place. In most of these countries, inflation continued to be a factor working against the restoration of balance-of-payments equilibrium, and in only a few—notably Japan where, as in Germany, there had been a radical change in occupation policy—was the improvement attributable to increased production.[13]

[13] For the major developments in international payments during this period see International Monetary Fund, *Annual Report of the Executive Directors for the Fiscal Year Ended April 30, 1950* (1950), pp. 16–21; *Annual Report of the Executive Directors for the Fiscal Year Ended April 30, 1951* (1951), pp. 1–13; and U.S. Department of Commerce, *Balance of Payments of the United States, 1949–1951*, pp. 1–3.

Marshall Plan and
Work of the United Nations

One of the first effects of the launching of the European Recovery Program was to relieve the Fund of pressure to use its resources in ways that were really inconsistent with its basic purposes. On April 20, 1948, the Executive Directors of the Fund decided that the members of the Fund that were also participants in the European Recovery Program could negotiate with the Fund for dollars only in exceptional and unforeseen circumstances. The purpose of this action was to conserve the resources of the Fund so that at the end of the recovery period, these members might have unencumbered access to them.[14] More important, from the long-range point of view, were the problems raised for the United Nations by the appearance on the scene of the Organization for European Economic Cooperation, entirely outside the jurisdiction of the United Nations, through which its Western European members were to co-operate to solve many of their monetary and trade problems on a regional basis.

The terms of reference of the OEEC on commercial policy required co-operation toward the objectives of reducing trade barriers between the participating countries and of establishing the world multilateral trading system contemplated in the Havana Charter for an International Trade Organization.[15] Inasmuch as nondiscrimination was a basic principle of the Havana Charter, these two objectives were, in the short run at least, potentially contradictory,[16] and this contradiction was not removed by the inclusion in the Charter of some ingenious devices for reconciling certain types of preferential trade arrangements with a world-wide effort to promote nondiscriminatory trade. It was almost inevitable, therefore, that as a result of the work of the OEEC, the difficulty of reconciling regional and world objectives in the field of trade, as in the monetary field, would assume serious proportions.

The OEEC had the advantage of being able to deal with European monetary and trade problems together on a regional basis, but the United Nations system was not in a position to do so on a world basis. It was handicapped from the outset by the dispersion of responsibility

[14] International Monetary Fund, *Annual Report . . . April 30, 1948*, App. IV, pp. 74–75.

[15] Great Britain, *Convention for European Economic Co-operation, Paris, 16 April 1948*, Cmd. 7388 (1948), Arts. 5 and 6.

[16] On this point see William Adams Brown, Jr., *The United States and the Restoration of World Trade* (1950), pp. 308–10.

for international co-operation on trade and payments among different international bodies. These handicaps were expected to be overcome in considerable measure by the creation of the ITO as a specialized agency. The responsibilities envisaged for this agency were considerably expanded during the course of the long negotiations for the ITO Charter, and one of the many ways in which the European Recovery Program influenced the future work of the United Nations was its important, although indirect, contribution to the success of these negotiations. Had there not seemed to be good prospects that the European Recovery Program would put Europe as a whole on a self-sustaining basis, the charter might have been so weakened as to prove unacceptable to the American negotiators. This was not a matter of transitory significance, ending with the abandonment of the ITO itself. Many provisions of the charter continued to influence international co-operation on trade and related problems, including co-operation through the United Nations, long after the ITO had been abandoned.

Sponsorship of ITO Negotiations

In making public the Anglo-American *Proposals for Expansion of World Trade and Employment* in November 1945, the United States Secretary of State announced that the United States representatives in the appropriate United Nations organs would urge that an International Conference on Trade and Employment meet under the sponsorship of the United Nations. It was proposed at the Preparatory Commission of the United Nations that the question of achieving "an equitable adjustment of prices in the world markets" be included in the scope of the conference.[17] It is significant that the very first issue thus raised in the United Nations concerning the proposed International Trade Organization was one of special interest to the underdeveloped countries. This issue was raised again when, at its first session (January–February 1946), the Economic and Social Council considered and adopted a resolution calling for the establishment of a Preparatory Committee of nineteen members. As introduced by the United States, this resolution proposed an agenda confined to matters dealt with in the proposals, but it was amended in the Council by requesting the Preparatory Committee to "take into account the special conditions which prevailed in countries whose manufacturing industry is still in its initial stages of

---

[17] U.N. Preparatory Commission, *Report of the Preparatory Commission of the United Nations*, Doc. PC/20 (Dec. 23, 1945), p. 22.

development, and the questions that arise in connection with commodities which are subject to special problems of adjustment in international markets."[18]

The resolution also reserved the right of the Council to make suggestions to the Preparatory Committee and so involved it in taking positions on substantive as well as procedural questions. The subsequent communications between the Preparatory Committee and the Council illustrated an important segment of a much broader problem confronting the United Nations, the appropriate allocation among all its agencies and organs of functions relating directly or indirectly to international trade and payments.

Allocation of Functions Within the United Nations System

In a *Report on Commercial Policy in the Post-War World*, published in 1945, the Economic and Financial Committees of the League of Nations had dealt with the relationship between commercial policy, production, and employment as follows:

> We are strongly of the opinion that the direct association of commercial policies with policies designed to secure an expansion of production and consumption and the maintenance of high and stable levels of employment is an essential prerequisite to progress towards international economic co-operation. The failure in the interwar years to emphasize the essential interdependence of these issues was indeed one of the reasons for the lack of success that was then experienced. We believe that . . . the most hopeful method of securing progress would be a general conference to deal *jointly* with commercial policy and the international aspects of employment policy.[19]

The thesis that an expanding economy and a high level of domestic employment are *prerequisites* for international economic co-operation has had a strong appeal to many Members of the United Nations. Nevertheless, it is open to question. When, however, the Secretary-General of the United Nations in his report to the second session of the General Assembly in 1947, quoted this view of the League of Nations commit-

[18] The nineteen members selected were Australia, Belgium, Brazil, Canada, Chile, China, Cuba, Czechoslovakia, France, India, Lebanon, Luxembourg, the Netherlands, New Zealand, Norway, South Africa, the Soviet Union, the United States, and the United Kingdom. Only the Soviet Union refused to serve. For the text of the resolution see United Nations, *Report of the First Session of the Preparatory Committee of the United Nations Conference on Trade and Employment* (October 1946), Annexure 1, p. 42.

[19] League of Nations, *Commercial Policy in the Post-War World: Report of the Economic and Financial Committees* (April 1945), p. 64. Italics supplied.

tees, he did so uncritically and without qualification. The advice of the League committees that a joint approach be made to commercial and employment policies had already been followed when the Economic and Social Council approved the agenda of the Preparatory Committee, but the Secretary-General was not content merely to emphasize the interdependence of commercial and employment policies. He took a position on the priorities that should be assigned to them by declaring that: "Unemployment in advanced industrial countries, and the underdevelopment of many areas of the world are much more serious and fundamental in their effect on the volume of world trade than the restrictive practices which are often merely the secondary phenomena of profound economic instability."[20] He thus gave his support to a body of opinion within the United Nations system that tended to minimize the positive contributions of a liberal commercial policy to high levels of employment and to economic development, even though these had been strongly emphasized in the basic instruments both of the Fund and the GATT.[21]

The Preparatory Committee found it difficult to reach agreement on what functions in the field of employment and economic development should be assigned to a trade organization, and what functions should be reserved for the Economic and Social Council, and how the two should be related. With respect to employment, the Preparatory Committee was confronted with the following dilemma. It recognized that preventing the international spread of depressions was beyond the capacities of an international trade organization. At the same time, it was made clear that some governments might not accept the commitments on commercial policy of the proposed ITO Charter unless there were firm assurances that some such continuing effort would be made either through the ITO or through the Economic and Social Council. To solve this problem, the Preparatory Committee decided that the future members of the ITO should be under obligation to co-operate with the Council on such matters as the assembling and dissemination of infor-

[20] U.N. General Assembly, Second Session, *Official Records*, Supplement No. 1, "Annual Report of the Secretary-General on the Work of the Organization" (1947), p. 26.

[21] See *Articles of Agreement*, Art. I(ii), p. 1; also, The Contracting Parties to the General Agreement on Tariffs and Trade, *General Agreement on Tariffs and Trade: Basic Instruments and Selected Documents*, Vol. I (May 1952), p. 13. The General Agreement was amended in 1955. With certain minor changes in the text, the preamble, which recognized explicitly the contribution of a liberal commercial policy to better standards of living, became Article I (Objectives). See *ibid.*, Vol. I (Revised, April 1955), p. 7.

mation relevant to the problem, and the initiation of various forms of consultation with intergovernmental agencies. Responsibilities for international co-operation to prevent the spread of depressions and to maintain full employment were left to the Council itself.

Another difficult problem before the Preparatory Committee was to determine what the functions of an international trade organization should be in the field of economic development, and how its responsibilities in that field should be related to those of the Economic and Social Council and of the many international agencies already concerned with economic development. At its first session (October 1946), the committee recognized the existence of a special relationship between economic development and the other objectives of the proposed charter, especially the expansion of trade, and in the final text of the charter, elaborate provision was made for co-operation within the organization and with the Economic and Social Council and other agencies to promote such development. This was in addition to many concessions made to underdeveloped countries in the commercial policy provisions of the charter—in particular, concessions regarding the use of quantitative restrictions for economic development purposes.[22]

In the field of commodity trade, the problem of allocating functions within the United Nations system was complicated by the fact that the Food and Agriculture Organization had a strong interest in any form of co-operation affecting trade in agricultural products. It was proposed, for example, early in the discussions of the Preparatory Committee, that commodity agreements on agricultural products should be placed under the FAO and not the ITO. In general, the representatives of FAO looked on commodity agreements as a desirable and constructive device for helping to solve the problems of primary commodities. In the Preparatory Committee and in the debates at the Havana Conference, therefore, the FAO often found itself in opposition to those who wished to treat international commodity agreements as necessary but essentially emergency exceptions to general rules of commercial policy. The United States supported the latter viewpoint, and it prevailed in the final drafting of the commodity chapter of the Charter.

At the time the Preparatory Committee first met, a number of international commodity discussions were already under way and the committee recommended that the Economic and Social Council establish

[22] For texts of the Charter and the resolutions of the Havana Conference, see United Nations Conference on Trade and Employment held at Havana, Cuba from Nov. 21, 1947 to Mar. 24, 1948, *Final Act and Related Documents* (March 1948).

an interim body to keep in touch with these developments. In March 1947, the Economic and Social Council adopted a resolution establishing the new agency under the resounding name of the Interim Coordinating Committee for International Commodity Arrangements.[23] This resolution recommended to governments that they adopt as a general guide in international consultations or actions with respect to commodity problems the principles laid down in the draft ITO Charter, and it directed the new interim committee to keep informed of, to facilitate, and to co-ordinate, such consultations or actions.[24]

Finally, the entire ITO negotiation was an attempt to allocate functions within the United Nations system in such a way as to provide a world-wide approach to many interrelated fields in accordance with certain agreed principles. To achieve this, it was necessary to compose conflicting viewpoints both among and within governments, some of which had been well developed in the interwar years and some of which were brought to the surface by the dislocations of the war itself. The United States negotiators, for example, while striving to assert general principles of multilateralism and nondiscrimination and to keep the use of restrictions other than tariffs to a minimum, also found it necessary to insist on provisions that would safeguard the subsidies and import quotas required by American domestic agricultural policy. A large group of the underdeveloped countries strongly urged that they be given special rights to introduce new preferential arrangements and import quotas in the interests of economic development.

The European countries, in general more susceptible than the United States to balance-of-payments difficulties and more accustomed to governmental controls and to the regulation of foreign trade, insisted that provision should be made for enabling them to deal with their balance-of-payments difficulties through the use of such methods. In addition, rules had to be devised governing trade carried on partly or—as in the case of the Soviet Union—wholly by the state, and trade carried on by international cartels.

The final text of the Havana Charter therefore contained many escape clauses, reserved rights, and transitional arrangements. It reflected the dislocations not only of the Second World War but also of a whole generation. Nevertheless, it contained specific commitments in eight different fields as well as many undertakings for consultation.

[23] Res. 30(IV), Mar. 28, 1947.
[24] U.N. Interim Coordinating Committee for International Commodity Arrangements, *Review of International Commodity Arrangements* (1947), pp. 7-9.

The charter recognized that the employment policies of its members were of vital concern to other members and contained certain broad commitments in regard to such policies. It also recognized economic development as a vital factor in the expansion of trade and in raising standards of living, and provided for co-operation in this field. It committed its members to negotiate for reductions in the general level of tariffs and for the elimination of preferences and the avoidance of other forms of trade restrictions and discriminatory trade practices except in agreed circumstances or conditions. It obligated its state-trading members to conduct their operations on commercial principles and to negotiate their margins between cost and selling price in the way other members negotiated duties. It permitted countries in balance-of-payments difficulties or in process of economic development to use quantitative restrictions but specified the conditions under which they could be used. It committed its members also to reduce the harmful international effects of restrictive business practices through a procedure of complaint investigation and recommendation, to eliminate export subsidies if possible, and to refrain from using any form of subsidy to increase their shares in world markets. Intergovernmental commodity agreements in primary and related commodities were to be used only for defined objectives and under specified conditions.

Many compromises had been made concerning all these commitments, but the basic principles of the charter as a whole were those set forth in Article VII of the mutual aid agreements. The charter was an attempt to achieve co-ordinated action on a number of interrelated and extremely complex problems through a single international agency, at a time when the world was still struggling with the problems of basic reconstruction. It was criticized in the United States on three main grounds: that it was too strong, that it was too weak, and that it dealt unsatisfactorily with employment and investment policies. It was criticized also, even by its drafters, because of its extreme length and complexity, which were due both to the scope of the subjects covered and the compromises required by the special interests of the large number of countries represented.

Although the ITO failed to come into existence, in the field of commercial policy most of the provisions intended for the ITO were applied through the GATT.[25] The Economic and Social Council became the residuary legatee of responsibilities for international co-operation in-

---

[25] See William Diebold, *The End of the ITO*, International Financial Section, Department of Economics and Social Institutions, Princeton University (1952).

cluded in the ITO Charter with which no other agency was competent to deal. At the same time, the Council fell heir to the tentative and hard-won solutions worked out in the draft charter on a great many problems, of which restrictive business practices affecting international trade and international commodity agreements were the most notable. These were fairly substantial offsets to the fragmentation of the work of the United Nations in the field of trade and related problems that was one of the consequences of the failure to bring the ITO into existence. To some extent the provisions of the Havana Charter on co-operation between the Fund and the proposed ITO, which were carried over into the GATT, compensated for difficulties caused by wartime decisions to assign international responsibilities in the field of foreign exchange and in the field of trade to different agencies.

GATT Negotiations

The Fund and the GATT have considered many problems relating to trade and payments restrictions together, and the GATT to some extent has filled the gap left by the failure of the ITO to come into existence as a specialized agency of the United Nations. For these reasons, and because the United Nations Secretariat has continued up to the present to render certain administrative services to the secretariat of GATT on a reimbursable basis, it has become customary to speak of the GATT loosely as if it were part of the United Nations system.

The General Agreement on Tariffs and Trade was negotiated in 1947 at a meeting of the members of the Preparatory Committee of the United Nations Conference on Trade and Employment. Although this meeting was held in Geneva, Switzerland under the sponsorship of the Preparatory Committee in connection with and as part of its second session, it was the United States and not the Preparatory Committee that invited the participants to attend and negotiate multilaterally for the reduction of tariffs. The Agreement was, and remains a multilateral tariff agreement among sovereign states. The obligations it imposed were all related to the tariff concessions contained in it, and it was completely independent of the proposed ITO, which contained many obligations of quite a different kind. Had this not been the legal status of the GATT, it would have been impossible for the United States to become a contracting party under the Trade Agreements Act of 1934 without special legislation by Congress.

The seven-month long tariff negotiations carried on at Geneva were conducted under the bilateral-multilateral procedure worked out in the

Anglo-American trade and financial negotiations and elaborated by the Preparatory Committee. The multilateral part of this procedure required a pooling of information among all participants, which many countries found hard to accept. There was a strong tendency therefore to fall back on straight bilateral bargaining. Fortunately, this was successfully resisted.[26] The bilateral-multilateral method prevailed with only minor modifications, and mutual tariff concessions covering some 45,000 tariff items relating to about half of world trade were negotiated.

The General Agreement was signed on October 10, 1947, by the representatives of the twenty-three countries participating in the negotiations. It was given provisional application on January 1, 1948, by nine of these countries under a Protocol of Provisional Application, and by September 1948, all the original signatories had, by adhering to this protocol or in other ways, become contracting parties.[27] The tariff schedules negotiated at Geneva were made an integral part of the Agreement (Part I, Article II) and became effective with respect to each country as soon as it became a contracting party. When acting collectively under the Agreement, these countries were known as the Contracting Parties.[28]

Like other tariff agreements, the General Agreement contained general clauses dealing with nontariff barriers to trade and trade discrimination. Most of these were adaptations of draft provisions of the proposed ITO Charter, and the decision on how much of the charter should be incorporated in the Agreement was a difficult one. The final selection was restricted to provisions designed to protect the value of the tariff concessions included in the Agreement, mainly because the United States delegation did not have congressional authority to go beyond this. The Agreement was, however, sufficiently liberal to con-

[26] See William Adams Brown, Jr., *The United States and the Restoration of World Trade* (1950), pp. 131–33. Another important technical problem, that of preventing governments from attempting to improve their bargaining position by new tariff and other restrictive measures in preparation for the negotiations, was also successfully overcome.

[27] Australia, Belgium, Brazil, Burma, Canada, Ceylon, Chile, China, Cuba, Czechoslovakia, France, India, Lebanon, Luxembourg, Netherlands, New Zealand, Norway, Pakistan, South Africa, Southern Rhodesia, Syria, United Kingdom, United States.

[28] Technically, GATT is an agreement, not an agency. Correct usage requires that the contracting parties, when acting collectively under the Agreement, be identified as the CONTRACTING PARTIES. In the interests of readability, however, Contracting Parties (initial capitals only) is used in this study to mean the adherents acting in their collective capacity. Moreover, at times the term GATT will be employed in this study not only as an abbreviation for the Agreement but also in an organizational sense.

stitute a comprehensive international code of conduct in the field of commercial policy.[29]

Under this code, the contracting parties are obligated to observe two basic rules of conduct: (1) to accord to each other most-favored-nation treatment on tariffs, and national treatment on internal taxation and charges, and, as a corollary of this, not to introduce new or increase existing preferences; and (2) not to initiate or maintain prohibitions or restrictions other than duties, whether made effective by quotas, import or export licenses, or other measures, on imports from or exports to each other. Aside from the rule against new or increased preferences, these obligations are subject to numerous but carefully defined exceptions, including the formation of customs unions or free-trade areas, and the use of quantitative restrictions in connection with agricultural stabilization schemes, for economic development, and for balance-of-payments reasons. The Agreement also includes many so-called technical articles covering a wide range of practices affecting imports and exports. If any contracting party believes the benefits accruing to it under the Agreement have been nullified or impaired by the action of another, it has rights of complaint, and remedies are provided.

The negotiation of mutual tariff concessions, the settlement of differences, and the application to particular cases of the rules governing quantitative restrictions under the balance-of-payments exception were from the beginning the three principal activities of the Contracting Parties. The last of these required the active co-operation of the Fund.

In the words of Article XV of the General Agreement, it was necessary to ensure that the contracting parties would not "by exchange action frustrate the intent of the provisions of [the] Agreement, nor by trade action, the intent of the provisions of the Articles of Agreement of the International Monetary Fund." This was difficult because the Articles of Agreement of the IMF gave considerable freedom to its members to use exchange restrictions, both discriminatory and non-discriminatory, during a transitional period, while the General Agreement laid down specific substantive standards and rules governing the conduct of its members in the application of quantitative trade restrictions. To meet this problem, an elaborate formula was included in the GATT, which, it was hoped, would prevent frustrations of this kind. Both instruments also contained detailed provisions for consultation with members looking toward the relaxation of restrictions in their own fields, and these also had in some way to be dovetailed. The General

---

[29] Brown, *op. cit.*, pp. 234–59.

Agreement therefore provided for co-operation between the Fund and the Contracting Parties in co-ordinating their policies, and it further provided that on all matters concerning monetary reserves, balance-of-payments or foreign exchange arrangements, the Contracting Parties would consult with the Fund and accept all findings or other facts presented by the Fund relating to such matters.

Role of the Fund

While the ITO Charter was being negotiated, the Fund arrived at a number of basic policy decisions in addition to those affecting the use of its resources that have already been mentioned. Under the Articles of Agreement of the Fund, members are permitted, during a transitional period to maintain restrictions on transfers and payments for current international transactions and to adapt their restrictions to changing circumstances. Even during this period, however, a small degree of initiative is given to the Fund: it is authorized in exceptional circumstances to make representations to any member that conditions are favorable for the withdrawal of restrictions. The Articles of Agreement did not set a fixed date for the end of the transitional period, but they required members to consult with the Fund annually, beginning in March 1952, concerning the further retention of those restrictions still being applied on the basis of the transitional provisions.

So long as most members of the Fund continued to run heavy current account deficits with the United States, the Fund did not feel justified in exercising even the small amount of initiative concerning exchange restrictions reserved to it, although it suggested technical improvements. These limitations, however, did not apply to its responsibilities concerning par values, which were not limited by any transitional provisions.

One of the main purposes and obligations of the Fund is "to promote exchange stability, to maintain orderly exchange arrangements among members, and to avoid competitive exchange depreciation."[30] The Fund is not authorized formally to propose to any member a change in its par value, but its concurrence is required both for the establishment of "initial par values," and for subsequent changes (beyond a 10-percent limit) proposed to it by members.[31] The executive directors made it clear that the Fund would not resist justifiable proposals for changes

---

[30] *Articles of Agreement*, Art. I(iii), p. 1.
[31] *Ibid.*, Art. XX, Sec. 4, pp. 38–41, and Art. IV, Sec. 5, pp. 5–6.

in par values, that it considered stability and rigidity as two different concepts, and that stability implied that when changes in par values were necessary, they should be made in an orderly manner.[32]

The exchange arrangements existing among its members were far from orderly at the time the Fund began operations. The first problem presented to the Fund was, therefore, whether it should use the authority given to it in connection with the establishment of initial par values to bring about a general adjustment. On this question, the decision of the Fund was that the time was not yet ripe for such action. The Fund had the right to reject initial par values proposed to it by members if it thought they could not be maintained without causing excessive recourse to the Fund, but it accepted in December 1946 initial par values based on existing exchange rates proposed to it by thirty-two of its members. Consideration of initial par values for eight other member countries was postponed at their request. Whether any proposed initial par values were rejected has not been made known.

In almost all cases, the rates accepted by the Fund overvalued the currency of the member in terms of dollars and were being maintained under the protection of restrictive mechanisms. The Fund recognized that many of these rates would later have to be adjusted,[33] and in the summer of 1949 developed, for the first time, an argument in favor of a general adjustment of exchange rates accompanied, both in deficit and surplus countries, by policies necessary to make the new rates effective. The Fund held that inflated prices in countries that did not customarily settle their international transactions in dollars were one of the major reasons for the failure of exporters in Europe, the Middle East, and the Far East to offer their exports in larger part to the Western Hemisphere countries, and that this difficulty could be removed only as the general pattern of exchange rates was adjusted to relative prices and demands.[34] At this time, American official opinion was strongly in favor of early devaluations of most European currencies, especially sterling, and this view must have been expressed in the Fund by the American executive director. There is, however, in the nature of the case no direct evidence that the Fund pressed its members on this issue prior to the devaluations of September 1949.

[32] International Monetary Fund, *Annual Report . . . April 30, 1948*, p. 21.

[33] International Monetary Fund, *Annual Report . . . June 30, 1947*, App. X, Statement Concerning Initial Par Values, pp. 70–71.

[34] International Monetary Fund, *Annual Report of the Executive Directors for the Fiscal Year Ended April 30, 1949*, (1949), pp. 15–16, 29. This report took account of developments up to July 1949.

The following conclusions, made public in 1950, concerning the role of the Fund in these devaluations appear to be well-grounded:

Because of the confidential nature of the Fund's operations, an outsider cannot know whether the September devaluations were taken with no more than perfunctory references to the International Monetary Fund. The Fund officially stated at the time that the devaluations were taken through its machinery, but the statements of officials of several governments—especially the French and the British—strongly suggest that consultations with the Fund were no more than token and that the crucial devaluation, that of sterling, was sprung on it without observing more than a semblance of consultation. And to many outsiders it appears that other devaluations sprang in considerable measure out of efforts, after Britain had acted, to adjust to a *fait accompli*. At the same time it must be recorded that its Fourth Annual Report showed the Fund was alert to the possibility and was not taken by surprise. It should also be recognized that, of necessity, devaluations must be handled quickly; it is, therefore, the Fund's responsibility to be fully prepared to consider proposals on short notice. Further, it is possible that the Fund's staff may have held confidential discussions with individual member governments and exerted some influence on their final action, but there is no evidence that such was the case. The Fund did state that the devaluations were in conformity with its views, but this can be true even though the decisions were taken unilaterally.[35]

Within the space of four days, from September 18 to 21, 1949, the Fund had considered and concurred in proposals for changes in the par value of thirteen of its member countries and of some of their dependent territories, and had also approved exchange rates for several other member countries that had no agreed par values.[36] In no case did it withhold its approval. The devaluation of sterling was the key to the almost world-wide readjustment of rates, and it was not to be expected that the United Kingdom would relinquish to the Fund its freedom of action on such a vital matter as the sterling-dollar rate, or that other important trading nations would do so.

The basic conception of exchange stability under the Fund agreement was that of fixed exchange rates adjusted from time to time by international consultation and agreement. The Fund was therefore opposed in principle to freely fluctuating exchange rates and to any practices that tended to move the actual exchange rates of its members away from their declared par values. This was the basis of its opposition in principle to the multiple exchange rate practices of many of its Latin American and some of its other members; and although, on this issue, it pursued a

[35] International Finance Section, Department of Economics and Social Institutions, Princeton University, *Survey of United States International Finance, 1949* (1950), pp. 115–16.
[36] International Monetary Fund, *Annual Report . . . April 30, 1950*, p. 28.

liberal policy, its influence was exerted toward a simplification and integration of multiple exchange rate systems.[37]

While the Fund was thus developing its basic policies, two very important questions concerning its role became the subject of extensive international discussion: (1) How could the Fund help prevent the international spread of economic depressions? (2) How should it be related to the European Payments Union? The first of these questions was raised in an important report on full employment made in December 1949 by a group of experts appointed by the Secretary-General of the United Nations, and is discussed at a later point in this study.[38] The second was raised by the turn of events in Europe and required the Fund to give immediate consideration to the formulation of its own position.

When improvements in intra-European payments arrangements were first under discussion by the countries participating in the European Recovery Program, the Fund was consulted concerning these arrangements. Although sympathetic to the aim of multilateralization of European payments, the Fund was also concerned with the possibility that "prolonged dependence on restrictions and discriminations would be likely to divide the world economy into economic blocs, each with its own price structure, each tending increasingly to insulate itself from the rest of the world by the necessity of protecting its own inconvertible currency system by trade restrictions and exchange controls."[39] The fear that the European Payments Union contemplated by the OEEC countries might contribute to the formation of a permanent soft-currency area in Europe was shared by the National Advisory Council on International Economic and Financial Problems of the United States, the body from which the American executive director of the Fund received his instructions. These apprehensions, together with the opposition of some important OEEC members to close relationships between the Fund and the European Payments Union, made it difficult to find a basis for co-operation between them. Although some highly technical proposals were put forward to place their relationships on a formal basis, none was accepted, and it was not until June 1952 that any of the resources of the Fund were used to facilitate the operation of the Union.

[37] An elaborate statement of IMF policy on multiple exchange rates was communicated to members on June 18, 1947. International Monetary Fund, *Annual Report . . . April 30, 1948*, pp. 65–72.

[38] See below, Chap. V.

[39] International Monetary Fund, *Annual Report . . . April 30, 1949*, p. 19.

Role of the GATT

Inasmuch as the European Payments Union (EPU) combined a program of intra-European currency convertibility with a program of intra-European trade liberalization, the issue raised by establishment of the EPU was fundamental not only for the Fund but also for the GATT. The EPU was widely regarded, especially in the United States, as being at one and the same time a step toward European economic integration and a transitional arrangement through which European countries could move away from bilateralism and toward general convertibility of currencies and nondiscrimination in trade. If these two aims could not be reconciled, there would be a clear conflict between the regional objectives of the EPU and the world-wide objectives to which the United Nations system was committed through the Fund and the GATT.

So far as the GATT was concerned, the EPU was welcomed as an important step toward convertibility and toward the realization of one of the basic principles of the GATT—namely that tariffs should resume their traditional role as the principal instrument of commercial policy.[40] For countries entitled to use discriminatory quantitative restrictions under the balance-of-payments exception, the relaxation of such restrictions in intra-European trade while they were maintained against dollar imports did not constitute a violation of the Agreement. Members of the EPU in over-all international balance, however, would be violating the GATT by discriminating in this way against dollar imports.

A more serious problem of conflicting obligations was raised by other plans for European integration that were proposed and discussed during the summer of 1950, of which the Schuman plan for a European Coal and Steel Community was the most important. All such proposals, whether for a large European preference area or for open-market "communities" for particular sectors of the European economy, were incompatible with obligations assumed under the General Agreement. If any of these proposals matured, as the Schuman proposal did, the Contracting Parties would, in the words of their third annual report, "have to steer a difficult course between the rigid application of the rules of the Agreement, with the risk of frustrating what might be a promising initiative for the recovery and strengthening of the European economy and acceptance of regional arrangements, which would weaken the basic principle of equality of treatment."[41]

[40] Interim Commission for the International Trade Organization, *GATT in Action*, Third Report on the Operation of the General Agreement on Tariffs and Trade (1952), p. 24.

[41] *Ibid.*, p. 28.

While the GATT was being confronted with ticklish problems of reconciling its world-wide objectives with European economic regionalism, it was expanding its own membership by new multilateral tariff negotiations at Annecy, France in 1949, which resulted in the accession of Denmark, the Dominican Republic, Finland, Greece, Haiti, Italy, Liberia, Nicaragua, and Sweden. Italy thus became the first ex-enemy to take its place in the GATT family, but active consideration was being given also to the future accession of Germany and Japan.

In September 1948, a protocol, entirely separate from the General Agreement, had been drawn up by the Contracting Parties on the initiative of the United States, providing most-favored-nation treatment for Germany by the countries acceding to it, and by August 1949, fourteen countries had assumed this obligation. The next step was to include Germany in the list of countries to take part in the next round of tariff negotiations to be held at Torquay, England, in 1950. In the case of Japan, similar action was much longer delayed. The United States had proposed extension of most-favored-nation treatment to Japan, but encountered such strong opposition that it withdrew the suggestion. The root causes of this opposition had by no means been removed when, in July 1952, Japan made a formal request to enter into tariff negotiations with a view to accession.

It is not necessary to labor the point that the new emphasis on European regionalism and the new economic relations being established with former enemy states were matters heavily charged with political implications. Yet the Contracting Parties dealt with them primarily, if not exclusively, as economic problems. There was one area, however, in which such an approach was not possible—East-West trade. American controls on exports to communist countries had been under attack in various organs of the United Nations, and during the Annecy negotiations, Czechoslovakia charged that the United States was violating the General Agreement by imposing export restrictions on Czechoslovak trade.[42] Two years later, on September 27, 1951, the Contracting Parties officially declared that the United States and Czechoslovakia would be free to suspend the obligations of the Agreement with respect to each other on the purely political ground that, as the United States contended, the general deterioration of relations between the two countries made it impossible to fulfill them.[43]

[42] Interim Commission for the International Trade Organization, *The Attack on Trade Barriers* (1949), p. 19.
[43] "Actions Taken on Strengthening Administration of GATT," U.S. Department of State *Bulletin*, Vol. 25 (Nov. 19, 1951), p. 830.

Concern of FAO and
Regional Economic Commissions

The inherent difficulties of international economic co-operation through many agencies are further illustrated by the general work of the FAO and the United Nations regional commissions in the field of trade and payments. In his early reports to the Council and the Conference of FAO, the Director-General of that agency placed great stress on such problems as the effect of hard and soft currencies on commodity trade; the decline in the volume of world trade in food as compared to prewar; and the difficulty of finding a basis whereby the surplus food-stuffs of North America could be exchanged for other commodities— the last being a euphemistic way of expressing the interest of the FAO in American tariff and price-support policies. The fifth Conference of the FAO asked the Director-General to make a selective study of meas-ures taken by governments to maintain or achieve certain price rela-tionships between commodities, especially import and export com-modities,[44] and the organization has since continued to place great emphasis in its research program on studies of international trade in food and agriculture.

It has tended, however, to overestimate the practical possibilities of effective co-operation in the control and distribution of agricultural products. Such overestimates had been made when proposals were ad-vanced for a World Food Board and an International Commodity Clearing House.[45] After these were rejected, the FAO appointed a Com-mittee on Commodity Problems to operate in a much narrower field. Initially, the main function of this committee was to deal with surplus commodity situations in food and agriculture arising from balance-of-payments difficulties. After attempting unsuccessfully to interest other governments in the purchase of certain surplus commodities held by the United States, it tried to lay down the general principles that should govern the distribution of food on special terms for the development of nutrition programs.[46]

The FAO continued to be a strong advocate of the type of interna-tional commodity arrangements it had supported during the ITO negotiations. It did not, however, become the major link between the

[44] Food and Agriculture Organization, *Report of the Fifth Session of the Conference, 21 November–6 December 1949* (March 1950), p. 10.

[45] See above, Chap. II.

[46] Food and Agriculture Organization, *Work of FAO, 1949/50: Report of the Di-rector-General* (October 1950), p. 40. See also Chaps. V and VII below.

United Nations and the various international commodity councils and committees such as the International Sugar Council, the International Wheat Council, the International Wool Study Group, and the Rubber Study Group. The main instrument of co-operation between the United Nations and these groups was the Interim Coordinating Committee for International Commodity Arrangements, which, as noted above, was established in 1947 to carry out the procedures laid down in the Havana Charter concerning international study groups and conferences in anticipation of the ITO. The continued functioning of this "interim" body served to fill a gap in international co-operation that would otherwise have been left by the demise of the ITO.

The interest of the FAO in international trade problems was also shown by the co-operation between its secretariat and the secretariats of the regional economic commissions of the United Nations. The commissions for Latin America and the Far East, in particular, became important forums for the discussion of regional aspects of world trade and payments problems. Before the regional commissions could devise methods of effective co-operation in the field of trade and payments, however, certain preliminary questions had to be answered. What was the economic basis for regional co-operation in these fields? What were its potentialities and limits? What forms should it take?

The first of these was the most fundamental. The economies of the Latin American countries were not, like those of Europe, closely bound together by an intricate network of trade, communications, and payments. Most of them were relatively insensitive to economic and financial developments in other Latin American economies. Almost all of them were dependent on world markets for the sale of a relatively few products. All shared a common desire for economic development leading to an intensive demand for imported capital goods and frequently to differential treatment of imports according to a judgment of essentiality. In many of these countries inflation was endemic, with resultant adverse effects on their balances of payments. Intra-Latin American trade was much smaller than Latin American trade with other areas and in order to overcome the exchange controls extensively used in the area, a substantial part of it was carried on by barter arrangements.

Most of these generalizations are applicable, although with some qualifications, to many countries in Asia and the Far East. In the Far East, as in Latin America, the exchange of primary products for capital goods with other areas was far more important than intraregional trade. Many Far Eastern countries continued to maintain close financial links with Europe—India, Pakistan, Burma, Ceylon, Hong Kong, and Malaya with the sterling area; the Associated States of Indo-China with France; and Indonesia with the Netherlands.[47]

In both regions there was a strong feeling that their trade patterns were of a colonial type, and that much could and should be done to change them. This was especially true of Far Eastern countries whose independence had been but recently achieved, and for whom the expansion of trade with their neighbors was for the first time an important objective of economic policy. Consequently, the United Nations commissions, like the regional meetings of the FAO, emphasized intraregional trade expansion. But trade with other areas, which was part of the world problem being dealt with by other agencies, continued by force of circumstances to be their major concern.

During the period under consideration, the work of the Economic Commission for Latin America (ECLA) with respect to international trade and payments was almost entirely exploratory. An analysis of the possibilities of multilateral compensations of Latin-American trade and payments was prepared by the Fund and considered by the commission at its second session (May–June 1949), but conditions were deemed not favorable to such a project. At its third session (June 1950) the commission was still of this opinion, but with the example of the European Payments Union before it, it asked the Fund to explore the possibilities of partial multilateral clearings within the region. The commission also asked its executive secretary to undertake, with the executive secretary of the Economic Commission for Europe (ECE), a study of ways and means of expanding Latin American trade with Europe, and to study the possibilities of expanding intra-Latin American trade. It is noteworthy that the latter subject was a late arrival on the agenda of the commission, which gave priority to the Latin American role in the network of world trade.

The emphasis of the Economic Commission for Asia and the Far East (ECAFE) on intraregional trade and payments was, from the beginning, stronger than that of the ECLA, but ECAFE was far from neglecting trade with nations outside the Asian region. At its third session (June 1948), the commission considered a report from its secretariat outlining the possibilities for developing intraregional trade and urging the establishment of a permanent trade promotion branch in the secretariat. The recommendation was approved, and the commission soon became very active in this field.

[47] Even after it became independent, Indonesia continued to make its European settlements through the European Payments Union via the Netherlands.

At the fifth session of the commission (October 1949), the Fund presented an extensive study, which it had been requested to make on intraregional trade. It had also been asked to consider the desirability of a regional multilateral clearing arrangement, a matter on which it reserved its position. ECAFE itself concluded, however, as ECLA had done a few months before, that the time was not propitious for such a project.[48] Thereafter, the Fund co-operated actively with the ECAFE secretariat in joint studies on the financing of trade and the mobilization of domestic capital—a subject that was given top priority at the sixth session of the commission in May 1950.

Although the Economic Commission for Europe was no less interested in the trade and payments problems of its members than the other two commissions, its work in this field was of quite a different order. In view of the fact that the major intra-European trade and payments problems were dealt with by OEEC, of which the Soviet Union and its satellites were not members, it was almost inevitable that the interests of the ECE, in which the Eastern countries were participants, would be concentrated on East-West trade.

The commission was from the beginning engaged in three operations that directly affected the flow of trade within Europe—the allocation of solid fuels among European consuming countries, the allocation of scrap produced in Europe, and the establishment of "buying limits" for timber-importing countries. These allocations were part of an extensive program of co-operation in increasing availabilities and improving productive methods, but with the restoration of better balance in supply and demand in 1949, they were terminated. The commission also touched on many matters directly affecting the international flow of European goods through its Inland Transport Committee, which dealt with such matters as international highways, customs formalities, road and rail transport, and inland waterways and seaports.

At its third session (April–May 1948), the commission, after prolonged East-West debate, set up an Ad Hoc Committee on Industrial Development and Trade to examine the functions it might appropriately undertake in order to promote the industrial reconstruction and development of war-devastated and underdeveloped countries and to expand international trade between the countries of Europe and also

[48] U.N. Economic and Social Council, Ninth Session, *Official Records*, Supplement No. 13, "Report of the Economic Commission for Asia and the Far East," p. 18; and U.N. Economic and Social Council, Eleventh Session, *Official Records*, Supplement No. 8, "Report of the Economic Commission for Asia and the Far East," pp 16–17.

between European countries and countries outside Europe.[49] In September 1948, this committee recommended that a Committee for the Development of Trade be established, but agreement on its terms of reference was reached only over vigorous opposition of the countries in the Soviet bloc. In the debate, the Eastern European nations took the position that a satisfactory increase in East-West trade was dependent on the development of production in their countries, and they clearly implied that this development should in large measure be financed by the West. The Committee on the Development of Trade, thus brought into being in an atmosphere of strife between East and West, met in May 1949 primarily to consider ways and means of expanding East-West trade. It was completely deadlocked, however, and rendered no report to the commission.

In November 1949, the Executive-Secretary sent an *Aide Memoire* to participating governments suggesting an entirely new approach involving (1) relatively long-term purchase commitments by Western European nations, formed on the model of the International Wheat Agreement, for cereals and other supplies from Eastern European nations, and (2) use of the proceeds by the Eastern European nations for purchases from an agreed list of Western products.[50] This initiative was followed by a long series of negotiations between the secretariat and interested governments, which culminated in an *ad hoc* meeting of these governments in Geneva in November 1950 and annual trade consultations thereafter.

These efforts were characteristic of the ECE secretariat. It was not content merely to analyze, but it also made strenuous efforts to achieve practical results through facilitating and encouraging international negotiation on concrete problems. General analysis of European trade and payments problems in all their aspects was, moreover, provided in the annual *Economic Survey of Europe* begun in 1948, and in the *Quarterly Bulletin* of the commission, which first appeared in 1949.

Economic and Social Council and General Assembly

Prior to the Korean crisis, questions of international trade and finance were discussed in the Economic and Social Council and its Economic

[49] U.N. Economic and Social Council, Seventh Session, *Official Records*, Supplement No. 10, Annex 1.
[50] U.N. Economic Commission for Europe, *Report to the Fifth Session of the Economic Commission for Europe, by the Executive Secretary, on the Future Work of the Commission*, Doc. E/ECE/114/Rev. 1 (April 1950), p. 57, and App. IV

and Employment Commission in connection with the annual economic surveys and special economic reports submitted by the Secretariat. In these documents attention was increasingly devoted to current international relationships in the field of commerce and finance, especially in the report on *Major Economic Changes in 1948*.[51] The Council discussions on them were, however, often diffuse and desultory, ranging over such topics as the general obstacles to trade, the desirability of long-term agreements on trade in essential products, the dollar problem, and suggested revisions of the Articles of Agreement of the International Monetary Fund to make it more effective in helping other countries to deal with balance-of-payments fluctuations without resort to deflationary measures or trade restrictions.

In the General Assembly in November 1948, Poland attacked the United States for using export controls to deny a broad range of items to communist countries on security grounds, for according priority to countries participating in the Marshall Plan for goods in short supply, and for including provisions covering East-West trade in the bilateral agreements between the United States and the Marshall Plan countries. A Polish resolution, strongly supported by the Soviet Union, Czechoslovakia, and Yugoslavia, launched a debate that was carried on in the Second (Economic and Financial) Committee and in the plenary meetings.[52]

American practices were vigorously defended by the United States, with support from many other countries. Discrimination was defended on two grounds: first, that it was necessary to assure the rapid recovery of Western Europe by giving the co-operating countries priority for commodities in short supply, and second, that the United States could not furnish materials for building up the military potentials of Eastern European countries in view of their aggressive tendencies. Western nations also pointed out that the nations in the Soviet bloc could and regularly did engage in trade discrimination on political grounds under their system of bilateral agreements. They challenged the communist bloc to accept the most-favored-nation principle with the exceptions so painfully agreed upon in the ITO negotiations.

The differences of view between East and West were irreconcilable,

[51] U.N. Secretariat, Department of Economic Affairs, *Major Economic Changes in 1948* (January 1949), pp. 20–31.

[52] U.N. General Assembly, Third Session, Second Committee, *Official Records*, 69th Meeting (Nov. 2, 1948), pp. 154–60, and 71st–76th Meetings (Nov. 4–12, 1948), pp. 185–278. For text of Polish resolution, see p. 159. See also U.N. General Assembly, Third Session, Plenary, *Official Records*, 164th–65th Meetings (Nov. 26, 1948), pp. 592–609.

and the Polish resolution was finally rejected in the General Assembly.

In its annual summary of economic changes during the 1949–50 period, the Secretariat reached the conclusion that the trade and payments setback of 1949 demonstrated anew that progress in solving the difficult and long-run structural problems underlying the imbalance in international transactions could be made only in a context of full employment in more highly industrialized countries and progressive economic expansion in underdeveloped areas.[53] It was in this context that international trade and payments policies were most intensively canvassed in debates of the General Assembly and the Council.

Following the receipt of the report of a group of experts on full employment in December 1949,[54] the Council debated international trade policies as part of its general discussions on employment. The recommendations of the experts affecting international trade, the reception given to their report at the tenth and eleventh sessions of the Council in 1950, and the lengthy resolution on full employment, which was adopted by the Council and which included sections dealing with trade and payments, are all discussed later in this volume.[55] It should be noted here, however, that in this major resolution, the basic commercial policy principles and objectives of the Havana Charter were reasserted in substance, although not by direct reference.[56]

The work of these experts was to be supplemented by further studies on trade and payments questions of particular concern to underdeveloped countries under a resolution of the Council of August 1950. This resolution requested the Fund and the Bank to assemble data on the absorption of foreign exchange resources of such countries by the service of foreign investment, and it requested the Secretary-General to study "the relation of fluctuations in the prices of primary products to the ability of underdeveloped countries to obtain foreign exchange."[57] The new study of price relationships was begun at a time when the terms of trade were turning strongly in favor of the underdeveloped countries under the impact of the crisis in Korea. In many ways, this crisis represented a turning-point in the consideration of trade and payments problems by the Council and the Assembly, and it had significant effects on the work of all other parts of the United Nations system in this area.

[53] U.N. Secretariat, Department of Economic Affairs, *World Economic Report, 1949–50* (March 1951), pp. 5–10.

[54] U.N. Department of Economic Affairs, *National and International Measures for Full Employment* (the Kaldor Report), Doc. E/1584 (December 1949).

[55] See below, Chap. V.

[56] Res. 290(XI), Aug. 15, 1950, para. 9(a).

[57] Res. 294B(XI), Aug. 12, 1950.

After the Invasion of South Korea

The dislocation of the world price structure during the two years immediately following the invasion of a small country whose independence had been recognized by the United Nations appears in retrospect as a temporary interruption in world progress toward a better international equilibrium. It accentuated, however, many of the interests of special concern to the underdeveloped countries and had a great effect on the approach of the Economic and Social Council and of the regional commissions. The resumption of progress toward international equilibrium that followed also raised certain major long-range problems for the Fund and the GATT.

Economic Impact of
Invasion of South Korea

The most lasting economic consequence of the reaction to Communist aggression in Korea was the large-scale diversion of additional material and man-power resources to rearmament, but the effects of this increased diversion were felt only gradually. In contrast, the price effects were immediate and spectacular as a result of the intensive demand for industrial raw materials and other primary commodities, both from governmental and private sources. There was a world-wide speculative effort, first in the United States and later elsewhere, to build up inventories of such commodities far beyond current requirements as a protection against future shortages.

The general upward movement of commodity prices reached its peak in February 1951 when raw material prices were on the average 45 per cent above the level of June 1950.[58] The balance-of-payments position of the countries producing raw materials was greatly eased, and their gold and dollar reserves, particularly those of Latin American countries, were increased. Despite the deterioration in the terms of trade of European countries, which imposed a severe burden on them estimated by the International Monetary Fund to be at an annual rate of $2 billion, almost all the countries belonging to the OEEC were also able to improve their reserve position.

Late in 1950, American consumer demand began to decline, and the United States Government took various steps to reduce the prices paid for certain important raw material imports. The course of the Korean

[58] Bank for International Settlements, *Twenty-Second Annual Report* (1952), p. 72. A comprehensive survey of the price developments of 1950–52 is given on pages 68–89 of this report.

war also took a turn favorable to the United Nations forces, and it became clear that the level of raw material prices was fast becoming untenable. The International Index of Raw Material Prices fell from the February 1951 level of 145 (June 1950 being taken as 100) to 108 in February 1952, and in May 1952 it returned to the June 1950 level.[59]

For the underdeveloped countries, especially of Southeast Asia, the sharp fall in export prices disappointed many hopes and raised many new difficulties. The imports of these countries continued to expand after the raw material boom had subsided, with the result that their reserves were rapidly depleted. At the beginning of 1952, many countries producing raw materials were in serious balance-of-payments difficulties and had to adjust their development programs to a lower level of imports.

In the first part of 1952, the countries of the outer sterling area began to draw heavily on their sterling balances. This added to the difficulties of the United Kingdom. Sterling area reserves suffered their third and most serious contraction since the war, falling from $3.8 billion in June 1951 to a low point of $1.7 billion in June 1952. On three occasions, November 1951, January 1952, and March 1952, the United Kingdom imposed a series of new import restrictions, mainly against dollar trade but also against the trade of the continental members of the European Payments Union.

France was also in balance-of-payments difficulties in the winter of 1951–52, due mainly to continued inflation, and restrictive measures taken by France and the United Kingdom together constituted a serious setback to the trade liberalization program of the OEEC.

Industrial production in Europe in 1952 failed for the first time since 1945 to rise above the level of the preceding year, and in the first part of that year the exports of continental Europe, like those of the United States and the United Kingdom, declined substantially. After taking into account private capital movements and remittances, the world dollar deficit with the United States rose from $0.3 billion in 1950 to $3.2 billion in 1951. The "dollar shortage" again appeared to be as formidable as ever.

In the latter part of 1952, the situation began to change for the better. Industrial production in Europe began to rise again, and in most European countries, there was a revival of monetary policy as a major

---

[59] *Ibid.* For a comprehensive discussion of the readjustment period following the boom, see The Contracting Parties to the General Agreement on Tariffs and Trade, *International Trade 1952* (1953), Pt. I, pp. 1–54.

weapon of internal stabilization. This was true also of the United Kingdom.

At the end of the year, sterling reserves had begun a slow but steady rise. Although still substantial, the deficits of continental Western Europe vis-à-vis Canada and the United States were being reduced. The improvement was sufficient to permit some of the European countries, including the United Kingdom, to relax their trade restrictions somewhat, although a notable exception was France, which continued to intensify them. There was also an improvement in the position of the countries producing raw materials, although there were some important exceptions, such as Brazil. Moreover, the declining trend in United States "commercial" exports, which had been a feature of the American balance of payments since the beginning of the European Recovery Program, was resumed, while imports continued to increase gradually. The current account deficit of the rest of the world with the United States declined in 1952 to $1.8 billion. The trend in the latter part of the year was sharply downward, and at the end of the year the deficit had disappeared entirely.

The generally favorable development of international trade toward a more balanced position in 1953 was summarized by the United Nations Secretariat as follows:

International trade reached a high point in 1953; the value of world exports (excluding those of eastern Europe and mainland China), measured in constant prices, rose above the preceding peak in 1951. In the first nine months of 1953 the export quantum was 15 per cent above the average for 1950, or about 40 per cent above 1948 or 1937. In the same time a substantial improvement was attained in the regional pattern of world exports. United States foreign aid was not only significantly reduced, but there was in fact a flow of gold and dollars of a similar magnitude from the United States to the rest of the world. An important factor contributing to this change was the rise in exports of the rest of the world while commercial exports of the United States fell sharply from 1952 to 1953.[60]

This did not mean, of course, that all transitional problems had been solved. Nevertheless, from 1953 on, the United Nations system as a whole was less influenced than at any previous time by emergency situations left by the Second World War. Reconstruction in the physical sense was approaching completion; prices of internationally traded goods were relatively stable; and the extreme dependence of other countries on dollar sources of supply was being gradually reduced. The

[60] U.N. Secretariat, Department of Economic Affairs, *World Economic Report, 1952–53* (1954), p. 75.

abnormal inventories built up after the Korean crisis had been worked off, and it became possible to regard the price dislocations of 1950–51 merely as a historical episode. Nevertheless, these dislocations left their mark on almost every aspect of the work of the United Nations system in the field of international trade and payments.

Responses of the Economic and Social Council and the Assembly

When the Economic and Social Council at its twelfth session in February-March 1951 reviewed the world economic situation, plans for large-scale rearmament were being pushed forward, the boom in commodity prices had about reached its peak, and inflationary forces were still strong. In making its recommendations to governments on policies to be followed in these circumstances, it gave priority to three matters of primary concern to the underdeveloped countries. These countries tended to look on Western rearmament as a threat to their development programs. They were concerned lest exceptional demands for capital goods in the industrialized countries deprive them of what they regarded as an equitable share in the international distribution of such goods. They were also afraid that their command over such goods would be diminished if inflation continued unchecked in industrialized countries, with a consequent fall in the purchasing power of their rapidly rising reserves. Both fears had been expressed by the Latin American countries at the Inter-American Conference on War and Peace held in Mexico City in 1945, and were ingrained in the thinking of many representatives of underdeveloped countries. At the same time, these countries wished to preserve the advantages of the favorable terms of trade that were the consequence partly of demand created by rearmament and partly of inflation.

It is somewhat of an understatement to say that these views, even though not wholly consistent, were reflected in the resolution adopted by the Council on March 20, 1951, on the world economic situation. This resolution was, in turn, a reflection of concerns that were being expressed by underdeveloped countries also at meetings of two of the regional economic commissions, the Economic Commission for Asia and the Far East, and the Economic Commission for Latin America.[61]

[61] See, for example, U.N. Economic and Social Council, Thirteenth Session, *Official Records*, Supplement No. 7, "Report of the Economic Commission for Asia and the Far East," p. 48; U.N. Economic and Social Council, *Annual Report of the Economic Commission for Latin America*, Doc. E/2021. E/CN 12/266 (June 15, 1951), pp. 20, 110–14, and 147.

Although the concept of rearmament as a common effort to safeguard international peace and security was incorporated in the resolution of the Council, at least by implication, its wording left no doubt that the primary purpose of the resolution was to safeguard the economic interests of the underdeveloped countries. All members of the United Nations were called upon: first, to take special measures—during the period of general shortage of goods—to bring about adequate production and equitable international distribution of capital and essential consumer goods and raw materials especially needed for the maintenance of international peace and security, the preservation of standards of living, and the furtherance of economic development; second, to take measures, direct or indirect, to regulate at equitable levels and relationships the prices of essential goods moving in international trade; third, to maintain this equitable regulation of distribution and prices as long as strong inflationary pressures persisted, in order to minimize changes in the purchasing power, in terms of imports, of current earnings from exports as well as of monetary assets. There was a fourth recommendation that was not open to the charge of special pleading, that all members take all steps in their power to prevent the development of inflationary pressures, thereby preventing speculative profits and maintaining the purchasing power of the poorer sections of the population.[62]

The recommendation of the Council on equitable allocation did not differentiate between the types of allocation that might be feasible for capital goods and for raw materials. Nor did it assign responsibility for taking action to any United Nations agency. So far as capital goods were concerned, it was essentially a plea to the industrialized countries not to allow their defense programs to interfere with the plans of the underdeveloped countries. Although the recommendation that steps be taken to increase the production of goods especially needed for the maintenance of international peace and security might be interpreted to imply that the underdeveloped countries should give greater emphasis to the production of strategic materials, this was not the spirit of the resolution. The underdeveloped countries strongly insisted on their right to determine their development programs without interference, and they were inclined to argue that economic development as such, without any emergency deviations from long-range plans, was their best contribution to peace and security.

The anxieties of the underdeveloped countries about the availability of capital goods were probably somewhat exaggerated. At the time they were given formal expression in the resolution of March 20, 1951, many

[62] Res. 341(XII), Mar. 20, 1951.

special measures were being taken by the industrialized countries to increase the production of capital goods to meet the combined demands of their domestic economies, their export markets, and their rearmament. Indeed, the whole concept of the equitable distribution of capital goods once produced was extremely vague, and it is difficult to visualize what general measures could have been taken to ensure it. The nub of the problem was the scarcity of raw materials entering into the production both of capital and consumer goods, and it was to the conservation and effective utilization of such raw materials that the export controls and domestic allocation machinery of the industrialized countries were directed.

These measures did raise problems of equitable international allocation capable of being dealt with through an international agency. On these problems also, the United Nations could take no effective action, because the intensification of the East-West conflict made it impossible to entrust international allocation functions to a United Nations agency as had been done immediately after the war when the Food and Agriculture Organization, a specialized agency of which the Soviet Union was not a member, fell heir to certain functions of the wartime Combined Food Board.[63]

In January 1951, when the allocation problem was being discussed in the Economic and Social Council, the United States, Great Britain, and France agreed that international action should be taken entirely outside the United Nations to deal with the world scramble for raw materials. The method chosen was the creation of a new agency called the International Materials Conference, comprised essentially of commodity groups representing the producing and consuming countries of the free world having a substantial interest in the commodities involved. Quarterly allocations for a number of raw materials in short supply, particularly metals, were worked out and accepted through these commodity groups, and the position in cotton and wool was kept under review by them. Some major commodities, such as tin and natural rubber, however, of interest especially to underdeveloped countries, remained outside the jurisdiction of the conference.

Many of the contracting parties to the GATT participated in the International Materials Conference. In accordance with recommendations of the conference, they introduced new controls over trade in materials for industry, and the conflict between these measures and the basic principles and objectives of GATT was underlined by the Contracting Parties in the following terms:

[63] See above, Chap. II.

. . . these [measures] may be but the forerunners of further controls on an international scale stemming from other factors such as the economic and financial plans of the North Atlantic Treaty Organization. These new controls will almost inevitably run counter to the progressive removal of controls on international trade which is one of the principal aims of the General Agreement. But the Agreement recognizes the possible need for such exceptional measures, and lays down the condition of equality of treatment for the international distribution of scarce products. While progress towards the early attainment of the objectives of the Agreement will thus be interrupted, the very existence of its principles and the pursuit of its objectives become all the more important in the long run, because in the absence of limitations these temporary distortions would be even more harmful to trade. Governments will also be able more easily to withdraw emergency measures if these measures are regarded from the beginning as agreed departures from normal rules.[64]

This reaction to the International Materials Conference was in strong contrast to that of many underdeveloped countries in the principal organs of the United Nations. In their view, the work of the conference did not constitute an adequate response to the resolution adopted by the Economic and Social Council on March 20, 1951, because it dealt neither with the problem of equitable distribution of capital goods nor with that of long-range price stabilization at equitable levels and relationships. This was made clear by a resolution of the General Assembly of January 12, 1952, which urged all members to continue to make every effort to carry out the four recommendations of the resolution adopted by the Council in March 1951.[65]

The drastic decline in the prices of raw materials in 1951 greatly intensified the concern of the principal organs of the United Naions with the second major theme of the resolution of the Council of March 20, 1951—the regulation of the prices of essential goods moving in international trade at equitable levels and relationships. So great was this concern that from this time onward it dominated the approach of the Council and the Assembly to problems of commodity trade and became a central feature of their efforts to promote greater stability in the world economy.[66] As will be shown later in this study, the United Nations continued to issue reports and pass resolutions that contained a measure of good advice with respect to their trade and commodity policies not only for the industrialized countries but also for the underdeveloped

[64] Interim Commission for the International Trade Organization, *GATT in Action*, *Third Report on the Operation of the General Agreement on Tariffs and Trade* (January 1952), p. 25.

[65] Res. 523(VI), Jan. 12, 1952.

[66] For this reason, further consideration of this aspect of United Nations activities in the field of trade is discussed in this study in the general context of full employment and stability. See below, Chap. V.

countries. The advice to the former, however, was concerned mainly with their duty to take account of the special problems of the latter. This set the general tone, but the balance was to some extent redressed by the revival of the cartel issue at the thirteenth session of the Council (July–September 1951).

Revival of the Cartel Issue in the Economic and Social Council

The problem of restrictive business practices having harmful effects on international trade was of primary interest to the industrialized countries. As pointed out earlier, the United States and the Western European countries were divided on this question during the interwar years. Their viewpoints were compromised in Chapter V of the Havana Charter, and it was the principles of that chapter that were incorporated in a resolution of the Economic and Social Council adopted in September 1951.[67]

The initiative on this matter was taken by the United States delegation. Commitments to follow the principles of the Havana Charter on restrictive business practices had been included in the bilateral agreements negotiated by the United States with countries in the European Recovery Program, and at this time the so-called Benton Amendment to the Mutual Security Act of 1951 requiring that American aid be used to promote private competitive enterprise in the participating countries was under active debate in Congress.[68] The United States delegation felt that it would be desirable to generalize these principles through action by the Council, and at the same time to fill an obvious gap in international economic co-operation by reviving a part of the Havana Charter that had never been severely criticized in the United States.

The resolution passed by the Council was in harmony with these views. It recommended that Member states should take appropriate measures and co-operate with one another to prevent business practices affecting international trade that restrain competition, limit access to markets, or foster monopolistic control, when such practices have harmful effects on the expansion of production or trade, on the development of underdeveloped countries, or on standards of living. This was a repetition of the language of the Havana Charter, except that the reference to economic development was made more explicit.

---

[67] Res. 375(XIII), Sept. 13, 1951.
[68] *Congressional Record*, Vol. 97, Pt. 8, 82 Cong. 1 sess., pp. 10943–52.

An *Ad Hoc* Committee on Restrictive Business Practices was established to report on methods of giving effect to this recommendation.[69] Early in 1953, this committee agreed on a final report that contained twenty draft articles of agreement covering international co-operation in this field. These were based on Chapter V of the Havana Charter, with only minor changes. The report also outlined the structure and internal procedures of an agency that might implement these substantive proposals.

At its sixteenth session (June–August 1953), the Council received the report of the committee and remanded it for further study by Member governments, nongovernmental organizations, and the Secretariat. This action is to be explained mainly by a change in the attitude of the United States, which both surprised and disappointed many other countries. It was taken at a time when the United States Government was greatly influenced by a strong movement in favor of a constitutional amendment (the Bricker amendment) to limit the treaty powers of the President. There is some ground also for supposing that under a new administration, the United States Government had become more sensitive to the views of a few strong opponents of action in this field, and the most active supporters of the recommendation were no longer in its service. The government was beginning to feel that the kind of international obligations that the United Nations was tending to impose were those that would be enforced more strictly by the United States than by other governments, and that no real changes in the cartel practices of foreign countries would in fact result from giving effect to the recommendation. Whatever the reasons for the waning of American enthusiasm, the subject was for all practical purposes removed for some time to come from further consideration by the principal organs of the United Nations.

Fund and GATT: Operations, Policies, and Problems

One of the consequences of the Korean crisis was to accentuate certain differences between the views of the Economic and Social Council, the General Assembly, and the regional commissions on the one hand, and the GATT and the Fund on the other. For example, the concept of "equitable" international distribution of capital goods according to

[69] U.N. General Assembly, Seventh Session, *Official Records*, Supplement No. 1, "Annual Report of the Secretary-General on the Work of the Organization, 1 July 1951–30 June 1952" (1952), p. 69.

some criterion of need, which was upheld by many underdeveloped countries in the Assembly, the Council, and the regional commissions for Latin America and for Asia and the Far East, was different from the concept of equal (nondiscriminatory) treatment in the market place to which the GATT was committed. An example of a different kind is a difference of opinion that developed between the Fund and the secretariat of the Economic Commission for Europe on the proper foreign exchange policy to be followed during the period of inflation after the invasion of South Korea.

In 1951, the secretariat of the Economic Commission for Europe presented an elaborate argument in favor of a general appreciation of European exchange rates in terms of dollars as a means of checking inflation in Europe, the principal cause of which—in its opinion—was the rise of import prices.[70] This argument for exchange appreciation as an anti-inflationary device was considered and rejected by the Fund, which reached the conclusion that "widespread appreciation would be as ineffective for solving [the problem of inflation] as widespread depreciation was for solving the problem of deflation in the thirties."[71]

Whatever the merits of these views, the point to be stressed is that they were in conflict and were not "co-ordinated" in advance of publication. In view of the fact that the initiative on exchange rates rests in any case with the governments, a service was probably rendered by the raising and analysis of this entire issue by competent international civil servants.

During the post-Korea inflation, the Fund received no proposals for the appreciation of the exchange rate of a member, but on the closely related issue of fluctuating or "floating" rates, it had to take action. On September 30, 1950, Canada, with the approval of the Fund, suspended its fixed par value in order to counteract a speculative inflow of capital from the United States. Because the purpose of this suspension was not to improve the Canadian balance-of-payments position, the Fund chose to regard this as an exceptional case. In giving its approval, it was careful to take note of the Canadian intention to remain in consultation with the Fund and to re-establish an effective par value as soon as circumstances warranted.[72] The Fund strongly maintained its general

[70] U.N. Department of Economic Affairs, Economic Commission for Europe, *Economic Survey of Europe, 1950* (1951), pp. 157–64.

[71] International Monetary Fund, *Annual Report . . . April 30, 1951*, p. 36.

[72] International Monetary Fund, Press Release No. 145 (Sept. 30, 1950).

INTERNATIONAL TRADE AND PAYMENTS   137

position that "a system of fluctuating exchange rates is not a satisfactory alternative to the par value system."[73]

There were in fact few changes in par values in 1950–51, and the Fund held that the new structure of rates established in the earlier devaluations had largely eliminated disparities in price levels.[74] In other respects, progress toward "orderly" exchange arrangements, as these were conceived by the Fund, was very slight. There was no pronounced trend toward reducing multiple exchange rate practices, although the Fund was able to report some desirable modifications in a few countries during the upward swing of prices. This slight improvement was counterbalanced by the development, especially by European countries, of "new competitive exchange policies involving the use of retention quotas or special facilities for the acquisition of import rights." These were designed to stimulate exports to the dollar area mainly, but the Fund believed that they had much in common with multiple currency practices and that if extensively used they could readily be employed as weapons of economic aggression.[75]

During this period also, the Fund became engaged in the development of a new lending policy. As early as September 1946, the authority of the Fund to use its resources had been interpreted by a decision of its Board as being restricted to "temporary assistance in financing balance of payments deficits on current account for monetary stabilization operations."[76] This principle called for further elaboration, and procedures announced in 1951 and 1952 were designed to give confidence to member countries undertaking practical programs of action to help achieve the purposes of the Fund—especially those members willing to run graver risks because of the availability of assistance from the Fund. Members whose programs were found acceptable were to be assured that the resources of the Fund would be available, if required, to carry out such programs under a stand-by credit arrangement. This policy was approved and put into effect by a series of decisions in May

[73] International Monetary Fund, *Annual Report . . . April 30, 1951*, p. 39. For the economic considerations accepted by the Fund as justification for its action in making the exception in the Canadian case, which are of major importance in the development of the policy of the Fund, see *ibid.*, pp. 44–45.

[74] *Ibid.*, p. 33.

[75] International Monetary Fund, *Annual Report of the Executive Directors for the Fiscal Year Ended April 30, 1952* (1952), p. 62.

[76] On this question see International Monetary Fund, *First Annual Meeting of the Board of Governors: Report of the Executive Directors and Summary Proceedings, Sept. 27 to Oct. 3, 1946* (November 1946), pp. 23–27, 106.

1951 and in February and October 1952. Although these decisions provided for a more liberal lending policy, they also stressed the importance of preserving the revolving character of the resources of the Fund. The exchange purchased from the Fund was not to be outstanding beyond the period reasonably related to the payments problem for which it was purchased—a period falling within the outside range of three to five years.[77]

At the end of 1952, therefore, the Fund was prepared to consider requests by members for stand-by credit arrangements designed to give assurance that, during a fixed period of time, transactions up to a fixed amount would be made whenever a member requested, and without further consideration of its position.[78] The size of stand-by credits available under this policy was still limited by the restrictive provisions of the Articles of Agreement, and this was quite different from the large-scale stabilization credits that might be required for a collective return to convertibility.

During the fiscal year ended April 30, 1954, only four stand-by credits, amounting in all to $90 million, were arranged, of which only $25.5 million was utilized. One such credit amounting to $35 million was granted in the fiscal year ending April 30, 1956, but no drawings were made under any stand-by credit during the fiscal years 1955 or 1956. This record reflected the general improvement in the balance-of-payments positions of the members, which was reflected also in the substantial amount by which repurchases from the Fund exceeded new drawings in these two fiscal years. Of the total of $1,236.4 million drawn from the Fund from the beginning of its operations to April 30, 1956 only $187.3 million had not been repurchased or otherwise offset. This moderate use of the revolving fund provided for by the IMF was reversed in late 1956. In October 1956, France made a stand-by arrangement permitting it to purchase, with French francs, up to $262.5 million in foreign currencies from the Fund during the ensuing twelve months. This was followed in December 1956 by an arrangement under which the United Kingdom was authorized to purchase foreign currencies with sterling up to the full amount of its quota, $1,300 million. Of this,

[77] International Monetary Fund, *Annual Report . . . April 30, 1952*, pp. 40–51, and App. IV, pp. 87–90.

[78] International Monetary Fund, *Annual Report of the Executive Directors for the Fiscal Year Ended April 30, 1953*, pp. 50–51 and 95–96. The time limit for stand-by credits was fixed at six months with the possibility of renewal for another six months by a decision of the Executive Board. In a later decision of December 23, 1953, the Fund declared itself willing to give sympathetic consideration to stand-by arrangements of more than six months "in the light of the problems facing the member and the measures being taken to deal with them." *Annual Report . . . April 30, 1954*, p. 131.

$561.5 million was added directly to the United Kingdom monetary reserves, and $738.5 million was in the form of a twelve-month stand-by credit which required a waiver of the standing rules of the Fund.[79]

The new lending policy did not mean that the Fund was willing to extend its concept of temporary assistance to include very large-scale advances in periods of widespread recession or depression. The Fund did not support the recommendation of the report of the experts to the Economic and Social Council on *Measures for International Economic Stability* for an enlargement of its resources so as to increase the effectiveness of its activities in such circumstances.[80] The Fund was, in fact, no more willing than the Bank to support the more exuberant proposals for anticyclical action put forward in the Council and General Assembly by those who had little or no responsibility for their execution. Such differences of approach have an important bearing on the question of co-ordination and the autonomy of specialized agencies within the United Nations system, and in this context the reasons for the unwillingness of the Fund are especially significant. These were stated by the Fund in a published report:

The basic problem of depression cannot . . . be overcome by the availability of international short-term credit to be repaid in the next boom. The cure for a depression will require national measures to stimulate effective demand, especially in the great industrial countries. It may take time, however, before these measures bring recovery. The Fund can assist members which in the meantime may be faced with serious balance-of-payments difficulties, and by so doing reduce the deflationary pressure on the world economy as a whole. . . . The Fund has for some time had under consideration the question of increasing the members' quotas, having in mind such factors as the magnitude of possible balance-of-payments deficits in a depression and the fall in the purchasing power of money since 1946. It has, however, concluded that an increase in its resources is not a question for action at the present time. Its existing resources are by no means small as a source to finance cyclical balance-of-payments deficits. The Fund's resources, moreover, are secondary reserves, and the ability of countries to maintain import demand in a depression will depend also on the size of their reserves. It is important, therefore, that countries follow policies that will enable them to build up reserves in periods of prosperity which would provide a first cushion to absorb the shock of a recession.[81]

While the Fund was preparing itself for the time when it could fulfill one of the major functions for which it had been established, the GATT was also giving consideration to some basic long-range problems. A

[79] International Monetary Fund, *Annual Report . . . April 30, 1954*, pp. 106–08; *Annual Report of the Executive Directors for the Fiscal Year Ended April 30, 1956* (1956); pp. 120–25, and International Monetary Fund Press Release, Dec. 10, 1956.
[80] See below, Chap. V.
[81] International Monetary Fund, *Annual Report . . . April 30, 1952*, pp. 45–46.

third series of multilateral-bilateral tariff negotiations was completed at Torquay in April 1951. The resulting concessions were bound for three years, and the earlier Geneva and Annecy concessions were re-bound for the same period. As a result, more than 58,000 tariff rates covering a large part of world trade were stabilized till the end of 1953.[82] This was a great accomplishment, but it was an open question whether a further extension after 1953 would be possible.[83] One of the reasons for this was a growing conviction that the negotiating procedures thus far followed might have outlived their usefulness.

The results of the Torquay tariff negotiations were not as extensive as had been hoped, partly because the negotiations coincided almost exactly with the great upsurge of prices after Korea, and partly because of special bargaining difficulties that had not been present to the same degree at Geneva and Annecy. The United Kingdom, Australia, and New Zealand were not willing to reduce margins of preference in return for tariff reductions or bindings by the United States, and as a result no concessions were exchanged between these important countries. More important for the whole bargaining technique of the GATT were the difficulties caused by the disparities in European tariff levels.

Under the GATT rules, the binding of a low tariff was treated as equivalent to the reduction of a high one. The low tariff countries of Europe, having used up their bargaining power in the earlier negotiations urged that this principle be stretched to make the mere prolongation of a low tariff binding the equivalent of a reduction in a high tariff. The high tariff countries felt that this would require them to give unrequited concessions and refused to agree. This put the low tariff countries at a disadvantage. The reduction of quantitative restrictions under the trade liberalization program of the OEEC was at this time increasing the importance of tariffs, and this made the disadvantage of the low tariff countries even greater.

Two remedies were suggested: one by the Benelux countries that the disparity in tariff levels should be reduced by unilateral action by the high tariff countries; and one by France that all participating countries should, over a period of three years, reduce their tariffs by 30 per cent. Both were carefully examined by the Contracting Parties, and the French proposal underwent many refinements, including the incorpora-

[82] Interim Commission for the International Trade Organization, *GATT in Action*, p. 8.
[83] The Contracting Parties to the General Agreement on Tariffs and Trade, *International Trade 1952* (June 1953), p. 100.

tion in it of some features of the Benelux plan. By the end of 1952, how-ever, there was no agreement except that more study was required.[84]

There was one serious obstacle to the progressive reduction of tariffs through the GATT procedures that was not squarely met by either the Benelux or the French proposals. This was the difficulty of applying to underdeveloped countries the basic principle of GATT that such reductions should take place on the basis of an exchange of roughly equivalent concessions. The exports of many such countries were pre-dominantly primary products that were admitted free of duty by highly industrialized countries. The latter were consequently not in a good position to offer equivalent tariff concessions in exchange for the re-duction of the often highly protective duties applied by the under-developed countries to the processed or manufactured goods of which they were heavy exporters. This difficulty was compounded by the drive for industrialization in the underdeveloped countries, which had become convinced exponents of the infant-industry argument. The search for some method of making membership in the GATT more attractive to underdeveloped countries without a complete surrender of basic principles had become a major preoccupation of the Contract-ing Parties by the time of the Torquay meeting. Subsequent annual reports of the Contracting Parties show that almost complete liberty of action in imposing quantitative restrictions in the interests of eco-nomic development was retained by underdeveloped countries despite membership in the GATT.[85]

In addition to the long-range problems of stabilizing tariff rates and devising new negotiating procedures, the Contracting Parties were at the time of the Torquay meeting also confronted with the difficult ques-tion of Japanese adherence to the Agreement. The problem was how to provide safeguards against the revival of certain prewar Japanese trade practices and against a flood of extremely low-cost Japanese goods without attaching conditions to Japanese adherence that would discriminate against Japan. In July 1952, Japan formally requested an opportunity to enter into tariff negotiations with a view to adherence, but the Contracting Parties remained divided on this issue and only a provisional solution was reached in 1953.[86] It was not until the sum-mer of 1955 that these negotiations were held. In September 1955,

---

[84] *Ibid.*, p. 99.

[85] The Contracting Parties to the General Agreement on Tariffs and Trade, *International Trade 1953* (June 1954), pp. 105–06.

[86] *Ibid.*, pp. 122–23.

Japan became a contracting party, but fourteen of the thirty-four contracting parties, including the United Kingdom, withheld application of the Agreement to their relations with Japan.[87] The problem basically remained unsolved.

Meanwhile precedents for the application of the General Agreement to a great variety of concrete situations were being established.[88] Many of the problems were settled by diplomatic action, but many others were brought formally before the Contracting Parties. Some complaints were rejected; others were sustained and some form of remedial action taken. Other differences were mediated and thereafter settled directly by the parties, as in the notable case of the India-Pakistan dispute over the license fee imposed by Pakistan on raw jute. Still others were carried forward from session to session in the hope that the countries complained of would sooner or later change their practices. A case in point was the vigorous complaint of many countries against import quotas imposed by the United States under Section 104 of the Defense Production Act.[89]

The basis of all these complaints was that one or more contracting parties felt they had been deprived of benefits under the Agreement by the action of another. On certain issues involving the general clauses of the Agreement this basis was not available. The most important of these was the application of quantitative restrictions for balance-of-payments reasons, an issue in which the Fund was also deeply involved.

As noted earlier, the United Kingdom and other Commonwealth countries agreed in July 1949 to intensify their import restrictions in order to halt a severe drain on sterling area reserves. The Contracting Parties, however, did not call them immediately into consultation, preferring to wait until they could appraise the economic effects of the currency devaluations of September 1949. Consequently, the first full-dress consultations were held at the Torquay meeting of GATT with Australia, Ceylon, India, New Zealand, Pakistan, Southern Rhodesia, and the United Kingdom, and also with Chile, which had imposed new

[87] Article XXXV of the General Agreement permits a contracting party to withhold application of the Agreement from another contracting party with which it has not entered into tariff negotiations.

[88] The third annual report of the Interim Commission for the International Trade Organization listed ten different kinds of disputes that had come before the Contracting Parties. *Gatt in Action* (January 1952), pp. 13–14.

[89] For an evaluation of the record of the Contracting Parties in the settlement of differences, see Raymond Vernon, *America's Foreign Trade Policy and the GATT*, Essays in International Finance, No. 21, Princeton University, Department of Economics and Sociology (October 1954), pp. 15–18.

restrictions. Several hard-currency countries (Belgium, Cuba, Canada, and the United States) contended that the time had come when the Commonwealth countries other than India and Pakistan might begin a cautious but progressive relaxation of restrictions. This was also the view of the Fund, which submitted a report and background paper on each of the consulting countries, and participated actively in the consultations.

The respresentatives of Australia, Ceylon, New Zealand, Southern Rhodesia, and the United Kingdom argued that the Fund had not taken account of certain adverse factors already operating, including rearmament, the full force of which would not be felt until 1951. They strongly opposed any relaxation in spite of the improvement in their reserves during the post-Korean price rise.[90]

The consultations therefore had no visible result, except that all were agreed that no relaxation was feasible for India, Pakistan, and Chile. This outcome was perhaps fortunate in view of the serious fall in sterling area reserves a few months later when commodity prices began to decline drastically. The Fund can be fairly criticized, without having recourse to hindsight, for not having taken this possibility sufficiently into account in tendering its official advice. A miscalculation of this magnitude was in fact very likely to give aid and comfort to those who favored a rigid application of the principle of noninterference by international bodies in matters of domestic jurisdiction.

To check the drain on sterling reserves, the United Kingdom, in November 1951, imposed the first of a series of new restrictions, but again the Contracting Parties took no immediate action. On this occasion, an important reason for postponement was that the restrictions affected principally the countries with which the United Kingdom was in regular consultation in the OEEC. The United Kingdom was not alone in intensifying old and imposing new restrictions on balance-of-payments grounds, and in October 1952, after the effects of the Korean crisis had worked themselves out, the Contracting Parties in co-operation with the Fund consulted with Australia, Ceylon, France, Italy, the Netherlands, Pakistan, and the United Kingdom. In these consultations, more attention was paid to the protective effects of the restrictions, and all the consulting countries acknowledged the importance of applying them in such a manner as to avoid unnecessary

---

[90] For the text of the communiqué on these consultations issued by the Contracting Parties on December 13, 1950, see International Monetary Fund, *Staff Papers*, Vol. 1 (April 1951), p. 442.

damage to the commercial and economic interests of other contracting parties.[91]

In 1952, general consultations were begun by the Fund on the need of its members for continued exchange restrictions, and by the Contracting Parties on the need for discriminatory application of restrictions on trade. Because most of the GATT adherents were permitted under the General Agreement to discriminate in trade in a manner having equivalent effect to exchange restrictions they might apply as members of the Fund, the GATT had a major interest in the outcome of the Fund consultations. During the first year of consultations, this outcome was disappointing, and the Fund had to report that "although some countries were applying policies designed to produce favorable conditions for the removal of restrictions, most countries were so preoccupied with their immediate problems that any substantial withdrawal of restrictions was impracticable."

These annual and other less formal consultations kept the Fund in contact with all of its members except Czechoslovakia. They were for the most part confidential, but they were one of the most important contributions of the Fund during the period when little use was being made of its resources. For example, in the year ending April 30, 1953, forty-three members of its staff were sent to meet officials and technicians of member countries, often on narrow technical problems, but sometimes on more fundamental problems involving a reform or a reorganization of the exchange system of the member. In the spring of 1954, the second series of annual consultations with Fund members on exchange restrictions was completed, and it became evident to the Fund that a considerable number of major trading countries regarded as possible both relaxation of restrictions and progress toward convertibility. There had been, in fact, a considerable relaxation of exchange restrictions, notably against the dollar area, while these consultations were in progress. The Fund expected this trend to continue and was able to report in the spring of 1956, after the fourth series of consultations, that very few countries had intensified their restrictions and a large number had found it possible to reduce them. With wider transferability of currencies in international payments, there had been a corresponding lessening of emphasis on discrimination and strict bilateralism and some simplification and decline in the use of multiple currency practices.[92]

[91] The Contracting Parties to the General Agreement on Tariffs and Trade, *International Trade 1952*, p. 106.
[92] International Monetary Fund, *Fifth Annual Report on Exchange Restrictions* (1954), p. 2; and *Seventh Annual Report on Exchange Restrictions* (1956), p. 2.

As in the case of the consultations with the Fund on the exchange adjustments of 1949, there is no direct evidence to show whether, or in what degree, these consultations influenced the action of the countries concerned. In the nature of the case, national consultations with international agencies could not bring about the abolition of restrictions that were symptoms of basic structural disequilibrium. The frequent warnings in the reports of the Fund against inflationary practices of all kinds suggest that this institution may have placed too much reliance on the elimination of international price disequilibria as the main, if not the sole, prerequisite for the elimination of restrictions. Nor could it be expected that sovereign states would follow a course recommended by an international institution unless they were convinced that it would serve their national interest as well as the interest of the world community.

Still the Fund was in a position, after reviewing the situation and policies of many of its members, not only to make constructive technical suggestions but to point out ways in which unnecessary and often unintended damage to other members could be avoided without sacrifice of national interests and objectives. There is reason to think that advice of this kind was frequently accepted, especially after 1952 when the basic causes of chronic disequilibrium were being gradually overcome and when sterling convertibility became an objective of practical policy to be achieved by gradual but persistent relaxation of controls.

One of the most perplexing aspects of the sterling convertibility problem was the working out of a smooth transition from the regime established in Europe under the European Payments Union to a regime in which some, but not all, European currencies would become convertible. The consultations of the Fund and the GATT on exchange and trade restrictions, the policies of the Fund on the use of its resources, the complaint procedures of the GATT and its techniques of tariff negotiation, were all affected in one way or another by the fact that some Fund members and contracting parties were also members of this Union. The postponement by the Contracting Parties of action on the trade restrictions of the United Kingdom of November 1951, pending their discussion in the more suitable forum of the OEEC, and the relation of the GATT tariff negotiations to the trade liberalization program of the OEEC have already been referred to. Other aspects of the problem may be illustrated by the growing creditor position of Belgium in the European Payments Union.

In September 1951, the Belgian Government introduced several measures to deal with this problem. In accordance with suggestions from the EPU, Belgium restricted dollar imports on the theory that reduced purchases from the United States would mean increased purchases from European countries and better balanced accounts with them. The United States and the Canadian governments lodged a complaint with the Contracting Parties on the ground that this violated the obligations assumed by Belgium under the GATT, and requested authorization to take compensatory action. The Contracting Parties did not pursue the question immediately "in view of the many serious problems" it presented for governments and the prospects for early removal of the restrictions. [93]

While this complaint was pending, Belgium asked the Fund for a stand-by credit. This was the first such request, and in granting it, the Fund was influenced by the fact that the payments position of Belgium in the European Payments Union "was the key to a significant part of the payments problem of a number of other Fund members." It was in fact the key to the continued existence of the Union. As a result of its large surpluses with other EPU countries, Belgium had extended to the Union more than twice the amount of credit it had originally agreed to. This exposed the Belgian economy to inflationary pressures, and the price of Belgian consent to the extension of the Union for another year was a settlement of the excess credit. As part of this settlement, it was agreed to request the Fund to give Belgium a stand-by credit of $50 million, while the European Payments Union would make five annual payments of $10 million to Belgium to put that country in a position to repay the Fund. This was an effective form of co-operation between the Fund and the European Payments Union, despite the fact that no continuing formal relationship between the two bodies had been worked out. In the reports of the Fund, it was treated as if it were an entirely independent transaction between the Fund and one of its members. [94]

In October 1952, the American-Canadian complaint against Belgium was again reviewed by the Contracting Parties, but action was again deferred pending the outcome of the forthcoming consultations of Belgium with the Fund. After these consultations, the Fund found that relaxations of the discriminatory restrictions might be feasible and requested Belgium to reconsider the necessity of such restrictions. The

[93] Interim Commission for the International Trade Organization, *GATT in Action*, pp. 17–18.

[94] International Monetary Fund, *Annual Report . . . April 30, 1952*, pp. 43–44. In this report the Fund stated that it was still considering the problem of how to develop closer relations with the European Payments Union (*ibid.*, p. 80).

complaint was not pressed, and the restrictions were modified early in 1953.[95]

This was a happy outcome, but it was due to a fortunate change in the Belgian position in the European Payments Union coinciding with an improvement in its dollar position. For a year and a half, Belgian necessities as a member of a regional organization and its obligations as a member of a world organization were reconciled only by recourse to the rights of Belgium to impose discriminatory restrictions under Article XIV (transitional arrangements) of the Fund Agreement. This temporary expedient did not represent any real solution to the problem of reconciling regional and world-wide obligations.

The question of possibly conflicting regional and general international obligations was posed even more sharply for the GATT by the European Coal and Steel Community. There was nothing in the GATT that expressly covered this case, but in November 1952, the Contracting Parties examined the treaty establishing the Coal and Steel Community, found that its objectives were broadly consistent with those of the GATT, and granted a waiver of GATT obligations to the six countries in the Community. This waiver allowed them to act as if they were a single country as far as coal and steel were concerned, and stipulated that their barriers to imports should not be more restrictive than when the waiver was granted. The members of the European Coal and Steel Community also agreed that they would seek to avoid unreasonable barriers to exports to nonmembers and would abide by the decisions of the Contracting Parties in disputes that might arise over commercial policy matters within the jurisdiction of the GATT. This was the middle course that the Contracting Parties felt impelled to follow, but it did not relieve them of difficulties. At subsequent sessions, serious questions were raised about the precise obligations imposed by the waiver, the binding nature of the assurance given by the High Authority, and the extent to which the interests of third countries had, as required by the waiver, been protected and taken into account.

Although, as the foregoing review has shown, the work of the Fund and the GATT was considerably influenced by the economic repercussions of the Korean crisis, their principal concern during this troubled period was with the continuing long-range problems of co-operation in their respective fields, the major problem of the Fund being related to the use of its resources, and the major problems of the GATT centering

[95] The Contracting Parties to the General Agreement on Tariffs and Trade, *International Trade* (1952), p. 94.

around its negotiating procedures, the wide scope of the exceptions to its general rules, and its provisional status.

It was only with difficulty that the consent of all but one (Brazil) of the contracting parties was obtained in 1953 for extending the validity of the assured life of the GATT tariff schedules from January 1954 to July 1955. This gave the Contracting Parties an eighteen-month respite for a further examination of the new methods of tariff reduction that had been proposed. When, however, a fourth round of tariff negotiations was carried on at Geneva from January to May 1956, the established procedures were adhered to. These negotiations were entered into in a generally pessimistic mood by the twenty-two contracting parties participating, chiefly because of the very limited negotiating authority of the Americans.[96] Although the results were considerably better than were expected, they were by no means spectacular.

Before these tariff negotiations were held, there was a general review of the Agreement as a whole in accordance with a decision reached by the Contracting Parties at their eighth session (September–October 1953). This review was completed on March 7, 1955, and protocols were opened for acceptance by the contracting parties covering revisions to the Agreement and the creation of a new body, the Organization for Trade Cooperation (OTC), to administer the revised agreement.[97]

The principal results of this review were a reaffirmation of the basic objectives and obligations of the General Agreement; an extension of the firm validity of the tariffs bound under it indefinitely, subject to their withdrawal at three year intervals or with the consent of the OTC;

[96] The major provision of the Trade Agreements Extension Act of 1955 authorized tariff reductions to a maximum of 15 per cent from rates existing January 1, 1955 and no more than 5 per cent in any one year.

[97] The possibility that the OTC, if it comes into being, will become a specialized agency of the United Nations appears at present to be ruled out by the provisions of the draft legislation authorizing the membership of the United States in the OTC. Section 351(e) of H.R. 5550, as submitted to the Congress by the Administration in early 1956, read as follows:

"In adopting this Section, the Congress does so with the understanding

"1. that the functions of the Organization for Trade Cooperation will be limited to (a) the administration of the General Agreement on Tariffs and Trade and (b) facilitating intergovernmental cooperation solely in the field of trade, and

"2. that, therefore, the Organization for Trade Cooperation will not be an intergovernmental organization having wide international responsibilities in the economic field as described in Article 57 of the Charter of the United Nations (relating to specialized agencies).

"Accordingly, it is the sense of the Congress that the Organization for Trade Cooperation shall not be brought into a specialized agency relationship with the United Nations under the permissive language of Article 11(b) of the Agreement on the Organization for Trade Cooperation."

a new procedure for the review of quantitative restrictions for balance-of-payments purposes; and a fresh set of rules giving underdeveloped countries greater freedom to impose quantitative restrictions for the establishment of new industries, subject to a new review and consultation procedure. At the same time, by separate action, the Contracting Parties granted waivers on matters of vital importance to the United Kingdom, Germany, and the United States.

The establishment of the OTC would not, however, resolve the still unanswered question whether more effective methods of continuous collaboration between the Fund and the GATT could be devised. This question has been intensively discussed in the OEEC, in the annual meetings of the Fund and the Bank, and in the GATT itself. It is a difficult one because of the basic differences in the nature of the two agencies, which have been brought out in the preceding discussion. Although the provisions of the General Agreement requiring consultation with the Fund were intended to bring the two agencies together, these differences of objective and procedure have made effective coordination of effort between them extremely difficult. There has therefore developed in some quarters a strong desire to strengthen the liaison arrangements, so as to bring the objectives of both the GATT and the Fund to bear when a country consults with either.

Fund, GATT, and
Commissions of the Council

As has been indicated earlier, the decentralization of the United Nations system led to a considerable amount of co-operation and consultation between the specialized agencies and the commissions of the Council in the field of trade and payments, as in other fields. Much of this was due to the efforts of the three regional commissions to fulfill their mandate to strengthen the economic relations of countries in their areas with each other and with other countries of the world. The two parts of this mandate—the stimulation of trade with the rest of the world, and the stimulation of intraregional trade—could not be entirely separated, and both were of direct concern to the Fund, the GATT, and the FAO. Although the approach of the three regional commissions to this part of their mandate had certain common features, there were some significant differences both on priorities assigned to different parts of the problem and on action taken.

At its fifth session in April 1953, the Economic Commission for Latin America considered an analysis by its own secretariat of the characteristics of the intraregional trade of seven important Latin American countries. The difficulties of reconciling commercial policies that would help Latin American countries to sustain their raw material exports to the world market and restrict the import of certain kinds of manufactured products to protect their nascent industries, with commercial policies that would promote intraregional trade, were explored in connection with this report. Further studies were requested.[98] At the same time the commission considered two other important studies on trade and payments. One was a study undertaken jointly by the secretariats of ECLA, FAO and ECE on trade between Latin America and Europe, a subject on which the commission also requested further studies. The other was a report prepared by a member of the staff of the Fund, acting as a consultant, on the problem of effecting multilateral compensatory settlements between Latin American countries through the European Payments Union. No action on the clearing proposal was taken by the commission at this time, but further studies were requested on this matter also.[99]

The problems and prospects of expanding trade between Europe and Asia and the Far East were explored in a joint ECAFE/ECE/FAO report considered in February 1954 by the Committee on Industry and Trade of the Economic Commission for Asia and the Far East. The committee commended its suggestions for consideration by the governments concerned, and at the same time took a number of positions on the foreign trade problems of the area that were both moderate in tone and constructive in content.[100] The committee acknowledged that the apprehensions of the commission concerning the supply of capital goods had not been fully justified and dropped further work on the subject. It emphasized the importance of intraregional trade, but stated that this should not prejudice the trade of the countries concerned with the rest of the world. It made a number of constructive suggestions for the expansion of trade between Asia and Europe, which it felt was entirely consistent with a general expansion of international trade.

The Economic Commission for Asia and the Far East was not content with studies and reports, but engaged actively in trade promotion. Its secretariat became a clearing-house for trade information, and the

[98] U.N. Economic and Social Council, Sixteenth Session, *Official Records*, Supplement No. 3, "Economic Commission for Latin America, Annual Report (15 February 1952–23 April 1953)," pp. 22–23.

[99] *Ibid.*, pp. 12, 18, and 26.

[100] U.N. Economic and Social Council, Seventeenth Session, *Official Records*, Supplement No. 3, "Annual Report of the Economic Commission for Asia and the Far East," pp. 6 and 7.

commission held regular trade promotion conferences, which increasingly included business representatives in their membership. It also developed training programs for personnel in trade promotion. All of these activities concerned both intraregional trade and trade with the rest of the world, and in carrying them out, the co-operation of the secretariat of the Economic Commission for Europe was enlisted.

In its efforts to expand trade between Eastern and Western Europe, the Economic Commission for Europe was, as already noted, also not content with studies and reports. The executive secretary continued to convene East-West Trade Consultations and some trading opportunities were undoubtedly disclosed in the annual consultations. Until the death of Stalin, the continued participation and interest of Western European countries in these talks, however, was probably due mainly to a feeling that they were a means of somewhat diminishing international tension. They continued to look to the OEEC and to the European Coal and Steel Community, and more recently to a proposed "common market," as the principal instrumentalities for expanding intra-European trade. The ECE, however, was able to be helpful in working out some of the trade problems that followed the expulsion of Yugoslavia from the Cominform.

In regulating the arrangements between the GATT and the Commission on International Commodity Trade established by the Economic and Social Council in 1954, obstacles were encountered.[101] The Contracting Parties were given an opportunity by the Economic and Social Council to consider to what extent the problem of instability in primary commodity prices should be worked out under the auspices of the GATT, but no firm stand on the question could be taken by them, due largely to the opposition of the United States to the assumption of any price stability functions by the GATT.

The Parts and the Whole

Up to the present time, the structure of the United Nations system of specialized agencies has been incomplete because of the absence of an agency or agencies in the field of trade, including in that term commercial policy, cartel policy, and commodity policy. Within the United Nations system, primary responsibilities for foreign exchange policy, which is intimately related to trade policy, have been assigned to an agency with no direct responsibilities for trade policy—a circumstance for which the United Nations Organization cannot be held responsible.

[101] See below, Chap. V.

Within the system, responsibilities in the field of commodity policy have been divided between an interim organization with very limited authority (the Interim Coordinating Committee for International Commodity Arrangements), the FAO as an incident to its major activities, and—more recently—a new Commission on International Commodity Trade established by the Economic and Social Council.

The Fund, the interim committee, the new commission, and—to a lesser extent—the FAO, all have a legitimate concern with commercial policy, or at least with the results of commercial policy, and therefore with the work of the GATT, the main international instrumentality operating in this field. The GATT is a multilateral trade agreement and not an organization, although it may soon be administered by the Organization for Trade Cooperation which, it now seems, is not destined to become a specialized agency of the United Nations. The accomplishments of the GATT cannot be put to the credit of the United Nations, but the accomplishments of the United Nations system as a whole in the field of trade and payments cannot be evaluated without reference to the record thus far made under the GATT, which, like the Fund, was designed to contribute to the primary and global economic objectives laid down in the United Nations Charter.

The Fund

The Fund has been true to the basic concepts written into its charter. It has agreed to most, but not all, of the changes in par values proposed to it by members. It has opposed in principle freely fluctuating rates, multiple exchange rates, broken cross-rates, and gold sales at prices involving deviations from agreed par values. It has resisted pressures for the use of its resources for purposes for which they were not intended in order to conserve them for purposes for which they were intended. For the seasonal or cyclical difficulties that the Fund was intended to meet, its contribution to international liquidity has, by force of circumstances, been modest. The capacity of the Fund to respond to a balance-of-payments crisis of quite a different kind has been demonstrated by its response during the closing of the Suez Canal after November 1956.

The Fund has tried to hasten the return to currency convertibility by emphasizing the inherent disadvantages of exchange controls and the possibilities of relaxing them at a faster rate than member governments have been inclined to adopt. In contrast to the Economic and Social Council and the General Assembly, the Fund has emphasized the need for domestic monetary and fiscal policies that would promote a return to international equilibrium, even though it has been prevented by its Articles of Agreement from withholding its consent to proposed changes in par values on the ground that a change in domestic policies of the member states might render them unnecessary. The Fund has regularly reviewed the exchange policies of its members in consultation with them; has made constructive technical suggestions; and has pointed out ways in which unnecessary damage to other members might be avoided without sacrifice of national interests and objectives.

The Fund has co-operated actively with the GATT, and although in one instance at least it appears to have given bad advice, it has endeavored to see that the work of the GATT has not been "frustrated" by exchange restrictions permitted under the Articles of Agreement of the Fund. This co-operation, however, still leaves much to be desired, and its improvement is at present a matter under active discussion.

The Fund has preserved the revolving character of its assets in order to remain at all times in a position to fulfill the function of extending temporary assistance in financing balance-of-payments difficulties on current account for monetary stabilization purposes, despite the fact that this, prior to the Suez crisis, meant that only a small portion of its resources was made available to members. Between 1952 and 1956, it prepared itself for a more liberal use of its resources in conditions that for the first time approximate those under which it was supposed to function, by introducing a system of stand-by credits and using its waiver powers to overcome some of the rigidities surrounding access to its resources. These policies enabled the Fund to act boldly during the Suez crisis.

The record of the Fund has been severely criticized on several scores. It has been criticized by economists and public officials who are in basic disagreement with the concept, held by the Fund, of orderly exchange arrangements. To many who believe that flexible exchange rates are a prerequisite for the full convertibility of sterling and other major currencies, the Fund has appeared outdated, old-fashioned, and unrealistic. The Fund has been criticized on the other hand by those who believe its principal defect has been its ineffectiveness in persuading member governments to put its basic tenets into action.

When countries such as Canada and Peru felt that flexible exchange rates were in their interest, the Fund has found reasons for going along with them. These were such good reasons that the Fund has not been greatly reproached on this account. Many critics feel, however, that the Fund has been far too complacent in the matter of multiple exchange rates. This "complacency" has been due in part to a realistic recognition of the fact that multiple exchange rates have been used frequently to accomplish domestic objectives by countries that did not have the monetary and fiscal equipment and the administrative competence of the major trading countries of the world.

The Fund has been unfavorably compared to the European Payments Union on the ground that the EPU has been able, by the close and continuous consultation of its members, to influence greatly their monetary and other internal policies in the interests of Europe as a whole; whereas the Fund, partly because of its cumbersome organization and partly because of its world-wide membership, has no similar record to boast of.

Perhaps more fundamental than any of these criticisms are the three following: (1) Major changes in exchange rates have not been made since the war by international agreement in any real sense; the world is not ready to accept this principle, and the Fund therefore has become an artificial construction through which changes in par values are recorded but not decided upon. (2) The Fund has not adjusted its thinking to the realities of a world that has forever turned its back on nineteenth century methods of reaching international equilibrium. (3) The Fund has not been able to perform the role intended for it and has not to date been able to discover any other role.

It is not the function of this study to pass judgment on the validity of these criticisms, especially those that rest on doctrinal grounds, such as the relative merits of fixed and flexible exchange rates. It is rather to reach some general conclusions whether the record of the Fund thus far has made a contribution to the objectives of the United Nations Charter.

International agreement on "orderly exchange arrangements" is clearly in accordance with these objectives because the disorganization or disruption of foreign exchange relationships can, as the experience of the depression showed, have disastrous effects on almost any other form of international co-operation. Opinions may and do differ on what should constitute orderly exchange arrangements, but on this question, the burden of proof must rest on those who believe that the Fund has been mistaken in its basic concepts, inasmuch as it has for a decade been a forum for international consultation and discussion on this problem. There can be no doubt, however, that the Fund has not been and is not likely to be a forum in which the crucial decisions on changes in par values, especially those of major currencies, are made.

The objectives of the United Nations are global objectives, and the Fund has been a force working against their undue subordination to regional ones. The moderation of cyclical disturbances and the prevention of the international spread of economic depressions have become major objectives of the United Nations in which the Fund has been expected to play a significant role. It has resisted pressures to play this role in a manner favored by majorities in the Council and by some of the expert advisers to the Council. It is preparing to act with greater boldness in the use of its resources whenever conditions become ripe for the fulfillment of its stabilization functions.

The GATT

Like the Fund, the GATT was in the first instance designed to promote the objectives of Article VII of the mutual aid agreements, in this case by making a contribution to the elimination of all forms of discriminatory treatment in world commerce and to the reduction of tariffs and other trade barriers. In the system of priorities developed in the Council and the General Assembly, the reduction of trade barriers and the removal of discriminations in trade did not occupy a very prominent place and were in fact subordinated to other values. This may have been due in part to the very success of the GATT, as well as the lack of interest of the Soviet Union in tariffs and related trade problems. For those who attach great importance to trade barrier reduction, it may appear fortunate that the Contracting Parties were not obliged to make reports to the Council and the Assembly and to submit to pressures of the kind to which the Fund and the Bank were subject. The pressures to which the GATT has recently been subjected are of a different kind. Since about 1952, its work has had to be carried out against the resistance of mushrooming protectionist demands. The impression has been growing that little further progress in reducing tariff levels is likely to be made by the use of its special methods of negotiation.

Like the Fund, the GATT has been a force tending to prevent an undue emphasis on regional at the expense of global objectives. Furthermore, the Contracting Parties have, like the executive directors of the Fund, although on a more extensive scale, met some of the special problems of individual members or groups of members by the use of waiver provisions in the Agreement. The most important of these have been the waiver granted in 1952 to members of the European Coal and Steel Community to act as one country in the application of tariffs and a group of waivers granted during the renegotiation of the Agreement in 1954 and 1955. Among the latter were two which, although surrounded by administrative safeguards, allowed the United Kingdom to introduce new preferences that were justified on technical grounds.[102] Another was the waiver granted to countries no longer able to justify quantitative restrictions on balance-of-payments grounds, which allowed them to continue such restrictions for a time in order to provide a period of adjustment for certain interests that had been protected by them as an incident to their main function. Far the most important was the waiver granted to the United States, which permitted it to apply quotas under Section 22 of the Agricultural Adjustment Act. This flexibility must be counted among the accomplishments of the GATT, for no international agency dealing with economic matters can accomplish very much if it attempts to bind its members to courses of action that they regard as contrary to their vital interests. It has not resulted in a retreat from the basic objectives of the Agreement, but rather has marked out the area in which these objectives can be pursued with maximum prospects of success.

While the GATT provides for the sponsorship of negotiations for tariff reductions and recognizes that the success of such negotiations, if multilateral in character, will depend on the participation of all major trading countries, no contracting party is specifically obligated to participate in such negotiations. All are, however, obligated to accord to each other most-favored-nation treatment on tariffs, and national treatment on internal taxation and charges, and as a corollary of this, not to introduce new or increase existing preferences. The rehabilitation of the most-favored-nation clause, which was an important objective of the efforts of the League of Nations in the interwar period, could hardly be more complete as a general rule of international conduct. Deviations from this rule by the principal trading countries now have to be justified and accepted as in the general interest by an international body.

Moreover, the GATT has provided an element of stability in tariff rates that was lacking in the interwar years by binding these rates for successive three-year periods. At present, they are bound until December 31, 1957, and there is provision for automatic extension for further three-year periods subject to the renegotiation of individual items.

The principle that, when benefits under the Agreement have been impaired or nullified by the action of a contracting party, remedies must be found by the withdrawal of the measures complained of, the

---

[102] See George Bronz, "An International Trade Organization: The Second Attempt," *Harvard Law Review*, Vol. 69 (January 1956), p. 449.

granting of compensatory benefits, or equivalent retaliatory action by the injured country has been applied successfully in most cases. Even though some of these disputes have remained unsettled and some of the practices complained of have not been altered, the Contracting Parties have felt increasingly that retaliation is not an adequate remedy, because it merely increases the number of restrictions and works against the central purpose of the Agreement. They have therefore placed increasing reliance on consultation, discussion, advice, and persuasion. As a result, the GATT has become an international forum for the adjustment of disputes on commercial matters for which there is no previous parallel.

It must be admitted that the exceptions to the rules governing the conduct of contracting parties leave a wide area for the use of quantitative restrictions and other nontariff barriers to trade and that the good will of underdeveloped countries toward the GATT has recently been purchased at the price of making it much easier for them to follow a policy of protection. On this score, the GATT has been severely criticized, especially in the United States. There has also been a considerable amount of criticism emphasizing not the weakness of the GATT but its strength. This has come chiefly from supporters of the Commonwealth preference system and from those who fear that through the GATT other countries will be able to dictate the foreign trade policy of the United States. This latter argument, although politically powerful, is based on a misunderstanding of the Agreement itself.

To all this there is a major offset—the agreement of countries, however powerful, to take account of the effects of their trade policies on other countries and to justify them before an international body. To this must be added one further consideration. The contribution of the GATT to the expansion of trade has been as much what it has prevented as what it has positively achieved. In a recent study of the GATT, this point has been effectively made as follows:

> There is nothing rash in the conclusion that the General Agreement and its enforcement methods have helped measurably in the development of rules of the game among trading nations. This does not mean that the Agreement has necessarily brought peace to areas where economic warfare was consciously desired. GATT or no GATT, nations which had the desire to engage in economic warfare with one another during the period would have done so; witness the deterioration of our [United States] trade relations with Czechoslovakia, one of the original signers. But the converse is equally true; nations with a reasonable desire to avoid trade warfare with their neighbors might none-

theless have been at each other's throats in the absence of standards of international behavior such as the GATT. For governments are under constant
pressure from their domestic interests to take measures which injure the trade
of their neighbors. Where there is no code for distinguishing the actions that
are justified from those that are not, a lapse from grace is easy. And once the
cycle of recrimination and counterretaliation begins, no self-imposed standard
of reasonable conduct can long be maintained.[103]

United Nations System as a Whole

The United Nations system as a whole has been attempting to deal
with several major issues in the field of trade and payments: the relation
of commercial policy to employment and development policy; the
potential conflicts between global and regional approaches to trade
and payments policies; the relation of commodity trade to economic
stability; and the role of short-term credit from international sources
in preventing the international spread of depressions.

Although such a formulation of major issues greatly oversimplifies the
over-all picture of United Nations activities in this area, it serves as
a basis for drawing some general conclusions.

1. The failure of key governments to ratify the proposed Charter for
an International Trade Organization demonstrated that an inter-
locking series of commitments by a large number of countries in so
vast a field is not, and is not likely to be, within the feasible limits of
co-operation through any international agency.

2. The overwhelming importance attached to employment and
development and the subordination of commercial policy to these objectives by majorities in the Council and the Assembly have led these
organs to underestimate, and at times to ignore, the contributions that
the reduction of trade barriers can make to the raising of standards of
living, and the dangers involved in the failure of Member governments
to adopt domestic policies that will promote international equilibrium.

3. The conflict between regional and global approaches to trade
and payments problems has been dealt with by the United Nations
system as a whole and by the GATT with flexibility and moderation
and without sacrifice of global objectives. There has been good co-
operation between the Fund and the regional commissions in the study
of both the intraregional and the world trading problems of their
respective areas, and two of the commissions have engaged in active
trade promotion (the ECE on east-west trade, and the ECAFE on

[103] Vernon, *op. cit.*, p. 18.

trade within its area); but there has not been any substantial change in the pattern of world trade as a result of these efforts. Schemes for regional payments arrangements that might have strengthened existing tendencies to divide the world into regional groupings have been explored and rejected. The relationship between the Fund and the GATT and regional organizations outside the United Nations—the EPU and the European Coal and Steel Community—has been such that neither agency has impeded constructive solutions (in the case of EPU, transitional ones) of European problems; but both have continued to exert their influence against regional as opposed to world-wide solutions of international trade and payments problems.

4. There has been a tug-of-war between the Economic and Social Council and the Fund on the amount and use of its resources. This has not been due to any difference of opinion regarding the need for adequate international reserves and the functions of the Fund as a source of secondary reserves needed to provide international liquidity. It has been due to much more fundamental questions, such as the responsibilities of creditor countries for helping debtor countries to solve their balance-of-payments difficulties by providing through the Fund or otherwise the credits necessary to sustain the volume of their imports; the extent to which monetary and fiscal policy should be relied on to correct balance-of-payments difficulties of a cyclical character without undue recourse to international short-term credit; and the question whether the Fund has been unduly zealous in guarding against the use of its funds by countries that are in need not of short-term accommodation but of long-range assistance.

It is a good thing that these issues have been raised and debated within the United Nations system, and that the boldness of the majority of the members of the Council and some of the experts reporting to the Council has been matched by the caution of the Fund. With the completion of the major work of reconstruction, the rediscovery of the role of monetary policy, the steady increase in the transferability of major non-dollar currencies, and their *de facto* convertibility at a modest cost, the tide is now running in favor of the general principles upheld by the Fund.

If the record of the United Nations system as a whole is judged in the light of the extraordinary complexity of international trade and payments relationships and of the long list of international disagreements and conflicts inherited by the United Nations, it is a record of progress on all but the most intractable problems.

CHAPTER IV

Production and Investment*

A NUMBER of the problems in the field of trade and payments that have come before the United Nations during its first ten years are fundamentally production problems. At the end of the Second World War, the productive capacity and other economic resources of the world were heavily concentrated in the United States. Unless a better pattern of world production evolved, other nations, it was feared, might be confronted not with a temporary but with a chronic dollar shortage, regularly tending to spend more dollars for purchases in the United States than they could earn in sales to the United States or in third markets. Recent events, in particular the experience of 1953–54 when an American recession coincided with a vigorous expansion of production in Europe, have cast doubt on whether the underlying structural disequilibrium is as acute or as permanent as it seemed to be during the early postwar years. Whether the adjustments already made in terms of production and trade, however, are sufficient to banish the prospect of a chronic dollar shortage is still an open question.

The efforts the United Nations has made to expand industrial and agricultural output and to mobilize investment for productive undertakings, like the work in trade and payments, may be divided for purposes of analysis into two time periods: a "formative period" lasting from 1946 to mid-1950, and an "operating period" extending from mid-1950 to date. During the formative period, the reconstruction of war-devastated areas had top priority, and the spotlight was on Europe. By the end of the period, the raising of standards of living in the underdeveloped areas of Asia, Africa, and Latin America had become the central economic aim of the United Nations. Activities during the operating period were consequently world-wide in scope.

The International Bank for Reconstruction and Development during the formative period mobilized sizable resources, developed its loan principles and procedures, completed the reconstruction phase of its work, and made a start on the long-term job of helping underdeveloped countries prepare and realize programs of development. The formative

* By Robert E. Asher.

period in the life of the International Bank was paralleled by exploratory work in the field of production and investment by other agencies of the United Nations, most notably the Food and Agriculture Organization, the Economic and Social Council, the Economic and Employment Commission of the Council, and the regional economic commissions. Shortages of food, fuel, and capital equipment characterized the period, and much attention was given to methods of overcoming temporary deficits. Various types of inter-agency collaboration were developed, although none was as formal as the procedures employed after 1950 for carrying out the Expanded Programme of Technical Assistance.

The realization that important increases in production could be obtained through exchanges of know-how, with comparatively insignificant expenditures of capital, lay at the heart of the technical assistance program. Although the program as a whole is analyzed and appraised at a later point in this study,[1] certain aspects of the work intimately affecting output in industry and agriculture are discussed below.

The inauguration of the Expanded Programme of Technical Assistance was recognized by both developed and underdeveloped countries as a landmark in international economic co-operation under United Nations auspices, but the underdeveloped countries continued to feel that shortage of capital was the main obstacle to a more rapid improvement in their living standards. Many heated discussions arose in United Nations forums regarding the scale and terms on which loan capital should be provided, the measures required to increase the flow of private international investment, the methods of mobilizing domestic capital in underdeveloped countries, and the need for public grants-in-aid from abroad to supplement other sources of development funds. Solution of these problems was made more difficult by conflicting national attitudes concerning intergovernmental versus private lending and investment, and the respective rights and obligations of the receivers and providers of international investment. Some of these same conflicts of attitude arose during the complex negotiations to implement an American proposal for promoting the peaceful uses of atomic energy through the establishment of a world bank for fissionable materials.

The dissatisfaction of many underdeveloped countries with their share in the expansion of world production, and their passionate desire for rapid economic development, inevitably involved the United

---

[1] See below, Chap. X.

Nations in the removal of obstacles to economic development within the underdeveloped countries themselves. Among these were lack of technically trained man power, chronic underemployment in agriculture, immobility of labor force, lack of knowledge of potential resources, lack of administrative organization and skills, traditional systems of land tenure, lack of adequate domestic savings and of means of directing them into productive channels, inadequate communications, and shortage of social capital generally.

The attention given to underdeveloped areas in the present discussion of production and investment issues, as elsewhere in this study, is necessitated both by the intrinsic importance of their problems and by the increasing emphasis given to them in the work of the United Nations. It should be borne in mind, however, that the objectives of the Charter in the field of production and investment, as in other fields, were originally conceived of as world-wide objectives, and that the economic, social, political, and cultural aspirations dependent for realization on an expansion of production are not confined to any particular group of countries.

Formative Period: 1946–50

The idea that the international community as a whole and, more specifically, the inhabitants of the wealthier nations, have a responsibility for the welfare of their fellow men in remote, poorer nations is relatively new in international affairs. Although it has gained ground during the postwar years, especially since 1950, it remains far from a self-evident truth. The idea that the members of a victorious wartime coalition have a collective responsibility for helping to repair war damage to the worst-devastated areas within the alliance is also new, but has won much wider acceptance. Even before the Charter of the United Nations had been ratified, the wartime coalition had assumed a responsibility in connection with relief, rehabilitation, and reconstruction by establishing the United Nations Relief and Rehabilitation Administration (UNRRA) and approving the Articles of Agreement of the International Bank for Reconstruction and Development (IBRD).

Development of Loan Principles and Procedures by the International Bank

Whereas UNRRA was an emergency organization dominated by humanitarian considerations, the International Bank was envisaged as a permanent organization operating more or less on business principles. UNRRA, already in being at the time of the Bretton Woods Conference, was to meet immediate relief and rehabilitation requirements—primarily through grants. Once emergency needs were met, countries would presumably be in a position to borrow. Loans for the medium-term job of reconstruction and the long-term job of economic development, if not obtainable in the private capital market on reasonable terms, would be available through the Bank.[2]

Subscriptions to the capital fund of the Bank were to be made by all of the members, roughly in accordance with their economic capacities. Under the Articles of Agreement, the capital subscription required of each member is divided into three parts. A small fraction, 2 per cent, is paid in gold or United States dollars, and may be used freely by the International Bank for any of its activities. Another 18 per cent is payable in the currency of the subscribing country—in pounds, francs, guilders, etc.—and may be used for lending only with the consent of the subscriber. The remaining 80 per cent is, in fact, only a guarantee fund. It is not available for direct lending, but is subject to call if and when it is required to meet obligations of the Bank arising out of its borrowing or guarantees.

The capital structure of the Bank was thus designed to provide it with some loan resources of its own (the 20 per cent of their capital subscriptions that members would pay in), and a guarantee fund four times as great (the other 80 per cent) to enable the Bank to mobilize private capital, either through the sale of its obligations to private investors or by guaranteeing international credits privately financed. The emphasis in the Articles of Agreement was on facilitating investment by others, not on investment by the Bank itself. When private capital was unavailable on reasonable terms, however, the Bank was "to supplement private investment by providing, on suitable conditions, finance for productive purposes out of its own capital, funds raised by it and its other resources."[3]

The Secretary of the United States Treasury who was President of the Bretton Woods Conference, described the central aim of the Bank in his closing address to the conference:

[2] For a useful history of the Bank, from which this analysis has borrowed liberally, see *The International Bank for Reconstruction and Development, 1946–1953,* prepared by the Staff of the Bank (1954). (Hereinafter cited as *The International Bank, 1946–1953.*)

[3] United Nations Monetary and Financial Conference, Bretton Woods, N.H., July 1 to 22, 1944, *Articles of Agreement, International Monetary Fund and International Bank for Reconstruction and Development* (1945), Art. I(ii), p. 51. (Hereinafter cited as *Articles of Agreement.*)

... The chief purpose of the International Bank for Reconstruction and Development is to guarantee private loans made through the usual investment channels. It would make loans only when these could not be floated through the normal investment channels at reasonable rates. The effect would be to provide capital for those who need it at lower interest rates than in the past, and to drive only the usurious money lenders from the temple of international finance.[4]

Before the resources of the Bank could be put to effective use, a number of policy issues concerning the scope and character of its operations had to be settled. To raise funds in the private capital market, the Bank would have to win the confidence of the investing community. To win the confidence of the investing community, it would have to hew closely to the line of standard banking practices. Yet if it were really to assist as expected in "raising productivity, the standard of living and conditions of labor,"[5] it would inevitably have to take certain risks that private enterprise would not take. Which risks should these be?

The desperate need for reconstruction funds in Europe and the rising demand in other areas for more rapid economic development called for speedy action. These strong external pressures had to be reconciled with the injunctions in the Articles of Agreement that the Bank act "prudently" and "pay due regard" to the prospects that the borrower would repay the loan. An "equitable" division of limited resources had to be made between the vast but probably finite claims of reconstruction and the vaster and almost infinite need for development funds.

The promotion of a climate favorable to private foreign investment had to be reconciled with the national sensitivities of countries that were in fact hostile to private foreign investment. The Bank had to refrain from interference in the political affairs of any member, but it was expected to satisfy itself that its loans would be put to productive use and that the economic house of the borrower was in reasonably good order.

Knowledge that the authorized capital of the Bank was $10 billion, of which more than $8 billion had been subscribed by mid-1947, could give a misleading impression of the resources at its disposal. The 20 per cent represented by paid-in capital amounted to $1.6 billion. Only

---

[4] Closing address to the United Nations Monetary and Financial Conference by Henry Morgenthau, Jr., July 22, 1944, U.S. Department of State *Bulletin*, Vol. 2 (July 30, 1944), p. 113.
[5] *Articles of Agreement*, Art. I(iii).

$727 million was in gold or United States dollars, and the balance was in the currencies of other member countries. For all practical purposes, the resources of the Bank for direct loans were limited initially to the $727 million, for its clients needed supplies obtainable in 1947 only in the United States market, with gold or United States dollars.[6]

The founders of the Bank, as noted earlier, assumed that the guarantee provisions, behind which stood the other 80 per cent of the American subscription and that of other members, would enable the Bank to mobilize private capital without great difficulty. Just as the founders underestimated the magnitude of European reconstruction requirements, they underestimated the damage wrought by depression and war on the pattern of international trade and payments and on the psychology of private investors. Private investors, mindful of earlier experiences with defaulted foreign loans and distrustful of governmental and intergovernmental institutions, were not interested in lending money to foreign borrowers, even with the safeguard of a guarantee by the Bank. Marketing the bonds of European, Latin American, and Asian borrowers, backed by the guarantee of an institution whose credit was not yet established, therefore could not be adopted as a major fund-raising technique.

The Bank, on the advice of its management and without objection from its membership, decided instead to sell its own bonds and to devote the proceeds to project loans. This, too, proved more difficult than anticipated. The psychological barriers of investors' reluctance to engage in foreign lending, ignorance concerning the Bank and the resources behind it, and opportunities for profitable investment in the domestic market, were reinforced by a major legal barrier. The most likely purchasers of Bank securities at the time—institutional investors in the United States—were subject to state and federal laws that did not authorize investment in the Bank type of security. An extensive tour of state capitals by representatives of the Bank and a publicity campaign, which continued to the summer of 1949, were necessary to obtain legislation and rulings in the various states that would qualify bonds of the International Bank as appropriate investments for national banks, commercial and savings banks, and insurance companies.

In July 1947, the Bank made the first public offering of its own bonds: $100 million in ten-year, $2\frac{1}{4}$ per cent bonds, and $150 million

[6] International Bank for Reconstruction and Development, *Second Annual Report, 1946–1947*, p. 15.

in twenty-five-year, 3 per cent bonds. Both issues were substantially oversubscribed, and the bonds immediately sold at a premium over the public offering price. This was, of course, gratifying to the management of the Bank. On the other hand, making such bonds eligible and attractive to the most conservative American investors, however important to the longer-run operations of the International Bank, reinforced the pressures toward caution inherent in any organization dominated by officials of treasuries and central banks. Procedural safeguards that delayed the granting of loans, or limited the purposes for which they could be granted, or required ancillary domestic reforms as the price of their approval, could all be justified as essential in order to gain and hold the confidence of private investors. The alleged dependence of the Bank on "Wall Street" consequently became the target of much criticism.

In material terms, what the world outside of North America needed and wanted at the close of the war was the largest possible increase in output, telescoped into the shortest possible period of time. The Bank was certain to be judged in the light of the contribution it could make to this objective. It was therefore under great pressure to give prompt approval to meritorious projects, provided it could satisfy itself on what constituted a meritorious project.

The project approach was intended to avoid the kind of unproductive loans for ill-defined purposes that had been made at high rates of interest during the 1920's and followed by wholesale defaults. If applications were tied to the financing of specific power plants, railroad lines, and irrigation facilities, there would be a better opportunity to judge the amounts needed, the goods and services for which the sums would be expended, and the prospects of repayment. Hence the requirement limiting loans to specific projects except in unusual circumstances.[7]

Proper evaluation of proposals for specific projects, however, required information regarding the over-all prospects and policies of the borrowing country. Regardless of the caliber of the technical designs and specifications, a power plant proposed to the Bank as a specific project would represent a waste of valuable resources if its initial capacity were greatly in excess of foreseeable requirements for electricity. Scaled down to its proper proportions, the plant might appear as an unqualified boon to industrial and agricultural production in the area, but the benefits could be reduced by tax and credit

---

[7] *Articles of Agreement*, Art. III, Sec. 4 (vii).

policies that discouraged enterprise. To assure the most productive use of the total resources of a nation, the Bank at an early stage began encouraging member governments to formulate long-term investment programs within the framework of which individual project proposals could be more intelligently assessed.

Under its Articles of Agreement, the Bank was expected to finance only those productive projects for which other financing was not available on reasonable terms. Surveying the field during its formative period, the Bank assumed that private capital would be most readily available for the development of export products such as tin, rubber, and petroleum. It hoped that light manufacturing industries such as textiles, which required smaller amounts of capital and which were traditionally private enterprise activities, would continue to be financed privately. On the other hand, large amounts of capital would be required for basic facilities—transportation, communications, and power projects—no longer attractive to private capital, but prerequisites for the attraction of private capital to other fields.

Public utilities had attracted private foreign capital to underdeveloped countries in prewar days, but it would have been unrealistic to expect them to continue doing so after the war on any appreciable scale. The investment was too large, the return too small, the prospect of government intervention too great. Projects to develop electric power and transport facilities were accordingly judged appropriate for Bank financing, although not without some audible expressions of misgiving on the part of the American financial community.

At the same time, and not without equally audible expressions of concern in some other parts of the world, the Bank was led to eschew a field traditionally reserved for public investment even in the highly developed, free enterprise economies: namely, investment in sanitation, education, and health work. These so-called "social overhead investments" were widely recognized as fundamental to other development work. Their contribution to increased production was less measurable and direct, however, than that of a railroad or power plant, and they could be completed without large expenditures of scarce foreign currencies. It therefore seemed logical to consider projects for eliminating malaria, wiping out illiteracy, building elementary schools, or establishing clinics, as unsuitable, in normal circumstances, for financing by the International Bank. Still, the crying need for such projects, and the paucity of domestic resources to finance them, helped in later years to fan the flames for grant-aid programs to supplement loan aid.

Affecting somewhat more subtly the types of projects for which loans would be desired, was the government-guarantee requirement. The Bank could make loans only to governments or in cases where repayment of both principal and interest were fully guaranteed by the government of the area in which the project was to be located. Yet the group most likely to invigorate the climate for private enterprise in underdeveloped countries, the persons desirous of establishing privately owned manufacturing or processing plants, would be least likely to seek Bank financing for fear that the government guarantee demanded by the Bank would subject them to closer government scrutiny and interference than would otherwise be the case. Governments, for their part, would be reluctant to criticize this hesitancy because lack of proposals from the private sector would relieve the government of charges of favoritism for having placed its guarantee behind the borrowings of particular private groups within its borders. Moreover, the governments would then be freer to submit proposals of their own for government-owned facilities that would enhance the prestige of the state. It was the government-guarantee requirement, and the inability of the Bank to supply equity capital, that prompted later proposals for an International Finance Corporation.

So long as currencies remained inconvertible, the requirement of the Bank that repayment must be made in the currency that was borrowed operated as a further barrier. It meant that a project financed by a dollar loan normally had to contribute directly or indirectly to the dollar earnings of the borrowing nation. The availability of Bank financing only for the foreign exchange costs of approved projects was intended to limit to the minimum the future foreign exchange burden of servicing the debt. It meant, moreover, that borrowers would have to meet their own local currency costs, *i.e.*, the funds required for the payment of local labor and domestically produced supplies as contrasted with the currencies needed to pay for the capital equipment obtainable only from abroad. This arrangement, it was believed, would test the sincerity of the interest of a nation in more rapid development and give it an incentive to mobilize its own resources. To many, who were troubled by the relative absence of local savings to mobilize, it seemed an arbitrary limitation. Supporters of the view that IBRD loans should cover the total costs of development projects argued that if British investors in the nineteenth century had limited their investments in Argentina or British Dominion railway projects to the value of the imported equipment required for building the railways, the projects would have remained dead letters.[8]

As reported earlier, the Bank was clearly intended, when making loans to cover the foreign exchange costs of proposed projects, to assume some risks that private banks would not assume, but at the same time to limit itself to investments that were reasonably likely to be repaid. The special risks that it was willing to assume included world war and widespread depression. In other respects, it was determined to make a conscientious assessment of the prospects of repayment. The scope of its conscience is revealed in the following quotation:

. . . The assessment of repayment prospects involves an exercise of judgment after consideration of a multitude of factors. The availability of natural resources and the existing productive plant within the country are the obvious starting points, but equally important is the capacity of the country concerned to exploit its resources and operate its productive facilities effectively. This involves, among other things, an evaluation of the effectiveness both of the government administration and of the important private enterprises operating within the country, the availability of managerial, supervisory, and technical skills, the types of investment which are proposed to be undertaken both with domestic resources and with funds borrowed from the Bank, and the economic and financial policies which are likely to be followed, particularly insofar as they affect the levels of consumption and of domestic savings and the flow of foreign private capital. The probable impact of all these factors upon the country's future balance of payments position must then be assessed in the light of such considerations as the likely course of prices for the country's principal exports and imports, the stability of export markets, the essentiality of imports, and the effect of population increases. Moreover, in a world of inconvertible currencies, it is not sufficient simply to consider how much over-all foreign debt the borrower can service, it must also be determined in what currencies such a service obligation can be met.

Complicating judgment in every case is the fact that credit-worthiness is not determined by economic forces alone; within fairly wide limits it is determined, too, by the intangible factor of the country's traditional attitude towards its foreign debts. A country which shows a willingness to maintain debt service at the expense, if necessary, of short-term domestic interests is plainly a better credit risk than a country, even with a potentially somewhat stronger economy, which does not treat its foreign obligations with equal seriousness and which may therefore be unwilling, in times of stringency, to make sacrifices in consumption standards to maintain debt service. In this connection, the past debt record of the country is significant.[9]

[8] This was said, for example, by Nicholas Kaldor, a principal author of the report of the experts on "National and International Measures for Full Employment." U.N. Economic and Social Council, Eleventh Session, *Official Records*, 385th Meeting (July 12, 1950), pp. 78–79.
[9] *The International Bank, 1946–1953*, pp. 42–43.

The breadth of the concern of the Bank with the affairs of its borrowers precluded prompt conclusion of loan negotiations. Instability in a borrowing country would jeopardize the prospects for repayment of loans made by the Bank, would alarm purchasers of Bank securities, and would frighten away the private investors for whom the Bank was supposed to prepare the road. A demand for the correction of unsound financial practices as a condition for the granting of a loan consequently seemed to the Bank management to be entirely justifiable. The difficulty was that what was unsound in the eyes of the Bank was not universally recognized as such. Moreover, where it was recognized, correction was not always politically practicable. The delays of the Bank, its stress on "fair and equitable settlements of outstanding debts," "balanced budgets," "sound tax systems," "sound monetary systems," "avoidance of inflation," etc., gave rise to much debate when the representatives of underdeveloped countries became more vocal in international forums.

The determination of a reasonable rate of interest on Bank loans was likewise a controversial issue. Prewar loans were believed to have been made at exorbitant rates. To members in need of credit, "reasonable" at the close of the Second World War meant rates appreciably lower than those charged at the close of the First World War. The appropriate rate, in the view of the Bank, was the estimated cost to the Bank of a comparable borrowing in the United States market, plus a margin to cover operating expenses and build up a reserve. The resultant 4 per cent or more seemed high to many prospective borrowers, influenced by the knowledge that the American Export-Import Bank was making loans at interest rates of $2\frac{1}{4}$ to $3\frac{1}{2}$ per cent and that large-scale intergovernmental grants were still being made for reconstruction purposes. Their dissatisfaction with the rates charged by the International Bank gave rise to a persistent clamor for additional United Nations machinery to provide "low-interest" loans for "low-yielding, slow-yielding" projects.[10]

There were other issues concerning the scope and character of operations of the Bank that had to be resolved, temporarily at least, before actual loans could be made, but they were minor in comparison with the problems of mobilizing loanable resources, determining the types of projects for which loans would be made, and fixing appropriate terms. All of the loan principles and procedures of the Bank could be

[10] In 1956, the interest rate on loans of more than fifteen years was raised to 5 per cent (including the controversial commission of 1 per cent required by the Articles of Agreement during the first ten years of the life of the Bank).

justified as logical outgrowths of one or more requirements of its
Articles of Agreement. They were intended to enable the Bank to
borrow successfully in the private market, to pave the way for a revival
of private international lending, to limit the use of public funds to
public purposes, and to break with the Lend-Lease and UNRRA
concepts by re-establishing the old-fashioned notion that international
finance is business, that a borrower should be a good risk, and that he
should not only be capable of repaying the funds he borrows, but
also be of a mind to do so. In total, they constituted a fairly formidable
set of hurdles to be cleared before a loan could be obtained. It remained
to be seen whether the erection of such a set of hurdles to meet specific
provisions in the Articles of Agreement could be reconciled with the
larger objectives implicit in the Articles as a whole: the speedy reconstruction of war-devastated areas and the triggering of the longer-term
process of satisfying in some measure the pent-up aspirations of the
peoples in underdeveloped countries.

The dual purpose of the Bank—reconstruction and development—is
clear from its name. Thanks to the work of the Leith-Ross committees
in London and to the operations of UNRRA, more was known at the
Bretton Woods Conference about the reconstruction needs of war-
devastated Europe than about the capital requirements of underdeveloped countries, although in both cases the knowledge was pitifully
deficient. The underdeveloped countries, particularly in Latin America,
were fearful that the Bank "would allocate too large a share of its resources to reconstruction and that not enough would be left for development."[11] Discussion of the relative emphasis to be placed on reconstruction and development was heated. The kind of compromise language that has so frequently enabled international meetings to surmount difficulties without resolving them was finally adopted. "The
resources and the facilities of the Bank shall be used," said the Articles
of Agreement, "with equitable consideration to projects for development and projects for reconstruction alike."[12]

[11] Antonin Basch, "International Bank for Reconstruction and Development,
1944–49: A Review," *International Conciliation*, No. 455 (November 1949), p. 794.
[12] Art. III, Sec. 1(a). The word "equitable," brimming with high moral connota-
tions and never defined, later performed similar service in Article XX(II) of the General Agreement on Tariffs and Trade (countries "are entitled to an equitable share
of the international supply" of scarce products); in the Economic and Social Council
(the regulation "at equitable levels and relationships" of the prices of essential
goods, Res. 341(XII), Mar. 20, 1951); and in the General Assembly ("the establishment of fair and equitable international prices for primary commodities," Res.
623(VII), Dec. 21, 1952). It seemed to afford at least as much satisfaction to the
underdeveloped countries as the term "sound," in "sound" projects and "sound"
financial policies, gave to representatives from the more advanced free-enterprise
economies.

In practice, "equitable consideration" meant reconstruction first, then development. The requirements for European reconstruction—urgent, visible, basic to the re-establishment of a functioning world economy—turned out to be far in excess of the ability of the Bank to meet them. They claimed not only the first $500 million loaned by the Bank and sales by its companion institution, the International Monetary Fund (IMF), of more than $500 million in dollar exchange to European members of the Fund, but also many billions from the United States in the form of post-UNRRA relief, credits connected with the settlement of lend-lease obligations, loans from the Export-Import Bank of Washington, and grant assistance under the European Recovery Program. Not until after Marshall Plan funds began flowing to the countries in the Organization for European Economic Cooperation (OEEC) did the IBRD begin making loans to other areas for economic development purposes. In this uncharted, post-reconstruction field, however, the Bank did its trail-blazing at a more dignified pace.

It opened its doors on June 25, 1946. Within a few months, applications for more than $2.5 billion in dollar loans had been received from nine countries. The first loan was made in May 1947 to France—$250 million to the *Crédit National*, guaranteed by the French Government. The original application was for $500 million, but the Bank decided to limit its commitment to the immediate future, saying it would be willing to consider a further application later in the year.[13] Fortunately, the United States Secretary of State in June 1947, in a speech at Harvard University, introduced what became known as the Marshall Plan or—more formally, the European Recovery Program—thereby enabling France to look elsewhere than to the IBRD for help in meeting its reconstruction requirements.[14]

The Netherlands had applied to the IBRD for an even larger sum than France—$535 million—to help cover its reconstruction requirements for 1947–49. The Bank, limiting its commitment to the 1947 portion of the program, approved a loan of $195 million in August 1947. These were followed promptly by loans of $40 million to Denmark and $12 million to Luxemburg.

[13] International Bank for Reconstruction and Development, *Second Annual Report, 1946–1947*, p. 18.

[14] Only eight months earlier, U.S. Secretary of the Treasury Snyder had said to the First Annual Meeting of the Board of Governors, of which he was chairman: "As we all know, the International Bank must now assume responsibility for underwriting reconstruction loans to countries otherwise unable to borrow on reasonable terms." International Bank for Reconstruction and Development, *Proceedings and Related Documents* (Oct. 29, 1946), p. 6.

The plight of Western Europe in 1947 was desperate. The Bank courageously cast its resources into the breach. It functioned as one of the lifelines to a sinking Europe until Marshall Plan grants were mobilized. Its first four loans were not for specific productive projects but for the "general purpose" of financing a variety of essential dollar imports. It then withdrew from the reconstruction field although Czechoslovakia and Poland, prevented by the Kremlin from participating in the European Recovery Program, still had loan applications totaling $1 billion before the Bank.

The factors militating against approval of the Czech and Polish loan applications were, of course, political. But intergovernmental agencies are not supposed to discriminate on political grounds. The economic justification for the position of the Bank was set forth in its annual report for 1948:

It is unfortunate but nonetheless true that the existing political difficulties and uncertainties in Europe present special problems which have thus far prevented the Bank from making loans in those countries. The Bank is fully cognizant of the injunction in its Articles of Agreement that its decisions shall be based only on economic considerations. Political tensions and uncertainties in or among its member countries, however, have a direct effect on economic and financial conditions in those countries and upon their credit position.[15]

Unable to obtain a loan and not in a position to participate constructively in the work of the Bank, Poland withdrew in 1950. Czechoslovakia, also unable to obtain a loan, and unsuccessful in its quest for a further period of grace in which to pay that part of its capital subscription due in gold or United States dollars, was suspended from membership as of December 31, 1953, and membership was formally terminated at the close of 1954.

In addition to the unapproved applications from Poland and Czechoslovakia, the Bank had applications on file from Chile, Iran, and Mexico. The first development lending—$16 million to Chile, of which $13.5 million was for hydroelectric development and $2.5 million for the production of agricultural machinery—was not undertaken until March 1948.

The record of approximately $500 million loaned for reconstruction as compared with $16 million for development purposes during its first two years in business made the Bank vulnerable to the charge of insensitivity to the urgency of raising living standards in underdeveloped

[15] International Bank for Reconstruction and Development, *Third Annual Report, 1947–1948*, p. 14.

countries. The desire of these countries for capital, however, was not
matched by any corresponding ability to prepare properly documented,
technically sound project applications. The underdeveloped countries
were underdeveloped as respects administrators and technicians, as well
as natural resources. Before they could absorb large amounts of capital,
they needed technical assistance.

Although technical assistance was subsequently to become one of the
most important activities of the Bank, nothing is said in the Articles of
Agreement about this form of aid. Nevertheless, in its first annual report, the Bank indicated its willingness to consider furnishing technical
assistance in the preparation of loan applications. Gradually, the technical assistance concept was broadened, from helping a prospective borrower find competent technicians to prepare necessary engineering and
financial data for specific projects, to full-scale surveys of economic conditions in member countries. By mid-1948, such surveys had been made
or were in process in a number of areas, chiefly in Latin America, in
response to requests from governments. The job of missions organized
by the Bank was to survey the potentialities and problems of the
countries to which the missions went and to help the countries formulate
realistic, long-term development programs.

Meanwhile the granting of Bank loans for development purposes was
necessarily slow. In the Latin American region, Mexico and Brazil obtained loans in early 1949. The first loans to Asia, $44 million to India
for railway rehabilitation and the improvement of agricultural production, were approved during the second half of 1949. The first loans to
the Middle East and Africa (to Iraq and Ethiopia, respectively) were
not approved until 1950. Despite growing pressure for greater assistance
to underdeveloped areas, total Bank loans to non-European nations as
of mid-1950 amounted to only about a quarter of a billion dollars. Of
this sum, less than $100 million had actually been disbursed.

An important broadening of the principle that loans would be made
only for specific projects took place in 1950, however, with the approval
of a dollar loan to Australia to finance the purchase of assorted capital
goods and equipment "needed for development projects, both private
and governmental."[16] The specific project concept was further broadened
by the approval in October 1950 of a loan to a new Turkish Industrial

[16] International Bank for Reconstruction and Development, Press Release No.
205 (Aug. 22, 1950), p. 1. The extensive investment requirements of Australia arose
in part from its acceptance during the postwar period of large numbers of immigrants
n relation to its population.

Development Bank. Prior to this, the International Bank had not been equipped to assist small- and medium-sized private undertakings, partly because of the government-guarantee requirement, partly because of the inability of the Bank to make equity investments, and partly because of the impracticability of employing the resources of a large international agency to investigate applications for small loans. The establishment of a local institution that could carry out the necessary financial and technical investigations, and make either loans to or equity investments in private domestic enterprises provided an answer to these difficulties. Private Turkish interests subscribed equity capital for the Industrial Bank, the Central Bank of Turkey furnished additional capital on a loan basis, and the International Bank provided a dollar loan as well as technical assistance in bringing the new institution into being.

The inability of potential borrowers in underdeveloped countries to submit approvable loan applications during the early years of the Bank or, as those borrowers sometimes viewed it, the slowness of the Bank in approving applications, made it unnecessary for the Bank to expand its own public borrowing at a rapid rate. The first borrowing in a currency other than United States dollars occurred in 1948 when the Bank sold about $4 million worth of 2½ per cent Swiss Franc Serial Bonds. A second issue, somewhat larger than the first, was sold in 1950.[17]

The development of a broader market outside the United States was hampered by obstacles analogous to those previously encountered by the Bank within the United States. The status of Bank obligations under the investment laws of different countries was unclear. Legislation was required in order to classify Bank securities as eligible investments for banks, insurance companies, and similar institutions within member countries. Action was also required before dollar bonds could be traded on local stock exchanges. Some progress had been made as of mid-1950, however, in Chile, Cuba, Mexico, and the Netherlands.

Meanwhile, the Bank management continued its attempts to acquire interest-free funds by persuading member governments to release additional portions of their capital subscriptions. In March 1947, the United States had released unconditionally the 18 per cent payable in the currency of the subscribing country and employable only with the consent of that country. Canada had rather promptly released Canadian dol-

[17] A second public offering of bonds in the United States market was made in 1950. The purpose was not to obtain additional capital but rather to redeem an earlier $100 million issue of 2¼ per cent bonds and effect a savings in interest payments. It was notable as the first issue of the Bank bonds sold by competitive bidding to underwriters.

lars for purchases in Canada but not for purchases anywhere in the world. Efforts to secure the consent of other members were comparatively unsuccessful though partial releases had been obtained by mid-1950 from a handful of European and Latin American nations for goods and services to be purchased within the territory of the lender. With this qualification, the funds were of little use so long as borrowers wanted capital goods obtainable only in North America.

By mid-1950, the formative period of the Bank may be regarded as having ended and the main lines of its work as fairly well defined. Until 1947, attention had been devoted to problems that had to be resolved, at least in a preliminary way, before any borrowing or lending could be undertaken. The period from mid-1947 to mid-1950 included these major developments: (1) completion of the reconstruction phase of the work of the Bank, *i.e.*, the extension of loans to help four Western European nations carry on until the European Recovery Program came to their rescue; (2) the approval of one or more development loans to other major regions of the non-Communist world; (3) the emergence of technical assistance as an important aspect of IBRD activity, and survey missions as effective devices for focusing expert analysis on the problems of particular countries; (4) a broadening of the specific project provision to the point where the requirement meant no more than there should be advance agreement on the manner in which loan proceeds would be expended; (5) successful small-scale efforts to obtain capital, public and private, outside of the United States; (6) the solidifying of the credit position of the Bank and general satisfaction on the part of the private investment community with the "soundness" of its management; and (7) growing impatience in many other circles with the rate and volume of its lending.

Concern of Other Agencies with
Production and Investment

While the International Bank was developing its operating techniques, other agencies within the United Nations system concerned with production and investment issues were undergoing a similar evolution. But the Food and Agriculture Organization (FAO), the Economic and Social Council, the Economic and Employment Commission and the three regional economic commissions of the Council were not equipped, as was the Bank, with funds for large-scale investment in productive projects and were not confined within pre-established frameworks as detailed as the Articles of Agreement of the Bank. For the agencies lacking capital endowments, "operating techniques" tended to mean the compilation of reports and analyses and, through subsequent discussion of their implications at intergovernmental meetings, the stimulation of appropriate action by national governments.

Pending the completion of studies that would outline the main problems in need of attention at the international level—and the consent of governments to a concerted attack on such problems—these United Nations agencies were feeling their way, probing for vacuums to fill, groping for methods of being useful. In this spirit, they embarked on a series of projects, seeking to overcome specific shortages in the supply of food, fuel, power, and transportation, while gathering the facts required for an analysis of the more intractable longer-term problems. "Breaking bottlenecks," it was called in the literature of the day, although this now sounds curiously unconstructive for such nobly conceived agencies. But even in the earliest dealings with shortages, there were undercurrents of fear regarding future surpluses. If the longer-range analyses and forecasts revealed potential surpluses, however, such reports usually went on to explain that the excess related only to "effective demand," to what people could afford to buy, not to what they needed. To meet real needs and provide twentieth century standards of decency, it was rightly reported, would require levels of production far higher than any that were likely to be achieved.

Another feature of the early work in production and investment was that the agencies began spilling over into each other's fields of interest and working out various forms of interagency co-operation on an *ad hoc* basis. The FAO, for example, would encounter obstacles that could not be overcome without the collaboration of other international agencies. It found that the biggest impediment to increased rice production in Thailand was the prevalence of malaria, and it called the attention of the World Health Organization to the situation. The key to greater food production in the Near East lay in large-scale investments in irrigation and reclamation projects of a kind that might be eligible for IBRD financing.

To the Economic Commission for Europe (ECE), the FAO recommended certain steps to increase the availability of timber for European reconstruction. The ECE, in helping to implement these recommendations, established a pattern of co-operation with the FAO that served as a model for FAO collaboration with the other regional commissions. The ECE and the FAO together then went on, with the International

Bank, to work out the main lines of a complicated short-term loan by the Bank to help Finland and Yugoslavia increase their timber exports to Belgium, Denmark, France, Italy, the Netherlands, and the United Kingdom.[18]

Although the General Assembly and the Economic and Social Council were concerned at an early date with such production problems as the reconstruction of war-devastated areas and the attainment of an increase in the world's food supply, they imposed relatively little coordination from above, and merely ratified the practical forms of inter-agency co-operation worked out at the regional and country levels by agencies with overlapping interests. Gradually, however, the Council and the Assembly became more assertive in the establishment of priorities on a global basis and concerned with the form and substance of agency efforts to attack problems in the order of their importance.

The main directions of the early explorations of the United Nations in the field of production and investment appear to have been the following:

1. The provision, on a limited basis, of a wide variety of technical services. The early United Nations activities thus laid the foundations for the expanded and co-ordinated program of technical assistance initiated in 1950.

2. The development of regional approaches to economic problems. Although the number of economic problems suitable for handling on a regional rather than on a global or national basis is fairly limited, the regional approach, tried initially as an experiment in Europe, took firm root during the 1947–49 period in other regions where it had much less chance of flowering than in Europe. For better or for worse, it became a permanent feature of the United Nations landscape.

3. At the country level, further impetus was given to the formulation of national development programs establishing investment targets and priorities. The formulation of such programs seemed essential to the rendering of intelligent decisions concerning the relative merits of urgent, competitive claims on limited investment resources. Yet international encouragement of national planning inevitably tended to strengthen national governments, both *vis à vis* private and local interests within their boundaries and *vis à vis* the emerging international machinery for co-ordinating the economic activities of member states.[19]

[18] For details, see International Bank for Reconstruction and Development, Press Release No. 171 (Feb. 8, 1950).

[19] For an interesting elaboration of this point, see Gunnar Myrdal, *An International Economy: Problems and Prospects* (1956), Chap. 4. "National political machin-

4. On a global basis, the investment problem was gradually broken into functional segments that lent themselves to more intensive analysis: the mobilization of domestic capital in underdeveloped countries; the stimulation of private foreign investment; the role of public loan capital from abroad; and the need for grant aid.

Initially, however, the food crisis was virtually at the top of the list of urgent economic problems. Supplies of cereals, meats, fats and oils, and sugar were woefully inadequate and ill-distributed among nations. Rationing schemes were in operation in all the industrialized countries. There they succeeded, by and large, in preventing starvation or wholesale undernourishment and, in some cases, in providing a better balanced diet for low-income groups than had been available in prewar days. The plight of the underdeveloped countries where starvation, undernourishment, and incredibly monotonous diets had been the lot of the people for generations, was more critical. It was in these areas, least able to feed their prewar inhabitants, that population was thought to be increasing at the most rapid rates. The world was unanimous in desiring a greater output of food.

Among the international agencies, primary responsibility for increasing the production of foodstuffs, fibers, and forest products rests with the Food and Agriculture Organization. The efforts of the FAO to alleviate the postwar world food shortage, first by continuation of wartime allocation arrangements and then by more imaginative schemes for building up reserves against future famines and stabilizing trade in foodstuffs, have been described earlier.[20] Although the ups and downs of agricultural output during the period were noted, the emphasis in that discussion was largely on courses of action to be pursued during periods of crisis. To round out the earlier picture, some indication should be given of the development of international co-operation between the FAO and other parts of the United Nations system for the purpose of obtaining long-term increases in supply.

The General Assembly at its first session, it will be recalled, had urged

---

ery ... has a firm basis in people's attitudes of allegiance and solidarity; this machinery is getting stronger and its psychological basis firmer every year. It is used in the service of interests that are felt to be commonly shared within the nation. Machinery for international cooperation is, by contrast, weak and ineffective, and it lacks a solid basis in people's valuations and expectations. Even without any real inherent conflict between the two goals, this tremendous and steadily increasing preponderance of national political machinery has deflected—and, if a radical change of the trend is not induced, will continue to deflect—the development of practical policy towards economic nationalism." (Pp. 33-34.)

[20] See above, Chap. II.

all governments and peoples to take immediate and drastic action, both directly and through the international organizations, to secure an adequate collection of crops from producers, to avoid waste, to reserve grain supplies for direct human consumption, and to secure increased production.[21] The FAO was requested to publish full information on the world food position and outlook. According to the FAO, no such survey on a country-by-country basis had ever been made before.[22] The appraisal of the world food situation in 1946 indicated that shortages of certain essential foodstuffs would continue for another three or four years. It also warned that unmarketable surpluses of farm products might suddenly appear.

The Conference of the FAO that year recommended a series of measures for the best use of the 1946 harvest and the attainment of maximum output in 1947. The FAO emphasis on the scarcity of fertilizers as a limiting factor in raising output foreshadowed some of its later technical services to increase the availability and expand the use of fertilizers. Similarly, the FAO stressed the enormous waste, running into millions of tons per year, caused by insects, rodents, and fungi. The introduction of relatively simple precautions, not requiring large capital investments, could reduce this damage substantially. The FAO therefore began promoting the adoption of such measures.

The limited output of chemical fertilizers in Europe was due not to the ignorance or the perversity of manufacturers but to inadequate allocations of coal, which was also very scarce. Low production of farm machinery was due to the steel shortage. The movement of food from farm to market was hampered by lack of transport. The responsibility of the FAO for stimulating an increase in world food production could not be met without the co-operation of other international agencies.

Accordingly, the Economic and Social Council, in early 1948, considered an agenda item proposed by the FAO concerning co-ordinated action to meet the world food crisis. The Council invited the specialized agencies and the regional economic commissions, in consultation with the FAO, to study ways and means of increasing food production by eliminating shortages of oil, coal, steel, and power that were directly or indirectly affecting the production of fertilizers and agricultural machinery, and the availability of transport.[23]

[21] Res. 27(I), Feb. 14, 1946.
[22] Food and Agriculture Organization, *First Annual Report of the Director-General to the FAO Conference* (July 5, 1946), p. 10.
[23] Res. 103(VI), Mar. 2, 1948.

The FAO, having solicited and obtained a broad "hunting-license" from the Council, then tried to concentrate on a limited number of the most essential production and supply problems in each region. In the Far East, a Working Party on Agricultural Requisites serving both the FAO and the Economic Commission for Asia and the Far East (ECAFE) had been formed to consider short-term needs for chemical fertilizers, pesticides, irrigation and drainage equipment for small projects, and other requisites. Nothing very concrete seems to have resulted from this initiative, and the 1948–49 report of the Director-General of the FAO records a decision of the working party to the effect that "at the present time no scope for international action is apparent from the recommendations on fertilizers and agricultural requisites."[24] This did not, of course, mean satisfaction with the situation, but rather that technical assistance at the country level might be more effective than further intergovernmental consultation at the regional level. Food production in the Far East continued to lag. Restoration of at least prewar per-capita levels of consumption continued to be a main preoccupation of the region and to introduce a depressing note of realism into the ambitious plans for industrialization.

The most serious food deficit in the Far East was in rice. The negotiations that ultimately led to the establishment of the International Rice Commission in Bangkok in 1949 began with the convocation of an FAO study group in India in 1947. The study group surveyed the rice situation and predicted a continued grave shortage for another five years. Many of its recommendations for increasing production involved costly, long-term investments, which the FAO was in no position to implement. In addition to irrigation and drainage programs, rehabilitation of the transport system, and the like, for which the extension of international credits was recommended, there were suggestions for other, more immediate measures—in particular an active campaign to reduce the estimated 12 million tons of rice per year lost as waste. Here the FAO could and did provide technical assistance.

The permanent International Rice Commission set up in 1949 was given the assignment of formulating a world rice policy based on human needs, and of promoting a program of rice production, distribution, conservation, and consumption that would utilize fully advanced research and technology.[25] Meanwhile, however, the nature of the deficit

[24] Food and Agriculture Organization, *Report of the Director-General: Work of FAO, 1948–49* (October 1949), p. 15.
[25] *Ibid.*, pp. 9–10.

had changed. In 1947, Far Eastern nations were prepared to buy more rice than was available on the world market and foresaw a continuation of this situation for another five years. By 1949, the region was nearly self-sufficient again "so far as effective demand for rice was concerned,"[26] although the extent to which technical aid from the FAO contributed to the attainment of this new equilibrium is not clear. In any event, the FAO felt that further increases in rice production were needed, but that agricultural development must be accompanied by simultaneous industrial development in order to provide the purchasing power that would render them marketable.

In Africa, as well as in the Far East, livestock production was unnecessarily low because of the prevalence of rinderpest, a cattle disease the spread of which could be checked by a virus vaccine developed in Canada during the war. Here was an ideal field for technical assistance, an area in which dramatic results could be obtained in short order at low cost. Since 1946, therefore, FAO experts have initiated or participated in immunization campaigns and given advisory assistance to underdeveloped countries in the production of vaccines for reducing the ravages of rinderpest.

The general experience of the FAO in the Far East and Africa was duplicated in the Near and Middle East. Large-scale, long-term investments in agriculture would be needed if food production were to keep pace with population growth, but the techniques employed in the area were so primitive that low-cost, simple improvements could make an important immediate difference. In the arid regions, the crying need for large investment was in irrigation facilities.

In Latin America, as in Asia, FAO personnel worked with the secretariat of the regional economic commission in developing programs and recommendations in the fields of agriculture, fisheries, and forestry. A Joint Working Party of the FAO and the Economic Commission for Latin America (ECLA) made recommendations for increased food production in each of the Latin American countries. FAO forestry experts helped actively to focus the attention of Latin American governments on the potentialities of their own vast forest resources. In all of the underdeveloped regions, discussions and reports sponsored by the FAO publicized the institutional barriers to increased production, which reinforced the technical barriers. Antiquated systems of land tenure, exorbitant interest rates, the absence of agricultural extension services

[26] *Ibid.*, p. 16.

to speed the diffusion of know-how, the lack of marketing facilities—
these were obstacles as formidable as ignorance concerning the use of
steel-tipped plows, disease-resistant seeds, or nitrogenous fertilizers.

In Europe, technical advice from the FAO on how to increase food
output was less necessary than in the underdeveloped regions, and more
attention could be given to increasing the availability of timber for
housing and reconstruction purposes. At the time the Economic Commission for Europe was holding its first organizational session in Geneva,
the FAO was sponsoring a timber conference in Marianske Lazne,
Czechoslovakia. The data assembled for this conference forecast a deficit in 1948 large enough to reduce housing programs in European
timber-importing countries by 600,000–750,000 dwelling units. The
conference recommended modification of established conservation
practices to permit an increase of 10 per cent in cuttings of saw timber
and thus to reduce the anticipated deficit by a third.

The Marianske Lazne conference recognized that some countries
would need foreign aid in order to increase their timber output. Pursuing this question, the ECE Timber Committee was able to obtain a
commitment from Sweden to increase its timber exports in exchange
for an increased coke allocation, which, in turn, was arranged by the
ECE Coal Committee. Later the ECE and the FAO laid the groundwork for the timber loan to which reference has already been made—
the short-term loan of the International Bank to Finland and Yugoslavia.

Decentralization of certain United Nations work to the regional level
undoubtedly had great advantages. The measures agreed upon tended
to be more concrete than those discussed at world-wide gatherings.
Global forums were relieved of burdensome details, and a series of
training schools was provided in which extreme nationalist views might
be toned down in the common interest. Opponents of any kind of
autarky, however, might find reason to be disturbed by the flavor of
regional autarky in some of the early United Nations actions. European
self-sufficiency in timber and coal was frequently cited as a desirable
goal without serious reference to cost or efficiency of production. Asia
strove in similar fashion for self-sufficiency in rice. The FAO Latin
American Commission for Forestry and Forest Products called various
"principles" to the attention of ECLA, including the principle that, in
procuring equipment for modernizing their forest industries, the countries of the region should give preference first to Latin American na-

tions, second to countries offering favorable rates of exchange, and third to countries requiring payment in dollars.[27] These developments, coupled with current investigations of regional payments schemes,[28] could hardly fail to arouse some uneasiness and fears of discrimination in Canada and the United States.

The decentralization of FAO activities did not stop at the regional level. Technical assistance was provided directly to national governments at a very early stage. An FAO mission that went to Greece in 1946 produced a long-term development plan and called it to the attention of the Economic and Social Council and the International Bank.[29] More specialized FAO missions went to Thailand to see what could be done to expand the production of rice and forest products and improve the management of livestock; to Poland to advise on problems connected with the rehabilitation and improvement of agriculture, forestry, and related industries; and to Venezuela to advise on the production of edible oils. Joint missions of the FAO and IBRD also went to several other Latin American countries.

Although the reconstruction of devastated areas had immediately been recognized by the General Assembly as a matter of vital importance, no United Nations agency was concerned with industrial rehabilitation in the broad manner in which the FAO was concerned with agricultural rehabilitation. A Temporary Subcommission on the Economic Reconstruction of Devastated Areas was, however, established in 1946 under the Economic and Employment Commission of the Economic and Social Council. The "devastators," as the subcommission members were familiarly known, subdivided into two working groups: one for Europe and Africa, and one for Asia and the Far East.

Their bulky report on Europe described the extent of war devastation, the progress of recovery, and the nature of the short-term and long-term problems confronting European industry and agriculture. Discussion of it led the Economic and Social Council to request the Secretary-General to undertake forthwith special studies of the needs of devastated areas for long-term and short-term financing of their urgent reconstruction requirements, on favorable terms; to review the means for meeting these needs; and to call attention to cases where the existing means were inadequate. The reference to "favorable conditions" of financing occurs frequently in later United Nations resolutions, and

[27] *Ibid.*, p. 35.
[28] See above, Chap. III.
[29] See below, Chap. X.

always means terms favorable to the borrower. Sometimes it means loans at rates of interest lower than those of the IBRD, or at longer maturities; sometimes it means loans with waiver provisions suspending repayments when conditions are "unfavorable"; sometimes it is merely a euphemism for grants.

More importantly, the report of the "devastators" led to the establishment in 1947 and 1948 of the regional economic commissions whose collaboration with the FAO has already been mentioned. In the industrial as in the agricultural field, the early work of these commissions—the ECE in Europe, ECAFE in Asia and the Far East, and ECLA in Latin America—consisted in part of breaking bottlenecks and in part of studies and discussions devoted to longer-term problems. For example, the Steel Committee of the ECE, in co-operation with the Coal Committee, arranged for an allocation of metallurgical coke that is reported to have permitted a 400,000-ton increase in European steel production in the second quarter of 1948. ECLA, with the help of the IBRD, surveyed the cotton textile industry of Latin America and found that the backwardness "which was usually attributed solely to the existing equipment" was "due to a great extent to inefficient organization and management of the factories."[30] ECLA also began studies of the legal and economic factors affecting investment, public and private, foreign and domestic, in Latin America. ECAFE, with the help of the International Bank, studied the need for long-term and short-term capital for rehabilitating the economies of Far Eastern countries and for developing new industries there, as well as the regulations affecting foreign investments in the region. Both ECAFE and ECLA, particularly the former, began studying the possibilities of mobilizing domestic capital through savings banks, savings bonds, improved tax collections, agricultural banks, and other institutional arrangements.

At Lake Success, then the headquarters of the United Nations Organization, the possibilities of increased production through the more efficient use of existing resources were discussed at a unique United Nations Scientific Conference on the Conservation and Utilization of Resources, suggested by the United States, and held in 1949. Although no Soviet scientists participated, seven hundred experts from fifty other nations joined the discussion groups in their individual capacities, not as government representatives. They met at a time of widely publicized,

---

[30] U.N. Secretariat, Department of Public Information, *The Economic Growth of Twenty Republics, The Work of the Economic Commission for Latin America* (1954), pp. 11–12.

gloomy predictions concerning the ability of the world to support a growing population on a shrinking base of natural resources. They discussed techniques susceptible of more widespread use in the fields of minerals, fuels and energy, water, forest, land, and fish and wildlife resources.

According to the postmeeting report of the Secretary-General, the experts tried to address themselves to such questions as: "What are the costs of applying these techniques measured in terms of money or human effort?" and "What returns can be expected from a given method, either in the form of increased yields, reduced expenditures per unit of production, or in the elimination of waste?"[31] Their papers made clear that it was technically possible for the world to achieve substantially higher standards of living, provided that institutional and other obstacles to the use of better techniques could be overcome, and provided that war could be avoided. Again and again, they brought out the interdependence of different resources and the need for integrated development. The effect of the exchange of know-how at the conference was to provide a kind of preview of the range of projects that might later be undertaken on a country basis under the Expanded Programme of Technical Assistance of the United Nations.[32]

The conference was a discussion session with no attempt made to reach agreement on resolutions and recommendations. Although the Secretary-General believed, and was not alone in his view, that this approach resulted in a more fruitful conference, five years were to pass before another large group of experts was brought together under United Nations auspices solely for an exchange of views.[33] Meanwhile, the art of moving from one agenda item to the next without pausing for intervening resolutions was almost forgotten.

Increasingly, the development of underdeveloped countries became the major economic preoccupation of the United Nations agencies. The

[31] U.N. Economic and Social Council, Tenth Session, *United Nations Scientific Conference on Conservation and Utilization of Resources, Report by the Secretary-General to Tenth Session of ECOSOC*, Doc. E/1579 (Dec. 28, 1949), p. 4.

[32] As the United States Representative reported at the tenth session of the Economic and Social Council in a comprehensive review of the conference, "The United Nations Scientific Conference on the Conservation and Utilization of Resources had constituted a prologue to the expanded programme of technical assistance, presenting its problems and its possibilities." U.N. Economic and Social Council, Tenth Session, *Official Records*, 349th Meeting (Feb. 13, 1950), p. 28.

[33] In August 1954, a World Population Conference was held in Rome and in August 1955, an International Conference on the Peaceful Uses of Atomic Energy was held in Geneva.

problems of Europe faded into the background as economic activity there returned to or surpassed prewar levels. The Marshall Plan, to be sure, was much discussed at United Nations meetings. Long and vitri-olic attacks were launched on it by delegates from the Soviet bloc, largely for the purpose of creating friction and division between the United States and its Western European allies, partly for the purpose of misrepresenting the program to the nonparticipating nations, and occasionally—in the case of spokesmen from the Soviet satellites—for the purpose of demonstrating to watchful delegates from the Soviet Union their devotion to the party line. Underdeveloped countries at times expressed a sense of grievance as a result of the large-scale aid given to Europe on a priority basis under the European Recovery Pro-gram. Western delegates defended the Marshall Plan, and made coun-terattacks on various aspects of the Soviet economy. Nevertheless, the entire battle was a propaganda side-show, not expected by any of the major participants to affect directly the levels of production and invest-ment in Europe.

There was, however, real hope that the concerted attention of the United Nations to the problem of economic development could affect the production and investment levels in underdeveloped countries. Ac-cordingly, the Economic and Social Council, in 1949, asked the Secre-tary-General to prepare a report on "methods of financing the economic development of underdeveloped countries, including methods of stimu-lating the international flow of capital for this purpose."[34]

The Secretary-General's report illustrated the confusion, the lack of co-ordination, and the deep cleavages of opinion prevalent at the time in this field.[35] It was a symposium containing the report of the third session of the Subcommission on Economic Development; critical com-ments on the report of the subcommission by the parent body, the Eco-nomic and Employment Commission, in terms amounting almost to a repudiation of the work of the subcommission; and memoranda of vary-ing quality from the FAO, the IBRD, the IMF, and the International Labour Organisation (ILO). The contribution of the Department of Economic Affairs of the United Nations Secretariat consisted primarily of comments on the contributions of the other agencies.

All the interrelated issues that continued to divide the delegates in later discussions were foreshadowed in this report. Included among

[34] Res. 179(VIII), Mar. 4, 1949.
[35] U.N. Secretariat, Department of Economic Affairs, *Methods of Financing Economic Development in Under-developed Countries* (1949).

them were: (1) the role of national versus international action in mobilizing capital for economic development; (2) the importance of applying available capital to industry versus agriculture or, within the industrial sector, to heavy versus light industry; (3) whether the basic obstacle to more rapid development was lack of capital or whether other factors were even more fundamental; (4) whether loan capital should be provided on terms more liberal than those offered by the International Bank; (5) whether large-scale, grant aid should be made available through the United Nations to finance non-self-liquidating projects; (6) what inducements could and should be offered to private investors.

There was general agreement that domestic finance would have to cover the bulk of investment requirements. There was also agreement that domestic savings in underdeveloped countries were very low, very unevenly distributed, and frequently employed for very unproductive purposes from the point of view of the underdeveloped country— hoarded in the form of gold chains and bars, invested in urban real estate and high-rental apartment buildings, devoted to the construction of monumental government edifices, or exported to safe havens in the more developed countries. There was agreement that by reorganizing their domestic banking and investment machinery and tax systems, underdeveloped countries could do more to finance their own development programs, but there were differences of view about how much more.

The extent to which nations would put their domestic houses in order would itself affect the volume of foreign capital that they could attract. Most of the agency reports recognized that, to enlarge the flow of private investment, substantially greater incentives would have to be offered, but as the Secretary-General's summary stated it, divergent conclusions were drawn from this common premise.[36] The International Bank and the spokesmen for developed, private-enterprise economies stressed the methods by which existing deterrents to private investments might be overcome. Spokesmen for underdeveloped countries, dubious about the likelihood of attracting private capital on an adequate scale for investments essential to their national development programs and in some cases not greatly interested in doing so, emphasized alternative methods of financing. These included the extension of loans on better terms than those offered by the Bank and the provision of grant aid.

The symposium also contained a brief summary of postwar attempts

[36] *Ibid.*, p. 24.

to clarify the private investment picture through the development of a multilateral code of fair treatment for foreign investors. The critical issues, as summarized by the Secretary-General, had been: (1) the treatment to be accorded to foreign investors with respect to taxation, the repatriation of their earnings, the participation of domestic nationals and domestic capital in their enterprises, and similar matters, and (2) the methods of determining the compensation due to foreign investors in the event of expropriation or nationalization.[37]

The drafters of the Havana Charter for an International Trade Organization had already foundered on these issues. According to United States standards, the investment provisions were perhaps the weakest feature of the proposed charter put forward in April 1948, and one of the major reasons for the failure of the United States to ratify the document. The Economic Agreement signed in May 1948 at the Conference of American States in Bogota seemed to represent an improvement by providing for "prompt, adequate and effective" compensation in the event of nationalization or expropriation, but the provision was virtually nullified by reservations, which, as the Secretary-General of the United Nations reported, rejected any notion that "fair" compensation should be determined by courts or agencies other than those of the capital-importing nation.

Given this background, it is understandable that the United Nations Subcommission on Economic Development was unable to suggest acceptable formulae for the nondiscriminatory treatment of foreign investors. Reviewing the postwar record of private international investment early in 1950, the subcommission, in the only session it held after publication of *Methods of Financing Economic Development in Under-developed Countries*, was pessimistic. The United States was the only important exporter of private capital. Dollarwise, its net outflow of private capital in the highest postwar year, 1948, was hardly more than the corresponding figure in 1928, and, in terms of actual purchasing power, was probably little more than half the value in the peak year of the 1920's. The 1949 outflow was below that in 1948. Portfolio investments, which were substantial in the 1920's, were no longer viewed with favor by private investors. Direct investments in underdeveloped countries were overwhelmingly concentrated in a few oil-producing areas.[38] The

[37] *Ibid.*, p. 29.
[38] U.N. Economic and Social Council, Economic and Employment Commission, *Report of the Fourth Session of the Subcommission on Economic Development*, Doc. E/CN.1/ 80 (May 19, 1950), pp. 10–11.

prospect for a broadly-distributed, substantial increase in private foreign investment was, in the opinion of the subcommission, dim.

The subcommission concluded that codes and treaties would not substantially promote the flow of private foreign investment because what was really needed was good faith and confidence. If there were mutual confidence, the code would be superfluous; in the absence of such confidence, the code would not lead to greater investment.[39] The truth seemed to be that multilateral negotiation of an investment code would succeed only in codifying the lowest common denominator; interested governments felt that they could obtain better deals for their nationals through unilateral declarations or bilateral negotiations.

The result of the discussion of private foreign investment in the subcommission was the disassociation of the Indian chairman and the Mexican vice chairman from the rather moderate, formal proposals for stimulating private investment offered to the Economic and Social Council by the subcommission.

With no disagreement however, the subcommission asserted, in more positive fashion that any earlier United Nations organ, that the United Nations and the specialized agencies had a responsibility to go out and help underdeveloped countries prepare economic development programs. Such programs, said the subcommission, would necessarily contain a proportion of "low-yielding and slow-yielding projects" in which capital would have to be invested before other projects would appear attractive. These low-yielding and slow-yielding projects constituted essential "social and economic overhead capital." Investments for the promotion of health, education, and housing were classifiable as "social overhead," and those for the improvement of transport, communications, and power as "economic overhead."[40] Because it was difficult for underdeveloped countries to finance these projects from their own meager resources, it was important that foreign capital be available for the purpose. Investment in overhead projects would broaden the base for later investment in more directly productive undertakings. Because of the non-self-liquidating character of the social overhead projects, a strong case could be made for grants, or loans at nominal rates of interest, to finance them.

Given the limited prospects for an enlarged flow of private investment, the trickle of public loans at the interest rates charged by the International Bank, the scarcity of domestic resources to tap, and the

[39] *Ibid.*, p. 14.
[40] *Ibid.*, p. 21.

political necessity for raising living standards in underdeveloped areas, the creation of a United Nations Economic Development Administration (UNEDA) to provide long-term loans at nominal rates of interest was again suggested.[41] In view of the fact that the main burden of financing UNEDA would clearly fall on the United States, and that an agency financed by a single nation could not be truly international, the subcommission did not recommend its creation. It did, however, urge the Council to consider the problem.

The May 1950 report was the swan song of the Subcommission on Economic Development, whose members were expected to serve in their individual capacities instead of as government representatives. The pretense that the financing of economic development could be regarded primarily as a technical economic issue was abandoned. It quickly became a burning political issue in the Economic and Social Council and in the General Assembly.

Work of the United Nations System Since 1950

So far as production and investment are concerned, the United Nations system since 1950 has continued to function as a somewhat inconsistent fount of policy guidance; as an increasingly effective instrument of co-operation in the solution of technical problems; and as a modest source of capital funds. The main areas of activity have been the following: (1) the provision of technical assistance to underdeveloped countries on an augmented basis within the framework of the Regular and the Expanded Programmes of Technical Assistance of the United Nations (2) outside of this specialized framework, the focusing of international attention on, and the development of international co-operation with respect to, a host of technical problems affecting production and investment in both developed and underdeveloped countries; (3) the loan, through the International Bank, of about $2.2 billion during the period January 1, 1950–December 31, 1956; (4) continued debate concerning the measures needed to expand and stabilize the international flow of private investment; (5) the elaboration of schemes and the effort to mobilize support for new international financing agencies to supplement the loans of the International Bank: specifically, for (a) an International Finance Corporation to invest in private enter-

[41] It had first been put before the subcommission by its chairman, the Indian expert, in 1949 at the third session.

prise without governmental guarantees, and (b) a Special United Nations Fund for Economic Development to make long-term, low-interest loans and grants-in-aid to underdeveloped countries; (6) negotiations—conducted primarily in the political and security framework rather than in the economic and social framework of the United Nations—to establish a new agency of vast potential economic significance: the International Atomic Energy Agency.

There was a narrowing of activities at the top and a broadening at the base. At the sessions of the General Assembly and of the Economic and Social Council—the more political forums—the economic debates tended increasingly to concentrate around the drive of the underdeveloped countries for a grant-aid agency within the United Nations framework. The developed countries, unwilling to establish costly, new operational arms of the United Nations, resisted this drive. They compromised on resolutions calling for more studies and reports concerning the role and operations of such an agency when circumstances would permit its establishment. Almost imperceptibly, the issue became not whether a grant-aid agency should be established but when. The developed countries also tried to deflect the drive for capital by highlighting the institutional obstacles to development. They advocated productivity programs, land reform, and similar activities that could be stepped up by the underdeveloped countries themselves, with relatively little capital from abroad. It was much easier, however, for the underdeveloped countries to say that the General Assembly and the Economic and Social Council should establish a grant-aid agency than for the developed countries to say what the General Assembly and the Economic and Social Council should do about land reform. Antiquated systems of land tenure, low industrial productivity, lack of esteem for private initiative and enterprise are the product of long-standing cultural, economic, political, and social conditions that cannot be changed by resolutions adopted at lofty levels.

The almost exclusive preoccupation with the grant-aid issue, which characterized the discussion of economic development in the Assembly and the Council, was not reflected in the debates of the regional forums. The Latin Americans, the most persistent proponents of grant-aid at United Nations headquarters, displayed more interest at the regional commissions of the United Nations, as did the Asians, in discussions of technical aspects of forestry and fishery development, exploration of mineral resources, improvement of transport facilities, expansion of electric power production, and the establishment of manufacturing industries. However, the precise role of regional co-operation in the solution of production and investment problems was not greatly clarified during the period.

At the country level, the variety of activities was immense. It was limited only by the imagination of governments in submitting technical assistance proposals, the availability of experts to implement the proposals, and—more recently—the availability of funds to finance eligible projects.

Technical Assistance and Technical Co-operation

In listing above six main areas of United Nations activity since 1950 in the field of production and investment, a distinction was made between technical assistance offered under either the Regular Programme or the Expanded Programme of Technical Assistance of the United Nations and other technical co-operation developed within the United Nations system. Although the distinction has organizational validity, it is artificial in other respects. Both technical assistance and technical co-operation have as their objective the more efficient employment of the human and material resources of the world. Illustrative of the work of the United Nations in this field during the period are the activities of the system with respect to the conservation and use of mineral resources, the control and utilization of water resources, the release of technical data concerning the peaceful uses of atomic energy, and the provision of technical assistance to stimulate agricultural output.

The successful conference of 1949 on the Conservation and Utilization of Resources seemed for a brief period to presage further action on a global scale to facilitate the efficient use of mineral resources. The Secretary-General, pursuant to a request by the Economic and Social Council, studied the conference proceedings and proposed to the Council in 1950 an international program, the main elements of which were to be the systematic survey and inventory of nonagricultural resources on the one hand and, on the other, international conferences on particular resource problems. Authorized to go ahead,[42] the Secretary-General selected iron ore as the first subject for a particular resource survey. He appointed a committee of experts and, in 1954, issued a report under the impressive title, *Survey of World Iron Ore Resources: Occurrence, Appraisal, and Use.* This was to have been followed by similar

[42] Res. 345(XII), Mar. 9, 1951.

reports on coal and lignite, and other important nonagricultural resources. No such reports were issued, however. The world as a whole
might benefit from up-to-date information on the location, extent, and
quality of its major mineral deposits, but the value of the global surveys
to any individual country was marginal compared to the value of
surveys of the resources within its own territorial borders.

Interest consequently shifted to regional and country studies. The
Economic Commission for Asia and the Far East published a report on
the coal and iron resources of the region,[43] sponsored a regional Conference on Mineral Resources in Tokyo in 1953 (the first United Nations meeting in Japan), and issued documents concerning the utilization of lignite in ten Asian countries. The Economic Commission for
Europe gathered data on the energy resources of Austria and Yugoslavia and the feasibility of exporting power across international
boundaries to Italy, Germany, and Switzerland. The Economic Commission for Latin America ran an Iron and Steel Seminar in Bogota at
which experts from North America and Europe joined Latin Americans
in frank analyses of the problems involved in establishing an efficient
steel industry in Latin America.

At the country level, technical assistance was obtained both for general purposes such as exploring the mineral resources of Tanganyika,
and for specific purposes such as exploiting marble quarries in the
Philippines, advising on the cutting of quartz crystals in India, and reorganizing the salt industry in Ceylon. Given international acceptance
of the authority of the United Nations system to furnish technical assistance on a retail basis, the chief policy problem raised by projects of the
types mentioned is to ensure that they fit logically into the long-term
economic development program of the requesting country, that they
cannot be completed without external aid, and that they consequently
represent a valid claim on the resources of the international community.

In the case of mineral resources, the top organs of the United Nations
stimulated interest by the summoning of a large international conference that helped launch a variety of projects at the regional and country
levels. Within the complicated structure of the United Nations, however, the flow of activity and interest is a two-way affair. Discussion of
an issue at the top levels stirs up activity at lower levels; conversely,
activity initiated at lower levels frequently points to the need for policy
pronouncement or for program co-ordination at the top.

[43] U.N. Economic Commission for Asia and the Far East, *Coal and Iron Resources
of Asia and the Far East* (1952).

The Conference on the Conservation and Utilization of Resources stimulated interest in water development as well as in mineral development. At the same time, the variety of regional and country responses to pressures to control floods, irrigate crops, develop hydroelectric sites, deepen river channels, eliminate stream pollution, and discover new sources of water in arid lands underscored the need for greater co-ordination and more integrated planning. The consequence was a resurgence of concern at the top.

One of the first acts of ECAFE had been the establishment of a Bureau of Flood Control. The United States, in commenting on the work of the bureau at meetings of ECAFE and of the Economic and Social Council, consistently stressed the need for viewing the problem not solely in terms of flood control but also in terms of multiple-purpose river basin development. While ECAFE was concerned with flood control, the United Nations Educational, Scientific, and Cultural Organization (UNESCO) developed a lively interest in the special problems of arid zones. The FAO was interested in irrigation and in fisheries; the IBRD in hydroelectric power development, navigation, and irrigation projects; the World Health Organization (WHO) in stream pollution.

The United States, as a nation aware of the potential benefits of the multipurpose approach to river valley development and as the Member of the United Nations most concerned with procedural and organizational issues, circulated a note to the Economic and Social Council in early 1951 pointing out that segments of the water resource problem came within the competence of various agencies but that no single agency had a co-ordinating responsibility in this field. The note suggested a survey by the Secretary-General and the specialized agencies that could serve as the basis for a better organized effort to promote efficient use of the world's water resources.

The United States suggestion was adopted, and the Secretary-General prepared a report summarizing the activities of some thirty international organizations concerned with one phase or another of water control. After consideration of his report in 1952, a resolution endorsing the multipurpose approach to water resource development was adopted by the Council.[44] More importantly, the resolution vested the Secretary-General with co-ordinating responsibility; asked him to promote the development of basic water resource data and the international exchange of information and experience; and invited him to make recommendations for further international activity in this field.

[44] Res. 417(XIV), June 2, 1952.

To date, however, little co-ordination or stimulation appears to have been provided by United Nations headquarters. The interest of the United States Government in giving the Secretary-General a more active role in connection with water resource development declined with the change in domestic administration, and the support and resources required from Member governments for effective discharge of the Secretary-General's new responsibilities were not forthcoming.

On the other hand, it was the initiative of the United States that led the United Nations during the period 1954–56 to assume new roles in promoting the peaceful uses of atomic energy. American initiative was responsible for two related lines of action. One—the complex negotiations arising out of President Eisenhower's suggestion that the United Nations establish a kind of world bank for fissionable materials—is discussed later. The second—the convening of a technical conference on the peaceful uses of the atom—is mentioned here because it is comparable in character to the Conference on the Conservation and Utilization of Resources.

The suggestion for a major scientific conference to consider the development of atomic energy through international co-operation was put forward by the United States Secretary of State in his address to the General Assembly on September 23, 1954.[45] It was referred to the First (Political and Security) Committee, where there was extensive and inconclusive discussion concerning the functions and structure of the proposed International Atomic Energy Agency but general approval of the holding of a conference in 1955 for the exchange of scientific information. Upon emergence from the First Committee, the proposal was unanimously endorsed by the Assembly.[46]

Held in Geneva, Switzerland, during August 1955, the ensuing International Conference on the Peaceful Uses of Atomic Energy was the largest and probably the most important international technical gathering under United Nations auspices during the entire postwar period. In the diplomatic terminology of the Secretary-General, "a great deal of important data hitherto restricted for reasons of security was made public for the first time at this Conference."[47] In the American press it was said that "so much information had been dammed up on that topic [atomic power] for ten years that the resulting flood turned Geneva

[45] U.N. General Assembly, Ninth Session, Plenary, *Official Records*, 475th Meeting (Sept. 23, 1954).

[46] Res. 810(IX), Dec. 4, 1954.

[47] U.N. General Assembly, Eleventh Session, *Official Records*, Supplement No. 1, "Annual Report of the Secretary-General on the Work of the Organization, 16 June 1955–15 June 1956," p. 3.

into the greatest scientific irrigation project of modern times . . . the competition generated a friendliness that had been unknown between East and West since wartime days."[48]

Seventy-three nations sent delegations. In addition to more than 1,400 delegates, there were 1,350 observers, principally from academic institutions and industrial enterprises, and 900 representatives of public information media. In contrast to the many meetings of the United Nations of benefit primarily to the underdeveloped countries, this conference had relevance for the production and investment plans of developed and underdeveloped countries alike. It covered economic as well as technical aspects of nuclear energy, and among other things, helped make plain that atomic power was as yet no panacea for the ailments of underdeveloped nations.

The conference began with general sessions. These were followed by three parallel sets of specialized sessions dealing broadly with (1) physics and reactors; (2) chemistry, metallurgy, and technology; and (3) medicine, biology, and radioactive isotopes.[49] The 1,050 papers submitted at the conference, the text of the oral presentations, and the record of the discussions have been published by the United Nations in sixteen printed volumes, which constitute the greatest single collection of information yet made available on the peaceful uses of atomic energy.[50] The "impressive results" of the conference were noted at the tenth session of the General Assembly, and a decision was made that a second scientific conference on atomic energy should be held in two to three years time.[51]

The more prosaic job of keeping agricultural output in line with demand, a task that had required a massive production drive during the initial postwar years, assumed new dimensions in the 1950's when surpluses again made their appearance. To date, both national governments and international agencies have been more successful in dealing with acute shortages than with unsalable surpluses. The shortages have occurred in wartime or as a result of other catastrophes and crises during which the spirit of sacrifice and compassion has remained strong. The shortage is invariably expected to be temporary. Meanwhile, consumers are asked to endure for a time a rationing scheme based on need rather

---

[48] John Lear, "Ike and the Peaceful Atom," *The Reporter* (Jan. 12, 1956), p. 21.

[49] U.N. General Assembly, Eleventh Session, *Official Records*, "Annual Report of the Secretary-General on the Work of the Organization, 16 June 1955–15 June 1956," p. 3.

[50] United Nations, *Peaceful Uses of Atomic Energy—Proceedings of the International Conference in Geneva, August 1955*, Vols. 1–16 (1956).

[51] Res. 912(X), Dec. 3, 1955.

than ability to pay. Producers are exhorted to increase supply and are frequently aided by governments in doing so.

Surpluses emerge in a very different psychological setting. The existence of a surplus is evidence of a soft spot in the economy. The situation may grow worse before it grows better. The remedies are far from self-evident. Allowing prices to fall means hardship for producers. Buying up the surplus and holding it off the market requires large sums of money. Disposing of accumulated supplies without disrupting normal marketing arrangements is exceedingly difficult. Stepping up consumption is a gradual process.

So long as the FAO could campaign for greater production, it was superficially on safe ground. In 1951, it could still report that food production was about 9 per cent above the 1934–38 average, but population was up more than 12 per cent. The increases in food production, moreover, were concentrated largely in the developed areas, particularly in North America. The FAO Conference in Rome, in late 1951, decided that the whole effort of the FAO should be directed toward obtaining a greater output of food. A goal was set and publicized: food production should increase by at least 1 or 2 per cent more than the annual population increase. Agricultural development plans should be drafted, and technical assistance should be sought in executing agreed plans.

The production target first set by FAO was warmly endorsed by the Economic and Social Council in 1952.[52] By 1953, it was clear that the world as a whole had overshot the mark. Per-capita consumption in important areas was still below prewar levels, but in a number of commodities embarrassing surpluses were being accumulated. As the London *Economist* stated: "What began as a straightforward crusade for higher production everywhere of practically everything eatable has turned, with the reappearance of agricultural surpluses, into a somewhat bewildered search for a 'selective' policy of expansion—which FAO is much less well fitted either to devise or encourage."[53]

The FAO has been unable to prevent surpluses from being accumulated, to police their distribution, or, in pursuit of its policy of "selective expansion," to obtain in food-deficit areas the desired increases in output of products needed for nutritional purposes. More technical assistance, however, has been devoted to agriculture than to any other sector of the economy, and the FAO has unquestionably made effective use of the funds available.

[52] Res. 424(XIV), June 19, 1952.
[53] *The Economist*, Vol. 170 (Jan. 2, 1954), p. 31.

In the early days of the United Nations, "industrialization," symbolized by the desire for a steel mill regardless of the accessibility of iron ore or metallurgical coke, was the aim of almost every underdeveloped country. After 1950, however, "balanced development" became the watchword, and the importance of modernizing agriculture began to be more widely appreciated. With FAO aid, new tools and implements have been introduced, better seeds developed and supplied, crop rotation taught, pastures improved, irrigation programs developed, locust control projects initiated, reforestation undertaken, and forestry and fishery services strengthened.

Rice-breeding and rice-processing experiments organized by the International Rice Commission are conducted by national experiment stations in a number of Far Eastern countries. Great progress is being made in rendering rice cultivation less laborious and more efficient. Ironically, however, the volume produced by the cumbersome methods currently employed seems to be more than consumers in the low-income areas of the Far East can afford to buy. Stocks in 1953 reached a point that found Thailand and Burma facing real difficulty in disposing profitably of their crops and making no secret of their concern about American surplus-disposal programs.

Although stressed by FAO, the vast potentialities of the oceans, lakes, and streams as sources of food supply have hardly begun to be tapped. The problem is a two-fold one of educating the public that fish is a nutritious food on the one hand and, on the other, improving the methods of catching, chilling, transporting, and distributing fish. UNESCO is assisting in the educational program. The technical assistance projects of the FAO include simple undertakings such as the establishment of hatcheries, the stocking of canals and rice paddies with fish, and the improvement of primitive fishing vessels and equipment. They also include advanced undertakings such as demonstrations of the latest electronic devices for locating schools of fish.

Provision of Public Loan Capital

The disclosure, through productivity campaigns and other technical assistance measures, of ways to increase output without important new capital investment has in no way blunted the desire for fresh loan capital as a means of stepping up production and productivity. This desire, moreover, was satisfied only to a modest extent by the scale of IBRD lending during the period 1950–56.

In May 1951, an international group of experts appointed by the United Nations Secretary-General in response to an invitation from the

Economic and Social Council issued a provocative and widely-discussed report on economic development.[54] The pages on "Government Lending" were more flattering to the United States Export-Import Bank than to the International Bank for Reconstruction and Development, although no details concerning the work of the former institution were supplied. The experts merely said that they were "impressed by the job which the [Export-Import] Bank is doing, and wish to recommend that other developed countries might well establish similar institutions."[55]

The International Bank, according to the experts,

> . . . has not adequately realized that it is an agency charged by the United Nations with the duty of promoting economic development. It should do everything that lies in its power to break down the obstacles to sound investment in the under-developed countries. The Bank should set itself to reach, within five years, some such target as an annual rate of lending of not less than $1 billion to the under-developed countries. If it shows no signs of approaching this target, the whole question of the proper international organization for the provision of adequate amounts of loan capital to the under-developed countries should be reviewed by the United Nations.[56]

The International Bank at the time was lending to the underdeveloped countries at a rate below $200 million annually. The authors of *Measures for the Economic Development of Underdeveloped Countries* were not unmindful of the difficulties confronting the Bank and the progress made since 1946 in overcoming these difficulties. Throughout their report, however, they appear to have grossly overestimated the capacity of the underdeveloped countries to absorb capital rapidly. They tended to assume that the majority of countries were either on the threshold, or could readily be brought to the threshold, of a vast new era. Only a minority, in their view, were unprepared for more rapid development, unable to put forward adequate plans, or utterly lacking the nucleus of trained workers necessary to put approved plans into operation.

The Economic, Employment and Development Commission, the first organ in the United Nations to consider the report of the experts, decided, at the urging of the representatives of the industrialized nations, that no useful purpose would be served by reference to the lending target of $1 billion per year. The Economic and Social Council agreed.

---

[54] U.N. Department of Economic Affairs, *Measures for the Economic Development of Underdeveloped Countries*, Report by a Group of Experts Appointed by the Secretary-General of the United Nations, Doc. E/1986 (May 3, 1951). (Hereinafter cited as *Measures for Economic Development*.)

[55] *Ibid.*, p. 82.

[56] *Ibid.*, pp. 83–84.

Its resolution on the report simply recommended that the existing lending agencies continue to expand their operations.[57]

The expansion hoped for had not occurred by the end of 1954, although more favorable terms of trade provided the underdeveloped countries with the equivalent of several billion dollars in purchasing power during the raw material boom that followed the outbreak of war in Korea. For the period 1950 through 1954, no clear trend is discernible, either in total lending by the Bank or in its lending to underdeveloped countries. Total lending fluctuated between $200 million and $300 million per year; loans to underdeveloped countries, between $150 million and $212 million. The figures for 1955 and 1956 indicate that the corner may have been turned. The rate of lending rose sharply, but much of the increase went to Europe and Australia.

INTERNATIONAL BANK LOANS BY CALENDAR YEARS, 1950–56[a]

Year (1)	Number of Loans (2)	Number of Countries Obtaining Loans (3)	Total Loans (In thousands) (4)	Loans to Underdeveloped Countries[b] (In thousands) (5)
1950	17	10	$ 279,230	$ 179,230
1951	17	11	208,408	158,408
1952	16	12	292,483	212,004
1953	22	13	256,900	156,700
1954	16	15	282,700	171,700
1955	27	20	406,500	204,500
1956	24	17	507,408	270,150
1950–56	139	41[c]	$2,233,629	$1,352,692

[a] Compiled from "Chronological List of Loans," unnumbered, undated press release from International Bank for Reconstruction and Development; *Eleventh Annual Report*, 1955–56, pp. 28–37; and Memorandum of Dec. 20, 1956 from Office of Information of International Bank.

[b] The Bank does not attempt to segregate loans to underdeveloped countries. The figures in column 5 have been derived by subtracting from the official totals in column 4 amounts indicated below for loans to countries that, because of their per-capita income levels, are not usually regarded as underdeveloped:

    1950: $100 million (to Australia)
    1951: 50 million (to South Africa)
    1952: 80.5 million (to Australia, Finland, and the Netherlands)
    1953: 100.2 million (to Japan and South Africa)
    1954: 111 million (to Australia, Austria, Belgium, and Norway)
    1955: 202 million (to Australia, Austria, Finland, Italy, Japan, Norway, and South Africa)
    1956: 237.25 million (to Australia, Austria, Finland, Italy, Japan, and Norway)

[c] Because some of the same countries obtained loans in different years, this total is less than the sum of the figures in the column.

From its inception through December 31, 1956, the Bank has made loans totaling nearly $3 billion to more than forty different countries. More than 35 per cent of this total has gone to Europe, with Finland

[57] Res. 368C(XIII), Aug. 22, 1951.

and Yugoslavia the only European recipients that were not participants in the Marshall Plan. About 25 per cent has gone to Latin America, with Brazil, Colombia, and Mexico together accounting for nearly two-thirds of the Latin American total. South Africa and Australia account for about 15 per cent. The remaining 25 per cent has gone to Asia and to African areas other than the Union of South Africa; among these, India has been by far the heaviest borrower.

The classification of loans by purpose is necessarily somewhat arbitrary. The Bank has, however, made such a classification, and the resultant distribution is shown in the accompanying table. Excluding the early reconstruction loans, about two thirds of the $2.9 billion loaned as of December 13, 1956, has been allocated to electric power and transportation projects.[58]

Reconstruction.....................	$ 497,000,000
Electric Power.....................	886,000,000
Transportation.....................	686,000,000
Communications...................	26,000,000
Agriculture and Forestry............	274,000,000
Industry..........................	369,000,000
General Development...............	140,000,000
Total...........................	$2,878,000,000

To date, all service charges and principal repayments have been met. As yet they remain modest offsets against new lending, but they will increase steadily. Whether the burden of the service charges on the operations of the Bank will become large enough to constitute a serious drain on the foreign exchange resources of the underdeveloped countries depends in part on the relationship between the amount of new lending and the size of the service charges, and, more importantly, on the cumulative and indirect effects of the loans by the Bank on the general economies of underdeveloped countries. The loans of the Bank can contribute to capital formation in the underdeveloped countries, irrespective of the increase in charges they give rise to, so long as lending continues. Nevertheless, the contribution of the Bank is unlikely to be great enough to reduce the pressure for additional sources of development funds.

The improvement in general economic conditions during the postwar period has spared international institutions the added strain of having to operate in bad times. In the United Nations discussions concerning

[58] Source: International Bank for Reconstruction and Development, *Facts About World Bank Lending* (Dec. 13, 1956).

the role of the Bank in promoting international economic stability, three types of action have been suggested:

1. It has been proposed that targets, considerably above present levels, be set in advance for the total outflow of long-term capital from developed to underdeveloped countries. As private investment will fall off sharply in periods of depression, public lending should be increased reciprocally in order to maintain a stable total flow. The Bank should be reorganized to enable it to make up the shortfall and ensure stability.[59]

2. In a more flexible fashion than mechanically maintaining some target level, the Bank should reach advance agreements with countries on their development programs and be prepared to expand promptly its rate of lending in times of recession or depression. In other words, there should be a shelf of public works ready for prompt execution.[60]

3. More modest than either of the above, the Bank, if it cannot vastly increase its lending during periods of recession, should at least ease the burdens of borrowers at such times by declaring a moratorium or a partial moratorium on repayments of outstanding loans.

The first form of activity has generally been regarded as overly ambitious, impractical, and because of the assurance of increased public funds to compensate for any decrease in the private flow, likely to reduce the incentives of borrowers to attract private capital. The second runs afoul of political realities in assuming, as does the first, that the Bank can defer the financing of desirable projects in good times merely in order to have them ready for execution when times are less good. Times are perpetually hard in the underdeveloped countries, and they would be the first to balk at the prospect of temporarily shelving mature and well-conceived development projects.[61] The Bank, for its part, has steadfastly maintained that the modest level of its lending has been due to the lack of appropriate projects and the limited capacity of potential borrowers to service additional loans, not to a desire to conserve resources for times of increased need.

[59] See U.N. Department of Economic Affairs, *National and International Measures for Full Employment*, Report by a Group of Experts Appointed by the Secretary-General, Doc. E/1584 (Dec. 22, 1949), pp. 54–58, 90–92.

[60] See U.N. Department of Economic Affairs, *Measures for International Economic Stability*, Report by a Group of Experts Appointed by the Secretary-General, Doc. E/2156 (Nov. 27, 1951), pp. 28–30.

[61] In depression periods, however, the Bank might help finance the completion of projects that had been started without recourse to the Bank but could not be finished during a period of declining export proceeds without outside aid.

It seems plain that the Bank is not at present equipped or prepared to act as a countercyclical lending agency. Neither has it yet indicated the extent to which it might, in a period of deflation, mitigate the burden of servicing existing loans. Under the Articles of Agreement, a member suffering "from an acute exchange stringency," may ask for a relaxation of the conditions of payment.[62] In these circumstances, the Bank may accept service payments in the currency of the borrowing nation (rather than the currency in which the loan was made) for a period of not more than three years, or the life of the loan may be extended, or the amortization terms modified. The Bank, having struggled to establish the concept that loans are business, not charity, and that repayments are expected to be made as scheduled, has been reluctant to indicate in advance how liberal it might be during a depression. If it is to function as a bank, it must, in so far as it can, behave like a bank.

Although the volume of Bank lending has been slow to rise, the Bank has nevertheless become a more influential factor in the field of investment. Further broadening of the specific project concept has permitted funds to be advanced for a greater variety of activities. Additional survey missions have uncovered investment opportunities in areas about which little was previously known.

The loan by the Bank in 1950 to the Turkish Industrial Development Bank was mentioned earlier as an example of the broadening of the specific project concept with which the Bank commenced its operations. A second loan was made to the Turkish Industrial Development Bank in 1953, after which that institution successfully marketed a new issue of its own stock. However, despite the fact that the IBRD made a total of six loans to Turkey between 1950 and 1954 and stationed a high-level representative there, relations between the IBRD and the Turkish Government were not always harmonious. As time went on, IBRD officials became increasingly critical of the accumulation of short-term debt by Turkey and of its failure to curb the inflationary pressures that made it a chronic debtor to the European Payments Union. The Turkish Government claimed the Bank was overly orthodox: as the investments of the postwar period began to bear fruit, more goods would become available both for domestic consumption and for export; inflationary pressures and balance-of-payments deficits would then be overcome. Meanwhile, said the government, the delay of the Bank in granting further credits to Turkey was inexcusable, and its representative in Turkey—a former Finance Minister of the Netherlands—had no business discussing the financial problems of Turkey with the officers

[62] *Articles of Agreement*, Art. IV, Sec. 4(c).

of the European Payments Union. In a formal letter, the Premier demanded withdrawal of the representative, throwing in for good measure a complaint illustrative of a long-standing grievance of the underdeveloped countries: the Bank had loaned more than $225 million to the Netherlands, a developed country, and only $63 million to Turkey, an underdeveloped country.

The dispute is indicative of the differences of view in different parts of the world concerning the economic policies appropriate for nations promoting more rapid economic development, specifically the strictness with which inflation should be controlled. It is also a wholesome reminder that international agencies as well as individual foreign governments can be accused of intervening in the domestic affairs of a country.

On the theory that local institutions like the Turkish Industrial Development Bank are better equipped than the International Bank to investigate the credit-worthiness of and to extend credit to small domestic enterprises, development financing institutions have been established, with the aid of the Bank, in Ethiopia and, more recently, in India. The Industrial Credit and Investment Corporation of India is a complex financial partnership. The initial capital consists of $10.5 million of equity money subscribed by private investors, British and American as well as Indian, and $25.75 million in loan capital subscribed by the International Bank and the Government of India. The loan of the Indian Government is in rupees derived from the sale of a grant of steel by the United States Foreign Operations Administration. The International Bank loan is a fifteen-year loan of $10 million at $4\frac{5}{8}$ per cent interest, with amortization to begin after a five-year period of grace. The representatives of the $10.5 million of share capital will manage the Bank and arrange its loans to and equity investments in private Indian undertakings.

The original policy of the International Bank, it will be recalled, was to limit developmental loans to the foreign exchange costs of equipment imported for specific productive projects. This policy was frequently criticized in the Economic and Social Council and elsewhere both because it failed to cover the full cost of capital equipment even for specific projects and because it appeared to prohibit lending for general developmental purposes. Roads, schools, hospitals, and other social and economic overhead investments may require large local currency expenditures, which in turn may increase the demand for imported goods, but they do not themselves require foreign equipment nor do they earn foreign exchange. In at least a few cases, the Bank has been willing to make general-purpose loans to finance undertakings of this kind, confident that the over-all improvement in the economy of the borrower would make repayment possible. Thus the Bank has made several loans to a development corporation in Italy, the *Cassa per il Mezzogiorno*, to meet the increased demand for dollar imports generated by the development program for southern Italy. In Iran, the Bank, having reached agreement with the government on the over-all magnitude of a development program for the years 1955–62, is financing the anticipated deficit during the first three years of the program.

The first loan entirely in a currency other than United States dollars was a very small one in sterling and three other European currencies made to Iceland in 1951. Pakistan obtained one in 1954. Again, the amount was small—£5 million—to help finance the foreign exchange costs of a natural-gas pipeline to be constructed in Pakistan, but the arrangements are interesting. The borrower was a new company, the Sui Gas Transmission Company, three quarters of whose shares were held by private investors in Pakistan and the United Kingdom and one quarter by the Pakistan Industrial Development Corporation. The Transmission Company was to be operated by the Pakistan subsidiary of the Burmah Oil Company. Six British Banks participated in the loan, in small amounts, without a guarantee by the Bank.[63]

As the free world economy has improved, more of the loan capital of the Bank has been raised in the private market outside the United States; more of its disbursements have been made for purchases outside the United States; and a progressive internationalization of its resources has occurred. Bank disbursements, of course, lag well behind loan commitments and by June 30, 1956, less than $2 billion of the $2.7 billion loaned as of that date had been expended. Of this amount, however, nearly 40 per cent had been expended for purchases outside the United States in nations able to supply, on a competitive basis, the equipment and other items needed by borrowers.[64]

Mobilization of Private Capital for Investment Purposes

Classification of the International Bank as a public lending institution tends to understate its role as a promoter of private investment. More and more, the Bank has become a kind of international invest-

[63] International Bank for Reconstruction and Development, *Ninth Annual Report, 1953–1954*, p. 17.
[64] International Bank for Reconstruction and Development, *Eleventh Annual Report, 1955–1956*, p. 17.

ment fund, raising money in the private capital markets of the United States, Canada, and Western Europe for investment in underdeveloped countries. The projects in which it invests, primarily electric power and transportation facilities, are prerequisites for the attraction of private capital to underdeveloped areas. The specific techniques used by the Bank to promote private foreign investment, however, can best be understood in the light of certain general developments in this field since 1946.

Much of the essential background for understanding the approach of the United Nations toward international investment problems is contained in a report of the Secretariat on the international flow of private capital during the period 1946 to 1952.[65] In this report, the main trends in the international movement of private capital are summarized as follows:

The floating in international capital markets of foreign government bonds, once so important in international financing, is now limited to special cases of loans between countries maintaining close commercial or political relations with each other.

Similar floating of shares and debentures of business enterprises, and trade in outstanding securities, have also declined to minor importance, except when the transactions are related to so-called direct investments, involving managerial control through enterprises in the investing country. Such investments accordingly account for the great bulk of private long-term capital moving between countries.

The growth of direct investments does not result principally from the transfer of fresh funds from the capital exporting countries, but from the reinvestment of a large proportion of the profits earned.

Under-developed countries in Latin America derive most of their inflow of foreign private capital from the United States, and dependent territories from their respective metropolitan countries in western Europe. (This does not apply to investments in the petroleum industry.) Relatively little capital is flowing to the independent countries in South-eastern Asia.

There is no flow of private capital to countries with centrally planned economies in eastern Europe and Asia.

New private foreign investments in public utilities have been more than offset by the liquidation of such investments, particularly in railway properties; the outstanding amount of such investment has accordingly tended to decline.

The petroleum industry accounts for a large proportion of foreign direct investments in recent years.

In other extractive industries, foreign direct investment has expanded, particularly in the dependent territories of western European countries.

[65] U.N. Secretariat, Department of Economic Affairs, *The International Flow of Private Capital, 1946–1952*, Doc. E/2531 (Jan. 18, 1954).

Most of the foreign direct investment in manufacturing has been made, not in under-developed, but in economically advanced countries. Nevertheless, certain Latin American countries have received considerable amounts of United States capital for investment in manufacturing.[66]

The report points out that the volume of private capital exports during the period under review corresponded in real terms to about half of the volume during the 1920's. Because populations have increased in both capital-importing and capital-exporting countries, the decline in capital movement per capita has been still greater. Basic to any significant increase in the flow of private capital to underdeveloped countries, however, is the creation of a climate more hospitable to economic growth.

Climates in which custom and tradition are the prime regulators of human behavior are hostile to economic growth. For growth to occur, the climate must be receptive to change, hospitable to innovations that increase productivity and enlarge total output. It must be capable of generating further innovations. For the growth to be balanced, the desire for continuous improvement must permeate all sectors of the economy and the whole of society.

The creation of such a climate is a complex and subtle process. It involves more than the negative function of removing obstacles. Enterprise in underdeveloped countries is not just chafing under restrictions; it is frequently nonexistent. Many members of the United Nations have tended to assume that the positive key to the process is finance. Financing has been thought of in terms of (1) mobilizing domestic capital in underdeveloped countries; and (2) increasing the flow of international capital from the more developed to the less developed nations by means of private loans and equity investments, public loans, and public grants.

The rate of domestic capital formation in underdeveloped countries is painfully low. Except for a few rich citizens, the inhabitants cannot reduce consumption in order to release resources for investment. The underdeveloped countries, it has been observed before, cannot save because they are so poor, and remain so poor because they cannot save. The inability of the masses to reduce consumption, however, does not completely close the circle.

The surplus income of the favored few can be tapped for public investment by tax systems that are more progressive than at present, but not so progressive as to discourage savings and investment. Better op-

[66] *Ibid.*, pp. 27–28. Since the above-cited report was published, there has been some revival of the floating of foreign government bonds in international capital markets, but the totals remain small.

portunities for investment in local enterprises can be provided through the establishment of development banks, savings institutions, and stock markets. Surplus labor, more plentiful in underdeveloped countries than surplus capital, can be employed in community development programs to increase the capital stock of the community. Although present consumption levels, by and large, cannot be reduced, increases in output can, to a considerable extent, be channeled into investment rather than into consumption.

Foreign capital is necessary, both to stimulate the process of domestic capital formation and to add to the available supply of capital in underdeveloped countries. Where national income is low, small amounts of outside capital can make a great difference in the local capital supply.[67] The risks to private foreign investors, however, are so much greater today than before the First World War, and the rewards so much smaller, that such investors remain cautious. At the receiving end, nationalist ambitions and vivid memories of past exploitation keep the welcome cool.

The factors limiting the flow of private investment have been summarized in various United Nations reports.[68] Underdevelopment is itself a major obstacle. The lack of skilled labor, public utilities, and transportation systems limits the field for investment, and low per-capita income limits the market for goods and services. International tension, persistent inflation, and political instability seal off large areas. In industrialized countries such as the United States and Canada, domestic investment continues to be highly profitable. Moreover, in the event of difficulties, investors are more confident of their ability to obtain relief from their own governments than from the governments of foreign countries. In the so-called capital-importing countries, the following specific obstacles have been noted:[69]

1. Legal restrictions on the entry of foreign capital and the control

---

[67] See Eugene Staley, *The Future of Underdeveloped Countries* (1954), pp. 260–62.

[68] See, for example, U.N. Secretariat, Economic and Social Council, *Survey of Policies Affecting Private Foreign Investment*, Doc. E/1614/Rev. 1 (Mar. 8, 1950); International Bank for Reconstruction and Development, *Report on the Proposal for an International Finance Corporation*, Doc. 2215 (April 1952); U.N. Secretary-General, *International Flow of Private Capital for the Economic Development of Underdeveloped Countries*, Doc. E/2546 (Feb. 19, 1954); U.N. Secretariat, Department of Economic Affairs, *The International Flow of Private Capital, 1946–1952*.

[69] The listing is virtually verbatim from U.N. Secretary-General, *International Flow of Private Capital for the Economic Development of Underdeveloped Countries*, Doc. E/2546. As pointed out in the Secretary-General's memorandum, some of these restrictions are "symptoms of underlying economic conditions rather than the expression of policy towards foreign capital as such." P. 46.

and operation of foreign-owned enterprises. Among such restrictions are: exclusion of foreign capital from particular industries or types of economic activity; restriction of entry of foreign capital on a case-by-case basis; requirements for minimum financial or other participation by nationals of the capital-importing country in all business enterprises or in selected types of economic activity; stipulations regarding participation by nationals in the labor force of enterprises established within the country; regulations governing the exploitation of minerals and natural resources; official fixing of prices and rates, particularly in the public utility industry; and official regulation of labor relations.

2. Exchange restrictions, quantitative restrictions on imports and exports, and other types of control over international transactions.

3. Fiscal measures such as the imposition of taxes that may be non-discriminatory in form but are discriminatory in substance.

4. Policies concerning nationalization, expropriation, and public ownership of industry.

Reduction of these obstacles by resolutions of either the Economic and Social Council or the General Assembly has proved just as impractical as reduction by multilateral investment treaties. At the Council and the Assembly, the United States has taken the lead in keeping the private investment issue alive, partly as an offset to the mounting pressure for public funds and partly to express its own deeply felt convictions about the role of private enterprise in the development process. In most of the rest of the world, enthusiasm for free private enterprise is clearly more restrained than in the United States and in some of the free world nations there is considerable distrust, not just of private foreign investments but of private enterprise generally. Nevertheless, all nations outside the Soviet bloc and Yugoslavia reiterate in the United Nations their desire for private foreign capital and their interest in giving adequate assurances to potential investors. Still, there remains a gap between the maximum that it is politically possible for most of them to offer by way of assurances and the minimum that is necessary to attract capital on a significant scale.

The resolutions of the principal organs of the United Nations are, on the whole, confined to generalities. In them, governments commit themselves, not to eliminate, but rather to *try* to eliminate certain obstacles or establish certain facilities. Each remains judge of the adequacy of its efforts.

Even if the resolutions were to be more concrete—if, for example a firm twenty-five-year moratorium on further nationalization of industrial enterprises were negotiated—the effects on the flow of private international capital would be uncertain. Individual investors might or might not be moved to invest larger sums in distant places. Whereas the decisions of governments regarding the provision of grant and loan aid can be affected directly and immediately by debates at intergovernmental forums, the decisions of private investors can only be indirectly influenced.

Nevertheless, the debates reveal a growing sophistication on the part of both capital-importers and capital-exporters about the role of private investment, and the resolutions include numerous recommendations regarding the kinds of action that should be taken to promote its flow. The improved climate that resolutions, such as the one adopted by the Council in August 1951,[70] both create and reflect, is from time to time worsened by a resolution like the one on "the right of economic self-determination" introduced by Chile and accepted by the Commission on Human Rights in 1952,[71] or the one adopted by the General Assembly in late 1952 on the "Right to Exploit Freely Natural Wealth and Resources."[72] The latter resolution, widely publicized in American business and financial circles, arose out of an attempt by Uruguay and Bolivia to have the United Nations recognize anew the right of Members to nationalize their domestic resources. As introduced, it was conspicuously one-sided in emphasizing the rights but not the obligations of governments that nationalize industries. Strongly opposed by the United States as a deterrent to private investment, it was ultimately amended into less offensive form and adopted by a vote of 36 to 4 with

[70] Res. 368B(XIII), Aug. 22, 1951—opposed by the Soviet Union and Poland as a one-sided interference in the domestic affairs of Member nations but accepted, after negotiation, by the rest of the Council—recommended that capital-exporting nations provide potential investors with the fullest possible information on foreign investment opportunities; undertake measures for the avoidance of double taxation; be prepared to negotiate treaties to ensure conditions favorable to the investment of private foreign capital; provide, to the extent desirable and feasible, guarantees to potential investors against certain nonbusiness risks affecting foreign enterprise; impress on investors the importance of serving the economic and social welfare of the capital-receiving countries. Parallel recommendations were made to capital-importing nations. The latter were urged specifically to provide adequate assurances, through treaties or otherwise, regarding the treatment to be accorded to foreign investors in the operation, management, and control of their enterprises; in the remittance of earnings and the withdrawal of capital; in the protection of their persons and property; and in the matter of compensation in the event of expropriation.

[71] See the monograph in this Brookings series, *The United Nations and Human Rights*, Chap. I.

[72] Res. 626(VII), Dec. 21, 1952.

20 abstentions.[73] The negative votes, due more to the legislative history of the resolution than to its final provisions, were cast by the United States, the United Kingdom, South Africa, and New Zealand, whereas Canada and most of the countries of Western Europe abstained.

It is obvious that nationalization is an extremely sensitive subject. No underdeveloped country will go on record against it in a United Nations forum. On the other hand, the action of the Assembly in 1952 in response to the Uruguayan-Bolivian initiative marked no real shift in policy or emphasis on the part of United Nations Members. Better balanced and more comprehensive resolutions on private investment issues, clearly more indicative of the considered views of the Members, were passed both before and after the 1952 session.[74]

The blunting of extreme views that has become evident in debates and resolutions is in part due to plainer speaking in United Nations publications. The following quotation from a 1955 report is a far cry from the tone of some of the earlier reports issued by the United Nations:

> . . . Under-developed countries in other words, are competitors for foreign capital, and in so far as market forces prevail, investment is likely to be made in that field and in that country which, comparative risk being taken into account, appear to offer the highest prospective rate of return over a reasonable period of time. The under-developed country is in effect entering a competitive market as a buyer; it cannot dictate both the volume of capital and entrepreneurial ability it is proposing to absorb and the price and conditions it is prepared to offer. Difference in potential reward is one of the principal reasons why in the international movement of private capital, most of the industrial investment has taken place in more advanced countries while investment in under-developed countries has been very largely in primary activities producing raw materials and foodstuffs for markets abroad.[75]

At the same time, spokesmen for the more developed countries have come to recognize that private investment in underdeveloped countries cannot be a substitute for public investment and is more likely to follow it than to occur without it. Consequently, the gap between the views of capital exporters and capital importers—a gap that has defied bridging by multilateral treaties and codes—is being bridged repeatedly in bi-

---

[73] U.N. General Assembly, Seventh Session, Plenary, *Official Records*, 411th Meeting (Dec. 21, 1952), p. 495.

[74] See, especially, Economic and Social Council Res. 512B(XVII), Apr. 30, 1954, "International Flow of Private Capital for the Economic Development of Underdeveloped Countries," the recommendations of which were endorsed by the General Assembly in Res. 824(IX), Dec. 11, 1954.

[75] U.N. Department of Economic and Social Affairs, *Processes and Problems of Industrialization in Under-developed Countries*, Doc. E/2670 (December 1955), p. 86.

lateral negotiations.[76] In a number of countries, mutually satisfactory arrangements have been made, and the International Bank, as well as other informed sources, has noted a distinct improvement in the private investment climate.

The International Bank, in addition, has contributed directly to this improvement. The regular long-term loans of the Bank are financed, to an increasing extent, from capital raised in the private markets of member countries. The total of outstanding bonds of the Bank as of mid-1956 amounted to $850 million, and of this total, an estimated $380 million—or 45 per cent—was held by investors outside the United States.[77] The President of the Bank has stressed that it also offers a vehicle for short-term capital in the form of loan participations and sales of securities of borrowers from its portfolio.[78] Loan participations are being arranged whereby private investors take short-term and medium-term maturities, without an IBRD guarantee but with the protection inherent in retention of the longer maturities by the international agency. This development is still insignificant in terms of the total flow of international investment, but is nevertheless encouraging. In the year ending June 30, 1955, the Bank for the first time raised nearly $100 million, or more money from the sale of the obligations of borrowers than from the sale of its own bonds.[79]

In addition to sales to private investors of its bonds and sales of the securities of its borrowers, the International Bank has been instrumental in a further move to re-establish private portfolio investment. Combined operations have been arranged under which loans by the Bank have been made at the same time that foreign dollar bonds of the borrowing governments were offered to the public through groups of American underwriters. In this manner, for example, $50 million was obtained by Belgium, $20 million as a loan from the Bank, and $30 million by a simultaneous offer of Belgian bonds on the New York investment market.

[76] See U.N. Economic and Social Council, Twentieth Session, *Recent Governmental Measures Affecting the International Flow of Private Capital, A Report Prepared by the Secretary-General in Accordance with General Assembly Res. 824(IX)*, Doc. E/2766 (June 2, 1955).

[77] International Bank for Reconstruction and Development, *Eleventh Annual Report, 1955–1956*, p. 16.

[78] International Bank for Reconstruction and Development, *Summary Proceedings*, Ninth Annual Meeting of the Board of Governors, Washington, D.C. (1954), p. 9.

[79] Address of Eugene R. Black, President to the Boards of Governors of the International Bank for Reconstruction and Development and the International Monetary Fund, Sept. 12, 1955, *International Financial News Survey* (Sept. 23, 1955), pp. 99–103.

In the receiving countries, as has been noted earlier, the Bank has been instrumental in the establishment of national development banks equipped to finance local private undertakings; has made country surveys that have brought to light new opportunities for private investment; has itself financed the foreign exchange costs of public utility and transportation services needed by private industry and agriculture in underdeveloped countries; has stimulated the mobilization of local capital by requiring the other-than-foreign-exchange costs of approved projects to be raised domestically; and has strongly advocated orthodox policies designed to improve the climate for private capital.

The experience of the postwar years in promoting the flow of private international investment indicates that a good deal of time was wasted in premature efforts to develop multilateral codes and treaties in forums in which a handful of capital-exporting nations were negotiating with a very much larger number of capital-importers. Such codes are more likely to reflect the climate already in existence than to create a different one and consequently could not be developed when views were as polarized as they were during the early postwar years. Opinions have mellowed since then, mutual understanding has grown, and techniques have been found for associating public and private funds and management in ways that make the earlier one-or-the-other approach obsolete. Private investment alone will rarely suffice to stimulate economic growth in areas that have long been stagnant. Recent history suggests, however, that as public projects for the development of power and transportation facilities are completed, as production for the local market becomes feasible and attractive—in short, as development itself occurs—a broad field for domestic and foreign private investment in manufacturing, distribution, and extractive industries opens up.[80]

Establishment of the International Finance Corporation

United States concurrence, after more than three years of fence-sitting, has made possible the establishment of an International Finance Corporation (IFC). In the field of public-versus-private financing of economic development, the proposed corporation is another half-way house. Its initial capital consists of funds subscribed by member governments. These are public funds, but they will be used for financing—in association with private investors and without the requirement of a

---

[80] For a brief, readily understandable analysis of the major legal, political, and economic issues currently involved in the promotion and protection of private foreign investment, see Seymour J. Rubin, *Private Foreign Investment* (1956).

governmental guarantee—the establishment and expansion of private undertakings, particularly industrial enterprises in underdeveloped countries. Sales of IFC holdings in successful ventures are expected to provide a revolving fund for reinvestment.

The merits of the IFC were never a subject of real controversy in the United Nations. Developed countries did not publicly oppose the idea, but insisted that more study was necessary before conclusions regarding its practicability could be reached. The consistent support of the underdeveloped countries seems to have been due less to convictions about this particular technique for stimulating development than to enthusiasm for anything that would give them access to more capital without jeopardizing their independence. There is no evidence, therefore, that creation of an International Finance Corporation will reduce the pressure for a grant-aid agency.

An International Finance Corporation with a capital fund of $400 million was first publicly suggested in March 1951 in a report to the President of the United States by the International Development Advisory Board, of which Nelson A. Rockefeller was chairman.[81] The Board recommended that "the United States take the initiative in creating an International Finance Corporation, as an affiliate of the International Bank, with authority to make loans in local and foreign currencies to private enterprise without the requirement of government guaranties and also to make nonvoting equity investments in local currencies in participation with private investors."[82] Within a few weeks international status was given to this idea by the group of experts appointed by the United Nations Secretary-General to prepare *Measures for the Economic Development of Underdeveloped Countries*. Their report, issued in May 1951, commended the proposal to the United Nations for study.[83] No detailed consideration was given to this recommendation at the ensuing session of the Economic and Social Council although in its omnibus resolution on financing economic development, the Council requested the International Bank to prepare a report on the contribution that an international finance corporation could make.[84]

The report by the International Bank concluded that an international finance corporation could fill an important gap in the existing ma-

[81] The proposal actually originated with the staff of the International Bank for Reconstruction and Development and was publicized by the Board after consultation with the Bank.

[82] U.S. International Development Advisory Board, *Partners in Progress: A Report to the President* (March 1951), p. 84.

[83] *Measures for Economic Development*, p. 82.

[84] Res. 368(XIII), Aug. 22, 1951.

chinery for economic development, but went to great pains to make clear that the views being expressed were those of the staff of the Bank, not of its Executive Directors or member governments.[85] The report stressed the importance of private investment, particularly equity capital, in the development field and noted reasons for the low level of the postwar flow of private capital. It mentioned as two major limitations on the ability of the Bank to contribute directly to the growth of private investment: (1) the requirement that loans made by the Bank be guaranteed by the government of the country in which the project to be financed is located; and (2) the fact that the Bank does not engage in equity financing. It did not suggest modifying the Articles of Agreement of the Bank in order to overcome these difficulties, for this would have required resubmitting the Articles to the parliaments of Member countries for ratification.

The International Bank reported that an international finance corporation could make three important contributions. First, it could provide funds to enable private investors, both domestic and foreign, to undertake promising projects otherwise held back for lack of sufficient capital. Second, it could direct the attention of private investors to profitable opportunities abroad and induce them to enter the foreign investment field by an offer of financial participation in sound proposals. Third, it could encourage investors to embark on projects from which they might be deterred by lack of confidence rather than lack of capital.

The report was discussed by the Economic and Social Council in 1952. At that time, several Member states indicated their willingness to participate in the proposed corporation, but the key country—the United States—was cool to the proposal and reluctant to discuss it in detail. The year 1952 was a presidential election year; the initial reaction in some American business circles had been hostile; the precise outlines of the proposal were still somewhat hazy; and the International Bank was in any event better qualified technically to clarify the outline than was the Council. Moreover, the United States voice in the Bank, where weighted voting prevailed, was a great deal more powerful than its voice in the Economic and Social Council.

Consequently, in deference to the United States view, the Council merely noted that the Bank was continuing its study of the proposal and asked that the Council be kept informed of the results of such further

[85] International Bank for Reconstruction and Development, *Report on the Proposal for an International Finance Corporation* (April 1952).

explorations.[86] There was actually little to study; the real issue was always the willingness of the United States to participate. Despite evidence of increasing support for the proposal on the part of the American business community, the United States Government remained uncommitted until November 1954 when the Secretary of the Treasury announced the willingness of the Government to solicit congressional approval for United States participation to the extent of $35 million in an International Finance Corporation having an authorized capital of $100 million.[87] The ninth session of the General Assembly then approved without dissent a resolution initiated by the United States requesting the International Bank to prepare draft statutes (articles of agreement) for the new corporation.[88]

In April 1955, the Bank submitted to its member governments proposed articles of agreement for the new International Finance Corporation, to become effective after formal acceptance by at least thirty governments whose combined subscriptions amounted to not less than $75 million.[89] In the space of a little more than a year, the necessary acceptances were obtained. The IFC which came into being in mid-1956, however, differs in some important respects from the organization envisaged in 1951. The authorized capital is $100 million, not $400 million. The entire subscription, however, is payable in gold and United

---

[86] Res. 416(XIV), June 23, 1952. The seventh session of the General Assembly, n Res. 622(VII), Dec. 21, 1952, endorsed the action of the Council. For information on the situation in 1953 and 1954, see U.N. Economic and Social Council, Sixteenth Session, *Report of the International Bank for Reconstruction and Development on the Question of Creating an International Finance Corporation*, Doc. E/2441 (May 25, 1953); and International Bank for Reconstruction and Development, *A Second Report on the Status of the Proposal for an International Finance Corporation* (June 1954).

[87] Inter-American politics undoubtedly played a role in the timing of the United States announcement. It was made on the eve of the departure of a high-level American delegation to a special economic meeting in Rio de Janeiro at which the United States might otherwise have appeared singularly empty-handed.

[88] Res. 823(IX), Dec. 11, 1954, adopted by a vote of 50 in favor, none against, and 5 abstentions (Soviet bloc). See U.N. General Assembly, Ninth Session, Plenary, *Official Records*, 510th Meeting (Dec. 11, 1954), p. 479.

[89] For the text of the Articles of Agreement, see *Message from the President of the United States Urging Enactment of Legislation Permitting the United States to Join With the Other Free Nations in Organizing the International Finance Corporation*, H. Doc. 152, 84 Cong. 1 sess. (1955). For summary and explanatory information, see International Bank for Reconstruction and Development, Press Release No. 397 (Apr. 15, 1955); International Bank for Reconstruction and Development, *The Proposed International Finance Corporation* (May 1955); and Statement on the International Finance Corporation, by Robert L. Garner, Vice-President, International Bank for Reconstruction and Development, at the Tenth Annual Meeting of the Board of Governors, Istanbul, Sept. 15, 1955.

States dollars (and therefore fully convertible), and the corporation is empowered to raise additional funds.

More puzzling, in view of the desire to provide a mechanism that could supply equity financing to private industrial undertakings, is the absolute prohibition against the best-known form of equity financing, the holding of common or preferred stock. This prohibition apparently grew out of the belief of certain officials of the United States Government that the possession of capital stock, even nonvoting shares, in private enterprises would somehow involve the IFC in ownership or management responsibilities inconsistent with the private character of the enterprises it would assist. Despite the prohibition against holding either common or preferred stock, the IFC will be able to supply venture capital without offending American sensitivities. "It may, for instance, buy securities which give it the right to participate in the profits of an enterprise and which, when sold, can be converted by the purchasers into capital stock." [90]

Even assuming that the IFC gets under way more rapidly and more smoothly than any predecessor international agency, its contribution within the foreseeable future cannot possibly be substantial enough to dampen the drive for grant aid.

The vigorous and as yet unsuccessful campaign of the underdeveloped countries for the establishment of international machinery to provide additional investment assistance in the form of grants and very long-term, low-interest loans has continued unabated since 1951. That campaign, however, is analyzed at a later point in this study, in connection with the special problems of the underdeveloped countries, because it is in the latter context that the issue has been debated in the Economic and Social Council and the General Assembly. [91]

A World Bank for Fissionable Materials?

A new kind of international bank—dealing not in dollars, pounds, and francs but in fissionable materials—was suggested to the United Nations in a dramatic address by President Eisenhower on December 8, 1953. He proposed that governments possessing the secret of atomic development (the Soviet Union, Great Britain, and Canada as well as the United States)

> . . . to the extent permitted by elementary prudence, should begin now and

[90] International Bank for Reconstruction and Development, *Tenth Annual Report, 1954–1955*, p. 27.
[91] See below, Chap. X.

continue to make joint contributions from their stockpiles of normal uranium and fissionable materials to an international atomic energy agency. We would expect that such an agency would be set up under the aegis of the United Nations.

The more important responsibility of this atomic energy agency would be to devise methods whereby this fissionable material would be allocated to serve the peaceful pursuits of mankind. Experts would be mobilized to apply atomic energy to the needs of agriculture, medicine and other peaceful activities. A special purpose would be to provide abundant electrical energy in the power-starved areas of the world.

Thus the contributing Powers would be dedicating some of their strength to serve the needs rather than the fears of mankind. [92]

At the time of the President's proposal, it was legally impossible for the United States, under the Atomic Energy Act of 1946, to release fissionable material to a foreign government. Consequently, new domestic legislation as well as protracted and difficult international negotiations extending over a period of nearly three years were required before the proposal could be translated into a convention likely to be ratified by a significant number of governments. The issues raised during these negotiations transcend economic and social policy and extend deeply into the realm of political and security policy. Analysis of these issues in a discussion of production and investment would therefore be inappropriate.

Necessary amendments to the Atomic Energy Act of 1946 were obtained in 1954, and a bilateral program of assistance to foreign governments was initiated by the United States in 1955. The negotiations for a multilateral agency began inauspiciously with private discussions between the United States and the Soviet Union. When these bogged down because of Soviet unwillingness to discuss the American proposal unless the United States would first agree to an unconditional ban on the use of nuclear weapons, the United States proceeded to discuss with seven other nations plans for an international atomic energy agency of considerably more modest scope than the atomic bank outlined by the President in 1953.

The proposed scope of the agency was enlarged again, however, as a result of thorough discussion at the ninth session of the General Assembly in 1954; circulation, in August 1955, of the draft statute prepared by the United States and seven other nations to the eighty-four states Members of the United Nations or of a related specialized agency; further debate of the tenth session of the General Assembly in 1955;

[92] U.N. General Assembly, Eighth Session, Plenary, *Official Records*, 470th Meeting (Dec. 8, 1953), p. 452.

the deliberations of a committee of twelve nations in February–April 1956, and a major international conference in September–October 1956. Finally, on October 23, 1956, eighty-two nations, including the Soviet Union, voted unanimously to approve the twenty-three articles of the statute (constitution), which will come into force as soon as instruments of ratification have been deposited by eighteen nations, including at least three of the following five: Canada, France, the Soviet Union, the United Kingdom, and the United States.[93]

The statute of the agency provides authority for an extremely broad program. The International Atomic Energy Agency can become not only a medium of substantial economic and technical assistance to member nations in building atomic power plants, but also a control organ administering world-wide safeguards on the use of nuclear energy. It is empowered to receive and store fissionable materials in different regions of the world and to make them available to nations whose atomic energy projects have been approved.

The terms on which materials will be sold or leased to members will depend on the cost of the materials to the agency. In a message to the final meeting of the conference of eighty-two nations in New York in October 1956, the President of the United States promised to make available,

. . . on terms to be agreed with the Agency, 5,000 kilograms of the nuclear fuel uranium 235 from the 20,000 kilograms of such material allocated . . . by the United States for peaceful uses by friendly nations. . . . In addition to the above mentioned 5,000 kilograms of uranium 235, the United States will continue to make available to the International Atomic Energy Agency nuclear materials that will match in amount the sum of all quantities of such materials made similarly available by all other members of the International Agency,

[93] See U.N. General Assembly, Ninth Session, Plenary, *Official Records*, 475th–76th, 479th, 481st–92nd, 498th, 503rd Meetings (Sept. 23–Dec. 4, 1954); U.N. General Assembly, Ninth Session, First Committee, *Official Records*, 684th–85th, 687th, 690th, 707th–25th Meetings (Oct. 8–Nov. 23, 1954); U.N. General Assembly, Ninth Session, *Official Records*, Annexes, Agenda item 67: "International Co-operation in Developing the Peaceful Uses of Atomic Energy," Res. 810(IX), Dec. 4, 1954; U.N. General Assembly, Tenth Session, First Committee, *Official Records*, 757th–72nd Meetings (Oct. 7–28, 1955); U.N. General Assembly, Tenth Session, Plenary, *Official Records*, 550th Meeting (Dec. 3, 1955); U.N. General Assembly, Tenth Session, *Official Records*, Annexes, Agenda item 18: Peaceful Uses of Atomic Energy; and Res. 912(X), Dec. 3, 1955. See also U.N. General Assembly, Eleventh Session, *Official Records*, Supplement No. 1, "Annual Report of the Secretary General on the Work of the Organization, 16 June 1955–15 June 1956," pp. 3–6. For text of statute of the International Atomic Energy Agency, see U.S. Department of State *Bulletin*, Vol. 35 (Nov. 19, 1956), pp. 820–27.

and on comparable terms, for the period between the establishment of the Agency and July 1, 1960.[94]

Small pledges of fissionable materials have been made also by the Soviet Union and the United Kingdom.

"The cost of fuel is only one part, and a comparatively small part, of the investment involved in an atomic energy program. Reactors, processing plants, and installations to house them are the expensive items."[95] Despite the efforts of certain underdeveloped countries, the role of the new agency in helping members to acquire these items is strictly limited. It may assist any member or group of members to make arrangements to secure necessary financing from outside sources, but it may not provide financial guarantees or assume financial responsibility itself.[96]

The precise role to be played by the new agency thus remains to be seen. Negotiations among the members of the European Community for Coal and Steel for establishment of a supra-national atomic energy agency, EURATOM, are well advanced. The United States program of bilateral agreements includes arrangements with thirty-seven other nations. The bilateral programs of other atomic powers provide further competition for the new agency. Even if the sale and lease of fissionable materials continues to be handled primarily on a bilateral basis and the banking role of the global agency is minimized, it can make a major contribution to the general welfare through fostering the exchange of scientific and technical information, encouraging the training of experts, developing health and safety standards, and administering safeguards against the military use of fissionable materials.

The Balance Sheet

The most striking feature of the United Nations attack on production and investment problems has been diversity. This applies to the general approach, to specific projects undertaken, and to practical results obtained. A multitude of organs and agencies have given attention to fundamental issues such as the mobilization of domestic capital for pro-

[94] "Letter and Statement by President Eisenhower," U.S. Department of State Bulletin, Vol. 35 (Nov. 19, 1956), pp. 814–15. The value of 5,000 kilograms—11,000 pounds—at the price of $16 per gram currently charged by the United States Government for U-235 is $80 million.

[95] William R. Frye, "The UN and the Atomic Revolution," Foreign Policy Bulletin (Sept. 1, 1956), p. 190.

[96] Statute of the International Atomic Energy Agency, Art. XIB.

ductive purposes, the stimulation of private foreign investment, the use of public funds so that they will have maximum impact, and the creation of a climate in which experimentation and initiative will flourish. Factors inhibiting and stimulating productivity in agriculture, mining, and manufacturing have been debated *in extenso*. At the same time, the special investment requirements, production potentials, and market outlooks for a host of particular industries, particular enterprises, and particular localities have been analyzed. The variety of activities undertaken in local communities and national capitals, in regional forums, and in the more rarified atmosphere of the General Assembly, tends to obscure the pattern of this intricate mosaic.

Initially, the reconstruction of war-devastated areas had top priority. The United Nations Relief and Rehabilitation Administration operated between 1945 and 1947, primarily in eastern and southern Europe, but also in some of the war-devastated areas of Asia. In 1947, the International Bank for Reconstruction and Development made a series of reconstruction loans to certain nations in western and northern Europe. The reconstruction job, however, soon proved to be beyond the resources— and probably beyond the capacity—of the United Nations. After the Soviet Union rejected the Anglo-French invitation to join in working out a new European Recovery Program, European reconstruction went forward with Marshall Plan aid, almost entirely outside the framework of the United Nations.

Within the United Nations, the economic and social development of underdeveloped countries—the raising of standards of living in Asia, Africa, and Latin America—became the central economic aim of the system. There was agreement that lack of know-how was a formidable obstacle to progress in these regions, and that important increases in production could be obtained with comparatively insignificant expenditures of capital. In recognition of this fact, the Expanded Programme of Technical Assistance was established by the United Nations, largely on the initiative of the United States. The underdeveloped countries recognized the inauguration of the program in 1950 as a landmark in international economic relations, but continued to feel that shortage of capital was the main obstacle to their more rapid development. By providing some of the *expertise* necessary for translating grandiose schemes into concrete projects, and by steadily uncovering new opportunities for capital investment, the technical assistance program reinforced these feelings.

Governments of underdeveloped countries were eager for public loan capital on a more liberal scale and on better terms than could be obtained from the International Bank. They exerted unending pressure for more activity and greater flexibility on the part of that institution. The Bank responded by a fairly rapid expansion of its technical services and a much more gradual stepping-up of its lending and spending. The total of IBRD loans to underdeveloped countries, $150-to-$270 million per year during the period 1950–56, has seemed modest in the eyes of developed as well as underdeveloped countries.

On private investment, the underdeveloped countries have been ambivalent, stressing their desire and need for it but unable or unwilling to offer incentives sufficient to attract capital in significant volume. The International Bank has been ingenious in developing techniques for associating private with public capital and paving the way for a revival of private international investment. The lengthy debates and many reports of the United Nations on the private foreign investment problem have shed a good deal of light on the issue and have helped to narrow the differences separating capital importers from potential exporters. The improved climate, noticeable since about mid-1952, has not yet, however, significantly enlarged the flow of funds.

As the underdeveloped nations have seen it, their problems are almost insoluble without additional government aid from abroad, particularly for non-self-liquidating projects like schools, hospitals, and roads, that are nevertheless basic to development. Since 1951, the establishment of a United Nations fund to make grants-in-aid has become the primary economic objective of the underdeveloped countries in the United Nations. Spokesmen for the Soviet bloc until recently have repeatedly claimed that foreign funds from capitalist sources, whether public or private, would bring exploitation and enslavement, but the drive for greater aid has continued.

The United States, which would be the main contributor to a grant-aid fund, first opposed and lately has sought to postpone its establishment.[97] American representatives have emphasized instead what the underdeveloped countries could do with their own resources and by using established forms of international assistance. The preparation of national development plans has been encouraged, and excessive concentration on industrialization at the expense of agriculture has been discouraged. The possibilities of utilizing the spare time of villagers on community improvement projects of their own choosing have been publicized. Antiquated systems of land tenure have been criticized and a wholesome impetus given to broad, democratically-conceived, land

---

[97] See below, Chap. X.

reform programs. Better machinery for mobilizing domestic capital has been advocated, along with the removal of obvious barriers to foreign private investment. Agreement has been reached on the statute of an agency to promote the development of atomic energy for peaceful purposes.

Ten years of running debate on production and investment problems has highlighted and perhaps intensified differences between countries on a few issues. Grant aid for economic development is the outstanding case. On many other matters agreement has been reached, and concrete programs of action have been initiated. The mutual education of delegates in developed, underdeveloped, and intermediate countries has been furthered by a long series of reports and studies. The technical assistance program has captured the imagination of millions. The Food and Agriculture Organization has operated effectively in a sector of the economy in which small investments can make large differences in output and in which the increased output can provide an important offset to the inflationary pressures generated before longer-term investments pay off. To the growth of industrial establishments in underdeveloped countries an additional fillip may now be supplied by the International Finance Corporation, an affiliate of the International Bank.

The direct contribution of the United Nations system to the impressive increase in world output that has occurred since the end of the war has necessarily been modest. The broad economic objectives of the United Nations have at the same time, of course, been the objectives of Member governments, many of which have vigorously pursued programs of their own—frequently drafted with assistance from agencies of the United Nations—for enlarging agricultural and industrial output. Within each nation, innumerable nongovernmental groups have worked toward these same ends. Moreover, on the international side, United Nations activities have been paralleled, and in some cases dwarfed, by programs conducted outside the framework of the United Nations, most notably the foreign economic programs of the United States Government. Nor should the contribution of completely unplanned and unprogramed factors be forgotten.

In these circumstances, it becomes almost impossible to isolate and measure separately the effect of United Nations activities. The combined result of the United Nations and other influences, national and international, has not only been the attainment of record levels of output during the first postwar decade, but the establishment of a foundation for a much larger and better-balanced growth during the second decade.

CHAPTER V

Full Employment and Economic Stability*

THE various United Nations programs designed to help repair the ravages of war, to promote the development of under-developed countries, and to stimulate production, investment, and trade have had a common purpose—to foster conditions of full employment and steadily rising standards of living. The counterpart of the efforts to attain higher levels of productive employment and economic activity has been the consideration of measures for avoiding reverses involving mass unemployment and cumulative deflation. Noteworthy attempts have been made to build into the United Nations system additional anti-depression safeguards and comprehensive arrangements for the co-ordination of national full-employment policies.

The attainment and maintenance of full employment—important as it has come to be—is not an end in itself and is by no means the sole economic objective of governments. Apparent and, in the short run at least, frequent real conflicts between full employment and other objectives of economic policy have arisen, and the need for reconciling these conflicts both domestically and internationally has had to be faced. Accordingly, the analysis below, after tracing briefly the origins of today's preoccupation with full employment, mentions the related aims with which full employment has had to be reconciled and the general approach of Members of the United Nations to this task. Identified next are the interests of certain specialized agencies: of the International Monetary Fund and the International Bank in economic stability, of the International Labour Organisation in full employment, and of the Food and Agriculture Organization in more stable commodity prices and in the constructive use of agricultural surpluses. For the most part, attention in this analysis is focused on the consideration of problems of full employment and economic stability in the United Nations itself, where the evolution of postwar thinking on these matters is vividly illustrated.

The analysis is divided into two time periods, with a dividing line drawn at the close of 1949. By that time, the accumulated inflationary

* By Robert E. Asher.

pressures of the Second World War had worn off, pockets of unemployment had begun to appear, and a reversion to the nationalistic policies of the 1930's was feared. In December 1949, far-reaching proposals for strengthening the ability of the international economy to resist depression were put forward by a group of experts appointed by the Secretary-General of the United Nations. By the time their recommendations reached the Economic and Social Council, however, the American economy was again surging forward. Governments rejected the major innovations suggested by the experts. Nevertheless, the discussion of their proposals at the 1950 session of the Council represented a high-water mark in United Nations consideration of full employment and economic stability.

Thereafter, other groups of experts were commissioned by the Council and the General Assembly to prepare further reports, both on the general problem of stabilizing the international economy and on the more specific problem of stabilizing the prices of primary commodities moving in international trade. Although these reports, too, became subjects of intense discussion at United Nations meetings, they did not bring about international co-ordination of national full-employment policies, the provision of new sources of credit for meeting temporary setbacks, the completion of a network of commodity agreements, or adequate measures to prevent surplus agricultural products from being utilized in a destabilizing fashion.

Despite much talk and many studies, the international community therefore remains almost entirely dependent on nationally devised and nationally executed safeguards against recession. The ability of the major industrial nations to avoid deep and prolonged depression has, of course, increased greatly during the past two decades. Nevertheless, if a serious depression should begin, it would be rash to assume that the United Nations would make any greater contribution to checking its spread than did the League of Nations.

General Background

The abiding fear of large-scale unemployment and deflation, which characterized the 1930's and to which the "freedom from want" clause of the Atlantic Charter was a response, shaped the postwar aims, aspirations, and programs of peoples and governments everywhere. At the same time,

... a great transformation was taking place in economic thought. The economy was no longer regarded as being fundamentally self-directing and capable of maintaining continuous full employment except for periodic crises. Instead, the possibility of an equilibrium at a low level of employment for an indefinite period of time had been recognized. Economic analysis had now become engaged in critical enquiry into the determinants of the general level of employment.[1]

This critical inquiry was epitomized in John Maynard Keynes' *General Theory of Employment, Interest and Money*, published in 1936, which was in large measure responsible for the "great transformation" in economic thought.

Because depression anywhere threatens prosperity everywhere, and because national antidepression policies also have international repercussions (the "export of unemployment" is a tempting form of foreign trade in a depression), international discussions during the war inevitably became concerned with questions of employment and stability in the postwar world.[2] These discussions culminated at the San Francisco Conference in the inclusion in the United Nations Charter of Article 55 explicitly requiring the new Organization, "with a view to the creation of conditions of stability and well-being," to promote "higher standards of living, full employment, and conditions of economic and social progress and development."

A similar policy declaration is contained in the United States Employment Act of 1946, although it speaks of "maximum" rather than "full" employment. The Canadian White Paper on *Employment and Income* presented to Parliament in 1945, the several declarations by the British Government on the subject, the postwar French Constitution, and other national undertakings following the close of the Second World War make similar references to "full employment" or high and stable levels of employment.

Basic National Attitudes

Although the great depression that began in 1929 made the elimination of unemployment the paramount social problem and the maintenance of full employment the dominant economic objective of governments, the need for reconciling this objective with other objectives of economic policy has posed numerous dilemmas. Like any individual nation, the United Nations has had to recognize that promotion of the general welfare involves a delicate reconciliation of aims that are not wholly consistent. Within the United Nations, moreover, national

[1] International Labour Organisation, *Fourth Report of the International Labour Organisation to the United Nations* (1950), pp. 25–26.
[2] See above, Chap. I.

governments, reflecting divergent social and economic philosophies, have differed importantly in their approach to the full-employment problem. Broadly speaking, four basic national attitudes toward full employment have been reflected in United Nations debates. The United States, Canada, and a few European countries have held that high and stable levels of employment can best be achieved through market forces and free enterprise, with the role of government more or less limited to compensatory action in the event of recession or excessive boom, mainly through monetary and fiscal policy, but also through building into the economy various "stabilizers" such as unemployment compensation, progressive taxation, bank deposit and mortgage insurance, and agricultural price supports. The viewpoint presented by the United Kingdom and shared by many other countries has been that government should at all times play a more positive role in maintaining full employment. For the underdeveloped countries, the main problem has not been unemployment, but underemployment, and its chief cure rapid economic development. The position of the Soviet Union and its satellites has been that unemployment is an insoluble problem under capitalism and a nonexistent problem under communism. The differences between the first two groups are matters of degree; reconciliation with the third viewpoint presents far greater difficulties but is by no means impossible; the introduction of the fourth point of view makes for propaganda instead of economic analysis and cacophany instead of harmony.

Effective reconciliation of full employment, economic stability, and other objectives of the United Nations Charter has inevitably required extensive consideration of methods of achieving agreed goals, in particular the respective spheres for national and for international action. This line is, however, difficult to draw. Basically, the maintenance of total demand at a level sufficient to absorb a growing labor force in productive employment has been accepted as a national responsibility, and the principle was early established that there should be no interference by international organs, in the interest of other objectives, with the discharge by a member country of this responsibility.

A ruling of the executive directors of the International Monetary Fund at their first meeting made it clear that if, while pursuing a full-employment policy, a country found itself in balance-of-payments difficulties that threatened the success of this policy, it could—without interference by the Fund—relieve the external pressure by a change in its exchange rate, even though the Fund might hold that a change in the internal policy could in the long run prove a more constructive solution.[3] Similarly, it was provided in the draft charter for an International Trade Organization that no member should be required to withdraw or modify restrictions that it was applying under the article dealing with balance-of-payments restrictions on the ground that a change in its domestic policies devoted to maintaining full employment and development would render these restrictions unnecessary. Yet there can be no doubt that employment and stability in other countries might be affected by the consequences of the policies thus protected against interference by specialized agencies.

Major International Problems

The question regarding international economic stability that has been of constant concern to Members of the United Nations other than the United States has been what to do in order to prevent balance-of-payments crises and other disastrous effects from occurring because of temporary failure on the part of a major industrialized nation like the United States to maintain full employment and a high level of effective demand at home. Assume, for example, as the European nations have been wont to do, that the American economy should suffer a substantial setback. In the ensuing recession, United States imports would fall, and exports, in theory at least, would tend to be pushed more vigorously. What courses of action would then be open to a nation whose exports to the United States would decline, whose marketings in third countries might encounter heavier competition from United States exports, and whose reduced foreign exchange earnings would threaten such balance-of-payments equilibrium as it might have attained?

If the nation had ample reserves, or adequate sources of credit, it might survive the strain without reducing its imports. If not, and if demand were sufficiently elastic, it might depreciate its currency in order to improve its export prospects and discourage imports. Or it might impose direct controls on its imports and foreign exchange transactions in order to conserve funds for the purposes it regarded as most essential. Finally, it might accept wage cuts and unemployment in its export industries, and deflation generally until its import re-

[3] For the text of this ruling made pursuant to a request from the United Kingdom for an interpretation of Article IV, 5(f) of the Articles of Agreement, see International Monetary Fund, *First Annual Meeting of the Board of Governors, Report of the Executive Directors and Summary Proceedings, September 27 to October 3, 1946* (1946), pp. 105–06.

quirements were reduced to a level that could be financed from current export earnings.

The underdeveloped countries, even more than the countries of Western Europe, have emphasized their vulnerability to external forces. Possessed of undiversified economies, they have felt excessively dependent on the vicissitudes of world demand for a few export products such as tin, copper, coffee, rubber, or sugar. In 1952, there were thirty-two nations in which two commodities accounted for over 50 per cent of total export earnings. There are at least six countries that regularly earn from 50 to 90 per cent of their dollars from coffee exports to the United States. Such nations are unable to obtain whatever stability benefits may be obtainable from averaging the price movements of a number of different exports; yet the orderly execution of their development programs depends heavily on greater regularity in current export earnings.[4]

The range of short-term fluctuations in the prices of most internationally traded primary products is wider than that of prices in general. The downturns are, therefore, more disastrous for primary producers than for others. At the same time, primary producers in underdeveloped countries appear to benefit less from an upswing of export prices than they lose during comparable downswings. Because the economies of underdeveloped countries have very limited absorptive capacities, the advantages accruing from sudden increases in export earnings are likely to be partially dissipated in inflation or else lost in the initiation of development projects that the country is unable to complete or maintain when the boom is over.

Some of these difficulties might be avoided if increased earnings could be sterilized during boom periods and released during downswings, but such action requires greater political maturity and administrative skill than is usually available in an underdeveloped nation. The impact on the economies of underdeveloped countries of short-term fluctuations in demand for raw materials in the industrialized nations could also be made less severe by international commodity agreements, if these would limit the range of fluctuations, and by programs of economic diversification, which would reduce the vulnerability of underdeveloped countries to particular fluctuations. Diversification requires considerable capital, takes long years to accomplish,

[4] U.N. Department of Economic Affairs, *Commodity Trade and Economic Development*, Report by a Committee Appointed by the United Nations Secretary-General, Doc. E/2519 (Nov. 25, 1953), para. 24.

and in some cases, would be an uneconomic expedient because the area is uniquely equipped to continue as a highly specialized producer. The demand for international commodity agreements consequently cannot be regarded as transitory.

From this brief statement of the problem and catalog of alternatives open to developed and underdeveloped countries, it should be clear why United Nations discussions of full-employment and stability inevitably became concerned with the adequacy of domestic full-employment programs in major trading nations; the degree to which failure to maintain full employment at home should carry a responsibility for making good the foreign trade losses caused elsewhere; the adequacy of national and international monetary reserves; the use of trade restrictions and exchange controls; the mitigation of fluctuations in primary commodity markets; and the regularization of the flow of long-term investment capital. Although the inability of labor to cross frontiers because of immigration barriers has added to the instability of the international economy, it has, by and large, been accepted in United Nations economic discussions as a fact of contemporary life. Migration from lands of lesser opportunity to lands of greater opportunity has been given relatively little emphasis as an equilibrator in the international economy.

Concern of the Specialized Agencies

The concentration of attention in this study on discussions of full employment and economic stability in the Economic and Social Council and other organs of the United Nations tends to obscure the continuing concern of a number of specialized agencies in this area. It is desirable at the outset, therefore, to give some indication of the interests of the International Monetary Fund (IMF), the International Bank for Reconstruction and Development (IBRD), the International Labour Organisation (ILO), and the Food and Agriculture Organization (FAO).

Fund and Bank

The International Monetary Fund, as conceived at Bretton Woods in 1944, was to be concerned primarily with problems of exchange stability and related questions arising out of international trade and payments. Its first and third purposes, according to its Articles of

Agreement, were "to promote international monetary cooperation" and "to promote exchange stability." Its second purpose was "to facilitate the expansion and balanced growth of international trade, and to contribute thereby to the promotion and maintenance of high levels of employment and real income and to the development of the productive resources of all members as primary objectives of economic policy."[5] The emphasis at the Bretton Woods Conference, as distinct from the emphasis at the San Francisco Conference, was not on full employment *per se*, but on the expansion and growth of international trade; not on economic stability, but on the development of productive resources as "primary objectives of economic policy." These are significant distinctions. Moreover, the Articles of Agreement of the International Monetary Fund speak of "high levels of employment," not "full employment."

These differences in terms of reference help to explain the divergent policies at times recommended by the Fund and the United Nations Organization. There is, moreover, a fairly sharp distinction between the generally conservative outlook of central bank presidents and monetary experts, comprising the Board of Governors and Staff of the Fund, and the more pragmatic viewpoints of the delegates to the principal organs of the United Nations and of the experts commissioned to prepare special reports for their consideration. As has been pointed out,

... One cannot believe in full employment or free trade as desirable economic objectives exclusively on economic grounds. ... Emphasis on employment, and even more on unemployment, conveys the idea that there is an urgent social problem to be solved, whereas emphasis on monetary factors may create a very different impression—as it did during the nineteenth century.[6]

Perhaps the differing economic philosophies of the Fund and the United Nations Organization, although they tend to complicate harmonious co-operation between the agencies, are not altogether lamentable. The more conservative approach of the Fund and its emphasis on monetary factors help to keep certain indispensable objectives of economic policy—the expansion of international trade, the development of productive resources, and the importance of a relatively

[5] United Nations Monetary and Financial Conference, Bretton Woods, N.H., July 1 to 22, 1944, *Articles of Agreement, International Monetary Fund and International Bank for Reconstruction and Development* (1945), Art. I(ii), p.1.
[6] Arthur Smithies, "Economic Welfare and Policy," *Economics and Public Policy* (1955), pp. 1–2.

stable price level—from being subordinated in the United Nations to full employment as an objective. Vice versa, the concentration of the United Nations on full employment and the maintenance of effective demand provides a counterweight to the preoccupation of the Fund with monetary factors and exchange and budgetary policies.

Whereas the International Monetary Fund was intended to serve as a source of credit for members in temporary balance-of-payments difficulties, the International Bank for Reconstruction and Development has been concerned with stability from a longer-range point of view. Article I(iii) of the charter of the Bank charged it with promoting "the long-range balanced growth of international trade and the maintenance of equilibrium in balances of payments by encouraging international investment for the development of the productive resources of members, thereby assisting in raising productivity, the standard of living, and conditions of labor." As pointed out earlier in this volume, the Bank has inevitably become deeply concerned with the prospects for stability, avoidance of inflation, and attainment of balance-of-payments equilibrium on the part of potential borrowers.[7] It has been less concerned with stability problems from the global, theoretical point of view.

ILO and FAO

The International Labour Organisation antedates the Bank and Fund by twenty-five years. Its views on the unemployment problem illustrate the profound changes in economic thinking that have occurred since 1919. When the ILO was founded, the prevailing view was that the economy was basically self-directing through the operation of the natural forces of supply and demand. Governmental activity was looked upon mainly as interference with natural forces, and the sphere within which it was expected to operate was confined primarily to a compensatory public works policy. The ILO Constitution consequently provided simply that "the prevention of unemployment" should be one of the major objectives of the agency.[8]

A quarter of a century later, the emphasis had shifted, and the 1944 Declaration of Philadelphia recognized "the solemn obligation of the International Labour Organisation to further among the nations of the

[7] See above, Chap. IV.

[8] International Labour Organisation, *Fourth Report . . . to the United Nations*, pp. 22–23.

world programmes which will achieve full employment and the raising of standards of living." The statements on full-employment policy approved by the International Labour Conference in 1944 and 1945 contrast sharply with the more limited view taken after the First World War, and opened the doors to a far wider range of activities.[9]

The ILO in recent years has given consideration to the statistical and institutional requirements for carrying out a policy of full employment. It has consistently emphasized that modern economic analysis distinguishes three major types of unemployment: (1) frictional and seasonal unemployment—inevitable in any economy where consumers are free to change their tastes, producers are free to improve their methods of production, and workers may move from one job or industry to another; (2) unemployment arising from shortages of raw materials and capital—either from short-run shortages as an aftermath of war destruction and disorganization, or from more persistent capital shortages, as in the underdeveloped countries; and (3) general unemployment arising from a deficiency in aggregate demand.[10] Discussions in the United Nations have emphasized the third type of unemployment, characteristic of the major industrial countries in the 1930's, although the underdeveloped countries have been concerned primarily with the second kind. The ILO has made modest but useful contributions to the diagnosis and treatment of all three types of unemployment.

Apart from its general policy statements on full employment, the ILO has pioneered in the adoption of concrete measures, which, although subsidiary, can contribute to the maintenance of employment at a high level. These relate to the organization of the labor market and include such questions as the organization of employment services, vocational training, vocational guidance, and migration. In each of these fields the International Labour Conference has adopted international conventions, recommendations, or resolutions that have facilitated the spread of successful techniques from the more advanced to the less advanced countries.[11]

The particular concern of the Food and Agriculture Organization with problems of economic stability, apart from its general concern with the attainment of a proper balance between agricultural and

[9] *Ibid.*, pp. 22 and 26.
[10] *Ibid.*, p. 29.
[11] For a full description of these ILO activities, see the ILO reply to the United Nations questionnaire on "National and International Action to Achieve or Maintain Full Employment and Economic Stability," Doc. E/1111/Add. 1 (Feb. 16, 1949). Also, see below, Chap. VII.

industrial development, arises from "excessive" fluctuations in the availabilities and prices of agricultural commodities. Mitigation of these fluctuations involves consideration of such measures as buffer-stock maintenance, production and consumption controls, surplus disposal schemes, and other commodity control arrangements.

At the discussions of the Preparatory Committee for an International Trade Organization, consideration was given to proposals for vesting in the FAO the responsibility for commodity agreements on agricultural products. The decision of the committee, however, was that commodity agreements should be handled in the context of general commercial policy and allocated to the prospective ITO. Pending establishment of the ITO, the interim arrangements described elsewhere in this study were made, and the FAO was brought into the picture through its authority to nominate one of the members of the Interim Coordinating Committee for International Commodity Arrangements.[12] More recently, the FAO interest in international economic stability has taken the form of a lively concern with surplus disposal arrangements, both from the point of view of the threat to stability posed by ill-considered schemes and the opportunity to promote the general welfare by a constructive disposition of accumulated surpluses.

Although a number of agencies have thus been concerned with aspects of the stability problem, over-all responsibility for developing recommendations to prevent the international spread of recessions has been left to the United Nations Economic and Social Council.

Consideration of Employment and Stability Problems in the United Nations, 1946–49

Eager to implement the full-employment provision of the Charter, the United Nations Economic and Social Council, at its first session in January–February 1946, established an oddly named subsidiary, the Economic and Employment Commission. At its second session in mid-1946, the Council made the new, fifteen-man commission responsible for advising it on "the prevention of wide fluctuations in economic activity and the promotion of full employment by the coordination of national full-employment policies and by international action."[13]

[12] See above, Chap. III.
[13] U.N. General Assembly, First Session, Second Part, *Official Records*, Supplement No. 2, "Report by the Economic and Social Council to the General Assembly," p. 8.

Subcommission on Employment and Economic Stability

The Economic and Employment Commission, in turn, was directed by the Council to establish a Subcommission on Employment and Economic Stability. After some difficulty, it was decided that the subcommission should have seven members, and that they should serve as "individual experts." The instructions that the commission gave them merit quoting in full:

1. To report to the Commission as early as possible on current world economic conditions and trends, giving particular attention to any factors that are preventing, or are likely to prevent in the near future, the maintenance of full employment and economic stability, together with analyses indicating causal factors involved and recommendations as to desirable action.

2. To report to the Commission at its early convenience on:

(a) The preliminary views of the Sub-commission concerning the kinds of international action which are likely to be feasible and of assistance in maintaining economic stability and full employment. In this connexion the Sub-commission should bear in mind important links between stability and development and should examine such proposals as:

(i) The concerted timing, to the extent which might be appropriate and practicable in the interests of employment policy, of national and international measures to influence credit conditions and the terms of borrowing;

(ii) National or international arrangements, in suitable cases, to promote due stability in the real incomes of producers of primary products, taking account both of the interests of consumers and producers regardless of country;

(iii) The timing, to the extent appropriate and practicable in the interests of employment policy, of capital expenditures on projects that are either of an international character or are internationally financed; as well as the expansion of investments in less developed countries as measures designed to maintain stability of employment during periods of depression in more highly industrialized countries.[14]

Noteworthy in these instructions are several themes that recur, with variations, throughout the life of the commission and its subcommission, as well as in the Council and the General Assembly. One is the importance of international action, the assumption that new kinds of international action would be desirable and feasible in maintaining economic stability and full employment. Another is the stress on "important links between stability and development." That the economic development of underdeveloped areas can contribute to the maintenance of stability and full employment in the industrialized areas is

[14] U.N. General Assembly, Second Session, *Official Records*, Supplement No. 3, "Report by the Economic and Social Council to the General Assembly," p. 9.

usually conceded. It may reasonably be doubted, however, whether the two are as inseparably linked, from a strictly economic point of view, as they are made to appear in United Nations reports and debates.

Illustrative of the overlapping interests of different international agencies and the compromises of national viewpoints that result in ambiguous, if not meaningless, language is paragraph 2(a)(ii) giving the subcommission a role in the commodity agreement field. Atypical in United Nations literature, it should be added, is the apparent taking for granted in paragraph 2(a)(iii) of "periods of depression in more highly industrialized countries." Although delegates fully expected a recurrence of depression, they preferred in their resolutions to speak of "recession," "decline in effective demand," or "undue fluctuations."

Most of the first formal report of the Subcommission on Employment and Economic Stability to the commission and the Council was devoted, not to the long-term problem of maintaining effective demand, but to the more immediate problem of inflation. In the years 1946–48, the control of accumulated inflationary pressures and the restoration of wartime devastation were the most pressing issues. Although the report of the subcommission contributed but little to either the economic analysis of inflation or the knowledge of techniques for dealing with it, the report did help to focus the attention of the United Nations on the problem.

By 1948–49, the inflationary threat was beginning to subside, and pockets of unemployment were appearing in various countries. Enthusiasm for international action was likewise waning in some of the key areas. The report drafted by the subcommission in April 1949 was pessimistic about both the psychological climate and the economic outlook. It recalled the magnificent efforts made before the end of the war to establish effective machinery for international economic collaboration and concluded on the nostalgic note that such movements are likely to occur "only on rare occasions such as the union of nations in a war for all they hold dear."[15]

The subcommission was troubled by certain evidences of disillusion and return to nationalistic policies. First, the replies to an employment questionnaire circulated by the Secretary-General convinced the subcommission that "few nations now put their main reliance on international cooperation in the event of serious depression." Second, most

[15] U.N. Subcommission on Employment and Economic Stability, *Report of the Third Session*, Doc. E/CN.1/66 (Apr. 26, 1949), para. 27.

nations at that time envisaged a resort to import restrictions, although outlawry of this form of beggar-my-neighbor policy had been a basic objective of postwar planners. Third, despite wartime efforts to assure that remedial measures would be of an expansionist character serving to increase demand rather than restrict supply, other parts of the world could be expected to parallel American agricultural restrictions should the oversupply of primary products become general.[16] Discussions on the problem of primary products had been "disappointing." The International Bank seemed to the subcommission "a useful but a minor addition to existing financial machinery at a time when world uncertainty makes venture capital extremely unventuresome."[17]

To correct the situation, the subcommission recommended vigorous efforts to negotiate commodity agreements, reconsideration of the Articles of Agreement of both the Bank and Fund, and new international consultations at the highest level to review the activities and policies of all the organizations involved in maintaining full employment.

Economic and Employment Commission and the Council

The Economic and Employment Commission, more sensitive to jurisdictional issues than the experts on the subcommission, commented to the Economic and Social Council that the desirability of revising the Articles of Agreement of the Bank and of the Fund was, in its view, a question to be dealt with only by those specialized agencies. The Economic and Employment Commission also rejected the proposal for early high-level consultations, and suggested instead that the Council consider convening special sessions of the commission should the world economic situation warrant it.[18]

The employment situation was on the agenda of the Council in 1949, not only via the reports of its subsidiaries, but also because the Communist-controlled World Federation of Trade Unions (WFTU) had proposed as an agenda item "Unemployment and Full Employment." The motivation behind the action of the WFTU was obvious, and the opportunity was fully exploited by the spokesmen of the Soviet bloc.

[16] *Ibid.*, para. 31.

[17] *Ibid.*, para. 32.

[18] U.N. General Assembly, Fourth Session, *Official Records*, Supplement No. 3, "Report of the Economic and Social Council Covering the Period from 30 August 1948 to 15 August 1949," pp. 24–25.

All members of the Council agreed that there had been some increase in unemployment, but there was considerable difference of opinion regarding the importance and the causes of the increase. The majority, led by the United Kingdom, felt that although the decline in employment might be of a temporary character, countries should be prepared to deal with it promptly if the necessity for action arose; at the first sign of a recession the United Nations should be prepared to review the situation. Some members, including the United States, stressed that unemployment in their countries reflected a healthy readjustment to peacetime conditions and was purely temporary. Others, led by the Soviet Union, considered that unemployment was already critical and that concrete measures should be taken immediately by the Council to restore full employment and "to protect workers from the effects of unemployment."[19]

Following this inconclusive debate, the Council adopted a noncommittal resolution recommending to the General Assembly the inclusion on the agenda of its next session of an item on measures for promoting full employment and economic stability.[20] More important, the Council invited the Secretary-General to appoint a small group of experts to prepare a report on national and international measures required to achieve full employment.[21] This was to result in the significant and controversial document discussed below. The Council also adopted a resolution urging governments to give any anticyclical measures they might adopt a form that would promote the economic development of underdeveloped countries—once again linking full employment with economic development, primarily to satisfy the demands of the underdeveloped countries.[22]

In addition, the Council considered recommendations from the Economic and Employment Commission on organizational matters. The commission recommended that the Subcommission on Employment and Economic Stability, as well as the Subcommission on Economic Development, be abolished. Instead, the Secretariat should assist the commission directly and should be strengthened by *ad hoc* groups of experts and by individual experts selected by the Secretary-General. The commission complained that it had been handicapped by inadequate contact with current developments and concrete prob-

[19] *Ibid.*, p. 25.

[20] Res. 221F(IX), Aug. 11, 1949.

[21] Res. 221E(IX), Aug. 11, 1949.

[22] Res. 221D(IX), Aug. 10, 1949. A similar resolution was adopted by the General Assembly at its fourth session, Res. 308(IV), Nov. 25, 1949.

lems. The recommendation for abolition of the laboriously created subcommissions was tabled for a year, but was accepted by the Council in 1950.

The dissatisfaction of the commission with the work of its subcommission stemmed in part from the original illusion that members nominated by governments would act as "experts" rather than as representatives of governments. In fact, of course, many of them did not—and perhaps could not—act in such fashion, and even their *expertise* was dubious in some cases. The decision to substitute *ad hoc* groups of bona fide experts selected by the Secretary-General raised the possibility that the experts would reflect the biases, if any, of the secretariat, but nevertheless was a move to obtain reports of a higher order of economic analysis, relatively unmarred by the intrusion of political considerations. At the same time, the disappointment of the commission with its subcommission was to some extent a function of its own naiveté. The commission, for example, had directed its subcommission to give particular attention to the problem of recognizing incipient downturns in economic activity, and had been annoyed by the inability of the subcommission to prepare promptly a significant report on the subject. Yet economists have long been baffled and continue to be baffled by the difficulty of determining which are the key economic indicators, when changes in those indicators presage a downturn, and whether the downturn, if it occurs, will be long and deep, short and sharp, or long and mild.

Regional Commissions

The complaint of the commission about its own "inadequate contact with current developments and concrete problems" touched upon a real weakness of the world-wide functional commissions.[23] Their deliberations too often appeared to take place in a vacuum, where they dealt with abstract conceptions, divorced from firm connections with the pressing issues in specific countries or regions. While the Economic and Employment Commission and its subcommissions were withering on the vine, the United Nations regional commissions, with their larger and more active secretariats, were deepening their roots and flourishing.

In fact, some of the most concrete and specific contributions to the discussions of full employment and economic stability were prepared by the secretariats of the Economic Commission for Europe (ECE)

---

[23] U.N. General Assembly, Fourth Session, *Official Records*, Supplement No. 3, p. 26.

and the Economic Commission for Latin America (ECLA). Their annual economic surveys quickly became authoritative source books, rich in data, penetrating in analysis, provocative, sometimes irritating, and usually more influential than the *World Economic Report* issued by the headquarters office. Although the *World Economic Report* also provided information on employment and unemployment, prices and wages, trade and balances of payments, it concentrated more on description than analysis, tended to accept official statistics at their face value somewhat more readily than did the regional surveys, eschewed forecasts, and avoided evaluations of the efficacy of economic policies being pursued by governments.

The *Economic Survey of Europe in 1949*, compiled by the ECE secretariat, brought to light a formidable array of data, analyzed in stimulating fashion, on the situation and prospects of the European economy. Characteristically pessimistic in tone was the lengthy chapter entitled "The Continuing Problem of International Equilibrium," bearing the main message of the volume. Looking ahead to 1952 and the scheduled end of United States aid under the European Recovery Program, the authors foresaw trouble for the rest of the world. Achievement of equilibrium at a high and expanding level required more foresight and planning than was likely to be forthcoming. Balance at a lower level would jeopardize living standards and probably require trade and payments restrictions on a sizable scale. This view was both challenged and supported in plenary meetings of the commission.

The *Economic Survey of Latin America, 1949*, similarly brought together information dealing with employment and unemployment in Latin America, and the relations of fluctuations in production and exports of Latin American nations to recessions elsewhere. The main thesis of the survey was that the exports of Latin American countries were not in 1949, and were not likely to become, great enough to provide for the expected increases in population and to pay for the imports needed for economic development. The conclusion drawn from this thesis was that there would continue to be a persistent tendency toward disequilibrium in Latin America, a generalization that the survey found it necessary to qualify when it came to analyze economic conditions in specific Latin American countries. Moreover, as the United States delegation pointed out when the survey was under discussion at the Economic and Social Council, it tended to postulate a rapid rate of economic development in Latin America and to take for granted a high rate of population growth instead of investigating what the rates might be if economic development in Latin America were to proceed in a fashion more analogous to that of Western Europe and the United States.[24]

The situation with respect to full employment and economic stability problems in the United Nations as of the close of 1949 may be summarized briefly as follows:

1. The architects of the postwar international structure, working in the long shadow of the 1929–32 depression, had been preoccupied with the avoidance of cumulative deflation, but the initial postwar years were in fact characterized mainly by persistent inflationary pressures.

2. The subsidiary structure created by the Economic and Social Council to advise it on employment and stability questions—an Economic and Employment Commission of government representatives and a smaller "expert" Subcommission on Employment and Economic Stability—was proving unsatisfactory and destined soon to die.

3. By way of replacement, provision had been made for an *ad hoc* group of experts appointed by the Secretary-General to prepare a special report on *National and International Measures for Full Employment*, the first of a distinguished series of United Nations reports to be issued by such groups.

4. Basic information on economic conditions throughout the world was being provided by the regular Secretariat, most notably in the annual economic surveys of the regional commissions and in the *World Economic Report*.

5. By 1949, inflationary pressures were subsiding and signs of deflation were appearing. There was little confidence in the ability of the international economy to withstand even minor shocks and great pessimism abroad about the ability of the United States to avoid depression. Between June 1948 and June 1949, industrial production in the United States fell 12 per cent, and unemployment increased by 1.5 million. Between the fourth quarter of 1948 and the second quarter of 1949, the value of United States imports fell by 15 per cent, thus substantially reducing the dollar earnings of a dollar-short world.[25]

---

[24] U.N. Economic and Social Council, Eleventh Session, *Official Records*, 401st Meeting (Aug. 7, 1950), pp. 230–32.

[25] U.N. Department of Economic Affairs, *National and International Measures for Full Employment*, Report by a Group of Experts Appointed by the Secretary-General, Doc. E/1584 (Dec. 22, 1949), pp. 8, 9. (Hereinafter cited as *Measures for Full Employment.*) Shortly after publication of these figures, a less disquieting and better-balanced review of 1948–49 developments in the United States economy was given to United Nations Members by the United States representative to the tenth session

This gave rise to demands in the United Nations for improved international machinery to help nations withstand cyclical fluctuations and, in the absence of any steps to meet those demands, to the threat of a return to more narrowly nationalist policies.

6. In retrospect, the skepticism of the United States delegates concerning the need for immediate measures to strengthen the international institutional framework was vindicated by the course of events. The United States recession was short-lived, and the economy had regained its momentum even before the added stimulation of the Korean boom took effect. The pockets of unemployment in member countries vanished as well, and the Soviet announcement of a new and worse capitalist depression turned out, once more, to be premature.

Consideration of Employment and Stability Problems Since 1950

In the consideration of full employment and economic stability problems by organs of the United Nations, a high-water mark was registered in 1950 in terms of comprehensiveness of proposals considered, eminence of the group that put forward the proposals, and level of the debate concerning them. In the end, governments rejected the specific innovations that were suggested, but enlarged the area of consultation and raised their sights in the process.

The discussions during 1950 were based on a report prepared by five distinguished economists appointed by the United Nations Secretary-General pursuant to a resolution adopted by the Economic and Social Council during the preceding summer.[26] This report, which was entitled *National and International Measures for Full Employment*, soon became known as the Kaldor Report. Its recommendations were discussed with more than customary frankness in the United Nations because of the absence of delegates from states in the Soviet bloc, which were protesting the continued recognition of the National Government of

---

of the Economic and Social Council. In his statement on the World Economic Situation, he included data on total United States production as well as industrial production and on exports and aid as well as imports. See United States Mission to the United Nations, Press Release No. 812 (Feb. 21, 1950), p. 4.

[26] Res. 221E(IX), Aug. 11, 1949. The five economists were: John Maurice Clark, Professor of Economics at Columbia University, who worked in association with Arthur Smithies, Professor of Economics at Harvard; Nicholas Kaldor, Fellow of King's College, Cambridge; Pierre Uri, Economic and Financial Adviser to the *Commissariat Général du Plan*, Paris; and E. Ronald Walker, Economic Adviser to the Australian Department of External Affairs.

China. This made it feasible for representatives of the free nations to air differences of view that they would have been reluctant to expose to Soviet exploitation. Moreover, these representatives at the 1950 sessions of the Economic and Employment Commission and the Economic and Social Council were themselves more competent in the field of economics than their colleagues at other sessions. The Soviet boycott of the United Nations had ended, however, when the Economic and Social Council held its debates on full-employment during the years 1951–54. For this and other reasons brought out later, the debates of the Council on the subject never resulted in the systematic international review of national policies and programs for which a groundwork had been established in 1950.

After the rejection of the bold recommendations of the Kaldor Report, alternative measures for cushioning the international impact of recessions were proposed, and the report of a second group of experts was published in late 1951. This second report, which was entitled *Measures for International Economic Stability*, became known as the Angell Report and was considered by the Economic and Social Council in 1952.[27] The report proposed international action to complete a series of long-term commodity agreements, to enlarge the flow of international capital, and to increase the monetary reserves of countries other than the United States.

The recommendation for renewed efforts to negotiate multilateral commodity agreements coincided with the collapse of the post-Korean boom in raw material prices and precipitated a comprehensive discussion of general commodity problems. The quest for greater stability in primary commodity trade continued to occupy a prominent place on the international agenda from 1952 on, but the problem remains unsolved.

National and International Measures for Full Employment

The authors of the Kaldor Report painted with broad strokes and avoided qualifying details. They placed primary reliance on quantita-

[27] U.N. Department of Economic Affairs, *Measures for International Economic Stability*, Report by a Group of Experts Appointed by the Secretary-General, Doc. E/2156, ST/ECA/13 (Nov. 27, 1951). (Hereafter cited as *Measures for Economic Stability*.) The experts were: James W. Angell of Columbia University; G. D. A. MacDougall of Oxford University; Javier Marquez, Alternate Executive Director, International Monetary Fund, and formerly Professor at the National School of Economics, Mexico; Hla Myint, of Oxford University, and formerly of the University of Rangoon; Trevor W. Swan, Australian National University.

tive indicators. Their great fear was that action to correct unemployment would be delayed disastrously if it were not triggered automatically. Their aim, accordingly, was to identify the signals for automatic corrective action and the type of action to follow once the alarms were sounded. They were far more concrete regarding measures to avoid deflation than they were regarding measures to avoid inflation. The effect of their recommendations was to place on the United States chief responsibility for the maintenance and underwriting of stability.

The experts included recommendations for domestic and for international action, with primary emphasis on the former. As a first line of defense against unemployment, they recommended that each government establish and announce a full-employment target and a program to maintain employment at the target level. The second line of defense was to be a set of automatic countermeasures for application if the maintenance program failed. The third was an elaborate international scheme to sustain foreign trade and investment if the domestic countermeasures did not succeed in doing so.

It was urged that in industrialized countries the full-employment target be stated in terms of the smallest percentage of unemployment among wage-earners that the country could reasonably hope to maintain in the light of seasonal movements and structural changes in the economy. If the full-employment program of a government failed to prevent unemployment from exceeding the target percentage by a predetermined amount for three successive months, compensatory measures should be applied automatically. The measures should be capable of raising effective demand promptly and throughout the economy. The case the experts made for automatic action was that government officials would otherwise wait too long and do too little. Furthermore, the guarantee of countermeasures would promote confidence, which, in turn, would contribute to stability.

The international recommendations of the experts were conceptually more novel. They were designed to eliminate the "structural disequilibrium in world trade"; to establish a stable flow of international investment to underdeveloped countries; and to stabilize the flow of international trade.

The Kaldor Report did not explain what it meant by the establishment of a new equilibrium in world trade. What it advocated was a more orderly arrangement, through international meetings of an Expert Advisory Commission under the Economic and Social Council, for harmonizing the import and export, and the lending and borrowing, plans of governments. Deficit countries (*i.e.*, countries that were unable to finance imports from export earnings) would declare the amounts by which they desired to raise their earnings from exports or reduce their expenditures for imports. Surplus countries (*e.g.*, the United States, which was then enjoying a substantial excess of exports over imports) would declare the amounts by which they would raise their disbursements for imports, the extent to which they would curtail their exports, and the amount of long-term lending they would undertake. By an undefined process of mutual adjustment, a new balance at a high level of trade would be negotiated.

The program for stabilizing the flow of long-term lending would require the lending countries to fix annual targets for their long-term international investments for five years ahead. Shortfalls on the part of private investors would be offset by contributions of public funds. Unless loaned directly by governments, those public funds would be placed at the disposal of the International Bank. The Bank would set up a new department for lending them to underdeveloped countries.

International trade would be stabilized in somewhat similar fashion. If, in any given year, the imports of a particular country fell because of a decline in effective demand within its borders, and this fall were not fully offset by a decline in the value of its current exports of goods and services, it would deposit with the International Monetary Fund an amount equal to the fall in its imports less the fall in its exports in the given year as compared with a reference year, which would normally be the preceding year. The Fund would lend these deposits to the affected countries in appropriate amounts so that the latter would not be forced willy-nilly to curtail their imports. This would prevent the cumulative contraction that occurs when country A, because of failure to maintain full employment at home, reduces its imports, thereby reducing the export earnings of countries B, C, and D, which might in turn be forced to contract their own imports and thus add to the difficulties of country A.

The Economic and Employment Commission, meeting only a month after publication of the Kaldor Report, reviewed it in a preliminary way and, without making substantive recommendations to the Economic and Social Council, posed a number of searching questions. The Council, at its tenth session in February–March 1950, heard some additional comments and urged governments to study the report further so that they would be ready to express their considered views at the eleventh session in the summer of 1950. By that time, the Council had before it a 225-page report from the ILO, which was designed to complement the Kaldor Report.[28] Whereas the recommendations of the Kaldor Report dealt mainly with measures to stimulate effective demand, the ILO report reminded the Council that "full employment is likely to intensify certain economic problems, notably how to maintain flexibility and efficiency in production and how to avoid inflation."[29] It also included advice on the reduction of seasonal unemployment, the transfer of workers to new jobs, and the special employment problems of underdeveloped countries.

The proposals of the Kaldor Report were hotly debated from the point of view of technical adequacy, economic desirability, and political feasibility. Among the major issues raised were the following:

1. Automaticity versus discretion. Is it possible to rely on formulae to the extent that the experts did? Is the advantage of a precisely formulated series of commitments regarding steps to be taken illusory and, in the words of a leading American economist, likely to be offset by the disadvantage of "substantial uncertainty as to the economic consequences of these steps in relation to the fundamental objective of preventing serious unemployment"?[30]

2. Freedom versus controls. Would the network of regulations required to implement the plan of the experts discourage initiative and sacrifice important freedoms? Would countries make adequate efforts to export if trade deficits were covered semi-automatically? Would countries in need of foreign investment try to attract private funds if the governments of creditor nations were committed to make up with public funds any shortfalls in private foreign investment?

3. Relationship between full employment and other United Nations objectives. The United Nations Charter grouped three related objectives: "higher standards of living, full employment, and conditions of economic and social progress and development."[31] Did the experts give primacy to full employment to the detriment of other objectives, such as economic expansion, economic efficiency, and the establishment of a multilateral trading system? Was too little attention given to the dangers of inflation, particularly suppressed inflation, and to the relations between wages, prices, and profits?

4. Allocation of responsibility to the United States and the rest of

[28] International Labour Organisation, *Action Against Unemployment*, Studies and Reports, New Series, No. 20 (1950).

[29] *Ibid.*, p. 3.

[30] Jacob Viner, "Full Employment at Whatever Cost," *Quarterly Journal of Economics*, Vol. 64 (August 1950), p. 395.

[31] Art. 55(a).

the world. Was solution of the dollar problem primarily the job of the United States? Was it realistic to expect the United States, if it proved unable to stabilize its own economy, nevertheless to provide other countries with the sizable sums they might in more prosperous years have earned from sales to the United States?

The representatives of the United States, the United Kingdom, and Canada were most prominent in the debates. Important roles were played also by the representatives of Denmark and France; by the representative of Australia who had served as one of the five experts; by another of the experts, Nicholas Kaldor, who, although lacking any authorization to speak on behalf of the experts as a group, was invited by the Council to participate in a personal capacity; and by representatives of the Bank and the Fund. The underdeveloped countries, some of which had also discussed the experts' report at the Economic Commission for Latin America, considered the key recommendations inapplicable to them, and this point was conceded by the United States, the United Kingdom, and Canada.

In so far as recommendations for domestic action were concerned, the United Kingdom delegation fully accepted the report of the experts. The representatives of the British Labour Government declared that: "The maintenance of full employment was not just a desirable aim; it was the cornerstone of its [Britain's] whole economic policy, a top priority objective which it must achieve by every means consistent with the preservation of the country's freedoms."[32]

The Canadians were more cautious, on both philosophic and technical grounds. They said they were unwilling to overemphasize full employment at the expense of stability and other objectives of the Charter. Moreover, they could not accept the recommendation for establishing a maximum percentage of unemployment as the triggering device for a host of compensatory measures because they could not put it into effect. In similar vein, the Danish representative suggested that the experts might advantageously have paid greater attention to the pursuit of full employment as a means of securing maximum production and income rather than as a goal in itself. In his opinion, the strong influence of Keynes had led the experts to overemphasize the need for expansion and confine themselves too exclusively to the negative question of how to avoid unemployment. He praised the ILO report for having placed greater stress than did the United Nations experts

[32] U.N. Economic and Social Council, Eleventh Session, *Official Records*, 390th Meeting (July 17, 1950), p. 113.

on the profit expectation and, therefore, on wage-price relationships as a main factor in determining private investment. He stated that he had received the impression that the experts at times had been less concerned with correcting the disequilibrium of which unemployment was a symptom "than with the suppression of that symptom alone, and indeed in such a manner that real adjustment of the underlying factors or of the structure of production was unlikely to take place."[33]

The mechanical nature of the proposed compensatory arrangement was criticized by the United States on the ground that every economic crisis has its own characteristics. "In . . . a complex economy, where unemployment can arise from a multiplicity of causes, simple mechanical devices, however ingenious, are not likely to do the job. Rather than solve the problem by a formula, we propose to place our major reliance upon the preparation of a variety of programs for adoption in appropriate combination in the case of threatening recession or depression."[34]

Although official representatives of the Soviet nations were not present during the 1950 discussions, their viewpoint was expressed by the representative of the World Federation of Trade Unions. According to the WFTU, the Charter required the United Nations to promote full employment, meaning zero unemployment. Therefore, when the experts recognized an unemployment rate of some 2 to 5 per cent of the labor force as a reasonable minimum, they were in effect advocating a violation of the Charter. The problem of full employment, according to the WFTU, had been solved only "in the Soviet Union and the people's democracies, where the harmonious development of planned economy was accompanied by a constant rise in income, productivity, and employment."[35] In stark contrast to this idyllic condition stood the worsening situation under capitalism.

This was the line consistently taken by delegates of the Soviet bloc in United Nations discussions of full employment and economic stability, and it was one of the reasons later discussions proved so frustrating.

The international measures proposed by the experts, involving novel

[33] U.N. Economic and Social Council, Tenth Session, *Official Records*, 357th Meeting (Feb. 20, 1950), pp. 85–86.
[34] Statement by United States Representative on the U.N. Experts Report on Full Employment, U.S. Delegation, U.N. Economic and Social Council, Eleventh Session, Press Release No. 2 (July 17, 1950), p. 11.
[35] U.N. Economic and Social Council, Eleventh Session, *Official Records*, 391st Meeting (July 18, 1950), p. 143.

and intricate arrangements for stabilizing the flow of investment and trade, were also vigorously debated. By stressing technical difficulties in implementing these proposals, speakers kept the debate on a high, nonpartisan plane. Equally apparent, however, was the fact that the nations on which the main financial burdens would fall (primarily the United States) were not prepared to underwrite what seemed to them questionable and costly schemes for maintaining international stability.

By far the most important feature of the international program advocated by the experts was the proposal for stabilizing the flow of international trade. The United States delegation said it was unable to accept the proposal that countries suffering depression be obliged automatically to deposit with the International Monetary Fund currency to which others would have automatic drawing rights. In its view, there was no simple method by which the Fund would be able to determine to what extent a reduction in imports in any one country was the result of a decline in effective demand and to what extent it might be due to changes in technology, inappropriate exchange rates, or restrictive policies abroad. Early introduction of a trade stabilization plan might merely aggravate the existing disequilibrium by enabling deficit countries with inconvertible currencies to continue to import goods without making the readjustments necessary for balancing their economies and trading levels. Even the Australian Government, the delegate of which to the Economic and Social Council had served as one of the experts, found that the particular scheme he had helped to draft raised "a number of practical difficulties."[36]

The United Kingdom preferred measures whereby a country suffering from a fall in effective demand would take special steps to stimulate imports, thus maintaining employment levels in the export industries of other countries. However, it was prepared to support a scheme along the lines of the experts' proposal whereby the depression country would enable other countries to maintain their imports despite declines in their export earnings.

The proposal for stabilizing foreign lending by stepping up the public contribution to offset any decline in private lending ran into numerous objections from potential lenders, although it was naturally approved by the underdeveloped countries. The remaining international recommendation of the experts was for the creation of an advisory commission to establish a new structural equilibrium in world trade. This recommendation came at a moment when the Council was determined to

[36] *Ibid.*, p. 137.

reduce and consolidate its subsidiary structure, and neither among the underdeveloped countries nor among the industrialized nations was there active support for the proposed commission.[37]

In the lengthy, four-part resolution finally adopted by the Council, earlier American-British-Canadian differences were compromised, and none of the rigidity of the recommendations of the experts was incorporated.[38] The first two parts of the resolution, dealing with domestic full-employment standards, however, broke new ground in formalizing the obligations of Member governments to subject their domestic policies to international scrutiny. An American proposal for the annual consideration by the Council of the problem of achieving and maintaining full employment and balance-of-payments equilibrium was adopted, effective in 1951. Each government was urged: (1) to publish annually a statement of its economic objectives, accompanied wherever practicable, by a statement of quantitative goals or forecasts relating to employment, production, consumption, investment, and other pertinent measurable, economic factors; (2) to publish its full-employment standard; (3) to formulate, announce, and periodically review the policies, programs, and techniques that it intended to pursue for the purpose of achieving its objectives. The Secretary-General was asked to obtain by questionnaire full information concerning the above matters, and to assemble and analyze the information for the consideration of the Economic, Employment and Development Commission and the Council. The International Labour Organisation was encouraged to continue its efforts to facilitate international comparability of employment and unemployment data.

The international provisions in the third and fourth parts of the resolution included a series of general exhortations to governments to achieve and maintain equilibrium in their balances of payments, at high levels of trade and investment, and with minimum restrictions; to avoid actions adversely affecting the economies of other countries; to provide statistical information to the Secretary-General; to co-operate in investigating ways and means of preventing domestic recessions from

[37] At its eleventh session, the Economic and Social Council abolished the Subcommission on Employment and Economic Stability and the Subcommission on Economic Development, and renamed the Economic and Employment Commission the Economic, Employment and Development Commission. Res. 295(XI), Aug. 12 and 16, 1950.

[38] At the outset of the discussion at the eleventh session of the Council, separate draft full-employment resolutions had been introduced by the representatives of the United States, the United Kingdom, and Canada. Res. 290(XI), adopted Aug. 15, 1950, borrowed from all three drafts.

spreading internationally; and to facilitate migration and the international mobility of labor. At the same time, the International Bank was urged to achieve and maintain a high and stable rate of lending in ordinary circumstances and, if possible, to expand the volume of its lending in periods of recession. The International Monetary Fund was urged to make its resources available to members to meet needs arising from economic recessions "as fully and readily as its Articles of Agreement permit."

These two parts of the resolution also opened employment opportunities for three new groups of "independent experts": one to prepare a special report on unemployment and underemployment in under-developed countries; another to analyze government replies to a special balance-of-payments questionnaire called for in the resolution but, by later action of the Council, postponed indefinitely; and a third to formulate and analyze "alternative practical ways of dealing with the problem of reducing the international impact of recessions."[39]

The resolution adopted by the Council in 1950 was believed at the time to represent a significant step toward fulfillment of the full-employment pledge in Article 55 of the Charter. The Secretary-General was accordingly asked to give wide publicity to this resolution. It should be noted, however, that the chief obligation that it placed on Members was the obligation to provide information for review and comment by the Secretariat, by independent experts, and by delegates of other governments. The success of the exercise would depend both on the degree to which nations filed meaningful data and on the degree to which common standards of value, common objectives, and homogeneity of outlook in other respects were shared by the parties engaged in the collective review.

Measures for International Economic Stability

The 1950 resolution on full employment provided no real guidance for the new group of experts commissioned to devise alternative practical measures for cushioning the international impact of domestic recessions. An amendment to that resolution adopted at the twelfth session of the Economic and Social Council proved no remedy for this deficiency. It asked the new group to include in its report recommendations for establishing and maintaining "appropriate relations between

[39] Res. 290(XI), Aug. 15, 1950, para. 19.

prices of raw materials, on the one hand, and essential manufactured goods on the other, and thus to ensure greater economic stability."[40] This reflected the deep concern of underdeveloped countries on account of declining raw material prices, their desire for an international parity scheme, and their growing power in United Nations forums. In view of the known opposition of industrialized countries to any parity scheme, however, the amendment could hardly be regarded as pointing the way to feasible and acceptable methods for mitigating the international impact of recessions.

Although the new report—the Angell Report—which was published in late 1951, was favorably received by many who were sharply critical of the Kaldor Report, its specific recommendations cannot be said to have fared with notably greater success. The document opened with a timely summary of the problem:

> It is now generally accepted that the major countries have both the will and the means to avoid deep and prolonged depressions. The full employment pledges embodied in the United Nations Charter, and in other national and international instruments, reflect the fact that in one decade the world has taken a long step forward in social attitudes and economic techniques. But we are still living in the shadow of the great depressions of the past. Full employment commitments cannot wipe out overnight the ingrained distrust of dependence upon a many-sided international system, and do not themselves create the complex institutional and economic framework which such a system requires for its working.[41]

The experts recommended international action of three types: the negotiation of multilateral long-term commodity agreements; an expansion of the flow of international capital; and an increase in the monetary reserves of countries other than the United States. Their recommendations in the financial field indicate that the experts shared the dissatisfaction of the Kaldor group with the roles that the Bank and the Fund were then playing, but were less concerned than their predecessors with ensuring absolute stability in the flow of international payments.

As summarized by the Angell Report, the upshot of the recommendations of the Kaldor Report on foreign investment and trade would have been to ensure the availability of a steady flow of foreign exchange on both current account and long-term capital account, the former being protected by supplementary deposits against recessions of effective demand that would reduce the flow of foreign exchange

---

[40] Res. 341A(XII), Mar. 20, 1951, para. 5.
[41] *Measures for Economic Stability*, para. 1.

below its previous annual peak, and the latter against fluctuations within five-year periods. The Angell group were convinced that some new international provisions working in this general direction were essential.[42]

With respect to the flow of long-term capital, the experts provided fresh support for the advocates of low-interest loans and grants, by stating that a strong case could be made for loans to some of the under-developed countries on especially easy terms as well as for grants. Rigid stabilization of the total flow of long-term capital, however, was neither practicable nor desirable. Nevertheless, the International Bank should be prepared to expand greatly its rate of lending in the event of recession. To be able to do so and to help, as recommended by the experts, in financing buffer stocks set up pursuant to international commodity agreements, the International Bank would need a more reliable source of loan funds than the private investment community. To this end, the experts suggested: (1) increasing, above the 20 per cent authorized by its Articles of Agreement, the portion of the subscribed capital of the Bank actually available for making loans; (2) increasing the total capital itself; or (3) setting up arrangements under which governments or central banks could purchase the securities of the Bank if the need arose. Effective use of the additional capital would, of course, require projects that could be initiated or expanded at the onset of recession. The Bank, it will be recalled, consistently shunned the role of anticyclical safeguard and maintained that it had no business deferring the financing of desirable projects in prosperity in order to execute them in adversity.[43]

The proposal in the Angell Report for helping countries overcome temporary declines in foreign trade earnings,

. . . unlike the scheme recommended in *National and International Measures for Full Employment,* is basically the equivalent of a once-for-all increase in its members' foreign exchange reserves, which can do no more than enable them to smooth out temporary fluctuations in the availability of foreign exchange. It cannot repeatedly make good the full losses of recession years, and so will not permit any country's payments for imports to exceed in the long run its actual exchange earnings on current and capital account. . . .[44]

The group analyzed in a stimulating and constructive manner the need for reserves in terms of current trade levels and probable swings.

[42] *Ibid.*, paras. 20 and 21.
[43] See above, Chap. IV.
[44] *Measures for Economic Stability*, para. 36.

It concluded that in 1951 the gold and dollar reserves of most countries, together with the "comparatively trivial" supplements available through the International Monetary Fund, were totally inadequate to meet the kind of decline in dollar earnings that could occur during a recession in the United States. Price rises since the creation of the Fund had greatly diminished the real value of its resources. Access to those resources in the event of recession should be greatly liberalized, especially by waiving the rule limiting annual drawings to 25 per cent of the quota of a member, and the resources themselves should be increased. Practical, *i.e.*, political, difficulties might prevent an over-all increase in Fund subscriptions, in which case the Fund ought to be able to rely on borrowing from the country experiencing the major recession, *e.g.*, the United States.

That country might well take a liberal view of lending its currency to the Fund as a means of preventing unemployment in its export industries, of reducing the need for other countries to take new discriminatory measures against its exports, and of giving effect to the spirit of its international full employment commitments.[45]

In 1952, during consideration of the Angell Report by the Economic and Social Council, there was a large measure of agreement that existing monetary reserves were seriously inadequate. There was agreement that a larger volume of resources and a greater willingness on the part of both governments and the International Monetary Fund to use them freely could help offset the international repercussions of recessions. But the United States, for example, pointed out that the mere availability of additional resources offered no guarantee that a disequilibrium would be corrected. "In the absence of domestic monetary and international trade policies designed to correct the disequilibrium, such additional resources could be very rapidly dissipated."[46] The representative of the Fund reported that the existing resources of the IMF, if regarded as secondary reserves, were not small; that the question of increasing government quotas had been considered but was regarded as premature; and that the Fund believed it could operate with sufficient flexibility to be helpful in a depression with no change in its Articles of Agreement.

Although it is doubtful whether the view presented by the Fund

[45] *Ibid.*, para. 34.
[46] Statement by U.S. Representative in the Economic and Social Council on Agenda Item 4—Report of the Experts on International Stability, U.S. Mission to the United Nations, Press Release No. 1508 (June 30, 1952).

representative was widely shared, the resolution of the Economic and Social Council on the Angell Report,[47] in so far as the Fund and the Bank were concerned, was not essentially different from what the Council had already recommended two years earlier, following its discussion of the Kaldor Report. The Fund was urged to apply its rules flexibly, to give careful consideration to the suggestions made in the Angell Report, to use its resources as promptly and fully as consistent with its Articles of Agreement, to keep under continuing review the question of adequacy of reserves, and to furnish the Economic and Social Council an analysis of this question in 1953.

Although the preamble of the 1952 resolution seemed to support the case for stronger international facilities to mitigate the repercussions of depression, the operative portions foreshadowed no early strengthening. The net effect, therefore, of United Nations consideration of the second report by experts was to leave countries as dependent as before on domestic resources and nationally devised safeguards against depression.

Annual Full-Employment Review

The annual full-employment review, regarded in 1950 as perhaps the most constructive provision of the resolution of the Council on full-employment, appears to have had very little direct influence on policy making at the national or international level. Since 1954, full employment has been dropped as a separate item on the agenda of the Council, although the secretariat has continued to collect information on the subject by questionnaire and to use the replies both for circulation to other governments and for preparation of the annual *World Economic Report*.

During the period 1951 to 1954, the full-employment questionnaire required the submission of narrative as well as statistical information in forms not easy to summarize and evaluate. Governments were slow to respond and on the ground that statements of economic objectives, summaries of plans for preventing undue increases in unemployment, and explanations of inflationary pressures do not change significantly from year to year, merely referred in later years to their early replies to certain questions. The Secretariat's analysis was seldom available soon enough to be of use during the full-employment debate in the Council. The debate took place at the height of the cold war in a public,

[47] Res. 427(XIV), July 10, 1952.

political forum. A similar annual economic review undertaken outside the United Nations framework by a more homogeneous group of nations—the member countries of the Organization for European Economic Cooperation—has been much more fruitful.

At the Economic and Social Council, delegates from the Soviet bloc consistently used the full-employment discussion to exaggerate grossly the levels of unemployment in free-world nations; to predict further worsening of the situation, culminating in collapse at an early date; to charge that rearmament represented a vain attempt to stave off inevitable depression; and to attack, as causes of instability, unemployment, and lower standards of living, the export controls adopted by the West for security reasons. In this atmosphere, hindsight proved as hard to exercise as foresight, and other delegates found themselves fully occupied setting the record straight or redressing it in their favor. They stressed auspicious developments within their domestic economies, minimized weaknesses, and publicized the current economic difficulties of nations in the Soviet bloc. There was no systematic and sympathetic review of the employment problems of different Member governments; no effort to ascertain, through orderly discussion, the pros and cons of alternative solutions; no serious attempt, within the United Nations, to synchronize national employment policies.

To date, the United Kingdom remains the only nation having a specific full-employment standard in strict accord with the recommendations of the Council in 1950. A number of other industrialized nations have fulfilled the recommendation in spirit, if not in letter, but almost certainly in response to domestic rather than international pressures. The United States, for example, explained that although it could fix no definite and unalterable percentage of the labor force as its maximum unemployment level, it made (up to and including 1953) annual announcements of employment goals that served as guides for economic policy. Australia, Canada, Belgium, Denmark, France, New Zealand, and Sweden also advised the Secretariat that they had not adopted fixed, quantitative, full-employment standards, in some cases because of the manner in which their external payments situation had conditioned their ability to maintain high levels of employment at home.

In 1953, the non-Communist, pro-Western International Confederation of Free Trade Unions (ICFTU), fearful that reductions in rearmament expenditures might result in unnecessary unemployment and hardship, asked the Council to give special consideration to "reconversion after the rearmament period." The ICFTU fears were echoed by many delegates to the Council, and there was some sentiment for discussing reconversion policies as a special aspect of the full-employment problem. The United States and the United Kingdom, however, viewed the reconversion problem as basically no different from the problems caused by changes in demand in other sectors of the economy. Consequently, the techniques available for maintaining employment at high levels could be used in the event of reconversion difficulties in the same manner as in the event of difficulties arising from other causes. This view was ultimately accepted by the Council.[48]

In 1953, at the same time that the specter of deflation was being raised by the ICFTU, the Swedish Government was reviving a plea made a year earlier that the Council consider concrete measures for dealing with the inflationary threat implicit in full-employment programs. Sweden had proposed the appointment of a committee of experts to make recommendations for national and international measures designed to reconcile the attainment and maintenance of full employment with the avoidance of inflation. The Council, in 1952, had preferred to turn the job over to the Secretary-General,[49] who presented the 1953 session with an inconclusive paper. The Council then decided to solicit further information from governments.[50] No new measures have been proposed although over the course of the years, the United Nations in its global and regional surveys, country studies, and quarterly bulletins has circulated a number of analyses of inflation. The maintenance of full employment admittedly carries risks of inflation and the techniques for eliminating these risks have not been mastered.

From the foregoing review of the full-employment discussions in the Economic and Social Council after 1950, it is clear that the delegates ranged over a wide field without coming firmly to grips with the problems touched upon. Conscious of this deficiency and of "the need for more constructive discussion of important questions," the Council decided, in 1954, to eliminate full employment as a separate agenda item and to discuss it as part of the regular review of the world economic situation. The United Nations Secretary-General, "assisted by appropriate officials of the Secretariat, including the executive secretaries of the regional economic commissions," has been made responsible for introducing the discussion of the world economic situation. The execu-

[48] See Res. 483B(XVI), Aug. 4, 1953, and Res. 531B(XVIII), Aug. 4, 1954.
[49] Res. 426B(XIV), July 10, 1952.
[50] Res. 483A(XVI), Aug. 4, 1953.

tive heads of the interested specialized agencies have been invited to participate actively.[51] These procedural modifications are serving at least to start the discussion on a higher plane, but it remains to be seen whether they will succeed in making the discussion as a whole more rewarding.

International Commodity Arrangements

The drastic decline in the prices of raw materials during 1951, after their sharp rise following the outbreak of the Korean war, intensified the long-standing desires of most Members of the United Nations for assurances of greater stability in primary commodity trade. This limited objective assumed increased importance as more ambitious schemes for stabilizing total international trade, for increasing monetary reserves through planned international transfers, or for greatly expanding the flow of investment funds were rejected one by one. The high priority assigned to the regulation of the prices of essential goods moving in international trade at equitable levels and relationships was manifested in two principal ways. One was the multiplication of studies and reports on international price relationships. The other was a growing emphasis on the price objectives of intergovernmental commodity agreements.

Before the post-Korean price rise, the primary impetus for the negotiation of commodity agreements had been the fear that burdensome surpluses would develop, and it was to deal with this problem that provision was made for commodity "control" agreements in the Havana Charter for an International Trade Organization. As early as March 1947, the Economic and Social Council had endorsed the principle that such agreements were justified only when a burdensome surplus had developed or was expected to develop, by recommending to governments that they be guided by the principles and objectives of this part of the draft Havana Charter.[52] The first suggestions by a United Nations agency that these principles should be modified were made on procedural rather than substantive grounds. In its review of international commodity problems for 1949, the Interim Coordinating Committee on International Commodity Arrangements (ICCICA) reached the conclusion that in some cases it would not be either necessary or desirable to delay discussion about the basis for an agreement until the

[51] Res. 557B(XVIII), Aug. 5, 1954.
[52] See above, Chap. III.

stage when burdensome surpluses were present.[53] Its chairman consequently urged the Council to lay down procedures under which the committee might convene commodity conferences without undue delay. This suggestion was, with a minor modification limiting the initiative of the committee, adopted by the Council in August 1950.[54]

These principles were again recommended as a guide to governments in a resolution approved by the Council in September 1951, but by that time a change was in the making.[55] The authors of the Angell Report, as noted earlier, had had their terms of reference modified by the Council in 1951 to include the preparation of recommendations

> . . . concerning the appropriate national and international measures required to mitigate the vulnerability of the economies of underdeveloped countries to fluctuations in international markets, including measures to adjust, establish, and maintain appropriate relations between prices of raw materials on the one hand, and essential manufactured goods on the other.[56]

A major portion of their report, which was submitted to the fourteenth session of the Council (May–August 1952), was devoted to proposals for international commodity arrangements. It precipitated "the first major international discussion of general commodity problems . . . held since the drafting of the Havana Charter."[57]

According to the experts, the growing belief in the likelihood of an expanding world economy had removed one fundamental obstacle to commodity agreements. They noted that when the Havana Charter was negotiated, such agreements were considered almost wholly in the context of burdensome surpluses, but felt that it was now possible to view them in quite a new light. They therefore considered the potentialities of such agreements in the general context of long-range price stabilization. The serious disadvantages of violent price fluctuations for countries dependent mainly on exports of primary commodities were analyzed sympathetically along familiar lines and, in addition, a somewhat new note was struck by a thorough examination of the problems created for industrialized countries by such fluctuations. From this, the experts concluded that the time was ripe for governments "to reconsider the case for a series of commodity arrangements of various types

[53] U.N. Interim Coordinating Committee on International Commodity Arrangements, *Review of International Commodity Problems, 1949* (1950), p. 16.
[54] Res. 296(XI), Aug. 2, 1950.
[55] Res. 373(XIII), Sept. 13, 1951.
[56] Res. 341A(XII), Mar. 20, 1951.
[57] U.N. Interim Coordinating Committee on International Commodity Arrangements, *Review of International Commodity Problems, 1952* (1953), p. 3.

as a means of keeping short-run movements of primary product prices, both upward and downward within reasonable bounds, and of helping to stabilize the international flow of currencies."[58]

This sharp break with concepts that had been vigorously advocated by the United States in the negotiation of the Havana Charter found wide support in the Council itself, in the Economic Commission for Latin America, in the FAO, in the Interim Coordinating Committee, and in the General Assembly. There were, however, some notable differences between the attitudes of the principal organs and the subordinate agencies.

The Interim Coordinating Committee for International Commodity Arrangements strongly emphasized that the difficulties envisaged in the Havana Charter might come either from a condition of surplus or from one of shortage, and that commodity agreements should aim at price stability—but not price rigidity—in both situations. It also pointed out, however, that the practical obstacles to the conclusion of commodity control agreements were such that in recent years only one—the International Wheat Agreement—had entered into force. It concluded therefore that it was "too much to expect a series of commodity agreements which might achieve a measure of price stability substantially throughout the field of primary commodities."[59]

The principal organs of the United Nations were more ambitious and less restrained in their approach to the whole question of price instability. It was, in fact, a characteristic of the economic work of the United Nations that the closer a United Nations agency was to operations and to concrete, day-to-day problems, the less inclined it was to underestimate practical difficulties and encourage extravagant hopes. The further it was removed from operations, the greater the tendency to multiply resolutions and reports analyzing a given problem in very general terms or emphasizing those aspects of special interest to a numerically strong group of Members.

The aspect of the problem that especially interested the underdeveloped countries—fluctuations in the terms of trade—was dealt with in a special report submitted by the Secretariat to the Council.[60] This

[58] *Measures for Economic Stability*, pp. 17–26, quotation from p. 25.

[59] U.N. Interim Coordinating Committee for International Commodity Arrangements, *Review of International Commodity Problems, 1952*, pp. 1, 6.

[60] U.N. Department of Economic Affairs, *Instability in Export Markets of Under-Developed Countries in Relation to their Ability to Obtain Foreign Exchange from Exports of Primary Commodities 1901–1950*, Doc. E/2047/Rev. 1, prepared in response to Res. 294 (XI), Aug. 12, 1950.

report was concerned with the long-term problem of the relation between fluctuations in the prices of primary commodities and the ability of the underdeveloped countries to obtain foreign exchange. It pointed out that the instability caused by fluctuations in raw material prices was accentuated rather than modified by the behavior of other items in the balances of payments of raw-material producing countries, and that "the interaction of these destabilizing factors produces extreme instability in the capacity of underdeveloped countries to finance imports of necessary commodities by means of their own exports, and in general to finance their economic development."[61]

This special study was completed before the major break in prices in 1951, and the underdeveloped countries, whose terms of trade were improving while it was in preparation, were not satisfied with its broad generalizations. Consequently, under pressure from these countries, the Council, in July 1952, requested that the Secretary-General prepare a new study of the relative movements of prices of various classes of goods moving in international trade.[62] This request was symptomatic of a view widely held in many countries producing raw materials—that over the years such countries had suffered not only from price instability but had also been systematically exploited by the industrialized countries through having to accept adverse terms of trade. This view had been expressed, for example, in the 1950 survey of the Economic Commission for Latin America, which included a theoretical explanation of the allegedly inevitable deterioration of the terms of trade of primary producing countries.[63] Its argument was countered in the Angell Report.[64] Although both sides of the question were thus presented in United Nations reports, the notion of exploitation of underdeveloped countries as a result of unfavorable terms of trade has persisted and demands for more favorable terms continue to be made in the Economic and Social Council and the General Assembly.

It was, in fact, in the Assembly that the concern of the underdeveloped countries with the terms of trade found its most robust expression, and that the conflict of views between them and the industrialized

---

[61] U.N. General Assembly, Sixth Session, *Official Records*, Supplement No. 1, "Annual Report of the Secretary-General on the Work of the Organization, 1 July 1950 to 30 June 1951" (1951), pp. 90–91.

[62] Res. 427(XIV), July 10, 1952.

[63] U.N. Department of Economic Affairs, *The Economic Development of Latin America and Its Principal Problems*, Economic Commission for Latin America, Doc. E.CN. 12/89/Rev. 1 (1950), pp. 8–14.

[64] *Measures for Economic Stability*, paras. 42–47.

countries was most irreconcilable. Stabilization of commodity prices was discussed as one of the principal means of financing economic development, and it was quite clear that this "means of financing" was to be provided by the industrialized countries. The general approach of a majority of the Assembly is shown by the title of a resolution adopted in 1952, namely, "Financing of Economic Development Through the Establishment of Fair and Equitable International Prices for Primary Commodities and Through the Execution of National Programmes of Integrated Economic Development."[65]

When this resolution was drafted, international price relationships had once more become approximately those prevailing before the invasion of South Korea, and the Members of the United Nations were just emerging from the shock of a major dislocation in the world price structure. Yet the terms of the resolution suggested that existing price relationships were neither just nor equitable and that the industrialized countries should revise their policies to remedy the situation. As originally proposed by Argentina in the Second Committee of the Assembly, the resolution made drastic suggestions for changes in these policies, in the form of a recommendation to all Member states that:

(a) Whenever governments adopt measures affecting the price of primary commodities entering international trade, they should duly consider the effect of such measures on the terms of trade of countries in the process of development in order to ensure that the prices of primary commodities *remain* in an adequate, just and equitable relation to the prices of capital goods and other manufactured articles so as to permit the more satisfactory formation of domestic savings in the countries in process of development and to facilitate the establishment of just wage levels for the working population of these countries with a view to reducing the existing disparity between their standards of living and those in the highly industrialized countries;

(b) Their governments should refrain, unless unavoidably required by national security in times of war and without prejudice to technological research and progress, from encouraging the production of any synthetic or substitute materials that unnecessarily affect the international demand for natural primary commodities;

(c) Their governments should intensify their efforts to reduce restrictions on imports of primary commodities.[66]

The first two of these proposed recommendations were strongly opposed by the industrialized countries. The second did not command the solid support of the underdeveloped countries and was replaced in

[65] Res. 623(VII), Dec. 21, 1952.
[66] U.N. Department of Public Information, *Yearbook of the United Nations, 1952* (1953), p. 374. Italics added.

committee by an Indian amendment for further study of the synthetics problem. All the underdeveloped countries, however, supported the first recommendation, which was the heart of the resolution, and all attempts by the industrialized countries to amend it were voted down. Indeed, the only amendment accepted was an inconsequential one replacing the word "remain" by the phrase "are kept."

The grounds on which the strong opposition of the industrialized countries was based have been summarized as follows:

... (1) that a system of international parity prices such as that implied in the draft could not be instituted unless foreign trade were controlled by the State; (2) that such a system would make the economic structure more rigid and would not be conducive to increased productivity; (3) that there were no objective criteria for determining an "adequate, just and equitable" relationship between prices of primary commodities and those of capital and other manufactured goods; and (4) that it would be better to deal with the problem through individual commodity agreements as the need arose.[67]

As finally passed by the General Assembly, the resolution did contain a recommendation on commodity agreements, which was the result of several amendments by underdeveloped countries, but it bore little resemblance to the proposals of the Havana Charter and was closely tied in with the main price objectives of the resolution as a whole. It was recommended that governments co-operate in establishing multilateral as well as bilateral international agreements or arrangements relating to individual primary commodities as well as to groups of primary commodities and manufactured goods, for the purpose of achieving appropriate relationships. In the light of obstacles to commodity agreements but recently reported on by ICCICA, this was indeed optimistic.

The resolution also asked the Secretary-General to prepare a report on the financial repercussions that changes in the terms of trade between primary commodities and capital goods produced on the national incomes of countries in the process of development, and to appoint a small group of experts to report on practical means to ensure stable and equitable price relationships in international trade. It was characteristic of the attitude of the majority that the Secretary-General was not asked to examine the financial effects of adverse terms of trade on industrialized countries even though these countries had had to bear heavy burdens from this cause only a year and a half before.

The resolution was adopted by the General Assembly by a vote of 35

[67] *Ibid.*, p. 375.

to 15 with 9 abstentions.[68] It did not command the support of a single industrialized country and thus represented a signal failure of the United Nations in harmonizing national viewpoints on a matter of vital importance. The long struggle about commodity policy continued thereafter with some clarification and improved understanding of the separable issues that had become confused in the 1952 debates but without satisfactory reconciliation of the views of the United States, as the nation most cool to the commodity-agreement approach to stability, and its Latin American neighbors, as the nations most vocal in their advocacy of agreements.

At its fifteenth session, March–April 1953, for example, the Council recommended that the membership of ICCICA be strengthened by the addition of a person of wide experience in the problems of underdeveloped countries. This appointment was duly made, and the ICCICA continued to take part in intergovernmental commodity negotiations, which resulted in 1953 in a renewal of the International Wheat Agreement and the preparation of new agreements in tin and sugar. But the headway being made through the commodity-by-commodity approach was regarded by the underdeveloped countries as inadequate and their dissatisfaction was reflected in the decision of the General Assembly, in late December 1952, to appoint a new group of experts to report on the international measures that would be feasible to achieve stable and equitable price relationships in international trade.[69]

The report of this group of experts was submitted in November 1953.[70] Although it was a document of high quality, it received less attention from the Council and the Assembly than the Kaldor and Angell reports, in part because of its more specialized subject matter, and in part because the publication of reports prepared by outside experts for organs of the United Nations was no longer a novelty. The report stressed the benefits to be derived from greater stabilization of commodity markets and recommended a flexible "multiple approach" combining over-all stabilization policies with specific measures for individual commodities. It examined existing evidence on long-term trends

[68] U.N. General Assembly, Seventh Session, Plenary, *Official Records*, 411th Meeting (Dec. 21, 1952), p. 490.

[69] Res. 623(VII), Dec. 21, 1952.

[70] U.N. Department of Economic Affairs, *Commodity Trade and Economic Development*, Submitted by a Committee appointed by the Secretary-General, Doc. E/2519 (Nov. 25, 1953). The experts were Charles F. Carter of the Queens University, Belfast; Sumitro Djojohadikusumo of the Djakarta School of Economics, University of Indonesia; J. Goudriaan of Pretoria University; Klaus Knorr of Princeton University; and Francisco Garcia Olano, *Escuela Superior de Economica*, Buenos Aires.

in terms of trade and decided that the evidence of the past offered no help in predicting future movements of a secular character. It opposed stabilizing the terms of trade. It was forthright on the problem of synthetics and came out firmly against retarding technological progress for the sake of avoiding the pains of adjustment that inevitably attend progress. It analyzed alternative stabilizing devices, with particular sympathy for international buffer-stock arrangements.

It concluded that there was no ground for confidence that agreements for single commodities would be made in sufficient number to meet the more general demands of underdeveloped countries for stability of earnings, and that there was no effective international procedure for discussing and proposing action on the general problem of stabilization—a matter that transcended the problems of particular commodities. The experts suggested, therefore, that the Economic and Social Council establish an intergovernmental commission, advisory in nature, the main tasks of which would be to consider and make recommendations to the Council on general proposals for stabilization and, when the stability of the markets of the world appeared threatened, to make prompt recommendations to the Council for appropriate intergovernmental action.[71]

The Council at its seventeenth session decided by a vote of 12 in favor, 5 against, and 1 abstention to establish a Commission on International Commodity Trade, but postponed activating the commission until the eighteenth session (July–August 1954).[72] At that session, over the strenuous opposition of the United States and the United Kingdom, an Argentine resolution launching the commission was adopted by a vote of 12 to 3, with 3 abstentions.[73]

The main function of the new commission as set forth in its terms of reference was "to examine measures designed to avoid excessive fluctuations in the prices of and the volume of trade in primary commodities including measures aiming at a just and equitable relationship between the prices of primary commodities and the prices of manufactured goods in international trade, and to make recommendations."[74] The commission was to maintain relations with all international organizations having anything to do with international trade. Inasmuch as there

[71] Ibid., pp. 81–84.

[72] Res. 512A(XVII), Apr. 30, 1954. U.N. Economic and Social Council, Seventeenth Session, Official Records, 791st Meeting (Apr. 30, 1954), p. 234. In opposition were Belgium, France, Norway, the United States, and the United Kingdom. Australia abstained.

[73] Res. 557F(XVIII), Aug. 5, 1954; U.N. Economic and Social Council, Eighteenth Session, Official Records, 829th Meeting (Aug. 5, 1954), p. 257.

[74] Res. 512A(XVII), Apr. 30, 1954, and Res. 557F(XVIII), Aug. 5, 1954.

were a number of agencies having such an interest, a new problem of overlapping jurisdiction was raised for the United Nations system. This was recognized in the resolution quoted above, which instructed the commission to consult with the FAO Committee on Commodity Problems and indicated the willingness of the Economic and Social Council to take into account the views of the contracting parties to the General Agreement on Tariffs and Trade (GATT) regarding the extent to which the problem of instability in primary commodities should be dealt with under that Agreement.

Accordingly, at the 1954–55 negotiations for the revision of the GATT, a working party considered proposals for international action to overcome problems in primary commodity trade and submitted for governmental review the draft of a new International Agreement on Commodity Arrangements. The proposed agreement was intended to provide the main co-ordinating mechanism for all commodity arrangements and to be allied in appropriate fashion to the GATT. In November 1956, however, the Contracting Parties decided to abandon the project,[75] largely because skepticism concerning the value of international commodity agreements had grown more pronounced than ever in official United States circles.

Meanwhile, the Commission on International Commodity Trade of the Economic and Social Council, in which the United States has refused to participate, has held lengthy meetings and laid out a program of work. Any effort to dissolve it is likely to be strongly opposed by countries like Argentina that are not contracting parties to the GATT and that prefer to see commodity problems considered in the context of economic development instead of in the framework of commercial policy.

International action in the field of commodity arrangements has, in the words of a perceptive writer on trade problems, been "haphazard, opportunistic, and lacking in any apparent systematic framework." The major improvement in principle introduced during the postwar period, equal representation for consumers (*i.e.*, importing countries) in the negotiation of individual commodity agreements, has vastly complicated the completion of agreements but has not ensured adequate representation of the public interest. The delegations of both importing and exporting nations have commonly been dominated by wheat, sugar, and tin specialists

[75] General Agreement on Tariffs and Trade, Press Release GATT/324, Nov. 21, 1956, p. 13.

. . . skilled in the problem of producing and marketing their particular products and responsible in their respective governments for these commodities
alone. As officials whose responsibilities are confined to specific commodities,
these representatives have naturally been more concerned with rendering a
good account of developments in those commodities than with worrying about
such larger issues as the optimum use of the nation's total resources, or the
precedent-making implications of any particular arrangements. From the nature of their position, the problems of their particular commodities have had
to be considered by these officials as unique situations, entitled to any solution
which empirically seemed to fit.[76]

On the other hand, the officials at the Economic and Social Council or
General Assembly level, theoretically equipped with the necessary
breadth of view, have persistently underestimated the politico-economic
and technical difficulties that invariably arise when the discussions
move from broad principles to concrete commodity negotiations.

Surplus Disposal Problems

The absence of international arrangements to ensure greater stability in primary commodity prices increased the anxiety of United
Nations Members over the possible destabilizing effects of programs for
the disposal of agricultural surpluses—surpluses accumulated, in large
measure, as a result of domestic stabilization policies. These anxieties
related primarily to the intentions of the United States, possessor of the
most gargantuan stocks in the world.

The surplus disposal drive of the United States began to gather force
in 1953–54. Of total United States exports of agricultural commodities
amounting to $3.14 billion in 1954–55, 43 per cent, or $1.34 billion,
were aided by government programs of one kind or another.[77] All of
the sales, subsidies, grants, and barter arrangements were subject to the
principle that they would not be allowed to disrupt normal trade, but
this did not quiet the fears of other United Nations Members dependent
on the export of primary products.

These fears were expressed in various United Nations forums, no-
where more vigorously than in the address of the spokesman for
Australia before the annual meeting of the International Monetary
Fund in September 1954:

From the viewpoint of Australia and other primary producers of foodstuffs
and raw materials there is a[n] . . . immediate and dangerous threat. It is of

[76] Raymond Vernon, "Organizing for World Trade," *International Conciliation*, No.
505 (November 1955), p. 180.
[77] Interagency Committee on Agricultural Surplus Disposal, *Prospects of Foreign
Disposal of Domestic Agricultural Surpluses* (1956), pp. iii–iv.

course the growing surplus of agricultural products in the Western world, many of them stimulated by uneconomic subsidies in the large producing countries. In compiling their Annual Report the Executive Directors appear to have paid scant attention to this critical factor. Subsequently, Congress has, however, provided funds and taken other steps which revive in our minds the ugly specter of subsidized exports to other countries. No words, no lip service to the commercial interests of allied countries, however genuine and well meant, can obscure the actual threat to the livelihood of thousands of agricultural producers in other parts of the world. As one who is responsible to a great number of these producers, I say earnestly, but without rancor, that such policies may do the world a great disservice. We, in common with many others, lack the power and the long purse with which to withstand such overwhelming competition—at least within the framework of the liberal, nondiscriminatory, world trading system which it is our common purpose to attain. We cannot compete on equal terms if U.S. domestic surpluses are to be sold abroad from the bargain basement.[78]

In the Fund, delegates could do little about the surplus problem except give vent to their emotions. The FAO, however, had for several years been actively involved in the development of constructive solutions.[79] Its Committee on Commodity Problems, first established in 1949 after rejection of the proposals for an International Commodity Clearing House, proved to be a useful forum for consultation on commodity matters and in 1954 drafted a statement of FAO Principles of Surplus Disposal[80] that has been formally accepted by the United States and a majority of FAO members as a code of international behavior. The principles are necessarily general, however, and difficult to enforce.

At the request of its Committee on Commodity Problems, the FAO staff began making pilot field surveys in the underdeveloped countries likely to receive surplus supplies. A potentially important study of the manner in which surplus farm products might be used in India to finance additional development, without competing with sales of domestic Indian agriculture and without displacing the normal marketings of other nations, was published in 1955.[81] The study reported that

[78] International Monetary Fund, *Summary Proceedings of the Ninth Annual Meeting of the Board of Governors, September 1954* (1954), pp. 72–73.

[79] See above, Chaps. II and III.

[80] Food and Agriculture Organization, *Report of the Twenty-fifth Session of the FAO Committee on Commodity Problems,* Doc. C/55/22 (July 1955), App. A. The Committee also established in 1954 a Consultative Subcommittee on Surplus Disposal, which has met periodically in Washington, D.C.

[81] Food and Agriculture Organization, *Uses of Agricultural Surpluses to Finance Economic Development in Under-developed Countries—A Pilot Study in India,* Commodity Policy Studies No. 6 (June 1955).

to meet the standards for surplus disposal suggested at international conferences, surpluses should be used for financing development only if they meet two basic conditions. First, the country must already be doing all that it can without the surpluses to carry out economic development, so that the surpluses make possible additional development. Second, the new projects using the surpluses must expand domestic consumption of the surplus products to the full extent of the surpluses added to the supply. Introducing an element of specificity that had previously been lacking, the study went on to calculate the proportion of the wage payments to extra labor that could be expected to reappear as increased demand for surplus products, to examine how the rest of the cost of the additional projects might be met, and what effect that decision, in turn, would have on the consumption of surplus foods.[82]

While FAO was engaged in probing the feasibility of utilizing surplus commodities to improve nutritional standards, relieve famine, and promote economic development, the contracting parties to the GATT continued to be concerned from the viewpoint of possible harmful effects on the trade of third countries. In March 1955, at the ninth GATT session, the Contracting Parties passed a resolution recommending that countries, when disposing of surplus agricultural products, undertake to consult with the principal suppliers in other interested countries, with a view to an orderly liquidation of the surplus and the avoidance of prejudice to the interests of other countries. At the tenth session, in December 1955, a number of countries reported that the consultation procedures under the resolution had helped to reduce the disruption of international trade, but most delegations "also expressed the view that consultations had not been as effective as they would have wished."[83] The surplus disposal problem, it would appear, must be added to the list of difficult problems for which the United Nations has not yet found a satisfactory solution.

The Record in Review

The determination of every major government to attain and maintain full employment and to avoid depression became plainly apparent during the 1945–55 decade. For the achievement of these common pur-

[82] In this connection, see also Food and Agriculture Organization, *Functions of a World Food Reserve—Scope and Limitations*, FAO Commodity Policy Studies No. 10 (1956), pp. 29–41.

[83] General Agreement on Tariffs and Trade, Press Release 266 (Dec. 6, 1955), p. 15.

poses, however, the international economy remains almost wholly dependent on domestic efforts, domestic resources, and domestic stabilizers—some of which have introduced new rigidities into the economy and increased the danger that countries will either run into balance-of-payments difficulties themselves or create such difficulties for others.

The many United Nations activities of aid to specific sectors of the economy or to specific geographic areas do not add up to a co-ordinated international program for maintaining an expanding world economy or for preventing the international spread of deflationary pressures should they make their appearance in a major industrial nation. The development, through the General Agreement on Tariffs and Trade, of a code of conduct in the trade field represents an important net gain, but in most other respects international machinery for preventing the spread of unemployment has not been notably strengthened since the Bretton Woods Conference of 1944.

The experts at Bretton Woods were deceived in more than the scale of the problem. Its essential nature was not clearly foreseen. Preparation was made to cover a brief reconstruction period, mainly by loans of the [International] Bank, and then to face the deep-seated problems of development on the one hand and of recurring trade dislocation on the other. The development problems were handed to the Bank. For the cyclical crises, the [International Monetary] Fund's articles laid down certain rules: ... Provision was made for a five-year period of transition which was to elapse before the rules took effect. Thereafter, however, the long-run problem of development and the cyclical problem of temporary dislocation were regarded as separate and distinct. ... No provision was made for the contingency that the business cycles were organically related to the deep-seated developmental forces, and that most cycles would operate in the same direction.[84]

The successive groups of experts commissioned by the Economic and Social Council and the General Assembly to make proposals for strengthening the international system have recognized the relationship. Their proposals have been designed both to establish a better long-term equilibrium and to reduce the amplitude of periodic departures from the equilibrium position. Although much of their analysis of the problem has been accepted, and a number of their prescriptions for domestic action have been endorsed, their most important recommendations for international action have been rejected. The international community has not been willing to guarantee the maintenance of a given level of international trade or flow of investment funds, to

[84] Charles P. Kindleberger, "Bretton Woods Reappraised," *International Organization,* Vol. V (February 1951), pp. 34–35.

increase vastly the volume of international reserves available for meeting short-term requirements, to negotiate a series of commodity agreements to stabilize the prices of internationally traded raw materials, or to set up international machinery for disposing of surplus agricultural products without disrupting normal trade.

The United States has been instrumental in bringing about this situation. It has contributed massive sums to the reconstruction of the world economy but the contributions, for the most part, have been direct rather than through international agencies. The United States has been reluctant to entrust sizable additional resources to international management for use as antidepression insurance, especially when existing resources have not been seriously taxed. Noting the freedom of sovereign nations to pursue domestic policies that keep them in or on the verge of balance-of-payments difficulties—and the persistence of a number of countries in following such policies—the United States has suspected that the insurance might be dissipated without correcting the maladjustments for which it was intended.

Recently, the international economy has shown itself to be better disciplined, less fragile, and more resilient than many believed possible. In 1949, when the world was still quite vulnerable, a minor recession in the United States precipitated a payments crisis in a number of foreign countries. In 1953–54, during an American recession of comparable magnitude, Europe enjoyed outstanding prosperity. Fortuitous factors unquestionably played a role, but there is also no doubt that nearly all countries in 1956—at least until the Suez Canal crisis—were in a stronger position than at almost any time since the end of the Second World War.[85]

In 1954, the volume of world trade was about 65 per cent larger than prewar. At the same time, the abnormally large proportion of world exports supplied by the United States and Canada declined from 30 per cent of the total in 1948 to 25 per cent of the much larger total in 1954. The rest of the world added about $2.5 billion to its gold and dollar reserves in 1953 and $1.7 billion in 1954.[86] Commodity prices, on the average, remained relatively stable. Employment levels remained high during the first half of the 1950's, and there has consequently been little pressure on nations to "coordinate" their employment policies—

---

[85] International Monetary Fund, *International Financial News Survey* (Sept. 13, 1955), pp. 103–07.

[86] *Ibid.* In 1955, however, while foreign countries were adding another $1.7 billion to their gold and dollar reserves, British reserves declined by about $640 million.

an undertaking that is inherently much more difficult than it was assumed to be in the early postwar years.

Despite the encouraging progress toward equilibrium, the world at large is not confident of its ability to withstand the impact of fluctuations in the American economy or of the ability of the United States to maintain prosperity. The American economy, because of its sheer size, is far and away the most important single element in the world picture.

Rich in resources, immensely diversified, comparatively self-sufficient, the United States is able to take in stride shocks that would paralyze less hardy victims. It has performed remarkably well during the postwar period. It has weathered demobilization and disarmament, the Korean conflict and the rearmament build-up, and, more recently, substantial cutbacks in the defense program. Consumer demand has remained high. United States foreign trade has been concentrated more heavily than before the Second World War on Canada and Latin America with the result that Europe, comparatively speaking, has become less vulnerable to fluctuations in United States import demand. The import demand itself has grown more stable because food has become a larger element in the import total.

A battery of stabilizers has been built into the economy since 1932. These built-in stabilizers can be depended upon to retard deflation, but they are not capable of preventing a depression or reversing it once it gets under way. Positive antirecession measures would doubtless be invoked, however, regardless of the party in power.

Would they be invoked promptly enough to avoid difficulties for the more precariously balanced economies of other nations, and would other large nations likewise manage their affairs with the necessary skill and dispatch? This is the current dilemma of the United Nations system. If the major industrial nations, and above all the United States, can be trusted to maintain relatively full employment at home, the need for elaborate international antidepression safeguards will be greatly reduced. If they cannot be relied upon to protect their home fronts, they will hardly be foresighted enough to commit themselves to appropriate international defenses. But if the international community waits until the emergency is upon it to strengthen its defenses, it may find it has waited too long.

CHAPTER VI

*Transportation and Communications**

IN DEALING with economic problems of the type discussed earlier in this study, the United Nations has had to improvise machinery, to test it on unfamiliar terrain, to raise sizable sums of money, and to face many controversial political and social issues. Its work in the field of transportation and communications—confined on the whole to the provision of long-range, well-recognized, technical services through genuinely specialized agencies and organs—has proceeded more tranquilly than its other economic activities.

International co-operation to facilitate postal deliveries, weather observations, and telegraphic communication has a long history. It antedates by many years the establishment of both the League of Nations and the United Nations. Since ratification of the United Nations Charter, however, the older, world-wide, technical agencies (as well as the newer International Civil Aviation Organization) have been brought officially into the United Nations system as specialized agencies. The bulk of their work has continued to be based on reciprocal exchanges of a technical, non-controversial character, which it has not been thought necessary to analyze in detail for purposes of this study.

In one notable respect, however, intergovernmental activity in transport and communications during the postwar period has differed from work during earlier periods. Through the International Bank for Reconstruction and Development and the Expanded Programme of Technical Assistance, the United Nations and its related agencies have been able to help nations directly in planning and building the railroad lines, highways, airports, telephone systems, port improvements, and other concomitants of the higher standards of living to which the peoples of the less developed areas so ardently aspire.

In recent years, innovations in transportation and communications have greatly accelerated the pace at which men have been able to overcome barriers of space and time that during most of the world's history have kept nations apart. Further developments already on the horizon promise to make the world still smaller as aeronautical science and

* By Wilfred Owen, William Adams Brown, Jr., and Priscilla St. Denis.

telecommunications accelerate the rate of innovation and make the air, rather than earth and water, the medium through which international relations are effectuated.

Modern transport and communications also serve to promote economic development and the general welfare by making it possible in many areas of the world to use resources that until now have remained either undiscovered or that have been deemed useless because the cost of making them available has been prohibitive. Undertakings now technologically possible in these areas can bring about improved social and economic conditions by facilitating internal trade and travel and by promoting international trade and cultural relations.

Unfortunately, however, the role of transport and communications has not been confined to what is favorable to the general welfare. On the contrary, these instrumentalities have also helped to create some of the conditions leading to international friction and to provide the vehicles and weapons of international conflict. To prevent the use of these tools for warfare and to direct their use wisely in the interest of social and economic objectives, is a major challenge to international organization today.

Nature of the Problem

Adequate transportation and communication are essential ingredients of economic growth and development. The improvement of agricultural yields, for example, presupposes the means to permit effective distribution of perishables and the movement of surplus foods to areas of short supply. Utilization of mineral resources involves the ability to haul bulk materials at costs that make mining operations economically feasible. Improvements in health, education, and government operations all depend on communications and access to remote areas. The conduct of private business and trade likewise relies to an important degree on the availability of rapid and low-cost transport and communications. These objectives require the construction of all-weather roads, waterways, railroads, airways and airports, the installation of communications facilities, the provision of needed equipment, and the training of personnel. Technically and financially such objectives are difficult to meet, but they are essential first steps in the improvement of the general welfare.

In much of the world today, the isolation resulting from primitive methods of transportation and communications is a principal factor in the retarded development of areas that might otherwise be sources of substantial wealth. This is illustrated by the problem of transport modernization in Africa.

In southern Africa, railroad lines extending far into the interior carry out copper, wood, and other raw materials to the coastal ports. The financial strength of the rail system and the cost of transport out of the interior are dependent on the availability of traffic in the reverse direction, but the poverty and primitive levels of living among the interior population create little demand for the manufactured goods that might be exchanged. Vast distances, widely separate cities, and scarcity of fuel combine to create transport difficulties of great magnitude. In other parts of Africa, the large number of small autonomous political units reduces efforts to solve national transportation and communication problems to a local and un-co-ordinated basis. Finally, low levels of national income make impossible the domestic supply of capital required to develop facilities that can break the interrelation of under-development and lack of adequate transport and communication. Without substantial foreign capital, the possibilities of opening up this vast continent and applying the wealth of its forests and minerals to the improvement of levels of living seem remote.

Even in those countries that have been able to develop substantial transport services, the available facilities have frequently been geared to strategic rather than economic objectives. Railroads, for example, often provide no direct connections between economically important points, and where economic factors have influenced transport development, primary emphasis has been given to serving major heavy industries rather than agriculture. One of the reasons for the relatively slow progress of many countries has been the lack of a balanced transportation system.

The world transportation and communications setting in which the United Nations operates is predominantly one of growth and change, but is also one of startling contrast. Rising population, expanding consumer requirements, and higher levels of production in many parts of the world have been both cause and effect of a steadily increasing volume of passenger travel and goods movement both within national boundaries and internationally. Along with growth in volume, there has been a shift in the geographical patterns of transportation as a result of changing postwar political ties and shifting material sources and markets. Changes in method of movement have also altered the picture as the volume of motor transport has multiplied, and as air transport has accounted for a major share of international passenger traffic. Another factor has been the increasingly vital role of communications for both private and official purposes as radio and television have made possible a volume and excellence of communications hardly dreamed of a few years ago.

Some $75 billion of goods move annually in international trade, and the world tonnage of ocean-going vessels is 45 per cent above the prewar total. On the world's 10 million miles of highways, there are now 100 million motor vehicles, more than double the 1940 figure, and the airlines of the world are carrying 85 million passengers a year.

But the growth, change, and technical progress of transport and communications that have been so spectacular in the western world are in sharp contrast to the scientific lag typical of the less developed areas. Asia, with more than 50 per cent of the population of the world, has less than 9 per cent of the highways of the world, 22 per cent of its railway mileage, and 3 per cent of its motor vehicles. In contrast to North America, where there is one motor vehicle for every four people, in Asia there is only one motor vehicle for every 689 inhabitants. In India, the figure is one vehicle for every 1,194 people. The population of India is more than twice that of the United States; yet it operates only 90,000 trucks compared with 10 million trucks serving the United States.

In the United States, a powerful railroad locomotive is capable of hauling a ton of materials one mile with the energy from two teaspoonsful of diesel oil, but in vast areas of the world, it is still the human back along with the pack animal, the bullock cart, and the crude hand-propelled water craft, that support the commerce of nations. One modern jetliner passing overhead may utilize more power than all the mechanical energy available for transportation in vast areas of the earth below.

In these circumstances, many of the economic and social goals toward which the underdeveloped countries are working cannot be realized without substantially greater advancement than has been made to date in the provision of transport facilities. The question what the United Nations is doing to help make such facilities available has broad significance because success in this field may affect the results of other activities designed to promote the general welfare.

International machinery and agreement are necessary if international transportation or communication is to be possible. International movement and message transmission tend to be contemptuous of national boundaries, whereas national sovereignty imposes conditions that must be dealt with realistically and patiently if the possibilities of transport and communications are to be realized at all. The nature of these problems has been undergoing rapid change with advancing technology. The United Nations has been concerned with the changing character of these problems, and also with problems relating to the lack of technological progress in the underdeveloped areas and the close interrelation between the conditions of transportation and communications and the conditions of economic progress and general welfare. In many parts of the world, the United Nations has been called on to assist in developing needed facilities, domestic and international, in areas where the problem is not one of co-ordinating facilities that already exist but rather of laying the groundwork for the minimum levels of transport and communications essential to social and economic progress. The United Nations has had to face these two aspects of the problem in almost all the fields of transportation and communications.

Impact of Communications Developments

Among the international problems deriving from modern technology, those having to do with modern methods of message transmission introduce many new and challenging difficulties. Electromagnetic waves travel great distances and in doing so, cross national boundaries. There is a limit to the number of electromagnetic waves that can be received without interference, and the limited radio spectrum must be shared by all the nations of the world. Inasmuch as the medium through which these waves travel is the public domain, the rapidly growing demand for radio services must be adjusted to the limited capacity of the spectrum through common consent.

Today, the achievement of satisfactory working relations in the field of telecommunications under conditions of rapidly changing technology requires continual international adjustments. The international aspect of radio has developed to the point where "almost no major frequency allocation can be made without considering world-wide usage."[1] Foreign merchant ships entering New York harbor, for example, cannot use the same bands for radar as New Yorkers use for television, and because certain parts of the radio spectrum are best adapted to aviation radio purposes and to radiotelephone and radiotelegraph, these limited

[1] U.S. Federal Communications Commission, *Sixteenth Annual Report, Fiscal Year Ended June 30, 1950*, p. 163.

bands must be shared by all nations to preserve equity and to achieve effective use of available frequencies with a minimum of congestion. International treaties and agreements are necessary to allocate frequencies and to settle equipment and interference problems. In addition, there must be agreement on telephone and telegraph rates and other matters.

Special Problems of Aviation

In the field of aviation, the problem is essentially that each of the nations of the world has sovereign control over the air space above its territory. This principle was established before it was imagined that mechanical contrivances might travel beyond the atmosphere of the earth. International agreement may soon be needed on the use of the outer space by the nations of the world. But leaving aside this emerging problem, the principle of air sovereignty means that international flights are possible only through bargaining among nations regarding the reciprocal rights for air carriers. No world-wide agreement has been possible on the kinds of commercial air transport rights that should be exchanged multilaterally, so that a great number of bilateral agreements provide the basis on which international air traffic rests. These bilateral treaties represent varying degrees of departure from the goal of providing the world with the most efficient and low-cost air transport service.

International agreement has to be reached on many other aspects of aviation, of course, to make flying from one country to another possible. Because the air space and available airport facilities must be used jointly by the aircraft of all participating nations, there must be general agreements on types of navigation and landing aids, competence of personnel, emergency procedures, certification of aircraft, and other standards. And the desirability of preventing unfair or destructive competition has led to agreement on matters involving both service and rates.

Technical and economic problems are complicated, however, by factors that underlie the whole question of freedom of the air. Participation in air operations is not conditioned merely by the desire to provide air services, but by considerations of national security and prestige that have impelled nearly every nation to seek a place in the world air transport system regardless of economic justification. This has frequently resulted in excess capacity, duplicating services, and resort to competing subsidies to preserve uneconomic operations. The problem has been to arrive at an acceptable compromise between the goal of meeting world needs economically and the objective of respecting the rights of all nations wishing to participate in the provision of air services.

Water and Land Transport
Problems

Merchant shipping involves many of the same problems encountered in the air, for in this sphere, too, the role of commercial transportation is closely related to national defense and national prestige. The resultant dimensions of merchant marine operation by the various maritime nations frequently lead to an oversupply of shipping capacity, the intensification of competition on shipping routes of the world, and the necessity of arriving at international agreement on discriminatory practices.

Problems associated with rail, inland water, and road transport, while less spectacular, are equally vexing. In rail transport, international operations are complicated by the need for standardization of track gauge and equipment, the need for arrangements to permit the interchange of cars moving from one country to another, and the question of through routes and rates. Waterway transport requires agreement on freedom of movement and maintenance of facilities, while international road transport raises issues regarding type and size of equipment, permissible weights, payments for use of the road system, operating standards, insurance provisions, and the like. The problem of establishing international agreement on standards and procedures for road transport has encountered many obstacles stemming from the relative newness of motor transport, the many separate operating units involved, and the competitive struggle between road and rail.[2]

In all fields of transport, there is the problem of establishing rules and regulations for commercial transport, and of minimizing international barriers to the movement of people and goods through the simplification of customs and immigration formalities, visa requirements, health and police procedures, and monetary transactions.

[2] Even in the United States, without the complication of international boundaries, problems of motor transport regulation and the relation between road and rail transport have not been satisfactorily resolved. Differences in allowable loads and in methods of paying for the use of the highways of the several states through which interstate shipments pass have not been eliminated by interstate agreement. In the matters of driver licensing, rules of the road, and signs and signals, there is still little uniformity among the several states, and in matters of road design and financial policy, wide variations continue to exist.

As indicated in the foregoing discussion of the nature of the problems of international transport and communications, those created by national boundaries are not only technical and economic but are also problems affected to an important degree by political and security considerations that often overshadow other obstacles to the realization of satisfactory transportation services.

Organizational Arrangements of the United Nations

The continuity of international work initiated before the end of the Second World War in the field of transportation and communication was assured when the Preparatory Commission of the United Nations suggested that the Economic and Social Council establish a Temporary Transport and Communications Commission to advise the Council in its relations with the intergovernmental organizations already operating in the field.[3] The Temporary Commission met in 1946 and set up the framework of the future permanent Transport and Communications Commission.

The Transport and Communications Commission, which came into being the following year, is the transport advisor to the Council. Its task is to promote the study and solution of international transport and communications problems and to co-ordinate the activities of the various international organizations dealing with these matters.

The commission deals in addition, on a world-wide basis and for all means of transport, with the problems of passport and frontier formalities and barriers to the international transport of goods, and as noted below, with certain relatively minor features of international road transport and shipping relations.

Significant contributions to the study of transportation problems are made through the efforts of the United Nations to collect, standardize, and make available statistics on transportation and communications as a basis for research and policy determination. Today much more is known about the problems encountered in these areas because extensive data have been made available through international organizations.

Co-ordination of activities in various fields is provided to some extent through relations of the commission with nongovernmental organizations having consultative status in the field of transport and communica-

[3] U.N. Preparatory Commission, *Report of the Preparatory Commission of the United Nations*, Doc. PC/20 (Dec. 23, 1945), pp. 28, 38.

tions.[4] Contacts have also been maintained with certain intergovernmental organizations outside the United Nations framework, for example, the Central Office for International Transport by Rail and the Central Commission for the Navigation of the Rhine.

The commission, however, maintains its contacts with major fields (aviation, telecommunication, postal and weather services) mainly through international organizations that were already in existence before the commission was itself established. These agencies are the International Civil Aviation Organization (ICAO), the International Telecommunication Union (ITU), the Universal Postal Union (UPU), and the World Meteorological Organization (WMO), all of which have been brought into relationship with the United Nations as specialized agencies.

The United Nations has recognized the competence of each of these agencies in its own field, but whenever a problem is the concern of two or more specialized agencies, there is a need for co-ordination. This is one of the functions of the Transport and Communications Commission. In the case of safety at sea and in the air, for example, it is necessary to bring together ICAO, the ITU, the WMO, and maritime authorities. In the transportation of explosives and other dangerous goods, the organizations involved also include the International Labour Organisation (ILO), the Universal Postal Union, and a number of interested intergovernmental and nongovernmental organizations.

The scope of transport and communications problems considered by the United Nations system is indicated by the fact that four of the ten specialized agencies deal with these matters. Establishment of the Intergovernmental Maritime Consultative Organization, not yet operative, will raise the total to five. In addition, both the International Labour Organisation and the International Bank for Reconstruction and Development are active in the transport and communications field. The ILO is concerned with wages, hours, occupational hazards, and other conditions of work, and with the training of skilled personnel in the underdeveloped countries. The Bank has directed a large part of its resources to the financing of transportation facilities and has made a number of comprehensive country studies for the development of long-range transportation plans.

[4] Among the nongovernmental organizations which have made useful contributions to the work of the United Nations are the International Chamber of Commerce, International Road Federation, International Air Transport Association, International Chamber of Shipping, International Transport Workers Federation, International Union of Official Travel Organizations, and International Union of Railways.

The Transport and Communications Commission could rely on no specialized agencies, however, to deal with problems of inland transport. A survey of these problems led to the early conclusion that circumstances governing railroad, inland water, and highway transport were so different in different parts of the world that these methods of transport should be dealt with regionally. The commission, however, reserved to itself certain functions in this field.

On its initiative, a Road and Motor Transport Conference was convened at Geneva in 1949 to deal with technical matters governing road transport, including standards for driver licensing, traffic regulations, vehicle registration, and signs and signals. The conference concluded a new world-wide convention on road and motor transport, which provides for the international recognition of operators' licenses issued by any contracting state to persons over eighteen years of age who have given proof of driving competence. This action has since been followed by recommendations for minimum requirements for the licensing of motor vehicle drivers, so that all countries can ultimately have the assurance that foreign drivers on their highways have met reasonable standards of training and competence. Out of the 1949 meeting also came a study of signs and signals that may eventually lead to a single standard incorporating the best elements of existing practices.[5]

The commission also took the initiative on one other road transport problem. Although it was decided, on the one hand, that the problem of customs formalities for commercial road vehicles and for the transport of goods by road should be dealt with on a regional basis, on the other hand, problems of customs formalities for the temporary importation of private motor vehicles and their equipment and for the personal effects of tourists traveling by all methods of transport were considered to be world-wide in scope. A special United Nations conference in New York in 1954 prepared and opened for signature two conventions, one concerning customs facilities for touring and the other on the temporary importation of private road vehicles.

These were minor exceptions to the principle recommended by the commission that the problems of inland transport be dealt with through the regional commissions, and the latter were organized to discharge this function. The Economic Commission for Asia and the Far East established an Inland Transport Committee. Although some of its member countries had participated in the transportation work of the League

---

[5] H. H. Kelly and W. G. Eliot, "The Growing Structure of International Motor Traffic Agreements," U.S. Department of State *Bulletin*, Vol. 30 (Jan. 25, 1954), pp. 117–20.

of Nations, there were in this area few existing organizations operating
in this field.[6] The special function of the Inland Transport Committee
was to provide technical assistance and to plan and develop transport
facilities, rather than to co-ordinate existing facilities. The Economic
Commission for Latin America was confronted with a situation somewhat comparable to that in Asia, but there were some existing Pan-
American technical organs concerned with rail and road transport, and
the establishment of a separate transport committee under the regional
commission was not deemed necessary.

The problems to be met in Europe were rather different, and arrangements were made to deal with them through an Inland Transport Committee within the framework of the Economic Commission for Europe
(ECE).[7]

European Inland Transport

The field of inland transport has been the subject of extensive international co-operation in Europe for many years, through both governmental and commercial organizations. The idea of freedom of navigation of the international rivers was formulated as early as 1792, and by
the middle of the nineteenth century binding agreements had been
made by interested European nations. The Danube was placed under
international administration one hundred years ago, and the Rhine was
regulated by the Mannheim Convention a dozen years later. These conventions provided for freedom of navigation to vessels of all nations and
promoted uniformity of maintenance and policing of waterways. After
the First World War, commissions were established for the Danube, the
Elbe, and the Oder.[8]

International arrangements governing railroad freight transportation
were established by the Berne Convention of 1890. In 1924, this convention was revised to include passenger traffic, and further revisions have
produced the conventions in effect today. The Central Office for International Railway Transport, which was set up by the Berne Convention, has been concerned with the conditions under which goods and
passengers are carried in international railway transport and has established relations with a number of railroad organizations dealing with

[6] U.N. Economic and Social Council, Fourth Session, *Official Records*, Supplement
No. 8, "Report of the Transport and Communications Commission" (1947), pp.
56–60.

[7] *Ibid.*

[8] H. Osborne Mance, *International River and Canal Transport* (1945), pp. 1–79.

international transport law, commercial and technical matters, and conditions governing operation and exchange of rolling stock.[9]

Highway transportation activities on an international scale were of much more limited scope. A European Convention on Motor Transport was signed, however, as early as 1909, and the question was later studied by the Transit Committee of the League of Nations.[10]

In the prewar period of international co-operation on transport questions, the only activity ostensibly on a world level consisted of the Organization for Communications and Transit of the League of Nations and a number of rail, road, and navigation associations, but their work was concentrated on European inland transport and closely related problems.

During the war, discussions took place on the problem of meeting postwar European transport requirements, and to deal with this situation, the European Central Inland Transport Organization was established in 1945 to aid in reconstruction work.[11] When this emergency organization was terminated in 1947, the transport systems in Europe had to a large degree been restored to fair working order, and its unfinished business was left to the Inland Transport Committee of the ECE.[12]

Difficult problems still stood in the way of a satisfactory rehabilitation of European inland transport. Many of them were posed by the international character of the boundaries, and by the great need for husbanding resources while achieving an integrated system of transportation that makes economic sense. Moreover, there was no organization dealing with international road transport, and this part of the transport system, badly needed to supplement the disorganized rail system, was suffering from retarded highway development and a variety of obstacles to free movement. The problem of standardizing railroad rolling stock had assumed major proportions, and better utilization of rail cars serving in international traffic was a compelling requirement. The need for prompt action to support the general program of European economic

[9] Hans Hunziker, "The Berne Conventions and the Central Office for International Railway Transport," *Transport and Communications Review*, Vol. 2 (January–March 1949), pp. 10–15.

[10] H. Osborne Mance, "International Inland Transport in Europe: Recent Developments in Organization," *Journal of the Institute of Transport*, Vol. 25 (March 1954), pp. 337–42.

[11] For further information on prewar and wartime co-operation, see above, Chap. I.

[12] "European Inland Transport Since the End of the War," *Transport and Communications Review*, Vol. 1 (October–December 1948), pp. 14–26.

recovery was obvious, and measures aimed at this goal were needed.

The ECE Inland Transport Committee prepared draft conventions for the simplification of European frontier formalities for rail transportation of passengers and of goods, both of which have been adopted. On the recommendation of the committee, an agreement was concluded between international agencies and nongovernmental railway organizations aimed at avoiding duplication of functions; and the committee has also dealt with tariff and monetary problems and the possibilities of a uniform system of accounts for main railway lines. Improvement in commercial transport by roads was accomplished under the ECE through agreements in 1947, which lifted restrictions on the freedom of the road, and an agreement in 1954, relating to economic regulation of road carriers.

United Nations activity in Europe has met with special difficulties, partly because of the East-West split and partly because of the dominance of state railway administrations in the European transport field. Solutions have also been sought outside the framework of the United Nations. The Council of Europe, for example, has suggested a supranational European Transport Authority with powers similar to those of the European Coal and Steel Community. In the special field of rail transportation of coal and steel, three major problems have been faced by the High Authority of the European Coal and Steel Community: elimination of discrimination in rates between domestic and foreign shippers; the establishment of international through rates; and the harmonization of national structures of rail rates. The first two problems have been fully met, and some progress has been made on the third. Other organizations have adopted different approaches to the tasks first attempted by the European Central Inland Transport Organization.[13] Among these was the formation of a European Conference of Ministers of Transport, in October 1953, by the countries belonging to the Organization for European Economic Cooperation (other than Iceland and Ireland), and Spain.[14]

[13] E. R. Hondelink, "Transport and Communications Problems in Development Programmes," *Transport and Communications Review*, Vol. 6 (July–September 1953), pp. 11–20. See also L. A. Lewis, "Coordination of European Inland Transport," U.S. Department of State *Documents, State Papers*, Vol. I (October 1948), pp. 451–99, and "Transport in the Common Market," *Bulletin from the European Community for Coal and Steel* (February–March 1955), pp. 1–4.

[14] For the background and work of this Conference, see *The Present State of Economic Integration in Western Europe*, Report by the Research Directorate of the Secretariat-General of the Council of Europe, Strasbourg, Doc. SG/R(55)3/Rev. (July 1955), pp. 31–35.

International Civil Aviation Organization

Although technical co-operation in the field of aviation was initiated as early as 1919 by the Paris Peace Conference, the first attempt to take international action on such questions as transit rights, international routes, and air transport services was not made until the International Civil Aviation Conference met in Chicago in 1944. This conference sought to fill one of the major gaps in the structure of international co-operation as it had developed during the interwar years.[15] It laid the groundwork for most of the principles that still apply to international civil aviation, except of course for the basic principle that each nation has sovereignty over its own air space. This principle has long been generally accepted and was explicitly reaffirmed in the convention drafted at the Chicago conference, which provided that no scheduled air services may be operated over the territory of a contracting party without the permission of that state.[16]

The permanent international organization, which was planned at this conference to promote the application of these principles, was the International Civil Aviation Organization. It came into existence in 1947 and became the first of the specialized agencies in the field of transport and communications to become associated with the United Nations.

The objectives of ICAO are to develop the principles and techniques of international air navigation and to foster the planning and development of international air transport to ensure the safety and orderly growth of international civil aviation. This includes the improvement of aircraft design and operation for peaceful purposes; the development of airways and facilities; the provision of efficient and economical air transport; the prevention of waste caused by unreasonable competition; the assurance that nations have a fair opportunity to operate international airlines without discrimination; and the promotion of safety of flight and the general development of all aspects of international civil aeronautics.

[15] See above, Chap. I.
[16] U.S. Department of State, *International Civil Aviation Conference, Chicago, Illinois, November 1 to December 7, 1944: Final Act and Related Documents*, Publication 2282 (1945), Art. 6, p. 60. Article 5 of the Convention, however, required a contracting party to allow the entry of private and nonscheduled flights of foreign aircraft of other contracting parties, subject to such regulations, conditions, and limitations as it might unilaterally impose.

As was expected, ICAO has been concerned with the continuation of prewar co-operation in such matters as airways systems, aeronautical communications, rules of the air and air traffic control, licensing of aeronautical personnel, log book requirements, air-worthiness, aircraft registration and identification, aeronautical meteorology, aeronautical maps and charts, customs procedures, search and rescue, and accident investigation. It has been, however, confronted with broader problems, including that of striking a balance between subsidies, on the one hand, and restrictions of commercial rights, on the other, in order to ensure a trend toward lower costs, better service, and further development of air transport. In these matters, it has co-operated with a nongovernmental organization, the International Air Transport Association, to which all the largest international airlines belong. The International Air Transport Association has as one of its principal functions the development of agreement on international tariffs.

One of the earliest tasks of ICAO was to attempt to draw up a multilateral agreement to regulate commercial rights and to replace the multiplicity of bilateral agreements. The hope that such an agreement would be provided by the International Air Transport Agreement (Five Freedoms Agreement) drawn up at the Chicago conference was dashed by the failure of the principal carrier nations other than the United States to accept this agreement.[17] Consequently, it was renounced by the United States in July 1946, but the foundations for a new approach had been laid by the Bermuda Agreement between the United States and the United Kingdom signed on February 11, 1946. Up to that time, the United Kingdom had negotiated bilateral agreements based on the economic principles that it had supported in the Chicago conference. These provided for a definite division of frequencies of landing, plus control of rates, while the United States negotiated agreements in which there was no control of frequency, capacity, or rates.

The Bermuda Agreement provided for reciprocal United States-United Kingdom air services, fixed the routes to be operated by the respective services, adopted certain principles to govern capacity, and set up machinery for intergovernmental agreement on rates. It represented a shift in United States policy to the extent of the United States

---

[17] For a discussion of the five freedoms and the instruments in which they were incorporated, see above, Chap. I. The first two freedoms permitted flying across the territory of another nation and landing there for nontraffic purposes only; the third and fourth freedoms permitted the discharging and loading of passengers, mail and cargo coming from or destined for the home nation of an aircraft; the fifth freedom permitted the discharging or loading of passengers and cargo destined for and coming from any other nation.

concurring that if the rates charged were not agreeable to both governments, the question could be referred to ICAO. Each government would then use its best efforts to put into effect any advisory rate decisions made by ICAO. The agreement also set up certain principles to cover traffic capacity that involved a shift in the British position, particularly by including the amount of fifth freedom traffic, which each country could pick up in the other country while en route to foreign destinations. But the agreement did not seek any specific division of frequency or capacity.

Subsequent to the Bermuda Agreement, the United States negotiated other bilateral agreements in some of which it went even further than in the Bermuda Agreement in deferring to international authority. It expressed a willingness to use its best efforts to make effective the advisory opinions rendered by ICAO in disputes concerning frequency, capacity, and other economic problems as well as in disputes concerning rates. The United States then joined with other members of ICAO in urging the adoption of a multilateral agreement, and ICAO convened a conference at Geneva, in 1947, for this purpose. This project appeared promising owing to the Anglo-American compromise developed at Bermuda, but agreement was not reached.

With respect to the third and fourth freedom rights, there were differences of view at Geneva over what constituted an adequate provision against destructive competition. The main reason for the failure, however, was inability to reach agreement on the fifth freedom. The states with highly developed transport systems debated violently with the smaller states on the issue whether and to what extent limitations should be placed on the number of passengers and amount of freight an airplane should be allowed to carry between two points neither of which was in the country of the airline operating the plane. The smaller countries insisted that principles governing such fifth freedom traffic under the general Bermuda type of agreement were insufficient to protect local services and that any country had the right to refuse fifth freedom traffic to foreign air services. Twelve countries supported a Mexican resolution to this effect, while the United States, Great Britain, France, the Netherlands, and certain other countries insisted that whenever a route is negotiated, the countries on the route must allow fifth freedom traffic. There was a complete deadlock on this issue.

This was not the only issue. The United States indicated its willingness to agree to principles along the lines of the Bermuda Agreement regarding capacity, frequency, and rates and to accept decisions of the International Court of Justice under Article 36(2) of the Statute of the

Court or, alternatively, on specific agreement of both parties, to accept binding arbitral decisions in case of dispute. The United States was unwilling, however, to agree that routes should be fixed under multilateral agreement or that the granting or refusal of a route or any matter in connection therewith should be the subject of international decision or of arbitral awards, as desired by a number of other countries.

As a result of these basic differences, the conference decided that it was unjustifiable to submit an agreement for signature, with the result that routes for international flying and commercial rights exercised on the routes continued to be determined by bilateral agreements.[18]

These problems, however, remained on the agenda of ICAO, and at its fourth session in the summer of 1950, the ICAO Assembly requested member nations to place at the disposal of the organization the full benefit of their knowledge and experience in international air transport in order to make possible a satisfactory multilateral agreement that would define the exchange of commercial rights in international civil aviation.

These matters were debated at length by the assembly in June 1953, but it was concluded that the time had not yet arrived when it would be possible to obtain world-wide agreement concerning exchange of commercial rights in international air services. It was noted that at that time there existed over three hundred agreements between different pairs of governments on this question. It was agreed, however, that the ICAO Council should study what might be achieved by partial solutions, and a suggestion by the Council of Europe that a regional agreement on the question might be evolved was approved by the ICAO Assembly. Special attention was given to the needs of nonscheduled international air services, but the assembly felt it was too early to expect universal freedom for this type of transportation. The ICAO Council was requested, however, to study the question further to see how charter operations could be distinguished from regular services, and which charter operations could be given general freedom to operate internationally without encroaching on the traffic of regular services.

It was not until a year later that the ICAO Council decided to call the first meeting of a European Air Transport Conference and to cooperate in the drafting of multilateral agreements dealing with (1) the establishment of conditions leading to progressive liberalization of air transport on scheduled carriers undertaken by European operators in

[18] George P. Baker, "The Bermuda Plan as a Basis for Multilateral Agreement," McGill University (mimeo. speech, Apr. 18, 1947).

European regions, and (2) the establishment of parallel conditions for nonscheduled air service.

By that time, most of the countries belonging to ICAO were freely exchanging the rights of nonstop passage and the stopping for refueling or other noncommercial purposes, and some forty countries had accepted the International Air Services Transit Agreement. It was, however, on the issue of violation of the commitments under this agreement and of the convention itself, that the first dispute between members was submitted to ICAO. The complaint was made by India against Pakistan in the summer of 1952, and in January 1953, the ICAO Council was able to announce amicable settlement of the dispute by an agreement permitting Indian civil aircraft to fly over Pakistan territory to Kabul through two twenty-mile-wide corridors without having to follow the lengthy detours that had previously been required by Pakistan.

Efforts of the International Civil Aviation Organization in the technical field of air navigation have been more successful than in the economic field. Differences in languages, technical, economic, and social developments, operational experience, and educational standards among the nations operating aircraft necessitate uniform international standards to make international air operations practical. Among the accomplishments of ICAO has been the addition to the 1944 Chicago convention of fifteen international standards and recommended practices, which are designated as "annexes." Of this number, fourteen are concerned with standards and recommended practices for technical matters such as personnel licensing, rules of the air, meteorological codes, aeronautical charts, operations of aircraft, aeronautical telecommunications, and search and rescue. Only one is concerned with economics.[19]

These annexes were subject to continuous amendment and improvement. In June 1953, however, the ICAO Assembly, feeling that the basic text of the various international standards and procedures had reached a sufficient state of stability, decided that more emphasis should be placed on implementation. In the case of international standards for air-worthiness, however, the assembly felt that more work should be done to develop comprehensive international standards. Great emphasis has also been laid on the development of the five regional offices

[19] Annex 9, "Standards and Recommended Practices—Facilitation of International Air Transport." In January 1949, the Director of ICAO reported that the most significant achievement of the organization during 1948 was the adoption of standards controlling six different technical aspects of international flight. See U.S. Department of State, *International Civil Aviation, 1949–1950*, Publication 3915 (1950), pp. 4–7.

of ICAO (in Paris, Cairo, Bangkok, Lima, and Montreal) to enable regional representatives to assist national administrations more effectively, and in order to plan the provision of air navigation services for international civil aviation. Regional air navigation meetings are convened periodically by ICAO in each of eight regions.

The relation of civil aviation to peace and security, which had been raised at the Chicago conference, was again debated at the fifth assembly of ICAO.[20] The United States then proposed that in the light of the resolution of the United Nations General Assembly on "Uniting for Peace" and subsequent recommendations by the Economic and Social Council, the agreement between the United Nations Organization and ICAO be revised. This proposal was rejected by the Executive Committee of the ICAO Assembly on the ground that revision of the basic agreement was undesirable. Instead, the executive committee approved for submission to the assembly a revised United States proposal constituting a declaration of support of the "Uniting for Peace" resolution. This declaration was interpreted as meaning that ICAO would render all possible assistance within its competence to the principal organs of the United Nations on matters directly affecting world security.

International Telecommunication Union

During the war, rapid technological improvements and the increase in aeronautical, navigational, and broadcasting activities made the structure of the existing International Telecommunication Union clearly inadequate to deal with emerging problems, particularly in the field of radio.[21] Among these, were the allocation of radio frequencies and the bringing of radio regulations into line with recent technical developments. To meet this situation and to alter the structure of the Telecommunication Union so that it could be more readily brought into formal relation with the United Nations, were matters of urgent concern to the Economic and Social Council.

Accordingly the Council suggested the convening of international telecommunication conferences, which met in 1947 at Atlantic City. An agreement establishing the relationship between the International Telecommunication Union and the United Nations was approved at that time. The conferences completely reorganized the structure of the outdated International Telecommunication Union and achieved gen-

[20] See above, Chap. I.
[21] *Ibid.*

eral acceptance of a new frequency allocation table. This was to correct the situation that had developed under the old regulations adopted at a Cairo Conference in 1938, under which each country could simply decide on the wave lengths it wished to use, and inform the Union. The consequence of the Cairo regulations had been that many countries used the same frequencies, disregarded the separation of the frequencies, and reserved frequencies without using them. The frequency spectrum had become too crowded, and steadily growing interference increasingly endangered the reliability of telecommunications.

In view of the complexity of the problem of implementing the new frequency allocation table, the conferences provided for a series of special meetings in several regions of the world, an International Conference on High-Frequency Broadcasting, an International Administrative Aeronautical Radio Conference, and others. Originally, it was planned that the frequency lists resulting from these conferences would be incorporated with the master list prepared by a Provisional Frequency Board for final approval by an Extraordinary Administrative Radio Conference. However, the task of the Provisional Frequency Board was much more difficult than had been expected at the Atlantic City conferences.

For example, the International High Frequency Broadcasting Conference in Mexico City lasted over five months, from October 22, 1948 to April 10, 1949, in an attempt to put an end to the anarchy prevalent in high-frequency broadcasting. A majority voted down a proposal to complete the allocation plan at a later date, and only fifty of the sixty-nine countries participating signed the agreement reached. The United States and the Soviet Union were among those that did not sign.

In general, countries submitted frequency requirements far in excess of foreseeable needs, and total requests went well beyond the capacity of the frequency spectrum. As a result, the Extraordinary Administrative Radio Conference, which was scheduled for 1950, was postponed, for it became obvious that the objectives of the conference could not be achieved or any substantial agreement reached. The United States urged that the work accomplished at the Atlantic City conferences not be scrapped and the conference be held when conditions had become more favorable. It was subsequently held successfully in 1951.

The task of this conference—the fitting into the radio frequency spectrum of all radio stations of the world—was extraordinarily complex. It included broadcasting stations, airplane, ship, telegraph and telephone systems, land mobile stations, coastal stations, and radio location, direction-finding, navigation, beacon, experimental and amateur stations. The agreement signed by sixty-three members of the ITU represented a major step toward implementing a new table of frequency allocations. The conference adopted frequency allocation plans designed ultimately to provide for some 80,000 frequency assignments to specified stations. Although one of the most comprehensive agreements ever negotiated in the field of telecommunications, the agreement did not solve the difficulties inherent in the detailed assignments of the frequencies, and reliance was placed on a gradual implementation based on actual frequency use.

A Plenipotentiary Conference of ITU held in Buenos Aires in 1952 reaffirmed the decisions of the Extraordinary Administrative Radio Conference. It made a number of modifications in the convention designed to facilitate the working of the Union.

Although the most significant developments in communication technology have involved radio communications, there have been considerable advances in techniques in the fields of telephony and telegraphy and a greatly increased demand for international facilities as standards of living have risen. The International Consultative Committees of the International Telecommunication Union have done much work on the integration of the European telephone and telegraph systems and on the interconnection of the telephone and telegraph systems of Southern Asia and the Middle East with those of Europe and the Mediterranean basin.

Intergovernmental Maritime
Consultative Organization

The concern of the United Nations in shipping problems has taken several forms. On the initiative of the International Labour Organisation, international conferences have been convened for the purpose of improving living conditions aboard ships and a Conference for the Revision of the Convention on Safety of Life at Sea was convened in London in 1948 by the United Kingdom. The Transport and Communications Commission has been concerning itself with the immediate tasks of arriving at the unification of maritime tonnage measurement and controlling the perennial problems of sea water pollution. But the major United Nations interest has been the attempt to reach agreement for the first time on a world-wide public agency in the field of shipping.

World shipping problems have over a long period been handled by rate conferences of organizations of private shipowners. These international cartels, designed to control competition by regulation of schedules, pooling of cargo, and control over rates, had their origin in the compelling need for self-regulation in an industry the financial position of which was frequently imperiled by cut-throat competition. The shipping conferences are mainly conferences of liner operators, and one of their purposes is to protect the services of liners—which due to their regularity may have to bear higher costs—against competition from outsiders, who may take the cream of the traffic when it suits them.[22]

The importance of merchant fleets to national defense has also introduced a wide variety of subsidy policies and practices among the maritime nations, which have intensified shipping rivalries. Despite some more general forms of co-operation referred to earlier in this study,[23] and the postwar proposals for an Intergovernmental Maritime Consultative Organization, the shipping conferences have remained the principal basis of international co-operation.[24]

During the war, centralized control of allied shipping was provided by the Allied Shipping Adjustment Board (1942–45). It was recognized that for some time ahead centralized control for at least part of the shipping of the world would be needed to provide necessary tonnage during the demobilization and early rehabilitation period. To this end and to pave the way for an orderly return of shipping to normal commercial operations, a United Maritime Authority was set up, including the representatives of nine maritime nations. This body was succeeded by a United Maritime Consultative Council in 1946 to draft recommendations for a permanent peacetime organization in the shipping field.

In the meantime, a number of nations that had never possessed merchant marines of any size undertook to build and operate their own fleets. Countries with adequate financial reserves at the end of the war were offering to place substantial orders with European nations on condition that at least half of the traffic would move in national vessels. Countries that had changed from colonial or dominion status to independence announced their intention to create their own national fleets. States that had no fleets but were dependent to a large extent on shipping, saw in the United Nations framework opportunities to appeal against what they considered to be oppressive practices on the part of the shipping lines that served them.

[22] Daniel Marx, Jr., "Shipping Conferences," *Transport and Communications Review*, Vol. 6 (October–December 1953), pp. 14–24.
[23] See above, Chap. I.
[24] Louis Delanney, "The United Nations Maritime Conference," *Transport and Communications Review*, Vol. 1 (July–September 1948), pp. 17–21.

There was growing sentiment consequently for a permanent governmental maritime agency at the time that the United Nations Transport and Communications Commission was organized in 1947. The commission was confronted with the existence of a great number of international conventions and agreements in the field of ocean shipping and several international organizations were dealing with aspects of the problem. The absence of a central organization meant that there was no intergovernmental agency comparable to the ITU or ICAO to represent shipping interests, as telecommunication and aviation were represented, in the discussions of problems of common interest. Examples of such problems are safety at sea and in the air and the application of radio aids in navigation.

In May 1946, the Transport and Communications Commission recommended that an intergovernmental body be established to fill this gap, but that it be limited to dealing with technical matters. In October 1946, the United Maritime Consultative Council completed a draft for a permanent organization that went far beyond technical co-operation. Its proposed functions included encouragement of the removal of all forms of discriminatory action and unnecessary restrictions affecting shipping engaged in international trade. The purpose was to promote the availability of shipping services to the commerce of the world without discrimination and permit the consideration by the organization of shipping problems of an international character. Pending the establishment of a permanent organization, a Provisional Maritime Consultative Council was established.

These developments were duly noted by the Transport and Communications Commission and by the Economic and Social Council. The latter convoked a United Nations Maritime Conference, which was given, as a basis of discussion, the draft completed by the United Maritime Consultative Council. This conference, which met in Geneva in 1948, adopted a Convention on the Intergovernmental Maritime Consultative Organization (IMCO). It also adopted a resolution establishing a preparatory committee to prepare for the first session of the new organization when the necessary support was achieved. The intended role of this organization was to provide for consultation on technical matters affecting international shipping, to promote safety and navigation standards, and to encourage the removal of discrimination and unfair restrictive practices by shipping concerns and governments.

It was over the inclusion of the economic problems of the industry that serious international differences developed. In the deliberations in Washington in 1946 on the draft of the United Maritime Consultative

Council, the Scandinavian countries had agreed to the inclusion of these matters, but at the Geneva conference, they favored restricting the new organization to technical matters alone. The United States was in a delicate position on the inclusion of provisions relating to unfair or discriminatory practices. It was using government-owned ships in private operations, operating government-owned vessels as a government project, subsidizing both construction and operation of private vessels, and even controlling allocation of cargoes in certain cases. In these circumstances, the United States proposed that in matters of unfair practices, the proposed IMCO should recommend that those matters capable of settlement by the normal processes of international shipping should be so settled. It proposed that matters concerning unfair restrictive practices of private shipping concerns be considered by IMCO only after the parties themselves had failed to reach an adjustment. Furthermore, the United States view was that if and when IMCO did take jurisdiction, such matters should be considered in the light of the applicable principles and precedents established by the specialized agencies having responsibility in the field of restrictive practices (*i.e.*, the proposed International Trade Organization). There was a clear danger that in this area of restrictive practices a body of doctrine might be developed in the shipping industry that would differ from that to be developed by the International Trade Organization.

The withdrawal of its proposals by the United States led to the adoption of a compromise proposed by the United Kingdom providing for the consideration by the maritime organization of matters concerning unfair restrictive practices by shipping concerns and of any matters concerning shipping that might be referred to it by any organ or specialized agency of the United Nations.

The British proposal, however, included two major limitations affecting the consultative and advisory functions of the organization on these economic matters. One of these was a provision that assistance and encouragement given by a government for the development of its national shipping and for purposes of security do not in themselves constitute discrimination, provided that such assistance is not designed to restrict the freedom of shipping of all flags to take part in international trade. All efforts to expand the definition of discrimination and unfair practices were unsuccessful. The second major limitation was that, in those matters that appeared to the organization capable of settlement through normal processes of international shipping business, the organization should so recommend. When in the opinion of the organization any matter concerning unfair restrictive practices was incapable of settlement in this way, and after an attempt to negotiate directly had failed, the organization should, at the request of one of the disputants, consider the matter.

The provision of the final draft concerning the removal of discriminatory action and unnecessary restrictions by governments affecting shipping engaged in international trade was thus surrounded by severe limitations. The function of providing machinery for co-operation among governments in technical matters and the encouragement of the general adoption of the highest practical standards in matters concerning maritime safety and efficiency of navigation appear therefore to be the most important and generally acceptable provisions of the convention as a whole.

The Intergovernmental Maritime Consultative Organization will be activated as soon as twenty-one countries have ratified the convention, including seven with merchant fleets of over a million tons. To date, seventeen nations, including the United States and the United Kingdom, have taken this step, but in other areas opposition to ratification has persisted. The Scandinavian nations, with their maritime economies and powerful shipping interests, would like to confine the new agency to technical matters so that the shipping industry would be left to regulate economic matters itself. In contrast, emerging and underdeveloped nations, desirous of establishing themselves in world shipping operations, wish to be free to provide such government aids as their aspirations would—at least in the early stages—require, and they do not feel sufficiently safeguarded by the reservation in the text of the convention on subsidies for promoting national shipping and national security.

Universal Postal Union

A common meeting ground for the solution of postal problems was provided by the establishment of the Universal Postal Union eighty years ago. The first International Postal Treaty established the concept that all member countries comprised a single postal territory for the reciprocal exchange of mail. Previously each country had entered into bilateral agreements for sharing the cost of mail transportation, and an intermediate country that handled the mail in transit could charge whatever it could arrange through negotiation.[25]

When the Universal Postal Union was established, uniform rates were

[25] A. Muri, "The Origin, Development and Activities of the Universal Postal Union," *Transport and Communications Review*, Vol. 1 (July–September 1948), pp. 22–25.

made applicable throughout the Union, and it was agreed to abolish payments by a sending country to the receiving country on the theory that a letter dispatched would generally call for a letter in return. Costs of carriage and delivery incurred by the two countries would thus balance out. The problem of compensating intermediate countries led to the adoption of a system of weighing shipments and estimating the amount of payment necessary to compensate for transit costs.[26] Over the years, due to changes in postal service, rates, and transportation charges, the Universal Postal Convention was revised and brought up to date at the postal congresses normally held at intervals of approximately five years. Although the continuity of these meetings was broken by the two world wars, the Union itself survived and in 1947, was brought into relation with the United Nations as a specialized agency.

Since that time, the Union, in order to keep pace with changing conditions and the steady increase in international correspondence, has added new services and revised regulations in the light of changing needs. The Thirteenth Postal Congress of the Union in 1952, for example, adopted a uniform scale of transit rates. It also adopted a more detailed scale of distances, with the corresponding transit rates, both for land and sea carriage. Airmail rates, which had been the subject of extensive study between the Union, the International Civil Aviation Organization, and International Air Transport Association, were fixed.

The Union has adopted provisions regulating the transmission of all types of international mail and fixed maximum and minimum rates, weight limits, and dimensions. It not only provides for transmission of international mail but prohibits certain articles, such as opium and other narcotics, and explosives, from being moved by mail across international boundaries.

World Meteorological Organization

Another early beginning of international co-operation is found in endeavors to provide information about the weather. A century ago an international conference dealing with a program for collecting meteorological observations by ships at sea was held in Brussels. During the next quarter century, additional international meetings were held, and in 1878, the International Meteorological Organization was established. Its members were the directors of the meteorological services of the various countries throughout the world, and although it did not have

[26] Fulke Radice, "The Problem of the Payment for Mails in Transit: A Historical Survey," *Transport and Communications Review*, Vol. 4 (April–June 1951), p. 27.

the full official backing of governments, it nevertheless carried out significant programs of perfecting and standardizing meteorological activities, especially services to maritime navigation, agriculture, and more recently, to aviation. In 1947, the agency was reorganized as a formal intergovernmental organization known as the World Meteorological Organization, and its operation as a specialized agency of the United Nations began in 1951.[27]

The organization is concerned with establishing networks of stations for making meteorological observations and setting up meteorological centers throughout the world. It has prepared a set of technical regulations relating to meteorology to serve as a guide to meteorological services and has standardized meteorological observations. Weather information is gathered by 2,500 volunteer merchant ships representing thirty countries. The organization has worked to further the application of meteorology to aviation and shipping, and agreements with appropriate agencies in these fields have been negotiated. It has prepared thunderstorm frequency maps in different parts of the world. One of the most important observations reported from weather stations is the type of cloud. To ensure uniformity in methods of reporting clouds, it has prepared an International Cloud Atlas. The World Meterological Organization is also participating in the preparations for International Geophysical Year (1957–58), a period of intensified world-wide study of the earth and its upper atmosphere.

Technical and Financial Assistance

Many needs for technical assistance have arisen in the field of transport and communications. They include advice on the organization or reorganization of private transport companies, government administration, public regulatory policy, maintenance and repair of railroad and motor vehicle equipment, sanitary measures at ports and airports, the installation of railway signals and aids to aerial navigation, the design of inland water transport craft, the development of road and bridge construction techniques, and the construction, modernization, and operation of maritime ports. The United Nations Technical Assistance Administration provides assistance in fields not covered by the specialized agencies, including road, rail, inland water transport, and shipping, as well as problems of transportation in general.

[27] "The International Meteorological Organization," *Transport and Communications Review*, Vol. 3 (April–June 1950), pp. 1–14.

The World Meteorological Organization conducts a wide variety of studies aimed at improving weather knowledge and applying meteorology to the problems of underdeveloped areas. On the basis of requests received under the Expanded Programme of Technical Assistance, the WMO has given attention to the organization and development of national meteorological services, and training has been provided for local personnel in underdeveloped countries. Technical assistance projects in 1955 involved agricultural, maritime, and aeronautical applications of meteorology in twenty-three countries. The WMO has operated projects to provide advice in synoptic meteorology and on the technique of obtaining meteorological information from the upper air. It has dealt also with water resource problems, including the prevention of floods and the provision of water for irrigation, electrical energy, and industrial uses.

The International Telecommunication Union, in conjunction with the Technical Assistance Administration, has sent experts to aid in setting up a telecommunications training center for radio, telegraph, and telephone personnel in Ethiopia. It has operated projects to study problems and provide advice on reorganization of telecommunication services in Iran and aided Pakistan in telephone and short-wave radio communication problems. Experts were sent to Afghanistan to study problems arising out of the installation of a telecommunications network.

The primary importance of civil aviation to an underdeveloped area is to provide a means of transport that can surmount geographical barriers, provide travel for great distances over land and sea in a short time, and pioneer inaccessible land areas without the large initial investment required for surface transportation. Aviation is also of value to agriculture and public health programs through dusting and spraying operations, mapping, and surveying. A report of the Technical Assistance Board points out that although the International Civil Aviation Organization "has been able to render some small assistance" in helping nations to establish air services, lack of funds has held the level of help far below the volume of requests.[28]

The International Civil Aviation Organization has placed primary emphasis on the development of aviation ground services, particularly air traffic control, communications, and meteorological services. Fellow-

---

[28] U.N. Economic and Social Council, Eighteenth Session, *Official Records*, Supplement No. 4, "Sixth Report of the Technical Assistance Board," p. 75. The share of ICAO in the budget of the Expanded Programme of Technical Assistance averaged about $800,000 per year during the period 1953–55.

ships have been granted for this type of training and for commercial pilot training; experts have also been sent to the recipient countries to provide such training together with guidance in improving the techniques of the local personnel in such operations as the repair and maintenance of aircraft engines, airframes, and airborne equipment.

The technical assistance extended by the International Civil Aviation Organization has also provided advice on the organization of government departments of civil aviation and the preparation of air laws and regulations; the conduct of air transport surveys; the establishment of statistical and accounting systems; airline organization and operation; the location, construction, and improvement of airports; the installation and operation of air navigation facilities and services; and the opening, in co-operation with the Mexican, Egyptian, and other governments, of civil aviation training centers in their countries.

Technical assistance in the field of inland transport has been facilitated by the regional economic commissions. Recommendations by the Singapore conference on inland transport arranged by the Economic Commission for Asia and the Far East in 1949 led eventually to a series of studies on road, rail, and waterway problems; and arrangements were made for the collection and dissemination of transport statistics and the establishment of a technical library service. Experts from Burma, India, Indonesia, Pakistan, Thailand, and Viet Nam have visited Europe and the United States to study technological improvements in inland transport, and railway personnel from sixteen countries have visited Europe, North America, and Japan to study modern railway operations. One result has been the establishment in Pakistan of a regional training center for railway operating and signaling officials.

Highway transport problems that have received special attention from United Nations agencies include economical methods of constructing, repairing, and maintaining highways; improvements in the use of existing road transport equipment; design of wheels and axles for animal-drawn vehicles to minimize road damage by iron-tired wheels; the development of international highway connections; and preparation of simplified manuals of instruction for motor vehicle drivers.

Through the co-operation of the Technical Assistance Administration, the Economic Commission for Latin America has undertaken the study of such problems as development and integration of the transport systems of the Central American countries. A technical commission was sent to that area for an intensive survey of the transport situation, and its work has contributed to the creation of a regional conscience and a sense of urgency concerning the role of transport as a factor in the integrated development of the region.[29] A treaty recently negotiated by the Central American republics under the auspices of the commission greatly simplifies automobile travel in the area and if, as is confidently expected, the treaty is ratified, it should be a boon to users of the Inter-American Highway. Studies are also being carried out on the working conditions and mechanization of Latin American ports and their comparative operating costs.

Technical assistance activities in the field of transport and communications, as elsewhere, have been limited by lack of funds. The need for capital to carry out desirable programs of transport development poses even greater problems.

The International Bank has provided significant financial support for self-liquidating projects. Activities engaged in by the Bank have included general economic surveys that include analyses of transportation, and loans for transportation development. More than $650 million —or nearly one third of the total amount loaned by the Bank through June 30, 1956 for developmental work—has been for the improvement of transport services. Of this sum, about $350 million has been for railroads and $160 million for highways. Highway construction has been financed in Colombia, Ethiopia, Guatemala, Haiti, Honduras, Nicaragua, Panama, and Peru. Railroads have been rehabilitated in Australia, Brazil, Burma, India, Pakistan, Thailand, and the Union of South Africa. Port development projects have been undertaken in Burma, Pakistan, Peru, South Africa, Thailand, and Turkey.[30]

Results of United Nations Action

In the work of the United Nations, the promotion of satisfactory transportation and communication services has encountered two major difficulties that are frequently present in the provision of these services both domestically and internationally.

First is the tendency in the field of transportation to consider each form of transport separately, or, conversely, the failure to take a comprehensive view of transportation as a whole. This situation stems from the fact that developments in technology have appeared at different periods

[29] "Survey on Transport in Central America," *Transport and Communications Review*, Vol. 6 (October–December 1953), pp. 34–49.

[30] See above, Chap. IV, for further information on the work of the International Bank and the volume of loans made for the development of transportation and communication facilities.

of history, so that each new and competing invention has given rise to new policies and methods, new governmental machinery, and new private and quasi-public agencies and associations. The result has been a proliferation of organizations in and outside government that makes comprehensive plans and policies substantively and administratively hard to come by. Separate agencies of transport come to be looked upon as rivals rather than related parts of the whole. Scattered organization is often an obstacle to the careful weighing of alternative transport possibilities and the effective physical co-ordination of facilities. Desirable standards of economy and service, however, are often dependent on careful selection of alternatives, joint use of facilities, satisfactory physical co-ordination, and uniform policies and procedures.

The second problem is the tendency to consider transportation and communications as something apart from the social and economic goals they are intended to support. This weakness appears to result from the highly technical nature of transport and communications and the natural preoccupation of experts with operational problems. The fact that transportation is the means by which social and economic objectives may be accomplished is sometimes lost sight of in the complex of scientific and engineering problems and the intensity of interagency rivalries.

The framework in which the transport and communications work of the United Nations is accomplished provides an organizational basis for overcoming these two difficulties, but in practice the results have been limited. The establishment of a Transport and Communications Commission in the United Nations has provided a focal point where problems common to all methods of transportation could be given proper attention, and where points of impact or relationship among the several transportation and communications media could be recognized and dealt with. To date, however, the potential of the system has not been realized.

The fact that the Transport and Communications Commission is part of the Economic and Social Council has likewise been a salutary arrangement, providing machinery by which it would be possible to consider these programs in relation to broader objectives. Transport services and communication facilities have an indispensable role in the economic development of communities and nations, in the conduct of trade, and in the achievement of economic and cultural goals. But actually the provision of transportation and communication facilities is carried on without a close relationship to economic and social development. This means that the opportunity to use transportation to accomplish broader objectives of economic development is in constant danger of being lost.

The influence exerted by the world organization has differed widely with different kinds of transportation and communications and with differing geographical situations. In cases where the scope of operations is world-wide, and therefore where world-wide co-operation has been needed from the beginning, fairly effective devices to cope with these problems were already established before the United Nations Organization was formed. This has been true particularly of the postal and weather services. In more recent times, the solution of aviation problems has not been noticeably furthered by the inclusion of the International Civil Aviation Organization in the United Nations system. The negotiation of agreements making international bodies in these areas specialized agencies of the United Nations has merely ensured that the official agencies dealing with these problems are part of the world system, and—what may in the long run prove to be of considerable importance—provided the opportunity for them to share in the Expanded Programme of Technical Assistance. Affiliation with the United Nations to date has had only a minor impact in bringing related transport and communications agencies to bear on a single problem, in overcoming the duplications and overlappings of international organizations, or in focusing attention on the economic and social implications of transportation and communications policy.

It was never intended, of course, that the United Nations Organization would displace existing agencies, and bringing the specialized agencies into relation with the Organization has not altered the nature of the predominantly technical work they were already undertaking. But where the need for a unified approach has been manifested, the Transportation and Communication Commission has been somewhat disappointing in meeting the need.

On the positive side, the United Nations Organization has resulted in the sponsorship of the new Intergovernmental Maritime Consultative Organization, and in isolated cases the Transportation and Communications Commission has provided integrating machinery that has aided the specialized agencies in reaching the solution of common problems. The most active operations of the United Nations Organization, however, have been in the fields of road, rail, and inland waterways, where regional rather than world-wide problems predominate. It was in this area that the largest organizational vacuum existed at the time the United Nations was established. But even in the case of regional activity most of the attention has been directed to the problems of European inland transport, largely because of the need for restoration and realignment of European facilities at the end of the war.

The accomplishments of the Inland Transport Committee of the Economic Commission for Europe have been substantial, and it has served in addition as a forum for discussion, which foments ideas that have led to action by the railroads, truckers, and other transport interests outside the commission itself. Much remains to be done, however, to overcome the barriers to freedom of movement that still interfere with the European transport system.

In other regions of the world where transportation patterns have not been crystallized, as they have in Europe and North America, the regional commissions uncover areas requiring technical assistance and facilitate the obtaining of such assistance. As yet there are no regional arrangements, however, in either Africa or the Middle East. In the underdeveloped areas, the necessity of relating transportation to economic development is more apparent than elsewhere, yet difficulties have been encountered by the United Nations in the meager financial support for technical assistance relative to the need. Furthermore, the difficulties to date of obtaining the necessary capital to finance large-scale investment have meant that accomplishments have lagged far behind urgent need.

In addition to further financial aid, there is also a need—as well as an opportunity—for the Economic and Social Council, through its Transport and Communications Commission, to sponsor comprehensive studies of transport requirements in the various underdeveloped areas in order to provide the guidance for technical assistance and investment and to ensure the most practicable plans in the light of local conditions and modern technology. Despite an organizational setting that permits a broad approach to the planning of transport and communications developments by the United Nations, a piecemeal approach by individual projects is still the rule in the requesting countries.

The great economic potential of modern transportation development is being demonstrated in many parts of the world today as transportation and communications facilities open the way to new wealth and higher standards of living. The United Nations Organization has not yet seized on the opportunity that lies in a concerted attack on inadequate transportation and communications as a means of opening the door to economic growth and development.

CHAPTER VII

Social Action to Improve Levels of Living*

I T IS an outstanding characteristic of the present age that for the first time in history human society has dared to think of the welfare of the entire human race not as a dream but as a practical objective. Modern science and engineering, it is widely believed, have provided the tools to eradicate from the face of this earth hunger, want, and disease.

For these purposes, the economic programs discussed earlier in this study are essential, but they are not enough. Social action on a broad front is also required to help bring the benefits of scientific advance and of modern technology to the largest number of people in the shortest time and at the lowest cost.

One broad group of social programs—the group discussed below—has as its central purpose the promotion of higher levels of living for the population as a whole. Another group—analyzed later—tends to be concerned with special categories of the population such as mothers and dependent children, the handicapped, the refugees and migrants.[1] The latter approach frequently, but not always, puts the emphasis on defense, on protection, and on remedial action.

The programs discussed here, however, place the accent on development, both economic and social. They represent a dynamic approach. Under the aegis of the United Nations and its affiliated agencies, this approach is being internationalized.

The present analysis of the process of internationalization begins with a discussion of the problem of defining and measuring an individual's level of living—of selecting the key components that together comprise the level of living, and of choosing appropriate indicators of progress with respect to each component. Certain landmarks in the evolution, within the United Nations system, of the social approach to the improvement of levels of living are then noted. With a chronological frame of reference thus established, it becomes possible to review in a more meaningful way the many specific activities of the United Na-

---

* By Walter M. Kotschnig.
[1] See below, Chap. VIII.

tions aimed at improving the health, nutrition, housing, employment arrangements, and working conditions of the people in Member states. These activities have involved the Social Commission of the United Nations, the World Health Organization (WHO), the Food and Agriculture Organization (FAO), the International Labour Organisation (ILO), as well as other organs and agencies.

Definition and Measurement of Levels of Living

A clear grasp of what is meant by standards or levels of living, and of methods by which they can be measured, is essential to the development of purposeful action programs to improve such standards. During recent years, international concern with the problem of definition and measurement has been reflected not only in the deliberations of the Economic and Social Council and its Social Commission, but also in the discussions of the Seventh International Conference of Labour Statisticians of the ILO (1949), and the Rural Welfare Panel of the General Conference of the FAO (1949). An important report on defining and measuring levels of living, published in 1954, reflects the thinking both of the United Nations experts who drafted it and of the personnel of the United Nations Educational, Scientific and Cultural Organization (UNESCO), the ILO, FAO, and WHO, which participated actively in its preparation.[2]

The report suggested a distinction between the terms "standard of living" and "level of living." It recommended that in future discussions the expression "level of living" be employed when referring to actual conditions of life, as contrasted with aspirations or ideas of what ought to be. The latter concept involves judgments on which it is difficult to reach international agreement. The report of the experts therefore confined its analysis to the problem of definition and measurement of actual levels of living.

General agreement was reached on certain major conclusions: (1)

[2] United Nations, *Report on International Definition and Measurement of Standards and Levels of Living*, Doc. E/CN.5/299 (1954). (Hereinafter cited as *Report on Standards and Levels of Living*.) See also U.N. Statistical Office, *Survey of Social Statistics*, Statistical Papers, Series K, No. 1 (December 1954). Chapter VI (pp. 16–19) gives a brief summary of the report together with the comments of the Statistical Commission, which reviewed it in April 1954. It also contains a comprehensive review of the statistical activities of the United Nations and the specialized agencies as they relate to levels of living, as well as to the more traditional social welfare activities.

No single index can be devised to measure differences in levels of living between countries. (2) No type of monetary index as a general international measure of levels of living can be recommended. (3) The problem of measuring levels of living should be approached by analyzing many "components" representing generally recognized values and by the use of various "indicators" for the many types of components. (4) The statistical analysis of "indicators" and "components" should be accompanied by background information of a descriptive nature. (5) In addition to current efforts in the field of economic and social statistics to improve the factual basis for intercountry comparisons, family-living studies should be undertaken for the purpose of obtaining more comprehensive information on the actual conditions of life and work of individuals and families.

Much of the report was devoted to a discussion of "components" and "indicators." Components, as defined by the experts, are clearly delimited aspects or parts of the total life situation such as health, nutrition, education, etc., that are amenable to quantification. Indicators measure some aspect of a component—in the sense in which, for example, calorie consumption measures an aspect of nutrition and literacy rate measures an aspect of education.

The report suggested the following classification of *components* as suitable for international reporting on levels of living: (1) health, including demographic conditions; (2) food and nutrition; (3) education, including literacy and skills; (4) conditions of work; (5) employment situation; (6) aggregate consumption and saving; (7) transportation; (8) housing, including household facilities; (9) clothing; (10) recreation and entertainment; (11) social security; (12) human freedom.

In addition, the report urged the use of certain macro-economic items to indicate available or potential means for better satisfaction of needs. Among recommended indicators were percentage of the national income spent on the basic needs of life (food, clothing, shelter, and fuel); output of electric power per 100,000 of population; output plus import of steel and coal per 100,000 of population.

The experts recognized that an international analysis of levels of living, in terms of the components and indicators proposed, would fall short of giving a complete and balanced picture. They stressed, therefore, the importance of descriptive materials and background information, particularly in the form of social and cultural analyses, *i.e.*, studies of the conditions of living of special groups, and of social and cultural patterns. The report concluded, moreover, that an adequate over-all picture of levels of living would not be obtainable except through a very considerable expansion of studies of family living, that is, studies of actual conditions of life of families as directly observed and recorded in surveys. It suggested that as a next step, international organizations should undertake an examination of the possibility of developing relatively uniform techniques and schedules for family living studies in different parts of the world.

In this area, the International Labour Organisation had already done pioneering work, in particular, in its surveys of urban wage earners' families. Revised and extended recommendations on the conduct of family living studies were adopted by the aforementioned Seventh International Conference of Labour Statisticians, on the basis of a study prepared by the International Labour Office.[3] In underdeveloped areas, a rather considerable number of studies had been completed, as shown by a survey undertaken by the United Nations.[4] This survey showed, however, that much remained to be done in these areas because, with a few exceptions, the studies undertaken were on a very small scale and lacked comparability with regard to definitions, classifications, and presentation.

In summary, important progress is being made in defining and measuring levels of living, thus helping to bring into clear focus the major elements to be taken into account in any practical program for the improvement of levels of living.[5]

Development of Program of Social Action

When the Economic and Social Council, in June 1946, adopted terms of reference for its Social Commission, it did not make the pro-

[3] International Labour Office, *Methods of Family Living Studies*, Studies and Reports, New Series, No. 17 (1949).

[4] U.N. Department of Social Affairs, *Enquiries into Household Standards of Living in Less Developed Areas*, A Survey of the Organization and Geographic Range of Field Investigations of the Income, Expenditure, and Food Consumption of Selected Households in Africa, Asia, the Caribbean, Latin America, and the Pacific, 1930–1950, Doc. ST/SOA/1 (July 6, 1950).

[5] For recent information on this problem, see U.N. Economic and Social Council, Statistical Commission, *Comments of Governments on the Report on International Definition and Measurement of Standards and Levels of Living* (*A Summary Prepared by the Secretary-General*), Doc. E/CN.3/213 (Jan. 20, 1956). Observations by the interested specialized agencies are contained in *addenda* to Doc. E/CN.3/213. The Secretary-General's *General Conclusions Concerning Statistical Aspects of International Definition and Measurement of Levels of Living* are given in Doc. E/CN.3/214 (Feb. 2, 1956). Re-

motion of higher levels of living a specific function of the commission.[6] In the introductory portion of the resolution establishing the commission, however, the Council did mention that "the raising of the standard of living and the welfare of the peoples of the countries of the United Nations, which should include not only wages and income but all kinds of social services, is an important task of the United Nations." The very vagueness of this statement is significant. It shows that the raising of standards of living was not considered essentially a social problem. At best, social action was to be secondary in the promotion of better standards of living.

This is borne out by the fact that on the same day, the Council approved the terms of reference of the Economic and Employment Commission, the first paragraph of which stipulated that "the Commission shall advise the Economic and Social Council on economic questions in order to promote higher standards of living." The underlying assumption was clearly that economic development *per se*—improved methods of production, industrialization, larger trade, increased national incomes—would result in improved standards of living. There is, of course, justification for this assumption, and it is certainly true that there can be no substantial improvement in general levels of living without economic development. History, however, abounds in examples showing that economic development does not automatically result in a general improvement in the level of individual welfare. Not infrequently, existing inequalities in the distribution of wealth are increased, at least for a time, and periods of social instability and strife precede the attainment of stability at a higher level of individual welfare.

Several factors help to explain the initial lack of focus on the promotion of higher levels of living as a function of the Social Commission. First, the momentum of the social welfare activities of the League of Nations carried over into the United Nations. The social welfare activities of the League (though not those of the ILO) were aimed more at the protection of vulnerable groups in the population than at the active promotion of higher living levels for the population as a whole. Second, in its early economic and social activities, the United

cent work of the ILO in the field of family studies is summarized in *Report on Family Living Studies*, Doc. E/CN.3/215 (Jan. 19, 1956). The conclusions of the Statistical Commission are contained in U.N. Economic and Social Council, Statistical Commission, *Report of the Ninth Session*, Docs. E/2876 and E/CN.3/225, pp. 19–21.

[6] Res. 10(1), June 21, 1946.

Nations gave primary attention to the problems of the war-devastated countries. In the social field, this meant an emphasis on social rehabilitation, the rebuilding of social services, child and family welfare programs, and similar matters. Third, there were in existence or in process of creation a number of specialized agencies with operational functions in the social field and their respective roles were not yet clear. The International Labour Organisation had long been concerned with the improvement of labor conditions, the development of social security systems, and related matters. In spite of the Declaration of Philadelphia, it was not clear at the time to what extent the ILO might assume the major responsibility for promoting social action to improve standards of living.[7] In the field of health, an important component in the level of living, plans were under way for the creation of the World Health Organization. The proposed United Nations Educational, Scientific and Cultural Organization was also expected to contribute to higher standards of living. In these circumstances, the Social Commission appeared to be left with a residuum of social problems.

In 1947, the Economic and Social Council formally requested the Secretary-General to report to a future session of the Social Commission on the extent to which questions within the terms of reference of the commission had been or were being studied by the specialized agencies and intergovernmental organizations, and to suggest measures enabling the commission effectively to carry out the tasks entrusted to it, in particular, the study of standards of living in underdeveloped countries and areas.[8] At its third session in April 1948, the Social Commission had before it a report of its Advisory Committee on Planning and Co-ordination.[9] This report marked an important step forward in emphasizing the indivisibility of the social and economic aspects of promoting better standards of living and the need for co-ordinating both aspects.

---

[7] This declaration, adopted by the International Labour Organisation in 1944 (see Chap. I, above), affirms that all human beings, irrespective of race, creed, or sex, have a right to pursue both their material well-being and their spiritual development in conditions of freedom and dignity, of economic security and equal opportunity. The declaration asserts the need for effective national and international action, including measures to expand production and consumption, to promote the economic and social advancement of the less developed regions of the world, and to improve the health, education, and well-being of all people.

[8] Res. 43(IV), Mar. 29, 1947.

[9] U.N. Economic and Social Council, Social Commission, Third Session, *Report of the Advisory Committee on Planning and Co-ordination*, Doc. E/CN.5/46 (Mar. 23, 1948).

In establishing its own program, however, the Social Commission at that time developed a list of priorities on which work on "standards of living" appeared sixth and last after such items as social welfare services, prevention of crime and of prostitution.

In 1948 and 1949, some field inquiries into the living conditions of selected social groups in various parts of the world, particularly the less developed areas, were undertaken. The year 1950 marked a more decisive step forward in the social approach to the improvement of levels of living. That year the Council, on the recommendation of the Social Commission, adopted a resolution by which it requested the Secretary-General to submit to the Social Commission and to the Council a report on the world social situation to parallel the *World Economic Report* published annually, since 1947, by the United Nations.[10] In spite of misgivings on the part of many members of the Council about the feasibility of such an undertaking, the report, first published in 1952, became a real landmark in the development of the social work of the United Nations. Also in 1950, the Population Commission paid special attention to the interrelationship between population and economic development. It suggested that technical assistance be rendered to governments for surveys of the demographic situation of their countries as a part of broader surveys of economic and social conditions affecting development plans. It also suggested special studies of such subjects as the effects of changing social and economic conditions on birth and death rates; the influence of migration on population trends and on economic development; the estimation of future changes in population size and composition; and the effects of such changes on labor supply, utilization of resources, capital formation, consumption, production, and the standard of living.

The most important decision in 1951, involving the recognition of social action, provided that additional technical assistance activities undertaken for the benefit of underdeveloped countries in the field of social welfare should be considered under the Expanded Programme of Technical Assistance (EPTA) in cases where such work could not be financed from the regular budget of the United Nations.[11] Ever since, substantial social activities have been carried on under EPTA. In 1951, moreover, the Social Commission considered two papers on community welfare centers as instruments for the promotion of eco-

[10] Res. 309F(XI), July 13, 1950.
[11] This was recommended by the Economic and Social Council in Res. 399(XIII), Sept. 20, 1951, approved by the General Assembly in Res. 518(VI), Jan. 12, 1952.

nomic and social progress.[12] These papers helped to open the way for the adoption at a later stage of a program of community development that is proving an increasingly effective means of advancing levels of living.[13]

Potentially more important than these papers was the publication in 1951 of the report of a group of experts appointed for the purpose of exploring unemployment and underemployment in the underdeveloped countries, and the national and international measures required to reduce such unemployment and underemployment. Their report not only offered an extensive set of recommendations regarding measures for economic development, but contained also an incisive discussion of "Pre-Conditions of Economic Development."[14] It brought out with admirable clarity that economic development cannot be considered as a purely economic phenomenon but must be viewed in the context of social, political, cultural, and religious ideas, facts, and institutions.

Four outstanding events characterized developments in 1952. First, was the publication of the *Preliminary Report on the World Social Situation*, which brought together in a concise and purposeful way world-wide data on living conditions in both the developed and the underdeveloped countries.[15] It brought order into a welter of facts and figures out of which emerged an impressive picture of needs and aspirations. Second, the Economic and Social Council, explicitly recognizing the essential interdependence between the improvement of social conditions and the raising of living standards, transmitted the report to the specialized agencies for appropriate action and invited their recommendations on the development of programs of practical action in the social field.[16] Third, the Council requested the Secretary-General, in co-operation with the specialized agencies and appropriate nongovernmental organizations, to prepare for publication in 1954 a companion volume to

[12] U.N. Economic and Social Council, Social Commission, *Use of Community Welfare Centres as Effective Instruments to Promote Economic and Social Progress throughout the World—Report by the Secretary-General*, Doc. E/CN.5/244 (Feb. 28, 1951), and *Use of Community Welfare Centres as Effective Instruments to Promote Economic and Social Progress throughout the World—Document Submitted for Information by the United States of America*, Doc. E/CN.5/L.118 (Mar. 22, 1951).

[13] See below, Chap. X.

[14] U.N. Department of Economic Affairs, *Measures for the Economic Development of Under-Developed Countries* (1951), Chap. II, pp. 13–16. For a discussion of this report, see below, Chap. X.

[15] U.N. Department of Social Affairs, *Preliminary Report on the World Social Situation*, Doc. E/CN.5/267/Rev. 1 (Sept. 8, 1952). (Hereinafter referred to as *Report on the World Social Situation*.)

[16] Res. 434A(XIV), July 28, 1952.

the *Report on the World Social Situation*, this companion volume to survey national and international measures taken to improve social conditions throughout the world. It also arranged for publication, in 1956, of a second edition of the *Report on the World Social Situation*. Finally, the Council requested the Secretary-General, in co-operation with the ILO and other appropriate specialized agencies, to convene a small group of experts to prepare a report on the most satisfactory methods of defining and measuring standards of living and changes therein in various countries.[17] This undertaking, to which reference has already been made, was to lay the foundations for a systematic approach to the problem.

A pioneering study on the *Determinants and Consequences of Population Trends* was published in 1953.[18] It brought into focus the impact of changes in the size and structure of population on economic development and standards of living. In 1953 also, the Economic and Social Council, on the recommendation of the Social Commission, adopted a resolution setting forth a Program of Concerted Practical Action in the Social Field covering both the promotion of higher levels of living and the more traditional programs of social welfare.[19] In the preparation of its recommendations, the Social Commission had at its disposal an analysis by the Secretariat of social problems lending themselves to international action, and of the development of policies and activities relating thereto.[20]

The program as approved by the Council set forth a number of general principles, the first of which was that "economic and social development should go hand in hand with a view to improving standards of living." It stipulated that primary emphasis should be given by the United Nations system to projects that: (a) improve health and nutrition by increasing food supply, improving food distribution and dietary practices; (b) strengthen national health services, improve

---

[17] Res. 434B(XIV), July 25, 1952.
[18] U.N. Department of Social Affairs, *Determinants and Consequences of Population Trends*, A Summary of the Findings of Studies on the Relationships between Population Changes and Economic and Social Conditions, Doc. ST/SOA/Ser.A/17 (1953). A brief summary was published in 1954; see U.N. Department of Social Affairs, *Population Growth and the Standard of Living in Under-Developed Countries*, Population Studies No. 20, Doc. ST/SOA/Ser. A/20 (1954).
[19] Res. 496(XVI), July 31, 1953.
[20] U.N. Economic and Social Council, Sixteenth Session, *Official Records*, Annexes, Agenda Item 10: "Program of Concerted Practical Action in the Social Field of the United Nations and the Specialized Agencies." (Hereinafter cited as "Concerted Practical Action in the Social Field.")

maternal and child health, and prevent and control major communicable diseases; (c) strengthen national family and child welfare services; (d) improve social security measures; (e) develop and extend services for the welfare of groups in need of special care; (f) promote fundamental education, introduce or develop free compulsory primary education for all, and encourage scientific training and research; (g) improve housing and community facilities; (h) increase employment opportunities and improve the social and economic status of workers.

The Council at the same time urged that, in carrying out this program, particular attention be given to the use of the following practical methods and techniques for assisting governments in executing their social programs: (a) promotion and implementation of community development projects; (b) development of programs and facilities for training both professional and technical personnel and auxiliary and community workers; (c) development and strengthening of national and local organizations necessary for administering social programs.

In March 1954, the results of the work of the above-mentioned committee of experts on the measurement of standards and levels of living appeared, and in March 1955, the Secretary-General published the survey of programs of social development that he had been asked in 1952 to undertake.[21] Because international measures in the social field had been outlined in the Program of Concerted Practical Action in the Social Field, the 1955 report was confined to national measures. It revealed an extraordinary range of programs and activities carried on by national governments, both with a view to raising levels of living and protecting or rehabilitating special groups of the population.

Thus, by the beginning of 1955, the attention of the United Nations had clearly been focused on the social aspects of improving levels of living. Studies had been undertaken to develop a better understanding of what is meant by standards and levels of living and methods for their measurement. The impact of changes in population had been investigated. A mass of relevant data on actual living conditions had been gathered and presented. A careful analysis of the development of international programs had been prepared. Agreement had been reached within the United Nations and with the specialized agencies on a concerted program of practical international action in the social field. In theory at least, the old dichotomy between economic and

---

[21] U.N. Secretariat, Bureau of Social Affairs, *International Survey of Programs of Social Development*, Doc. E/CN.5/301/Rev. 1 (Mar. 31, 1955). (Hereinafter cited as *Survey of Programs of Social Development*.)

social objectives was resolved. The combination of the Economic and and Social Departments of the Secretariat of the United Nations into one department at the end of 1954 was more than a symbolic gesture.

With this as background, a more detailed analysis may be made of the insights gained as a result of studies and research, of the specific action programs evolved, and of the achievements registered.

Health

The objective of the World Health Organization is "the attainment by all peoples of the highest possible level of health."[22] Its constitution defines health as "a state of complete physical, mental and social well-being and not merely the absence of disease or infirmity."[23] Other agencies directly interested in health as here defined are the FAO (particularly with respect to nutrition); UNESCO (health education); and the United Nations Children's Fund or UNICEF (health of children and expectant mothers).

So important is the health component and so great was the need for international action that the World Health Organization was compelled to assume important operational and other functions even before it was permanently established. The Final Acts of the International Health Conference, which were signed on July 22, 1946, included an arrangement establishing an Interim Commission, which performed certain essential international health functions until the permanent organization was established on September 1, 1948. The Interim Commission re-established the epidemiological reporting services of the League of Nations and revived the technical work of that organization in such fields as vital statistics, the standardization of drugs and biologicals, the fight against important epidemic diseases, the supervision of international quarantine measures, and the adaptation of international sanitary conventions to conform with modern scientific knowledge and to meet new needs. In the autumn of 1947, it was called upon to help the Egyptian Government combat a major cholera epidemic. In the discharge of this task, it succeeded in getting Soviet planes to fly serum from Moscow and United States army planes to fly serum from Shanghai.

Since then the work of the World Health Organization has been developing in three major areas: the provision of central services, the

---

[22] United Nations, *Final Acts of the International Health Conference*, Constitution of the World Health Organization, Doc. E/155 (October 1946), Art. I.

[23] *Ibid.*, Preamble.

campaign against communicable diseases, and the development and strengthening of national public health services.

Central Services

Basic to the entire work of WHO are the functions that may be grouped under the general title of "central services." These include the stimulation and co-ordination of research and the broadening of the statistical frontiers of medical knowledge. Much of this work is carried on with the help of some thirty expert advisory panels composed of specialists in subjects ranging from alcoholism to zoonoses. These specialists supply the organization with technical advice by correspondence and provide the membership for its expert committees on antibiotics, biological standardization, drugs liable to produce addiction, health statistics, international pharmacopoeia, mental health, midwifery training, nursing, and other major fields.

Epidemiological bulletins are broadcast daily from Geneva (on six wave lengths in English and two in French), weekly from Singapore, and twice weekly from Alexandria. Closely related to this activity is the formulation of health and sanitary regulations. The publication of *Regulation No. 1 Regarding Nomenclature with Respect to Diseases and Causes of Death*[24] was followed in 1952 by the adoption of *Regulation No. 2: International Sanitary Regulations*. The latter are particularly important for purposes of standardizing national and international quarantine measures while expediting travel and trade.

The establishment of international pharmaceutical standards that facilitate and encourage the manufacture of drug products of uniform strength and potency throughout the world is another current activity of WHO. The first volume of the first *International Pharmacopoeia (Pharmacopoeia Internationalis)* setting uniform standards for two hundred important drugs was published in 1951 and a second volume in 1955.

Communicable Diseases

Of more immediate importance for the raising of levels of living are the large-scale campaigns carried on by the World Health Organization, frequently in co-operation with the Children's Fund, against certain endemic and other communicable diseases. This drive has benefited both from the work of many predecessors and from four developments

[24] See the volume in this Brookings series, *The United Nations and Promotion of the General Welfare*, Part One.

of the last ten years.[25] First, the general efforts undertaken since the Second World War to improve social and economic conditions have had important consequences for disease control through improvements in housing, nutrition, personal hygiene, environmental sanitation, general education as well as health education, and better medical care and health services. The World Health Organization itself has had a large share in some of these developments. Second, laboratory facilities have improved as a consequence of the increased demand from medical practitioners and health officers, so that diagnosis has become more adequate, and preventive measures can be applied earlier. Third, active immunization against specific diseases, although not new, has been undertaken on a larger scale since the war. Vaccination against yellow fever has been widely used for two decades and more recently vaccination against typhus has become a practical proposition; immunization against diphtheria and pertussis has become in many countries as widely accepted as small pox vaccination. Fourth, the greatest change in communicable disease control has been brought about by the development of three new types of products that have revolutionized the public health approach to different diseases: chemotherapeutic drugs, antibiotics, and insecticides.

A few examples of successful programs against communicable diseases will illustrate the dramatic effectiveness of modern medical means and the remarkable results achieved by governments working in co-operation with WHO.

Malaria is chiefly a rural disease, which has a severe adverse influence on agricultural and food-producing activities, reduces family income, prevents exploitation of fertile areas, and jeopardizes labor on large construction projects. Fortunately, the application of insecticides such as DDT to the walls of houses has made the control of rural malaria an economically feasible task even for countries that can afford little for public health budgets. Until recently, there have been approximately 300 million cases of malaria each year, with 3 million deaths. As a result of anti-malaria campaigns inspired or aided by WHO, approximately 229 million people, particularly in Asia and Latin America, but also in European countries such as Greece and Italy, have been protected against that disease. Ceylon is a striking example of what can be done. In that country, where work had been conducted on a demonstration basis for many years, a national malaria campaign was

[25] *Survey of Programs of Social Development,* pp. 27–28,

started in 1946. Whereas in that year there were 413 cases of malaria per 1,000 inhabitants, the rate dropped to 5 per 1,000 in 1954. In Latin America, Venezuela, also in 1946, initiated an anti-malaria program involving DDT spraying; 3.8 million people were directly protected in 1956; and malaria mortality, which was 173 per 100,000 inhabitants during the period 1941–45, dropped to 19 deaths among the entire population during 1955.

Extensive use has been made by teams from WHO, and by national teams guided by WHO experts, of penicillin in the treatment of syphilis, yaws, and related infections. The cost per person examined has been approximately ten cents. In Thailand, a campaign for the control of yaws has been in operation since May 1950. Of the 10 million Thais living in affected areas, 7.6 millions had been examined by the end of 1955, and more than a million cases had been treated.

Wide-ranging campaigns against tuberculosis have blunted the threat of that disease. These campaigns have included assistance to and the development of tuberculosis clinics, case finding, X-ray programs, training of specialized personnel, and vaccination with BCG (anti-tuberculosis vaccine). Under the nation-wide BCG vaccination program in India, initiated with assistance from WHO and the Children's Fund, nearly a million and a half persons are now being tested every month, and one third of these are being vaccinated. In Japan, a carefully planned and thorough tuberculosis control program, involving compulsory examination, immunization, reporting and registering of cases, clinical care, and home treatment, has been associated with a drop in deaths caused by tuberculosis from 187.2 per 100,000 inhabitants in 1947 to 62.3 in 1954.

Similar campaigns involving vaccination, environmental sanitation, and other procedures are being carried on against smallpox, yellow fever, typhus, diphtheria, and trachoma.[26]

Public Health Services

The World Health Organization itself considers its work on behalf of the development of public health services its most important task. It has defined the term public health as follows:

Public health is the science and the art of preventing disease, prolonging life, and promoting physical health and efficiency through organized com-

[26] Such campaigns not only save and enrich human life but bring tangible economic benefits as well. For information on the economic aspects of health programs, see C.-E. A. Winslow, *The Cost of Sickness and the Price of Health* (1951).

munity efforts for the sanitation of the environment, the control of community infections, the education of the individual in principles of personal hygiene, the organization of medical and nursing services for the early diagnosis and preventive treatment of disease, and the development of the social machinery which will ensure to every individual in the community a standard of living adequate for the maintenance of health.[27]

In approaching this objective, the first task is the strengthening of national health services, and the second is the establishment and integration of local health services. The activities of WHO and other organs and agencies in the United Nations system can be grouped as follows:

1. Assistance to governments in the preparation of long-term national plans for health;

2. The setting up of model local health services or health demonstration areas in which both international and national personnel participate;

3. Emphasis within these health services on the improvement of environmental sanitation;

4. Health education of the public.

In promoting these objectives, all the known methods of international assistance, including the provision of advisers and of expert field workers, have been employed. Among the most important activities has been the development of facilities for the training of medical and paramedical personnel. The shortage of such personnel has been the greatest handicap in the development of adequate medical services. While Austria and the United States in 1952 had one physician for 650 and 770 inhabitants respectively, India had one physician for 5,700 inhabitants; Haiti, one for 10,000; and Nigeria, one for 58,000. This situation cannot be remedied overnight, but WHO is rendering substantial assistance by helping in the planning of medical schools, the occasional provision of teachers, and the granting of scholarships and fellowships.

In view of the time required to train physicians, high priority has been given also to the training of auxiliary personnel such as assistant doctors, nurses and nurses aides, assistant midwives, and sanitary inspectors. The periods required for such training are more limited and much can be achieved through the organization of short-term courses and on-the-spot training, particularly in connection with the development of local health centers or the work of health teams in the campaign against specific diseases.

The international activities relating to communicable diseases and

[27] World Health Organization, *Health Is Wealth* (1953), p. 14.

the development of public health services are so manifold and varied, and extend over so many territories, that it is quite impossible within the available space to give an adequate impression of their scope. A few statistics, however, may be of help. Between 1947 and the end of 1955, WHO awarded 5,355 fellowships, of which 1,103 were given in 1955. The beneficiaries of these fellowships were not only from the under-developed countries but also from Canada, the United States, and most of the nations of Western Europe. The weight attached to the several fields of activity is to some extent revealed by the fact that of the 1,103 fellowships given in 1955, 129 were awarded for study and training in public health; 151 for sanitation; 202 for nursing, maternal and child health; 186 for other health services; 303 for the study of communicable diseases; and 132 for clinical medicine and health education.[28]

During 1954—a typical recent year—WHO engaged in 337 work projects, most of them in the field, including both developed and under-developed countries.[29] Assistance to governments offered through these projects included expert advice in the development of national health plans and the establishment of national and local health services; assist-ance of individuals and teams in health campaigns, vaccination opera-tions, and application of insecticides; training assistants to nurses and midwives; and a multitude of other training activities at all levels. Such work is contributing greatly to human happiness and well-being, to hope and faith in the future, to the determination to build steadily and persistently the basis for a better life.

Food and Nutrition

In 1951, the Director-General of the Food and Agriculture Organiza-tion remarked about the food supply:

Grim is still the word for the world food situation. . . . In spite of the dark facts I find myself with the feeling of hope and confidence. This is because nations seem at last to be preparing for a genuinely large-scale world war against want. . . . This is essentially a movement to wipe out mass hunger and lift the burden of hopeless poverty from men's shoulders by applying modern scientific knowledge to the development of the earth's resources.[30]

[28] U.N. Technical Assistance Committee, *Eighth Report of the Technical Assistance Board*, Doc. E/2842; E/TAC/REP/66 (Apr. 10, 1956), p. 104.
[29] World Health Organization, *Official Records*, "The Work of WHO, 1954: An-nual Report of the Director-General" (1955), pp. 127–89.
[30] Food and Agriculture Organization, *The Work of the FAO, 1950/51, Report of the Director-General* (1951), pp. 3–4.

The cautious note of optimism reflected in this passage has been justified by substantial improvements in the international food situation.[31] Not only are more people getting enough food, but more and more of them are beginning to enjoy the right food; real advances have been made both in the volume of food production and the level of nutrition. Internationally, the leading role in this battle against want has been played by the FAO, working in co-operation with WHO, with UNICEF, and UNESCO, as well as with other specialized agencies and the United Nations itself.[32]

What has been done thus far is only a beginning. A study prepared by the FAO for the Rome Conference on World Population in 1954 concluded that world production of cereals and many other crops could be at least doubled without assuming anything like the full application of technical knowledge; or alternatively, current production could be obtained from half or less than half of the present area under cultivation. In the case of livestock, the study concluded that the resources and technical basis exist for a level of production of animal products not less than five times the present world output. Fish production could be increased two or threefold without using more than a fraction of the productivity of the seas and inland waters.[33]

Even if these estimates are overoptimistic, they hold out real hope that levels of food consumption may before long become much more adequate than they are now. Recent statistics from a large number of countries on daily supplies of calories per capita (January 1952 or 1952–53) place those countries in the following broad categories:[34]

3,000 calories or over: Argentina, Australia, Canada, Denmark, Finland, Iceland, Ireland, New Zealand, Norway, Sweden, Switzerland, United Kingdom, and United States.
2,800–2,999 calories: Belgium-Luxembourg, France, Germany, Netherlands, and Uruguay.
2,600–2,799 calories: Austria, Cuba (1948–49), Czechoslovakia (1948–49), Turkey, and Union of South Africa.

[31] See above, Chaps. II and IV.
[32] The best accounts of the work of the Food and Agriculture Organization are to be found in Gove Hambidge, *The Story of FAO* (1955), and in Food and Agriculture Organization, *So Bold An Aim, Ten Years of International Cooperation Toward Freedom from Want* (1955).
[33] W. H. Pawley, *et al.*, *Possibilities of Increasing the Supply of Food and Agricultural Products by Exploitation of New Areas and Increasing Yields* (August 1954), 27 pp. (mimeo.).
[34] U.N. Department of Economic Affairs, Statistical Office, *Statistical Yearbook 1954*, pp. 272–75.

2,400–2,599 calories: Cyprus (1948–49), Greece, Israel, Italy, and Southern Rhodesia.
2,200–2,399 calories: Brazil, Chile, Colombia (1948–49), Egypt, Japan, Mauritius (1948–49), Portugal, and Venezuela.
2,000–2,199 calories: Honduras and Pakistan (1948–49).
Under 2,000 calories: Burma (1947–48), Ceylon, and India.

The deficiencies in caloric intake are, by medical standards adjusted to the conditions of the various countries, close to 20 per cent of requirements in parts of Southeast Asia and of Africa. This makes it imperative that every effort be made to provide not only *enough* but the *right kind* of food. This, in turn, raises the problem of nutrition, and of what the United Nations system is doing by way of studies, surveys, and action programs to improve the level of nutrition.

The central objective in nutrition is to make food production and consumption yield the best return in terms of individual health and well-being. Pioneering work in this field was undertaken by the Health Section of the League of Nations.[35] These early activities, together with progress made in such countries as the United States, offered a firm basis, by the end of the Second World War, for further international action. The promotion of nutrition became particularly promising when in 1953, as a result of the general increase in food production, the FAO could turn to the selective expansion of agricultural production, stimulating the output of foods in short supply or of special nutritive value.

The FAO and WHO are collaborating closely in this type of work. A Joint FAO/WHO Expert Committee on Nutrition has been in existence since 1950 and has provided effective co-ordination. The two organizations have fostered extensive studies of food needs in terms of human requirements for calories and nutrients. They have compared estimates of requirements against estimates of consumption, to determine whether the food supplies of countries are sufficient for their needs and whether existing food habits are satisfactory. A continuing task of the Nutrition Division of the FAO is to help countries to improve and refine national food balance sheets, which show the quantities of different food groups and the calories, proteins, and other nutrients available per head of population.

In recent years, on-the-spot surveys of food consumption and habits have not only added new knowledge of deficiencies in rice and maize diets but have led also to more important insights into protein malnutri-

[35] See above, Chap. I.

tion, which appears to be even more serious, particularly for children, than malnutrition resulting from vitamin or mineral deficiencies. World attention was focused on the widespread incidence of protein malnutrition by a study prepared jointly by the FAO and WHO in 1952 on this condition in Central Africa, where it is known as kwashior-kor.[36] During recent years, reports from all parts of the world have told of the same disease taking its toll of children, but under a great many different names, which by their variety had previously obscured the common cause—protein malnutrition. Further extensive surveys were made in Latin America in 1953. Conferences on the subject were organized jointly by the Food and Agriculture Organization and the World Health Organization in 1952 and 1953 in Gambia, Africa, in Java for South and East Asia, and in Venezuela for Latin America. These activities helped prepare the way for effective measures to meet this threat to the health and well-being of millions of young people.

The most direct way of meeting food deficiencies is by supplementary feeding. Such feeding programs were started by the United Nations Relief and Rehabilitation Administration (UNRRA) and later continued by the Children's Fund in co-operation with WHO and the FAO. School feeding programs with emphasis on protein-rich skimmed milk have by now become accepted practice in a number of countries, and many of these programs can be traced directly to international initiative. Special feeding programs are also being developed for plantation and industrial workers with remarkable results in terms of increased productivity.

In countries where milk is in short supply, the FAO has not only assisted in the development of the dairy industry but, under its leadership, successful experiments have been made in developing substitutes for animal milk and other foods of high nutritive value. To provide a protein-rich food, soy milk has been produced for some years in a factory in Hong Kong. Active experiments with soy and peanut preparations are being carried on also in other parts of Asia, particularly in the Philippines, Indonesia, and India. Fish is another protein-rich food, and the FAO has played a considerable part in advising on methods of increasing world fish yields from both fresh and salt water. It has pioneered in the stocking of rice paddies with fish and has promoted the development of the manufacture of fish flour that has no objectionable flavor. Similarly, new processes in the milling of rice

[36] J. F. Brock and M. Autret, *Kwashiorkor in Africa*, FAO Nutrition Studies, No. 8 (March 1952), 78 pp.

have been inspired by FAO-sponsored activities and experiments aimed at avoiding the almost complete loss of thiamine (Vitamin B-1) that occurs in the traditional milling of rice and is the major cause of beri-beri. In the Philippines, rice is being "fortified" on a large scale by vitamin additives.

In addition to developing substitute foods that are rich in protein, the FAO has made an outstanding contribution to the well-being of millions of people in the Middle East and Southeast Asia by saving the "natural" producers of protein-rich foods, i.e., livestock. As described earlier, the FAO since 1946 has co-operated with, and in many cases initiated, campaigns to immunize livestock against rinderpest, a disease that formerly killed millions of head of cattle per year.[37] It has also stimulated the production of other animal vaccines.

Next in importance to improving the production of nutritious food, is the preservation of perishable food of high nutritional value. Here again the FAO has engaged in extensive activities to improve storage facilities, canning, and the development of preserving additives. The Children's Fund has done outstanding work in the establishment of milk-processing plants.

Education in nutrition and the training of nutrition personnel are other subjects that hold a high priority in the FAO/WHO programs. One of the most important aspects of these educational campaigns is the attempt to modify food habits in order to make the best use of available foods. International assistance in the field of education in nutrition has included the publication of a guide that is being widely used in interested countries.[38] International aid also includes the provision of technical advisers to government departments to assist in the development of appropriate national education programs in the field of nutrition. Finally, direct assistance in furthering the supply of trained workers extends to the provision of fellowships, the conduct of regional and national nutrition training courses, in-service training, and the organization of workshops.

More and more of these activities are being carried on and co-ordinated by national nutrition organizations. The creation of such organizations was recommended as early as 1943 by the Hot Springs Conference, which established the Food and Agriculture Organization. At the end of the Second World War, actively functioning nutrition organ-

[37] See above, Chap. IV.
[38] Food and Agriculture Organization, *Teaching Better Nutrition—A Study of Approaches and Techniques*, FAO Nutritional Studies, No. 6.

izations existed in only a few countries, mainly in North America, northern Europe, and Oceania. By 1953, nutrition organizations had been established in India, Indonesia, Japan, Thailand, the Philippines, Malaya, and Singapore. An Institute of Nutrition for Central America and Panama, founded in 1946 under the sponsorship of the Pan American Sanitary Bureau, has been serving the entire Central American region.

Housing

The *Preliminary Report on the World Social Situation* concluded that there is no country without a housing problem.[39] It estimated that as many as 150 million families in the less developed areas required more adequate homes in better physical surroundings. In the industrially advanced countries, the housing deficit was estimated to be more than 30 million family dwelling units. Housing that was poor before the war has become worse as a result of rapid urbanization, population increases, war devastation, and economic dislocations. At the same time, standards for adequate housing have risen.

The socio-economic implications of the situation have become a matter of concern to the United Nations and several of its specialized agencies. The importance of the housing component in determining levels of living was clearly set forth in connection with proposals for an integrated program in the field of housing and town and country planning:

Housing is a most important element in standards of living. On the quantity and quality of the housing available, on the environment in which such accommodation is set, on the cost of housing in relation to family needs, and on the collective amenities made available to the community in the form of facilities for health, education, cultural and recreational services, depends to a large extent the well-being of the community. It is thus clear that the provision of adequate and healthy housing in a suitable environment at the lowest possible cost should constitute an important element in the promotion of " . . . higher standards of living . . . and conditions of economic and social progress and development," with which the United Nations is charged under Articles 55 and 56 of the Charter.[40]

In view of the vast destruction wrought by the Second World War, it is understandable that as early as 1946 a resolution was presented by Australia to the Preparatory Commission of the United Nations in

[39] See Chap. V, "Housing," pp. 53–59.
[40] U.N. Economic and Social Council, *Housing and Town and Country Planning*, Report of the Secretary-General, Doc. E/1343 (June 8, 1949), p. 6.

London requesting the establishment of a commission to deal with questions of housing and town planning. The proposal, however, was considered premature. The problem of housing was taken up later in 1946 by the Temporary Subcommission of the Economic and Social Council on the Economic Reconstruction of Devastated Areas. It presented a survey of immediate housing needs in Europe and drew attention to the fact that the common obstacles to speedy reconstruction were shortages of timber and coal, of skilled labor, and, in some countries, of manufactured goods. The main objective, it indicated, should be to carry out reconstruction conforming to modern social and technical requirements. The subcommission also associated itself with the report of a special meeting on emergency housing problems held in Brussels, in July 1946, under the auspices of the Emergency Economic Committee for Europe, which recommended that the Economic and Social Council sponsor a permanent international housing organization.

No such organization has been created. The idea was abandoned because (1) several existing agencies already included within their functions various aspects of housing, and a new agency might have led to duplication; and (2) it was believed that housing problems could best be handled on a regional basis. Therefore, from 1946 onward, stress was laid on the development of co-ordinated rather than centralized action, and emphasis was placed on regional activities.

Between 1946 and 1952, the General Assembly and the Economic and Social Council passed a series of basic resolutions that gave form and direction to intergovernmental action in the field of housing.[41] As a result of these resolutions and of practical experience gained over the years, co-ordinating responsibility in the field of housing has been assigned to the Social Commission. The Population Commission, which has been interested in housing in so far as fluctuations in the density of population may affect housing conditions and vice versa, has been supplying interested organizations with the population figures required to permit a better evaluation of housing problems. The Commission on Human Rights has been concerned with adequate housing as a "right," while the Commission on the Status of Women has been concerned with those aspects of housing that make life easier for the housewife, improve the health of the family, and provide children with the opportunity for safe and full development.

[41] See U.N. General Assembly Resolutions: 53(I), Dec. 14, 1946; 537(VI), Feb. 2, 1952. U.N. Economic and Social Council Resolutions: 50(IV), Mar. 28, 1947; 122D(VI), Mar. 1, 1948; 155F(VII), Aug. 13, 1948; 243D(IX), July 23, 1949; 434I(XIV), July 28, 1952.

Co-operation between the interested specialized agencies and the United Nations has been facilitated through a "Technical Working Group on Housing and Town and Country Planning" set up by the Administrative Committee on Coordination. Among the participating agencies, the FAO has been concerned primarily with housing standards for rural areas. It has been interested in addition in standardizing construction methods and timber materials in order to economize on these items. The ILO has been concerned not only with the working conditions of labor in the building industry but also with the availability of good housing for all workers. The problem of reducing production costs in the building industry and of subsidies to the industry to facilitate the provision of cheaper housing, have been subjects of extended study by the International Labour Organisation. UNESCO has been concerned with the improvement of the technical education of architects and planners, the development of technical schools, and the popularization of better housing through literature, films, and exhibitions. WHO has, of course, been interested in the health aspects of housing and housing standards, and particularly in better sanitation.

Within the Secretariat of the United Nations a Housing, Building and Planning Branch, as well as a Housing Reference Center, have been functioning since the early days of the Organization. The Secretariat publishes a bulletin that contains a great deal of technical information on housing, although some of it is highly specialized and, at times, academic.[42] The United Nations Technical Assistance Administration is concerned with technical assistance projects in the field of housing.

The programs and activities set forth in a report by the Secretary-General in 1949,[43] as revised by the Economic and Social Council in 1952[44] and developed in subsequent practice, lend themselves to discussion under four headings: housing conditions and planning; building materials and the construction industry; financing; and self-help housing.

Housing Conditions and Planning

Housing conditions are kept under review by the several regional commissions, particularly the Economic Commission for Europe (ECE) and the Economic Commission for Asia and the Far East (ECAFE).

The ECE, building on preliminary work of the Emergency Economic Committee for Europe, concentrated from the start on housing needs

[42] *Bulletin on Housing and Town and Country Planning.*
[43] U.N. Economic and Social Council, *Housing and Town and Country Planning.*
[44] Res. 434I(XIV), July 25, 1952.

and programs in Europe for the years 1948–55, requirements for building materials, and measures to economize in the use of scarce materials. The secretariat of the ECE publishes annual reviews of the European housing situation, in addition to a *Quarterly Bulletin on European Housing Statistics*, started in 1953. A major achievement of the ECE in the field of housing has been the establishment of the International Council for Building Research and Documentation, a European regional council of national research centers, which is in no way dependent on the United Nations for financing.

Work in Asia and the Far East was stimulated by a mission of experts on tropical housing that visited South and Southeast Asia in 1950 and 1951.[45] The United Nations Regional Seminar on Housing and Community Improvement held in New Delhi in 1954 was a direct consequence of the work of that mission. Government officials, representatives of the United Nations and the specialized agencies, and housing and planning experts attended this seminar, as well as the Regional Conference of the International Federation for Housing and Town Planning organized in conjunction with it. The seminar was followed by a session of the ECAFE Working Party on Housing and Building Materials, which helped to translate the findings of the seminar into recommendations to governments of the area.

As a result of these and other activities, plans are maturing for the establishment of two regional housing centers under the guidance of ECAFE in co-operation with the governments concerned, and with the assistance of the United Nations and interested specialized agencies. A center in Indonesia is expected to deal with housing in humid tropical areas; while a second center in India studies similar problems in dry tropical countries. The main task of these centers will be the co-ordination of studies, research, and developmental work carried out in the region on the economic, social, technological, and administrative aspects of housing, building, and planning.

The Economic Commission for Latin America (ECLA) has paid less attention to housing problems because housing has been a matter of special concern to the Organization of American States and its Inter-American Council on Housing. Both ECLA and the United Nations headquarters, however, had a share in the establishment in 1951 of the Inter-American Housing Center in Bogotá, which serves all of Latin America. The major function of the Center is to offer a

---

[45] U.N. Secretariat, *Low Cost Housing in South and South-East Asia*, Doc. ST/SOA/3/Rev. 1 (July 16, 1951).

one-year graduate course in housing that emphasizes the interrelationship of architecture, engineering, and the economic and social aspects of the housing problem.

Building Materials and Industry

To be economical, building activity has to be based essentially on local building materials. The United Nations has been able to encourage research regarding such materials by the provision of experts and of fellowships, by demonstration projects, and by help in the establishment of research and training centers such as those mentioned above.

Related to this problem of building materials is the problem of standardization, which is, of course, of importance both to developed and underdeveloped countries. In the economically less developed countries, there is generally a serious lack of standardization of building materials and construction methods. In the postwar period, however, there has been increasing experimentation, fostered partly by the United Nations, with basic housing designs and with a better use of readily available local building materials. Some of the results of these efforts were illustrated at the International Exhibition of Low Cost Housing staged in 1954 by the Government of India with the help of the United Nations. Eighty houses for the lower-income groups, built with different materials and designed in several countries, were exhibited there.

With a view to reducing the cost of building in Europe, the ECE has been investigating on a continuing basis the rationalization of building methods. On an even broader basis the Secretariat of the United Nations has been encouraging general building research, some of the results of which have been reproduced in the *Bulletin on Housing and Town and Country Planning.*[46]

Financing

Attention was given to the financing of housing in 1952 by the General Assembly, the Economic and Social Council, and the Social Commission. Although local financing was emphasized as practically the exclusive source of capital for housing purposes, sufficient pressure was generated by the representatives of the underdeveloped countries for the General Assembly to include a request to the Economic and Social Council to give urgent attention to "assistance to governments in

[46] Bulletin 8 (1953).

developing practical methods for financing housing programs from domestic *or external sources*."[47] The Social Commission at its eighth session also urged an exploration of the possibilities of external financing.

In the course of these discussions, it was suggested that the International Bank for Reconstruction and Development ought to extend its loan activities to the financing of housing. The Bank gave little encouragement to this suggestion. It indicated that the basic test of any project to be financed by the Bank was its contribution to productivity and that the relation of housing to increased productivity was most apparent in cases where housing development was an integral part of a directly productive project—for example, workers' housing for an industrial plant. In other cases, the most effective and economic way of stimulating more housing was investment in basic industries such as steel, power, transportation, and the like, that support an active building industry. Another basic requirement was that Bank loans are normally made to cover only foreign exchange needs rather than local currency needs. In summary, the aid of the Bank to housing would most likely take the form in the future, as in the past, of investment in basic utilities and industries, thus helping to build economies in which housing industries could become progressively more efficient.[48]

While the underdeveloped countries frequently reiterated their desire for international financing for housing purposes, the work of the United Nations, in research and in technical assistance, has emphasized the development of domestic resources. Recent reports, for example, contain valuable data on government housing schemes and subsidies, and on the methods employed in different countries to overcome the discrepancy between the "social rent" (what the consumer can afford to pay for adequate housing) and the "economic rent" (what the consumer should be charged according to actual costs.)[49]

Self-help Housing

In view of the inadequacy of available capital, the promotion of "self-help housing" has assumed increasing importance. Such self-

[47] Res. 537(VI), Feb. 2, 1952. Italics supplied.

[48] U.N. Economic and Social Council, *Housing and Town and Country Planning*, Statement by the Representative of the International Bank for Reconstruction and Development on Financing of Housing, Doc. E/CN.5/284 (May 23, 1952).

[49] U.N. Economic and Social Council, *Financing of Housing and Community Improvement Programs*, Report by the Secretary-General, Doc. E/CN.5/307 (Mar. 7, 1955). See also *Survey of Programs of Social Development*, Chap. IV.

help housing makes maximum use of underemployed labor and of materials available locally. In 1953, a self-help housing workshop and seminar was convened in Puerto Rico, sponsored jointly by the Caribbean Commission, the United States Foreign Operations Administration and the United States Housing and Home Finance Agency, and assisted by the Technical Cooperation Office of Puerto Rico. The seminar suggested that aided self-help be employed as a basis for providing adequate housing and other community facilities for low-income groups, in view of the advantages to the families concerned and to the government that could be derived from this method. A seminar on housing through nonprofit associations was organized by the United Nations and the Danish Government in collaboration with the Organization of American States. The seminar, which was held in Denmark in 1954 with the participation of thirteen Latin American countries, was a good example of the contribution that one geographic region can make to another. A similar seminar, again in Denmark but for countries from Asia, was held in 1956.

It is difficult to gauge the results of the activities of the United Nations system in housing. Despite what has been said and done, the progress made has been small compared with existing needs. It should, however, not be forgotten that most of the programs are long-range programs, the effects of which will be felt only during the years to come. In many parts of the world, real progress in housing depends on over-all economic development. Headway in housing can undoubtedly be speeded, however, and this is being done by the mobilization of domestic resources, both material and human—a mobilization that, at least to some extent, is being inspired and guided by international agencies.

Home Economics

Home economics represents another of the social approaches to the raising of levels of living. It is concerned with numerous aspects of family life, including home management, child training and care, cleanliness and elementary sanitation, the choice of foods, the preparation of family meals, the domestic production, storage, and processing of foods, and the provision and care of clothing and household furnishings. The purpose of education in home economics is to funnel the advances of science and management into the service of the individual family, especially through the education of women in the better use of family resources. Home-making is the chief full-time occupation of women throughout the world and adequate education in this field can contribute importantly to the attainment of higher levels of living.

The scope of international programs in this field is indicated in the following passage:

> In particular, assistance is being rendered to governments in the following ways: providing technical advisers to government departments to assist in promoting education in home economics at all levels and in establishing training centres for home economics teachers and rural leaders; participating in rural demonstration, production and training centres where the education of women is a significant part of the total programme; holding regional meetings for government officials and other leaders responsible for the promotion and development of home economics education and extension; participating in meetings of international nongovernmental women's organizations whose programme and activities centre around the problems of the rural family; providing a home economics information exchange for the use of member governments and country leaders in home economics education and extension.[50]

A few illustrations may be helpful. Home economics work by the FAO was initiated in the Caribbean area in 1949. A technical meeting on nutrition and home economics held in 1952 gave direction to the program and resulted in the establishment of an Advisory Council on Home Economics for the British West Indies, a three-months training course in home economics at the University of Puerto Rico, and the evaluation and further development of home economics curricula in public schools in the area. Another six-weeks training course on nutrition and home economics, sponsored jointly by the FAO, the Organization of American States, and the Government of Ecuador, was held in Quito in 1954. Home economics projects are under way also in Egypt, and an extension of this type of work to the Far East is planned by the FAO.

This work is not confined to underdeveloped countries. FAO is active in Working Group No. 10 on Rural Home Economics of the Food and Agriculture Committee of the Organization for European Economic Cooperation. It thus collaborates with OEEC in planning training programs and special home economics projects in countries that are members of the OEEC.

Employment and Working Conditions

High levels of employment and equitable working conditions, including adequate wages and reasonable hours of work, are basic to the

---

[50] "Concerted Practical Action in the Social Field," p. 28.

achievement and maintenance of satisfactory levels of living. Such adjectives as "equitable," "adequate," "reasonable," and "satisfactory," can be defined only in terms of evolving social concepts.

Various economic policies and measures to attain and maintain high levels of employment have already been discussed in this study.[51] The present discussion is concerned with action aimed at improving the working conditions of individual workers, at setting and achieving standards of wages and hours that will permit "satisfactory" levels of living. Among other things, this requires a discussion of measures for making optimum use of available labor resources, since improved levels of living are contingent on increased productivity. In this context, such matters have to be considered as: vocational guidance and training; employment services; occupational health and safety; the protection of young workers and of women; and industrial relations.[52]

Although the International Labour Organisation has made some outstanding contributions to economic research, it has in recent years concentrated on labor issues as such. Broad economic policy issues have been left to the United Nations, but the ILO has continued to be the major agency in setting labor standards through conventions and recommendations, while increasingly developing practical action programs aimed at assisting countries in attaining these standards.

Man-power Programs

Vocational guidance and training, and employment services, have the common objective of matching people and jobs. They thus contribute to the integration of the individual in society and help society to meet the needs for different types of labor. A prerequisite for these activitiee is adequate employment information.[53] The ILO therefore has been giving high priority to man-power surveys and the development of continuing machinery for obtaining current employment information. These matters were given special attention at the Asian Man-power Technical Conference in Bangkok in 1951 and at the Latin American Man-power Technical Conference in Lima in 1952.

[51] See above, Chap. V.
[52] For additional discussion see "Concerted Practical Action in the Social Field," Chap. 6, pp. 35–51; and *Survey of Programs of Social Development*, Chaps. VII and VIII. Especially helpful are the annual reports of the ILO submitted to the United Nations since 1947 in pursuance of Article V, paragraph 2(a), of the Agreement between the United Nations and the ILO. Even more comprehensive and authoritative information is to be found in the *International Labour Code 1951*, Vols. I and II.
[53] *Cf.* International Labour Organisation, *Seventh Report of the International Labour Organisation to the United Nations* (1953), pp. 27 ff.

In preparing and carrying out man-power studies and surveys, the ILO works with the three regional economic commissions of the United Nations. Surveys were made in collaboration with ECAFE in 1948 and with ECLA in 1949. A special ILO-UNESCO Working Party on Trained Personnel for Economic Development has for several years been working on a manual to assist Asian countries wishing to carry out man-power surveys.

In order to facilitate surveys and to render them internationally comparable—which is important for migration purposes—it is essential to establish common definitions and classifications of occupations. The most outstanding contribution of the ILO in this field has been the publication of an international classification, in which occupations are grouped according to similarities of skill requirements.[54] It is designed to facilitate the transfer of workers belonging to an occupation in one group to other occupations within the same group, with a minimum of retraining or adaptation and with a maximum of productive efficiency. Definitions of occupations are also included for each group and, in addition, tables of occupational comparability have been worked out, thus facilitating job comparisons between countries using different occupational terminologies.

The objective in vocational guidance has been to assist governments to establish and develop facilities for aiding individuals to choose occupations and to progress in these occupations, with due regard for the characteristics, aptitudes, and training of the individual on the one hand, and the available occupational opportunities on the other. One of the chief contributions of the ILO in this respect was the adoption, in 1949, of a Vocational Guidance Recommendation.[55] Its provisions are based on the experience and practice of the United States and Western Europe where up to 50 per cent of young persons ready to leave school are now receiving guidance offered either by special counselors attached to the schools or through employment offices. In many cases such offices or special guidance centers provide guidance on a continuing basis, irrespective of age.

The recommendation, coupled with expert advice to governments,

[54] International Labour Organisation *International Classification of Occupations for Migration and Employment Placement*, Vol. I, Occupational Titles, Codes and Definitions; Vol. II, Tables of Occupational Comparability (June 1952).

[55] For texts of this and other recommendations and conventions adopted by the International Labour Conference 1919-51, see International Labour Office, *International Labour Code 1951*. For texts adopted after 1951, see periodic issues of the ILO *Official Bulletin*.

fellowships, regional meetings, and vocational guidance "kits" prepared by the ILO and UNESCO, has in recent years stimulated and aided the development of guidance programs in all parts of the world, particularly in Asia and Latin America. According to the annual report of the Director-General of the ILO for 1954, growing interest in the use of vocational guidance services and the application of aptitude testing in relation to youth training and placement has recently been displayed in a number of countries in the process of industrialization, among them Brazil, Greece, Israel, and Indonesia.

Guidance has to be supplemented by training, and this has required assistance in the development of vocational schools, training centers, and facilities for in-service training to provide special skills. At the same time, it is essential that occupational training be so organized as to make for the adaptability of the individuals trained. Adaptability is important both for mobility of labor in the highly developed countries and for the integration of a growing industrial labor force in countries in the process of development. This is one aspect of the fundamental education programs developed by UNESCO, of which more will be said later.[56]

In training, the ILO has been active also in promulgating standards. It followed its Vocational Guidance Recommendation by a Recommendation, in 1950, on Vocational Training (Adults). Regional conferences such as the Asian Conference of Experts on Vocational Training in Singapore, 1949, have been organized to help governments apply such standards. Going beyond this, the ILO, particularly through its program of technical assistance, has set up regional field offices for manpower training, productivity centers, and apprenticeship institutes such as the Apprenticeship Training Institute for Asian Countries that was held at the end of 1952. The program of the institute provided for a study tour of national apprenticeship services by fifteen officials from nine Asian countries, to observe methods and techniques of proved value in France, the Netherlands, Switzerland, and the United Kingdom.

In addition, the ILO has helped individual countries carry out training programs. Most outstanding of these is the ILO vocational training project in Yugoslavia. In 1954, with the help of technical assistance funds, nearly four hundred Yugoslav worker-trainees had been or were at work in various industries all over Europe. Some thirty-five

[56] See below, Chap. IX.

instructor-foremen from ten different countries assisted in training activities in Yugoslavia itself. In addition, a course in management techniques was organized in France for a group of general and technical managers from some of the more important industries in Yugoslavia. Reports from factories, from instructor-foremen, and from trainees indicate that improvements of great economic value have been introduced by the trainees on their return and by the instructor-foremen in the course of their work in the Yugoslav industries.[57]

Another link in the chain of international activities for the rational use of man power is the promotion of employment services. As early as 1919, the Unemployment Convention—the second convention ever passed by the International Labour Organisation—provided for the setting-up of employment services assisted by advisory committees, including employers and workers. With the growing awareness of the importance of such services, more elaborate principles were adopted, first in 1944, particularly in the Employment (Transition from War to Peace) Recommendation, and then, in 1948, in the Employment Service Convention and Recommendation. These laid down basic principles to be followed in order that employment services might ensure the best possible organization of the employment market as an integral part of the national program for the achievement and maintenance of full employment and the development and use of productive resources. These general standards have since been further elaborated in Europe through the adoption by the Council of the OEEC, in July 1954, of a series of International Standards of Employment Service Organization, which was developed with the assistance of the ILO with a view to achieving general conformity in Europe over a five-year period.

The ILO is assisting less developed countries in establishing employment services, using mainly such devices as experts and fellowships. Efforts are being made to provide for clearance on a regional and national scale, through employment services, of job offers and applications for employment. This has proved of particular importance in such countries as Brazil, where a special placement service in the State of Sao Paulo is facilitating the large-scale movement of agricultural workers and their families from the overpopulated regions of the northeast to the south of the country.

In summary, man-power programs represent one of the important fields for technical assistance and technical co-operation in raising levels

---

[57] International Labour Organisation, *Eighth Report of the International Labour Organisation to the United Nations* (1954), p. 66.

of living. During the last few years, close to 60 per cent of all the technical assistance work of the ILO has been devoted to man-power problems.

Conditions of Work

International concern with conditions of work has been focused primarily on four areas: wages and earnings; hours of work and holidays with pay; occupational health and safety; and the protection of special categories of workers (*e.g.*, children).

The latest of the conventions and recommendations that have been adopted by the ILO concerning the protection of wages—and the only major convention concluded in this field since the end of the war—is the 1949 Convention on Protection of Wages. It provides that wages ordinarily be paid both regularly and in the legal tender of the country; defines permissible deductions from wages; and includes safeguards against exploitation in company stores.

Although the number of conventions and recommendations regarding wages is large, it goes without saying that the standards they set are less effective where trade unions are not in existence, are too weak to serve as real instruments of collective bargaining, or are exploited for ends other than those for which they were founded.

Many countries, therefore, including of late a number of underdeveloped countries, have found it necessary to establish statutory minimum wages. The Asian Regional Conference of the ILO in 1953 gave special attention to this problem. In the words of the Eighth Report of the ILO to the United Nations:

> The Conference unanimously agreed that collective agreements are normally the best means for the determination and adjustment of wages. But, while recognising that the rapid expansion of collective bargaining between adequately organised groups of employers and workers was the ultimate objective, the Conference recommended that, pending this development and as a preliminary step towards collective negotiation, statutory minimum wages should be fixed and regularly reviewed by tripartite machinery. The enforcement of statutory wage regulations should be the responsibility of an adequately staffed and equipped authority. Finally, the Conference recommended that the closest possible attention should be given to maintaining a relationship between wage regulation and the requirements of economic development.[58]

Thus, the conference recognized the pitfalls of wage policies that, inspired by a desire to improve wage levels rapidly, may result in in-

[58] *Ibid.*, p. 17.

flationary pressures and interfere with sound economic development. Similar reflections can be found in other ILO publications on wage policies in Asia and in Latin America.[59]

An increasing number of developed countries are confronted with a narrowing of wage differentials as a result of minimum wage fixing, full employment, technological change, social policies, and other factors. This raises a number of problems that are being given increasing attention by the ILO and, to some extent, by UNESCO. Some reduction in the gap between the wages of skilled and unskilled workers, and even professional workers, may be desirable. However, if wage differentials are narrowed too much by regulation, the result may be a loss of incentive to acquire or use socially needed skills. In this connection, the ILO has studied various aspects of the application of systems of payment by results. It has also shown a concern for the economic conditions of professional workers, their employment and income levels.

Another important issue in wage policy is the principle of equal pay for equal work. This has been a matter of interest to the Commission on the Status of Women, which has passed a series of resolutions on the subject. The principle that there should be "equal remuneration for men and women workers, for work of equal value," *i.e.*, rates of remuneration established without discrimination based on sex, is now contained in the 1951 Convention on Equal Remuneration for Work of Equal Value adopted by the ILO. The 1951 convention provides for gradual application of this principle in keeping with the gradualist approach that is characteristic of the ILO.

Not only wages, but hours of work as well, have been burning issues in labor relations ever since the industrial revolution, and one of the chief preoccupations of the ILO. In recent years, the problem has become much less acute as an international issue for reasons that are clearly set forth in the following quotation:

The excessive length of the working day and its ill-effects upon the health of workers, family life and productivity, have been among the first preoccupations of national and international action. International action in this field taken soon after the First World War resulted in the adoption of international standards limiting hours of work in industrial undertakings and in commerce and offices to eight a day and forty-eight a week, and fixing a minimum rest period of twenty-four consecutive hours per week in all public and private industrial undertakings. A trend towards a further reduction from the eight-

[59] International Labour Office, *Problems of Wage Policies in Asian Countries*, Studies and Reports, New Series, No. 43 (1956); and *Minimum Wages in Latin America*, Studies and Reports, New Series, No. 34 (1954).

hour day and forty-eight hour week led to the adoption of international regulations concerning the reduction of hours of work in particular industries or occupations but was interrupted by the Second World War and has since been held in check in many countries by various considerations connected with reconstruction or production requirements.

In the present circumstances international action in this field consists primarily in providing information on the regulation of hours of work and in assisting countries, on request, in drawing up laws and regulations in accordance with existing international standards.[60]

By contrast, international interest in the problem of holidays with pay has recently been much more pronounced. As early as 1936, the ILO had formulated international instruments setting forth minimum standards with regard to lengths of holidays, qualifying periods of continuous service, and similar questions, with a view to encouraging the introduction of annual holidays with pay in industrial and commercial establishments. A convention of the ILO, adopted in 1952, was designed to extend these principles to agriculture. It was followed, in 1954, by a recommendation concerning holidays with pay, providing that every person should be entitled after one year of continuous service with the same employer to an annual holiday with pay of not less than two normal working weeks. As a corollary to these developments, both the ILO and UNESCO have engaged in studies regarding better use of leisure time and the development of leisure time facilities.

Occupational health and safety is another field that has been of concern to the ILO since its inception. The objective has been to prevent occupational injuries and to protect the health of the workers in their places of employment. Occupational hazards have greatly increased in an increasingly industrialized world. With the growing mechanization of agriculture, a new element of risk has been added even in underdeveloped countries unaccustomed to the use of machines.

In this field, the setting of health and safety standards is one of the most important lines of attack. International standards of industrial safety are contained in comprehensive recommendations passed by the ILO prior to and since the Second World War. For example, a recommendation in this field, adopted in 1953, concerns "the protection of health of workers in places of employment" and deals with the control of health hazards, medical examinations, notification of occupational disease, and the provision of first aid facilities. It deals also in some detail with the ways in which environmental hygiene may be main-

[60] "Concerted Practical Action in the Social Field," p. 42.

tained in work places, the technical measures to protect workers from harmful agents, the use of protective clothing and equipment, the obligation to keep workers informed of any dangers arising from the nature of their work, and the periodic testing of atmospheric conditions to which workers are exposed.

International agencies have furthermore provided information on the health hazards of industrial and business life, and guidance for dealing with particular occupational diseases. The ILO publishes a periodical, *Occupational Safety and Health,* and has started revision of an earlier encyclopedia on *Occupation and Health.* Through technical assistance, advice and guidance is being offered to countries in safety and health matters, either by sending field consultants, granting fellowships for training, or on the basis of special research undertaken at the request of governments, safety associations, trade unions, and other groups.

For purposes of co-ordination, there is a Joint ILO/WHO Committee on Occupational Health. Partly as a result of the work of this committee, more and more emphasis is being placed on the health protection of workers in their places of employment, utilizing the latter as an avenue of approach to general health problems. At the same time, there has been a decided shift from emphasis on compensation in cases of occupational injury to emphasis on the reduction of occupational hazards.

In the promotion of better conditions of work for young persons and for women, the long record of the International Labour Organisation has been extended during the postwar period. Even in some economically advanced countries, but especially in the less developed countries, young children are still found at work in small-scale enterprises, handicrafts, and nonindustrial activities, including street trading and domestic service. In particular, great numbers of children are still working in agriculture under conditions detrimental to their health and well-being.[61]

The basic objectives of international action to provide for the protection of young workers in all countries, and particularly in technically less advanced countries, are to assist governments:

(a) to limit progressively child labour in all fields of occupation as rapidly as educational facilities are made available;

(b) to promote vocational guidance, vocational training and apprenticeship and placement services;

(c) to promote the extension of the protection of young workers to all occupations including employment in small-scale industrial enterprises, nonin-

[61] *Preliminary Report on the World Social Situation,* pp. 111–12.

dustrial occupations (including street trading), seasonal employment, and agriculture;

(d) to provide for adequate means of enforcing the legal provisions protecting young workers in all occupations.[62]

The international program of action to realize the above objectives has included many features such as guidance and training that have already been mentioned in this discussion. In addition, there are in existence ILO conventions, recommendations, and studies regarding minimum ages for admission to employment in industry, agriculture, and nonindustrial occupations; medical examination of young persons for employment; employment of young persons at night; and employment of young persons in nonmetropolitan territories. Most of these instruments lay down minimum standards for legislative action to provide for the protection of young workers; some include programs of general social protection, educational opportunity, and regulation of admission to employment and conditions of work, or set forth general principles concerning the administration of protective measures for children and young persons and the collaboration required on a national and international basis.

However great the educational value of these standards may be, their application remains a difficult question, particularly in agriculture and in the underdeveloped countries generally. Nevertheless, some real progress has been made as a result of this work, especially in Asia and the Middle East. New legislation regarding the employment of young people has been passed in recent years in India, Iran, Israel, Japan, and the Philippines.

An essential corollary to the setting of minimum ages for work is the development of free compulsory education. To the extent possible, legislation in both areas should be synchronized. An indication of the growing awareness of this need can be found in the conclusions of the ILO Asian Regional Conference that met in Tokyo in 1953. One of the main items on its agenda was the question of measures for the protection of young workers in Asian countries. The resolution adopted by the conference dealt in detail with the development of free compulsory education, vocational training, vocational guidance and youth employment services, and the extension of regulations for the restriction of child labor and the protection of young workers in employment.

Activities on behalf of women workers also have been extensive. Women workers have benefited, during the last fifty years, from the

[62] "Concerted Practical Action in the Social Field," p. 45.

progress of workers in general. Nonetheless, the participation of women in economic life has raised two related series of specific problems: those concerning equal opportunity for men and women regarding occupation and income; and those deriving from the maternal function of women and their role in society. The Convention on Equality of Remuneration approved in 1951 was the most important recent attempt to assure women equality of opportunity. Earlier conventions and recommendations provided for equality of opportunity for vocational training and employment services. The current efforts of UNESCO to promote equal educational opportunities for women attack existing inequalities in employment and remuneration at their root.

Other standards in the form of conventions and recommendations afford women workers the protection required for their biological and social functions as mothers and home-makers. Noteworthy in this context is the revision, effected in 1952, of the Convention on Maternity Protection originally adopted in 1919. Other related conventions cover such subjects as limitation of night work and of employment in unhealthy and hazardous occupations.

As one way of furthering the application of these standards, the ILO has promoted, by the usual methods of advice, training, publications, and international meetings, the development of legislation, including the establishment of women's bureaus in government departments of labor.

Although the progress made in protecting women and assuring them equality of opportunity with due regard for their biological and social functions is encouraging, it has raised new problems. Legislation on equal pay or on the provision of special protection for women may result in narrowing their opportunities for work and may make it more difficult for them to find employment. An answer to this problem is being sought in the enlargement of opportunities for vocational training for women and in providing for part-time work. The latter subject has been considered by the Commission on the Status of Women. The issue is still in the study stage, and the chief result to date has been a report on part-time employment prepared by the ILO at the request of the Commission on the Status of Women.[63]

Other groups of special concern to the ILO include agricultural workers and seafarers. Particularly in its technical assistance activities in the underdeveloped countries, the ILO has given attention to prob-

[63] U.N. Economic and Social Council, *Part-Time Employment, Preliminary Report Prepared by the International Labour Office*, Doc. E/CN.6/222 (Feb. 12, 1953).

lems of agricultural labor and has attempted to extend its standards, as far as possible, to agricultural workers. Some measure of success has been obtained with regard to workers on plantations, where approved standards can be most readily enforced. Working conditions on the land are, of course, only one aspect of levels of living of the agricultural population. Equally important are health, housing, and related matters. Substantial improvements in levels of living are contingent, therefore, not so much on special measures promoted by particular agencies or organs in the United Nations system as on the balanced development of the country as a whole.

Maritime conferences have been held periodically to establish and revise standards of employment and working conditions for seafarers. The conventions and recommendations of the ILO in this field have done much to equalize competitive conditions in the shipping industry.

Industrial Relations

The development and maintenance of sound relations between employers and workers constitute another essential element in achieving those higher levels of productivity on which improved levels of living to a large extent depend. They are equally basic to the existence of a "climate" in which men and women at work can pursue "both their material well-being and their spiritual development in conditions of freedom and dignity, of economic security and equal opportunity."[64] This explains the international concern for the promotion of freedom of association and the protection of the right to organize and bargain collectively.

With the adoption, in 1947, of a resolution concerning freedom of association and protection of the right to organize and bargain collectively, the International Labour Conference broadened its program for the improvement of industrial relations.[65] Prior to this date, the work of the ILO in the field of industrial relations had consisted of the development of techniques for intergroup discussion and negotiation, of giving a stimulus to the development of effective organizations of employers and workers in many countries and to the growth of systematic co-operation between such organizations, and of issuing numerous publications relating to industrial relations and cognate questions. The organization was eminently fitted for these tasks because of its tripartite composition.

[64] "Concerted Practical Action in the Social Field," p. 49.
[65] International Labour Office, *International Labour Code 1951*, Vol. I, p. 675.

The adoption by the conference, in 1947, of the above-mentioned resolution was followed by the adoption, in 1948 and 1949, of two conventions dealing with freedom of association and the protection of the right to organize and to bargain collectively. Other recommendations on collective bargaining, voluntary conciliation of industrial disputes, and consultation and co-operation between employers and workers at the job site were adopted thereafter.

Since 1949, considerable attention has been given to the "enforcement" of trade union rights. This has involved study and discussion, in the Economic and Social Council and the Governing Body of the ILO and subsidiary bodies, of allegations of violations of trade union rights.[66]

Quite recently, the ILO has broadened its concern with employment and working conditions to include the field known as human relations in industry. In 1955, the Director-General called for an international discussion of ways and means to create a more effective relationship between workers and employers. "Industrial democracy," in the words of the Director-General, "can never be an abstraction—it must be a living thing. The practice of labor-management relations in every day life is the key to its vitality."[67] The United States and a few other highly developed countries have made much progress in this field. The stimulation of similar progress elsewhere through the ILO involves a departure from its traditional emphasis on the setting of standards for legislation. The Director-General's willingness to adopt a new approach is clear from the following additional statement in the above-quoted report:

> Good industrial relations cannot be obtained through legislation. Legislation and administrative services are a necessary basic framework, but the working out of common problems of labor-management relations lies, inevitably, in the hands of the two parties most directly concerned.
> The mere fact that employers and workers agree to bargain collectively is not sufficient to insure satisfactory relationships. Much depends on the state of mind in which they engage in negotiations.[68]

In pursuing his subject, the Director-General pointed to the importance of joint labor-management committees, often also called works councils or works committees, both in private industry and in undertakings owned and operated by the state. He concluded that "a great deal more emphasis might well be laid on developing an understanding of

---

[66] See the monograph in this Brookings series, *The United Nations and Human Rights*, Chap. IV.

[67] International Labour Organisation, *Report of the Director General, International Labour Conference, Thirty-eighth Session* (1955), p. 8.

[68] *Ibid.*, pp. 63–64.

the human factors which make up the industrial society at the work level." And "solutions for many problems hitherto regarded primarily as concerning technical points or welfare may now be conceived with more explicit recognition of the psychological factors which lie at their roots."[69]

This new, more flexible conception of relations between labor and management is unlikely to win rapid acceptance. Employers may object to "interference" with what they consider their prerogatives of management. Workers may be uneasy and afraid of "psychological paternalism." They may consider their hard won right to collective bargaining an end in itself and may not be eager to accept a shift "from collective bargaining to collective thinking."

Nevertheless, the discussion has been opened, and it is likely to occupy the ILO and other international bodies for some time to come. It is probably no accident that it arose only a year after the Soviet Union and other Communist-dominated countries joined the International Labour Organisation. The promotion of human relations in industry and the harmonizing of labor-management relations may well prove to be an effective answer to some of the claims of Soviet Communism

Social Security and Income Maintenance

Social security means the provision of proper and sufficient benefits in a series of contingencies during which an individual may be prevented from earning his living, temporarily or permanently. It may also provide benefits for dependents deprived of the support of their breadwinner, and for medical care. In a broader sense, it may include assistance in the discharge of continuing family responsibilities in respect of which community aid may be considered expedient. Social security is a major element in maintaining incomes in times of adversity and old age and, in the case of unemployment benefits, has the incidental effect of mitigating economic recessions and depressions. It thus contributes indirectly to economic stability as well as directly to social stability. Social security may be achieved through social insurance, public services, and social assistance.

Social Insurance

The International Labour Organisation throughout its history has played a significant role in the development of social security, particu-

[69] *Ibid.*, pp. 77, 80–81.

larly through the promotion of social insurance. Under social insurance, individuals are entitled to benefits on the basis of contributions to an insurance fund paid by the beneficiaries, or by their employers, or by both; the state may also contribute a share to the fund or guarantee payment.

The adoption by the ILO of the first social security conventions in the late 1920's gave marked impetus to the world movement in this field.[70] For the first time, many governments began to consider the institution of social insurance plans. In increasing numbers, they turned to the ILO for information and help. The experts there were familiar with the best national practices as developed in countries such as Germany and the United Kingdom. They knew the mistakes to be avoided. The social security systems of many countries, including the United States, bear evidence of the help rendered by the ILO. Much of this work was carried forward on a regional basis through such bodies as the Inter-American Conference on Social Security, which was founded in 1942 with the assistance of the ILO and of the Inter-American Committee on Social Security.

Toward the end of and after the Second World War, there was an expansion of activities, studies, regional conferences, and seminars in this field. The Income Security and Medical Care Recommendations, approved by the International Labour Conference in 1944, played an important role in stimulating progress in social security based on insurance by laying down acceptable minimum standards and objectives adapted to present-day requirements of countries in different stages of economic development. They were a forerunner of the Social Security (Minimum Standards) Convention of 1952.

The ILO itself considers this last-named convention as the culmination of thirty years of work in the field of social security.[71] The convention covers nine different aspects of social security to be met primarily through insurance, namely, medical care, sickness benefit, unemployment benefit, old-age benefit, employment injury benefit, family benefit, maternity benefit, invalidity benefit, and survivors' benefit. It is framed in the light of the widely varying conditions in different parts of the world. Earlier international conventions on social security dealt with particular branches of social insurance. Most of them prescribed

---

[70] Cf. International Labour Office, *Lasting Peace the I.L.O. Way, The Story of the International Labour Organisation*, Second Edition (Revised) (1953).

[71] *Seventh Report of the International Labour Organisation to the United Nations*, pp. 41–42.

minimum conditions of entitlement to, and duration of, benefit, but they did not fix any rate of benefit, and their essential function was to provide the general legal framework for a social insurance system. The new convention starts from the conception of comprehensive social security. One of its leading features is that it prescribes rates of benefit for standard beneficiaries, such rates to be calculated, broadly speaking, either as percentages of the previous earnings of the beneficiary or breadwinner or as percentages of the average earnings of unskilled labor.

The convention has been characterized as follows:

> In the nature of the case, the Convention is a compromise. It represents the standards arrived at by fully authorised representatives of Governments, employers and workers, through free and democratic discussion. Like any agreement reached in this manner, it is the outcome of give-and-take. Like every other international labour Convention, it binds no one until the appropriate constitutional authorities in each country decide to ratify it. It is, moreover, a flexible instrument; States may become parties to it without accepting its provisions in respect of all branches of social security; in respect of each branch various alternatives are permitted, and some of these alternatives would not be regarded as appropriate in certain countries; temporary exceptions to certain provisions are allowed for States whose economy and medical facilities are insufficiently developed for the full application of the provisions of the Convention. The Convention is not intended to, and does not, interfere with voluntary private insurance in any way. It provides for a bed-rock of protection on which voluntary private insurance can and should build.[72]

Since the conclusion of this convention, the International Labour Organisation has pursued its work in the field of social security primarily along two lines: the preparation of studies and the provision of technical assistance. One study, which should prove of considerable value to less developed countries, concerns the different processes involved in administering social insurance and the techniques that may be used for making them effective. Attention is being given also to the costs of protection, and statistics pertaining to the cost of social security in different countries continue to be collected and analyzed.

The countries that constitute the Council of Europe have collectively sought the help of the ILO in working out a special Code of Social Security that recognizes the level of achievement typical of these countries and, to some extent, expresses their aspirations for improvement. Particularly interesting in this connection are the attempts at international co-ordination of social security schemes in the interest of foreigners and

[72] *Ibid.*, p. 42.

of migrants generally. The Committee of Ministers of the Council of Europe signed, in December 1953, two interim agreements on the equality of treatment for all nationals of members of the Council; both agreements were based on drafts prepared by the ILO.

In the last few years, a score of countries in the Near, Middle, and Far East, and in Latin America, have also been assisted by social security experts provided by the ILO. The ILO has in fact been directly involved in the planning of virtually all the new general schemes of social security that the less developed countries have introduced since the war.

Public Services

The ILO has frequently emphasized that it is primarily concerned with the ends of social security, *i.e.*, income maintenance and assured care in cases of illness, accident, and similar needs, and that flexibility is desirable in the choice of means. If less stress has been put on the public-service approach, it is due in part, undoubtedly, to the fact that it is much more controversial than social insurance.

The term *public service* is used here to designate schemes under which title to benefit is conferred on the population generally, or on a category thereof, at the expense of the community and without prior contribution by the beneficiaries (except in the form of taxes). The same benefit becomes available automatically to all who qualify (aged persons, families with children, maternity cases, etc.), and the possession of private means does not affect eligibility. The "public service" approach is perhaps best illustrated by policies in the Scandinavian countries (*e.g.*, the family-allowance system in Sweden), the United Kingdom (*e.g.*, the British Health Service), and Canada (*e.g.*, the Canadian automatic old-age pension).

In the Communist-controlled countries, public service appears to be the key to social security. Representatives of the Soviet Union and other Communist nations claim that their system assures their people of complete economic and social security without contributions from the workers. Theoretically, the system is based on insurance, with contributions coming entirely from the employer. Since the state is the only employer, however, it is the state that provides all the contributions and hence all the benefits.[73] These contributions, of course, are ultimately

[73] Benefits, however, are not in all cases automatically provided for a given category of the population, *e.g.*, those above a given age. Entitlement may depend on previous employment, and payments frequently vary with the type of such employment.

paid for by direct or indirect taxation, or by its equivalent, because real income transferred to the recipients must come from some elements of the public.

At the other end of the scale, is the United States with its emphasis on insurance financed by contributions from the workers, the employers, or both. In certain areas—for example, medical care—the United States has not accepted the principle of public insurance, and safeguarding against the cost of illness has been left to private insurance, with minimum provisions for public aid in the form of limited public health services and social assistance in cases of need.

There have been many statements but few debates in the United Nations on these issues. The "middle" countries have shown a marked reluctance to be drawn into political discussions initiated by Communist representatives. The debate that occurred at the Economic and Social Council, in July 1952, on the occasion of the discussion of the *Preliminary Report on the World Social Situation* soon developed into a controversy between the United States on the one hand, and the Soviet Union and its followers on the other, over Communist social concepts and organization as contrasted with those of a free society.[74] The resolution that was adopted following this debate did not refer in any way to the differences in basic concept.[75]

In practice, the public-service approach has most frequently been adopted by individual countries in the form of flat-rate, family allowances, as an integral part of population policies; of maternity benefits and old-age pensions; and of the provision of free medical care. These measures have usually been combined, in the free world, with social security schemes based on social insurance. In other words, social insurance and public service are not mutually exclusive, but to some extent are definitely complementary. The ILO has produced extensive studies in both areas and continues to provide technical assistance to governments on request.

Social Assistance

Social assistance comprises those forms of social security under which benefits at the expense of the community and without prior contribution on the part of the beneficiary are paid to individuals who, in terms of defined minimum standards, are "in need." A "means test" may be required before an individual becomes eligible for benefits.

[74] U.N. Economic and Social Council, Fourteenth Session, *Official Records*, pp. 547–90.

[75] Res. 434(XIV), July 25, 28, and 29, 1952.

In most of the countries with advanced systems of social security, assistance schemes serve as supplementary measures to provide for needy persons who are not covered, or are not adequately covered, by other forms of social security. Frequently, they come into operation when benefits under social insurance systems end because statutory or contractual time limits for the provision of such benefits have been reached, *e.g.*, in the case of unemployment insurance.

In many of the less developed countries, social assistance to the needy is offered, too often rather sporadically, in view of the obvious inadequacy of other social security measures. Although state and local authorities may have a share in such assistance, it is more often left to private agencies. Family and relatives and religious and other private groups remain the dominant means of assistance to the needy. Considerable effort has been made under the auspices of the United Nations and the ILO to stimulate, improve, and systematize social assistance programs in the underdeveloped countries.

The Trend to Date

Both in the thinking of the United Nations and the specialized agencies, and in their action programs for the promotion of higher levels of living, a large measure of "fusion" of the economic and social approaches has been attained. It has been recognized that the basic objective of any measures for economic development is the improvement of levels of living. There has also been a growing realization of the fact that the various social components that enter into the determination of levels of living have a direct bearing on economic development, and that better health, housing, and working conditions—to mention only a few—are essential to any acceleration of economic development. As a result of this acknowledged interaction of the economic and the social, the entire work of the United Nations and the specialized agencies in these fields has gained in realism and effectiveness.

The work has been focused increasingly on underdeveloped countries. This is only natural, considering their needs and the political implications of despair in the underdeveloped regions of the world. Moreover, even highly developed countries stand to gain indirectly by social improvements in the underdeveloped parts of the world. Elimination or control of communicable diseases in Asia or Latin America constitutes a shield for the protection of the population in the most highly developed countries. Improvements in wage levels, working conditions, and social security systems in the underdeveloped countries make for larger and more stable markets.

It may well be asked, however, whether there has not been over-emphasis on work in the underdeveloped regions of the world and a consequent neglect of some of the immediate needs of the more highly developed countries, particularly in health, nutrition, housing, and social security. The underdeveloped countries have a majority of votes, particularly in the General Assembly, but in an interdependent world in which the co-operation of all countries is essential, it would not appear to be in the best interests of the underdeveloped countries to limit the economic and social activities of the United Nations to their needs, to the detriment of international action to assist directly in improving levels of living in the more developed areas.

By and large, the activities of the United Nations and the specialized agencies designed to promote higher levels of living have been practical and down to earth. Efforts are being made to avoid vague generalities and to concentrate on concrete goals and ways and means of attaining them. Conventions and formal recommendations continue to set standards, but emphasis in recent years has shifted to the practical grass-roots approach in advising and otherwise helping governments improve the levels of living of their peoples. This requires patient, painstaking, arduous work on the part of those rendering and those receiving the advice and assistance. The progress that has been made during the past ten years, although limited and uneven, is nevertheless remarkable. The world is moving forward in improving the lot of the common man, and the United Nations and the specialized agencies are playing a vital part in the progress achieved.

CHAPTER VIII

Welfare and Social Defense*

IN DEVELOPING a broad social approach to the promotion of the general welfare, the United Nations has gone beyond the programs designed to obtain improvements in levels of living through making the environment more healthful, the diet more nutritious, the housing more suitable, and the working conditions more conducive to higher output with greater security and dignity for the wage-earner. In addition, the United Nations and the specialized agencies have actively promoted social work and welfare programs on behalf of specific groups that require special attention or protection—among them mothers and children, migrants and refugees, the physically handicapped, the drug addicts, and the offenders against the laws of society.

Despite the fact that the term "social welfare" has no exact counterpart in other languages and that there is no internationally agreed definition of the term "social work," there is widespread agreement among Member states in the free world that the outstanding characteristic of social work is its concern with the individual and his physical, mental, and emotional well-being.[1] Economic, medical, or other forms of personal assistance may be prerequisites for the achievement of such well-being, or it may be necessary to strengthen the social unit and groups—particularly the family—within which the individual seeks security. Not only may people need help in overcoming handicaps that militate against their full integration into society, but they also may have to be protected against social evils destructive of personality. The concern of social work, in brief, is with the total individual and his integration in society.

There are obvious difficulties in utilizing international machinery

---

* By Walter M. Kotschnig.

[1] During the preparation of a United Nations report entitled *Training for Social Work, An International Survey* (Doc. E/CN.5/196/Rev. 1, Oct. 23, 1950), Member governments were invited to submit definitions of "social work." The "definitions" ranged from descriptions of unorganized personal "charity," through organized activities for aid to the needy, to the most advanced types of "case work" employing the latest scientific discoveries in sociology, physiology, psychiatry, and related fields. Social work was described both as a means of dealing with "the poor" and as a profession providing services to and potentially required by all.

354

for the promotion of this many-faceted, individual approach—difficulties that are not apparent from a study of voting records on social problems raised at meetings of the United Nations. Most of the basic resolutions in the social welfare field were adopted by comfortable majorities, and many of them with no negative votes. The United States frequently took the lead in initiating action by the United Nations and was supported by most of the countries of Western Europe and of the Commonwealth. The underdeveloped countries supported every move for international assistance in the development of social welfare programs within their territories to the point at which, in the social as in the economic field, attention became focused increasingly on the underdeveloped areas.

Even the Communist-controlled countries, although they exhibited little enthusiasm for the social work approach, seldom engaged in outright opposition. Instead, they made speeches and proposals implying that most of the social work programs were at best palliatives and that the United Nations should turn instead to ensuring full employment, improved conditions of labor, guaranteed health services, and state-financed, state-controlled education schemes.

Although the voting record appears to reveal a remarkable degree of unanimity, co-ordinated progress in the social welfare field has been slow and painful, largely due to the confusion of ideas and concepts, aggravated by the enthusiasms of special interest groups and their desires to obtain international sponsorship for particular projects. Not all of the clamor of contending voices has disappeared, although the programs have become better co-ordinated and the work more effective.

These programs may be considered in four main groups: those designed to help in the organization of adequate national and local social welfare departments and services; those for the welfare and protection of the family as a unit, of children, and of the physically handicapped; those facilitating international migration and the protection and resettlement of refugees; and finally, those concerned with drug-addiction, prostitution, and the prevention of crime or treatment of offenders.

Organization and Administration of Social Welfare Services

The havoc caused by the Second World War immeasurably increased the need for assistance on the part of millions of poeple who had lost their homes, whose families had been dispersed, and who found it difficult to adjust to the dire conditions of postwar life. As mentioned earlier in this study, one of the functions of the United Nations Relief and Rehabilitation Administration (UNRRA) was the re-establishment of social welfare services in devastated areas.[2] Requests for help, however, were not confined to war-devastated countries. Beginning right after the war, the governments of many of the underdeveloped countries, desirous of improving the lot of their people, sought assistance in establishing national machinery for administering programs of social welfare and above all, in the training of social welfare personnel. The United Nations was thus confronted in the very first months of its existence with calls for a wide range of action in the social welfare field.

Advisory Social Welfare Services

When it was decided in 1946 to liquidate UNRRA, the General Assembly on recommendation of the Economic and Social Council, authorized the transfer to the United Nations of the social welfare functions that UNRRA had developed to assist in the rehabilitation of social services disrupted by the war. By a resolution adopted unanimously, the General Assembly authorized the Secretary-General, in consultation with the Economic and Social Council and with the co-operation of the specialized agencies, to provide "for the continuance of the urgent and important advisory functions in the field of social welfare carried on by UNRRA."[3] The resolution envisaged the provision of social welfare experts to governments desiring advice in this field; a program of fellowships to enable qualified social welfare officials from such nations to observe, and familiarize themselves with, the experience of other countries administering social welfare programs; advice, demonstration, and instruction in the field of the rehabilitation and vocational training of the physically handicapped; and the furnishing of technical publications helpful in the training of social welfare workers.

This action of the Assembly marked the birth of the first program of technical assistance undertaken by the United Nations. It has been functioning ever since under the name "Advisory Social Welfare Services." As originally conceived by the General Assembly, the program was to be limited in space, purpose, and time.[4] Intended for the war devastated countries, it was, however, quickly extended to other parts

[2] See above, Chap. I.

[3] Res. 58(I), Dec. 14, 1946.

[4] U.N. Economic and Social Council, *Evaluation of the Program of Advisory Social Welfare Services, 1947–1951*, Doc. E/CN.5/266 (Mar. 26, 1952).

of the world, particularly to the underdeveloped countries. Its purpose widened over the years to the point where the program embraced virtually all the social services not already within the scope of a specialized agency. During the period 1947 to 1949, the program was operated on a year-to-year basis. This proved unsatisfactory and inadequate. Three arguments in favor of permanency were advanced with increasing force in sessions of the Social Commission and of the Economic and Social Council. It was said that the number of requests for assistance received from all over the world showed that the program filled a real and permanent need. It was stressed that the operation of a program of this scope on a year-to-year basis was extremely difficult. Finally, it was emphasized that the work, in order to be done well and to be of lasting value, had to be concerned not only with the acute needs of the day but tied in addition to long-range action in the field of social welfare.

In 1950, the Assembly consequently made the program permanent and enlarged it.[5] It explicitly approved the shift in emphasis to underdeveloped countries. In 1951, the Assembly decided to make additionl funds available for the program of advisory services by authorizing the use, where necessary, of funds at the disposal of the Expanded Programme of Technical Assistance (EPTA).

At the beginning, the program consisted principally of the provision of fellowships, scholarships, and experts. To this were added, somewhat later, the organization of seminars and various other types of training facilities.

Between 1947 and the early 1950's, the number of awards per year under the fellowship program increased from approximately one hundred to nearly two hundred. After that, the number of awards for study abroad began to level off, due largely to the development of training facilities within the various countries seeking assistance. More striking is the increase in the number of recipient countries, from twelve in 1947 to forty-six in 1955, exclusive of non-self-governing territories.

There has also been a notable increase in the number of countries serving as hosts to persons awarded fellowships. There were eight countries in 1947 and twenty-eight in 1955. In the early years of the program, most of the fellows went to North America, particularly the United States, or to Europe. Of late, recipients coming to the United States have actually decreased in number as compared with the first year of the program. There has been some increase of fellows in Europe.

[5] Res. 418(V), Dec. 1, 1950.

More significantly, however, an increasing number of fellows have elected to go to countries similar to, and frequently only slightly more developed than, their own countries—to India, for example. This has enabled the fellows to study social welfare developments in a setting more like the one in which they must operate when they return, and it also has been less costly than study in North America or Europe. The granting of fellowships has been supplemented by the provision of scholarships, and in Europe, an exchange program was set up in 1950 to promote the intra-European exchange of social welfare personnel.

In 1947, out of nine countries receiving foreign experts under the program of Advisory Social Welfare Services, seven were European and two Asian. In subsequent years, there was a steady decline in the number of European countries and a gradual increase in the number of recipient countries in other regions of the world.[6] Latin America joined the program in 1948, followed by the Middle East in 1949, and finally by Africa in 1951. Whereas in 1947–48, Europe received approximately half the total number of experts provided by the United Nations in the field of social welfare, by 1951, its share had decreased to approximately 6 per cent of the total, and the Far East and Latin America together absorbed nearly 65 per cent of the experts nominated by the United Nations in that year. Similarly, there was a sharp decline in the number of experts coming from the Western world, particularly from the United States. In the latter case, one of the reasons for the decline was the difficulty encountered by the United Nations in obtaining American experts because of delays in security checks requested by the United States Government for its nationals. More fundamental, however, was the realization by the underdeveloped countries that experts from other underdeveloped countries frequently had a better understanding of their needs and of the methods of meeting those needs than experts from the more highly developed countries. The Soviet Union in 1947–48 provided three expert advisers. Since then, no Soviet experts have been made available under the program of Advisory Social Welfare Services to any country outside the Soviet orbit.

The first seminars on social welfare questions were held in 1947 in Latin America, followed by seminars in the Middle East on general

---

[6] The decline in the number of participating European nations was due, in part, to the establishment of direct contacts between European countries, resulting in the provision of experts through bilateral negotiations, although frequently with the advice of the Secretariat of the United Nations.

social welfare and rural welfare in 1949 and 1951 respectively. During the two years 1953 and 1954 alone, twenty-two seminars of different types were organized.[7]

More revealing than these figures is the fact that there have been considerable changes over the last eight years in the areas of interest of fellowship holders, and in the subject fields of experts requested by governments. Among fellowship holders, the figures indicate a sustained interest in such activities as the rehabilitation of the handicapped and the prevention of crime and treatment of offenders; and an increased interest in social surveys and statistics, the organization and administration of social welfare services, and the training of social workers and auxiliary personnel. With regard to requests for experts, changes in interest have been more marked. Although in previous years a majority of the requests from governments was concerned with special social problems, a significant number of requests were received in 1953–54 for assistance in the organization and administration at the national level of comprehensive social welfare programs. Requests of this kind were received from Burma, Gambia, Israel, Pakistan, the Philippines, Somaliland, Thailand, Turkey, and Yugoslavia. There has also been an increase in the number of requests for assistance in community development.[8]

Organization and Development of National Services

In response to the growing emphasis on the development of comprehensive long-range programs of social welfare, the United Nations, in co-operation with the International Labour Organisation (ILO), the World Health Organization (WHO), and the Food and Agriculture Organization (FAO), has assisted governments in strengthening or improving the organization and administration of their social services. The Economic and Social Council, as early as 1947, asked the Secretary-General to arrange for a study of methods of social welfare administration in use in different countries, and of methods of furnishing advice, information, and experts to countries requesting such assistance,

[7] For a complete list of these activities see U.N. Economic and Social Council, *Progress Made by the United Nations in the Field of Social Welfare During the Period 1 January 1953 to 31 December 1954 and Proposals for the Program of Work 1955–57*, Doc. E/CN.5/308 (Mar. 15, 1955), Annex B, pp. 1–2.

[8] See below, Chap. X.

with a view to helping them to organize the administration of their own social services.[9]

In response, the Secretary-General prepared a comprehensive survey covering thirty countries, which brought to light the great differences among them in social welfare methods and administration.[10] The introduction to the study mentioned that "in the light of the information here assembled, the Secretary-General feels that each country will be well advised to develop methods of social welfare administration in harmony with its own traditions and needs."[11] In 1952, the Secretary-General published a follow-up study of the situation in seven countries from five continents. This study covered the place of assistance to the needy within the social security structure; eligibility requirements; and the level of financing and administration of assistance.[12] References to problems of administration appear also in a large number of other publications.[13]

In addition to issuing publications that have served as guides and source material for governments and others interested in social welfare services, the United Nations has provided, as has already been noted, a large number of experts and fellowships in this area and organized various seminars and training centers. It has appointed regional advisers and established social welfare staffs in the major regions of the world in response to the growing preference both on the part of the Secretary-General and of the countries concerned for on-the-spot advice instead of studies prepared at headquarters.

There is evidence that progress is being made in practically all the underdeveloped parts of the world in the establishment of national welfare administrations. To what extent this is due to the stimulus and advice given by the United Nations is, of course, impossible to state with any certainty even though in some cases the tie-in is clear. The establishment of a Council of Social Service in Burma was a direct result of the work of several United Nations experts. Similarly, in Pakistan, a team of experts advised the government on the planning and organization of social welfare programs, including particularly the

[9] Res. 43(IV), Mar. 29, 1947. In this connection, see also Res. 390C(XIII), Aug. 9, 1951.
[10] U.N. Department of Social Affairs, *Methods of Social Welfare Administration*, Doc. E/CN.5/224 (Oct. 25, 1950).
[11] *Ibid.*, p. 2.
[12] U.N. Department of Social Affairs, *Methods of Administering Assistance to the Needy*, Doc. E/CN.5/273 (1952).
[13] U.N. Department of Public Information, *Ten Years of United Nations Publications, 1945–1955, A Complete Catalogue* (1955), pp. 7–8, 44–58.

the organization of social services at the national and local levels. Lebanon, Thailand, the Philippines, Turkey, Yugoslavia, and some countries in Latin America have also drawn heavily on the advice of experts from the United Nations in the organization and administration of their social services. The structure and working of the new social welfare administrations differ from country to country and frequently include in their scope not only social assistance of the type discussed below but also social security measures of the type described earlier in this study.[14] There appears to be, however, a fairly general recognition of the fact that too much centralization can militate against the achievement of the very purposes of personalized social assistance and can weigh too heavily on local drive and initiative. It is being realized that co-ordination and planning do not necessarily involve a high degree of centralized administration or exclusive governmental responsibility. A number of countries, including many that are less developed, are trying to reconcile effective co-ordination with maximum encouragement of local and voluntary initiative.[15]

Training of Welfare Personnel

The word "training" runs through every discussion of social work and social welfare. This is understandable. Public concern in these fields is of comparatively recent date, and many countries have few if any trained workers available. Moreover, social work by its very nature requires more than administrators and executives. It needs people capable of dealing on a person-to-person basis with the problems of individuals. This work normally has to be done in the local community and not from some national center. In other words, social welfare work requires a large number of people with special training, for the vital force is the trained individual rather than the system.

Although concerned from 1947 on with methods of assisting in the training of welfare personnel, it was not until 1951 that the Social Commission and the Economic and Social Council undertook to formulate principles for social work training.[16] These principles heavily empha-

[14] See above, Chap. VII.

[15] U.N. Bureau of Social Affairs, *International Survey of Programs of Social Development*, Doc. E/CN.5/301/Rev. 1 (Mar. 31, 1955), *passim*. (Hereinafter cited as *Survey of Programs of Social Development*.)

[16] Res. 43(IV), Mar. 29, 1947 and Res. 390B(XIII), Aug. 9, 1951 of the Council. See also U.N. General Assembly, Sixth Session, *Official Records*, Supplement No. 3, "Report of the Economic and Social Council Covering the Period 16 August 1950 to 21 September 1951," p. 83; and U.N. Department of Social Affairs, *Training for Social Work, An International Survey*, Doc. E/CN.5/196/Rev. 1 (Oct. 23, 1950).

sized that social work is a professional function to be performed by men and women who have received their professional training in recognized educational institutions. The stress on social work as a profession reflected primarily the views and aspirations of social workers in the United States, and the recommended standards proved too high for a large number of countries.

In 1952, the Council watered them down somewhat by recommending that training for social work take as many forms as appropriate to the needs of the various countries and that in-service training programs be regarded as essential for all categories of social welfare personnel, including persons who had not received formal training.[17] Subsequently, the emphasis shifted further—to the training of auxiliary personnel—because facilities for full professional and "on-the-job" training did not keep pace with needs. Moreover, at the local level, less than professional training was often all that the community could afford.

Currently, international assistance for the training of social welfare workers attempts to serve the following purposes:

(1) to make available information concerning the content and method or training key personnel and keeping such personnel up to date with new knowledge, and to promote expansion of facilities for such training;
(2) to assist governments in speeding up the recruitment and concentrated training of supplementary personnel, now called "auxiliary and community workers," by
    (a) examining and making known the variety of functions now being performed, or needed to carry social welfare programmes into practical effect in local communities;
    (b) making known the methods found most effective in attracting and preparing such persons for their duties;
    (c) assisting directly in the development of expanded training facilities;
    (d) co-operative efforts by the organizations belonging to the United Nations family in formulating basic principles for the training and use of social welfare personnel at all levels.[18]

To help realize these purposes, technical assistance is provided under both the program of Advisory Social Welfare Services and the Expanded Programme of Technical Assistance. Experts have been employed, field surveys made, scholarships and fellowships provided, regional seminars and technical groups organized, training equipment supplied

[17] Res. 434F(XIV), July 25, 1952.
[18] U.N. Economic and Social Council, Sixteenth Session, *Official Records*, Annexes, Agenda Item 10: "Program of Concerted Practical Action in the Social Field of the United Nations and the Specialized Agencies," p. 72. (Hereinafter cited as "Concerted Practical Action in the Social Field.")

(on a limited basis), and studies and reports on subjects pertaining to the training of social work personnel have been distributed. These activities have by no means been confined to underdeveloped countries. More seminars and expert meetings have been held in Europe on training than on any other social program of the United Nations.

The expansion of activities designed to increase the number of auxiliary workers has characterized much of the work in underdeveloped countries. A special *ad hoc* interagency meeting on the training of auxiliary workers was held in Geneva in July 1954, with representatives of the secretariats of the United Nations (including the United Nations Children's Fund, UNICEF), FAO, ILO, United Nations Scientific and Cultural Organization (UNESCO), and WHO participating. This meeting discussed the formulation of general principles concerning the training of auxiliary and community workers and the content and production of training materials, and selected a number of field projects suitable for joint demonstration purposes.[19] Prior to the Geneva meeting of experts, regional meetings of specialists in this subject had taken place in Gandhigram, India, for the Far Eastern region; in Beirut, Lebanon, for the Middle Eastern region; and in Bogota, Colombia, for the Caribbean and Central American region.[20]

Advances with respect to all levels of training have been made in many underdeveloped countries. In Asia, the number of professional schools or courses offering at least one year of training in social work increased from fifteen in 1949–50 to twenty-seven in 1953–54. The number of schools of social work in the Middle East increased during the same period from five to ten; in Latin America from forty-eight to sixty-four. In 1953–54 alone, experts to assist in training social welfare personnel were sent to fifteen countries and advice was given on surveys of existing training facilities; general questions of administration, curricula, field work, and selection of students for admission; and on the development of facilities for in-service training or for the training of auxiliary workers.[21]

In spite of these advances, the picture as a whole remains very un-

[19] See U.N. Economic and Social Council, *Seventeenth Report of the Administrative Committee on Co-ordination to the Economic and Social Council*, Doc. E/2659 (Oct. 15, 1954).

[20] A summary report on the training of auxiliary and community workers, including the discussions of the three regional meetings, can be found in U.N. Economic and Social Council, *Training of Welfare Personnel, Summary Report on the Training of Auxiliary and Community Workers*, Doc. E/CN.5/306 (Mar. 7, 1955).

[21] U.N. Economic and Social Council, *Training of Welfare Personnel, Training for Social Work: Second International Survey*, Doc. E/CN.5/305 (Apr. 8, 1955).

even. Not only are there still many countries without training facilities or with inadequate facilities, but there continue to be very wide divergencies in the content of training. In the United States and Canada, there is a full two- to three-year, post-graduate, professional course with emphasis on the "scientific approach." In the United Kingdom and many European countries, there are special "social science" courses, frequently with emphasis on nursing, as in France. In Asia, there is a growing emphasis on developing patterns of work and training in conformity with local conditions in the region. Finally, there is an attempt in Latin America to develop case work practices in a continent where cultural attitudes make for social work *for* rather than *with* people. In brief, social work practice and training continue on the whole to rest on a body of knowledge and skills less clearly defined and less generally agreed upon than that of the long established professions and occupational groups.

These variations indicate that not only methods of social welfare administration but also of training should be developed in harmony with the traditions and needs of each country. They do not diminish the importance of international consultations and mutual assistance, but they call for caution lest theory become the enemy of practical action.

Family and Child Welfare

From the early days of the United Nations, family and child welfare programs were linked together and given special attention. The United Nations International Children's Emergency Fund was established in 1946 to offer aid not only to children, but also to nursing mothers.[22] When the Economic and Social Council decided, in 1948, to resume publication of the Legislative and Administrative Series on child welfare begun by the League of Nations, it soon extended its coverage to include family welfare.[23] In 1952, the Economic and Social Council

[22] See above, Chap. II.
[23] Res. 122A(VI), Mar. 1, 1948. Following the practice of the League, the Legislative and Administrative Series was supplemented by another series of reports on child and youth welfare, summarizing existing legislation and including information on other measures taken by governments. The series was discontinued in 1954, on the understanding that governments would continue to report on family and child care measures, primarily to provide continuing information for inclusion in other publications such as the quadrennial *International Survey of Measures for Social Development*. The move represented more than a streamlining of the publications program. It reflected a conclusion that the publication of legislative texts and of other measures adopted by governments is not a very effective way of advancing practical action because the texts and measures may have very limited applicability abroad.

approved an integrated program for child welfare, which had been proposed by the Social Commission, and which stressed the need for specific measures essential to the social security of the family.[24]

The international program in the field of family and child welfare that emerged from these deliberations and resolutions is directed toward the following basic purposes:

(a) encouraging governmental and nongovernmental programs designed
    (i) to strengthen family life;
    (ii) to promote special programs for mothers and children;
(b) supplementing such national programs, in agreement with governments, by direct international assistance to mothers and children in devastated or underdeveloped areas where necessary.[25]

International efforts to strengthen the family have to date centered largely on income maintenance. The approach to that problem through social insurance, public services, and social assistance has already been described earlier in this study.[26] Unemployment and disability benefits, family allowances, and tax exemptions for large families all serve to strengthen the economic foundations of the family. Measures to protect women and young people in employment similarly affect the welfare of the family. In addition to these areas—of special concern to the ILO— home economics training offers another approach to the strengthening of the family.

On the subject of income maintenance, the United Nations published a comprehensive survey in 1952.[27] This was followed, in 1956, by a second study dealing with methods of administering assistance to the needy in less developed areas, with special emphasis on problems of income maintenance for families. It was based on a survey of existing approaches to public assistance and pensions in nine selected countries in the Middle and the Far East and Latin America.[28] In preparation is a study dealing with the factors governing formulation of a co-ordinated policy aimed at the maintenance of family levels of living, and the methods of giving such a policy practical effect.

In addition to promoting family welfare through publications of the foregoing character, the United Nations has encouraged the education of social workers, along lines that frequently include training in mar-

---

[24] Res. 434E(XIV), July 25, 1952.

[25] "Concerted Practical Action in the Social Field," p. 62.

[26] See above, Chap. VII.

[27] U.N. Department of Social Affairs, *Economic Measures in Favour of the Family,* Doc. ST/SOA/8 (Mar. 31, 1952).

[28] U.N. Department of Economic and Social Affairs, *Assistance to the Needy in Less-Developed Areas,* Doc. ST/SOA/28 (1956).

riage and family counseling. The question of family planning, relevant in this connection, is highly controversial. It has been raised obliquely on a few occasions in discussions of the Population Commission and in the Economic and Social Council. It took more concrete form in the 1952 discussions in WHO regarding the provision of expert assistance to the Indian Government in a sample population survey that extended to problems of birth control. For religious and other reasons, the great majority of governments either oppose policies designed to reduce birth rates or have no policies on the matter. Only a few—including Egypt, Japan, and India—are actively pursuing policies of this kind or have sought advice from the international community in this connection.

Also related to the protection of the family are several legal instruments prepared under the auspices of the United Nations. The first is the Convention on the Declaration of Death of Missing Persons. In 1948, the Economic and Social Council recognized the urgency and importance of mitigating the legal difficulties arising from the disappearance of numerous victims of war and persecution and expressed the view that these difficulties might best be met by an international convention.[29] This was a matter of considerable interest to large numbers of families from which some member had disappeared but despite the assumption of death, there was no adequate machinery to permit a legal declaration of death that would allow for property settlements or for remarriage. It was an international problem because many of the missing persons could be assumed to have met their death in foreign lands to which they had been taken as soldiers, slave laborers, or victims of concentration camps. The proposal for an international convention met with general approval in the Economic and Social Council and the Assembly except for the Communist bloc states, which were evidently opposed to investigations extending into their territories. Finally, in 1950, the General Assembly convened a plenipotentiary conference that adopted a convention prepared in the first instance by the Secretary-General and revised by an *ad hoc* committee of experts.[30]

In addition to the Convention on the Declaration of Death of Missing Persons, the United Nations has prepared a Model Convention on the

[29] Res. 158(VII), Aug. 24, 1948; see also Res. 209(VIII), Mar. 2, 1949, and Res. 249(IX), Aug. 9, 1949; General Assembly Res. 369(IV), Dec. 3, 1949.
[30] An essential element in the system provided by the Convention on the Declaration of Death of Missing Persons was the establishment of an International Bureau for Declarations of Death. The creation of such a bureau within the framework of the United Nations was approved by the Assembly in Res. 493(V), Nov. 16, 1950. The Convention entered into force on Jan. 24, 1952.

Enforcement Abroad of Maintenance Obligations.[31] The need for action in this area arose from a sharp increase in the number of cases in which a family found itself abandoned by the bread winner, who, having moved or been moved to another country, enjoyed virtual immunity from maintenance obligations by reason of legal obstacles to effective prosecution. In addition to cases of willful abandonment, instances of involuntary failure to provide support had arisen, because the restrictions imposed in a number of countries on the transfer of funds made it difficult for immigrants to remit money to their families.

A committee of Experts on the Recognition and Enforcement Abroad of Maintenance Obligations was set up by the Council in 1951.[32] It produced as a guide to governments for the preparation of bilateral treaties or uniform legislation not only the Model Convention on the Enforcement Abroad of Maintenance Obligations, but also a draft multilateral Convention on the Recovery Abroad of Claims for Maintenance. The Economic and Social Council decided, in the spring of 1955, to call a plenipotentiary conference to complete the draft, which was strongly supported by such countries as Belgium, Cuba, France, the Netherlands, and the Scandinavian countries. A universal convention in this field is, however, opposed by the United States as well as by some other federal states. On June 20, 1956, the United Nations Conference on Maintenance Obligations adopted and opened for signature the completed Convention on the Recovery Abroad of Maintenance.

In the early years of its existence, the Social Commission gave repeated attention to the drafting of a Declaration of the Rights of the Child, which was to replace the so-called "Geneva Declaration," originally drawn up by the Save the Children International Union in 1920, and subsequently endorsed by the League of Nations in 1924. In 1950, a draft completed by the Social Commission was referred to the Commission on Human Rights, but to date no agreement has been reached on the final text. The difficulties reside largely in the lack of enthusiasm or outright opposition to such a declaration on the part of a substantial number of governments that consider it undesirable to have "declarations" for special groups in addition to the Universal Declaration of Human Rights adopted by the General Assembly in 1948. There is also

---

[31] See the volume in this Brookings series, *The United Nations and Promotion of the General Welfare*, Part One, for additional discussion of this convention.

[32] Res. 390H(XIII), Aug. 9, 1951.

a feeling that the procedure is not particularly productive in terms of the protection of the interests of children.

In addition to drafting the ill-fated Delcaration of the Rights of the Child, the Social Commission has taken the lead in arranging for studies about special aspects of child care and protection.[33] Although undoubtedly useful in themselves, there is question whether studies of this specialized character are the proper responsibility of the United Nations, and no additional studies of this type are envisaged.

Of more direct impact on the development of action programs are the assessments of services for children such as were carried out in 1953 at the request of the governments of Burma, El Salvador, and Syria. Experience has shown that such surveys do stimulate practical action on the part of the countries surveyed. Further assessments in this field are therefore planned if requested by governments.

All this work is overshadowed both in scope and importance by the work of the Children's Fund. The story of the establishment of UNICEF and its work until it was made permanent in 1953 has already been told.[34] It will be recalled that even before the Children's Fund was made permanent, the Economic and Social Council and the General Assembly had agreed, in 1950, to a reorientation of the work of UNICEF. Emphasis was placed on long-range activities for children rather than on emergency action. At the same time, the Executive Board of UNICEF was reconstituted to consist of the eighteen members of the Social Commission plus eight additional member states, selected for a period of three years. This decision was taken to ensure the closest possible co-ordination and integration of the work of the Social Commission on the one hand and of UNICEF on the other, in so far as children were concerned. It was modified, in 1956, to permit direct election by the Economic and Social Council of all members of the Executive Board, irrespective of their membership on the Social Commission, after experience had demonstrated that some members of the Social Commission had little interest in the work of UNICEF and that almost all members were represented by different individuals in the Social Commission and in UNICEF.[35]

UNICEF has continued to provide aid, mostly in the form of supplies, for four major programs: the strengthening of maternal and child

[33] Among such studies are *Children Deprived of a Normal Home Life, Adoption of Children, Care of Children in Institutions, Day Care of Children*, and *Home Help Services*.

[34] See above, Chap. II.

[35] Res. 610B(XXI), May 1, 1956, recommending that the General Assembly amend para. 6(a) of its Res. 417(V), Dec. 1, 1950.

welfare services; the control of communicable diseases affecting children; feeding and nutrition programs; and emergency relief in disaster situations.

During the period 1951 through 1955, nearly 25 per cent of the program funds of UNICEF were devoted to maternal and child welfare services, and more than 10,000 maternal and child welfare centers were planned, established, or assisted. More than 37 per cent of the program funds were expended on mass health campaigns with the result that the total number of mothers and children tested for tuberculosis from the beginning of the program through December 1955 rose to 154.5 millions, and 59.9 millions received BCG vaccinations (antituberculosis vaccine), 56.5 millions have been examined for yaws, bejel, and syphilis, and 9.8 millions have been treated for these diseases.[36]

UNICEF works closely with the competent specialized agencies. For the mass health campaigns, WHO provides technical guidance and technical personnel who, under the arrangement of UNICEF with WHO, are to some extent financed by the Children's Fund. The nutrition work is carried on in co-operation with the FAO, and certain educational programs in co-operation with UNESCO. Under the nutrition programs, nearly 118 million pounds of dried skimmed milk, obtained free at the port of exit from the United States, were shipped during 1955. Moreover, to ensure better use of milk available locally for children, UNICEF continued to provide milk-drying and milk-pasteurization plants.

The funds at the disposal of UNICEF, consisting of voluntary contributions from governments and—to a small extent—of contributions from private sources, amounted to $70 million for the period 1951 to 1955. This was considerably less than was available during the emergency period, 1947 to 1950, when expenditures were concentrated overwhelmingly in Europe. The shift to the underdeveloped countries since then has been striking. Between 1951 and 1955, only 8.4 per cent of UNICEF aid went to Europe; 8.5 per cent to Africa; 40.8 per cent to Asia; 18.8 per cent to the Eastern Mediterranean region; 21.0 per cent to Latin America; and 2.5 per cent to activities benefiting more than one region.

UNICEF sets great store by the "matching" principle. This principle

---

[36] For details, see U.N. General Assembly, Tenth Session, *Official Records*, Supplement No. 6A, "United Nations Children's Fund: Financial Report and Accounts for the Year Ended 31 December 1954 and Report of the Board of Auditors" (1955); U.N. Children's Fund, *General Progress Report of the Executive Director*, Docs. E/ICEF/309 and E/ICEF/309/Add. 1 (Feb. 15, 1956).

strengthens the efforts of officials and national groups who are most actively concerned with child care programs and helps them obtain budgetary and administrative provisions for such programs, which otherwise would probably not be forthcoming. The utility of the matching principle is evident in reports that, for every dollar spent by UNICEF to the end of 1954, the governments receiving aid provided $1.66 in internal expenditures and commitments. This means that of each dollar spent, UNICEF contributed thirty-eight cents while the government assisted by the Children's Fund spent sixty-two cents. There is some doubt whether these figures can be fully sustained, because the matching expenditures include not only cash contributions, but also the estimated value of services that are difficult to evaluate in monetary terms. The fact remains, however, that the whole operation is thoroughly co-operative in character.

UNICEF represents the second largest action program of the United Nations, and it shares with the Expanded Programme of Technical Assistance the honor of being the most popular program of the United Nations. Deliberations in the Executive Board of UNICEF are as a rule smooth and noncontroversial. The annual review of the report of UNICEF by the Economic and Social Council is usually an occasion for unstinting praise.

The emotional appeal on behalf of children is strong, and this is, of course, all to the good. There are times, however, when this emotional drive tends to lead UNICEF into questionable fields. Thus, it has in recent years not only helped to create training facilities for child welfare workers but has gone so far as to pay to some extent the local expenses of trainees recruited from the very country in which they are trained. Except in the case of impoverished countries in the earliest stages of economic development, this kind of international "pump priming" should be unnecessary. More fundamental is the question whether broad supply operations necessitated by mass health campaigns or capital investments in penicillin factories and milk-processing plants should be continued indefinitely with funds raised on the basis of an appeal for aid to children. These operations obviously benefit not only children but also others. Anti-malaria campaigns or campaigns to eliminate yaws cannot distinguish between children and adults. In these circumstances, it might be proper to consider whether the terms of reference of UNICEF should be clarified to make it evident that in much of its work it acts as a supply organization in the execution of highly important functions serving the population as a whole and not just children and nursing mothers. Provided public opinion is properly educated, such an explicit recognition of the broad scope of the work of UNICEF need not weaken its "appeal" or reduce public support for its programs.

Rehabilitation of the Handicapped

Activities on behalf of the handicapped have been undertaken by the United Nations as an integral part of the program of Advisory Social Welfare Services. Adequate statistics are not available concerning the number of people in the world prevented by physical disability or defects from leading a normal and unaided life in their respective communities. Less highly industrialized countries have a lower incidence of handicap from such sources as industrial and traffic accidents, but a much higher incidence from disease. From the few figures that are available, it appears that in many countries 4 per cent to 5 per cent of the total population suffer from serious handicaps. Certain handicaps, such as blindness, are particularly prevalent in some of the underdeveloped countries. It is estimated that in India approximately 500 persons per 100,000 inhabitants are either totally blind or blind to the point of interfering seriously with their employment. In Libya, it is estimated that between 500 and 1,000 persons per 100,000 population are in the same category. The proportion of the deaf or hard of hearing to the point of serious handicap in learning and employment in both countries is also in the neighborhood of 500 per 100,000.

Modern programs aim at the prevention of handicaps due to accidents or disease, and at the rehabilitation and integration of the handicapped into the normal life of the community. Up to 1950, the United Nations system provided various types of assistance to nations establishing or expanding services to lessen the incidence of physical disability and to aid the physically handicapped.[37] These efforts were largely un-co-ordinated. The ILO continued its long standing activities for the reduction of industrial injuries and occupational diseases, for the vocational training and placement of handicapped persons, and for the social security of disabled workers and their families. The World Health Organization, through its campaigns to improve health and to limit disabling diseases, contributed much to the prevention of physical handicaps. UNESCO helped to promote the education of the physically handicapped, particularly the blind, and provided facilities for the

[37] *Cf.* U.N. Department of Social Affairs, *Services for the Physically Handicapped* (November 1953), pp. 24–25.

circulation of Braille materials. The United Nations itself, under the program of the Advisory Social Welfare Services, provided expert help and training programs on behalf of the handicapped in many nations.

Although the Social Commission dealt with these programs at almost every one of its sessions from 1946 onward, it was not until 1950 that a serious attempt was made to arrive at a co-ordinated program. In that year, the Economic and Social Council asked the Secretary-General to plan jointly with the specialized agencies and in consultation with the interested nongovernmental organizations, a well co-ordinated international program for rehabilitation of physically handicapped persons.[38] A program was then worked out by an *ad hoc* working group of the Administrative Committee on Coordination and submitted to and approved by the Social Commission in 1952. The program called for a new approach toward disability by setting forth the following six "theses," which indicate clearly the spirit and direction of the entire program.

Firstly, that the handicapped person is an individual with full human rights, which he shares in common with the able-bodied, and that he is entitled to receive from his country every possible measure of protection, assistance and opportunity for rehabilitation.

Secondly, that by the very nature of his physical handicap he is exposed to the danger of emotional and psychological disturbance, resulting from a deep sense of deprivation and frustration, and that he therefore has a special claim on society for sympathy and constructive help.

Thirdly, that he is capable of developing his residual resources to an unexpected degree, if given the right opportunities of so doing, and of becoming in most instances an economic asset to the country instead of being a burden on himself, on his family, and on the State.

Fourthly, that handicapped persons have a responsibility to the community to contribute their services to the economic welfare of the nation in any way that becomes possible after rehabilitation and training.

Fifthly, that the chief longing of the physically handicapped person is to achieve independence within a normal community, instead of spending the rest of his life in a segregated institution, or within an environment of disability.

Sixthly, that the rehabilitation of the physically handicapped can only be successfully accomplished by a combination of medical, educational, social and vocational services, working together as a team.[39]

[38] Res. 309E(XI), July 13, 1950.
[39] U.N. Economic and Social Council, *Report of the Secretary General on an International Program for the Rehabilitation of the Physically Handicapped*, Doc. E/CN.5/229 (Jan. 28, 1952), pp. 8–9.

Much of the work of the United Nations in this area and of the co-operating specialized agencies has been dedicated to obtaining general acceptance throughout the world of this new conception of physical disability. Instead of stressing separate facilities for the handicapped, every effort has been made to assist in the development of the necessary facilities as an integral part of services furnished in the field of health, education, social welfare, and employment, and not as an extraneous service for a particular class of the community.

The actual programs have been modest but quietly effective. No attempt has been made to develop a large-scale publications program as in certain other areas of social welfare. Instead a rehabilitation unit in the United Nations Secretariat has made available selected bibliographies on the rehabilitation of the handicapped, including a bibliography of films that are particularly helpful in rehabilitation work.[40] Technical assistance has been provided to a number of countries. For the most part, the experts have given advice to the governments concerned on administrative, legislative, and technical problems; others, serving on a short-term basis, have assisted in the integration and expansion of existing services.

In 1954–55, for example, sixty-four fellowships and scholarships were awarded for study abroad. The establishment of demonstration centers for physical rehabilitation also has proved to be an effective means of assistance. Such centers were established with technical assistance from the United Nations in Egypt, Yugoslavia, and Venezuela. Finally, regional meetings have been organized on the education and welfare of the deaf, the rehabilitation of the adult disabled, and the use of prosthetic devices. A regional center has been established in Indonesia. The specialized agencies have continued to work within their respective fields with the difference that their activities are now planned and carried out so as to help in the development of integrated services for the handicapped within broader systems of social insurance, public services, and social assistance.

Nongovernmental organizations have played a very active role in these programs, chief among them the International Society for the Welfare of Cripples and the World Council for the Welfare of the Blind, the International Union for Child Welfare, the World Veterans' Federation, and the World Medical Association. In 1953, these and other organizations combined in a Conference of World Organizations Inter-

[40] *Cf.* U.N. Department of Social Affairs, *Rehabilitation of the Handicapped*, Doc. ST/SOA/Ser. F/11: 2 (1953), pp. 26–85.

ested in the Handicapped, the purpose of which is to co-operate with the United Nations and the specialized agencies, particularly with the *ad hoc* Working Party on the Rehabilitation of the Handicapped. The co-operation developed between these nongovernmental organizations and the secretariats of various intergovernmental agencies is a good example of the way in which even a small international program can greatly increase its effectiveness by using to the full the knowledge and enthusiasm of nongovernmental groups. The United Nations system has thus been able to make a real contribution to the pioneering of new ideas and concepts, the establishment of facilities for rehabilitation, and the integration of the handicapped into normal life, with resultant benefits to the individuals concerned and to the economies of many countries.

Migrants and Refugees

Any consideration of international migration poses, in addition to social problems, extremely complicated demographic, economic, political, and legal issues. Despite the broad economic and political implications of migration, national and international action relating to migration has of late been concerned largely with the individual migrant, his selection, preparation for emigration, transport, placement, and adjustment to new conditions, as well as his protection as a worker and an alien. These matters require measures of the type analyzed below.

The coupling of activities relating to migrants and to refugees is a natural one because most refugees by definition are international migrants confronted, however, with special problems beyond those faced by other migrants.

Migration

The story of migration is as old as man, but the nature and conditions of migration have changed through the ages. Present day migratory movements and the problems surrounding them have certain characteristics that have to be mentioned in order to facilitate understanding of the activities of the United Nations and the specialized agencies in connection with migration.

In recent decades, millions of men, women, and children have been on the move. A substantial proportion of them have been refugees and displaced persons. In Europe alone, there were about 8 million displaced persons and refugees at the end of the Second World War to which were soon added some 8 million "expellees" from Eastern Germany and other parts of Eastern Europe. The establishment of India and Pakistan as independent states resulted in a move of approximately 9 million refugees from India into Pakistan and of about 5 million from Pakistan into India. The war in Palestine resulted in the movement of about 1 million Arab refugees from Palestine, and the war in Korea produced, at least temporarily, 4.5 million refugees and displaced persons in South Korea. Emergency measures taken on behalf of several of these groups have been discussed elsewhere in this study.[41]

The stream of migrants has been further swelled by the overpopulated countries of Europe—Italy, Germany, Greece, and the Netherlands. It was estimated, in 1952 by the ILO that the surplus working population in Italy was about 3.7 million persons and that a large proportion of these were prepared to emigrate. In the Federal Republic of Germany, the number of persons ready to emigrate was then estimated by the government to be 1.2 million. Even in the Netherlands, it was estimated that an annual emigration of 25,000 workers was necessary to maintain the economic and social balance of the country. Actual emigration has not reached these totals. As a matter of fact, in no year since the war has European overseas emigration reached the levels of the early 1920's, when in some years more than 1 million migrants left that continent for overseas destinations. The postwar peak was reached between 1949 and 1952 when upwards of 600,000 migrants per year, a large proportion of them refugees and displaced persons, left Europe.

Despite pressure for emigration, it has become increasingly difficult to find places of settlement. There is general agreement that certain underdeveloped countries would benefit from additional immigration, but such immigration is impeded to some extent by the lack of agricultural migrants for which the underdeveloped countries are most frequently looking and partly by the fact that land settlement in the economically competitive society of today, calling for better and more expensive equipment, has become a very costly process. As a result of this situation and the broader opportunities offered by more diversified economies, a large proportion of modern migration is directed toward industrialized rather than underdeveloped countries. This, in turn, requires different types of selection and better preparation of migrants to enable them to adjust to the working processes and the kind of life in highly industrialized countries.

[41] See above, Chaps. I and II.

As a result of these difficulties, plus the legal restrictions imposed on migrants for political and economic reasons, migration as a pioneering venture on the part of individuals has been largely replaced by migration organized by governments. Both the governments of the countries of origin (except, of course, in the case of refugees) and governments of the countries of reception play a key role in the selection, preparation, admission, transportation, and placement of migrants.

Although some international agencies, including the United Nations and the ILO, have concerned themselves with internal migrations, international migration still remains the primary objective of international attention. More than ever, it has become a problem calling for intergovernmental action. In the late 1940's, the General Assembly and the Economic and Social Council repeatedly, and the Trusteeship Council occasionally, took up migration issues. The ILO exhibited a growing concern with migration as a way to make better use of man power and stepped up those of its activities designed to protect the working conditions of migrants. The FAO gave consideration to migration in relation to land reform and the problems of rural settlement. UNESCO expressed its concern with the cultural assimilation of migrants, as well as with vocational guidance and training for prospective migrants. WHO centered its attention on health qualifications and examinations of migrants and the availability of the kind of health services required by migrants in the receiving countries. Meanwhile, the International Refugee Organization (IRO), as has been reported earlier in this study, carried the major burden of settlement of refugees both in Europe and overseas between 1949 and 1952.[42]

This mushrooming of interest in migration was bound to result in conflicts of jurisdiction. Much of the United Nations effort up to 1950 was directed at bringing some order into the international work in this field.[43] After several earlier attempts, the Economic and Social Council, in 1948, attempted to lay down a permanent pattern of allocation of functions.[44] It assigned responsibility for research on migration problems to the Population Commission, asking it to deal not only with the demographic aspects of migration but with the relationships between demographic, economic, and social factors in migration, and to give special attention to the over-all co-ordination of research and study in

---

[42] See above, Chap. II.

[43] In this connection, see U.N. Economic and Social Council Res. 42(IV), Mar. 29, 1947; Res. 85(V), Aug. 13, 1947; Res. 104(VI), Mar. 3, 1948.

[44] Res. 156(VII), Aug. 10, 1948.

this field by the United Nations and specialized agencies. The Social Commission was asked to advise the Council on the social aspects of migration, particularly the rights and benefits of immigrants, including those of indigent immigrants; family and community relationships of immigrants; and advance planning by government authorities with a view to the provision of social services and facilities for health and education for immigrants and their families after arrival in a new community.

The same resolution laid the basis for future interagency consultations by inviting the specialized agencies and the United Nations to submit to the Administrative Committee on Coordination any migration problems that might arise within their areas of interest in such circumstances that overlapping with other organizations might occur or that important aspects of problems of migration might be neglected. At the same time, the Council noted with approval the division of responsibility between the United Nations and the ILO agreed to in consultation between the Secretary-General of the United Nations and the Director-General of the ILO. Under this arrangement, the ILO was to deal with migrants as *workers*, including policies governing their recruitment and selection, vocational training, care during transportation, employment and working conditions, social insurance, formalities in connection with departure from the country of residence and admission to the country of destination, and such general assistance and advice to governments on migration schemes as the ILO might be able to give from its experience. The United Nations, on the other hand, was to center its attention on the problems of the migrant as an alien, including conditions of residence, expulsion, deportation and repatriation, naturalization, relief in case of indigency, and recognition and enforcement of maintenance obligations. In addition, the United Nations was to maintain not only its responsibility regarding demographic aspects of migration but was to concern itself also with the broad economic, financial, social, and legal aspects.

This action on the part of the Economic and Social Council brought some clarification into a confused situation. It was followed by direct consultations on an organized basis through an *ad hoc* Working Group on Migration established under the Administrative Committee on Coordination.[45] Starting in 1949, this Working Group helped gradually

---

[45] A first meeting of the Working Group, in which representatives of the United Nations Secretariat, ILO, WHO, FAO, IRO, UNESCO, and the International Bank participated, was held in March 1949, and resulted in a more detailed delimitation of responsibilities as set forth in U.N. Economic and Social Council, *Coordination of Migration Activities*, Doc. E/1341 (May 31, 1949).

to reduce overlapping and conflicts of jurisdiction, although to this day, work on migration is not as closely co-ordinated as is the work in other fields of interest of the United Nations. To some extent, this is, of course, due to the extreme complexities of the issues involved.

These complexities became more evident in 1950 and 1951 when the ILO attempted as part of its man-power program to develop concerted international action for the movement, care, and protection of migrants. The ILO had just completed a major revision of its 1939 Convention on Migration for Employment, which had been prepared by its Permanent Migration Committee. It was felt in the ILO that its activities relating to migration could no longer be limited to the "traditional" activities of the organization, that is, research and studies, compilation of statistics and legislation, and the drafting of international instruments designed to set standards. The movement for additional action gained strength with the impending liquidation of the International Refugee Organization.

A Preliminary Migration Conference was convened by the ILO in the spring of 1950. The conclusions of this conference, which covered the entire field from selection to settlement, and which were later endorsed by the Governing Body of the ILO, constituted a veritable code of rules for international technical assistance in the field of European migration. The success of this conference led the Organization for European Economic Cooperation to arrange for the placement of a fund of nearly $1 million (mostly of American origin) at the disposal of the ILO for financing some of the new activities.

The ILO appointed experts to advise governments on various migration problems. Migration field missions were established at Bonn, Vienna, and Rome and a special migration unit was attached to the ILO Manpower Field Office for Latin America at Sao Paulo. A number of Latin American countries were given technical assistance (in some cases provided jointly by the ILO and the FAO) in the estimation of immigration capacity, the formulation of immigration programs, the examination of specific immigration projects, and the establishment of employment services. A guide to employment service organization was prepared as well as a guide to vocational training of migrants. A study was initiated to facilitate comparisons between the occupational classifications used in the countries of emigration and immigration. Guides to the principal immigration countries were prepared giving essential information on living and working conditions.

This hopeful start led the ILO to convene a migration conference to examine an over-all plan for handling European migration.[46] The conference was held in October 1951 in Naples and had before it a comprehensive plan for the establishment and financing of an ILO Migration Administration.

When the conference convened, serious differences of opinion developed almost immediately concerning the extent and nature of the international assistance required. The United States made clear that it was not prepared to make a financial contribution to the proposed agency. This opposition, shared by Australia and a few other countries, was largely based on the fact that the ILO plan appeared grandiose and impractical in many of its aspects. Reluctance, particularly on the part of the United States, to create such a migration administration within the ILO was prompted also by the fact that the proposed administration would have to deal with refugees from Communist countries, and that Communist states, specifically Poland and Czechoslovakia, were members of the ILO. The power of this particular argument became evident while the conference was still in session. When the Congress of the United States, in approving the Mutual Security Act of 1951, allocated an amount not in excess of $10 million for the continued operation of a number of vessels utilized by the International Refugee Organization for the transport of displaced persons, it stated as its intent that "none of the funds made available pursuant to the proviso should be allocated to any international organization which has in its membership any Communist, Communist-dominated or Communist-controlled country, to any subsidiary thereof or to any agency created by or stemming from such organization."[47]

This stipulation was clearly aimed at the ILO. It undoubtedly contributed to the failure of the Naples conference to achieve its major objective. The conference did adopt certain basic principles and criteria, worked out in co-operation with WHO, for the medical examina-

[46] The emphasis of the international community on European migration is significant. During the nineteenth and early twentieth centuries, organized migration was viewed by the western world primarily as a European problem and scant attention was paid to migratory movements in other parts of the world. This tradition left its imprint on the international organizations interested in migration and left them ill equipped to render effective assistance in meeting the problems of non-European migrants, particularly those from Asia and the Far East. In so far as any assistance, other than emergency aid, is being given to non-European migrants as migrants, it is taking the form of technical assistance to governments in the utilization and organization of man power.

[47] *Mutual Security Act of 1951*, H. Rept. 1090, 82 Cong. 1 sess. (Oct. 2, 1951), p. 21.

tion of migrants, and these have proved useful. It also proposed the setting up of a Consultative Council on European Migration, but this was largely a face-saving device, and the proposed council never came into existence.

Shortly after the Naples conference, and on United States initiative, another intergovernmental conference on migration was held. Convened in Brussels in November 1951, this conference—to which no Communist governments were invited—decided to set up a Provisional Inter-Governmental Committee for the Movement of Migrants from Europe. Its proposed terms of reference included the organization of land, sea, and air transport for refugees and the charter of ships formerly under the auspices of the IRO. This Provisional Inter-Governmental Committee later became the Inter-Governmental Committee for European Migration (ICEM), which, after the liquidation of the IRO, became the operating agency for the transport of European migrants and refugees. Twenty-six governments interested in migration belonged to the committee in early 1956. Its budget for 1956 was set at more than $43 million. A large part of the budget is met by reimbursements from sending and receiving governments for actual transportation costs. The ICEM moved more than 400,000 refugees during the period 1952 through 1955.

The Inter-Governmental Committee for European Migration has never been a part of the United Nations system. It maintains close working relationships, however, with various organs of the United Nations such as the Office of the High Commissioner for Refugees and the Economic Commission for Latin America, and it benefits from the work of the United Nations and the interested specialized agencies in the field of migration.

Research and studies continue to bulk large in this work. The list of publications by the United Nations and the ILO is lengthening steadily, with the latter concentrating on man-power studies and the protection of the migrant as a worker. The United Nations has published such practical aids as a *Handbook of International Measures for Protection of Migrants* and a report on research activities in the field of migration undertaken from 1946 to the beginning of 1953 by the United Nations and the specialized agencies.[48] In addition, the United Nations has

---

[48] U.N. Department of Social Affairs, *Handbook of International Measures for Protection of Migrants and General Conditions to be Observed in Their Settlement*, Doc. ST/SOA/15 (Jan. 15, 1953); U.N. Department of Social Affairs, *International Research on Migration*, Doc. ST/SOA/18 (September 1953).

prepared studies on more specialized subjects—for example, *Simplification of Formalities and Reduction of Costs for Migrants*, and *Expulsion of Immigrants*.[49] Field activities, so far as the United Nations itself is concerned, have been very limited, however; a few experts have been provided and some fellowships granted. By contrast, the ILO has continued to give active attention to migration problems as part of its technical assistance work in the man-power field.

Yeoman work in the reception and care of migrants has been performed by nongovernmental organizations, which, following a suggestion of the Economic and Social Council, combined in a Conference of Non-Governmental Organizations Interested in Migration. The fifth meeting of the conference was held in May 1955 under the joint sponsorship of the United Nations and the ILO.

In the light of the developments outlined above, it is possible to draw one major conclusion. The political difficulties and the economic complexities of large-scale migratory movements have proved too much for the protagonists of centralized or even closely co-ordinated action, under United Nations auspices, in the field of migration. To the extent that migration is a technical problem, valuable assistance is being offered by the ILO. Practical help to individual migrants is frequently extended by nongovernmental organizations, national and international. Beyond this, multilateral action is strictly limited, even as regards European migration. Political considerations and differing needs and absorptive capacities of individual countries remain the determining factors in the organization of international migration. Even where governments combine in common action as in the case of ICEM, they are only willing to provide for a minimum of international machinery to aid them in achieving their national economic and political ends. Thus international migration, which, at first sight, would appear to be a problem eminently fitted for joint international action, continues to be dealt with essentially by national governments. It is significant that no important resolution on migration has been adopted either by the General Assembly or the Economic and Social Council since 1952. One of the

[49] A discussion of "Economic and Social Factors Affecting Migration" was included in U.N. Department of Social Affairs, *Determinants and Consequences of Population Trends*, A Summary of the Findings of Studies on the Relationships between Population Changes and Economic and Social Conditions, Doc. ST/SOA/Ser.A/17 (1953), pp. 98–133. Two studies have been prepared for the United Nations by the International Institute for the Unification of Private Law: *A Compilation of Legislative Texts on the Legal Status of Aliens*, and a *Compilation of International Instruments on the Legal Status of Aliens*. A *Migration Digest*, of which thirty-nine issues had appeared by 1954, has been discontinued by the Secretary-General.

last such resolutions recommended to "Member States and non-Member States, classified variously as countries of emigration and immigration, to conclude bilateral or multilateral agreements with a view to the equipment, transfer and resettlement of groups of emigrants, without racial or religious discrimination, as part of their general economic development."[50] The emphasis on direct agreements between governments rather than on international machinery is significant.

Refugees

First slated for termination by June 30, 1950, the International Refugee Organization finally closed its books in early 1952.[51] This did not mean that the refugee problem had been solved. The General Council of the IRO itself stated, shortly before its termination, that "although the problems inherent in the situation . . . are clearly not of sufficient magnitude to justify the maintenance of the IRO, they are so grave in terms of human suffering that they call for urgent consideration by the United Nations."[52]

In anticipation of this situation, the Economic and Social Council, as early as 1949, had asked the Secretary-General to prepare for the consideration of the General Assembly a plan for continuing machinery, either in the form of a High Commissioner's Office or of a service within the United Nations Secretariat.[53] The Assembly decided to establish as of January 1, 1951 a High Commissioner's Office for Refugees and, at the same time, outlined certain principles to govern its functioning.[54] It also requested the Council to submit more detailed plans to the Assembly. The Council then transmitted a draft "Statute of the High Commissioner's Office for Refugees."[55] Final action on this statute, which was taken by the General Assembly in 1950, provided for the appointment of a United Nations High Commissioner for Refugees and laid out in considerable detail his functions and the organization and financing of his office.[56] The General Assembly at the same session elected the first High Commissioner.[57]

The discussions preceding the approval of these arrangements were

---

[50] U.N. General Assembly Res. 624(VII), Dec. 21, 1952.
[51] See above, Chap. II.
[52] U.N. General Assembly, Sixth Session, *Problems of Assistance to Refugees: Communication from the General Council of the International Refugee Organization*, Doc. A/1948 (Nov. 10, 1951), p. 6.
[53] Res. 248A(IX), Aug. 6, 1949.
[54] See Res. 319(IV), Dec. 3, 1949, and Annex thereto.
[55] Res. 319A(XI), Aug. 11, 1950.
[56] Res. 428(V), Dec. 14, 1950.
[57] G. J. van Heuven Goedhart, who died in July 1956.

prolonged and heated. Major differences of opinion arose over the definition of the "refugees" who were to be brought under the mandate of the High Commissioner. Most of the Asian and Middle Eastern countries, and a few European and Latin American countries, wanted a liberal definition that would have included millions of non-European refugees such as Pakistanis moving into India and Indians moving into Pakistan. The United States, supported by such countries as the United Kingdom and Australia, took a much more restricted view. The United States wanted to avoid any general definition and preferred an enumeration of clearly defined categories of refugees, specifically those who had been considered refugees under the various arrangements and conventions concluded under the League of Nations and the constitution of the IRO, and any persons who, as a result of events before January 1, 1951, had become refugees. To be specifically excluded were persons recognized by the competent authorities of the country in which they had taken residence as having the rights and obligations of nationals of that country. This excluded all the expellees from Eastern Germany and other *Volksdeutsche* who had found refuge in the Federal Republic of Germany, as well as Pakistanis, Indians, and Chinese, who could look to the protection of their own governments. The Communist bloc countries maintained the astonishing thesis they had put forward at the time of the creation of the International Refugee Organization: that only the victims or opponents of one particular form of government— Nazi, Fascist or Falangist—could be refugees. Opponents of any other form of government were traitors and criminals, whose immediate repatriation for summary punishment was an international obligation.[58]

In the end, the General Assembly agreed on a compromise. It enumerated certain categories of refugees along the lines suggested by the United States but included a further paragraph bringing under the mandate of the High Commissioner:

. . . any other person who is outside the country of his nationality or, if he has no nationality, the country of his former habitual residence, because he has or had well-founded fear of persecution by reason of his race, religion, nationality or political opinion and is unable or, because of such fear, is unwilling to avail himself of the protection of the government of the country of his nationality, or, if he has no nationality, to return to the country of his former habitual residence.[59]

[58] Elfan Rees, "The Refugee and the United Nations," *International Conciliation* No. 492 (June 1953), p. 272. This is one of the best summary accounts of the refugee problem as dealt with by the United Nations.
[59] Statute of the Office of the United Nations High Commissioner for Refugees, Res. 428(V), Dec. 14, 1950, Annex, Chap. II, Art. 6B.

Under these provisions, the mandate of the High Commissioner extended to approximately two million people, almost exclusively of European origin.

An even sharper conflict developed over the definition of the functions of the High Commissioner. The United States took the lead in emphasizing as the primary and almost exclusive function of the High Commissioner the task of legal and administrative protection, such as assuring that governments issue identity and travel papers and work permits enabling refugees to move about and to obtain their livelihood. The United States position was prompted by the belief that the relief problems remaining after termination of the IRO were not of such a magnitude as to require international financing and that the countries of refuge should and could assume responsibility for relief and other material aid. By contrast, certain countries of first residence for refugees, particularly France, urged that the High Commissioner be entitled and equipped to continue to give material aid to individuals and groups of refugees.

In a number of close votes, the Assembly finally agreed that the High Commissioner should assume the function of "providing international protection" and "of seeking permanent solutions" for the problem of refugees by assisting governments and, subject to the approval of the governments concerned, private organizations to facilitate the voluntary repatriation of such refugees, or their assimilation within new national communities.[60] The High Commissioner was given the power to "administer any funds, public or private, which he receives for assistance to refugees," but at the same time was enjoined not to appeal to governments for funds or make a general appeal, without the prior approval of the General Assembly.[61] As a matter of fact, most of the residual funds of the IRO were not turned over to the High Commissioner but to voluntary organizations aiding refugees.

From 1950 to 1954 was a period of continuous struggle on the part of the High Commissioner to obtain the funds that he considered essential to the discharge of his functions. In 1952, he obtained authority to appeal for funds for purposes of emergency aid.[62] He then set up a United Nations Refugee Emergency Fund for which he hoped to obtain $3 million. During the two following years, less than $1 million was contributed. The United States did not contribute to the United Nations

---

[60] *Ibid.*, Chap. I, Art. I.
[61] *Ibid.*, Chap. II, Art. 10.
[62] U.N. General Assembly Res. 538B(VI), Feb. 2, 1952.

Refugee Emergency Fund, but channeled its material aid through ICEM and through the newly created United States Escapee Program, which began in March 1952 with an allocation of $4.3 million for aid to refugees in Western Europe who had escaped from countries behind the Iron Curtain after January 1, 1948. Thus, the United States continued to be the largest contributor to the cause of refugee aid but did not make its funds available through United Nations channels.

After a decision had been taken by the General Assembly to continue the Office of the High Commissioner for another five years, from January 1, 1954,[63] the High Commissioner redoubled his efforts to obtain additional funds not only for emergency aid but also to assist in the finding of permanent solutions. He was encouraged in this by a grant of $2.9 million from the Ford Foundation in 1952 and $200,000 in 1954 to assist in providing permanent solutions for the refugee problem. These were obtained through the efforts of four of the major voluntary agencies working on behalf of refugees, and the High Commissioner became the trustee and administrator of the fund. It was used to facilitate agricultural integration, housing, vocational training, education, employment counseling, youth and community centers, medical rehabilitation, and overseas resettlement. The results were sufficiently promising to give a new impetus to the High Commissioner's drive for additional funds from governments.

He attained his end when the General Assembly, in 1954, finally agreed to authorize use of the United Nations Refugee Emergency Fund for the purpose of facilitating permanent solutions as well as for emergency needs.[64] The High Commissioner was authorized also to obtain additional funds on the basis of a detailed program he had submitted. The plan provided for a four-year program at a cost of $16 million. For the first time since the liquidation of the IRO, the United States not only voted for the establishment of this enlarged United Nations Refugee Emergency Fund but promised to seek a contribution from the Congress of the United States. The budget for the first year's operation was set for $4.2 million, with approximately $3 million to be used for the attainment of permanent solutions. Subsequently, the United States Congress allocated $1.2 million for the year 1955, provided that the United States contribution did not exceed one third of the total contributions made. Contributions of other governments fell short of expectations. By the end of 1955, only $2 million had been made available by

[63] Res. 727(VIII), Oct. 23, 1953.
[64] Res. 832(IX), Oct. 21, 1954.

these other governments, and the United States contribution to that date, therefore, was limited to $1 million. In the administration of these funds, the High Commissioner is assisted by an advisory committee, set up originally in 1951, and reconstituted with executive powers by the Economic and Social Council in 1955, as the United Nations Refugee Fund (UNREF) Executive Committee.[65]

Parallel to these actions involving the appointment of a High Commissioner and the development of his functions, the United Nations attempted to provide standard legal protection by a convention embodying earlier refugee conventions concluded under the League of Nations but adjusted to contemporary conditions. In a series of resolutions, the Economic and Social Council with the help of an *ad hoc* committee and, finally, of the General Assembly, advanced the drafting of such a convention to the point where a plenipotentiary conference was held in Geneva in July 1951.[66]

The conference completed and opened for signature a convention on the status of refugees, which has come into force largely as a result of ratifications on the part of European nations.[67] In the drafting of this convention, the same difficulties arose in defining "refugees" as had arisen in the drafting of the statute of the High Commissioner's office. The definition in the convention did not include the generalized definition of refugees that was included in the statute and that was cited above. The convention selected "events occurring before 1 January 1951" as the *terminus ad quo* for a refugee situation and further limited even this by leaving it to individual governments to decide whether they wished to include only events "occurring in Europe" before that date or would also include events "occurring in Europe and elsewhere."

In substance, the convention provided for freedom from discrimination and dealt with the legal status of refugees and their rights with respect to work, housing, education, public relief, social security, free-

[65] Res. 565(XIX), Mar. 31, 1955. In November and December 1956, Soviet intervention to crush a revolt in Hungary resulted in a mass exodus from that country. The General Assembly requested the Secretary-General and the High Commissioner for Refugees to arrange for emergency assistance to refugees from Hungary, and urged governments and nongovernmental organizations to contribute to this work. As a result, these officers promptly issued a joint appeal for $10 million to help meet the minimum initial needs of the refugees.

[66] U.N. Economic and Social Council Res. 116D(VI), Mar. 1–2, 1948; Res. 248B(IX), Aug. 8, 1949; Res. 319BII(XI), Aug. 16, 1950; U.N. General Assembly Res. 429(V), Dec. 14, 1950.

[67] U.N. Conference of Plenipotentiaries on the Status of Refugees and Stateless Persons held at Geneva, Switzerland from July 2–25, 1951, *Final Act and Convention Relating to the Status of Refugees* (1951).

dom of movement, and access to the courts. These provisions, if accepted, go a long way in facilitating the assimilation of refugees within their countries of residence. The United States participated in the drafting of the convention, but made clear that it had no intention of signing or ratifying it, on the ground that noncitizens, including legally admitted refugees, in the United States have even greater privileges than those set forth in the convention. Except for a few specific rights such as the right to vote, their position is in effect that of United States citizens.

In international programs of refugee aid, the record of voluntary organizations during the postwar years is outstanding. They have concentrated in their work on welfare, spiritual care, emigration assistance, and experiments in integration. After the establishment of the High Commissioner's office, and while the High Commissioner was barred from operational functions, the voluntary agencies had to assume the major burden of material aid to refugees.

Under the new plan for permanent solutions developed by the High Commissioner and accepted by the General Assembly, the voluntary agencies continue to be the chief action bodies in the carrying out of the program. It has been repeatedly suggested that they can make a dollar go further than any intergovernmental organization. Moreover, they bring to their work the human approach, which means so much, particularly when funds are scarce. These agencies—nearly forty of them—have established a Standing Conference of Voluntary Agencies Working for Refugees that is in consultative relationship with the Economic and Social Council, with the UNREF Executive Committee, and with the Inter-Governmental Committee for European Migration.

It has been said that "the United Nations in its spasmodic consideration of the refugee problem has persistently displayed either incredibly naive optimism, or a willful blindness to reality, neither of which is consistent with statesmanship." This may be too harsh a judgment, although there is much truth in the further statement that "it is some time since so few have been asked to do so much for so many on so little."[68]

Even with the restricted means available, and thanks to the help of the voluntary organizations, large numbers of refugees have been given emergency aid. Signal success was achieved in the placing of hard core cases, i.e., the old, the sick, and the maimed. Outstanding contributions

[68] Rees, loc. cit., p. 309.

in this respect were made by Norway, which received many of the blind, by Sweden and Switzerland, which took in the tubercular, by France, which accepted many epileptics, and by Belgium, Ireland, the United Kingdom, the Netherlands, and Germany, which agreed to take care on a permanent basis of many of the aged. The problem of these hard core cases is not altogether solved but nears solution. Under arrangements made by ICEM, in co-operation with the High Commissioner, more than 83,000 refugees were moved overseas for permanent settlement between 1952 and 1955. Until May 1956, when the authorities on the Chinese mainland closed the branch office of the High Commissioner in Shanghai, the 15,000 White Russian refugees stranded in China after the First World War were gradually being moved out of Communist China, again with the help of ICEM. Above all, the High Commissioner has succeeded in keeping alive and awakening, when necessary, the conscience of the civilized nations on refugee questions.

Social Defense

The dark forces in human nature, greed or lust or simply weakness, can easily become destructive of human personality unless they are kept under control. Society has to defend itself against them. There are three major areas of social defense that for many years have been recognized as a legitimate concern of governments, acting separately and jointly: the control of the traffic in dangerous drugs; the suppression of prostitution and of obscene literature; and the prevention of crime and the treatment of offenders.[69]

Narcotic Drug Control

The United Nations inherited no less than six international conventions and agreements dealing with the control of narcotic drugs, chief among them the Geneva convention of February 19, 1925 instituting a system of import certificates and export permits without which no international transaction in narcotic drugs could be made legally, and the Convention for Limiting the Manufacture and Regulating the Dis-

[69] In the terminology of the United Nations and for purposes of internal organization of the Secretariat, the control of dangerous drugs is not considered within the area of social defense. The ultimate purpose of international control, however, is the protection of the individual against the dangers of drug addiction, and for that reason the control of narcotic drugs is discussed in this study as an aspect of social defense.

tribution of Narcotic Drugs signed at Geneva on July 13, 1931. The
United Nations also inherited two control organs, the Permanent Central Opium Board set up under the 1925 convention to "continuously
watch the course of international trade" in narcotic drugs;[70] and the
Drug Supervisory Body established under the 1931 convention to examine the estimates furnished annually by governments of their requirements of narcotic drugs for medical and scientific purposes. This
machinery had continued to function on a limited scale throughout the
Second World War, in itself a striking sign of the importance that
governments had come to attach to the international control of traffic
in narcotics.

The Economic and Social Council, by unanimous action on February
16, 1946, established the Commission on Narcotic Drugs. It has since
served as the focal point of intergovernmental consultation and action
in the field of narcotics control, as did the Advisory Committee on the
Traffic in Opium and other Dangerous Drugs set up by the League of
Nations in 1920. Also in 1946, the General Assembly unanimously
adopted a protocol approving the assumption by the United Nations of
the functions and powers exercised by the League of Nations in respect
to narcotic drugs.[71]

The Commission on Narcotic Drugs and the Permanent Central
Opium Board each present an annual report on their work to the
Council. These are published, as is the annual statement issued by the
Drug Supervisory Body on *Estimated World Requirements of Narcotic Drugs*.
Four further series of publications are produced.[72] Special studies on
particular questions or problems are also issued. Publicity is one of the
most effective means of enforcement of controls, and information on
measures taken by national governments is essential to effective international action.

The varied activities of the Commission on Narcotic Drugs can be
broken down into five major categories: suppression of illicit traffic in
narcotic drugs; control of synthetic and newly discovered drugs; control
of the production of natural raw materials; consolidation of international treaties and protocols; and prevention of addiction and rehabilitation of addicts. With respect to the first of these areas of activity, there

[70] International Opium Convention, signed at Geneva Feb. 19, 1925, Art. 24.
[71] Res. 54(I), Nov. 19, 1946.
[72] The *Annual Summary of Laws and Regulations Relating to the Control of Narcotic Drugs*,
the *Annual Summary of Annual Reports of Governments*, monthly *Summaries of Illicit
Transactions and Seizures* reported to the Secretariat of the United Nations, and the
quarterly *Bulletin on Narcotics*.

was general apprehension among experts during the war that after the war the illicit traffic in narcotics might get out of hand. These expectations fortunately did not come true, but the illicit traffic did reach substantial proportions and continues at a high level. Much of that traffic is aimed at the United States market where a few pounds of narcotics can bring large monetary returns. Moreover, the long frontiers of the United States make control extremely difficult.

Public debate in the Commission on Narcotics Drugs, frequently based on specific seizure reports transmitted by governments, is an instance in which necessity often overrides diplomatic niceties. The reports of the commission are replete with discussions of specific situations, with the origin of illicit drugs frequently and publicly traced to named countries of origin. The reports of the Permanent Central Opium Board sometimes also refer to specific instances of failure to comply with provisions of the relevant conventions. These reports and discussions as a rule do not result in pious resolutions but in effective national action in the form of the closing of factories, or of police or even military action to destroy illegal poppy plantings.

With the endorsement of the Economic and Social Council, special control measures were taken in Germany and Japan during the allied occupation. Further, when it was found that much of the smuggling of narcotics, particularly into the United States, was attributable to merchant seafarers and civilian air crews, the Economic and Social Council requested the Secretary-General to establish lists of persons who had been convicted of offenses against narcotic laws and recommended that governments revoke certificates and licenses held by such personnel.[73]

Increasingly effective steps have been taken over the last ten years, largely by way of persuasion, resolution,[74] and publicity, to prohibit completely the use of certain narcotics, particularly the smoking of opium, and thus to establish a precondition for the application of international laws and machinery to the suppression of illicit traffic. Opium smoking remains legal only in one of the traditional opium smoking countries, although transitional arrangements are in force in a number of others.

Further progress in the international control of the traffic in opium is being made through scientific research. In 1949, the United States

---

[73] Res. 436D(XIV), May 27, 1952.
[74] U.N. Economic and Social Council Res. 49(IV), Mar. 28, 1947; Res. 159IIB (VII), Aug. 3, 1948; Res. 505B(XVI), July 28, 1953.

offered, and the Commission on Narcotic Drugs accepted, the use of United States laboratory facilities to develop methods for determining by chemical and physical means the geographical origin of seized opium. The Economic and Social Council requested governments to send for purposes of laboratory research, samples of all opium seized in the illicit traffic. This research has proved successful. Because of the work of a Canadian chemist, it has now become possible to ascertain the country of original production of seized opium, and this is bound to make control measures more effective. A permanent United Nations Narcotics Laboratory is now scheduled to be established in Geneva.

A second series of measures is aimed at the extension of controls to synthetic and other newly-discovered drugs. A fresh threat to the health and well-being of millions of persons and to the entire functioning of international campaigns against drug addiction arose with the development of synthetic, addiction-producing drugs that threatened to flood the illicit market. On the initiative of the United States, rapid action was taken against this threat. The move to bring these drugs under international control resulted, in 1948, in the conclusion of a new protocol "to bring under international control drugs outside the scope of the Convention of July 13, 1931 for limiting the manufacture and regulating the distribution of narcotic drugs."[75] The protocol applies to all drugs "liable to the same kind of harmful effects as the drugs specified in Article I, paragraph 2 of the [1931] Convention." Accordingly, it makes it possible to place under international control not only existing synthetic drugs but also any other addiction-forming drugs, as rapidly as they are discovered.

Under the convention, it is for the World Health Organization to ascertain whether a particular drug is addiction-forming. Pending such determination, the protocol allows the Commission on Narcotic Drugs to take interim measures to place under control a drug considered by a state party to the protocol as likely to produce addiction or capable of being transformed into such a drug. The list of drugs being brought under control in this way is lengthening steadily.

In a third field of activities, the United Nations has made extensive efforts to bring under control the *production* of "natural" raw materials. Earlier conventions aimed at the control of the international *traffic* in raw materials used in the manufacture of drugs (Geneva convention of 1925) and the *manufacture* of such drugs (Geneva convention of 1931).

[75] U.N. Economic and Social Council Res. 159I(VII), Aug. 3, 1948; U.N. General Assembly Res. 211A(III), Oct. 8, 1948.

Beginning with the first session of the Commission on Narcotics Drugs in 1946, attempts were made to go one step further and to limit the production of "natural" raw materials. Opium, by far the most important of the raw materials concerned, was the subject of a series of meetings under the sponsorship of the United Nations, first among the major producing countries (India, Iran, Turkey, and Yugoslavia), then of the principal manufacturing countries (France, the Netherlands, United Kingdom, United States and, as observers, Belgium, Italy, and Switzerland) and, finally, by a joint meeting of the two groups.[76]

The purpose of these meetings was to establish an international public drug enterprise in the form of a monopoly for buying and selling opium in the legal trade. The proposed agreement provided for estimates of annual opium requirements, the establishment of export quotas, and an international agency for purchasing and selling opium. Each country party to the agreement was to create a national opium monopoly to control all stages of production and purchase the crop for resale to the international agency. The international agency thereupon was to sell the crop at a fixed price to the drug manufacturing countries, according to "advance" orders based on requirements. Provisions were included in the plan for inspection and for the imposition of sanctions for violations of the agreement.

The discussion of these proposals, originally advanced by the Secretariat of the United Nations, led to one of the few major disagreements among members of the Commission on Narcotic Drugs. Negotiations finally broke down on two key issues. No agreement could be reached on the price to be fixed by the international agency. It was also impossible to reach agreement on the question of international inspection, largely because some of the producing countries declared themselves unwilling or unable to permit inspection in their territories except on the basis of specific consent for each international inspection. Beyond these specific difficulties, negotiations were complicated by an undercurrent of reluctance, not only on the part of the manufacturers but also of some of the producers, to depart from the free market approach and to accept control of prices and of purchasing by the establishment of a monopoly system.

When these negotiations collapsed, attention was transferred to an alternative plan suggested by the French Government. This plan, after

[76] Recently Iran, in a far-sighted move taken on its own volition, has banned the cultivation of the opium poppy and the Economic and Social Council in Res. 626E(XXII) of Aug. 2, 1956, authorized the use of technical assistance to help Iran in enforcing this ban and bringing about necessary adjustments in the Iranian economy.

consideration by the Commission on Narcotic Drugs and the United Nations Secretariat, resulted in a draft protocol for limiting and regulating the cultivation of the poppy plant, the production of, international and wholesale trade in, and the use of opium. This draft was submitted to and, with amendments, approved by the United Nations Opium Conference convened at New York in 1953.[77]

The protocol, which in the absence of the stipulated number of ratifications has not yet come into effect, calls for the continuance of a free order system in international trade in opium, within which the production of opium is to be limited with a view to reducing the amounts harvested to the amounts needed for medical and scientific purposes. Indirect means are to be adopted to achieve this aim. Countries producing opium are to submit full statistics, and also advance estimates, of their production to the United Nations. Consuming countries are required under the 1931 convention to estimate their needs. Stocks of producing countries are to be limited to the equivalent of their exports of any two and one-half years since 1947, and the stocks of manufacturing and consuming countries are also to be limited. Individual governments of countries in which opium is produced, whether for export or not, undertake to establish national agencies to be the only legal purchasers of opium, and to carry into effect stringent measures of internal control, including the licensing of each grower and the supervision of the area cultivated. The number of countries authorized to export is limited to those presently producing opium.

International control is exercised not through an international monopoly but through the Permanent Central Opium Board and the Drug Supervisory Body. If a country fails to submit estimates, exceeds maximum stock limits, threatens to become a center of the illicit traffic, or otherwise fails to implement the protocol, the board is authorized to take a series of steps. In addition to consultation with the government concerned, publication and publicity, and local inquiry (with the consent of the government), the board can recommend an import and/or export embargo of opium, this last step being subject to appeal to a body set up within the framework of the International Court of Justice.

Parallel efforts were made to establish controls over the production of other "natural" raw materials used in the production of narcotic drugs, specifically cannabis and the coca leaf.[78] In the case of cannabis,

---

[77] United Nations Opium Conference, *Protocol and Final Act*, Doc. E/NT/8 (Sept. 28, 1953).

[78] Indian hemp, marihuana, and hashish are forms of cannabis.

which plays an important role in the fibre industry of a number of countries and which grows wild over many regions of the world, practical solutions sought under the direction of the Food and Agriculture Organization include encouraging the breeding of narcotic-free strains of the plant and also investigating the possibilities of replacement by other fibre crops having comparable industrial uses. This is an interesting example of co-operation between different United Nations organs and agencies. Where there is no production of fibre for industrial purposes, the view of the Commission on Narcotic Drugs is that the abuse of the plant should be prevented by all available means including prohibition of cultivation. The commission has expressed its formal agreement with the World Health Organization that the medical use of cannabis products is no longer necessary and should generally be prohibited. An exception would be made for a stated period of years for countries in which the use of cannabis is traditional in indigenous (*e.g.*, Ayurvedic) medicine.

A series of studies on the coca leaf was initiated by the request of the Government of Peru that a special commission of experts be appointed to study, in certain regions of the Andes, the effects of the chewing of coca leaf, the factors engendering the habit, the social and economic implications of the habit, and the measures that should be taken if this habit were proved to be harmful. In 1954, the Economic and Social Council was able to record the agreement of the Commission on Narcotic Drugs, the World Health Organization, and the governments principally concerned, including Peru and Bolivia, that the practice constituted a form of harmful addiction and that measures should be taken for its gradual suppression.[79] It recognized that in several countries suppression required far-reaching social and economic measures and would take a considerable period of time. Moreover, it recommended that the technical assistance services of the United Nations and specialized agencies aid in developing appropriate administrative or social measures for the gradual suppression of the chewing habit and urged that the governments concerned gradually limit the cultivation and the export of coca leaf to medical, scientific, and other legitimate purposes. Since then, an extensive program of technical assistance, including assistance in the development of substitute crops, has been established in the Andean *Alto Plano*.

The consolidation of international treaties and protocols relating to

---

[79] Res. 548(XVIII), July 12, 1954.

the control of dangerous drugs represents a fourth area of activity. On recommendation of the Commission on Narcotic Drugs, the Economic and Social Council decided in 1948 that work should be begun on the drafting of a new single convention to replace the existing multilateral treaties on narcotics control, not only in order to simplify existing international law and administrative machinery concerned with the control of narcotic drugs, but also to make the system of control stronger and more flexible.[80] This task has been a major preoccupation of the Commission on Narcotic Drugs ever since. Certain countries such as Canada lean toward a codification of existing conventions and agreements, while others favor not only codification but new steps to bring under control the production of "natural" raw materials; to forbid the non-medical use of opium, coca, and cannabis; to prohibit altogether the production of particularly dangerous drugs such as heroin, for which less dangerous substitutes have been found; to institute a system of international inspection; and to simplify existing machinery. Many of these proposals raise extremely difficult and complicated technical issues.[81]

There is some danger that the single convention might turn into a convention of the "lowest common denominator." This tendency has been a matter of concern particularly to the United States, and in the Commission on Narcotic Drugs, the United States has been advocating a strengthened, flexible instrument. Considerable further discussion on the basis of observations to be made by governments will be necessary before the present draft single convention will be ready for final action. In view of the large number of questions that remain unsolved, there is considerable doubt whether the convention will be completed and submitted to an intergovernmental conference in 1957.

In a fifth area of activity, growing attention is being given to the prevention of addiction and the rehabilitation of addicts. The following interesting section on the treatment of drug addiction was adopted by the Commission on Narcotic Drugs in 1954, for inclusion in the single convention:

The Parties are cognizant of the importance of creating means for the medical treatment, care and rehabilitation of drug addicts and undertake to use their best endeavours towards this effort, on a planned and compulsory basis, in properly conducted and duly authorized institutions in those States where

[80] Res. 159IID(VII), Aug. 3, 1948.
[81] For a thorough discussion of these technical issues, see Herbert L. May, "The Single Convention on Narcotic Drugs: Comments and Possibilities," *Bulletin on Narcotics* (January–April 1955), pp. 1–14.

the seriousness of the problem of drug addiction and their economic resources warrant such measures.[82]

This paragraph reflects the growing concern with a previously neglected aspect of the fight against drug addiction. It puts the emphasis on cure and rehabilitation, the idea being to help individual addicts and to weaken the market for illicit traffic. This emphasis on the medical and social aspects of the problem rather than on the "policing" of the traffic in drugs is reflected also in the action of the Economic and Social Council urging governments to consider setting up means for the treatment, care, and rehabilitation of drug addicts on a planned and compulsory basis in properly conducted institutions.[83]

In spite of continuing weaknesses in the system of control of the traffic in narcotic drugs, and even greater weaknesses in procedures for the cure and rehabilitation of addicts, the record of the United Nations in facilitating control of one of the most dangerous social evils is impressive. In the debates of the various organs concerned with drug control, political issues, generally speaking, are minimized.[84] By and large, the differences that developed have been technical in character although economic and political considerations at times have acted as a brake on attempts to establish firmer controls. The breakdown of the discussions aiming at the establishment of an opium monopoly is an example in point. It cannot yet be said that the production, distribution, and use of narcotic drugs has been effectively limited to medical and scientific purposes, but the United Nations is assuredly making an increasingly effective contribution toward relieving mankind from the scourge of drug addiction.

[82] U.N. Economic and Social Council, Eighteenth Session, *Official Records*, Supplement No. 8, "Commission on Narcotic Drugs: Report of the Ninth Session, 19 April to 14 May 1954," Annex D, Sec. 41.

[83] Res. 548I(XVIII), July 12, 1954.

[84] Exceptional in this respect were the bitter debates provoked by the revelation on the part of the United States representative on the Commission on Narcotic Drugs that Communist China had become a major source of the illicit traffic in narcotics and appeared to be making a deliberate attempt to flood certain parts of the world with illicit drugs. See, for example, U.N. Economic and Social Council, Eighteenth Session, *Official Records*, Supplement No. 8, paras. 184–92 and U.N. Economic and Social Council, Twentieth Session, *Official Records*, Supplement No. 8, "Commission on Narcotic Drugs: Report of the Tenth Session, 18 April to 12 May 1955," paras. 300–06.

*Suppression of Prostitution
and Obscene Publications*

The activities of the United Nations in connection with the suppression of prostitution and of obscene publications follow a pattern in many ways similar to developments in the field of narcotics control. The United Nations decided, in 1947, to assume the functions formerly exercised by the League of Nations under the conventions of 1921 and 1933 relating to the suppression of the traffic in women and children, and the convention of 1923 relating to the suppression of the circulation of, and the traffic in, obscene publications. The General Assembly adopted protocols to that effect, which were signed on November 12, 1947.[85] The United Nations, in 1948, similarly assumed the functions formerly exercised by the French Government under the agreement of 1904 and the convention of 1910 for the suppression of the white slave traffic and the agreement of 1910 for the suppression of the circulation of obscene publications.[86] The prewar international instruments relating to prostitution provided for the establishment of national authorities for the co-ordination of information relative to the procuring of women or girls for immoral purposes abroad, and for annual reports by governments. They also dealt with such issues as the repatriation of foreign prostitutes and the extradition and punishment of traffickers. The functions taken over by the United Nations were largely reporting functions.

The United Nations, furthermore, inherited from the League of Nations a draft convention prepared, in 1937, by the Advisory Committee on Social Questions of the League, designed to secure the prosecution and punishment of any person keeping or managing a brothel, or exploiting the prostitution of another person. Due to the outbreak of the Second World War, however, this draft convention was not completed. The draft, together with the other instruments relating to prostitution, served as a basis for the elaboration of a new consolidated convention that was intended to replace all preceding instruments on the subject, and was finally approved by the General Assembly, in 1949, as the Convention for the Suppression of the Traffic in Persons and the Exploitation of the Prostitution of Others.[87]

Several of the articles of the convention were passed by close votes,

[85] U.N. General Assembly Res. 126(II), Oct. 20, 1947.
[86] U.N. Economic and Social Council Res. 155D(VII), Aug. 13, 1948; U.N. General Assembly Res. 256(III), Dec. 3, 1948.
[87] Res. 317(IV), Dec. 2, 1949.

and in some cases positions were reversed at different stages of the discussion. Difficulties arose over the question of medical inspection and registration of known prostitutes. These were finally settled by omitting any reference to such inspection, over very strong opposition, particularly on the part of France. Another point of concern to a substantial group of countries was the deletion from the convention of a clause recognizing that a signatory might require that the motive of gain be established in the prosecution of procurers. The omission of such reference was strongly urged by Brazil, France, and the Soviet Union. The United Kingdom and several of the Commonwealth countries were in the forefront of those insisting on inclusion of such a clause on the ground that it would make it easier to define an offense under the convention.

Considerable controversy arose also over the question of a limitative "territorial article" sought by various administering powers, particularly the United Kingdom, on the ground that the far-reaching requirements laid down in the convention could not immediately be applied by legislation to various non-self-governing territories. The General Assembly decided not to include a territorial clause but made it quite explicit that "for the purposes of the present Convention the word 'State' shall include all the colonies and trust territories of a State signatory or acceding to the Convention and all territories for which such State is internationally responsible" (Article 23). Finally, the Assembly, over strong opposition from the United States and other federal states, decided to omit any "Federal-State clause," despite the fact that the Sixth (Legal) Committee of the General Assembly had voted for such a clause.

The divergences of view were reflected in the final vote of the Assembly; thirty-five states voted for acceptance, two (France and the United Kingdom) were opposed, and fifteen abstained. The abstentions included many developed states such as the United States, Denmark, New Zealand, and Sweden, that were as determined as any other states to suppress the evil of prostitution but could not accept some of the provisions of the convention. Although this convention was adopted more than five years ago, only seventeen countries have deposited with the Secretary-General instruments of accession or ratification.[88]

Two other approaches to the problem of prostitution have also failed

---

[88] It is in effect for Bulgaria, Byelorussian Soviet Socialist Republic, Cuba, Haiti, Hungary, India, Iraq, Israel, Norway, Pakistan, Philippines, Rumania, Poland, Ukrainian Soviet Socialist Republic, Union of South Africa, Union of Soviet Socialist Republics, and Yugoslavia.

to obtain adequate support. First, plans for the establishment of a special Far Eastern Bureau for the Suppression of Traffic in Women and Children, originally proposed in 1937 in the League of Nations, were abandoned due to the unsettled conditions in the region and the fact that the newly established governments of that part of the world did not believe a bureau would be of real assistance in their efforts to suppress the traffic. Second, various projected studies and action programs with respect to the traffic in women and children and the rehabilitation of prostitutes did not come to fruition.

At first sight, it would therefore appear that the United Nations has failed to make any real contribution in an area in which the League of Nations had been highly active. Any such assumption would miss the real point. What has happened is that the traffic in women and children has practically ceased to exist as an international problem. The introduction of rigid passport and visa regulations throughout the world, although imposed for reasons unrelated to the traffic, has proved more effective than the special international instruments created for its suppression. The problem of prostitution has thus become essentially a domestic one, dealt with by the various countries in their own way, just as they deal with the problem of the abuse of alcohol according to their own conditions and needs. It is generally recognized that such problems as the prevention of prostitution and the rehabilitation of prostitutes raise broad social issues toward the solution of which the United Nations is contributing indirectly through its various programs of technical assistance in social planning and development, including community organization and development, improvement of the status of women, and the strengthening of family life.

Prevention of Crime and Treatment of Offenders

In contrast to the decline in activities of the United Nations relating to traffic in women and children, there has been a marked increase in activities concerning the treatment of offenders and the prevention of crime. This has been due not only to an increase in criminality in many parts of the world but to circumstances and considerations largely unrelated to matters of crime and punishment and rehabilitation. It goes back to the drive in the late 1940's to absorb or to integrate into the United Nations, for the sake of "simplification," "avoidance of overlaps," and "economy," intergovernmental organizations outside the

United Nations but working in areas within the scope of Article 55 of the Charter.[89]

One of these organizations was the International Penal and Penitentiary Commission (IPPC) which, after prolonged negotiations, was absorbed into the United Nations following an independent existence of some seventy-five years. The plan of integration was approved by the commission on August 12, 1950, and by the General Assembly in December 1950.[90] The agreement reached provided for:

1. The appointment of national expert correspondents by the governments of Members of the United Nations, by states not Members of the United Nations that were members of the IPPC, as well as by other governments designated by the Economic and Social Council. By March 1955, eighty-one such correspondents had been appointed by the governments of forty countries.

2. The convening, on a biennial basis, of regional consultative group meetings of the national correspondents and other qualified persons. By the end of 1956, six such meetings had been held (three in Europe, and one each in Latin America, the Middle East, and Asia and the Far East).

3. The establishment of an international *Ad hoc* Advisory Committee of Experts to meet from time to time, preferably annually, at the headquarters of the United Nations to advise the Secretary-General and the Social Commission "in devising and formulating programs for study on an international basis and policies for international action in the field of the prevention of crime and the treatment of offenders, and also to advise on the co-ordination of the work of the United Nations consultative groups."

4. The organization of quinquennial congresses composed of members officially appointed by their governments, representatives of specialized agencies and nongovernmental organizations, and individual participants having a direct interest in the subjects to be discussed. The first of these congresses met in Geneva in the summer of 1955.

5. The publication by the United Nations of an international review. In implementing this provision, the United Nations issues, twice yearly, the *International Review of Criminal Policy*.

As was to be expected, these arrangements resulted in a considerable extension of activities on the part of the United Nations and, inciden-

---

[89] See the volume in this Brookings series, *The United Nations and Promotion of the General Welfare*, Part One.
[90] Res. 415(V), Dec. 1, 1950.

tally, in additional expenditure. The Social Defense Section in the Secretariat was enlarged, and the United Nations assumed full financial responsibility for meetings of the *ad hoc* Advisory Committee of Experts, including the expenses of its members. Previously, such expenses had been carried by the IPPC and participating governments. The United Nations also provided an increasing number of fellowships in this field and made itself responsible for the financing of various regional meetings, but it did not pay the expenses of individual participants.[91]

The program of studies and publications was stepped up. In addition to the *International Review of Criminal Policy*, studies have either been issued or are in preparation on such subjects as juvenile delinquency, probation and related measures, the indeterminate sentence, parole and after-care, criminal statistics, standard rules for the treatment of offenders (a revision of rules originally worked out by the IPPC), open penal and correctional institutions, and prison labor. Broadly speaking, these were also the major subjects dealt with at the various regional meetings and seminars and at the First United Nations Congress on the Prevention of Crime and the Treatment of Offenders in 1955.

After six years of operation under the 1950 agreement, there is no doubt that international action in the field has been increased, and its geographic scope has been greatly extended. The IPPC was essentially limited to Europe and North America. Under the United Nations, the work has been extended to all the major regions of the world and has evoked considerable interest, particularly in Asia where industrialization is leading to growing urbanization, the breaking of old family and community ties, and concomitantly to a rising tide of delinquency and crime. The regional approach has permitted the adjustment of programs and activities to regional, national, and local conditions. Parallel to the extension of the geographical scope has gone an extension in the substantive scope of the work, with more emphasis being placed on the prevention of crime and the rehabilitation of offenders and less on punishment.

All this is to the good. On the other hand, it is evident that far from resulting in "economies," as had been hoped by the protagonists of

[91] The Economic and Social Council has established consultative relationships with the principal nongovernmental organizations operating in the field of crime prevention and the treatment of offenders, including the Howard League for Penal Reform, the International Criminal Police Commission, the International Law Association, the International Society of Criminology, the International Union for Child Welfare, and the Society of Comparative Legislation. Meetings involving these organizations are held periodically.

402 ECONOMIC AND SOCIAL CO-OPERATION

integration, the collective bill for governments is very much higher than it was at the time of the independent existence of the IPPC. In itself, this is defensible so long as the program and activities do not become too divorced from the central purposes of the United Nations. In this connection, it is interesting to note that under the plans of the Secretary-General, the highly specialized criminological studies are in the future to be "farmed out" to outside institutions and organizations rather than to be undertaken by the Secretariat.

It also appears that a literal interpretation of the 1950 agreement may result in overorganization. The frequency of regional meetings is at present under discussion, for there is much evidence that an undue burden is being placed both on the United Nations Secretariat and on the governments in the various regions. Proposals for reductions in the number of meetings and publications have, however, given rise to misgivings on the part of some of the experts who were formerly members of the IPPC.[92] Only future experience can show whether these misgivings are justified. One conclusion would appear noncontroversial: any further attempts to absorb into the United Nations the functions of intergovernmental organizations operating in highly specialized fields will require most careful scrutiny. There is only a slim dividing line between purposeful integration serving the ends of the United Nations and integration that might result in weakening the central programing and activities of the Organization.

The Lessons of Experience

A few concluding observations may help to draw together the heterogeneous activities dealt with in the foregoing discussion of welfare and social defense.

The common denominator of most of the programs and activities in the field of welfare and social defense is the emphasis on assistance to the individual. This emphasis makes for an almost infinite variety of possible programs and approaches, dependent on the special needs of the individual and the social and cultural pattern in which he lives. The temptation to engage in activities beyond the scope and powers of an intergovernmental organization such as the United Nations is, there-

[92] See U.N. Economic and Social Council, *Progress Made by the United Nations in the Field of Social Welfare During the Period 1 January 1953–31 December 1954 and Proposals for the Programme of Work 1955–57*, Report by the Secretary-General, Doc. E/CN.5/308/Corr. 1 (Apr. 5, 1955), p. 94.

fore, great. The trend toward the dispersal of energies and efforts is accentuated by well-meaning "interest groups," which attempt to use the United Nations as a vehicle for the attainment of their special purposes and for technical studies and activities of limited international applicability that might better be carried out by nongovernmental groups. Good will tends to outrun a realistic estimate of what can be accomplished by intergovernmental action.

Considering these pressures, the United Nations has, on the whole, been surprisingly successful in developing basic programs and adapting them to national and local needs. Major requirements, such as the need for trained welfare personnel, have been ascertained and programs to meet them have been initiated. Long-range programs are increasingly taking the place of earlier short-term activities. The emphasis now is on assistance to governments in the development of integrated programs of their own. Brakes are being applied to the preparation of studies that are not essential to the formulation of policy recommendations on the part of the United Nations or are of only limited value to national governments as they confront their major tasks in improving the lot of their people.

The recognition of differences in cultural patterns and stages of development has led to a shift of work from headquarters to the field. Less time is being spent on the setting of international norms of achievement, and more attention is being paid to adjusting international assistance to the needs of specific regions and countries. The co-operative nature of the programs has been enhanced by the growing use of experts from underdeveloped countries.

It may still be felt by some that the United Nations is spending too much time, energy, and money on "unessential activities" concerned not with major problems of state but with the needs of the individual. This question cannot be decided on points of principle or by easy generalization. So long as governments ask for assistance in this area, there will be United Nations programs of social welfare. For anyone believing in the dignity and worth of the individual, it would be doubtful wisdom to discourage such work.

CHAPTER IX

Education, Science, and Culture*

P RACTICALLY all of the activities of the United Nations system that are designed to bring about economic and social advancement have educational, scientific, or cultural aspects. The stimulation of production and investment, the facilitation of transportation and communication, or the encouragement of social action to improve levels of living have usually involved educational programs, arrangements for the exchange of technical information, and efforts to introduce new methods and standards.

Within the United Nations system, however, general responsibility for promoting collaboration among nations through education, science, and culture has been vested in the United Nations Educational, Scientific and Cultural Organization (UNESCO). The drafting of its constitution in 1945 raised some difficult questions, but these were resolved with remarkable speed and without bitterness. The establishment of UNESCO, in fact, met with almost universal acclaim.

It proved easier, however, to agree on broad objectives than on methods to realize them. The debate on programs began at the first General Conference of UNESCO in 1946 and, save for minor lulls, has continued ever since. The constitution appeared to authorize programs in virtually every field of endeavor, and repeated efforts have been made to ensure that the limited resources of the agency would be concentrated on a manageable number of projects. The difficulties that UNESCO has encountered, the controversies it has engendered, its achievements and its failures, warrant considered analysis.

Establishment of UNESCO

The Conference for the Establishment of an Educational, Scientific and Cultural Organization met in London, November 1–16, 1945. The fact that it was able to draft the constitution of UNESCO in a little over two weeks is a tribute to the preparatory work of the Allied Ministers of Education, who had been meeting intermittently in London

* By Walter M. Kotschnig.

since 1942;[1] to extensive preparations made by the governments of France, the United Kingdom, and the United States; and to the work of many nongovernmental organizations and groups in these and other countries.[2]

The conference had to resolve a number of difficult issues.[3] One issue that might have proved troublesome had been settled prior to the conference by preliminary discussions among the Allied Ministers of Education and various foreign offices, including the United States Department of State. The question was whether the new agency should be a temporary organization to meet emergency needs arising out of the war or a permanent organization with long-term objectives. As a result of the preliminary conversations, an earlier proposal for the creation of a United Nations Organization for Educational and Cultural Reconstruction, made by the United States at a 1944 meeting of the Allied Ministers of Education, was abandoned in favor of the more permanent organization. It was understood, however, that the permanent agency would, in its early stages, pay special attention to reconstruction needs.

A more basic issue arose over the attempt to define the nature and character of the organization. One school of thought, led by the French delegation, held that the new organization should serve above all to facilitate contacts and co-operation among the intellectual leaders of the world.[4] It should bring together the intellectual elites of the various countries and assist them in their search for a peace based "upon the intellectual and moral solidarity of mankind," a phrase taken from the preamble of the constitution of UNESCO. Essentially, this was the concept that had led the League of Nations Assembly in 1921 to set up the International Committee on Intellectual Cooperation, a decision followed in 1925 by the creation of the International Institute of Intellectual Cooperation in Paris.

[1] U.N. Information Organization, *Allied Plans for Education—The Story of the Conference of Allied Ministers of Education* (1945).
[2] Walter M. Kotschnig, "Toward an IOECD: Some Major Issues Involved," *Educational Record* (July 1944), pp. 259–87.
[3] See U.N. Educational, Scientific and Cultural Organization, Preparatory Commission, *Conference for the Establishment of the United Nations Educational, Scientific and Cultural Organization*, Doc. ECO/Conf./29 (June 1946).
[4] In UNESCO, even more than in other international agencies, references to positions taken by particular delegations are likely to be oversimplifications. Delegations are as a rule composed of representatives of the educational, cultural, and scientific communities of Member countries, are frequently divided in their views, and may speak with different voices, although each delegation in the end has only one vote.

Neither the committee nor the institute had proved singularly successful. The committee, composed of such outstanding individuals as Henri Bergson, Madame Curie, Albert Einstein, Gilbert Murray, Rabindranath Tagore, and other leaders of thought, frequently operated at a level beyond the comprehension of the common man or lacked the background and experience to translate its conclusions into practical action. The institute accomplished useful work in such technical fields as co-operation among libraries and museums, the protection of copyrights, and the exchange and free entry of educational films. It attempted with some success to develop closer co-operation between the officials in charge of secondary and of higher education. Concern with elementary education was not considered appropriate for an organization interested in the promotion of intellectual co-operation. Efforts were also made to bring about bilateral agreements to eliminate chauvinistic and biased statements from history textbooks.

The protagonists of UNESCO as an organization for the promotion of intellectual co-operation admitted some of the weaknesses and failures of the prewar experience, but pointed out that, except for a few individuals, the English-speaking world had not actively participated in the intellectual co-operation activities of the League, and that with their participation and larger resources, past weaknesses could be overcome.

This view was not shared by the United States, which held that UNESCO should be concerned with all the people—not only the intellectual elites—and that there should be a direct approach to them through education, cultural exchanges, and the widest possible use of such mass media as the press, radio, and films. This approach met with substantial support in the conference, particularly from those who were concerned with the reconstruction of educational facilities destroyed by the war and the even more serious damage done by the perversion of education under the Nazi rule. The extent to which the American thesis prevailed is revealed in Article I (2) of the Constitution:

. . . The Organization will:

(a) collaborate in the work of advancing the mutual knowledge and understanding of peoples, through all means of mass communication and to that end recommend such international agreements as may be necessary to promote the free flow of ideas by word and image;

(b) give fresh impulse to popular education and to the spread of culture; by collaborating with Members, at their request, in the development of educational activites; by instituting collaboration among the nations to advance the ideal of equality of educational opportunity without regard to race, sex, or any distinctions, economic or social; by suggesting educational methods best suited to prepare the children of the world for the responsibilities of freedom;

(c) maintain, increase and diffuse knowledge; by assuring the conservation and protection of the world's inheritance of books, works of art and monuments of history and science, and recommending to the nations concerned the necessary international conventions; by encouraging co-operation among the nations in all branches of intellectual activity, including the international exchange of persons active in the fields of education, science and culture and the exchange of publications, objects of artistic and scientific interest and other materials of information; by initiating methods of international co-operation calculated to give the people of all countries access to the printed and published materials produced by any of them.[5]

At first sight, the language of this article appears to indicate an almost complete acceptance of the concept of UNESCO as an organization of the people and for the people. It stresses "mutual knowledge and understanding of peoples"; it speaks of "popular education" and of "equality of educational opportunity"; and it authorizes the use of "all means of mass communication." At the same time, however, it states that the organization will maintain, increase, and diffuse knowledge and to this end encourage co-operation "in all branches of intellectual activity" including science. To highlight this last addition to the subject matter to be dealt with by the organization, the word "science" was included in the name of the organization.[6]

The result of the compromise achieved—for a compromise it was— was an article of broad and ill-defined scope. It can be interpreted to cover almost any human interest or activity. The article appears to assume—and has been so interpreted—that any and all activities in the fields of education, science, and culture are equally apt to further "universal respect for justice, for the rule of law, and for human rights and fundamental freedoms," that any type of knowledge *per se* is bound to

[5] U.N. Educational, Scientific, and Cultural Organization, *Final Act, Constitution, Rules of Procedure of the General Conference* (1953). Article I(3) of the Constitution, prohibiting the organization from intervening in matters essentially domestic, was written into the constitution despite earlier suggestions, for instance by the Educational Policies Commission of the National Education Association in the United States, that the organization be given a role in appraising educational methods and materials in various countries and that it expose, through investigations and reports, countries using methods and materials that in their effect would be "aggressive, militaristic, or otherwise dangerous to the peace of the world." The stringent "domestic jurisdiction clause" in its constitution, however, did not protect UNESCO against later allegations of trying to take over and pervert the schools of its member states.

[6] The word was added to the name and functions of the organization on the initiative of the United Kingdom, warmly supported by scientists in many other delegations.

advance "the common welfare of mankind."[7] These are assumptions that have made it difficult for the organization to develop clear-cut, co-ordinated programs of work.

Closely related to the controversy over the character and focus of the organization, was the question to what extent representation in the directing organs of UNESCO should be determined by governments and to what extent by nongovernmental organizations and groups, primarily of intellectuals. There was general agreement that the organization should be intergovernmental in that it should be financed by governments. Regarding representation, however, the French Government proposed that the General Conference should consist of: (1) a maximum of three delegates of the government of each member state; (2) five delegates of each National Commission of Intellectual Cooperation (which had been established under the aegis of the Committee on Intellectual Cooperation of the League); and (3) a delegate of each intellectual association of a world-wide character admitted by the General Conference. This proposal was not accepted, and the constitution provides that: "The General Conference shall consist of the representatives of the States Members of the Organization. The Government of each Member State shall appoint not more than five delegates, who shall be selected after consultation with the National Commission, if established, or with educational, scientific and cultural bodies."[8] Elsewhere in the constitution much emphasis was placed on national commissions or other national co-operating bodies composed of representatives of the principal bodies in each country interested in educational, scientific, and cultural matters, together with representatives of government. Under Article VII, the organization can communicate directly with such national commissions or co-operating bodies, which "shall function as agencies of liaison in all matters of interest" to the organization. Thus, much was done to minimize the role of governments.

Most important, it was decided that the Executive Board of UNESCO, which acts on behalf of the General Conference between sessions, was not to be a board of government representatives but of individuals elected by the General Conference from among delegates to the conference to serve in their personal capacities. This decision led to considerable difficulty as time went on, because under the constitution, the Executive Board was charged with administrative duties and responsibilities that involved commitments on the part of governments.

[7] *Constitution*, Art. I(1) and Preamble.
[8] *Ibid.*, Art. IV, A.

The Soviet Union did not participate in the London conference. The generally negative attitude of the Soviet Union toward the specialized agencies was undoubtedly accentuated by the fact that the Government of the Soviet Union considered education and related matters to be of purely domestic concern, and had little sympathy for the individualistic and liberalistic approach of the protagonists of UNESCO to the problems of peace and human welfare. At the London conference, there was a strong undercurrent in favor of universality of membership, although the memory of the recent holocaust in education, science, and culture caused by Nazi and Fascist action prevented writing this principle into the constitution. There was widespread regret that the Soviet Union was not willing to assume membership. UNESCO, however, was among the first of the newly created international organizations to admit to membership such countries as Austria, the Federal Republic of Germany, Italy, Japan, and Spain.

Controversy Concerning Programs

Once created, UNESCO rapidly launched a vast number of projects. This action was fully understandable in the light of the broad statement of purposes and functions in the UNESCO constitution, and it was accentuated by the encyclopedic interests of its first Director-General, Julian Huxley. It is impossible to understand fully the development of UNESCO during the first four years of its existence without taking into account his drive and enthusiasm. His exceptional abilities, his catholicity of interests, and his knowledge opened up many new lines of action. In speaking at the first General Conference in 1946 about the cultural activities of UNESCO, he said: "We have to think about music and painting, about history and classical studies, about language and architecture, about theater and ballet, about libraries and museums, and art galleries and zoos, about the history of art and the world's different cultures, about creative writing and about philosophy."[9] Earlier, he had set forth his concept of UNESCO in an essay in which he defined a twofold aim for the organization: "In the first place, it is international, and must serve the ends and objects of the United Nations, which in the long perspective are world ends, ends for humanity as a whole. And secondly it must foster and promote all aspects of education, science,

[9] U. N. Educational, Scientific and Cultural Organization, First Session, Plenary, *Records of the General Conference*, Second Meeting (Nov. 20, 1946), p. 21.

and culture, in the widest sense of those words."[10] By promoting all aspects of education, science, and culture, Huxley then hoped that UNESCO would, as stated in the conclusions of his essay, help the "emergence of a single world culture."[11]

Under Huxley's leadership, UNESCO went through a period of rapid development, a pioneering period, with ever new projects taken up, developed, and—not infrequently—abandoned. They ranged from substantial efforts to aid in the reconstruction of schools and libraries to ventures in adult education and the teaching of the ideas and ideals of the United Nations; from the development of abstracts, catalogues, and bibliographies to proposals for the definition of high "C" in music and the study of biology at high altitude. This was the great period of the establishment of new learned councils and societies initiated and supported by UNESCO, a period of exhilarating creativeness, which did not, however, result in any cohesive, co-ordinated program.

A variety of requests from the United Nations to UNESCO did nothing to help solidify the program. UNESCO was asked by the General Assembly of the United Nations to consider engaging on a program of translation of the classics and did initiate work in this field.[12] At its second session, the General Assembly requested the agency to concern itself with the exchange of workers and, in another resolution, with the teaching of United Nations ideals.[13] At its third session, the General Assembly referred to UNESCO and to the Economic and Social Council a plan for establishing an international center for training in public administration.[14] A proposal raised in the Economic and Social Council as early as 1946 for the establishment of international scientific research laboratories was also transmitted to UNESCO for action.[15]

In response to this last request, UNESCO proposed the creation of

[10] U.N. Educational, Scientific and Cultural Organization, Preparatory Commission, *UNESCO, Its Purposes and its Philosophy* (1946), p. 5. The essay was so challenging, provocative, and controversial that the Executive Committee of the Preparatory Commission decided that it should be published as a separate signed document representing a statement of the personal attitudes and beliefs of the Director-General and should not be construed in any way as representing the views of the Preparatory Commission. The General Conference at its first session took the same stand.

[11] *Ibid.*, p. 61.

[12] Res. 60(I), Dec. 14, 1946.

[13] Res. 133(II), Nov. 17, 1947 and Res. 137(II), Nov. 17, 1947.

[14] U.N. General Assembly, Res. 246(III), Dec. 4, 1948. See also U.N. Economic and Social Council, Res. 123(VI), Mar. 2, 1948.

[15] Res. 22(III), Oct. 3, 1946.

such laboratories in the following fields: (1) chemistry and biology of self-reproducing substances, including cancer; (2) nutrition and food technology; (3) life and resources of humid tropic zones; (4) oceanography and fisheries; (5) antarctic research; and (6) ornithological research.[16] These proposals overlapped the interests of several other specialized agencies, and in 1949, UNESCO revised the list.[17] First priority was then given to the creation of an International Computation Center, an International Institute for Research on the Brain, and an International Institute of Social Science. It furthermore recommended a lower priority list providing for the establishment of an International Laboratory for Arid Zone Research, an International Astronomical Laboratory, an International Institute of the Chemistry of Living Matter, and an International Meteorological Institute.

The plethora of proposals and projects developed by UNESCO in its early years was baffling and irritating, especially to the governments of the major contributing countries, and moves were made repeatedly in the general conferences of UNESCO to bring about a concentration and co-ordination of effort.[18]

At the fifth conference of UNESCO in 1950, a serious attempt was made to bring about a limitation of activities and to reach agreement on a restricted number of major programs. The conference, largely under United States leadership, developed a "decalogue" to cover UNESCO activities under the following priority headings:

(1) To eliminate illiteracy and encourage fundamental education;

(2) To obtain for each person an education conforming to his aptitudes and to the needs of society, including technological training and higher education;

(3) To promote through education respect for human rights throughout all nations;

(4) To overcome the obstacles to the free flow of persons, ideas, and knowledge between the countries of the world;

(5) To promote the progress and utilization of science for mankind;

(6) To study the causes of tensions that may lead to war and to fight them through education;

(7) To demonstrate world cultural interdependence;

(8) To advance through the press, radio and motion pictures the cause of truth, freedom, and peace;

[16] U.N. Department of Public Information, *Yearbook of the United Nations, 1947–48,* pp. 556–58.

[17] U.N. Department of Public Information, *Yearbook of the United Nations, 1948–49,* p. 664.

[18] See Charles S. Ascher, *Program-Making in UNESCO, 1945–1951, A Study in the Processes of International Administration* (1951).

(9) To bring about better understanding among the peoples of the world and to convince them of the necessity of co-operating loyally with one another in the framework of the United Nations;

(10) To render clearing-house and exchange services in all its fields of action, together with services in reconstruction and relief assistance.[19]

This listing reflected a renewed emphasis on education, the development of mass media in greater freedom, and the promotion of international understanding.[20] At the same time, it covered the entire field of the sciences without any limitations, and the tenth point offered an escape clause that permitted an unlimited number of activities so long as they related to education, science, and culture. The 1950 program, therefore, proved little more than a way-station on the road to a greater concentration of effort and resources. After 1950, the funds at the disposal of UNESCO under the Expanded Programme of Technical Assistance tended to accentuate, within the over-all program of the organization, projects of assistance in the development of underdeveloped countries.

In 1954, the Executive Board submitted, and the General Conference approved, a new approach to program-making, which provided for a division of the program into "general" and "special" activities.[21] General activities were to represent the continuing functions of the organization and to include the collection and exchange of information; assistance to international collaboration among specialists; the preparation of international conventions and regulations; inquiries, research, and studies necessary as a basis for the special activities; and similar functions. Special activities meant field projects of limited duration and scope, designed to meet specific needs of member states. These special activities were to be developed in the light of priorities determined by the General Conference. At the same time, the General Conference selected as its priorities: free and compulsory education at the primary level; fundamental education; programs relating to racial, social, and international tensions; mutual appreciation of Eastern and Western cultural values; and scientific research for the improvement of living

[19] U.N. Educational, Scientific and Cultural Organization, Fifth Session, *Records of the General Conference* (1950), Resolutions, p. 16.

[20] The emphasis on education was due in part to the support given the educational programs by Jaime Torres Bodet, who succeeded Huxley as Director-General of UNESCO.

[21] U.N. Educational, Scientific and Cultural Organization, Eighth Session, *Records of the General Conference* (1954), Resolutions, pp. 49–50. By this time Luther Evans, a former Librarian of Congress, had succeeded Jaime Torres Bodet as Director-General of UNESCO.

conditions.[22] Without eliminating clearing-house and related functions, this new departure in programing shifted emphasis to the field, where the needs are greatest. It remains to be seen whether this new departure will increase the efficiency of the program; it does not become effective until the 1957–58 period.

Problems of Method and Organization

The secretariat of UNESCO is divided into separate departments, five of which were originally established to supervise the several major programs: education, natural sciences, social sciences, cultural activities, and mass communications. A Department of Technical Assistance was later added, and there is also within the secretariat an exchange of persons service, which does not, however, rank as a department.

In itself, a division into five major substantive areas would appear natural, although other patterns of organization might have been adopted, and indeed were suggested but were rejected. Because of the unique constituency of UNESCO and the all-inclusive character of its program, however, certain drawbacks have developed to the arrangement that was accepted.

There has been complaint that the department for each major substantive area has been an empire unto itself: that the natural scientists boost their own department; that the educators attempt to increase the budget and scope for educational programs; and that the librarians and museum experts, the musicians and artists urge an expansion of the cultural activities of the secretariat. This competition has been fostered not only by "constituents," *i.e.*, representatives of the various disciplines in national delegations at the General Conference and by members of the Executive Board serving in their individual capacities, but also by nongovernmental "interest" groups and by officials within the secretariat. The latter, frequently men of science or letters, or leaders in education, have considered it their mission to serve what they conceive to be the best interests of their own field—the advancement of their particular discipline. The secretariat lobbies thus, at an early date, became a major element at the UNESCO general conferences. Not infrequently, the pet project of some department head would re-emerge, after rejection by the Director-General in planning his program and budget, as a proposal by one of the delegations on the conference floor.

[22] *Ibid.*, p. 50.

Clearly, the difficulties involved in developing a co-ordinated pro-gram are great in an organization whose parts in certain respects have less in common than the subdivisions of other organizations and whose personnel are probably less accustomed to organizational discipline. For these reasons, UNESCO, perhaps more than any other international organization, requires strong leadership by its director-general and effective co-ordinating machinery within the secretariat itself.

Closely related to this organizational problem, is another basic issue regarding the way in which UNESCO can best carry on its work. Some-what fewer than half of the approximately nine hundred members of the secretariat are in the professional category. They are responsible for preparing the numerous periodicals and current publications issued by UNESCO, which as might be expected, is the most productive of the specialized agencies in terms of the written word. Many of these publi-cations fall under the general heading of clearing-house activities. They include science and education abstracts, indexes, bibliographies, cur-rent information bulletins, and similar tools of primary interest to schol-ars and others engaged in research or to technical personnel in libraries and museums. In a world in which in the field of natural science alone nearly one million papers are written each year, these activities are obviously of importance.

At the same time, it is clear that no one international organization, even with a central staff as large as that of UNESCO, can possibly render such services in all the fields embraced by the constitution of the agency. Furthermore, in order to provide for cross-fertilization of thought and achievement even within a single discipline, it is necessary to establish direct contacts between the individuals working in a given field. From the beginning, therefore, UNESCO has attempted to es-tablish close relations with and to assist professional societies and other organizations operating in areas of interest to the agency. When no such organizations existed, UNESCO started them or offered aid in their creation.

The International Council of Scientific Unions (ICSU) has been the major single beneficiary of UNESCO aid. With its eleven affiliated international societies in such fields as astronomy, pure and applied chemistry, the biological sciences (in turn subdivided into more spe-cialized associations and congresses), pure and applied physics, crystal-lography, etc., the ICSU received a first subvention of $275,000 in 1947. The amount was reduced gradually to an annual subvention of approximately $200,000. To fill gaps in the pattern of international voluntary organizations in the natural sciences, UNESCO assisted in the foundation and assured, by way of substantial subventions, the existence of a Council of International Organizations of Medical Sciences, a Union of International Engineering Organizations, and an International Union for the Protection of Nature.

Because the social scientists were less organized nationally and internationally than the natural scientists, UNESCO made special efforts to sponsor and aid in the creation of international associations of social scientists. In 1949, it helped establish four such organizations: the International Sociological Association, the International Political Science Association, the International Economic Association, and the International Committee of Comparative Law. By 1953, under the impetus of UNESCO, these organizations were linked in an International Social Science Council. The agency also aided in establishing an International Union of Scientific Psychology. The financial aid given these organizations and a few institutes and associations such as the International Institute of Administrative Sciences, established before UNESCO, rose from $10,500 in 1950 to nearly $60,000 in 1953, and to more than $75,000 in 1955 and in 1956.

Support given to international education associations has been much more modest. This may in part be due to a continuing preoccupation with the needs and aspirations of the scientific elite rather than with mass organizations. It is significant that in the field of education, UNESCO centered its organizing work on the universities, establishing the International Association of Universities, which, since 1951, has continued to receive the heaviest subventions from UNESCO ($23,000 in 1951 and an annual grant of $14,000 since then). Total subventions in the field of education rose from a low of $5,000 in 1950 to $29,600 in 1953, and to a little over $40,000 in 1955 and in 1956.

The list of societies in the cultural field initiated or aided by UNESCO is long and comprehensive. It includes one "umbrella" organization, the International Council for Philosophy and Humanistic Studies, composed of twelve learned societies; and, in addition, the International Theater Institute and the International Music Council; the International Council of Museums and the International Council on Archives; the International Association of Plastic Arts and the International Society for Education through Art; and several others. Subventions to these and related organizations have been steadily increasing and in 1955, reached nearly $200,000, of which $100,000 was for the International Council for Philosophy and Humanistic Studies. During the International Conference of Artists in Venice in 1952, an attempt sponsored by UNESCO to create an international council of arts and letters did not gather sufficient support among the assembled artists and writers. Repeated attempts by UNESCO to create an international press institute or association also failed and were abandoned when an independent International Press Institute was established in Zurich.

Financial support from UNESCO for international voluntary organizations, mostly nongovernmental, is not confined to subventions. Payments are also made on a contractual basis for carrying out specific projects included in the work program. Most of these contracts are for research and special inquiries, or for the organization of symposia, seminars, or exhibitions. In 1953, for example, thirty-eight contracts were concluded with twenty-six international nongovernmental organizations for a total of more than $166,000.

In total, the funds made available as subventions or contract payments are considerable. Scholars, scientists, and others are helped thereby to help themselves in developing their international contacts and advancing their studies and research. As they are helped, they assist UNESCO "to maintain, increase, and diffuse knowledge."[23] But there are also serious drawbacks to this policy. A review in 1954 of the employment of subventions by beneficiaries shows that a substantial part of the funds goes toward administrative expenses: the payment of salaries of secretaries and their travel, the administrative cost of organizing conferences and congresses as well as meetings of the administrative organs of the various councils, institutes, and organizations.[24] Another large portion of the funds is used for the publication of the proceedings of such meetings, many of which would appear to be of interest to only a very limited audience.

Although much of this organizational activity and financial help serves to promote international co-operation in fields that are of interest to UNESCO, it would seem that, at least in some cases, organizing activities *per se* have become the major purpose rather than creative study and research, or direct contacts among a widening circle of scholars, scientists, and practitioners of the arts. Furthermore, the channeling of the subventions through the various umbrella organizations means that, by the time the subventions have been divided among the organi-

[23] *Constitution*, Art. I.
[24] U.N. Educational, Scientific and Cultural Organization, General Conference, *Quadrennial Review by the Executive Board of the Employment of Subventions Granted to International Non-Governmental Organizations*, Doc. 8C/ADM/20 (August 1954).

zations affiliated with them, minute grants are made available for specific projects of a most highly specialized type. To those who hold that one of the primary tasks of UNESCO is to promote research—any type of research—this situation may be satisfactory. On the other hand, it certainly does not make for a concentration of resources and effort on major projects and programs.

The most basic objection to the policy of subventions that has been made by the United States and others at conferences of UNESCO is that it may prevent the international scientific and professional bodies from developing the strength and self-reliance that is characteristic of the best type of professional organization. When UNESCO sponsored and financed a large number of these organizations, the assumption was that aid was necessary to get the organizations started, but that it would be reduced as they got under way. Subsequent events did not bear out this assumption. In most cases, the original annual subventions were maintained, and in a number, they were increased. In many cases, the UNESCO subvention continues to be practically the sole major source of income. The agency finds itself, therefore, surrounded by a network of organizations many of which would virtually collapse if support were withdrawn.

The United States has repeatedly suggested that one way of meeting the problem would be to shift the emphasis from general subventions to payments made under contract for specific projects undertaken by nongovernmental organizations. This would counteract the tendency toward a splintering of projects and a diffusion of funds and would lead to greater self-reliance and viability on the part of the organizations concerned. To date, the idea has not met with sufficient support to carry it in sessions of the UNESCO General Conference. Whether the latest departure in program-making, *i.e.* the division into "general" and "special" activities, will lend new strength to this idea remains to be seen. The greater emphasis on activities designed to meet specific needs of member states may bring these needs into sharper focus and result in the application of more rigid criteria in granting subventions and in extending the grants under contract.

The national commissions, of which more than sixty have been created in member states, constitute another channel for the promotion of the objectives of UNESCO. There are great variations in the composition and character of these commissions. In some cases, they are primarily governmental bodies attached to the ministries of foreign affairs or of education, with all members appointed by the government.

More often, they are of mixed composition and are more directly representative of the educational, scientific, and cultural life of their countries. Commissions of this type appear best suited to the purposes of UNESCO. They can offer representative advice to their governments; carry knowledge and understanding of UNESCO to their people; help implement programs of the agency through studies and publications and the organization of meetings, festivals, and exhibitions; and promote travel and other means of communication with commissions in other countries. In other words, they give body and meaning to the work of UNESCO within their countries.

The agency assists in the development of national commissions by lending to the countries the services of some of its officials, or by enabling the organizers of the commissions to spend short periods at UNESCO headquarters. Despite the fact that a number of the commissions are dormant and only a minority are truly active, the effectiveness of national commissions is increasing.

Another problem of organization—the composition of the Executive Board of UNESCO—came to a head in 1954 at the General Conference in Montevideo. The United States, Australia, Brazil, and the United Kingdom introduced a constitutional amendment to make the Executive Board representative of governments. The amendment provided that the General Conference would continue to elect individuals rather than governments, but these individuals, in order to qualify as candidates, would have to be nominated by their governments and, after election, would be subject to the instructions of their governments.[25] Similar amendments had failed in earlier sessions, and at Montevideo, the issue proved to be the most controversial question of the conference. Those strongly opposed to this amendment, particularly France, argued that the true spirit of UNESCO as an educational, scientific, and cultural body would be lost; that political considerations would dominate; and that the intellectual stature of the organization would suffer.

The sponsors of the measure stressed the key role the Executive Board played in UNESCO, and argued that the change would increase the confidence of governments in the organization and their sense of responsibility for it. At the same time, the view was advanced that responsible governments certainly would, in view of the nature of the organization, consult with their national commissions and propose for

[25] U.N. Educational, Scientific and Cultural Organization, Eighth Session, *Records of the General Conference* (1954), Resolutions, p. 12.

appointment individuals who were truly representative of the educational, scientific, and cultural life of their countries. Despite a last-minute effort to postpone consideration for two years, the constitutional amendment was finally adopted by a vote of 49 to 9.[26] It is hoped that this change will help make the program more responsive to the educational and cultural aspirations of the peoples of the world, without reducing the intellectual stature of the organization. Much will depend, of course, on the extent to which representative national commissions succeed in impressing their views on their governments.

At the same session in 1954, the Soviet Union and the Byelorussian and Ukrainian Soviet Socialist Republics were admitted to membership; Poland, Hungary, and Czechoslovakia—which had left the organization in 1952—returned as active participants. The applications of Bulgaria and Rumania for membership were postponed, largely on the ground that the two countries had been condemned by qualified international bodies for their failure to observe human rights and to live up to treaty obligations. The delegations from the Communist-controlled countries took little part in the work of the Montevideo conference, but the longer-term effect of the participation of Communist-controlled countries on the organization remains a matter of speculation. It may be that the inevitable confrontation within UNESCO of the views and ideas of the free world with those of the Communist-controlled countries will not only help clarify basic intellectual and cultural problems of contemporary society but will give new strength to those who helped to establish UNESCO as a means "to further universal respect for justice, for the rule of law and for the human rights and fundamental freedoms which are affirmed for the peoples of the world, without distinction of race, sex, language or religion by the Charter of the United Nations."[27]

Achievements

Notwithstanding the conflicts and difficulties that have beset UNESCO from the outset, much has been achieved that is positive, constructive, and conducive to better relations among the peoples of the world. In each of the major areas of interest—education, the natural sciences, the social sciences, cultural activities, and mass communications—progress can be reported.

[26] *Ibid.*, Proceedings, pp. 177–78.
[27] *Constitution*, Art. I(1).

Education

In the realm of education, there have been four areas of concentration: educational reconstruction; fundamental education; formal education; and education for living in a world community.

In the field of educational reconstruction, UNESCO has acted as a catalytic agent rather than as an operating agency. Following the war, it surveyed needs and made available limited funds from its budget ($400,000 in 1947-48, and $155,000 in 1949) to stimulate broader international action. The bulk of the work was carried on by voluntary international organizations, which were brought together by UNESCO in a Temporary International Council for Educational Reconstruction. About thirty agencies participated in the Council and made available nearly $160 million, most of which was spent in Europe and the Middle East.[28]

The European reconstruction phase was completed in 1950. Acute need for help continued among the Arab refugees from Palestine, including some 200,000 children of school age. Largely with funds provided by the United Nations Relief and Works Agency for Palestine Refugees, UNESCO helped in building schools for the refugee children, providing teaching materials, and training teachers. By June 30, 1956, 350 such schools had been established.

The end of the conflict in Korea found that country with half of its schools and 80 per cent of the instruction materials destroyed. UNESCO contributed to the reconstruction effort chiefly by sending an educational mission to Korea, which reported on existing needs and made recommendations for a long-term plan of rehabilitation and educational development. The report of this mission played a major role in the formulation of the educational reconstruction program carried on by the Government of the Republic of Korea and the United Nations Korean Reconstruction Agency.

UNESCO has at no time, however, acted as a major operating agency in the field of educational rehabilitation. Its function has been to provide limited services and to stimulate and guide reconstruction efforts.

By contrast, the promotion of fundamental education has emerged as a major program of the organization. With more than half of the population of the world illiterate, the fundamental education program has been attempting to cope with a problem that is basic to human welfare and vast in scope. It is concerned with more than mere literacy.

[28] U.N. Educational, Scientific and Cultural Organization, General Conference, Fifth Session, Doc. 5C/OXR/15 (Apr. 20, 1950).

In 1952, the Director-General defined fundamental education as "that kind of minimum and general education which aims to help children and adults, who do not have the advantages of formal education, to understand the problems of their immediate environment and their rights and duties as citizens and individuals, and to participate more effectively in the economic and social progress of their community."[29]

It is evident that fundamental education means more than rudimentary instruction in the "three R's." It calls for the development of attitudes receptive to change in societies that are moving forward economically and socially—in many cases after centuries of standstill. It means the teaching of elementary concepts of hygiene, nutrition, and home economics, of improved agricultural methods, and of basic skills essential in industrial development. The concept is intended to permeate formal schooling at the elementary level, but more often it finds expression in a variety of ways in training adults, particularly at the village level.

The methods of fundamental education are, to a great extent, still in the process of being worked out. International programs attempt to awaken public interest in the aims and methods of fundamental education through pilot projects, publications, and similar means; through the development of teaching materials, including audio-visual aids; and through the provision of specialized staff. UNESCO is taking the lead in furnishing such aid, although other specialized agencies, particularly the World Health Organization, the International Labour Organisation, and the Food and Agriculture Organization, are co-operating.

UNESCO, for example, has been issuing the quarterly *Fundamental and Adult Education Bulletin* and other publications reporting on experiments made in various parts of the world. It also has assisted in the development of a number of national fundamental educational centers, and has established two international training centers, which play a major role in the development of the program. The first was established in 1951 in Patzcuaro, Mexico, to serve Latin America; the second in 1953 in Sirs-el-Layyan, Egypt, to serve the Arab states. Trainees from these centers have, on return to their home countries, played major roles in national efforts to promote fundamental education. The centers themselves have made a signal contribution in the development of teaching materials.

Fellowships, scholarships, seminars, and field work have also been

---

[29] U.N. Educational, Scientific and Cultural Organization, *Report of the Director-General to the United Nations, 1951–52* (1952), p. 14. See also, Brenda H. Tripp, "UNESCO in Perspective," *International Conciliation*, No. 497 (March 1954), p. 356.

employed to provide training in fundamental education. Finally, UNESCO has assisted in the creation of national committees for the promotion of fundamental education, committees in which governmental and nongovernmental groups co-operate. By the end of 1955, thirty-three such committees existed.

Although still in its experimental stage, the fundamental education program of UNESCO is a pioneering project, full of promise. It is more than an emergency substitute for the absence of formal schools, and its impact on human welfare should prove substantial.

Fundamental education, however, cannot take the place of formal systems of education on all levels. The promotion of such systems is another field of primary importance for UNESCO and has gained prominence within the over-all program in recent years. Effective aid has become possible as a result of the participation of UNESCO in the Expanded Programme of Technical Assistance and the use by UNESCO of the established methods of that program.

In this area, results are attained slowly. UNESCO has assisted in developing far-reaching plans for education in many underdeveloped countries, but the governments concerned are handicapped by insufficient funds to implement the plans. This has prompted the underdeveloped countries to urge the establishment of an international education fund. There is little indication that such a fund will be created, but it is hoped that, with the growing awareness in the underdeveloped countries of the need for comprehensive systems of formal schooling, increasing funds will be made available nationally.

In the promotion of formal education, UNESCO is assisted by the International Bureau of Education, a quasi-official organization founded before the Second World War with headquarters in Geneva, in which nearly seventy countries participate. UNESCO and the International Bureau jointly sponsor each year an International Conference on Public Education, which brings together key personnel from the various ministries of education throughout the world. These conferences and the staff of the International Bureau deal with the technical aspects of education such as teaching mathematics at the primary level, the techniques of reading, and educational administration.

In the field of higher education, UNESCO has promoted the exchange of university professors and has helped provide teachers for universities in underdeveloped countries. Much of this work is being carried on in co-operation with the International Association of Universities, which itself is a creation of UNESCO. In adult education, the efforts of UNESCO have centered on education for workers. It helped establish an International Center for Workers' Education in France in 1951. In addition, it has organized seminars dealing with such subjects as the administration and organization of adult education, new methods in adult education, and the development of international understanding through workers' education.

In the educational programs of UNESCO, the great emphasis on education for living in a world community has proved controversial.[30] Over the years, various programs for promoting international understanding through education have been developed under titles such as "education for international understanding" or "education for international co-operation." The 1952 program included the misleading term, "education for world citizenship." This was interpreted in some quarters, particularly among some groups in the United States, to mean that UNESCO was attempting to impose a common educational pattern aimed at developing allegiance to some world order or government. This was never in any way intended by the organization, although some passages can be found, in the mass of literature published by the agency and its friends, that might support such an interpretation.

UNESCO and the sovereign governments that are Members of it have been aiming simply at the promotion of better understanding among the peoples of the world. Their emphasis in the program has been on diversity rather than on uniformity; on a knowledge and understanding of the different mores, traditions, and attitudes of the various countries and their peoples, and of the variety of their cultural riches. As conceived by UNESCO, education for living in a world community means the promotion of respect for the fundamental rights of individuals and cultural groups. If the term "world community" is used, it does not mean the promotion of any form of world government but an appreciation of the interdependence of the countries of the world and an understanding of the international organizations that have become necessary as a result of this interdependence. Above all, education for living in a world community means the promotion of a better understanding of the United Nations.

In this context, textbooks, of course, play an important role. UNESCO does not in any way control what is published in textbooks, but it can stimulate consultation among the writers and can encourage voluntary

---

[30] This program (education for living in a world community) is not administered solely by the Education Department of UNESCO, but by that department in co-operation with other branches of the secretariat.

arrangements among countries in order to eliminate from textbooks material based on prejudice and faulty perspective instead of on fact. For example, after a seminar in Brussels in 1950, several committees were set up by professional groups and national commissions in Europe to improve history textbooks through bilateral consultation.[31] Other seminars have dealt with the improvement of syllabi in schools and with better methods of teaching.

UNESCO itself has published a number of pamphlets on race, human rights, and similar subjects. At the time of the Korean war, the agency published several pamphlets on collective security, as well as a more thorough-going study of the subject. These were prompted by the desire to demonstrate the meaning of collective security measures taken by the United Nations to ensure the national independence and integrity of Member states.

In addition to the material already mentioned, the organization produced other literature dealing with the activities of other specialized agencies; it assisted the World Federation of United Nations Associations in organizing regional seminars for teaching United Nations principles; and it organized meetings of youth leaders with a view to promoting international understanding. These efforts were useful, but in this area, a clearer definition of the tasks of UNESCO and of the methods of performing them is still needed. In its search for a more effective program, it established, in 1953, an Expert Committee to Study the Principles and Methods of Education for Living in a World Community. The committee made some recommendations on which the Director-General might base a program for 1955–56, but the recommendations were referred instead to the member states and the national commissions for their consideration. Thus, the search continues for a comprehensive program to promote education for living in a world community.

Natural Sciences

The natural science group in UNESCO is closely knit, comprising the Natural Science Department in the Secretariat, the natural scientists in the General Conference and the Executive Board, and the affiliated scientific councils, unions, and organizations—and it has effectively pursued its objectives. The clearing-house activities developed in this field, either within UNESCO or by nongovernmental organiza-

---

[31] Tripp, *loc. cit.*, p. 360.

tions with financial help from UNESCO, are more comprehensive than in any other area and are undoubtedly rendering important service to individual scientists and research institutions throughout the world.

Field science co-operation offices have been established in South Asia, Southeast Asia, in the Middle East, and in Latin America. Their purpose is to facilitate, among the scientists and technologists of these regions, the exchange of information, personnel, and material, as well as the co-ordination of research. The offices are staffed by two or three experts who travel extensively as liaison officers. Symposia are organized within the respective regions to consider problems of special importance to the scientific life and economic advancement of the countries within the region. The scope of these offices has been gradually enlarged to include the social sciences.

In recent years, particularly in the underdeveloped countries, the teaching and popularization of the sciences have been receiving increasing attention. To this end, teaching aids and expert advice have been made available. Science clubs have been established in a growing number of countries, and the formation of national associations of science writers has been encouraged. Traveling science exhibits have met with considerable success.

Beyond these services and projects designed to promote science on the broadest possible front, UNESCO has attempted to bring into focus specific fields pre-eminently fitted for international scientific inquiry. None of the proposed international laboratories and institutes is actually functioning. Plans for the establishment of a Hylean-Amazon Institute collapsed because the governments directly concerned were unable or unwilling to provide adequate funds. All the other projects on the priority list, prepared by UNESCO in 1949, of international research laboratories in the natural sciences were abandoned, except an International Computation Center. Such a center was approved by the General Conference in 1951, and a special convention provided for its establishment in Rome. The convention fell short of the required ten ratifications, and it is not now expected that the center will ever come into existence.

These failures did not deter the protagonists of international laboratories—a few scientists and a number of governments—from urging the creation of an international institute of oceanography and one for studying the growth of cells, the latter intended to assist in cancer research. The Montevideo Conference in 1954 authorized preliminary exploration into the research facilities in these fields, but past experience and present lack of enthusiasm among governments make early action to establish the laboratories improbable. The most potent argument against these ventures is that there are already in existence many national research centers in universities and elsewhere, which enjoy substantial financial support. In most cases, they are open to scientists from other countries, and their findings are made freely available.

An exception to the negative record on laboratory establishment was the creation, under UNESCO sponsorship, of a European Council for Nuclear Research, comprised of eleven European nations, which is building a European Center for Nuclear Research in Geneva, Switzerland. The progress made to date in the realization of this project is attributable to the intense interest in the development of nuclear research and the difficulties encountered by European countries in establishing their own facilities for such research.

That it may not be necessary to establish international laboratories or other new facilities for international collaboration on a research project was demonstrated by the successful initiative of UNESCO in stimulating and co-ordinating arid zone research, which is of great practical interest to the people living in the vast arid zones of the world, including parts of the United States. UNESCO appointed an Advisory Committee on Arid Zone Research, charged with the task of co-ordinating existing information and of formulating the precise problems in need of investigation. Under this program, a system of associated research centers has been established whereby institutes now working on arid zone problems are, in suitable cases, recommended by the Advisory Committee for inclusion in the program.[32] As a result, considerable headway has been made in research on such matters as underground water, plant ecology, and wind and solar energy. As part of this project, UNESCO has embarked on the production of homoclimatic maps of arid and semi-arid zones, and provided other research materials. These research activities have been supplemented by the application of tested findings through technical assistance provided by UNESCO and the Food and Agriculture Organization.

Social Sciences

In many ways, UNESCO activities in the social sciences are similar to those in the natural sciences. There is the same pattern of assistance to various learned councils and societies, many of which were created by

[32] See James Swarbrick, "The Arid Zone—An International Task," *Impact*, Vol. IV, No. 4 (1953).

UNESCO or with its help. There is also the same emphasis on clearing-house activities and technical services. Because most international organizations of social scientists are still in their infancy, UNESCO has, through its own publication services, provided abstracts, inventories, and repertories, as well as such quarterly publications as the *International Social Science Bulletin* and *Current Sociology*. It has produced publications designed to further the teaching of the social sciences and has organized seminars and missions to that end. An International Institute of Social Science has also been established at Cologne with the help of UNESCO.

In its efforts to stimulate research in the social sciences, UNESCO has been concentrating fairly consistently on major issues directly related to the improvement of human relations. Considerable time and effort have been expended on the study of tensions between individuals, groups, and countries, and their causes. This program has already produced a large number of reports and publications on such subjects as group tensions in India and in other parts of the world; the changing attitudes of Japanese youth following the war; social structure and personality in the city and in rural communities; and democracy in a world of tensions. In addition to the analysis of social tensions, research is being conducted on the application of scientific methods in influencing those factors that are known to have a bearing on the origin of conflicts.

Related to these tension studies are other research activities encouraged by UNESCO, such as research into the social impact of industrialization, particularly in underdeveloped countries. These studies have a direct bearing on the technical assistance activities of the United Nations.[33] They gain in authority by virtue of the fact that technical assistance experts of the United Nations and related organizations, speaking and writing from first-hand experience, have participated in their planning and execution. The present trend is to conduct further studies on a regional basis, to take full account of the peculiarities and special aspects of the problem in different parts of the world.[34]

Other research projects sponsored by UNESCO also relate to pro-

[33] Among the most important of these publications are Margaret Mead (ed.), *Cultural Patterns and Technical Change* (1953); and M. E. Opler, *Social Aspects of Technical Assistance in Operation* (1954). The volume edited by Mead was produced under a contract with the World Federation for Mental Health; the volume by Opler grew out of a Conference of Experts sponsored by the United Nations and UNESCO.

[34] For example, a Research Center on the Social Implications of Industrialization in Southern Asia was opened in Calcutta in 1955.

grams and activities of the United Nations. One example is a series of studies of the cultural assimilation of immigrants, including refugees, in Australia, Brazil, Israel, Belgium, and France. Further field studies are planned or are under way to ascertain the most suitable measures for facilitating the assimilation of immigrants. Related also to operating programs are projected studies regarding certain social aspects of land reform and some of the legal problems involved in the implementation of such reform. Most of these studies are delegated to nongovernmental organizations such as the International Cooperative Alliance and the International Association for Legal Science.

Much effort and energy has been expended on a series of reports and monographs on human rights, particularly racial discrimination, beginning with publications on the concept and scientific basis of race and racial differences. Dealing with issues that are highly sensitive in many parts of the world, some of these publications have proved not only stimulating but also controversial.

Cultural Activities

The term cultural activities, as used in UNESCO, covers an extraordinarily broad range of programs and projects. It includes the usual clearing-house activities and technical services as applied to the needs of museums and libraries—to bibliographical handbooks and inventories of documentation services; catalogues of recordings and color reproductions of paintings; the compilation, through co-operating organizations, of albums of reproductions and the organization of traveling exhibitions of such reproductions; and the publication of a multilingual dictionary of artistic and archaeological terms. UNESCO every year organizes or assists in the organization of large numbers of meetings, bringing together artists, painters, writers, philosophers, historians, and others representative of the cultural life of their nations. It extends technical assistance in the development of libraries and museums, and in the restoration of art treasures and ancient monuments and archaeological sites. All these activities, many of which go beyond the League of Nations concept of co-operation among intellectuals, help to raise the cultural level of the population. It is difficult, however, to avoid the impression that, in its desire to serve, UNESCO has engaged in too many projects to permit effective guidance toward common ends.

There are some achievements that deserve special mention. The conservation and protection of the inheritance of the world of books, works of art, and monuments of history and science is a task of UNESCO under its constitution. Modern warfare threatens that inheritance with total destruction. To meet that threat to the extent possible, UNESCO, at the initiative of the Netherlands, sponsored the drafting of a Convention for the Protection of Cultural Property in the Event of Armed Conflict.[35] The convention was completed in 1954 and signed by thirty-seven countries including France, the Federal Republic of Germany, Italy, the United States, and the Soviet Union. It provides for the establishment of an International Register of Cultural Property under Public Protection and a series of measures designed to protect such property in the event of military operations. An additional protocol stipulates that such cultural property shall never be retained as war reparations. This convention is not yet in effect because it has not been ratified by the required five parties.

Another important convention, drafted under UNESCO auspices, is designed to provide protection throughout the world to authors and other copyright proprietors of literary, scientific, and artistic works, including writings, musical and dramatic works, films, paintings, and sculpture. The Universal Copyright Convention was completed at an international conference held in Geneva, in September 1952, and signed by thirty-five countries.[36] It obtained the requisite number of ratifications, including that of the United States, and entered into force in September 1955. It ensures for foreign authors essentially the same protection and treatment that each signatory nation accords to its own authors.

UNESCO has made a further contribution to the dissemination of culture by assisting in the selection and financing of the translation of representative literary works. This proved a major and difficult enterprise, especially the selection of the books to be translated. For this purpose, the assistance of the national commissions of the appropriate member states and the Council for Philosophy and Humanistic Studies was enlisted. So far, four series of translations have been started: an Arabic series, a Latin American series, a Persian series, and an Italian series. An Asian series is envisaged. In addition, UNESCO is continuing the publication of the *Index Translationum*, first started by the Inter-

[35] U.N. Educational, Scientific and Cultural Organization, *Final Act of the Intergovernmental Conference on the Protection of Cultural Property in the Event of Armed Conflict* (1954).

[36] *Universal Copyright Convention, 1952*, U.S. Department of State Treaty Series 3324.

national Institute of Intellectual Cooperation under the League of Nations. The fifth volume of this index, for example, listed 16,130 translations published during 1952 in forty-nine countries.

Also in this area, UNESCO assumed responsibility for drafting two other international instruments. The first is the Agreement on Importation of Educational, Scientific and Cultural Materials; the second, the Agreement for Facilitating the International Circulation of Visual and Auditory Materials of an Educational, Scientific and Cultural Character. Both of these agreements, which are now in force, were intended to facilitate the movement of cultural materials across national frontiers.

A book coupon scheme was devised by UNESCO to help make books, films, and scientific materials actually available to countries that, because of currency difficulties, are handicapped in buying them from abroad. UNESCO serves as a clearing-house and provides coupons in convertible currency in exchange for local currency, which it can use in other parts of its program. By the end of 1955, $9 million worth of UNESCO coupons had been issued. As an extension of this undertaking, a travel coupon scheme, operating on the same principle, was added in 1954.

In its promotion of intercultural relations, UNESCO has in recent years given special attention to furthering mutual appreciation of Oriental and Occidental cultural values.[37] Through the organization of round-tables and through publications, UNESCO seeks to interpret the cultures of the East, particularly of the Indian subcontinent, to the West and vice versa. Two major publications have so far resulted from this effort.[38]

Finally, in an effort to demonstrate the interdependence of nations and cultures and their contributions to the common heritage of mankind, UNESCO is sponsoring the preparation and publication of a scientific and cultural history of mankind. An international commission of fifteen members has been entrusted with full responsibility in the name of UNESCO for the preparation and execution of the work. The commission in turn has appointed 112 corresponding members and twenty advisers from more than forty countries. This history is to be published in six volumes, but pending its completion individual contributions are published in the *Journal of World History*, a quarterly review, which

[37] U.N. Economic and Social Council, *Report of the United Nations Educational, Scientific and Cultural Organization*, Doc. E/2735 (May 17, 1955), pp. 28–43.

[38] U.N. Educational, Scientific and Cultural Organization, *Interrelations of Cultures* (1953); and *Humanism and Education in East and West* (1953).

also reproduces comments on and criticisms of such contributions. Whether this undertaking will result in a universally recognized and accepted history of man and his heritage, only the future will tell.

Mass Communications

For an organization concerned not only with co-operation among the intellectual and cultural elites but also with the promotion of understanding among the peoples of the world, the fullest possible development and unrestricted use of mass media for the transmission of information and ideas are basic needs. That is why the United States at the London conference in 1945 sought to ensure that relatively high priority would be assigned by UNESCO to the development of mass media and the promotion of the free flow of information.

Ambitious projects, such as a plan for the establishment of a worldwide broadcasting system suggested in the early days of UNESCO, were discarded without serious discussion, due partly to difficulties in financing and in reaching agreement on programs to be broadcast, and partly to a lack of understanding of the importance of mass media, or even a positive disdain for them on the part of intellectuals and governments in Europe and elsewhere. Instead, UNESCO has concentrated primarily on fact-finding and on studies relating to the special use of mass media in education and the dissemination of art and the sciences. By 1954, over forty publications had been produced by UNESCO, including general surveys of the availability of mass media in some 170 states and territories. Other special studies dealt with such matters as the production, distribution, and content of newsreels; with films on art, including catalogues of such films; with the structure and operation of existing national and international news agencies and with newsprint; with educational broadcasting and television. These were supplemented by publications on the professional training of film technicians, journalists, and radio program personnel in various countries.

Many of these studies revealed serious gaps in the availability of mass media and trained personnel and thus tended to stimulate action to fill the gaps. The studies have been basic to a developing program of technical assistance, first proposed by the United States and carried on jointly by the United Nations and UNESCO, to help countries in the development of their own press, news agencies, and radio facilities. Expert missions and grants of fellowships have been the tools most frequently used. In the program for 1955–56, the General Conference in

Montevideo provided for the direct award by UNESCO of fifteen fellowships in mass communication.

UNESCO has avoided undertaking studies of censorship practices that interfere with the free flow of news and ideas. It considers this problem a political matter to be left to the United Nations for exploration, study, and remedy.[39] This does not mean, however, that UNESCO has been unconcerned with measures to facilitate a free flow of news and ideas and various cultural materials. Mention has already been made of two international agreements, initiated by UNESCO, in this field.

Beyond this, one of its most interesting studies shows how the flow of news around the world is hampered by high or discrepant cost of communications, and by shortages of cable and radio facilities, and urges adoption of more uniform press rates and wider use of new methods of communication to overcome these obstacles.[40] Steps were taken jointly by the Economic and Social Council, UNESCO, and the International Telecommunication Union to transmit to governments recommendations for reductions in rates for ordinary press telegrams; for extended facilities and lower charges for radio-communications to several destinations; for the establishment of press telephone calls as a separate category, with reduced rates for such calls; and for the removal of apparent discrepancies in rates for leased teleprinter lines. In cooperation with the Universal Postal Union, recommendations were formulated to facilitate and to reduce the cost of transmission through the mails of books, newspapers, periodicals, and other publications, and to permit payment in national currency at local post offices for subscriptions to foreign newspapers and periodicals. By the end of 1954, twenty-nine states had taken some action on these proposals. The book-coupon scheme, mentioned earlier, and a gift-coupon scheme developed by UNESCO are further evidences of its concern for the free flow of ideas and information.

To complete the picture, it must be recalled that UNESCO itself is making a massive contribution to the wide dissemination of written and recorded materials. A great deal has already been said about the books and reports distributed by the organization. To these must be added a weekly *World Review* radio-script sent out in Arabic, English, French, and Spanish to 103 countries and territories, a number of films

[39] For an analysis of the efforts of the United Nations to promote freedom of information, see the monograph in this Brookings series, *The United Nations and Human Rights*, Chap. III.

[40] Francis Williams, *Transmitting World News* (1953).

and film strips about the work of the United Nations, the specialized agencies, and various educational, scientific, and cultural subjects; the *UNESCO Features*, a bulletin supplying educational, scientific, and cultural information to the press, sent to 1,500 editors; and several other periodicals and newsletters.

Unresolved Issues

There can be no doubt that UNESCO is fully aware of the scope of its responsibilities and opportunities. It considers itself at the heart of the postwar effort to build, through international co-operation, peace based not on force and armed strength but on mutual understanding and consent.

The range of possible activities in this area is almost unlimited, and UNESCO has found it difficult to select the most effective means for attaining its goals. If the various co-operating nongovernmental organizations, the scientific, cultural, and educational councils and congresses—many of which were started by UNESCO—should attain greater independence and self-reliance, UNESCO might find it possible to withdraw from certain of its current activities and to concentrate more on major programs. This could be achieved without totally abandoning the more specialized endeavors, and the specialized work of the related independent organizations could still be useful to the major programs of UNESCO. In other words, UNESCO does not and should not have a monopoly on the international promotion of the scientific method or of education. These are also the instruments of other agencies, including the Food and Agriculture Organization and the World Health Organization.

The major programs of UNESCO are still in the stage of development. The fundamental education program is a great pioneering venture, but the search continues for ways and means to progress beyond studies, pilot projects, and national and regional centers. Good foundations, however, are being laid, and it is perhaps only a question of time and greater concentration on the part of UNESCO, before this program becomes a living reality throughout the underdeveloped regions of the world. Encouraging headway is being made by the program of education for living in a world community, although this program still lacks a clear focus.

There has been no satisfactory solution to the conflict over UNESCO as an organization for co-operation among intellectuals, on the one hand, and on the other hand, as an organization for the promotion of international understanding and the utilization of the achievements of education, science, and culture for the advancement of the general welfare and the enrichment of all. Many well-meaning people distrust UNESCO and the big words and activities that are beyond their understanding. At the same time, there are signs that many of the leading intellectuals, writers, and artists are becoming indifferent to the organization and somewhat weary of the feverish activity of those they consider to be scientific and cultural bureaucrats. Persistence and patience may resolve that conflict. Moreover, a concentration on major programs might command the respect and support of both these groups. The scientists need the humanists lest the world become the victim of its own scientific progress; and both they and the educators are essential to the organization if the sights, the levels of living, and the cultural life of the common man are to be lifted beyond age-old drudgery, tension, and prejudice.

CHAPTER X

Problems of the Underdeveloped Countries*

IT was obvious before the end of the Second World
War that the problems of the underdeveloped countries would require
far more attention from the international community than they had
received from the League of Nations. Nevertheless, for the first three or
four years after the signing of the United Nations Charter, the problems of stricken Europe tended to dominate the economic and social
scene. The international agencies, when they were not preoccupied
with organizational issues, turned their main energies to the relief and
rehabilitation of needy people in war-devastated countries, to overcoming shortages attributable to the war, to re-establishing essential
social services, and to the development of appropriate long-term trade
and payments arrangements. The problems of the underdeveloped
countries were by no means ignored; in fact, they grew more prominent each year, but until the inauguration of the Expanded Programme
of Technical Assistance, they were indeed special problems.

At about mid-point in the first decade of United Nations history, the
special problems of the underdeveloped countries ceased being special
problems and became the stock in trade of United Nations economic
and social programs. The problems now occupying the center of the
world stage are very different in character, however, from those that
in preceding decades constituted the staple of international negotiation. The rising interest in the problems of underdeveloped countries
has involved more than a shift of geographic focus away from Europe
to other continents. It has tended to obliterate many of the traditional
distinctions between matters of international concern and matters essentially domestic.

The economic and social machinery of the United Nations, although it provided also for co-operation on educational, cultural, and
health matters, was designed primarily to facilitate the attainment
of agreements on matters that were international in the sense that
they affected directly the movement of goods, funds, or people across

* By Robert E. Asher. Portions of this chapter are based on materials prepared by
Louis Lazaroff.

international boundaries. This machinery, with the consent of all concerned, has become inextricably enmeshed in matters formerly regarded as domestic. The pressing problems of the underdeveloped countries have been elevated to the international level, not because they involve international transactions, but because they are common to a large number of countries, because those countries individually and collectively lack the resources to solve them, and because failure to solve them—or at least to move energetically and perceptibly in the direction of solutions—is widely believed to threaten the peace and security of the world as a whole.

The degree to which the United Nations system has, since mid-1950, been engaged in promoting the welfare of the people in underdeveloped countries will already have become apparent from preceding portions of this volume. It is not intended at this point to re-analyze programs that have already been analyzed, but rather to tie together some threads that have become separated and to separate certain threads that have become entangled. The first step in this process is to trace the development, as it unfolded throughout the United Nations system during the period 1946–49, of techniques suitable for dealing with the problems of the underdeveloped countries. Both the United Nations Organization and certain of the specialized agencies experimented during this period with the provision of individual experts and teams of experts, fellowships and other opportunities for training, and some supplies and equipment for demonstration purposes.

Activities of the United Nations Organization, 1946–49

The Expanded Programme of Technical Assistance (EPTA), begun in 1950, was the first major program of an operational character undertaken on a long-term basis by the United Nations and its related agencies to meet the special needs of the underdeveloped countries. It was, as its name indicates, an expansion of services developed in the period 1946–49. During these years, the term "technical assistance" came into general use in United Nations circles to describe a variety of services available from or through international agencies. Moreover, the available services—offered initially to developed and underdeveloped countries alike—came to be identified more exclusively as aids to the underdeveloped countries.

The salient characteristics of the underdeveloped countries are well known.[1] Two thirds of the world, roughly 1.6 billion people, live in nations in which the average annual income in 1950 was less than $150 per person. They produced only 17 per cent of the income of the world. The area they occupy includes all of Asia except Japan, all of Africa except the Union of South Africa, the bulk of Latin America, and the southeastern corner of Europe. In this broad belt, "poverty is old, but the awareness of poverty and the conviction that something can be done about it are new."[2] With the end of the war and the achievement of independence by hundreds of millions of people, this conviction, this revolution of rising expectations, gained explosive force.

General Assembly and Economic and Social Council

Although not adopted to meet the special needs of the underdeveloped countries, several resolutions approved by the General Assembly, at its first session in late 1946, were of special interest to them. The first concerned the need for relief after the termination of the United Nations Relief and Rehabilitation Administration (UNRRA), which provided supplies and technical assistance to China, Greece, Korea, the Philippines, and Yugoslavia, as well as to economically more advanced nations that had suffered devastation during hostilities.[3] It raised the hope—subsequently dashed—that large-scale relief programs might soon be undertaken within the United Nations system. The second resolution, in which the United Nations assumed a responsibility for carrying on the advisory social welfare functions of UNRRA, was a more direct forerunner of technical assistance.[4] It authorized the Secretary-General to include in the budget for 1947 funds for the provision of experts to advise governments, on request, on welfare services; to provide fellowships for the training of officials in social welfare; to provide specialized advice on the rehabilitation and training of the physically handicapped; and to provide technical publications for social workers.

Acting on a recommendation of the Economic and Social Council, the General Assembly created the United Nations International Children's Emergency Fund (UNICEF) and authorized it to receive contributions and to use them in arranging or providing for "supplies,

---

[1] See the volume in this Brookings series, *The United Nations and Promotion of the General Welfare*, Part One.

[2] Eugene Staley, *The Future of the Underdeveloped Countries* (1954), p. 20.

[3] Res. 48(I), Dec. 11, 1946.

[4] Res. 58(I), Dec. 14, 1946.

material, services, and technical assistance."[5] The establishment of
UNICEF as an operational arm of the United Nations, not financed
from the regular budget of the Organization, provided further precedents for the arrangements later made in connection with the Expanded
Programme of Technical Assistance.

In another of its decisions, the General Assembly at its first session,
took direct note of a special problem of the underdeveloped countries.
It observed that all Members of the United Nations were not equally
developed and that some were in need of expert advice on methods of
meeting the requirements connected with economic development.[6] It
called upon the Economic and Social Council to study the means by
which such advice in the economic, social, and cultural fields could be
provided to Members desiring it.

Prior to this, the Council had already assigned to its Economic and
Employment Commission responsibility for "the promotion of economic development and progress with special regard to the problems of the
less developed areas."[7] Under the Economic and Employment Commission, a Subcommission on Economic Development had been established to "study and advise the Commission on the principles and
problems of long-term economic development, with particular reference to the inadequately developed parts of the world."[8] In deference
to the widespread identification of industrialization with progress and
power, the terms of reference of the Subcommission on Economic Development included the function of "studying the effects of industrialization and changes of a technological order upon the world
economic situation."[9]

By the time the Council met in 1947, it had before it the observations
of three of its commissions (Economic and Employment, Social, and
Population), as well as a note from the Secretary-General. Out of
these came an instruction from the Council to the Secretary-General
to establish machinery within the Secretariat for helping Member
governments through experts, research facilities, and other resources
that the United Nations and the specialized agencies might make
available, including the dispatch of teams of experts to study specific
problems of underdeveloped countries.[10] This action provided the

[5] Res. 57(I), Dec. 11, 1946.
[6] Res. 52(I), Dec. 14, 1946.
[7] U.N. Economic and Social Council, First Year, Second Session, *Official Records*,
p. 392.
[8] Res. 1(III), Oct. 1, 1946.
[9] *Ibid.*
[10] Res. 51(IV), Mar. 28, 1947.

necessary legal authority for the mission to Haiti that the Secretary-General organized in 1948, and it served to put the United Nations actively into the business of providing technical assistance in the whole field of economic development rather than solely in respect of social welfare services.

Subcommission on
Economic Development

During the remainder of 1947 and throughout 1948, United Nations organs continued to accumulate information on the economic and social situation of underdeveloped countries, the specific needs of those areas, and the manner in which the burgeoning international machinery might help meet such needs. Although the Social Commission in the summer of 1947 discussed the special needs of underdeveloped countries in the field of social welfare, the Subcommission on Economic Development continued to think of development in economic and political terms. Its first report was in harmony with sentiments then prevalent in underdeveloped countries.[11] It stressed the importance of political independence and of freedom from foreign interference. It expressed the view that economic development must be thought of largely in terms of industrialization. "While economic development cannot be treated as identical with industrialization and due importance should be attached to agriculture in national development, it is nevertheless true that industrialization forms the decisive element of economic development."[12] It called for diversified economies, including diversification of the export trade of raw material exporters.

Touching on a theme that was to become familiar, the subcommission reported that recent rises in the prices of capital goods and transport services had greatly complicated the task of economic development. It therefore recommended a careful study of relative trends in the prices of capital goods and of primary products.[13] It advocated greater financial assistance, the provision of technical assistance on a broader scale, and a series of domestic actions by the underdeveloped countries, including the establishment of machinery for surveying their resources,

[11] U.N. Economic and Employment Commission, Subcommission on Economic Development, Report—First Session—17 November to 16 December 1947, Doc. E/CN 1/47 (Dec. 18, 1947).

[12] Ibid., p. 11. Reservations regarding the word "decisive" were later expressed at the Economic and Employment Commission by the representatives of Belgium, Canada, France, the United Kingdom, and the United States, but not by representatives of the less developed nations.

[13] Ibid., p. 22.

the setting up of targets and goals of economic development, and the examination of specified economic obstacles to more rapid advancement.

At its next session (June 1948), the subcommission examined in detail the types of technical assistance available through the United Nations system. A majority of the members, moreover, emphasized the need for special budgetary appropriations enabling the Secretary-General to provide technical assistance in larger measure.[14]

Technical Assistance for
Economic Development

At the regional level, the establishment in 1947 of the Economic Commission for Asia and the Far East (ECAFE) had provided the underdeveloped countries for the first time with a United Nations forum of their own. During its first two years, ECAFE issued its first economic survey of the region,[15] and gathered material for its second survey. Its reports helped to reveal the dearth of basic statistical data on the situation and progress of the Asian region.

In the Caribbean area, the Secretary-General responded, in the summer of 1948, to the request of the Government of Haiti for a team to assist in planning the economic development of the country. Teams of a more specialized character had been sent to other countries, most notably by the Food and Agriculture Organization (FAO), the International Labour Organisation (ILO), and the International Bank for Reconstruction and Development (IBRD). But the mission to Haiti was a more comprehensive undertaking involving the United Nations Organization, the World Health Organization (WHO), the United Nations Educational, Scientific and Cultural Organization (UNESCO), the International Monetary Fund (IMF), and the FAO in a joint effort that demonstrated both the feasibility and the utility of such interagency co-operation.[16]

Thus, by the time the General Assembly convened in late 1948, the the United Nations was engaged at all levels in furnishing technical assistance to underdeveloped countries, but without any specific budget

[14] U.N. Economic and Employment Commission, Subcommission on Economic Development, *Report—Second Session—14 June to 29 June 1948*, Doc. E/CN.1/61 (July 1, 1948), p. 17.
[15] U.N. Secretariat, Department of Economic Affairs, Economic Commission for Asia and the Far East, *Economic Survey of Asia and the Far East* (1947).
[16] U.N. Mission of Technical Assistance to the Republic of Haiti, *Mission to Haiti* (July 1949).

for the purpose. Principles and policies to govern the administration of technical assistance had been recommended by the Subcommission on Economic Development, an organ comprised of experts, but had not yet been reviewed by governmental representatives. Without waiting, however, for the reactions of intermediate levels, the General Assembly adopted a resolution introduced by Burma, Chile, Egypt, and Peru instituting a program of technical assistance for economic development, appropriating a small sum—$288,000—for the first year of the program, and making the Economic and Social Council responsible for reviewing the program at regular intervals.[17] The four types of assistance in which considerable experience had already been accumulated were, so to speak, legitimized. The Secretary-General, on the request of Member governments and in co-operation with the specialized agencies, was authorized to:

1. Arrange for the organization of international teams of experts to advise governments on their economic development programs;

2. Arrange for facilities for the training abroad through fellowships of experts from underdeveloped countries;

3. Arrange for the training of local technicians within the under-developed countries.

4. Provide facilities to assist governments in obtaining technical personnel, equipment, and supplies, and organize other services, such as seminars and exchanges of information, that would promote economic development.

In a separate resolution adopted on the same day, the Assembly—to help overcome the shortage of qualified officials in underdeveloped countries—authorized the Secretary-General to make arrangements for the establishment of an International Center for Training in Public Administration.[18] Moreover, the Assembly gave a rationale for the assumption by the United Nations of greater obligations on behalf of the underdeveloped nations.[19] It stated that the low standard of living in underdeveloped countries had "bad economic and social effects" on the world as a whole and created conditions of instability that could prejudice "peaceful and friendly relations among nations." It reminded Member governments that the Charter had bound them to promote higher standards of living. It therefore recommended "further and urgent consideration" by the Council and the specialized agencies

[17] Res. 200(III), Dec. 4, 1948.
[18] Res. 246(III), Dec. 4, 1948.
[19] Res. 198(III), Dec. 4, 1948.

of all aspects of the problem of economic development in underdeveloped countries.

Activities of the Specialized Agencies, 1946–49

In the specialized agencies during the years 1946–49, as in the United Nations Organization, the problems of the underdeveloped countries became matters to be reckoned with by the international community, and experimental efforts were made—largely through technical co-operation and technical assistance—to meet the needs that were daily becoming more apparent. Africa on the whole remained a dark continent, but the problems of Asia and Latin America began to assume more precise outlines.

Technical Missions and Surveys

In 1946, the most obvious need was for increased food supplies. The rendering of technical assistance in the field of agriculture was not controversial during the early postwar years, and the FAO could pioneer, at the international level, in this type of activity.[20]

Both the acquisition and the dissemination of technical knowledge must be reckoned more difficult in agriculture than in industry. As to acquisition . . . , industry has got itself organized into units large enough and rich enough to sponsor research from its own resources, whereas there are few farmers operating on a scale enabling them to contemplate anything of the kind. . . . As to the dissemination of knowledge, this too is more difficult in agriculture. So much of industry is built in large units which either carry on their own research or have on their staffs men whose job it is to keep informed of technical developments in the relevant field and who have the training to apply them to the needs of their firm. Farms are quite different from firms.

. . . The organization and financing of agricultural research has from the outset been a function of governments, supplemented of recent years by the useful research programmes of the industries manufacturing farm requisites. Governments, in countries where they can afford it, also have established extension or advisory services, whose staffs bring to farmers the practical application of the findings of the research workers. Expensive though this may be,

[20] In fact, the Constitution of the FAO, Art. 1(3) makes it a function of the Organization "to furnish such technical assistance as governments may request," and "to organize, in cooperation with the governments concerned, such missions as may be needed to assist them to fulfill the obligations arising from their acceptance of the recommendations of the United Nations Conference on Food and Agriculture" held in 1943 at Hot Springs, Virginia. Food and Agriculture Organization, *Constitution* (1945).

it has been found the most effective way of speeding technical progress among the hundreds of thousands of small-scale producers.[21]

The less fortunate nations were aided by the FAO in numerous ways. A mission of twelve experts was sent to Greece during 1946 to study agriculture, fisheries, and related activities. Illustrative of the catholic nature of the interests of the FAO as well as the inherent difficulty in segregating its work from other economic activities, the report emphasized that agricultural development could not occur without parallel developments in other sectors. Its eighty-nine recommendations therefore dealt with industrialization, taxation, and public administration, as well as with irrigation and more narrowly agricultural issues.[22] By the close of 1948, the FAO had sent missions also to Poland, Thailand, and Venezuela and individual experts to a number of other countries.[23]

The organization of field missions was likewise an important activity of other specialized agencies during this period. An official summary of measures devised by the United Nations and the specialized agencies for promoting the development of underdeveloped countries classified such measures in the following order: (1) technical missions and the provision of individual experts; (2) other technical advice and assistance, including research; (3) international conferences, committees, and seminars; (4) technical training and fellowships; (5) equipment and supplies; (6) loans; and (7) other financial assistance.[24]

The ILO, which had sent missions to a number of the Latin American countries between 1936 and 1946, greatly extended this work and in the process, accumulated information on conditions of employment, training problems, and training facilities in Asia and the Far East as well as in Latin America. It was also active in assisting governments in drafting social security plans appropriate to their different structures and stages of economic development.

In the field of health, the furnishing of technical assistance to governments was authorized by the constitution of the World Health Organi-

---

[21] Food and Agriculture Organization, *So Bold An Aim—Ten Years of International Cooperation Toward Freedom From Want* (1955), pp. 20–21.

[22] Food and Agriculture Organization, *Report of the FAO Mission for Greece* (March 1947).

[23] For additional information on the efforts of the FAO to alleviate the postwar world food shortage, to obtain a better long-term balance between demand and supply, and to improve standards of nutrition, see above, Chaps. II, IV, V, and VII.

[24] U.N. Secretary-General, *Measures Devised by the Economic and Social Council and the Specialized Agencies to Promote Economic Development and Raise Standards of Living of Underdeveloped Countries*, Doc. E/1345 (May 25, 1949), pp. 1–2.

zation. Pending the establishment of WHO, the advisory services of UNRRA were continued by the Interim Commission of the World Health Organization. With residual funds from UNRRA, a broad international program of medical missions, visiting lecturers, and fellowships was financed. Programs for strengthening national and local health services, and for controlling malaria, tuberculosis, and venereal diseases received major attention.[25]

The International Bank alone among the specialized agencies expressed skepticism about the value of technical aid. In reply to an inquiry from the Secretary-General of the United Nations, the Bank in mid-1947 reported that it had received no requests for technical assistance as such and, in any event, neither had nor expected to have the staff to provide technical advice and assistance on a wide scale. It opposed adoption by the Economic and Social Council of a comprehensive policy on the granting of technical advice on the ground that the Council had insufficient experience to determine either the type of assistance required or the manner in which it should be rendered.

The Bank felt that a technical mission to aid a government in taking a census, or technical assistance in combating a contagious disease, was quite different from a technical mission to prepare a comprehensive reconstruction or development program. The recommendations of a mission with respect to reconstruction or development would normally be regarded as having the official sponsorship of the international agency or agencies that sent the mission. If the recommendations were then approved by the government concerned, the sponsoring international agency and related agencies would be under some obligation to carry them out. Because most of the projects recommended by field missions were likely to require financial aid, the Bank would be the agency most likely to be embarrassed by the situation.[26]

In November and December 1948, however, the President of the International Bank himself visited a number of Latin American countries. Out of these visits, and other negotiations, came the arrangements for a series of missions to survey development potentialities and financial requirements, and a new appreciation by the Bank of the value of this form of aid. The nations in question were, of course, more eager for loans than surveys. Nevertheless, the series of country surveys

---

[25] See above, Chap. VII.

[26] U.N. Economic and Social Council, *Expert Assistance to Member Governments— Addendum to Interim Note by the Secretary-General*, Doc. E/471/Add. 2 (July 29, 1947), pp. 25–27.

begun by the Bank during this period helped to bring development planning out of the clouds and to translate ardent aspirations into integrated investment programs.

Other Forms of Aid

Like the country mission, the international conference, during the years from 1946 to 1949, became a popular technique for meeting special problems of underdeveloped countries. Europe and North America lost their monopoly as hosts for international conferences, and the convening of sessions in underdeveloped countries became common. Cairo, Istanbul, Kandy, Montevideo, Nairobi, and New Delhi joined London, Paris, Geneva, and New York as potential sites for international gatherings.

Supplementing missions, conferences, and fellowships were diverse other technical services of value to underdeveloped countries. The ILO established an Asian Field Office on Technical Training. UNESCO helped a group of governments conduct intensive campaigns in fundamental education. The International Civil Aviation Organization (ICAO) installed technical staffs at a series of regional offices to advise and assist member states in carrying out the standards and practices recommended by the organization to meet the needs of the rapidly growing aviation industry. The International Monetary Fund prepared a study of banking and financial institutions in Chile, Egypt, and Mexico for the consideration of those governments and of the Subcommission on Economic Development.[27]

Although there were numerous instances of informal collaboration among specialized agencies, and between the agencies and United Nations organs, each agency moved ahead, on the whole, in its own way, in its own field. There was as yet little co-ordinated effort directed toward the development and execution of balanced country programs.

The provision of equipment and supplies, a major activity under UNRRA, dwindled to almost nothing. Hybrid corn seed, as well as samples of other types of seed, were distributed by the FAO, some books and scientific apparatus by UNESCO, and a small amount of medical literature by WHO. UNICEF, then an emergency activity, and the International Refugee Organization were, to be sure, dispens-

[27] U.N. Secretary-General, *Measures Devised by the Economic and Social Council and the Specialized Agencies to Promote Economic Development and Raise Standards of Living of Underdeveloped Countries*, Doc. E/1345 (May 25, 1949), pp. 29–50.

ing relief in considerable volume but their activities were confined primarily to Europe.

The high hopes of underdeveloped countries for loans from the International Bank were not realized during the first three years of the operations of the Bank.[28] In contrast to its lending of nearly $500 million to European nations for reconstruction purposes before the close of 1948, the IBRD had by then loaned only $16 million for development. This sum, borrowed by Chile, in March 1948, for electric power and agricultural development, was to be increased, in January 1949, by a loan of $75 million to Brazil and $34.1 million to Mexico, both for electric power development. Nevertheless, to the underdeveloped countries, the Bank seemed overly interested in establishing its credit in the private investment market in New York and insufficiently sensitive to the requirements and potentialities of the underdeveloped countries. Their sense of frustration was plainly evident at the General Assembly in 1948, although transformed in the Assembly resolution on economic development to a polite hope that the IBRD would take "immediate steps to adopt all reasonable measures to facilitate the early realization of development loans, particularly in areas economically underdeveloped."[29]

The situation of the United Nations system, in so far as its handling of the problems of the underdeveloped countries was concerned, appeared at the end of 1948 to be as follows:

1. As the problems of war-devastated Europe were overcome or moved outside the framework of the United Nations, the special problems of the underdeveloped countries filled the incipient vacuum both in the United Nations itself and in the related world-wide agencies.

2. The most generally recognized problem was the need for expert advice, for demonstrations of new techniques, for scholarships and training facilities, for technical literature, and statistical data. Budgetary limitations precluded meeting this need on more than a token scale, but the potentialities of technical assistance were revealed and a "regular" program of technical assistance for economic development was inaugurated in 1948.

3. By and large, development was envisaged as an economic problem. The introduction of new seed strains and fertilizers, better equipment and machinery, power plants and transportation systems was expected to

[28] See above, Chap. IV.
[29] Res. 198(III), Dec. 4, 1948.

lead to higher trade and higher incomes. Campaigns to reduce disease and illiteracy were initiated, but there was little appreciation, particularly in the underdeveloped countries, of the extent to which advancement was impeded by other social obstacles—by antiquated systems of land tenure, immobility of the labor force, veneration of custom and tradition, inability of the individual to participate in decision-making, and absence of entrepreneurial talents.

4. There was a tendency to think of development as synonymous with industrialization. Disappointment was voiced because capital was not forthcoming in larger volume to build the steel mills and mammoth manufacturing plants that the underdeveloped countries hoped to establish.

5. The International Bank, lacking adequately prepared loan applications from underdeveloped countries, was unwilling to commit substantial resources to projects in those areas. It was, however, developing an appreciation of their problems, building a staff to cope with them, and acquiring a reputation for soundness among potential providers of capital in the industrialized nations.

Expanded Programme of Technical Assistance

On January 20, 1949, President Truman included in his Inaugural Address as Point IV, a call for a "bold new program" to assist the underdeveloped nations of the world. He urged that it be undertaken as "a co-operative enterprise in which all nations work together through the United Nations and its specialized agencies wherever practicable."[30]

The prospect of an expanded program of technical assistance fired the imagination and evoked the enthusiasm not only of government officials but of peoples as well. Part of this great enthusiasm, which was as widespread and genuine among would-be donors as among prospective recipients, may have been due to the fact that the program lacked precise definition and so carried the promise of bringing with it all desired things. Although apparently involving only the transfer of know-how, not supplies and equipment, it seemed to the underdeveloped countries to presage a marshaling for their benefit of the resources of the richest country in the world, with its unparalleled record of successful accomplishment. To the underdeveloped countries, it appeared that they might at last become the focus of an international effort

[30] *Congressional Record*, Vol. 95, Pt. 1, 81 Cong. 1 sess., p. 478.

destined to continue until their standards of living approached those of the more developed areas.

In preparation for the proposed larger role of the United Nations in the field of economic development, the Economic and Social Council early in 1949—on the initiative of the United States delegation—asked the Secretary-General, in consultation with the specialized agencies, to formulate "a comprehensive plan for an expanded co-operative programme of technical assistance for economic development through the United Nations and its specialized agencies, paying due attention to questions of a social nature which directly condition economic development."[31] Differences of opinion promptly arose between the United Nations Organization and the specialized agencies regarding the method of financing.[32] The desires of the agencies for autonomy ran counter to the desires of the Secretary-General for tighter co-ordination and more unified control. The compromise solutions to this problem of administrative co-ordination that were adopted by the Economic and Social Council and the General Assembly favored the specialized agencies during the early years of the program but later strengthened and clarified the role of the United Nations. These have been described elsewhere in this series.[33] In addition, technical assistance projects in various functional fields have been analyzed.[34] The scope, significance, and the limitations of the program as a whole, however, have not yet been dealt with, and are therefore analyzed below.

Secretary-General's Proposals

In his proposals for an expanded program of technical assistance, the Secretary-General reminded the Economic and Social Council that the concept of economic development was not subject to precise definition. Development was a continuing process nowhere complete and nowhere totally absent. It involved not only economic but also social change, and the two were closely related. The Secretary-General warned that

[31] Res. 180(VIII), Mar. 4, 1949.

[32] United Nations, *Technical Assistance for Economic Development: Plan for an Expanded Co-operative Programme through the United Nations and the Specialized Agencies,* Doc. E/1327/Add. 1 (May 1949), p. 40. See also letter of transmittal from Secretary-General to the President of the Council quoted in U.N. General Assembly, Fourth Session, *Official Records,* Supplement No. 3, "Report of the Economic and Social Council Covering the Period from 30 August 1948 to 15 August 1949," p. 16.

[33] See the volume in this Brookings series, *The United Nations and Promotion of the General Welfare,* Part One.

[34] See above, Chaps. IV–IX.

the character of the development of a country must be determined by the inhabitants of the country itself, that it could not be patterned solely on the experience of other more developed countries, and that development programs must be carried on primarily with local capital and resources, including human resources.

Social change would result from economic change, and social impediments would to some extent inhibit economic change. Difficult problems of personal adjustment would arise. The magnitude of the social problems was thus more clearly appreciated in this report from the Secretary-General than in any earlier studies prepared by the United Nations. In addition, proposals were made regarding sectors in which work might be undertaken, the forms that assistance might assume, and the methods of organizing and financing the program.

The cost of the expanded program proposed by the Secretary-General in 1949 would have approximated $36 million during the first year and $50 million during the second. In practice, the maximum amount obligated during any one of the first six years proved to be $26 million.

Action by Economic and Social Council

Following extensive discussion of the Secretary-General's report, the Economic and Social Council—in high hopes—adopted a monumental resolution on technical assistance.[35] The resolution recommended the organization of a Technical Assistance Board and a Technical Assistance Committee; called for a conference at which all Members of the United Nations and all other governments belonging to any specialized agency participating in the program could pledge contributions to the new, expanded program; proposed an allocation of funds among the participating organizations; and included basic observations and guiding principles to govern the program. These principles still rule. They fall into five major categories: those of a general nature; those governing standards of work and personnel; the participation of requesting governments; the co-ordination of effort; and the selection of projects.

The most important general principle was that the primary objective of participating organizations should be to help underdeveloped countries strengthen their national economies. This was to be accomplished

[35] Res. 222(IX), Aug. 14 and 15, 1949; subsequently approved unanimously by the General Assembly in Res. 304(IV), Nov. 16, 1949.

through the development of their industries and agriculture, with a view to promoting their economic and political independence in the spirit of the Charter of the United Nations, and to ensuring the attainment of higher levels of economic and social welfare for their entire populations. Distinctions arising from the political structure of the country requesting assistance, or from the race or religion of its population, were to be avoided. The kinds of services rendered to a country were to be decided by the government concerned, and aid was to be given only to or through governments. Although the strengthening of national economies was an objective that could conflict with, as well as contribute to, the development of a better-balanced and more integrated international economy, it was here assumed to be a prerequisite for world development along desirable lines.

The principles governing standards of work and personnel were designed to help obtain employees of the highest professional competence and personal integrity. It was recommended that, in addition, the experts be chosen "for their sympathetic understanding of the cultural backgrounds and specific needs of the countries to be assisted and for their capacity to adapt methods of work to local conditions."[36] The standards to be observed by participating governments were intended to ensure that such governments would provide essential information, would give proper consideration to advice received, would contribute at least those project costs payable in local currency, and would progressively assume greater financial responsibility for projects initiated with help from abroad.

In indicating criteria to govern the selection of projects, the Economic and Social Council followed the Secretary-General's advice in placing social objectives on a par with economic goals. "The services envisaged should aim at increased productivity of material and human resources and a wide and equitable distribution of the benefits of such increased productivity, so as to contribute to the realization of higher standards of living for the entire populations."[37]

Although technical assistance had been a feature of international co-operation from the beginning, the launching of the Expanded Programme gave it a new significance. The rendering of technical assistance now became a major operational activity, the first such function to be undertaken by the United Nations Organization as a long-term assign-

---

[36] Res. 222A(IX), Aug. 14 and 15, 1949, Annex I—Standards of Work and Personnel, para. 2.

[37] *Ibid.*, Selection of Projects, para. 1.

ment. Designed to help meet the most generally recognized special problem of the underdeveloped countries—the lack of knowledge permitting them to break through their circle of poverty, dependence, and stagnation—the program gave a fresh priority and importance to raising living standards where they were lowest. It added a new dimension to the work of the United Nations—the ability to get to the grass roots and to shape assistance to the specific needs of an area.

The inauguration of the Expanded Programme provided a unique opportunity for co-ordinating the activities of the United Nations and the specialized agencies. Similarly, it provided an opportunity to fuse the economic and social aims of the United Nations system, bringing both to bear in a co-ordinated manner on the problems of particular areas. Initially conceived as a method of imparting to the underdeveloped countries knowledge and experience gained in the highly developed countries, it soon revealed also the great possibilities of mutual aid among underdeveloped countries. Experts from intermediate and underdeveloped countries often proved better equipped to assist in other underdeveloped lands than their professional colleagues in the most advanced nations.

The Expanded Programme of Technical Assistance has to date passed through three main stages: an initial period of preparation, which lasted until the end of 1951; a period of acceleration, characteristic of 1952; and what might be termed a period of consolidation, from 1953 to the present. In a sense, of course, all such divisions are misleading, for the entire life of the program has been a period of "preparation," a planting of seeds whose fruits are yet to ripen.

Launching the Expanded Programme

As a result of the Technical Assistance Conference, which met in New York in June 1950, fifty-four nations subscribed approximately $20 million to cover operations for the eighteen-month period ending December 31, 1951. The United States pledged 60 per cent of the total. Although the amount thus obtained greatly disappointed those who had been inclined to think of a "bold new program" in terms of the magnitude of UNRRA or the European Recovery Program, the $20 million available for the Expanded Programme of Technical Assistance proved more than adequate for the first eighteen months.

The approval of projects and recruiting of experts progressed slowly. Nevertheless, during the period covered by the initial contribution, nearly eight hundred experts were recruited from sixty-one countries and sent to seventy-five different countries and territories. More than eight hundred recipients of fellowships, from eighty-six countries and territories, were sent to study in forty-five host countries.

A second technical assistance conference held in Paris in February 1952 resulted in pledges equivalent to approximately $19 million for the calendar year 1952. The third pledging conference set a precedent in that it was convened before the beginning of the financial year during which the contributions were to be used. This tended to ease programing considerably. For 1953, sixty-nine governments pledged the equivalent of $22.4 million. By the end of December 1953, however, the cumulative total of unpaid pledges amounted to over $4.5 million. Although these arrearages were to a large extent made good during 1954, the actual amount obtained during the first four years hardly exceeded the amount proposed by the Secretary-General for the initial twenty-four months, and the boundless hopes of the underdeveloped countries had to be scaled down sharply.

Whereas the underdeveloped countries had little question that a massive concentration of resources on their special problems was the most important economic and social function of the United Nations, the more restrained views of the developed countries were revealed by the modesty of their contributions. Nevertheless, in the absence of comparable achievements in other fields, the developed countries participated in inflating the significance of technical assistance, and in justifying the United Nations to the public in terms of this phase of its work. There was a tendency on the part of the more developed nations to feel that with technical assistance initiated and seemingly successful, they could in good conscience fend off mounting pressures for further aid to the underdeveloped countries.

In the first stages of EPTA, the lack of adequate planning on the part of many of the underdeveloped countries was reflected in a rash of ill-considered and ill-defined requests for assistance. Pressures for speedy action and dramatic results led to approval of a number of projects that, in retrospect, were not in accord with recognized needs and might well have been delayed until the receiving countries had reached a higher level of development—if not longer.

There was a struggle among specialized agencies, and between the specialized agencies and the United Nations Organization, for autonomy in programing, for the right to meet requests for project assistance, and for prestige within the program. The struggle extended beyond the confines of the United Nations system to include competing bilateral programs, particularly that of the United States, whose new bilateral Point IV Program was becoming embroiled in very similar difficulties.

In the absence of integrated national plans for economic development, the government agencies within a given country, which had established relationships with particular intergovernmental agencies, made requests to those agencies for assistance. Such requests, if not in conflict with requests being made from other local sources, were inadequately related to them. This, plus the desire to obtain the best possible bargain in an atmosphere of competition among the specialized agencies and between the United Nations and bilateral programs, resulted in the same or similar requests for assistance being made of different United Nations programs and of multilateral and bilateral programs alike.

Among the underdeveloped nations, there was considerable disappointment not only with the volume of aid offered and the slowness with which it was made available, but also with the kind of aid given. In the zeal of the receiving nations for rapid and wholesale industrialization, the appearance of an expert instead of an industrial plant was a blow in itself. To policy makers in underdeveloped countries not accustomed to the need for assembling all the available facts before taking action, and impatient to see final results, the arrival and departure of experts on assignments of three-to-six months and the subsequent receipt of assessments and recommendations—difficult to read and more difficult to understand—seemed a bitter anticlimax.

From the viewpoint of the United Nations, time had to be spent to set in motion the machinery of a technical assistance program, and too many of the projects submitted by requesting governments had to be rejected or delayed because of inability to locate experts, or because of the vagueness or even the absurdity of the request. Frequently, the United Nations agencies, nonplussed by what to do about an especially vague request, took the simplest course and sent an expert or two to make a survey.

Before the first eighteen months had ended, however, many of the more important problems were in process of solution. The competition among participating agencies—which threatened to atomize any efforts to establish integrated and well-rounded policies for national development within the receiving countries—had begun to yield to order. Information on requests received began to be exchanged within the United Nations system and between the United Nations and the bilateral programs. The requests received from the underdeveloped nations improved and were scrutinized more carefully under the aegis of the Technical Assistance Board.

Acceleration During 1952

Whereas the United Nations found it difficult, during the first year and a half of operations, to identify enough suitable projects to obligate the sums available for technical assistance purposes, the situation was reversed by the end of 1952. During 1952, the program moved forward at an increasingly high rate of speed. During most of 1952, however, the United Nations continued to allocate its funds on a functional basis, to agriculture, to health, to education, and so on, rather than on a country basis.

The United States, in connection with its own Point IV Program, had struggled earlier with similar efforts by government departments to exercise autonomous control of projects in their respective fields, and to program Point IV funds on a functional basis. The United States had early centralized responsibility for the major part of its program in the Technical Cooperation Administration, and by the middle of 1951, was programing its funds on an individual country basis, with financial and project targets set by the national programs of the host countries.

A similar evolution toward more centralized responsibility for program approval having occurred in the United Nations, its programing, during the latter half of 1952, also began to follow the more logical country-planning technique. To facilitate country programing, the United Nations Technical Assistance Board established, in the more important countries, the office of Resident Representative, with responsibility for co-ordinating the activities of the various participating agencies in the host country, stimulating necessary planning by local authorities, and assisting in the formulation of requests. Although co-ordination continued to be a problem, and the arrival of resident representatives in the field offered no guarantee of co-operative relations among the international agencies, the climate improved, and attention could be shifted from co-ordination within the family of the United Nations to co-ordination with parallel technical assistance programs.

The problem of relating multilateral and bilateral projects within an individual country was not too difficult. There was, however, keen competition for the limited number of experts available for overseas duty, and some competition for the right to meet requests. This problem was, for a time, especially troublesome in the relations between the programs of the United Nations and those of the United States, although the latter, by adopting, in 1953, the stringent rules and time-consuming security requirements governing United States nationals employed in both multilateral and bilateral activities, made the competition for available Americans distinctly less brisk.

More basic problems confronted the United Nations in carrying on its program during the period of "acceleration." One of the obstacles in this effort to promote and encourage long-range economic growth was the absence of a relevant theory and a body of reliable data on the co-operative process in promoting economic development. Experts knew only dimly the key factors to consider, how they must be inter-related, or the art of relating them to the peculiar economic, social, and political conditions prevailing in a particular nation at a given time. Whereas in the beginning it was the economist who was consulted for guidance in planning programs of technical assistance, the attempts to execute programs in relatively unknown societies had revealed complexities, rigidities, and unities that underscored the usefulness of the social scientist with broader training. In the evolution of a theory of economic growth, more attention began to be given particularly to the findings of the cultural anthropologists.

More adequate and more clearly-defined projects resulted in the selection of experts more likely to achieve success. Many requesting governments became less rigid in demanding the world's best malariologist, port engineer, and agronomist, and some became willing to accept less well-known and younger specialists. At the same time, however, the requesting governments remained prone to see, in the renown of the experts nominated to assist them, evidence of the esteem with which they were regarded by their fellow Members in the United Nations.

Consolidation of Activities

During the period of consolidation, which began in 1953, programing continued to be hampered because a number of pledges, including the all-important contribution of the United States, were paid late in the period for which they were intended, after the close of the period, or not at all. Those paid in inconvertible currencies were, of course, of limited usefulness. The result was that, despite the rising trend in total pledges, there was a slight drop in 1953 in obligations incurred, as compared with 1952, and a further fairly substantial decline in 1954 as compared with 1953.[38]

Some projects consequently had to be curtailed, postponed, or withdrawn entirely. For this purpose, an interim program review was undertaken and, in a number of cases, a better use of resources was achieved in 1953. This tightening up, however, came hard on the heels of a deterioration in the economic condition of many underdeveloped countries as a result of the collapse in raw material prices. In the year 1954, although the number of contributing governments and the amount of their pledges were greater than ever before, the timing of payments on pledges was such that "a considerable slowing down in the tempo of operation" occurred.[39] A sharp increase raised expenditures to record levels in 1955, however.

During the period 1953–54, the limits of technical assistance as a motivator of more rapid development were more clearly revealed, the gap between needs and resources seemed to be widening, and the demand for grant aid grew more insistent. From this point forward, the technical assistance program, in the thinking of participating governments, tended to fall into place as a highly desirable activity, of greatest importance during the earliest stages of economic development but of decidedly lesser significance thereafter in relation to requirements for capital and equipment. Even so, the program remained exceedingly popular. By mid-1953, it no longer seemed feasible to the Soviet Union to ignore it while at the same time professing an interest in the welfare of the peoples in underdeveloped countries. Therefore, the Soviet Union and Poland, with some fanfare, announced their intention to contribute to the program.

The decision of members of the Soviet bloc to share in the program did not materially increase the total resources available. The total amounts pledged, by the United States, and by all contributors combined, the total contributions paid, and the unpaid balances as of December 31, 1955, for the first five financial periods are shown in the accompanying table, in United States dollar equivalents. It should be borne in mind, of course, that contributions to the EPTA constitute a very incomplete measure of the total resources that the United

[38] Total obligations incurred were as follows: $6,436,251 (1950–51); $22,968,129 (1952); $22,810,400 (1953); $19,464,742 (1954). See U.N. Economic and Social Council, Twentieth Session, *Official Records*, Supplement No. 4, "Seventh Report of the Technical Assistance Board" (1955), p. 32. (Hereinafter cited as "Seventh Report of the Technical Assistance Board.")

[39] *Ibid.*, p. 1.

EXPANDED PROGRAMME OF TECHNICAL ASSISTANCE: PLEDGES AND CONTRIBUTIONS, 1950–55[a]
(U.S. dollar equivalents—in thousands)

	1950–51	1952	1953	1954	1955	Total 1950–55
Number of countries pledged..........	54	65	69	74	71	—
Amount pledged by the United States...	$12,008	$11,400	$12,767	$13,862	$15,000	$ 65,037
Total amount pledged................	20,036	18,797	22,321	25,021	27,883	114,058
Amount paid during period:						
July 1950–Dec. 1951...............	$17,354	$ 5	—	—	—	$ 17,359
Jan. 1952–Dec. 1952...............	2,381	16,206	—	—	—	18,587
Jan. 1953–Dec. 1953...............	151	1,581	$18,939	—	—	20,671
Jan. 1954–Dec. 1954...............	51	953	3,197	$24,416	$ 100	28,717
Jan. 1955–Dec. 1955...............	—	—	32	394	25,147	25,573
Total.........................	$19,937	$18,745	$22,168	$24,810	$25,247	$110,907
Balance unpaid, Dec. 31, 1955........	$ 99	$ 52	$ 153	$ 211	$ 2,636	$ 3,151

[a] Source: U.N. Economic and Social Council, Twenty-second Session, *Official Records*, Supplement No. 5, "Eighth Report of the Technical Assistance Board" (1956), pp. 75, 87; U.N. Economic and Social Council, Twentieth Session *Official Records*, Supplement No. 4, "Seventh Report of the Technical Assistance Board" (1955), p. 268.

Nations system devotes to technical assistance; much of the international co-operation financed under the regular budgets of the participating agencies is essentially technical assistance.

The technical assistance program that has emerged after several years of experimentation and trial and error contains at least a little of something for everyone. Among the participating agencies, FAO has received the most funds, with the United Nations, WHO, UNESCO, ILO, and ICAO following in the order mentioned.[40] The International Telecommunication Union (ITU) and the World Meteorological Organization (WMO) round out the list, but have received only small amounts. Regionally, Asia and the Far East regularly account for more than 30 per cent of so-called direct project costs, Latin America for more than 25 per cent, and the Middle East for more than 20 per cent.[41]

Regardless of the form in which technical assistance has been provided, its ultimate objective has been the same. Through a better utilization of human and material resources at all levels and stages, it has sought to obtain greater output from industry and agriculture; more adequate health, education, and welfare facilities; improved trans-

[40] Within the United Nations, the organizational unit receiving the funds has been the United Nations Technical Assistance Administration (UNTAA), established by the Secretary-General in July 1950.

[41] For details concerning direct project costs by region and by agency, see "Seventh Report of the Technical Assistance Board," p. 21.

portation and communication; more efficient public services; and a generally higher level of individual welfare. There has, however, been a shift away from survey and study to direct participation by the international expert in development projects, public administration, and training activities. Concurrently, there has been a movement away from *ad hoc* requests on the part of a country to a series of interrelated projects and a tendency to replace individual experts with teams of specialists, both at the survey and the active stage. The number of experts and fellowships in the field of public administration has risen steadily. In all of the technical assistance work, there has been a growing emphasis on training, and this is regarded by the United Nations as "perhaps the most important and, indeed, the most encouraging development in recent years."[42]

Among the noteworthy programs not previously analyzed in the present study are the efforts of the United Nations system to promote land reform along democratic lines, to develop "productivity-consciousness" in industry, to improve public administration locally and nationally, and to encourage programs of community development.

Land Reform

Land reform has been a controversial issue. It was not solely or even primarily for the purpose of enlarging agricultural output in underdeveloped areas that the United States introduced the land reform problem at top levels of the United Nations in 1950 and 1951. There were likewise compelling political and social reasons for bringing this issue to the fore. The effect of a democratically conceived and democratically executed program of land reform on the dignity, self-respect, and self-reliance of millions of individual farmers could, the United States believed, be even more electric than the effect on their productivity and output.

[42] These main trends are noted in: U.N. Technical Assistance Committee, *The Expanded Programme of Technical Assistance: A Forward Look*, Report of the Technical Assistance Board with the Comments thereon of the Administrative Committee on Coordination, Doc. E/2885, E/TAC/49 (May 11, 1956), pp. 16–19. As an example of a series of interrelated projects, the review cites the assistance provided by the FAO to Brazil for the development of the forest resources of the Amazon basin. The first year was spent largely on an aerial survey of the area. In the second and third years, help was given in the establishment of mechanical logging and sawmilling demonstration centers. With a number of Brazilians trained in methods of utilizing forest resources, collaboration in the establishment of a pulp and paper factory has become possible.

As far back as 1943, the United Nations Food and Agriculture Conference at Hot Springs had recommended that each nation study the land tenure system and other agricultural conditions within its boundaries and ascertain whether changes were needed to promote the productivity and efficiency of agriculture and the welfare of agricultural workers. The new permanent organization (FAO) was to give every assistance in such studies. In general, the governments of underdeveloped countries were slow to respond to this invitation.

The representatives of underdeveloped countries in United Nations forums were often themselves owners of large estates or allied with such owners. They preferred to use international machinery for ventilating their needs for external aid. So long as they were petitioning for grants and loans, they could be certain of backing from their home governments and support from other underdeveloped countries. On land reform, they might be on the defensive, compelled to explain why they had progressed so little.

Under the United States occupation authorities, far-reaching land reform programs had been introduced in Japan and South Korea. The United States Secretary of State could therefore speak with authority at the 1950 session of the General Assembly when he took the lead in urging the United Nations to adopt programs for aiding the landless to become land owners. He was in tune with the aspirations of the people in underdeveloped countries, although not in every case with the governments of the moment; he was resuming the initiative exercised by the United States in the early years of the United Nations; and he was addressing himself to a fundamental economic and social problem.

The General Assembly asked the Secretary-General, in co-operation with the FAO and other specialized agencies, to prepare, for the session of the Economic and Social Council to be held in the summer of 1951, an analysis of the degree to which unsatisfactory forms of agrarian structure, particularly systems of land tenure in underdeveloped areas, impeded development and depressed standards of living.[43] Accordingly, the Secretary-General presented to the thirteenth session of the Council a report, which—like many other documents published by the United Nations—had been given a deceptively ponderous title, *Defects in Agrarian Structure as Obstacles to Economic Development*. It discussed for different areas, conditions of tenancy, size of farms, access to credit facilities, and arrangements regarding legal title and water rights. It

[43] Res. 401(V), Nov. 20, 1950.

showed that interest rates paid by those who worked the land ranged from 20 to 100 per cent per year; that rental charges ran as high as 80 per cent of the annual crops; that land reform was not necessarily a matter of breaking up large estates but frequently a problem of consolidating fragmentary holdings into economic units.

There was a lively contest between the delegates of the United States and Poland for the opportunity to speak first on land reform. Resolutions on the subject had been introduced by both delegations. Over strong protests from Poland, the President of the Council ruled in favor of the United States. The ensuing United States statement again firmly equated land reform with a wide range of measures for improving the social and economic institutions connected with farm life. Land reform, said the United States delegate, should mean either the redistribution or the consolidation of holdings into farms of an efficient size; the reduction of unreasonable rental charges; the provision of security of tenure for the tenant; the improvement of working conditions for farm laborers; the supplying of agricultural credit on reasonable terms; the formation of voluntary co-operative societies for purchasing and marketing purposes; and the establishment of rural industries. Land reform should be regarded as an instrument for ensuring human dignity and social justice, and for easing social and political tensions, which might otherwise give rise to destructive violence.

The Soviet bloc accused the United States of insincerity, and espoused its own brand of land reform. Underdeveloped countries explained what their governments were doing. The final resolution, adopted by the Council with no dissent but with abstentions by the Soviet bloc, recognized that no simple nostrum was applicable.[44] It requested the Secretary-General to keep the problem under review, to give it high priority in the technical assistance program, to obtain comprehensive data from governments at least once every three years on progress made, and to keep the United Nations informed.

The FAO Conference approved an implementation program including further studies and a series of regional seminars, as well as assistance to individual governments. At its sixth session in 1952, the General Assembly approved the program undertaken. The regional seminars were serious meetings, remarkably free of propaganda overtones. Some of the headway made by individual countries in the past few years has doubtless been due to the discussions in the United Nations and specialized agencies. The prestige of local groups favoring action has been

[44] Res. 370(XIII), Sept. 7, 1951.

enhanced, and some general guidelines have been given to them. In Italy, Iran, Egypt, India, the Philippines, Taiwan, and many other areas, programs have been initiated or speeded up.

Productivity and Industrialization

Like the land reform problem, the productivity issue was introduced at the General Assembly and the Economic and Social Council by the United States. In the case of land reform, however, the Americans were riding a wave that had been gathering force for many years. In the case of productivity, they were trying to expand a ripple into a wave. Both issues were raised at a time of mounting pressure for grant aid, and both pointed to courses of action whereby the less advanced countries could make significant progress via the self-help and technical assistance routes.

The word "productivity" had only recently become popular outside the United States. Following the publicity given to the reports of the Anglo-American Council on Productivity in the early postwar years, productivity teams from other European nations visited the United States. The Organization for European Economic Cooperation (OEEC) began backing productivity campaigns, sponsoring productivity centers, and trying, with some success, to make workers and management productivity conscious. The sponsors of similar activity by the United Nations wanted to extend the effort to other areas of the world.

A beginning in this direction had already been made by the International Labour Office whose Director-General had included in his annual report in 1950 an excellent discussion of the need for and the obstacles to more rapid improvements in the productivity of labor.[45] This was followed by additional discussion in the 1951 report, referral of the matter to the various industrial committees of the ILO, the issuance of a series of reports by the committees, and the devotion of technical assistance funds to productivity projects in a number of countries.[46]

Although measurements and comparisons of productivity are diffi-

[45] See International Labour Conference, Thirty-third Session, *Report of the Director-General* (1950), Chap. III, "The Productivity of Labour."

[46] International Labour Organisation, *Productivity in Coal Mines* (May 1951); *Factors Affecting Productivity in the Metal Trades* (1952); and International Labour Office, *Practical Methods of Increasing Productivity in Manufacturing Industries*, Conclusion of a Meeting of Experts Communicated to the International Labour Conference at its Thirty-sixth Session as a Supplement to the Report of the Director-General (1953).

cult, the underlying concept, as used in the United Nations, is simple
enough: productivity means the output of goods and services for a given
input of labor. The special twist given to the concept in the OEEC and
the United Nations during the early 1950's was the emphasis on an
equitable sharing of the fruits of increases in industrial productivity by
the workers, the owners, and the consumers. The theory was that industrial workers would resist change if they felt that the only result
would be greater profits for owners. On the other hand, they might
welcome change and create a climate hospitable to continuous productivity improvements if they could expect to share in the benefits and
look forward to owning more of the things they produced.

Following the pattern developed in connection with land reform,
the General Assembly, in January 1952, asked the Economic and
Social Council

(a) To study the varying ways in which the productivity of peoples everywhere can be increased by the application of existing scientific and technological knowledge; (b) To recommend . . . methods by which the results of the
studies undertaken . . . can be made available to the under-developed countries at their request; (c) To report to the General Assembly at its seventh
[next] regular session on the progress made. . . .[47]

The Secretary-General furnished the Council a working paper, prepared by an American expert, describing briefly the various national
campaigns to raise productivity and suggesting areas for further study.
The International Labour Organisation presented an additional paper
summarizing its activities in the field of productivity, particularly its
concern with vocational training, industrial safety, the difficult problems involved in the measurement and international comparison of
productivity, and the linking of productivity efforts with an equitable
sharing of the gains.

The discussion at the Economic and Social Council was rather perfunctory. The Council recommended that governments consider problems of raising productivity, establish national productivity centers
where appropriate, and employ technical assistance to further their
efforts.[48] The emphasis on an equitable sharing of the benefits declined,
and the productivity campaign became part of the general drive of the
underdeveloped countries for more rapid industrialization.

The development of a more efficient agriculture requires the transfer
of large numbers of people to other occupations. Some of these can be

[47] Res. 522(VI), Jan. 12, 1952.
[48] Res. 416E(XIV), July 10, 1952.

absorbed in service activities, but many should and will move into industry. Although the underdeveloped countries have been inclined to underestimate the obstacles to rapid industrialization and to overestimate the benefits of large-scale production where there is no mass market, a substantial increase in industrialization is inevitable if the hoped for increases in real income per capita are to be realized. The widespread belief that economically advanced nations oppose industrial development in hitherto underdeveloped areas because of fears of competition from the emerging societies is not substantiated by the records of the Expanded Programme. The percentage of aid devoted to industrial development has been small, but the United Nations has assisted in establishing plants for manufacturing DDT, penicillin, surgical instruments, fertilizers, and building materials; it has helped establish cooperatives, and it has provided numerous other services to industry. In Egypt, Israel, India, and Pakistan, productivity institutes have been set up, and throughout the world nearly 1,000 engineers, foremen, and skilled workers have been trained on projects conducted within the framework of EPTA.[49]

The relatively small proportion of technical assistance devoted to industrial development is probably a reflection of two conditions. In the first place, for countries in the preindustrial phase of development, there are other fields in which technical assistance is likely to be more urgent and of greater immediate benefit. In the second place, to the extent that industry in underdeveloped countries is in the hands of private entrepreneurs, it lies outside the direct range of aid provided to or through governments.[50]

The expansion of industrial output is, of course, heavily dependent on the development of basic facilities in power, transportation, and communications. In the development of these large-scale economic overhead projects, it is to the International Bank rather than the technical assistance program that the underdeveloped countries have turned for help. The technical assistance program has, however, made it possible to supply experts to help with initial surveys of land, water,

[49] U.N. Economic and Social Council, Twenty-second Session, *Official Records*, Supplement No. 5, "Eighth Report of the Technical Assistance Board" (1956), p. 2. See also U.N. Secretariat, Economic Commission for Latin America, *International Co-operation in a Latin American Development Policy*, Chap. III, "Increased Productivity and Technical Assistance Policy," Doc. E/CN.12/359 (September 1954).

[50] U.N. Secretariat, Department of Economic and Social Affairs, *Processes and Problems of Industrialization in Under-Developed Countries* (1955), p. 98. (Hereinafter cited as *Processes and Problems of Industrialization.*)

and mineral resources; with structural designs and layout; with installation and maintenance of hydroelectric and irrigation equipment; planning and management of low-cost housing; and with facilities and opportunities for training the lock operators, cablemen, hydrographic engineers, and area planners needed in programs that require financial support from elsewhere for completion.

Public Administration

Related to industrialization, to land reform, and to numerous other problems of the underdeveloped countries is the inadequacy of their governmental and administrative services.

The public administration of most underdeveloped countries faces two major problems to which we ought constantly to address ourselves: (1) there is a historic distrust of governmental institutions despite a growing dependence upon government, and consequently there is a widespread evasion of administrative authority; (2) a great burden of governmental formalism often paralyzes administrative action.

The first problem—the tendency toward popular evasion of administrative authority—arises, in part, from the regressive distribution of governmental benefits and burdens between the many poor and the few opulent which typifies underdeveloped societies. This distribution raises delicate internal questions which international public administration experts can approach only indirectly.

The second difficulty of public administration in underdeveloped countries —the traditional emphasis on administrative formalities—can be dealt with more directly. The elaborate administrative formality of under-developed countries comes as a surprise to those who expect overly elaborate procedures to be a characteristic of mature rather than immature public administration. The fact is that underdeveloped countries often suffer from too much, not too little, of the "mechanics" of administration. . . .[51]

Although each of the specialized agencies has been concerned with improving the level of public service in its sector, the over-all improvement and development of public administration as such has been the concern of UNTAA. It has been estimated that some 10 per cent to 15 per cent of the experts assigned by the United Nations and the specialized agencies since 1952 have been working in the field of public administration, strictly defined.[52]

The program had its origin in discussions at the Economic and Social

[51] Albert Lepawsky, "Technical Assistance: A Challenge to Public Administration," *Public Administration Review*, Vol. XVI, No. 1 (Winter 1956), p. 22.

[52] *Ibid.*, p. 25. The estimate is based on a classification in terms of actual project content instead of formal project title.

Council in early 1948.[53] Later in the year, the creation of an international center for training in public administration was discussed at some length by the Fifth (Administrative and Budgetary) Committee of the General Assembly. Objections to the proposal were based primarily on financial grounds, but also on grounds that such a program might be outside the scope of the United Nations and that the training of civil servants was the responsibility of national governments. Supporters stressed the need to help underdeveloped countries overcome the shortage of trained civil servants.[54] Finally, the committee, by a narrow margin, decided to recommend a draft resolution, which the General Assembly then adopted without change. The resolution stated that "an International Centre for Training in Public Administration shall be established under the direction of the United Nations."[55]

The idea of a major International Centre in the sense of an institute or group of institutes was, however, gradually abandoned. The "Centre" became the name for a program of technical assistance in the field of public administration, including some financial support for the International Institute for Administrative Sciences in Brussels, for the preparation of documentation in various languages on different aspects of public administration. In 1950, the term "programme" replaced the term "international centre" and a resolution was adopted by the Economic and Social Council recommending that "additional activities undertaken in the field of training in public administration . . . should be considered under the Expanded Programme for Technical Assistance."[56]

Under UNTAA, several regional and national training centers have been established. Among them are a regional School of Public Administration in Rio de Janeiro; a Public Administration Institute for Turkey and the Middle East in Ankara; a National Institute of Public Administration in Cairo; an Advanced School of Public Administration for Central America in Costa Rica; and a training course for government accountants in Libya.[57] More unique, as an activity of the United Nations, is the public administration project undertaken in Bolivia.

[53] See Res. 132(VI), Feb. 24, 1948, "International Facilities for the Promotion of Training in Public Administration."

[54] U.N. Economic and Social Council, *International Facilities for the Promotion of Training in Public Administration*, Doc. E/1336 (May 18, 1949), pp. 4–5.

[55] Res. 246(III), Dec. 4, 1948.

[56] Res. 292(XI), July 5, 1950.

[57] U.N. Economic and Social Council, *Technical Assistance in Public Administration*, Report by the Secretary-General, Doc. E/2415 (May 1, 1953), p. 5.

An international team that surveyed Bolivia in 1950 made a number of recommendations for action on economic and social matters and, in addition, urged that high priority be given to the public administration of the country as a whole. From 1952 to 1953, six foreign experts were assigned to the Ministries of Agriculture, Finance, Labor, and Social Welfare, to the Central Bank, and to the Office of the Comptroller General, to serve as members of the Bolivian civil service in helping to improve the operations of the agencies in question. There cannot be many instances in which sovereign nations have invited and freely accepted from international agencies a comparable measure of intervention in their domestic affairs.

The arrangement had the advantage of placing United Nations experts in responsible working positions in key offices, but it had its disadvantages also. The responsibility of the foreign "civil servant" to the local supervisor was not sufficiently clear to protect the prestige or effectiveness of both or to ensure the adoption of the recommendations proposed. Nevertheless, this phase of the experiment was regarded as successful; the project was continued in 1954, but the foreign experts relinquished their administrative authority and began serving as technical consultants only.

Community Development

In the efforts of the United Nations to generate economic and social development along lines that correspond to the felt needs of the people and that tend to be cumulative and self-sustaining, community development programs—as they have come to be known—have grown increasingly important. They embrace the villages and rural areas in which 80 per cent of the people in underdeveloped countries dwell. In these areas, the presence of many more hands than are needed to reap the meager harvests, and the enforced idleness of all hands at certain seasons, combine to make underemployment chronic. The aim of community development programs is to release latent local leadership and to channel surplus local labor into projects considered urgent and useful by the local population, thus simultaneously strengthening the foundations of democracy and adding to the capital stock of underdeveloped countries.

The purpose is "not so much to remedy any particular situation or to promote public works for any immediate need as to start a chain reaction of discussion, organization, action, achievement and renewed discussion of the next phase in development. The connexion is close between community develop-

ment and the evolution of democratic local government . . . once the emerging
societies have reached a certain stage in their evolution towards self-expression
and self-government, their activities, whether directed through government
machinery, central or local, or through private societies, will cease to depend
on persistent stimulation from without. They will tend to rely increasingly on
the functioning of services established as a part of the framework of their local
institutions."[58]

In the late 1940's, both the Social Commission and the Economic and
Social Council attempted on various occasions to clarify the role that
local communities might play in improving the welfare of their people.
In 1951, the Council, acting on a recommendation of its Social Commission (which, in turn, had been prompted by the United States)
asked the Secretary-General to compile "full documentation" on the
varying objectives and scope of community welfare centers, the methods used in establishing and operating them, the success achieved, and
the difficulties met.[59] The report was to be submitted to the Social Commission in order that the commission might, "if possible, determine
some general principles which underlie successful techniques."[60]

This resulted in one of the most comprehensive fact-finding efforts
undertaken by the United Nations. Before the close of 1954, thirty-
four governments had submitted voluminous data on conditions in their
territories. Missions, jointly staffed by the United Nations and the
specialized agencies, made surveys of selected community development
experiments in the Caribbean area, in the Middle East, and in South
and Southeast Asia.[61] Fourteen country monographs were published
and four study kits issued, all in a United Nations series on community
organization and development.[62]

[58] U.N. General Assembly, Tenth Session, *Official Records*, Supplement No. 16, pp.
23–24. Quoted in Carnegie Endowment for International Peace, "Issues Before the
Tenth General Assembly," *International Conciliation*, No. 504 (September 1955), pp.
84–85.

[59] Res. 390D(XIII), Aug. 9, 1951.

[60] *Ibid.*

[61] United Nations, *Report of the Mission on Rural Community Organization and De-
velopment in the Caribbean Area and Mexico*, Doc. ST/SOA/Ser.O/7, ST/TAA/Ser.D/7
(March 1953); United Nations, *Report of the Mission on Community Organization and
Development in Selected Arab Countries of the Middle East*, Doc. ST/SOA/Ser.O/9,
ST/TAA/Ser.D/9 (November 1953); United Nations, *Report of the Mission to Survey
Community Development Projects in South and Southeast Asia*, Doc. ST/SOA/Ser. O/10,
ST/TAA/Ser. D/10 (December 1953).

[62] For a list of publications in this series issued between Jan. 1, 1953 and July 15,
1955, see U.N. Secretariat, Bureau of Social Affairs, *Social Progress Through Community Development*, Doc. E/CN.5/303/Rev. 1 (1955), Annex II. (Hereinafter cited
as *Progress Through Community Development*.)

The most recent report in the series makes it clear that the investigation went far beyond a study of "social welfare centers" as physical facilities. It included descriptive accounts of many types of community effort, including community schools and experiments in group living, and summaries of national community development programs. It reviewed the methods employed in various parts of the world at different stages of economic and social development; analyzed the interactions of self-help and external assistance, national and international; and concluded with a review of the need for and training of local leaders and auxiliary workers.

As part of the Secretary-General's inquiry, persistent efforts were made to arrive at a clearer definition of the subject under consideration. The earlier concept of "community centers"—with its connotation of buildings and grounds—was soon abandoned in favor of a broader definition intended to cover programs of rural reconstruction, village betterment, and mass education. Agreement was finally reached on the use of the terms "community organization" and/or "community development." More specifically:

Community development can be tentatively defined as a process designed to create conditions of economic and social progress for the whole community with its active participation and the fullest possible reliance upon the community's initiative. "Community development" implies the integration of two sets of forces making for human welfare, neither of which can do the job alone: (i) The opportunity and capacity for cooperation, self-help, ability to assimilate and adapt new ways of living that is at least latent in every human group; and (ii) the fund of techniques and tools in every social and economic field, drawn from worldwide experience and now in use or available to national governments and agencies.[63]

Community development, in short, is a technique for obtaining popular participation in the planning and execution of local programs of improvement. The employees of national governments or international agencies may stimulate local action by providing knowledge of improved techniques and tools and by training village workers, but leadership from outside should not replace local initiative. Depending on the felt needs of the community, the starting point may be a health project or the digging of some irrigation ditches. This experience may lead to community action to establish a school, a rural co-operative, or a village industry. The order in which projects are undertaken is less im-

[63] *Ibid.*, p. 6.

portant than the creation of a community spirit that will induce sustained self-help.

In addition to a tentative definition, the Secretary-General provided a summary of community action programs in different countries.[64] He described community development via simple work projects of local significance in Greece; community development in connection with large irrigation projects, land reform and resettlement schemes in the Belgian Congo; community development built around agricultural extension services in Pakistan; the establishment of rural welfare centers in Egypt; the development of community education in Puerto Rico; and the work of the Mass Education Council in Burma.

The most ambitious programs have been developed in India.[65] They have their foundation in the evolution of the Gandhian philosophy and the concept of village life that the disciples of Gandhi attempted to implement in experiments dating back as much as thirty years. These early experiments were followed by other multipurpose projects organized on a larger territorial scale, and evolved into a national program under the first Five-Year Plan published in 1952. By 1956, under this plan, 120,000 villages and 74 million people, or about one quarter of the entire rural population of India, were to be brought gradually under the influence of the scheme. Under the second Five-Year Plan— i.e., by 1961—the entire country is expected to be covered by the program.

The employment of technical assistance funds for the initiation and extension of community development programs has been encouraged by the principal organs of the United Nations. In 1953, as in 1952, the Economic and Social Council included in its program of concerted practical action in the social field the "promotion and implementation of community development projects."[66] At the same time, the Council authorized the Secretary-General

. . . to convene one or more small groups of senior policy making representatives of governments having similar social and economic problems and of representatives of the Secretariats of the United Nations and the specialized agencies concerned, to plan concrete programs for expansion of community development projects, including training facilities and the strengthening of or-

[64] *Ibid.*, Chap. III.
[65] *Ibid.*, pp. 66–72. For an additional discussion of the program in India and its significance, see Chester Bowles, *Ambassador's Report* (1954), Chap. 14, "Community Development—A Key to Village India," pp. 195–214.
[66] Res. 496(XVI), July 31, 1953.

ganizations for administering social programs related to community development in their respective countries.[67]

The first such meeting was held in 1954 in the Philippines, a country with a good record in the use of schools as the focal point for community development. During 1953 and 1954, experts on community development were made available to Afghanistan, Haiti, Iraq, Pakistan, Paraguay, Peru, the Philippines, and Yugoslavia, with a number of the experts for other Asian countries drawn from India. Aid from foreign experts has been supplemented by the granting of fellowships and scholarships to local personnel for study abroad.

The possibility of making significant economic and social progress through local action at the village level appears to be catching the imagination of underdeveloped countries. Inasmuch as surplus labor is far more plentiful than surplus capital, and self-help must in any event be the foundation for continuing economic and social advances, the rapid spread of community development programs should be regarded as one of the most encouraging phenomena in the contemporary world. The unleashing of local initiative in all its diversity could prove to be among the strongest forces for the promotion of democracy.

General Appraisal

Considered as a whole, the complex, extensive United Nations program for fostering economic and social development through technical assistance has been beset with difficulties of programing and recruitment, administration, finance, and philosophy that are only slowly being overcome.

The most pervasive difficulty, perhaps, is the lack of adequate understanding of the general problem of economic growth and development, and of the specific problems of individual underdeveloped countries that have reached different stages of development. This deficiency, of which more will be said later, means that there is no satisfactory method of deciding which projects merit approval because they can contribute significantly to the development of an area, and which projects should be deferred or rejected because their contribution is unlikely to be significant. To date, technical assistance appears to have been more successful in propagating technology in the narrow sense— *e.g.*, knowledge concerning seeds, fertilizers, tractors, or textile produc-

[67] *Ibid.*

tion—than in introducing social or administrative change. Projects designed to institute land reform, to promote taxation in accordance with ability to pay, or to ensure that government contracts are let on the basis of competitive bidding, have been undertaken only on a modest scale by underdeveloped countries.

Most projects are planned for one, two, or three years in the hope that by the end of the period enough local personnel will have been trained to permit the withdrawal of foreign personnel and the take-over by nationals of the country aided. Whether this is a legitimate expectation obviously depends on the project and on the country; in many cases, it is patently over-optimistic. Moreover, there is the question whether supplying experts should permanently be separated from supplying equipment. The cost of foreign experts is, after all, one of the smallest costs in a development program. After the value of this type of service has been demonstrated for a few more years, it may not be unreasonable to ask the countries that want experts to assume the cost themselves, perhaps using the United Nations as the employment agency that would unearth and nominate qualified technicians for participating governments to hire. Moreover, if foreign financial assistance becomes available on a larger scale in the form of loans and grants and private investments, an increasing volume of technical assistance will be provided as an integral part of the larger package.

The resources of EPTA for the last several years have proved too limited to finance valid projects that could otherwise be undertaken. In addition, the program has suffered from other financial difficulties. The practice of obtaining contributions for only one year at a time makes it difficult to organize and staff many projects of longer duration. Annual programs have to be altered, curtailed, or canceled if the annual pledges are not fully paid, or are paid late in the period. During 1954, for example, only one third of the total amount pledged had been collected by June 30, and nearly half of the total was still outstanding at the beginning of the last quarter of the financial year.[68] In 1955, however, the Congress of the United States appropriated funds not only for the calendar year 1955 but also for 1956, thus putting the program on a more stable basis. Additional attempts have been made to ease some of the financial difficulties of the program—the establishment of a $12 million reserve fund is an example—but it is too early to report that the uncertainties of financing have been overcome.

[68] "Seventh Report of the Technical Assistance Board," p. 4.

The technical assistance effort has posed a number of other problems in the fields of personnel, programing, evaluation, and administration. As has been noted above, experts are recruited from all over the world, from the less developed as well as the more developed countries, and tensions have in some instances arisen because of the differing backgrounds of members of the same team of experts. Yet it is on the human beings associated with the field operations of the program that the success of the effort largely depends. Nominations are obtained on an unofficial basis from governments, from educational institutions, professional associations, charitable foundations, and other sources. They are not always made in the best interests of the program. There is the competing pressure of home requirements and interests, and a scarcity of qualified individuals willing or able to accept arduous foreign assignments. There is the tendency to release the man who can most easily be spared without handicapping the operation of the local laboratory or department. And there is a readiness to nominate the friend or relative of the minister or the university president. The great preponderance of experts, however, have been well qualified for their tasks. Moreover, the Technical Assistance Board has begun the practice of retaining on a long-term basis a few experts who have demonstrated their capacity and versatility in several assignments. This may presage the development of a career service within the United Nations for technical assistance personnel.

Perhaps the most important problem in programing is the formulation of criteria for evaluating results. This problem, like others in the field of technical assistance, is not confined to the multilateral programs. Results may be measured in simple quantitative terms where projects are intended to increase the area of land under cultivation or the output of refined sugar, bituminous coal, or rice; or to reduce the incidence of trachoma, industrial accidents, or illiteracy. But statistics concerning the number of persons engaged in village health work, the number of villages reached by community development programs, or the number of textbooks prepared locally are inadequate indicators of the effectiveness of projects having broad social objectives. Standards for measuring the value of the economist who helps frame a new tax law or the cultural anthropologist who helps draft a national development program that will properly respect the cultural heritage of the area are still more difficult to establish. It is significant that many activities initiated as technical assistance projects have been taken over on a permanent basis by host governments, that others have been continued as projects despite major changes in the complexion of the governments of the countries in which they have been located, and that governments in host countries have been willing to increase the value of their local contributions to the program.

Several international agencies, among them WHO, ILO, and UNESCO, have studied the problems of evaluating technical assistance. A seminar was organized by UNTAA at McGill University in Montreal to undertake a preliminary consideration of the problems·involved in evaluating projects of UNTAA. The Technical Assistance Board (TAB) asked four economists who had had experience in various parts of the world to undertake a review of the activities proposed for 1953. After the program had been in operation for five years, the Administrative Committee on Coordination asked TAB to review the experience gained to date and to consider plans for the future development of the program. Completed by TAB in May 1956, this report provides valuable data on directions in which the program might grow if substantially greater resources become available.[69]

By an independent source, the Expanded Programme of Technical Assistance has been appraised succinctly, though necessarily inconclusively, as follows:

Inevitably the strengths of the Programme are its very weakness. Because it embraces the nations of the world, it must operate in all fields and its work must spread, even if thinly, into the remotest corners. Because it is international, it can draw upon skills and experience everywhere, but the problems of selection are magnified by that very fact. Because the political import of its activities is great it cannot escape the consequences of political pressures. Because the needs are urgent and the scope unprecedented it must sometimes act by trial and error.

Over and above the problems inherent in the form and content of its operations, there are financial questions. In terms of its objectives the Programme has had sorely inadequate funds and even these have not been guaranteed. At best it has only been able to be the "yeast in the dough" and for maximum effectiveness it has had to mesh its modest efforts into those of other foreign programs and of the recipient governments. "It would, therefore, be difficult to separate the results attributable to technical assistance from the total improvement made, even if the latter could be accurately measured."[70]

[69] U.N. Technical Assistance Committee, *The Expanded Programme of Technical Assistance: A Forward Look*, pp. 32–41.

[70] Carnegie Endowment for International Peace, "Issues Before the Tenth General Assembly," *International Conciliation*, No. 504 (September 1955), pp. 111–12. Quotations within the quotation are from "Seventh Report of the Technical Assistance Board," p. 7.

Beyond Technical Assistance

Technical assistance, in the view of the underdeveloped countries, is "not enough." Its major limitation, according to these countries, is that in the United Nations it is generally divorced from the provision of capital. Some capital needs are being met through the International Bank and other channels, but many are not. Where development is already being impeded by a shortage of capital, additional technical assistance may even aggravate the situation by enlarging the unsatisfied demand for improvements that are costly.

That technical assistance is a limited approach to the complex problem of stimulating economic growth has long been conceded by the Economic and Social Council. The lengthy resolution on technical assistance adopted by the Council in 1949 recognized the necessity also for "an expanded rate of international capital flow."[71] This formulation caused no difficulty because it did not specify whether the expansion should take the form of loans, grants, or private investment. Since the launching of the technical assistance program, the major drive of the underdeveloped countries at the Economic and Social Council and at the General Assembly has been to establish new international machinery for collecting and distributing aid in the form of grants and long-term, low-interest loans.

Over this proposal the nations of the world have been sharply divided. The underdeveloped countries, almost without exception, have believed that shortage of capital was the major impediment to their more rapid development, that such development would clearly serve the best interests of the international community as a whole, and that new avenues to capital for development purposes should therefore be opened. The developed countries have questioned whether shortage of capital was the barrier it was purported to be and whether, in any event, the remedy was to provide it in the form of internationally administered grant aid.

The more rigid positions initially assumed in the debates, largely on political grounds, have become somewhat less doctrinaire—partly in response to changes in the political climate, but partly, too, as deeper insights into the nature of the development process have been gained. Recent analysis seems to indicate that "pure" technical assistance is most valuable during the earliest stages of development. As primitive societies become ready for the installation of basic power, transporta-

[71] Res. 222D(IX), Aug. 14, 1949.

tion, health, and educational facilities, foreign loans and grants become increasingly important. Private investment is most likely to flow at the next stage of development, after completion of the so-called economic and social overhead projects. To this emerging understanding of the nature of the development process, the United Nations has made some noteworthy contributions.

Understanding the Process of Economic Growth

Perhaps the first major contribution from a United Nations source to an understanding of the institutional framework required for development came in 1951 with the publication of a highly controversial report, to which references have been made earlier in this volume, recommending national and international measures for the economic development of underdeveloped countries.[72] The experts responsible for the preparation of the report clearly saw the revolutionary implications of a sharp acceleration in the rate of development.

There is a sense in which rapid economic progress is impossible without painful readjustments. Ancient philosophies have to be scrapped; old institutions have to disintegrate; bonds of caste, creed and race have to be burst; and large numbers of people who cannot keep up with progress have to have their expectations of a comfortable life frustrated. Very few communities are willing to pay the full price of rapid economic progress.

In our judgment, there are a number of under-developed countries where the concentration of economic and political power in the hands of a small class, whose main interest is the preservation of its own wealth and privileges, rules out the prospect of much economic progress until a social revolution has effected a shift in the distribution of income and power.

There cannot be rapid economic progress unless the leaders of a country at all levels—politicians, teachers, engineers, business leaders, trade unionists, priests, journalists—desire economic progress for the country, and are willing to pay its price, which is the creation of a society from which economic, political and social privileges have been eliminated. On the other hand, given leadership and the public will to advance, all problems of economic development are soluble.[73]

[72] U.N. Secretariat, Department of Economic Affairs, *Measures for the Economic Development of Under-Developed Countries*, Report by a Group of Experts appointed by the Secretary-General of the United Nations (May 1951). (Hereinafter cited as *Measures for Economic Development*.) The experts were Alberto Baltra Cortez of Chile, D. R. Gadgil of India, George Hakim of Lebanon, W. Arthur Lewis of the United Kingdom, and Theodore W. Schultz of the United States. For earlier references to this study, see above, Chaps. IV and VII.

[73] *Ibid.*, pp. 15–16. In the view of the French delegation, "the experts had compiled a document in which technical considerations played their part, but which

In their analysis of the "pre-conditions of economic development"—
from which the above quotation is taken—the experts stressed that economic progress would not occur in the absence of an atmosphere favorable to it. An experimental and scientific attitude was, therefore, the
first pre-condition they mentioned.

In underdeveloped societies, acceptance of the *status quo* might be
due, in the opinion of the experts, to the prevalence of an other-worldly
philosophy that discouraged material wants. Alternatively, people
might be unwilling to make the effort to produce wealth if the social
prestige they desired were more easily obtained in other ways—through
the acquisition of military skill, or the skill of the lawyer or priest. Men,
moreover, would be unwilling to strive for progress where they could
not secure the fruits of their efforts. In some societies, the techniques
and rituals of agriculture were prescribed by law, and an innovator
would be committing sacrilege. In societies stratified by caste, color, or
creed, whole sections of the population were being deprived by the
social system of the opportunity to contribute to a rising national income. Rapid economic progress was seldom found in societies lacking
vertical social mobility.[74]

Thus, at its outset, the report of the experts sought to focus attention
on the critical social and political factors that tended to prevent or retard economic progress in the underdeveloped countries. This portion
of the analysis, despite its trenchancy, was generally welcomed.[75] Since
1951, the literature on economic development—both inside and outside the United Nations—has devoted vastly more attention to the
deeply rooted institutional obstacles to development.

The main body of the report of the experts was given over to a summary of measures, national and international, that might be taken to
accelerate development. The numerous concrete recommendations for
national action to promote development tended, however, to be lost
sight of in the consideration of the report by the Economic and Social
Council in 1951, when attention was focused almost exclusively on the
proposal for an International Development Authority to make grants-

---

appeared, in more than one respect, to be little more than a manifesto. It seemed,
indeed, like a sign of the times—men of science venturing to encroach on the field
of political action." U.N. Economic and Social Council, Thirteenth Session, *Official
Records*, 502nd Meeting (Aug. 15, 1951), p. 201.

[74] *Measures for Economic Development*, pp. 13–16.

[75] For a highly critical review, however, see S. Herbert Frankel, "United Nations Primer for Development," *The Quarterly Journal of Economics*, Vol. LXVI, No. 3
(August 1952).

in-aid and on the dubious estimates of the amounts of foreign capital required by the underdeveloped countries. In retrospect, it would appear nevertheless that the more permanent contribution of the report was its discussion of the nature of the development process and the domestic actions required to initiate and encourage it.

Following the clarion call of the experts, all levels of the United Nations became involved in more searching consideration of the factors that encourage and discourage economic growth. Although the debates at the Economic and Social Council and the General Assembly continued to center around the desire of the underdeveloped countries for new international institutions to step up the flow of foreign capital, many other problems were actively and usefully explored. Economic analysis of a high order, for example, was provided by the staff of the Economic Commission for Europe in its examination of the problems of the underdeveloped regions of southern Europe.[76] Similarly, the Economic Commission for Latin America (ECLA) provided valuable current data and theoretical analyses of the development process in Central and South America.[77] The problems of Asia and the Far East were analyzed maturely and incisively at a Working Party on Economic Development and Planning that met under the auspices of the ECAFE in November 1955.[78]

Drawing on such of the foregoing source material as was available at the time and many other sources as well, the Department of Economic and Social Affairs of the United Nations Secretariat, in late 1954, issued an analysis of the process of industrialization and economic growth generally in underdeveloped countries that represented another long step forward.[79] The report as a whole was written in the Economic Development Branch of the Bureau of Economic Affairs but was circulated to outside experts in a number of countries for comment and criti-

[76] U.N. Economic Commission for Europe, *Economic Survey of Europe in 1953*, Doc. E/ECE/174 (1954).

[77] *Cf.* U.N. Economic Commission for Latin America, *Economic Survey of Latin America, 1951–1952*, Doc. E/CN.12/291/Rev. 2 (1953); *Economic Survey of Latin America, 1953*, Doc. E/CN.12/358 (1954); *International Co-operation in a Latin-American Development Policy*, Doc.E/CN.12/359 (1954); *Analyses and Projections of Economic Development*, Doc.E/CN.12/363 (1955).

[78] United Nations, "Economic Development and Planning in Asia and the Far East," *Economic Bulletin for Asia and the Far East*, Vol. VI, No. 3 (November 1955).

[79] U.N. Secretariat, Department of Economic and Social Affairs, *Processes and Problems of Industrialization in Under-Developed Countries* (1955). Prepared in response to Res. 461(XV), Apr. 23, 1953, of the Economic and Social Council, which included in paragraph 3 authority for the Secretary-General to consult with experts in making the study.

cism before publication. This combination of reliance on permanent staff and *ad hoc* consultants proved fruitful: the result was a judicious, penetrating statement of the nature of the industrialization process, the obstacles to industrialization, the domestic and international measures conducive to it, and the implications of industrialization. By emphasizing and illustrating the interdependence of progress in industry, agriculture, transportation, and education, the report gave new content to the oft-used but ill-understood term "balanced" or "integrated" development.

Further insights are being gained through the establishment, within the framework of the United Nations, of centers for study and training in problems of economic development. One of the first such programs was initiated jointly by the Economic Commission for Latin America and the United Nations Technical Assistance Administration in 1952. It is designed primarily to train economists who will be capable of integrating the recommendations of technical specialists into realistic development programs. Each trainee spends approximately eight months in study and work at the site of the commission in Santiago, Chile. By July 1955, fifteen of the twenty Latin American republics had on duty one or more officials trained under the program. Despite some doubts whether governments were making full use of the trainees, the results to date are regarded as encouraging. [80]

Serving a wider geographic area than the Latin American program, and aimed at a more senior level of civil servants, is the Economic Development Institute organized in Washington, D.C. by the International Bank, with financial assistance from the Rockefeller and Ford Foundations. The Institute maintains a small, full-time staff to plan and lead discussions and seminars designed to increase "the number of trained administrators skilled in dealing with problems of economic policy and with the planning and administration of development programs." [81] The first group of government officials began their six-month course of studies in January 1956.

Institutes such as the two mentioned above, supplementing the practical experience being gained every day by policy makers and research personnel in underdeveloped countries, are resulting in more sophisti-

---

[80] See U.N. Economic Commission for Latin America, Sixth Session, *Report on ECLA/TAA Economic Development Training Programme*, Doc. E/CN.12/376 (July 30, 1955).

[81] International Bank for Reconstruction and Development, *Economic Development Institute, Prospectus* (September 1955), p. 3.

cated national development programs than the series issued during the early postwar years. The initial plans were often hardly more than announcements of goals. Certain of their features were intensely nationalistic and the content of industrialization proposals, in particular, tended to be determined more by notions of what would enhance the prestige of the government than by realistic analysis of resources and requirements.

The current national development programs, like their predecessors, start from the assumption that some governmental intervention in the economic process is necessary. Allowing natural forces to determine the pace of development will not produce a rate of progress that is politically tolerable, if indeed it results in any progress at all. Present plans differ considerably, however, both from their predecessors and from each other, in their views of the points at which governmental intervention is most appropriate, the nature of the intervention, and the timing most likely to induce in orderly fashion the myriad changes in social structure, motivation, and standards of value that lie at the heart of economic development.[82]

The transformation of a static, primitive society into a modern nation, it is now clear, is a slow, uneven process, which cannot be achieved merely by exhortation or the injection of capital.

Economic development is a whole complex of interdependent changes manifested simultaneously in the physical environment (new roads, buildings, harbors, machines, implements, chemicals), in the forms of association by which men live and work (growth of cities, changes in government, factory organization, business corporations, banking, readjustments in land tenure, family practices, even religion), and in the skills, habits, and thought patterns of millions of individuals (literacy, technical specializations, respect for scientific methods, ambition, the idea of progress). To pick out any one aspect of this interdependent complex and center attention on it involves a considerable danger of wrong analysis, out of which ineffective or even harmful policies may spring. If we must simplify, we are least likely to go wrong when we think of economic development as a massive problem in human education and social readjustment and only secondarily a problem in equipment.[83]

Within the framework of the Colombo Plan, the programs of certain Asian nations are from time to time subjected to constructive outside scrutiny, and opportunities are provided for co-ordinating offers of foreign assistance. Within the United Nations system, there is no organ or

[82] *Cf.* U.N. Secretariat, Department of Economic and Social Affairs, *United Nations Studies of the Technique of Economic Planning in Underdeveloped Countries*, Doc. RS/ Conf. 7/4 (Dec. 21, 1955).

[83] Staley, *op. cit.*, pp. 202–03.

agency responsible for receiving and analyzing national development plans as they are issued by governments; for maintaining current records regarding their fulfillment; or for co-ordinating domestic, bilateral, and multilateral efforts to stimulate growth in a given area.

Drive for Grant Aid

Despite a heightened awareness of the need for basic changes throughout the fabric of their societies, the underdeveloped countries, in the principal organs of the United Nations, have concentrated since 1950 on their need for capital from abroad. In the eyes of the majority of its Members, the United Nations system remains ill-equipped to stimulate development precisely where help is most needed: namely, financing the non-self-liquidating projects that constitute economic and social overhead capital. The missing component, in their view, is machinery for collecting and distributing assistance in the form of grants and long-term, low-interest loans. Since 1950, the major economic battles at the Economic and Social Council and the General Assembly have been fought on this issue.

The basic arguments have remained unchanged as the debates waged in the early years at the Subcommission on Economic Development and the Economic and Employment Commission have moved through the Economic Committee of the Economic and Social Council, the Council itself, the Economic and Financial Committee of the General Assembly, and the Assembly in plenary meeting. Each organ has tended to ignore the work of subsidiary organs and to confuse two separable issues: the volume of aid available or likely to become available, and the machinery for distributing such aid. The General Assembly, where emotions have been highest and where the underdeveloped countries have the strongest voice, has insisted on steady movement in the direction of establishing a grant agency under United Nations auspices, and has been most ingenious in devising means for keeping the issue in the foreground at successive sessions.

Chile, India, and Yugoslavia have been the leading proponents for the early establishment of a grant agency. They have had the solid support of underdeveloped countries, including some that are more likely to be net contributors to than beneficiaries of a grant program, plus support from a growing number of the more industrialized nations. The United States, on whom the major financial burden would fall, has led the opposition but has been increasingly isolated.

The arguments of the underdeveloped countries have been simple and moving. Living standards in two thirds of the world are intolerably low. Poverty, famine, and disease exact a fearful toll. The toll is unnecessary and can no longer be borne with resignation. People everywhere are demanding a real improvement in their standards of living and a greater share in the benefits of modern industrial society. Their rightful aspirations must be satisfied, or world peace and stability will be in constant jeopardy. Without a foundation of economic security, the superstructure of military pacts and armaments rests on quicksand.

The gap in living standards between the have and have-not nations is said to be widening rather than narrowing. Some of the underdeveloped countries argue that the gap must be closed, *i.e.*, that growth rates must be more rapid in the underdeveloped than in the more developed economies. The majority concede that the fundamental problem is progress at the lower end of the scale regardless of the rate of improvement at the upper end. The requisite progress, they say, cannot be achieved with the resources at present available or likely to become available. The best solution for the problem is to finance the construction of basic educational, health, highway, and other noncommercial facilities by grant aid or by loans on especially easy terms, administered by a United Nations agency, which will ensure that "conditions" are not unilaterally imposed by donors or lenders.[84]

Proponents of a grant agency, moreover, claim that the benefits to industrialized nations in terms of increased trade and better international relations would far outweigh the costs, which would be small, both in relation to what such nations can afford and what they are already spending for other activities that are no more urgent than economic development. To these economic and political reasons, they add humanitarian reasons. In an interdependent world, the more fortunate cannot isolate themselves from the less fortunate and, in fact, have an obligation to help them. Some representatives of underdeveloped countries have claimed that the obligation is more direct: industrialized countries have exploited the underdeveloped countries in the past and should now repay their accumulated debts.

The task of replying to the underdeveloped countries has fallen primarily on the United States. It has stressed the availability of substantial unutilized lending capacity in both the International Bank and the

---

[84] Such loans—repayable in local currencies, or obtainable at rates of interest lower than those charged by the established international lending agencies or on the basis of more liberal provisions concerning amortization—have been referred to by the developed countries as "soft loans."

Export-Import Bank, and the fact that loans have been and can be made for non-self-liquidating projects. It has not denied the case for grant aid on a temporary basis in isolated instances but has questioned the desirability, in present circumstances, of establishing new United Nations machinery for the purpose. Grants-in-aid, the United States has said, should not be regarded as a normal feature of international economic co-operation. To the argument that it has granted many billions to the relatively rich continent of Europe through UNRRA and the Marshall Plan and therefore should be willing to assist the infinitely needier nations in other areas, the United States has replied that there is a vast difference between reconstruction and development. The restoration of war damage involved a short-term commitment of measurable dimensions; the raising of living standards in underdeveloped countries implies a long-term commitment of unforeseeable magnitude.

Moreover, the United States declared, it has in fact been making substantial grants to underdeveloped areas without the prodding of a new international agency. The prewar members of the Commonwealth of Nations have referred in similar terms to the contributions they and others make through the Colombo Plan and in other ways. To step up the level of aid would be impractical in the face of the financial claims of rearmament and existing commitments. To channel the same amount through a United Nations agency would not alter the rate of development but might raise serious political problems in donor countries. If real disarmament were achieved and mutual trust increased, the situation might be altered. Meanwhile the difficulties encountered in financing such modest undertakings as the Expanded Programme of Technical Assistance should give pause to those advocating more ambitious ventures.

Proposals During 1950-52

In early 1950, at the Subcommission on Economic Development, the United States was able to fend off endorsement of a proposal by the Indian expert for a United Nations Economic Development Administration. The Indian expert recognized that the United States was the only likely source of funds, and the subcommission reported that an agency financed primarily by a single government could not be truly international. Nevertheless, it urged the Economic and Social Council to consider the grant-aid problem.

The Council considered the matter at great length as part of the question of financing economic development. It adopted a carefully worded compromise resolution that avoided any direct mention of grant aid but nevertheless strengthened the hands of those who were advocating it.[85] The resolution "recognized" that the domestic financial resources of underdeveloped countries, plus available international capital, had not been "sufficient to assure the desired rate of economic development," and that development at the desired rate required "not only a more effective and sustained mobilization of domestic savings, but also an expanded and more stable flow of foreign capital investment." The resolution of the Council further recognized that the initiation of non-self-liquidating as well as self-liquidating projects was "justified." Inasmuch as no one maintained that it was "unjustified," the only object of the reference was to direct public attention to the category of project for which funds were proving most difficult to obtain. In the operative portion of its resolution, the Council did not ask the General Assembly for guidance, but recommended that a subsidiary organ—the Economic, Employment and Development Commission[86]—keep under review the problems involved in financing economic development, and from time to time make recommendations to the Council.

The General Assembly missed the hint from the Council on procedure, and expressed itself more categorically and more impatiently than the Council. It was "convinced" that the "needs" of the underdeveloped countries could not be met without an increased flow of public funds. It recommended that the Economic and Social Council consider "practical methods . . . for achieving the adequate expansion and steadier flow of foreign capital, both private and public, and pay special attention to the financing of non-self-liquidating projects which are basic to economic development." It requested the Council to submit its recommendations to the next session of the General Assembly.[87]

Notwithstanding the warnings of United States delegates at United Nations meetings, the hopes of the underdeveloped countries for an internationally administered grant-aid program were fed from other sources in the United States. The first of a series of postwar reports on United States foreign economic policy, prepared under the direction of a Special Assistant to the President, Gordon Gray, appeared while the General Assembly was debating the resolution quoted above.[88] This so-called Gray Report recommended United States grants for both

[85] Res. 294(XI), Aug. 12, 1950.

[86] Successor to the Economic and Employment Commission after abolition of the Subcommission on Economic Development in 1950.

[87] Res. 400(V), Nov. 20, 1950.

[88] Gordon Gray and Others, *Report to the President on Foreign Economic Policies* (1950).

technical assistance and economic development. A few months later, in March 1951, the United States International Development Advisory Board, under the chairmanship of Nelson Rockefeller, reported the existence of

> ... many projects of basic importance to the development of underdeveloped countries that cannot be financed entirely on a loan basis. Our considered judgment is that *such public works can be most effectively financed and developed through a well-managed international agency*. ... The Advisory Board recommends the prompt creation of a new International Development Authority in which all free nations will be invited to participate.[89]

It suggested that the new development authority be set up with total initial funds not to exceed a half billion dollars.

The same group of United Nations experts that had picked up from this report the idea for an International Finance Corporation also commended the proposal for an International Development Authority. On the basis of a series of highly debatable assumptions, the five experts appointed by the United Nations Secretary-General to prepare proposals for the Economic and Social Council on the economic development of underdeveloped countries concluded that a 2 per cent increase in per-capita national income would require an annual capital import into the underdeveloped countries well in excess of $10 billion for investment in industry and agriculture alone. If social overhead investment were included, the total would be much greater. About 80 per cent of the $10 billion, said the experts, would be needed for South Asia and the Far East. They urged that the United Nations establish an International Development Authority capable of making grants-in-aid in amounts that would increase rapidly up to a level of about $3 billion per year.[90] The magnitudes in which they discoursed caused alarm in the areas expected to export the capital. Moreover, the experts submitted virtually no evidence concerning the ability of underdeveloped countries to put large amounts of imported grant capital to effective use.[91]

The recommendation for an International Development Authority was debated by various bodies of the United Nations. The Economic,

[89] U.S. International Development Advisory Board, *Partners in Progress* (1951), pp. 72–73.
[90] *Measures for Economic Development*, pp. 75–80, 84–85.
[91] For a brief critique of the experts' estimates (as well as a lucid analysis of the whole problem of development financing) see "Financing Economic Development" by Benjamin Higgins and Wilfred Malenbaum, *International Conciliation* (March, 1955), especially pp. 291–92.

Employment and Development Commission concluded once more that it was not feasible to establish the proposed international agency because few countries would make substantial contributions. A minority however, supported a resolution inviting the General Assembly to establish the agency and endow it with authority to make both grants and long-term, low-interest loans. From 1951 to 1955, advocacy of grant aid was coupled in the United Nations with advocacy of soft loans. It is not clear whether the underdeveloped countries were genuinely convinced that loans on special terms were widely needed, whether they preferred such loans to grants, whether some, whose eligibility for grants might be dubious, wanted to ensure their entree to the agency, or whether the less developed nations simply assumed that the United States would be more receptive to a combination loan-grant agency than to a straight grant agency. Within the developed countries, many felt that the combination of business and charity involved in soft loans was more likely to exacerbate than to improve international relations, and that loans that are not loans should not be called loans.[92]

When the Economic and Social Council met in the summer of 1951, the proposal for an International Development Authority was hotly debated in the Economic Committee and in the plenary meetings of the Council. Although all members of the Council are represented on the Economic Committee, and although the Economic Committee had agreed, with only three abstentions and no dissents, to a long resolution, the Council in plenary meeting considered amendments to every paragraph of the committee text. The Council rejected a Chilean amendment that would have required it to prepare a blueprint for the

[92] "But the very fact that these loans are made on especially easy terms and are still called loans should make us suspicious. . . . In the end, although some loans will turn out well and will be repaid, others will bring in their train, first, severe strain on the economy of the borrower and, finally, default. When this happens, there is likely to be ill will, rational and irrational, on both sides. The lender will resent the default on a loan made in good faith, the borrower will resent the years lost in abortive struggle to maintain payment on a debt, which he probably regarded in the first instance more as a promise of prosperity than as a serious financial obligation. The effect of such defaults is to destroy credit generally and to wither the integrity of all orthodox lending. In my opinion, when a country has a choice between making grants or quasi-loans of this kind, it pays in the long run to choose grants." International Bank for Reconstruction and Development, Press Release No. 237, address of Eugene R. Black, President, to twelfth session of the Economic and Social Council, Mar. 6, 1951, p. 7. President Black's expression of preference, in certain circumstances, for grants marked the beginning of a change in the attitude of the Bank, which was confirmed at the next session of the General Assembly when he more explicitly endorsed internationally administered grant aid.

establishment, as soon as circumstances permit, of a special fund for grants-in-aid and long-term, low-interest loans, but accepted other amendments that went further in this direction than the resolution approved by the Economic Committee.[93]

The Chilean amendment, which the Council rejected in August 1951 by a vote of 10 to 1, with 7 abstentions,[94] was accepted by the General Assembly in January 1952. A spokesman for the United States delegation stressed his conviction as a member of the Congress that "the United States was not prepared to pledge itself to make a financial contribution . . . immediately or in the near future."[95] Other potential contributors expressed similar views. Nevertheless, the Second (Economic and Financial) Committee of the General Assembly, by a vote of 28 to 20, with 9 abstentions, sent to the Assembly a resolution instructing the Council to submit to the next session of the Assembly a "detailed plan" for establishing the special fund "as soon as circumstances permit."[96] This was adopted in the plenary meeting of the Assembly by a vote of 30 in favor, 16 against, and 11 abstentions.[97]

Recognizing, after further reflection, that 1952 was an election year in the United States and a peculiarly unpropitious moment for obtaining long-term views about United Nations machinery, the underdeveloped countries took the initiative at the Economic and Social Council during the following summer in suggesting that the preparation of the "detailed plan" be delegated to an independent committee of nine to be appointed by the Secretary-General instead of being undertaken forthwith by the Council.[98] It was foreseen that this device would

[93] Res. 368(XIII), Aug. 21, 1951.

[94] U.N. Economic and Social Council, Thirteenth Session, *Official Records*, 511th Meeting (Aug. 21, 1951), p. 288.

[95] Representative Mike Mansfield, U.N. General Assembly, Sixth Session, Second Committee, *Official Records*, 164th Meeting (Dec. 11, 1951), p. 123. However, on the preceding day the President of the International Bank for Reconstruction and Development, Eugene R. Black, had advised the Assembly that grants were necessary to accelerate development programs. "The management of the Bank," he said, "believed that in some countries the rate of development could not be substantially accelerated if the only external capital they received was in the form of loans with a reasonable prospect of repayment. It strongly believed that any additional assistance given to those countries should be in the form of grants rather than of quasi-loans, that the grants should preferably be administered through international channels, and that, to the fullest extent practicable, the technical facilities of existing international agencies should be utilized for such administration." *Ibid.*, 163rd Meeting (Dec. 10, 1951), pp. 114–15.

[96] *Ibid.*, 166th Meeting (Dec. 13, 1951), p. 139.

[97] U.N. General Assembly, Sixth Session, Plenary, *Official Records*, 360th Meeting (Jan. 12, 1952); Res. 520A(VI), Jan. 12, 1952.

[98] Res. 416A(XIV), June 23, 1952.

delay consideration of the blueprint beyond the next session of the Assembly.

Focus on SUNFED

The report of the committee on a Special United Nations Fund for Economic Development (SUNFED) was issued in the spring of 1953.[99] It suggested that operations should not begin until the equivalent of $250 million had been pledged by at least thirty governments. Contributions should be voluntary but could be made in the currencies of the contributors. Control should be vested primarily in an Executive Board on which "major contributors" on the one hand, and "other members" on the other hand, would have equal representation and equal voting rights. In addition to these controversial recommendations concerning local currency contributions and the strong voice to be given to recipient governments in policy determination, the experts' criteria for the allocation of resources were fuzzy, both as between loans and grants, and as between competing projects. On loans, the committee of experts thought the Fund should not ask for interest or attempt to recover principal when this would jeopardize the economic development of a country. On the distribution of available funds, the committee referred repeatedly to "the maintenance of geographical balance."

Before the Economic and Social Council could meet to consider the report of the experts, President Eisenhower revived the hopes of the underdeveloped countries for United States participation in a grant-aid program by his speech on April 16, 1953, to the American Society of Newspaper Editors. He called first for a system of internationally supervised world-wide disarmament. Then, reviving a view expressed at the General Assembly a year and a half earlier by President Truman, President Eisenhower said:

> This Government is ready to ask its people to join with all nations in devoting a substantial percentage of the savings achieved by disarmament to a fund for world aid and reconstruction. The purposes of this great work would be to help other peoples to develop the underdeveloped areas of the world, to stimulate profitable and fair world trade, to assist all peoples to know the blessings of productive freedom. . . . We are ready, by these and all such actions, to make of the United Nations an institution that can effectively guard the peace and security of all peoples.[100]

[99] U.N. Department of Economic Affairs, *Report on a Special United Nations Fund for Economic Development, by a Committee Appointed by the Secretary-General*, Doc. E/2381 (Mar. 18, 1953).

[100] "The Chance for Peace," address by the President, Apr. 16, 1953, U.S. Department of State *Bulletin*, Vol. 28 (Apr. 27, 1953), p. 602.

The President, it will be noted, did not advocate a grant-aid agency nor in any way endorse SUNFED, but the spirit and timing of his address gave a lift to those who did. It was very much in the minds of the delegates to the Council when they assembled in Geneva in the summer of 1953. On the initiative of the United States, the Council recommended and the General Assembly overwhelmingly adopted a resolution declaring that when sufficient progress had been made toward internationally supervised, world-wide disarmament, Members would ask their peoples to devote a portion of the resources so saved to an international fund for economic development and reconstruction.[101] The underdeveloped countries were pleased to receive pledges that could lead to sizable contributions in the distant future but did not consider them adequate substitutes for lesser contributions at an earlier date. They refused to agree that rearmament deserved a priority of indefinite duration over development.

SUNFED is still in the blueprint stage. The Economic and Social Council in 1953 simply transmitted the report of the experts to the General Assembly, the organ that had first asked for the blueprints, with a request that the Assembly consider what other preparatory steps could usefully be undertaken. The Assembly proved its ingenuity by designating a roving ambassador to keep the subject alive. It appointed the Belgian President of the Economic and Social Council, Raymond Scheyven, to obtain and examine government comments on the experts' report and to submit his findings to the Council and the General Assembly in 1954.

Scheyven toured the major capitals and found industrialized countries divided in their views. The key countries—the United States, the United Kingdom, and Canada—as well as New Zealand, the Federal Republic of Germany, Sweden, and Switzerland, were still unprepared to contribute to a fund. Another group of economically advanced nations—Denmark, Italy, Norway, and the Netherlands— declared themselves, however, ready to give material support to the fund. A third group—Belgium, France, Japan, and Luxembourg— were prepared to do so under certain conditions. The underdeveloped countries, of course, wanted the fund established immediately. Scheyven did not confine his report to a summary of the reactions of potential contributors. He included a plea for early establishment of the fund with primary emphasis on what he termed "the moral imperative,"

---

[101] U.N. Economic and Social Council, Res. 482A(XVI), Aug. 4, 1953, and U.N. General Assembly, Res. 724A(VIII), Dec. 7, 1953.

and "the duty of nations to help one another on an adequate scale."[102]

In a resolution approved unanimously, the Economic and Social Council, in the summer of 1954, noted the "increasing moral" and "increased degree of material" support for the establishment of SUNFED and recommended another government review of positions as well as an extension of Scheyven's appointment.[103] This recommendation was accepted by the General Assembly,[104] another *ad hoc* group of experts was appointed, and a new plan for SUNFED was submitted to the Economic and Social Council and the General Assembly by Scheyven in 1955.[105] The new plan, the most modest and realistic in the series on this subject, goes a long way toward meeting objections raised to earlier versions.[106] Like its predecessors, it envisages grants-in-aid as the most important and preponderant method through which the Special Fund would commit its resources. It differs from earlier reports, however, in certain other respects.

1. It quietly buries the proposals for loans on indefinite, renegotiable terms and provides only for fixed-interest loans repayable in the currency of the borrowing country, thereby filling a gap left by the requirement of the International Bank that its loans must be repaid in the currency borrowed;

2. It provides for much closer administrative ties between the Special Fund and the International Bank so that grant aid may be closely co-ordinated with other forms of external financing;

3. On the question of policy formulation, it plainly hints that a controlling voice for major contributors can be arranged;

4. To overcome misgivings about the establishment of grant aid as a permanent feature of international economic co-operation, it suggests that the Special Fund be set up on a trial basis for a five-year period.

[102] U.N. General Assembly, Ninth Session, *Official Records*, Supplement No. 19, "Special United Nations Fund for Economic Development," Final Report by Raymond Scheyven, Prepared in Pursuance of U.N. General Assembly Resolution 724B(VIII), (1954), p. 4.

[103] Res. 532A(XVIII), Aug. 4, 1954.

[104] Res. 822(IX), Dec. 11, 1954.

[105] U.N. General Assembly, Tenth Session, *Official Records*, Supplement No. 17, "Special United Nations Fund for Economic Development," Report Prepared in Pursuance of U.N. General Assembly Resolution 822(IX), (1955).

[106] Paradoxically, the realism in terms of capital resources that makes SUNFED politically acceptable to potential contributors may render it unrealistic in terms of its capacity to affect the pace of development in recipient countries. The smaller the special fund, the more likely it is to meet with approval but the less likely it is to have a significant impact in underdeveloped countries.

None of the numerous special reports to the United Nations has yet provided adequate answers to two questions. How many underdeveloped countries are approaching the limits of their borrowing power but are nevertheless in a position to make productive use of additional funds? What would their annual requirements for grant aid from abroad amount to during the next five to ten years? While Latin American countries have been among the most persistent proponents of grant aid in the Economic and Social Council and the General Assembly, the secretariat of the Economic Commission for Latin America, which is highly respected in that region, has placed greater stress on the need for increased loans, more private investment, and better terms of trade. The Middle Eastern governments, likewise staunch supporters of grant aid, in some cases have treasuries bulging with oil royalties. Their development seems to be hampered by factors other than lack of capital, although additional capital applied to irrigation projects could unquestionably speed the process. It is in Asia, specifically in the Indian subcontinent, that the case for grant aid is best documented. If more searching examination reveals that only a handful of the underdeveloped countries in the United Nations are in a position to use grant aid effectively, would the United Nations be justified in creating international machinery to serve such a limited clientele? This question has never been faced squarely.

Nevertheless the United Nations appears to be inching toward the creation of a grant fund. Recent changes in the international situation, specifically the emergence of the Soviet Union as a potential supplier of aid to underdeveloped countries, could conceivably bring about an ironic shift in present positions. Underdeveloped countries that have hitherto been strong advocates of internationally administered grant aid may conclude that they can do better by jockeying individual foreign governments into outbidding each other in offering aid; developed countries, such as the United States, may be transformed into warm supporters of an internationally administered fund in order to avoid being whipsawed into an intolerable competition for the privilege of financing foreign development projects. Barring any such dramatic reversal of majority and minority positions, the campaign for grant aid will continue unabated.

Retrospect and Prospect

Viewed in the perspective of history, the long-gathering drive of the underdeveloped countries for a new status as peoples and nations may well constitute the major event of the second half of the twentieth century. The problems of underdeveloped countries are psychological and political as well as economic and social. Irrational factors loom large in the picture. It would be a gross oversimplification, therefore, to think of this vast awakening and turbulence solely as a demand for a better material standard of life. Where economic gain and national prestige have come into conflict, nationalism has frequently carried the day.

Nevertheless, the heart of the problem of the underdeveloped countries is how to lift themselves from stagnation at a bare subsistence level to a condition of cumulative, self-generating expansion. Must they lift themselves by their own bootstraps, or can they count on continued help from abroad? How great is the obligation of people in more fortunate areas to collaborate in raising the level of well-being of those in less fortunate lands? What forms, if any, should their help take? Conversely, what accommodation should the numerically strong but economically weak majority of underdeveloped countries make in the interests of greater international harmony with the more developed areas?

By every device at their disposal, the spokesmen for underdeveloped countries have sought to arouse the conscience of mankind to the plight of their peoples, and to gain universal acceptance of the view that the international community as a whole has a responsibility for the welfare of its poorest inhabitants. The issue they have posed is moral as well as economic.

Within the framework of the United Nations, moral issues, if they are resolved at all, are resolved in political terms and in political forums. Although there has been little disposition to dispute the paramount importance of satisfying in reasonable measure the revolution of rising expectations, there have been serious differences between developed and underdeveloped countries about the nature and extent of their respective obligations. Debates at the technical levels have been repeated, with added emotion, at the political levels. Appeals have been carried successively from subcommissions to commissions, to the Economic and Social Council itself, and finally to the General Assembly. The United Nations has become a major battleground in what has been described elsewhere as a "curious war in which everyone professes to be on the same side, marching under the same banner, toward the same goal."[107]

[107] Isador Lubin and Robert E. Asher, "The Struggle for a Better Life," Chap. IV of *The U.S. Stake in the U.N.*, The American Assembly (1954), p. 74.

In relation to the immensity of the problem of satisfying in adequate measure the revolution of rising expectations, the contribution of the United Nations must be regarded as modest. Broadly speaking, it falls into four main categories: the provision of technical assistance through both the United Nations and the specialized agencies; the extension of loans through the International Bank; the exploration of proposals for internationally administered grant aid and other devices for enlarging the flow of capital to underdeveloped countries; and the development of a better understanding of the process of economic growth.

The Expanded Programme of Technical Assistance has become the best known, most far-reaching, and—in some ways—most flexible instrument for helping to solve a major problem of countries in the earliest stages of development. Although an organized exchange of information can bring about significant improvements in economic and social well-being, without an accompanying flow of capital, it remains a limited approach. Given a firmer financial foundation and concentrated more heavily on community development and similar forms of social engineering, however, the technical assistance program of the United Nations could become even more effective than it has been.

Although the total volume of loans from the International Bank to underdeveloped countries—about $1.6 billion through December 31, 1956—remains well below the expectations of those countries, even the severest critics of the Bank agree that its loans have been generally well conceived and have made a distinct contribution to the economic development of the borrowing nations. In addition to loan assistance, primarily for the completion of basic power and transportation facilities, the Bank has made its influence felt in other ways, most notably in the creation of a better climate for private investment. It might be said, in fact, that the International Bank has made a place for itself as much for the principles it has espoused and the approaches it has explored as for the capital it has provided. In this connection, the reports of the survey missions of the Bank to underdeveloped countries occupy an important niche, both as contributions to investment planning in the areas in question, and to the general body of literature on economic development.

The contribution of the United Nations as a whole to economic analysis and to a better understanding of the process of development is impossible to assess with any degree of precision. It seems clear that the many reports published by the United Nations on problems and aspects of economic development have exercised a considerable intellectual influence. Studies prepared outside the framework of the United Nations but influenced by earlier publications of the United Nations, have in turn influenced later United Nations studies, which have steadily become more penetrating and more sophisticated. These maturer views are beginning to be reflected in decisions of policy makers in underdeveloped countries.

The drive of the underdeveloped countries to establish a United Nations fund from which they can obtain financing for schools, hospitals, highways, port facilities, and other non-self-liquidating undertakings continues strong. Partly to divert this drive and partly for other more fundamental reasons, the United States and the developed countries have stressed social and institutional barriers that hinder progress in underdeveloped countries and that can be reduced without injections of foreign capital. The result of this tug of war has been to bring into the international arena a host of problems once considered matters of exclusively domestic concern and to raise a number of searching questions about priorities for action, but not to still the demands for capital and equipment. For the last few years, the question has no longer been whether a capital fund would be set up within the framework of the United Nations, but when.

The test of the merits of proposals such as that for a Special United Nations Fund for Economic Development is in any event not the warmth of the initial official reactions of governments. The test is more likely to lie in the reception first by expert circles and later by segments of the general public. New ideas, especially if they involve expenditures of money, are bound to encounter resistance from those who would have to put up the funds. But if the ideas are good, they tend to survive the official frowns and gain ultimate acceptance.

Had there been no United Nations, the formation of a political bloc of underdeveloped countries might have been deferred. *Ad hoc* solutions for the problems of a few especially restive lands might have been negotiated—or imposed by force. The simmering sickness of other, seemingly more quiescent, lands might have been neglected for the time being. Without the United Nations, it is probable that the emphasis given to the special difficulties of the underdeveloped countries would have been less universal, the analysis less searching and objective, and the incentives to action less compelling. But the problems would nevertheless have worked their way to the center of the world stage, for their solution is by almost any standard the major economic and social challenge of the day.

CHAPTER XI

Summary and Appraisal*

T HE CHARTER of the United Nations emphasizes the responsibilities of the Organization for fostering economic and social progress, encouraging respect for human rights, and advancing the welfare of dependent peoples. To help realize these objectives, a broad range of activities has been undertaken since 1946 within the framework of the United Nations system. As the scope of activities to promote the general welfare has broadened, their structure has become more complex.

The scope has been enlarged primarily in response to new and insistent pressures connected with the emergence of 600 million people from colonial status, the addition of a score of nations to the international conference tables, the revolution of rising expectations that is sweeping across the underdeveloped areas, the determination of all nations to avoid depression and mass unemployment, and the inability of many nation states—despite the persistence of nationalism and xenophobia—to discharge effectively the functions they must perform to survive as sovereign entities. Expanded by these pressures, the efforts of the United Nations to promote the general welfare have been curtailed by continuous conflict over the extent to which international restraints on national freedom of action should be accepted, and by the wide gulf that has separated the Communist-controlled world from the free world. Within the free world, there have been stubborn differences concerning the priorities to be assigned to various goals, the methods to be employed in attaining them, and the pace best suited to a long forward march.

The structure of the activities has become complex not only because the problems themselves are complicated, but also because different methods are required to solve them; because different countries are interested in their solution; and because nations find it politically possible, technically desirable, or economically advantageous to co-operate in more thorough-going fashion in some fields than in others. Moreover,

* By Robert E. Asher. The contents of this chapter have been derived from preceding chapters of this monograph and from Part One of the forthcoming volume in this Brookings series, *The United Nations and Promotion of the General Welfare.*

some of the international machinery in the United Nations system antedates the United Nations and could be brought into the system only in
the form of autonomous units that do not mesh well together.

Appraisals of the manifold activities undertaken to date could be
made from many points of view. This appraisal is intended to review
the direction that the work has taken, to evaluate certain procedures
and methods, to note some of the areas in which international co-operation through the United Nations system has been fruitful, and to call
attention to the major limitations encountered. Finally, it is intended to
ascertain whether the organizational framework has facilitated the work
and, if it has not, whether changes in constitutional and organizational
arrangements are needed.

Perspective

The economic and social work of the United Nations is an operation
in depth. It touches the daily lives of millions of people and carries
employees of the United Nations and the specialized agencies, in their
regular lines of duty, to the most isolated communities. Whatever the
founders of the specialized agencies may have envisaged, it is indeed
questionable whether the founders of the United Nations foresaw such
a comprehensive operation.

The Charter authorized the Economic and Social Council to establish
commissions in economic and social fields and for the promotion of
human rights, but from the legislative history of the Charter, it would
seem that its drafters were thinking in terms of functional rather than of
regional commissions. Nor does it appear that extensive operations at
the country level were foreseen, although the Economic and Social
Council was authorized by the Charter to perform services at the request of governments. Nevertheless, before five years had elapsed, not
only eight functional commissions but also three regional economic
commissions were in active status. In addition, a series of operating programs involving the feeding of children, the provision of technical assistance, and the rendering of emergency aid to the needy were being
carried on as separately financed services of the United Nations.

The major techniques to be followed by the Economic and Social
Council in order to promote the objectives stated in Article 55 of the
Charter—higher standards of living, full employment, and conditions
of economic and social progress and development—were (1) fact-finding
and the preparing of recommendations to the General Assembly and to

Member governments, and (2) influencing the work of the specialized agencies. In line with the former, the Economic and Social Council was authorized to make studies and reports; to call conferences and prepare draft conventions; and to make recommendations on international economic, social, cultural, educational, health, and related problems. In line with the latter, the Council was authorized to negotiate agreements bringing existing specialized intergovernmental agencies into relationship with the United Nations; to initiate negotiations leading to the creation of additional specialized agencies; and to co-ordinate the activities of specialized agencies through consultation and recommendation. Thus both specialization and co-ordination were provided for in the Charter, but how far each should be pressed, and how the function of harmonizing conflicting national viewpoints should be divided between the United Nations proper and the specialized agencies was left to the test of experience.

Although the specialized agencies are vital parts of the United Nations system, each has its own constitution, budget, membership, secretariat, and headquarters office. Changes in the United Nations Charter unaccompanied by parallel changes in the constitutions of the specialized agencies would not modify the constitutional responsibilities of those agencies.

Eight of the existing ten specialized agencies were established before the United Nations Charter entered into force.[1] Two specialized agencies—the World Health Organization (WHO) and the United Nations Educational, Scientific, and Cultural Organization (UNESCO)—although projected by governments before the Charter entered into force, were in a true sense created by the United Nations to carry on and expand forms of co-operation on which pioneer work had been done during the interwar period. A projected International Trade Organization was stillborn although many of its proposed provisions on commercial policy were incorporated in the General Agreement on Tariffs and Trade (GATT). An Intergovernmental Maritime Consultative Organization will come into being if the underlying convention is ratified

---

[1] This total includes the World Meteorological Organization (WMO), which in 1950 inherited the functions of the long-established International Meteorological Organization, and which entered into agreement with the United Nations in 1951. The other seven agencies in existence before the Charter of the United Nations entered into force are: the International Telecommunication Union (ITU), the Universal Postal Union (UPU), the International Labour Organisation (ILO), the Food and Agriculture Organization (FAO), the International Bank for Reconstruction and Development (IBRD or the Bank), the International Monetary Fund (IMF or the Fund), and the Provisional International Civil Aviation Organization (which ceased being provisional in 1947 and became ICAO).

by four more states, at least one of which has a merchant marine of one million tons or more. The statute for an International Atomic Energy Agency, approved at a major international conference in October 1956, will enter into force on ratification by eighteen nations including at least three from among the following five: Canada, France, the Soviet Union, the United Kingdom, and the United States.

The broad economic and social objectives of the United Nations system are at the same time the objectives of most national governments. The United Nations supplements national action; it recommends, stimulates, facilitates, and co-ordinates. Moreover, it has no monopoly on international action; numerous multilateral programs operate outside the framework of the United Nations. In addition, the programs of the United Nations have been paralleled and, in some cases, dwarfed by bilateral programs, most notably those of the United States Government.

The impressive improvement that has occurred since 1946 in the economic and social health of the world—spectacular in the case of Europe, and substantial in Latin America, but meager in much of Asia —is thus attributable only to a limited degree to the efforts of the United Nations system. Despite the continuance of trends toward the fragmentation and disintegration of the self-balancing world economy of the nineteenth century, industrial and agricultural output during the postwar period, both in total and on a per-capita basis, have increased significantly. International trade has expanded markedly in volume as well as value. Gold and dollar reserves in the possession of countries other than the United States are more nearly adequate. Employment levels in the industrialized nations have remained high. Social services almost everywhere have been improved, literacy is on the increase, and mortality rates are down. The dazzling possibilities of harnessing the atom for peaceful purposes are being revealed. Hope is replacing despair in a number of the underdeveloped countries.

As a pulse-taker of the universe, the United Nations has recorded and analyzed its ups and downs. In addition, it has proffered advice, comment, and some material assistance. Its direct contribution to the promotion of the general welfare, however, cannot be isolated from national and from other international efforts.

Methods and Processes

In recommending policies and selecting methods of work in the economic and social field, the Members of the United Nations were confronted with a situation of almost infinite complexity. They had in the first place to provide the specialization necessary for effective action. Second, they had to consolidate the specialized components into an over-all effort to achieve common objectives and as a result, to embark on an almost constant search for means of achieving co-ordination. Third, they had to harmonize as far as possible national viewpoints within each of the specialized fields in such a way that they would contribute to the pursuit of the over-all objectives. The new organization therefore had to analyze economic and social problems and their interrelationships, to increase mutual understanding of national aims and aspirations, and to promote forms of political accommodation that would make it possible to deal with some acutely controversial issues.

This formidable task was begun at a time when the true dimensions of the postwar reconstruction problem had not yet been disclosed. The time and resources needed to solve this problem were generally underestimated. The extent to which the fledgling United Nations system would be called upon to wrestle with emergency problems for which it was not prepared was likewise unforeseen. This led to unexpected difficulties in harmonizing national attitudes toward some forms of longrange co-operation, because countries preoccupied with urgent shortrun problems would not, and often could not, commit themselves in advance to follow policies that were desirable and appropriate in normal times. This might not have been a major obstacle to the advancement of the objectives of the Charter if there had been a sufficient measure of international agreement on what was desirable and appropriate in the long run. Unfortunately, despite the compromises reached at the Hot Springs, Bretton Woods, Chicago, and San Francisco conferences, and during the commercial policy discussions under Article VII of the Anglo-American Mutual Aid Agreement, the Members of the United Nations remained divided on many important economic and social issues. Meanwhile, the drive of the underdeveloped countries for a new status as peoples and nations was gathering force with a speed that was unappreciated.

Evolution of Priority Programs

Within the United Nations system, the Economic and Social Council and the General Assembly, as the principal general policy-making bodies, were confronted first with the task of selecting, from the vast array of problems that were of concern to Member governments, those that were most significant and most suitable for consideration by a world organization. They had to establish some system of priorities. An attempt was made to do this in a formal way by the General Assembly in 1947, but the problem was not then susceptible to such treatment and has not yet become so. Gradually, a greater consensus has been reached regarding major problems in each functional area of work and in each geographic region. So-called priority lists have been adopted periodically as guides to a more effective concentration of effort and resources. To satisfy the varied and varying interests of three or four score countries, however, it has been necessary to couch these lists in such general terms as to limit their usefulness in specific situations. Working priorities were nevertheless established, partly in response to the pressure of events, and partly in response to the new forces stirring in the world, which were making full employment, economic stability, and economic development primary objectives of economic and social policy.

These working priorities were also influenced by the fact that some of the most urgent problems of the industrialized countries requiring international collaboration were, from 1948 on, tackled entirely outside the United Nations system. For this and other reasons, the industrialized countries—although they shared the common aspiration for full employment and economic stability—did not turn to the United Nations as a source of help and guidance to nearly the same extent as did the underdeveloped countries. There is evidence in the record, however, to show that the increasingly one-sided emphasis on the demands and interests of a numerically strong group of Member governments, those of the economically underdeveloped countries, was sometimes carried to extremes.

During the early years, the emphasis was overwhelmingly on reconstruction. The international community, operating largely with resources obtained from the United States, undertook to help materially in the repair of damage and the restoration of essential services in war-devastated areas. Geographically, Europe was the chief beneficiary. Between 1945 and 1947, the United Nations Relief and Rehabilitation Administration (UNRRA)—which, despite its name, was never formally brought within the United Nations framework as a specialized agency—devoted the major portion of its sizable resources to relief work in Europe. Anticipating the termination of UNRRA, the General Assembly in 1946 established two agencies, the United Nations International Children's Emergency Fund (UNICEF, or the Children's Fund) to continue certain services for needy children, and the International Refugee Organization (IRO) to carry on a program of care, repatriation, and resettlement of refugees. During its initial years, the Children's Fund functioned primarily as an aid program for Europe. The IRO, during its limited lifetime, performed a similar role although it incidentally enriched a number of non-European nations by providing them with settlers whose education, training, and skills had been acquired in Europe.

In 1947, the Bank made four important reconstruction loans to European nations. The Fund, although not intended to provide facilities for relief and reconstruction, did in fact do so by some important sales of dollar exchange to its European members. The magnitude of the reconstruction job, however, proved far beyond the resources of the United Nations system. After the Soviet Union, in 1947, rejected the Anglo-French invitation to join in working out a new European Recovery Program, European reconstruction went forward, with Marshall Plan aid, almost entirely outside the framework of the United Nations.

The incipient vacuum in the United Nations was quickly filled by the special problems of the underdeveloped countries. Their problems, although perhaps subordinated, had by no means been ignored during the early postwar years. The ILO had become concerned with labor standards and social security provisions in underdeveloped countries during the interwar period, and this concern was intensified after the Second World War. The world-wide food shortage that characterized the years 1945 to 1948 caused the FAO relatively early in its life to broaden its span of attention and to encompass in its activities numerous services to underdeveloped countries. With the inauguration of the Expanded Programme of Technical Assistance in 1950, the special problems of the underdeveloped countries became, so to speak, the stock in trade of United Nations economic and social programs.

The rising tide of concern with the problems of underdeveloped countries has not only submerged the problems of Europe and concentrated attention instead on those of Asia, Latin America, and—to a lesser extent—Africa, it has also involved changes in the scale, scope, and nature of the activities undertaken. Assistance in the form of expert advice and training facilities has become a major method of operation, although the mobilization of pressures for a larger measure of direct financial assistance has remained the chief preoccupation of the underdeveloped countries during economic debates since 1951 in the General Assembly and the Economic and Social Council. Deeply rooted social and institutional barriers to more rapid development have been explored and assistance in understanding and overcoming them has been given.

Interpretation of Domestic
Jurisdiction

In the process described above, many of the traditional distinctions between matters of international concern and matters essentially domestic have been obliterated. The pressing problems of the underdeveloped countries have been elevated to the international level, not because of their direct effect on the movement of goods, funds, people, and messages across international boundaries, but because the problems in question are common to a large number of countries, because those countries individually and collectively lack sufficient resources to solve them, and because failure to solve them—or at least to make perceptible progress in the direction of solutions—is widely believed to threaten the peace and security of the world as a whole. That the United Nations has helped to bring the problems of the underdeveloped countries to the forefront and has become concerned with the reduction of domestic as well as international obstacles to more rapid progress may be viewed by some as a perversion of its purposes, but has been regarded by an overwhelming majority as an indication of the responsiveness of the machinery to political and economic realities.

Legal interpretations of authority have not been sought. Article 2(7) of the Charter, prohibiting intervention by the United Nations in matters essentially within the jurisdiction of Member states, has almost never been invoked in economic and social discussions, although it has played a role in the discussions of human rights and problems of dependent areas. Instead, the limits of fruitful international co-operation are being discovered by experiment. The underdeveloped countries, eager to enlist the co-operation of the international community in solving their problems and sensitive to their unfavorable position in bilateral dealings, have tended to regard the United Nations system as a kind of protection and projection of their sovereignty. The industrialized countries have more often viewed the system as a potential restriction on their freedom of action, but they, too, have been willing for the area of international co-operation to be determined pragmatically, by probing the limits of mutual consent and common interest.

Discussion and Debate

Discovering the limits of mutual consent has required a vast amount of discussion. The multiplicity of forums available for the consideration of economic and social issues results in endless repetition of arguments copiously developed at earlier sessions of any one of the forums in question. At the same time, however, it sometimes provides a welcome opportunity for shunting around proposals while governments slowly make up their minds what to do about them. Discussions at working committee levels have been repeated at functional and regional commissions, redebated in the Economic and the Social Committees of the Economic and Social Council, and aired again in plenary meetings of the Council.

Council debates are frequently reconducted in the more political atmosphere of the General Assembly. The fifty or more nations not represented on the Council have been unwilling to accept as final recommendations that they regard as unsatisfactory in fields in which they are deeply interested. Afghanistan, Saudi Arabia, and Uruguay are not satisfied to the point of silence because, for a given three-year period, India, Egypt, or Venezuela happens to be serving on the Council. Even countries that are members of the Council may feel that their views will be received more sympathetically and will in any event be better publicized if repeated in the Assembly where the underdeveloped countries, if they vote together, command an impressive majority.

Some of the major economic and social issues of the day have heavy political overtones in the sense of involving important national interests: for example, the provision of efficient, low-cost air transport service between nations, or the exploitation of petroleum reserves and other natural resources. Some problems are posed as moral issues. What is the responsibility of the international community as a whole, or—more specifically—the inhabitants of the wealthier nations, for the welfare of fellow men in remote, poorer nations? Do refugees unable to find employment in the countries of refuge and unwilling to return to their homelands deserve help from the international community? If so, should the countries from which the refugees have come be expected to contribute to their maintenance? Should an international convention on forced labor deal only with its use in the production of goods entering into international trade, or should such a convention outlaw forced labor completely on the ground that it is wrong and reprehensible?

Within the framework of the United Nations, moral as well as political issues are resolved in political forums—if indeed they are resolved at all. It was, therefore, almost inevitable that the central position of the General Assembly would be underscored by the trend of events in economic and social affairs, just as it has been in peace and security affairs. Initially, there may have been ambiguity between Article 7(1) of the Charter bracketing the Economic and Social Council and the General

Assembly as "principal organs" of the United Nations and Article 60 placing the Council "under the authority of the General Assembly." If so, the ambiguity has by now been resolved in favor of Article 60. Continued reliance on the Assembly for broad policy guidance is essential, and the more fundamental the issues tackled by the Economic and Social Council the greater the involvement of the General Assembly will be. In a number of cases, however, the Assembly has gone well beyond the provision of policy guidance and substituted—as it can if it so desires—its own judgment on technical issues for the judgment of the Council.

Frequent repetition of debates has not improved their quality. The decline in the number of outstanding speeches, however, has probably been matched by a corresponding decline in the number of irresponsible speeches as all rely more and more for their basic facts on the same set of notes: namely, the documentation prepared and circulated by the secretariats. Speeches continue to be made for the press and for the record rather than for the purpose of influencing delegates whose freedom of action is in any event severely circumscribed by the instructions they carry from their governments.

The trend toward instructed, official, government representation in lieu of representation by experts serving in their individual capacities has facilitated the efforts of each government to assume mutually consistent positions in the different agencies of the United Nations system in which it participates. In the United Nations proper, two "expert" subsidiaries of the Economic and Social Council, the Subcommission on Economic Development and the Subcommission on Employment and Economic Stability, were abolished in 1950. As early as 1947, the constitution of the FAO was amended to eliminate a clause that stipulated that the members of the Executive Committee should exercise the powers delegated to them by the FAO Conference on behalf of the whole conference and not as representatives of their respective governments. In 1954, a similar amendment to the constitution of UNESCO changed its Executive Board into a body of government representatives.

When functional representation continues to be a feature—*i.e.*, in the ILO, which provides for representation from labor and management as well as from government in policy-making—the participation of totalitarian states has presented a knotty problem. Can the employee and management representatives of such states speak with the independence of employee and management representatives in democratic societies? Because the answer is "no," the probable effect in the free world will be to cast further doubt on the practicality of anything but government representation in intergovernmental policy-forming or administrative organs.

In these tumultuous times, however, high-level government representatives cannot be away from their desks for very many days at a stretch. Within the United Nations system, top-level government representatives still find it possible and useful to attend the annual meetings of the Bank and Fund, which are simultaneous, last less than a week, and are largely ceremonial in character. Outside the United Nations system, they attend the frequent meetings of the Council of the Organization for European Economic Cooperation as well as the more infrequent sessions of the Organization of American States and the Consultative Committee on Economic Development in South and Southeast Asia (the Colombo Plan).

Ministerial-level representation either at the Economic and Social Council or at the Second (Economic and Financial) and Third (Social, Humanitarian and Cultural) Committees of the General Assembly, for at least part of the time, is highly desirable both for prestige reasons and in order that recommendations to governments may be adopted more readily by governments. It should be possible to rearrange the agendas of these organs so that the most important business is concentrated in the first or last week of a session and is such as to justify the attendance of higher-ranking officials of Member governments than is now the case. Major issues will not be settled within the United Nations framework if the people best qualified to settle them do not attend meetings, and such people will not attend except for discussions of major issues.

Multilateral discussions uncover problems and help reveal areas of agreement and disagreement regarding their handling. Whether or not remedial action is taken, this is part of the process of establishing an international community, an aspect of the development of common values and standards. Governments participating for the first time in a sector of the economic and social work of the United Nations are usually surprised at the extent to which they have until then been isolated from what suddenly appears to be a mainstream of international thinking— how much "history" they have to catch up with.[2]

[2] Although the Organization for European Economic Cooperation is the only international agency specifically mentioned in the following quotation, the comment made is equally applicable to participation in the United Nations system: "The Spanish economy . . . is a living and irrefutable answer to the common criticism that committees, councils, international secretariats, studies and reports are a

International discussion forces governments, or at least some of the officials of governments, to look at issues from the point of view of other nations as well as from the viewpoint of their fellow nationals. No government wants to be charged publicly with being unsympathetic to the problems of others or, worse still, of pursuing policies that aggravate those problems. "If the experience of defending bad and unneighbourly policies before an alert and militantly inquisitive conference were made sufficiently painful to national spokesmen, some at least of their embarrassment would be transferred to their home ministries."[3] Not infrequently international discussion suggests ways in which potentially injurious actions by national governments can be taken without injuring others and without sacrificing the basic economic or social objective of the nation instigating the action.

Reports and Statistics

The vast documentation prepared by the Secretariat and *ad hoc* committees of experts provides a common take-off point for United Nations discussion. This documentation is somewhat more extensive than it would be were it not for the bad habit (not unknown to national governments) of ending inconclusive debates by requiring further studies. The Council and the General Assembly also have developed a habit of tacking on to almost any resolution calling for a study a requirement that the interests of underdeveloped countries should be given special consideration. Despite this distortion of the international perspective, the provision of basic information on world economic and social conditions has been one of the outstanding services of the United Nations system, particularly helpful to the governments that lack the resources and facilities for independent investigation of matters of interest to them.

waste of time. The contrast with Italy, also a poor backward Mediterranean country that was flat on its back in 1945, is striking.

"Two examples among many are economic statistics and the application of modern production methods in industry. Had Spain been a member of the Organization for European Economic Cooperation for five years, national pride, if nothing else, would have fostered and produced reliable and reasonably comparable statistics about such basic economic factors as national product, the balance of payments, cost of living and so forth. . . . Greece and Italy now do it. Seven years ago their statistics were certainly no better than Spain's.

". . . The exchange of technical information and above all of technical personnel among industries is regarded by many European business men as the most important single legacy of the Marshall Plan." Michael L. Hoffman, "Spain's Isolated Economy," *New York Times* (Sept. 30, 1955).

[3] "Baffled by Food Surpluses," *The Economist* (Jan. 2, 1954), p. 31.

Moreover, the fact that the United Nations reports are for the most part scheduled for consideration at an early meeting compels governments to scrutinize them promptly, while equally informative reports, prepared at home, may remain for months on the desks of busy officials before being transferred, unread, to their bookshelves.

The services of the United Nations system in compiling statistics—particularly in the fields of international trade, finance, and population—the annual summaries by specialized agencies of major developments in their respective fields, and the numerous compilations of laws and technical data, are generally conceded to be very valuable. The analytical reports vary more widely in quality and in impact. Reports on the world economic situation and on the world agricultural outlook are important for the education and orientation of the international community, but they are less likely to stimulate concrete action by Member governments than more searching analyses of narrower problems such as the obstacles to private foreign investment in specific areas, the methods of utilizing low-grade coal resources, the long-term outlook for pulp and paper, or the problems and processes of industrialization in underdeveloped countries.

The pioneering *Report on the World Social Situation* and the penetrating regional economic surveys of Europe, Latin America, and Asia, prepared by the Secretariat of the United Nations; the high professional level of the articles published in the *Staff Papers* of the International Monetary Fund; the annual analyses of developments in international trade prepared for the Contracting Parties to the General Agreement on Tariffs and Trade: the country reports by missions of the International Bank; certain teaching materials developed by UNESCO; reports from WHO on nutrition in different regions of the world; a provocative series of economic reports by *ad hoc* groups of experts appointed by the Secretary-General of the United Nations—these and many other reports have been hailed repeatedly by delegates and experts for the contributions they have made to the understanding of complex problems.

While generally deserving of high marks, the economic reports of the United Nations have also been criticized for certain shortcomings, more frequently by American economists than by those of nations in which government is expected to play a more positive role in economic affairs.[4] Although a measure of governmental intervention in the eco-

---

[4] See, for example, Raymond F. Mikesell, "Economic Doctrines Reflected in United Nations Reports," *American Economic Review*, Vol. XLIV (May 1954), pp. 570–71.

nomic process appears to be necessary in order for the economy to function at a rate that is politically tolerable, there has perhaps been a tendency in the literature of the United Nations to shy away from suggesting traditional methods of adjustment through the operation of the price system. In particular, there has been a tendency, at least until recently, to attribute the "dollar shortage" to causes almost entirely outside the control of countries in balance-of-payments difficulties, and to place disproportionate responsibility for its elimination on the United States. The rediscovery of the role of monetary policy and its relation to the balance of payments owes little to the analysis of international economic problems provided by the United Nations proper (*i.e.*, excluding the analyses of specialized agencies such as the Fund and the Bank).

Resolutions

Just as the take-off point for United Nations discussion of a problem is usually a report, the immediate end-product is a resolution. In order to evaluate, in the most general terms, the contributions made by formal resolutions to the promotion of the economic and social objectives of the Charter, it is necessary to slash through a jungle in which even the largest trees are surrounded by a thick growth of underbrush. In embarking on this task, it is helpful to distinguish between two types of resolutions: those designed to expand the structure of the United Nations system—chiefly through the creation of new agencies and organs—and those designed to transmit general policy guidance to Member governments.

Three major questions may be asked in evaluating the series of important resolutions responsible for the growth of the system itself to its present proportions. Did they expand the scope of United Nations activities in such a way as to promote the objectives of the Charter? Did the Council and the Assembly, before passing these resolutions, succeed in getting sufficient agreement on controversial issues to permit the proposed work to be carried out effectively? Did the Council and the Assembly, in passing these resolutions, arrive at a satisfactory solution of the dual problem of permitting both the specialization and the co-ordination needed for effective action?

An affirmative answer can be given to all three questions in the case of most resolutions of the type that extended United Nations activities on emergency problems, in the field of social welfare, and in the provision of technical assistance for economic development. The distribution of the health and social welfare activities of the League and of

UNRRA between WHO and other agencies was not highly controversial. The extremely controversial issue of involuntary repatriation of
refugees was fought out in the negotiation of the constitution of the
IRO. The emergency work for women and children carried on by
UNICEF commanded general approval, and this enterprise was not
made permanent until there was a genuine consensus in the Assembly.
The United Nations Relief and Works Agency for Palestine Refugees
and the United Nations Korean Reconstruction Agency were established, also in response to such a consensus, to perform a manageable
range of functions in specific localities. The two major resolutions on
technical assistance did raise controversial issues, but these were much
more in the realm of finance and administration than they were in the
realm of objectives.

In the establishment of UNESCO, in contrast, the specialization for
effective action was not provided. An almost unlimited range of activities was authorized, and many of its troubles stem from this source. Nor
was adequate provision for specialization made in the case of the proposed International Trade Organization (ITO). The Economic and
Social Council was partly responsible for this inasmuch as it was unable
or unwilling to give firm advice to the Preparatory Committee of the
ITO regarding those employment and development functions that
should properly be assigned to a trade organization. The resultant
Havana Charter, replete with provisions concerning employment, investment, restrictive business practices, and intergovernmental commodity agreements, as well as commercial policy, covered an excessively
broad range of controversial functions and failed of ratification. Up to
the present time, therefore, the structure of the United Nations system
of specialized agencies remains incomplete because of the absence of an
agency in the field of trade that could deal with problems of commercial
policy, cartel policy, and commodity policy. Moreover, foreign exchange policy, which is intimately related to trade policy, remains the
province of an agency—the IMF—that has no responsibilities for trade
policy.

The decision to establish an Economic Commission for Europe was a
natural outgrowth of the work of the Temporary Subcommission on
the Reconstruction of Devastated Areas set up by the Economic and
Social Council. Once made, it was inevitable that Member governments in other parts of the world should feel that what was good for
Europe was good for them. Consequently, not only an Economic Commission for Asia and the Far East but also an Economic Commission

for Latin America was established, despite the fact that the Inter-American Economic and Social Council of the Organization of American States was already in the field. Had it not been for the Arab-Israeli conflict, a regional commission in the Middle East would also have been established. Back of the drive for these commissions was the view that there are some economic problems that can be handled better on a regional than on a world basis. The Council, however, offered little guidance on what these problems were, nor—despite some prodding from the United States—did it think through the larger implications of economic regionalism and possible conflicts between a regional approach to economic policy and the global approach to which the United Nations appeared committed, especially through the Fund, the Bank, and the proposed ITO.

Despite numerous disagreements on points of detail and, in the case of the regional commissions, of a certain lack of understanding of the full implications of the action taken, this series of resolutions reflected a broad consensus within the Council and the Assembly. Also it opened up wide areas in which the system as a whole could effectively contribute to the promotion of the general welfare.

This cannot yet be said of the series of resolutions intended to equip the United Nations system for making grants-in-aid to underdeveloped countries, for maintaining an international parity price scheme, or for establishing stand-by machinery to meet famines and natural disasters. The thinking that gave rise to the proposals was unacceptable to a strong and powerful minority of industrially advanced nations. As yet, there is no real consensus on the respective roles of public and private investment for development, on the use of grants as a normal feature of international economic relations, or on the form, if any, that international action to reduce fluctuations in the prices of internationally traded primary commodities should take. Yet even here, the record is somewhat mixed.

There has been a long series of resolutions putting pressure on the Fund and the Bank to enlarge their resources, change their established practices, and conform their policies to the views recommended to them by the Council and the Assembly. Opinions will differ whether these pressures have been entirely without effect. The establishment of the International Finance Corporation, which was the subject of a series of resolutions of the Council and the Assembly, is at least partially attributable to them. This has been due, however, not merely to majority votes in these organs but also to a gradual recognition, particularly on

the part of the United States, that the general interest could be promoted by such an institution. No such meeting of minds has yet occurred with respect to a proposed Special United Nations Fund for
Economic Development. Even here, however, national differences have
been softened. The principal, though not the only, opponent of an
agency to provide grants for economic development—the United
States—has been put on the defensive by the intensity and persistence
of the drive for such an agency. Opposition on grounds of principle has
been abandoned and the debate has shifted to when, how much, and
under what conditions.

The chief lesson to be drawn from these resolutions expanding or
seeking to expand the framework of the United Nations system is a
simple one—that a prerequisite for effective co-operation among sovereign governments is not a preponderance of votes but a meeting of
minds. This is not to say that the minds of the minority will be unin-
fluenced by the votes of the majority, but rather that until the conver-
sion is genuine the co-operation will be minimal. The service that international agencies render is to bring to the foreground and to highlight
problems before they assume explosive proportions, to give key countries some indication of the kinds of action desired, and then to ratify
and generalize what the key countries have already accepted as the most
appropriate solution to a pending problem. Occasionally, too, they
succeed in catching and preserving that golden moment when the key
governments themselves are willing to subscribe to a standard of behavior or a code of conduct that is not only better than any they were
previously willing to subscribe to, but more exacting than what they
would accept a few years later.

The resolutions looking toward the creation of new machinery are
far outnumbered by the long series of resolutions containing recommendations to governments. Many of these have been compromises and
makeshifts, battered about in debate, and laying down no firm policy.
This defect, plus a penchant for sonorous preambles to introduce
"operative" sections addressing a few pious platitudes to governments,
have weakened the effect of United Nations resolutions. Practical solutions of such complex problems as the relative weights to be assigned to
industrialization and agricultural expansion in development plans, or
how best to promote the free exchange of information among nations,
cannot reasonably be expected to flow from highly generalized compromise resolutions addressed to more than seventy governments. The
spotlight can be focused on a problem like land reform or barriers to

private investment. However, the ability of governments to prevent depressions is hardly strengthened by exhortations from the Council and the Assembly to maintain full employment.

The conclusion to be drawn is that resolutions, with some honorable exceptions such as the Universal Declaration of Human Rights, are comparatively unimportant as sources of policy guidance—less important than the published studies and extensive discussions that precede them, and much less important than the advice rendered on the spot by the experts and technicians from the United Nations who visit the different countries. In many cases, the debates, the studies, and the surveys by experts have led to second thoughts and more moderate opinions. To some extent, these have been reflected in the resolutions themselves.

Conventions and Legally-Binding Agreements

The drafting of international conventions and instruments that become legally binding on ratification by signatory states was originally conceived as a major function of the Economic and Social Council, but has not in fact proved to be one. Conventions continue to be considered appropriate where action by a single nation would be ineffective without corresponding or complementary action of a binding character by other nations. But acute doubts have arisen concerning the value of conventions designed to universalize standards that do not depend on multilateral acceptance in order to be meaningful within particular areas. Thus, for purposes such as controlling the traffic in narcotic drugs, obtaining uniform safety regulations on the high seas and in the airways, and extending copyright protection internationally, a multilateral convention may be an appropriate method of securing adherence to necessary standards. On the other hand, uniform social security provisions among nations are not essential, and education is the chief value of conventions such as the Social Security Convention of 1952, which the ILO regards as the culmination of thirty years of study and discussion. Given the present range of differences among nations in standards of living, patterns of behavior, and social values, it is questionable whether the drafting of conventions is the most fruitful technique where uniformity among nations and reciprocity are not essential features.

Within the United Nations system, the greatest devotee of the convention technique has been the ILO, which by the end of 1955 had adopted and opened for signature 104 conventions covering different aspects of employment and working conditions. The record of ratifications and of implementation after ratification suggests that the technique has very definite limits. The result is that there has been a decided shift within the ILO from conventions to recommendations, technical assistance, and education at the grass roots.

Operational Functions

To the extent that operational functions in the economic and social field were foreseen at the San Francisco Conference, they were envisaged as functions of the specialized agencies rather than of the United Nations Organization. The creation of operating agencies within the United Nations Organization to provide technical assistance, emergency relief for the needy, and other forms of direct aid represents a departure from the original approach in favor of an organizational arrangement that permits more centralized policy control.

The establishment of operating agencies within the United Nations itself, however, has not limited participation in such agencies to the Members of the United Nations; it has not burdened the Economic and Social Council with administrative details, for these usually have been delegated to an executive director or a board; and it has given the United Nations flexibility to meet emergency situations. Had it been necessary, for example, to establish a specialized agency to deal with Korean reconstruction problems, protracted negotiations to draft and ratify a constitution would have been inevitable.

With the exception of the work of the Technical Assistance Administration, the operational responsibilities assumed by the United Nations proper have been undertaken initially as short-term assignments. Generally, the assumption of such functions has represented a humanitarian response to a situation of peculiar urgency or need. The response, however, has implied a more sustained interest on the part of contributors in the welfare of children than in that of adults. The Children's Fund has become permanent, but in relief and refugee work of the kind undertaken by the United Nations Relief and Works Agency and the United Nations Korean Reconstruction Agency, the sums needed and the time required for doing the job have repeatedly been underestimated. The system of voluntary annual contributions by which these agencies have been financed has prohibited necessary forward planning and fostered perpetual crisis within the agencies. It has been the most glaring weakness of the emergency programs, and budgetary procedures will sooner or later have to be modified to provide more stable financing for activities of this kind. A start has already been made in connection with the technical assistance program.

Although the primary difficulty has been to obtain total resources sufficient to complete the job, there has been a second difficulty, intimately related to the first. This has been to make the participation broad enough to be truly international. The proportion contributed by the United States has been decreasing in several of the programs, but even so, it continues to represent more than half of the total budget. Any international operation that depends on a single contributor, however rich that contributor may be, for the major part of its budget is likely to be international in name only. This may prove tolerable and even advantageous for a brief period, but it is almost certain to be unwholesome in the long run.

The transformation of the Children's Fund from an emergency operation to a permanent service raises the question whether what is essentially a long-range child health program should be carried on indefinitely as a function of the United Nations proper, while major responsibility for promoting international co-operation in the health field rests with a specialized agency, the World Health Organization. As good administration implies the grouping of closely related programs under unified direction, it would seem desirable, but not urgent, at some stage to consider a transfer of the Children's Fund to the World Health Organization. The sole objective, however, should be to provide for permanent, professional supervision and effective co-ordination with other health programs. The objective should not be to comply with any theoretical principle that the United Nations Organization must disengage itself from long-term operational functions. In the first place, the distinction between operational functions and functions not regarded as operational is frequently as unclear as the distinction between short term and long term. Even if the dividing line could be firmly drawn, the advantages of observing a hard-and-fast principle concerning the assumption of operational functions would probably be more than offset by loss of flexibility and reduced capacity to meet the ever-changing requirements of governments.

Relations with Specialized Agencies

The presence of a group of specialized agencies within the United Nations system raises at least two important questions: (1) which functions should most appropriately be assigned to the United Nations proper and which to specialized agencies; and (2) how to co-ordinate the activities of the constituent parts of the system. In so far as functions are concerned, there clearly are areas of economic and social co-operation that require a high degree of specialization and will continue to demand attention at international levels for long years to come. It would be a misfortune if each such area were not made the primary field of interest of a competent international agency enjoying a substantial degree of independence. In a world of problems as complex as those with which the United Nations system is trying to deal, there is much to be said for a system that provides generously for technical specialization, for freedom from central political control, and for opportunities to experiment. The urgent problems in the fields of health, education, exchange stabilization, aviation, and communications require different types of programs to meet them, different personnel, and different organizational approaches.

These differences cause understandable concern in some quarters. Administrative co-ordination in the sense of comparable salary scales, vacation privileges, budget practices, and central statistical services is being brought about by present machinery; but substantive co-ordination of policies and program priorities through the Economic and Social Council is still fairly nominal. The need for such substantive co-ordination, however, is to an important extent a function of the magnitude of the programs to be co-ordinated, and of the ability of governments to co-ordinate their own policies at the national level. Were the FAO and WHO each spending or supervising the expenditure of several billion dollars per year, co-ordination of substantive programs to maintain some parity between food supply and population would be much more important than when each is dispensing less than $11 million annually, spreading it thinly across several continents, and influencing only marginally the expenditures of national and local agencies.

At present levels of expenditure, problems of overlapping, jurisdictional disputes, and unclear lines of authority can be, and have been, met to a large extent by the unspectacular method of mutual accommodation, experimentation, and learning by experience. From the start, the specialized agencies have recognized, indeed in some cases have exaggerated, the interrelations of problems in their respective fields. The international meeting at which fraternal delegates from other international agencies almost outnumbered the official delegates from governments was a familiar spectacle in the early days of the United Nations. Knowledge of each other's activities has led to more fruitful forms of co-operation—the co-operation, for example, of teams of specialists, each member of which can bring to a co-operative endeavor the experience of a different agency.

The General Assembly is entitled and determined to give central political guidance to the economic and social work of the United Nations proper. An extension of this authority to the specialized agencies might eliminate such absurdities as the repeated consideration by health officers, economists, and educationists of motions to seat representatives of Communist China. The advantages of central political direction for the entire United Nations system at its present stage of development, however, appear to be more than offset by the loss of freedom to the constituent agencies.

The inauguration of the Expanded Programme of Technical Assistance provided an opportunity to integrate the programs of the agencies that comprise the United Nations system. This opportunity was seized only gingerly at first, but subsequent progress toward effective co-ordination has been steady, and there is no reason to believe that the process will be interrupted. The existence, however, of international programs of technical assistance outside the United Nations system (the United States Technical Cooperation Program and the Colombo Plan) has added to the complications arising from the existence of a number of autonomous specialized agencies.

The creation of additional specialized agencies obviously should not be undertaken lightly. Short-term services like the provision of emergency relief in the wake of local wars can be provided directly by the United Nations without the complications of establishing and disestablishing a specialized agency, but a relief undertaking of the magnitude of UNRRA would probably require the establishment of an independent agency. When sizable expenditures are involved, the price of participation by major donors is likely to be a greater voice than they have in the United Nations proper, in which each nation has an equal vote. The alternative at present is an independent agency such as the International Bank or the International Monetary Fund, where voting is weighted. Thus, the International Finance Corporation has been established as an affiliate of the Bank, and the odds are good that if a grant agency comes into being, it too will operate either as another affiliate of the Bank or under a charter that gives donors a controlling voice in policy formulation. It would seem in the general interest to keep the path open for the establishment and maintenance of agencies governed by weighted voting, or agencies such as the ILO in which important interest groups have a recognized voice. Insistence on greater control of specialized agencies by the United Nations will tend to seal off these possibilities.

The problem of UNESCO, whose field of specialization may initially have been too broadly and too vaguely defined, has already been mentioned. The remedy would seem to lie neither in closer supervision by the Economic and Social Council or the General Assembly, whose mandates are even broader and vaguer, nor in "co-ordination" with such unrelated activities as those of the Universal Postal Union and the International Civil Aviation Organization. It would seem to lie instead in continued reform from within, through delegates from governments determined to develop an effective work program.

Co-operation with Nongovernmental Organizations

Nongovernmental organizations (NGO's) have played a smaller role in the councils of the United Nations than they foresaw for themselves at the close of the San Francisco Conference. Despite the misgivings of some delegates about the desirability of including Article 71 in the Charter, the question was not extensively debated at San Francisco. In the lobbying of the NGO's, however, and in such discussion as occurred, a recurrent theme was that:

. . . NGO's with large international membership would bring to the deliberations of the UN a cross-section of world public opinion. A related hope was that on vital issues and by more or less direct means NGO's would represent constituencies of world-wide scope who were not fully vocal through member governments.

The implication of these hopes was that, in effect, Article 71 opened a new channel of communication between groups of private citizens and an intergovernmental organization. It raised possibilities of functional as well as geographical representation in the UN . . . [Nine years later] there is no noticeable impulse to extend consultative arrangements to give more scope to NGO's to present their members' views. The hopes at San Francisco that NGO's might ultimately become a kind of Second Estate of the UN have been largely quenched by the experience of the last nine years. Member states . . . have narrowed and not increased the scope of these arrangements since 1946.[5]

Nevertheless, the NGO's have had an impact on the emergency relief work of the United Nations in Korea and the Near East; they have participated constructively in the refugee and migration programs, par-

---

[5] Edwin A. Bock, *Representation of Nongovernmental Organizations at the United Nations* (1955), pp. 15-17.

ticularly in arranging for the reception and early care of immigrants; and they have been active in the technical work of organs and agencies in the transport and communications fields.

Role of Secretariats

In practice, the secretariats have become the chief repositories of *expertise*. As they have amassed information about problems, they have naturally accumulated views on how those problems should be solved, and have devised ways and means of gaining acceptance for their views. Recommendations are implicit in many of the reports prepared for delegates and Member governments, and there are increasing opportunities for top secretariat officials to participate directly in intergovernmental deliberations. Often, where progress is deadlocked for political reasons, the secretariat is able, on its own responsibility, to put forward acceptable compromise proposals that would be rejected as suspect if presented by participants to the controversy. In other cases (including some in which the purpose of the secretariat is self-aggrandizement as much as the solution of a political deadlock), the secretariat works through national delegations. Both among the sincere and conscientious delegates and among those looking for a painless passage to statesmanship, there are always some ready and willing to serve as stalking-horses for secretariat proposals.

The influence of the international civil servants is enhanced by the instability of government representation. Secretariats are permanent, but government representation rotates. If an organization is to function at all, there must be enough of a hard-core of participants to furnish tradition, a sense of shared accomplishments, and respect within national ministries for the views of the international community. Governments too often tend to make representation of their interests in a given international agency the private province of one or two officials comparatively isolated from the mainstream of government policy making, or to regard nomination to the delegation for an international conference as a sinecure that should be widely shared. Either view is unhealthy.

Although the initiative of secretariats in suggesting new approaches to problems in the economic and social fields, and their ability to issue reports without prior government clearance are resented in some quarters, circumstances appear to favor a further relative growth in secretariat influence. The decision in 1954, for example, to begin the annual discussion of the world economic situation in the Economic and Social

Council with statements from the Secretary-General and the executive secretaries of the regional economic commissions provides new opportunities for officers of the Secretariat to affect the approach to one of the major items on the agenda. The periodic visits to national capitals by officers of the United Nations Organization and of the specialized agencies give them a further chance to outline their ideas for new work, to discover common features of divergent national views, and to enlarge their knowledge vis-à-vis that of the delegates. To date, they have—on the whole—performed with objectivity and with a view to serving the interests of the international community as a whole. They can create mischief and may on occasion have done so. But there is little danger that secretariats will become too powerful. More likely, they will be kept too circumscribed to make the full contribution of which they are capable.

Generally speaking, whatever the constitutions say, the powers of the secretariat are never anything else than delegated and they are limited in time. In the final instance all the power belongs to the governments for the simple reason that the efforts of the secretariat cannot be directed toward anything else than the reaching of agreements between the governments, agreements which the governments can decline to make.[6]

Achievements and Frustrations

Constructive international co-operation requires a clear understanding of the problems to be attacked, a respect for the views of all countries that may be affected, and a down-to-earth appraisal of the obstacles to be overcome. It cannot be conjured into being by high-sounding phrases, unless these phrases really express widely-shared aspirations and unless promotion of the welfare of the world community is a positive element in prevailing concepts of national interest. It cannot be forced by majority vote.

The assumption that the economic and social objectives of the United Nations and its related agencies were in harmony with the concepts of national interest held by Member governments has now been tested by ten years of experience. The record shows that, except for the almost unbridgeable gulf that separates the Soviet bloc from the rest of the world, this assumption was valid.

The years of United Nations research, discussion, and negotiation

---

[6] Gunnar Myrdal, *Realities and Illusions in Regard to Inter-Governmental Organizations*, L. T. Hobhouse Memorial Trust Lecture No. 24 (1955), pp. 22–23.

have resulted in a large measure of agreement regarding which are the most urgent of the economic and social problems of the world. Unfortunately, the gap remains wide between recognition that something constitutes a problem and attainment of a consensus regarding the handling of that problem. The gap is smallest when the problem can be reduced to a technical issue, and greatest when the problem appears as a political or moral issue. There is a

> . . . clear inverse correlation between success in international co-operation and political importance. Indeed, the best method of reaching international agreement on an issue is most often to divest it so far as possible from political content by defining it closely and delimiting it narrowly, so that it becomes a question which has the appearance of being merely technical, and, in addition, to move it away from the public gaze.[7]

On technical issues the differences are likely to be differences of detail rather than principle. Political leaders are willing to defer to the experts, provided the experts can operate on a modest budget. The experts of the free world—if they are divided—tend to be divided along other than national lines. Within the United Nations, a number of matters that were initially political issues have become primarily technical matters, widely accepted as appropriate functions for the United Nations system; for example, the lending, but not the granting, of public funds for economic development, and the sponsorship of negotiations between Eastern and Western Europe for the promotion of trade in nonstrategic items. The more ingenious international secretariats have made conscious efforts to speed the evolution from political to technical. Thus, the maintenance of an independent secretariat, free to exercise a certain amount of initiative, is important. Greater opportunity for private sessions is likewise necessary. Open covenants secretly arrived at need not spell trouble. Public sessions tend to highlight divergent views, to lock negotiators into positions from which they cannot gracefully extricate themselves, and to put a premium on the scoring of debating points.

In the end, however, international agreement is possible only when governments and peoples decide that they have more to gain than to lose by co-operation. The area of potential co-operation therefore expands or contracts over time. It depends, too, on the kind of commitment involved and the extent to which action by national legislatures is required to implement it.

Commitments of funds are entered upon with understandable reluc-

[7] *Ibid.*, p. 18.

tance. Emergency assistance programs in a few specific areas or situations—such as Korea or Palestine refugees—in which the United Nations has assumed military or political responsibility, have been accepted as appropriate forms of United Nations activity. But the expenditure of large sums elsewhere has to date appeared to involve conflicting national interests that could not be ignored or reconciled. The establishment of an internationally administered fund to make grants-in-aid for economic development has been resisted and postponed, and the establishment of a similar revolving fund for the relief of future famines has been rejected. Proposals for preventing the international spread of depressions by stabilizing the flow of international trade, the level of international investment, or the prices of important internationally traded primary commodities likewise have proved unacceptable to the major creditor nation—the United States. In the only permanent organizations in the United Nations system endowed with substantial financial resources, the International Bank and the International Monetary Fund, the price of life has been continuous deference to the views of the United States.[8] Any other nation making a comparable subscription to the capital funds of these agencies, however, could command comparable deference to its views.

Binding commitments concerning behavior may also prove difficult to obtain. Treaties and formal agreements, even though not calling for any great expediture of funds, can involve knotty legal and administrative issues. In many cases, as already noted, action by one nation would be ineffective without corresponding or complementary action by other nations. This need for an agreed international framework has been the rationale for a series of international conventions in the economic and social field to limit or prohibit the passing across international frontiers of drugs, germs, locusts, slaves, obscene literature, or unsafe aircraft, ships, and motor vehicles. There are many other problems that lend themselves to solution within the framework of an international convention or agreement but remain unsolved because of sharp and stubborn clashes of interest. The assignment of radio frequencies is an example; unilateral action makes for mutual interference and confusion, but multilateral agreement has not been readily obtainable. In an era of widespread broadcasting for political ends, it is understandable that nations with competing political philosophies

[8] *Cf.* Raymond F. Mikesell, "Barriers to the Expansion of United Nations Economic Functions," *Annals of the American Academy of Political and Social Science*, Vol. 296 (November 1954), p. 45.

should be unable to agree on the division among them of a limited number of high frequencies. Finally, there have also been sharp differences of opinion regarding the need for conventions and covenants to generalize standards of behavior that do not need to be upheld by all civilized nations in order to be upheld by some.[9]

The major share of United Nations work in the economic and social field involves neither financial nor legal commitments, but at most a moral commitment. This is frequently expressed as an obligation to "take into account" the views expressed in debates, to make "every effort" to progress toward some stated objective, or to provide information "as appropriate" in response to requests.

Consultation, exchange of information and experience, and joint review of data provided by secretariats, by *ad hoc* experts, or by *rapporteurs* constitute the regular grist of the United Nations mill. The practice of convening periodically for serious consideration of common problems helps to establish standards, ethics, and patterns of performance that can be of the greatest importance for the future of democratic society. The larger the area in which suitable self-imposed standards of performance and behavior become prevalent—standards that have moral force—the smaller the area in which legal sanctions formally restraining individual liberty are likely to be required.

Opportunities offered by the United Nations system for the exchange of information among health officials, demographers, land reform experts, commodity specialists, housing administrators, statisticians, or fuel and power producers cost relatively little, often prove very beneficial, and are almost never harmful. Frequently, they accomplish more than the spread of know-how; real business is done in the corridors and hotel rooms, if not at the formal sessions, of timber, coal, steel, and electric power meetings. It is easy, however, for the convening of meetings and the issuance of conference papers to get out of hand. Little clubs whose members gain status at home because they attend international meetings, and are listened to at international meetings on the theory that they have status at home, continue to gather at public expense. Public funds get diverted to the support of what should be private professional or trade associations. Constant vigilance is therefore required to prevent the United Nations umbrella from being used to shelter a dubious array of gregarious, self-perpetuating societies.

[9] See the monograph in this Brookings series, *The United Nations and Human Rights*, especially pp. 37–68.

Economic Problems

In the ever-changing area that governments choose to consider within the scope of the United Nations system, what have been the major substantive problems dealt with to date, and with what degree of success?

In the economic field, the United Nations system as a whole has been attempting to deal with a long list of exceedingly complicated issues. Leading this list and cutting across many other issues, is the adoption of measures to speed the economic and social development of underdeveloped countries. In production and investment, the United Nations has been concerned with the revival and expansion of industrial and agricultural production in order to overcome the extreme dependence of most of the world on supplies from the dollar area during the immediate postwar period; with the restoration of an international capital market, the removal of obstacles to the international flow of private investment, and the determination of the functions and scale of operation of public international lending institutions. It has been concerned also with the desirability and feasibility of providing capital for development purposes by means of soft loans or grants.

In transportation and communications, the work of the United Nations system has been much less controversial. On the whole, it has been confined to the provision of well-recognized, long-range, technical services through genuinely specialized agencies and organs. In trade and payments, the United Nations has been concerned with the reestablishment of a functioning multilateral system of trade and payments; with the relation of commercial policy to employment and development policy; and with the potential conflicts between global and regional approaches to trade and payments problems. The obverse of the concern of the United Nations with the attainment and maintenance of high and stable levels of employment, trade, investment, and economic activity generally has been consideration of measures for the avoidance of depression and mass unemployment, the role of short-term credit in preventing the international spread of depressions, and the relation of commodity trade to economic stability.

This oversimplified summary of the major areas of United Nations economic interest provides a basis for some general conclusions.

The priority given to the whole subject of economic development has in itself been a constructive achievement because it has focused

world attention on newly liberated, latent forces of explosive potentialities. The fundamentals of the problem of development in its manifold
aspects have been exhaustively explored, although the whole process of
economic growth needs further study and understanding. The advocates
of massive investment in heavy industry as the key to development
in all cases and in all circumstances have become less numerous than
they used to be; the importance of investment in agriculture, education,
health, and public administration is more widely appreciated; balanced
growth has become the watchword. The attention of the General
Assembly, the Economic and Social Council, and other interested
organs and agencies has been directed increasingly to problems that are
both more concrete and more manageable than the elaboration of
general principles for the economic development of fifty countries in
markedly different stages of underdevelopment and with great variations in resources and potentialities.

The debates in the United Nations, the documentation provided for
them, and the work of the International Bank and the International
Monetary Fund have led to a much better understanding of the
conditions that must be present before the flow of private investment
can be greatly increased. Attempts to develop a multilateral code of
fair treatment for foreign investors have foundered, but mutually
satisfactory arrangements have in a number of instances been worked
out bilaterally. The net flow of private investment has not increased
significantly, but the climate for such investment has improved considerably, notwithstanding one or two well-publicized United Nations
resolutions that temporarily clouded the skies.

The International Bank has increasingly become a kind of publicly
managed investment fund whereby money raised in the private capital
markets of the United States, Canada, and Western Europe is invested for productive purposes in underdeveloped countries. The total
volume of its lending to underdeveloped countries through December
31, 1956—some $1.6 billion, at an average rate of interest of 4 to 5
per cent—has been modest. Governments of underdeveloped countries
have exerted unending pressure for loan capital on a more liberal scale
and on better terms than offered by the Bank, while the Bank has
stressed the lack of adequately planned, technically sound projects for
financing.

To appraise the Bank on the basis of the volume of its lending would
be an error. Its major contribution has been to re-establish the old-
fashioned notion that international finance is business; that a borrower

should be a good risk, that he should be capable of repaying the funds he borrows, and be of a mind to do so; that honest, competent management is essential in a business undertaking, and that similar standards are necessary in government. The International Bank, it may be said, has made a place for itself as much for the principles it has espoused and the approaches it has explored as for the capital it has provided.

The Expanded Programme of Technical Assistance has fired the imagination of millions, dramatized the improvements that can be made with comparatively insignificant expenditures of capital, and enabled the United Nations to help reduce social and institutional barriers to progress within the underdeveloped countries themselves. Among these barriers are lack of knowledge of potential resources; lack of technically trained man power; chronic underemployment; immobility of the labor force; antiquated, burdensome systems of land tenure; low rates of domestic capital formation and inadequate means for directing available capital into productive channels; poor transport and communications; and lack of educational and health facilities.

At first, technical assistance was concentrated rather heavily on the spread of technology in the narrow sense—knowledge concerning seeds, fertilizers, tractors, tube wells, or textile production. More recently, it has been devoted increasingly to so-called community development programs and other promising ways of generating a cumulative, self-sustaining expansion in keeping with the felt needs of the people in underdeveloped countries. At the same time, the crucial importance of improved public administration at all levels of government has received greater recognition.

Although the technical assistance program as a whole unquestionably represents one of the most successful undertakings of the United Nations, satisfactory criteria have not been devised for evaluating results project by project or country by country, or for determining the type of expert aid and training most suitable for provision by an international agency. The program, precariously financed and thinly spread, is at best a small-scale undertaking—the foreign funds involved have never exceeded $30 million per year. The payment of salaries and transportation for foreign experts is a minute fraction of the cost of a development program. After the value of this type of service has been demonstrated for another few years, it may not be unreasonable to ask countries desiring it to underwrite it themselves, perhaps using the United Nations as the employment agency that would unearth and nominate qualified technicians for participating governments to hire.

As the underdeveloped countries have seen it, their problems are insoluble without greater financial assistance from abroad, particularly for meeting the costs of non-self-liquidating projects such as schools, hospitals, and roads, which are nevertheless basic to development. The five-year-long campaign of the underdeveloped countries for the establishment of a United Nations fund to make grants-in-aid and loans at nominal rates of interest has to date been unsuccessful. An important by-product of the campaign, however, has been the establishment, as an affiliate of the International Bank, of an International Finance Corporation, equipped to invest risk capital in private enterprises in underdeveloped countries without the governmental guarantee required in connection with loans from the Bank. Although some of the draft proposals for a grant agency have given the preponderant voice in the setting of terms and conditions to recipients rather than donors, the alacrity with which Members of the United Nations accepted an International Finance Corporation in which policy control is weighted in the same fashion as in the International Bank indicates that egalitarian views will not be pushed to the point of checkmating practical action.

It is difficult in some ways to draw a clear line of distinction between discussions in the United Nations of economic development and of another international problem of prime importance—preventing the international spread of depressions—or, more generally, maintaining economic stability. Reducing sharp fluctuations in the prices of internationally traded primary commodities, for example, has been discussed on some occasions as a contribution to economic development and on other occasions as a contribution to economic stability. The unsolved problem of commodity price stabilization remains in the foreground of international discussion because unless practical solutions in the interest of industrialized and underdeveloped countries alike can be devised, an important cause of world economic instability in the past will continue to exist in the future. Intensive explorations of the means thus far adopted, available, or proposed have shown that no single area of international economic relations is more beset with technical, financial, and politico-economic difficulties.

The co-ordination of national full-employment policies for the purpose of maintaining international stability was one of the earliest objectives of the United Nations. The resolution adopted by the Economic and Social Council in 1950, after extensive discussion of the report of a group of experts on *National and International Measures for*

Full Employment put Member governments under obligation to provide information regarding their employment position and policies for review and comment by the Secretariat, by independent experts, and by the delegates of governments. The enthusiasm evoked by this rather mild resolution, which was regarded as having added real meaning to a key provision of the Charter, was one of the errors of optimism of the Council. The *co-ordination* of national employment policies has not become a feature of international life, although full employment and the elimination of unemployment continue to be almost universal objectives of national policy, as they would have been had there been no United Nations.

Although the problem has been discussed at length in the United Nations, there is as yet no agreement concerning contracyclical lending by creditor governments, and it would be rash to assume that, if a major depression gets under way, the United Nations will be more successful in checking its spread internationally than was the League of Nations. In this all-important matter, reliance must be placed on the antidepression measures that the governments of all economically important countries are now determined to take in their own interest, in response to new internal social and political forces, rather than in response to international agreements and recommendations.

The overwhelming importance attached to full employment and rapid economic development, and the subordination of commercial policy to these objectives by majorities in the Economic and Social Council and the General Assembly, have probably led these organs to underestimate both the dangers of inflation and the contribution that the reduction of trade barriers can make to the raising of standards of living. Substantial progress has been made through the GATT—which filled part of the gap left by the failure of ITO—in reducing trade barriers and obtaining observance of a code of trade rules, without sacrifice of employment and development objectives. The extension of the most-favored-nation treatment in international trade and the stabilization of tariff rates, objectives for which the League of Nations struggled in vain during the interwar period, have been realized to a large extent through the GATT.

Potential conflicts between regional and global approaches to trade and payments problems have been dealt with by the United Nations system as a whole and by the GATT with flexibility and moderation and without sacrifice of global objectives. There has been good co-operation between the Fund, the Bank, the FAO, and the regional economic commissions in the study of both intraregional and interregional trading problems. The regional commissions have engaged in active trade promotion, but the pattern of world trade has not been significantly affected by these efforts. Schemes for regional payments arrangements that might have strengthened existing tendencies to divide the world into regional groupings have been explored and rejected. The relationship between the Fund and the GATT on the one hand, and on the other, those regional organizations outside the United Nations—the European Payments Union and the European Coal and Steel Community—has been such that neither body has impeded constructive attacks on European problems, but both have continued to exert their influence against regional as opposed to world-wide solutions of international trade and payments problems.

There has been a running conflict between the United Nations Organization and the International Monetary Fund on the amount and use of the resources of the Fund. This has been due to differences on such fundamental questions as: the responsibilities of creditor countries for helping debtor countries to solve their balance-of-payments difficulties by providing, through the Fund or otherwise, the credits necessary to sustain the volume of their imports; the extent to which monetary and fiscal policy should be relied on to correct balance-of-payments difficulties of a cyclical character without undue recourse to international short-term credit; and whether the Fund has been too zealous in protecting its resources. The boldness of many members of the Economic and Social Council and some of its *ad hoc* experts has been matched by the caution of the Fund.

The approach of the United Nations system as a whole to these problems has been largely in the realm of ideas and, until quite recently, it remained to be seen whether the Fund would make the contribution to international liquidity of which it is potentially capable. That the Fund may now be prepared to play its full role is indicated by the announcements in late 1956 of arrangements authorizing France to purchase, with French francs, up to $262.5 million in foreign currencies and authorizing the United Kingdom to purchase, with sterling, up to $1.3 billion from the Fund.

Social Problems

It is difficult and probably unnecessary, for purposes of this analysis, to draw a clear line between the economic approach and the social approach to the attainment of conditions of stability and well-being, because there must be a large measure of fusion between the two approaches for either one to be fully effective.

A distinguishing feature of all social work, however, is its concern with the physical, mental, and emotional well-being of the individual citizen in his ever-changing environment. This focus makes for an infinite variety of programs and services. It has consequently been necessary for the United Nations to resist the temptation to embark on an unmanageable series of programs of insufficient impact and of questionable suitability for a large intergovernmental agency. This temptation, powerful in the atmosphere of good will that prevailed in the early postwar years, was aggravated by the pressures and enthusiasms of well-meaning special-interest groups and the unhappy political position in which critics of humanitarian undertakings are inevitably placed.

In addition to short-term relief services, a remarkable range of long-term social services has been provided. Just as some economic programs have been developed to promote higher levels of production, trade, and investment while other economic programs have had the negative purpose of preventing the spread of harmful practices or the occurrence of large-scale unemployment, so the social programs of the United Nations have had both positive and negative aspects. One broad group of social programs has had as its central purpose the promotion of higher levels of living for the individual members of the community. This range of work has involved the Social Commission of the United Nations, WHO, the FAO, the ILO, and other organs and agencies in both independent and concerted efforts to improve the health, nutrition, housing, employment arrangements, and working conditions of the inhabitants of Member states.

Another group of social programs has been oriented toward special categories such as mothers and dependent children, the physically handicapped, the migrants and refugees, and the delinquents and potential delinquents. This orientation often, but not always, has placed the emphasis on protection, defense, prevention, and remedial care. On the whole, both types of programs have been initiated and carried on without evoking serious controversy among Member governments, despite some inherent difficulties in determining the manner in which and the extent to which international machinery should be utilized for promoting social welfare.

If popularity may be used as an index of success, the Children's Fund probably has been the most successful single social program of the

United Nations. The underlying concept is simple, the humanitarian appeal is great, and the cost is low.

The care, movement, and protection of international refugees and migrants—at first appearance, an ideal field for intergovernmental co-operation—has been hampered and handicapped by political differences almost from the start. Despite persistent attacks by the Soviet bloc on its work, the International Refugee Organization was able to arrange for resettlement of the bulk of the refugees under its relatively narrow mandate. The Arab refugees from Palestine, on the other hand, have been kept alive by the United Nations but no noticeable progress toward their reintegration into society has been made or seems likely until there is greater mutual understanding among contending governments in the tense Middle East.

In the field of migration, much attention was given during the period 1946–50 to the allocation of functions among the organs and agencies that had a legitimate interest in facilitating international migration on an orderly basis. The substantial headway that was made in clarifying responsibilities turned out to be largely a labor of love. Because of American reluctance to give a voice in the process to any international agency in which Communist-controlled governments were participants, the United Nations system was never called on to play a major operational role in connection with migration. Outside the framework of the United Nations, assistance to European migrants has been provided by the Inter-Governmental Committee for European Migration.

In the field of education, science, and culture, the unlimited breadth of the constitution of UNESCO encouraged the initiation of an encyclopedic range of activities. The first result was an enthusiastic, disorderly "parade of hobby horses" ridden by scholars and educators, musicians and painters, librarians and museum experts. In the procession were some down-to-earth projects such as aiding the reconstruction of schools and libraries in devastated areas and encouraging scientific research on arid lands, but flanking them were many esoteric pursuits. There was, and still is, confusion over whether the primary efforts of UNESCO should be directed toward the promotion of co-operation among the intellectuals of the world or directed to grass-roots activities such as reducing illiteracy and promoting basic education. In reality the agency must do both, because the stimulation of international co-operation among intellectuals is needed in order to develop fresh ideas that can be introduced into mass education. The grass-roots approach, supported by the United States, has gained ground of late, and the effect has been to give increasing emphasis within UNESCO, as in other parts of the United Nations system, to work on behalf of underdeveloped countries.

In the social programs of the United Nations, a major long-range objective has been to facilitate the establishment of adequate health and welfare services, manned by trained personnel, at national and local levels. As in the shorter-range programs designed to combat specific diseases or increase the availability of specific commodities, the basic tools have been the temporary assignment of foreign experts; the operation of pilot projects, training centers, and seminars; the provision of scholarships and fellowships; and the preparation and distribution of documentation. Through an intensified use of these tools under the technical assistance program, areas hitherto isolated are becoming acquainted with techniques employed elsewhere and being encouraged to adapt them to local requirements.

When modern technology lends itself to fairly direct transfer—for example, spraying with DDT to reduce the incidence of malaria or vaccinating with BCG to protect against tuberculosis—spectacular results can often be achieved in short order at little cost. Enough opportunities of this type have been seized by WHO, UNICEF, and the FAO to justify the existence of these agencies many times over. Results are more difficult to appraise, however, when the objective is to improve vocational training and guidance, to focus attention on housing problems, or to strengthen civil service or social security systems.

As a result of the interest of international agencies in nutrition, important insights into the nature and extent of protein malnutrition have been gained, world-wide attention has been focused on the problem, and major remedial programs have been initiated. But it would be an exaggeration to report comparable achievements as a result of excursions by the United Nations into the fields of housing, town and country planning, and home economics. In these areas, it would appear that the role of international machinery has not yet been adequately clarified.

For the most part, the activities of the ILO represent an extension and intensification of types of work initiated during the interwar years. Recently, however, there has been a departure from its traditional emphasis on the setting of standards for legislation and a greater interest in the dynamics of labor-management relations, the improvement of productivity, and the promotion of a climate in which real income will grow. This is a salutary development.

To even the most casual reader of the daily newspaper, it will be clear that the production, distribution, and use of narcotic drugs have not yet been restricted to legitimate medical and scientific requirements. Nevertheless, the record of the United Nations in facilitating control of narcotic drugs is in most respects outstanding. In another area of social defense in which the League of Nations was also active—the suppression of prostitution and the international traffic in women and children— the discussions in the United Nations have contributed modestly, if at all, to the desired objective. The introduction of rigid passport and visa regulations, regrettable for many other reasons, has, however, had the incidental benefit of practically eliminating such traffic.

Among the least publicized and most useful activities of the United Nations and the specialized agencies in the social welfare field, have been the efforts to promote rehabilitation of the physically handicapped and to obtain general acceptance of a new and more wholesome attitude toward the disabled members of a community.

Collectively, the social programs of the United Nations system, like the economic programs, have become concentrated increasingly on the improvement of conditions in the underdeveloped areas of the world. In those areas, the interaction of the social and economic approaches has helped to modify the views of many who ten years ago regarded lack of capital as virtually the sole obstacle to more rapid development and who failed to appreciate the fundamental character of numerous social obstacles. Only as these obstacles, too, are overcome, can captial be productively employed and the potentialities of the individual citizens who comprise the nations of the world be fully realized.

Past as Prelude

In the promotion of the general welfare, the real job of the United Nations system is to nurture, through education and shared experience, the nascent sense of international community and to strengthen the responsible, forward-looking elements within each country. For this, community development programs and other forms of technical assistance, literacy and health campaigns, financial aid for specific projects, and all the other myriad activities that reach down into the community are more important than resounding pronunciamentos from the General Assembly of the United Nations or the comparable organs of the specialized agencies.

Insufficiently stressed perhaps, but not to be neglected in any appraisal, have been the innumerable occasions on which actions harmful to the general welfare may have been prevented. International agencies, by bringing additional data and differing viewpoints to the attention of member countries, modify assessments by members of their own national interests. The voice of the international community is weak and muffled in comparison with the powerful voices of domestic interests, but where it corresponds with conscience, it is nevertheless a formidable deterrent.

Every nation must come to terms with the fact that, though the force of collective self-interest is so great that national policy must be based upon it; yet also the sensitive conscience recognizes that the moral obligation of the individual transcends his particular community. Loyalty to the community is therefore morally tolerable only if it includes values wider than those of the community.[10]

The most rewarding areas for international economic and social co-operation—and the limits of such co-operation—are being discovered by experience. A continuation of this pragmatic, evolutionary approach seems preferable to legislative action for the purpose of modifying charters, constitutions, articles of agreement, and terms of reference. The basic instruments provide institutional frameworks within which multilateral discussion and negotiation may take place. They do not require governments to pursue courses of action that are contrary to their national interests, nor do they prevent them from adopting courses in line with such interests.

This is not to say that, if one could start afresh today, no changes in framework would be made. Whether a new charter for the United Nations would establish an Economic and Social Council, would assign to it the heterogeneous functions it now has, or would fix its membership at the present level, is questionable. Remedies for most of the existing weaknesses can be found, however, without resorting to amendment of the Charter. The Charter does not require the Council to meet, and sessions could be temporarily suspended or differently scheduled if there were a general desire to experiment with alternative arrangements.

[10] Reinhold Niebuhr, *The Irony of American History* (1952), pp. 36–37.

The record of the Assembly provides no basis for believing that the situation would be improved without the Council as an intermediary. Meaningful agreements are hard to negotiate in the atmosphere of the Assembly. The Assembly, moreover, has readily approved most of the actions of the Council. Even when it has overridden the Council, its decisions have probably been sounder because of the prior deliberations of the Council than they would otherwise have been.

New constitutions for specialized agencies might establish a more effective concentration of effort within agencies and more formal channels for obtaining co-ordination among agencies. But here again, if governments desired a more closely co-ordinated approach or a different scale of operation, they could obtain them without all of the complications that are involved in drafting or amending constitutions.

Economic, and perhaps political, conditions more favorable than those prevailing heretofore may narrow the area of apparent conflict and open opportunities for lengthening, broadening, and deepening the channels of voluntary co-operation among nations. If the experience of the first ten years is any criterion, future growth will be in the direction of intensified efforts to speed the peaceful development of underdeveloped areas. This is by common consent the outstanding long-range economic and social problem of the day. To its solution, the United Nations system has already made important contributions, but much more remains to be done. There is a respectable body of evidence, however, to indicate that only in the face of imminent common danger will sovereign governments make significant concessions for the common good. A less tense atmosphere would not necessarily presage major changes in the character or pace of international co-operation to promote the general welfare through the United Nations system.

In summary, the record of the United Nations system in harmonizing conflicts of view among Member governments, achieving the specialization necessary for effective international action, and contributing to economic and social progress, leaves much to be desired. Nevertheless, given the extraordinary complexity of the issues, the brief period during which economic and social problems have shared the limelight with political and military problems, and the paralyzing effect—during much of that period—of strife between the free world and the Communist world, the sum total of concrete achievements during the first postwar decade should afford a basis for qualified optimism about the future.

APPENDIXES

APPENDIX A

Charter of the United Nations[1]

WE THE PEOPLES OF THE UNITED NATIONS DETERMINED

to save succeeding generations from the scourge of war, which twice in our lifetime has brought untold sorrow to mankind, and

to reaffirm faith in fundamental human rights, in the dignity and worth of the human person, in the equal rights of men and women and of nations large and small, and

to establish conditions under which justice and respect for the obligations arising from treaties and other sources of international law can be maintained, and

to promote social progress and better standards of life in larger freedom,

AND FOR THESE ENDS

to practice tolerance and live together in peace with one another as good neighbors, and

to unite our strength to maintain international peace and security, and

to ensure, by the acceptance of principles and the institution of methods, that armed force shall not be used, save in the common interest, and

to employ international machinery for the promotion of the economic and social advancement of all peoples,

HAVE RESOLVED TO COMBINE OUR EFFORTS TO ACCOMPLISH THESE AIMS.

Accordingly, our respective Governments, through representatives assembled in the city of San Francisco, who have exhibited their full powers found to be in good and due form, have agreed to the present Charter of the United Nations and do hereby establish an international organization to be known as the United Nations.

---

[1] Source: Photographic reproduction of the text given in *Charter of the United Nations and Statute of the International Court of Justice*, U. S. Department of State Publication 2368 (1945), pp. 1–20, which is a facsimile of the printed Charter agreed to and signed at the San Francisco Conference.

CHAPTER I

PURPOSES AND PRINCIPLES

Article 1

The Purposes of the United Nations are:

1. To maintain international peace and security, and to that end: to take effective collective measures for the prevention and removal of threats to the peace, and for the suppression of acts of aggression or other breaches of the peace, and to bring about by peaceful means, and in conformity with the principles of justice and international law, adjustment or settlement of international disputes or situations which might lead to a breach of the peace;

2. To develop friendly relations among nations based on respect for the principle of equal rights and self-determination of peoples, and to take other appropriate measures to strengthen universal peace;

3. To achieve international cooperation in solving international problems of an economic, social, cultural, or humanitarian character, and in promoting and encouraging respect for human rights and for fundamental freedoms for all without distinction as to race, sex, language, or religion; and

4. To be a center for harmonizing the actions of nations in the attainment of these common ends.

Article 2

The Organization and its Members, in pursuit of the Purposes stated in Article 1, shall act in accordance with the following Principles.

1. The Organization is based on the principle of the sovereign equality of all its Members.

2. All Members, in order to ensure to all of them the rights and benefits resulting from membership, shall fulfil in good faith the obligations assumed by them in accordance with the present Charter.

3. All Members shall settle their international disputes by peaceful means in such a manner that international peace and security, and justice, are not endangered.

4. All Members shall refrain in their international relations from the threat or use of force against the territorial integrity or political independence of any state, or in any other manner inconsistent with the Purposes of the United Nations.

5. All Members shall give the United Nations every assistance in any action it takes in accordance with the present Charter, and shall refrain from giving assistance to any state against which the United Nations is taking preventive or enforcement action.

6. The Organization shall ensure that states which are not Members of the United Nations act in accordance with these Principles so far as may be necessary for the maintenance of international peace and security.

7. Nothing contained in the present Charter shall authorize the United Nations to intervene in matters which are essentially within the domestic jurisdiction of any state or shall require the Members to submit such matters to settlement under the present Charter; but this principle shall not prejudice the application of enforcement measures under Chapter VII.

CHAPTER II

MEMBERSHIP

Article 3

The original Members of the United Nations shall be the states which, having participated in the United Nations Conference on International Organization at San Francisco, or having previously signed the Declaration by United Nations of January 1, 1942, sign the present Charter and ratify it in accordance with Article 110.

Article 4

1. Membership in the United Nations is open to all other peace-loving states which accept the obligations contained in the present Charter and, in the judgment of the Organization, are able and willing to carry out these obligations.

2. The admission of any such state to membership in the United Nations will be effected by a decision of the General Assembly upon the recommendation of the Security Council.

Article 5

A Member of the United Nations against which preventive or enforcement action has been taken by the Security Council may be suspended from the exercise of the rights and privileges of membership by the General Assembly upon the recommendation of the Security Council. The exercise of these rights and privileges may be restored by the Security Council.

Article 6

A Member of the United Nations which has persistently violated the Principles contained in the present Charter may be expelled from the Organization by the General Assembly upon the recommendation of the Security Council.

CHAPTER III
ORGANS

Article 7

1. There are established as the principal organs of the United Nations: a General Assembly, a Security Council, an Economic and Social Council, a Trusteeship Council, an International Court of Justice, and a Secretariat.

2. Such subsidiary organs as may be found necessary may be established in accordance with the present Charter.

Article 8

The United Nations shall place no restrictions on the eligibility of men and women to participate in any capacity and under conditions of equality in its principal and subsidiary organs.

CHAPTER IV
THE GENERAL ASSEMBLY

Composition

Article 9

1. The General Assembly shall consist of all the Members of the United Nations.

2. Each Member shall have not more than five representatives in the General Assembly.

Functions and Powers

Article 10

The General Assembly may discuss any questions or any matters within the scope of the present Charter or relating to the powers and functions of any organs provided for in the present Charter, and, except as provided in Article 12, may make recommendations to the Members of the United Nations or to the Security Council or to both on any such questions or matters.

Article 11

1. The General Assembly may consider the general principles of cooperation in the maintenance of international peace and security, including the principles governing disarmament and the regulation of armaments, and may make recommendations with regard to such principles to the Members or to the Security Council or to both.

2. The General Assembly may discuss any questions relating to the maintenance of international peace and security brought before it by any Member of the United Nations, or by the Security Council, or by a state which is not a

Member of the United Nations in accordance with Article 35, paragraph 2, and, except as provided in Article 12, may make recommendations with regard to any such questions to the state or states concerned or to the Security Council or to both. Any such question on which action is necessary shall be referred to the Security Council by the General Assembly either before or after discussion.

3. The General Assembly may call the attention of the Security Council to situations which are likely to endanger international peace and security.

4. The powers of the General Assembly set forth in this Article shall not limit the general scope of Article 10.

Article 12

1. While the Security Council is exercising in respect of any dispute or situation the functions assigned to it in the present Charter, the General Assembly shall not make any recommendation with regard to that dispute or situation unless the Security Council so requests.

2. The Secretary-General, with the consent of the Security Council, shall notify the General Assembly at each session of any matters relative to the maintenance of international peace and security which are being dealt with by the Security Council and shall similarly notify the General Assembly, or the Members of the United Nations if the General Assembly is not in session, immediately the Security Council ceases to deal with such matters.

Article 13

1. The General Assembly shall initiate studies and make recommendations for the purpose of:
a. promoting international cooperation in the political field and encouraging the progressive development of international law and its codification;

b. promoting international cooperation in the economic, social, cultural, educational, and health fields, and assisting in the realization of human rights and fundamental freedoms for all without distinction as to race, sex, language, or religion.

2. The further responsibilities, functions, and powers of the General Assembly with respect to matters mentioned in paragraph 1(b) above are set forth in Chapters IX and X.

Article 14

Subject to the provisions of Article 12, the General Assembly may recommend measures for the peaceful adjustment of any situation, regardless of origin, which it deems likely to impair the general welfare or friendly relations among nations, including situations resulting from a violation of the provisions of the present Charter setting forth the Purposes and Principles of the United Nations.

Article 15

1. The General Assembly shall receive and consider annual and special reports from the Security Council; these reports shall include an account of the measures that the Security Council has decided upon or taken to maintain international peace and security.

2. The General Assembly shall receive and consider reports from the other organs of the United Nations.

Article 16

The General Assembly shall perform such functions with respect to the international trusteeship system as are assigned to it under Chapters XII and XIII, including the approval of the trusteeship agreements for areas not designated as strategic.

Article 17

1. The General Assembly shall consider and approve the budget of the Organization.

2. The expenses of the Organization shall be borne by the Members as apportioned by the General Assembly.

3. The General Assembly shall consider and approve any financial and budgetary arrangements with specialized agencies referred to in Article 57 and shall examine the administrative budgets of such specialized agencies with a view to making recommendations to the agencies concerned.

Voting

Article 18

1. Each member of the General Assembly shall have one vote.

2. Decisions of the General Assembly on important questions shall be made by a two-thirds majority of the members present and voting. These questions shall include: recommendations with respect to the maintenance of international peace and security, the election of the non-permanent members of the Security Council, the election of the members of the Economic and Social Council, the election of members of the Trusteeship Council in accordance with paragraph 1(c) of Article 86, the admission of new Members to the United Nations, the suspension of the rights and privileges of membership, the expulsion of Members, questions relating to the operation of the trusteeship system, and budgetary questions.

3. Decisions on other questions, including the determination of additional categories of questions to be decided by a two-thirds majority, shall be made by a majority of the members present and voting.

Article 19

A Member of the United Nations which is in arrears in the payment of its financial contributions to the Organization shall have no vote in the General Assembly if the amount of its arrears equals or exceeds the amount of the contributions due from it for the preceding two full years. The General Assembly may, nevertheless, permit such a Member to vote if it is satisfied that the failure to pay is due to conditions beyond the control of the Member.

Procedure

Article 20

The General Assembly shall meet in regular annual sessions and in such special sessions as occasion may require. Special sessions shall be convoked by the Secretary-General at the request of the Security Council or of a majority of the Members of the United Nations.

Article 21

The General Assembly shall adopt its own rules of procedure. It shall elect its President for each session.

Article 22

The General Assembly may establish such subsidiary organs as it deems necessary for the performance of its functions.

CHAPTER V
THE SECURITY COUNCIL

Composition

Article 23

1. The Security Council shall consist of eleven Members of the United Nations. The Republic of China, France, the Union of Soviet Socialist Republics, the United Kingdom of Great Britain and Northern Ireland, and the United States of America shall be permanent members of the Security Council. The General Assembly shall elect six other Members of the United Nations to be non-permanent members of the Security Council, due regard being specially paid, in the first instance to the contribution of Members of the

United Nations to the maintenance of international peace and security and to the other purposes of the Organization, and also to equitable geographical distribution.

2. The non-permanent members of the Security Council shall be elected for a term of two years. In the first election of the non-permanent members, however, three shall be chosen for a term of one year. A retiring member shall not be eligible for immediate re-election.

3. Each member of the Security Council shall have one representative.

Functions and Powers

Article 24

1. In order to ensure prompt and effective action by the United Nations, its Members confer on the Security Council primary responsibility for the maintenance of international peace and security, and agree that in carrying out its duties under this responsibility the Security Council acts on their behalf.

2. In discharging these duties the Security Council shall act in accordance with the Purposes and Principles of the United Nations. The specific powers granted to the Security Council for the discharge of these duties are laid down in Chapters VI, VII, VIII, and XII.

3. The Security Council shall submit annual and, when necessary, special reports to the General Assembly for its consideration.

Article 25

The Members of the United Nations agree to accept and carry out the decisions of the Security Council in accordance with the present Charter.

Article 26

In order to promote the establishment and maintenance of international peace and security with the least diversion for armaments of the world's human and economic resources, the Security Council shall be responsible for formulating, with the assistance of the Military Staff Committee referred to in Article 47, plans to be submitted to the Members of the United Nations for the establishment of a system for the regulation of armaments.

Voting

Article 27

1. Each member of the Security Council shall have one vote.

2. Decisions of the Security Council on procedural matters shall be made by an affirmative vote of seven members.

3. Decisions of the Security Council on all other matters shall be made by an affirmative vote of seven members including the concurring votes of the permanent members; provided that, in decisions under Chapter VI, and under paragraph 3 of Article 52, a party to a dispute shall abstain from voting.

Procedure

Article 28

1. The Security Council shall be so organized as to be able to function continuously. Each member of the Security Council shall for this purpose be represented at all times at the seat of the Organization.

2. The Security Council shall hold periodic meetings at which each of its members may, if it so desires, be represented by a member of the government or by some other specially designated representative.

3. The Security Council may hold meetings at such places other than the seat of the Organization as in its judgment will best facilitate its work.

Article 29

The Security Council may establish such subsidiary organs as it deems necessary for the performance of its functions.

Article 30

The Security Council shall adopt its own rules of procedure, including the method of selecting its President.

Article 31

Any Member of the United Nations which is not a member of the Security Council may participate, without vote, in the discussion of any question brough† before the Security Council whenever the latter considers that the interests of that Member are specially affected.

Article 32

Any Member of the United Nations which is not a member of the Security Council or any state which is not a Member of the United Nations, if it is a party to a dispute under consideration by the Security Council, shall be invited to participate, without vote, in the discussion relating to the dispute. The Security Council shall lay down such conditions as it deems just for the participation of a state which is not a Member of the United Nations.

CHAPTER VI
PACIFIC SETTLEMENT OF DISPUTES

Article 33

1. The parties to any dispute, the continuance of which is likely to endanger the maintenance of international peace and security, shall, first of all, seek a solution by negotiation, enquiry, mediation, conciliation, arbitration, judicial settlement, resort to regional agencies or arrangements, or other peaceful means of their own choice.

2. The Security Council shall, when it deems necessary, call upon the parties to settle their dispute by such means.

Article 34

The Security Council may investigate any dispute, or any situation which might lead to international friction or give rise to a dispute, in order to determine whether the continuance of the dispute or situation is likely to endanger the maintenance of international peace and security.

Article 35

1. Any Member of the United Nations may bring any dispute, or any situation of the nature referred to in Article 34, to the attention of the Security Council or of the General Assembly.

2. A state which is not a Member of the United Nations may bring to the attention of the Security Council or of the General Assembly any dispute to which it is a party if it accepts in advance, for the purposes of the dispute, the obligations of pacific settlement provided in the present Charter.

3. The proceedings of the General Assembly in respect of matters brought to its attention under this Article will be subject to the provisions of Articles 11 and 12.

Article 36

1. The Security Council may, at any stage of a dispute of the nature referred to in Article 33 or of a situation of like nature, recommend appropriate procedures or methods of adjustment.

2. The Security Council should take into consideration any procedures for the settlement of the dispute which have already been adopted by the parties.

3. In making recommendations under this Article the Security Council should also take into consideration that legal disputes should as a general rule be referred by the parties to the International Court of Justice in accordance with the provisions of the Statute of the Court.

Article 37

1. Should the parties to a dispute of the nature referred to in Article 33 fail to settle it by the means indicated in that Article, they shall refer it to the Security Council.

2. If the Security Council deems that the continuance of the dispute is in fact likely to endanger the maintenance of international peace and security, it shall decide whether to take action under Article 36 or to recommend such terms of settlement as it may consider appropriate.

Article 38

Without prejudice to the provisions of Articles 33 to 37, the Security Council may, if all the parties to any dispute so request, make recommendations to the parties with a view to a pacific settlement of the dispute.

CHAPTER VII

ACTION WITH RESPECT TO THREATS TO THE PEACE, BREACHES OF THE PEACE, AND ACTS OF AGGRESSION

Article 39

The Security Council shall determine the existence of any threat to the peace, breach of the peace, or act of aggression and shall make recommendations, or decide what measures shall be taken in accordance with Articles 41 and 42, to maintain or restore international peace and security.

Article 40

In order to prevent an aggravation of the situation, the Security Council may, before making the recommendations or deciding upon the measures provided for in Article 39, call upon the parties concerned to comply with such provisional measures as it deems necessary or desirable. Such provisional measures shall be without prejudice to the rights, claims, or position of the parties concerned. The Security Council shall duly take account of failure to comply with such provisional measures.

Article 41

The Security Council may decide what measures not involving the use of armed force are to be employed to give effect to its decisions, and it may call upon the Members of the United Nations to apply such measures. These may include complete or partial interruption of economic relations and of rail, sea, air, postal, telegraphic, radio, and other means of communication, and the severance of diplomatic relations.

Article 42

Should the Security Council consider that measures provided for in Article 41 would be inadequate or have proved to be inadequate, it may take such action by air, sea, or land forces as may be necessary to maintain or restore international peace and security. Such action may include demonstrations, blockade, and other operations by air, sea, or land forces of Members of the United Nations.

Article 43

1. All Members of the United Nations, in order to contribute to the maintenance of international peace and security, undertake to make available to the Security Council, on its call and in accordance with a special agreement or agreements, armed forces, assistance, and facilities, including rights of passage, necessary for the purpose of maintaining international peace and security.

2. Such agreement or agreements shall govern the numbers and types of forces, their degree of readiness and general location, and the nature of the facilities and assistance to be provided.

3. The agreement or agreements shall be negotiated as soon as possible on the initiative of the Security Council. They shall be concluded between the Security Council and Members or between the Security Council and groups of Members and shall be subject to ratification by the signatory states in accordance with their respective constitutional processes.

Article 44

When the Security Council has decided to use force it shall, before calling upon a Member not represented on it to provide armed forces in fulfillment of the obligations assumed under Article 43, invite that Member, if the Member so desires, to participate in the decisions of the Security Council concerning the employment of contingents of that Member's armed forces.

Article 45

In order to enable the United Nations to take urgent military measures, Members shall hold immediately available national air-force contingents for combined international enforcement action. The strength and degree of readiness of these contingents and plans for their combined action shall be determined, within the limits laid down in the special agreement or agreements referred to in Article 43, by the Security Council with the assistance of the Military Staff Committee.

Article 46

Plans for the application of armed force shall be made by the Security Council with the assistance of the Military Staff Committee.

Article 47

1. There shall be established a Military Staff Committee to advise and assist the Security Council on all questions relating to the Security Council's military requirements for the maintenance of international peace and security, the employment and command of forces placed at its disposal, the regulation of armaments, and possible disarmament.

2. The Military Staff Committee shall consist of the Chiefs of Staff of the permanent members of the Security Council or their representatives. Any Member of the United Nations not permanently represented on the Committee shall be invited by the Committee to be associated with it when the efficient discharge of the Committee's responsibilities requires the participation of that Member in its work.

3. The Military Staff Committee shall be responsible under the Security Council for the strategic direction of any armed forces placed at the disposal of the Security Council. Questions relating to the command of such forces shall be worked out subsequently.

4. The Military Staff Committee, with the authorization of the Security Council and after consultation with appropriate regional agencies, may establish regional subcommittees.

Article 48

1. The action required to carry out the decisions of the Security Council for the maintenance of international peace and security shall be taken by all the Members of the United Nations or by some of them, as the Security Council may determine.

2. Such decisions shall be carried out by the Members of the United Nations directly and through their action in the appropriate international agencies of which they are members.

Article 49

The Members of the United Nations shall join in affording mutual assistance in carrying out the measures decided upon by the Security Council.

Article 50

If preventive or enforcement measures against any state are taken by the Security Council, any other state, whether a Member of the United Nations or not, which finds itself confronted with special economic problems arising from the carrying out of those measures shall have the right to consult the Security Council with regard to a solution of those problems.

Article 51

Nothing in the present Charter shall impair the inherent right of individual or collective self-defense if an armed attack occurs against a Member of the United Nations, until the Security Council has taken the measures necessary to maintain international peace and security. Measures taken by Members in the exercise of this right of self-defense shall be immediately reported to the Security Council and shall not in any way affect the authority and responsibility of the Security Council under the present Charter to take at any time such action as it deems necessary in order to maintain or restore international peace and security.

CHAPTER VIII
REGIONAL ARRANGEMENTS
Article 52

1. Nothing in the present Charter precludes the existence of regional arrangements or agencies for dealing with such matters relating to the maintenance of international peace and security as are appropriate for regional action, provided that such arrangements or agencies and their activities are consistent with the Purposes and Principles of the United Nations.

2. The Members of the United Nations entering into such arrangements or constituting such agencies shall make every effort to achieve pacific settlement of local disputes through such regional arrangements or by such regional agencies before referring them to the Security Council.

3. The Security Council shall encourage the development of pacific settlement of local disputes through such regional arrangements or by such regional agencies either on the initiative of the states concerned or by reference from the Security Council.

4. This Article in no way impairs the application of Articles 34 and 35.

Article 53

1. The Security Council shall, where appropriate, utilize such regional arrangements or agencies for enforcement action under its authority. But no enforcement action shall be taken under regional arrangements or by regional agencies without the authorization of the Security Council, with the exception of measures against any enemy state, as defined in paragraph 2 of this Article, provided for pursuant to Article 107 or in regional arrangements directed against renewal of aggressive policy on the part of any such state, until such time as the Organization may, on request of the Governments concerned, be charged with the responsibility for preventing further aggression by such a state.

2. The term enemy state as used in paragraph 1 of this Article applies to any state which during the Second World War has been an enemy of any signatory of the present Charter.

Article 54

The Security Council shall at all times be kept fully informed of activities undertaken or in contemplation under regional arrangements or by regional agencies for the maintenance of international peace and security.

CHAPTER IX
INTERNATIONAL ECONOMIC AND SOCIAL COOPERATION
Article 55

With a view to the creation of conditions of stability and well-being which are necessary for peaceful and friendly relations among nations based on respect for the principle of equal rights and self-determination of peoples, the United Nations shall promote:

a. higher standards of living, full employment, and conditions of economic and social progress and development;

b. solutions of international economic, social, health, and related problems; and international cultural and educational cooperation; and

c. universal respect for, and observance of, human rights and fundamental freedoms for all without distinction as to race, sex, language, or religion.

Article 56

All Members pledge themselves to take joint and separate action in cooperation with the Organization for the achievement of the purposes set forth in Article 55.

Article 57

1. The various specialized agencies, established by intergovernmental agreement and having wide international responsibilities, as defined in their basic instruments, in economic, social, cultural, educational, health, and related fields, shall be brought into relationship with the United Nations in accordance with the provisions of Article 63.

2. Such agencies thus brought into relationship with the United Nations are hereinafter referred to as specialized agencies.

Article 58

The Organization shall make recommendations for the coordination of the policies and activities of the specialized agencies.

Article 59

The Organization shall, where appropriate, initiate negotiations among the states concerned for the creation of any new specialized agencies required for the accomplishment of the purposes set forth in Article 55.

Article 60

Responsibility for the discharge of the functions of the Organization set forth in this Chapter shall be vested in the General Assembly and, under the authority of the General Assembly, in the Economic and Social Council, which shall have for this purpose the powers set forth in Chapter X.

CHAPTER X
THE ECONOMIC AND SOCIAL COUNCIL

Composition

Article 61

1. The Economic and Social Council shall consist of eighteen Members of the United Nations elected by the General Assembly.

2. Subject to the provisions of paragraph 3, six members of the Economic and Social Council shall be elected each year for a term of three years. A retiring member shall be eligible for immediate re-election.

3. At the first election, eighteen members of the Economic and Social Council shall be chosen. The term of office of six members so chosen shall expire at the end of one year, and of six other members at the end of two years, in accordance with arrangements made by the General Assembly.

4. Each member of the Economic and Social Council shall have one representative.

Functions and Powers

Article 62

1. The Economic and Social Council may make or initiate studies and reports with respect to international economic, social, cultural, educational, health, and related matters and may make recommendations with respect to any such matters to the General Assembly, to the Members of the United Nations, and to the specialized agencies concerned.

2. It may make recommendations for the purpose of promoting respect for, and observance of, human rights and fundamental freedoms for all.

3. It may prepare draft conventions for submission to the General Assembly, with respect to matters falling within its competence.

4. It may call, in accordance with the rules prescribed by the United Nations, international conferences on matters falling within its competence.

Article 63

1. The Economic and Social Council may enter into agreements with any of the agencies referred to in Article 57, defining the terms on which the agency concerned shall be brought into relationship with the United Nations. Such agreements shall be subject to approval by the General Assembly.

2. It may coordinate the activities of the specialized agencies through consultation with and recommendations to such agencies and through recommendations to the General Assembly and to the Members of the United Nations.

Article 64

1. The Economic and Social Council may take appropriate steps to obtain regular reports from the specialized agencies. It may make arrangements with the Members of the United Nations and with the specialized agencies to obtain reports on the steps taken to give effect to its own recommendations and to recommendations on matters falling within its competence made by the General Assembly.

2. It may communicate its observations on these reports to the General Assembly.

Article 65

The Economic and Social Council may furnish information to the Security Council and shall assist the Security Council upon its request.

Article 66

1. The Economic and Social Council shall perform such functions as fall within its competence in connection with the carrying out of the recommendations of the General Assembly.

2. It may, with the approval of the General Assembly, perform services at the request of Members of the United Nations and at the request of specialized agencies.

3. It shall perform such other functions as are specified elsewhere in the present Charter or as may be assigned to it by the General Assembly.

Voting

Article 67

1. Each member of the Economic and Social Council shall have one vote.

2. Decisions of the Economic and Social Council shall be made by a majority of the members present and voting.

Procedure

Article 68

The Economic and Social Council shall set up commissions in economic and social fields and for the promotion of human rights, and such other commissions as may be required for the performance of its functions.

Article 69

The Economic and Social Council shall invite any Member of the United Nations to participate, without vote, in its deliberations on any matter of particular concern to that Member.

Article 70

The Economic and Social Council may make arrangements for representatives of the specialized agencies to participate, without vote, in its deliberations and in those of the commissions established by it, and for its representatives to participate in the deliberations of the specialized agencies.

Article 71

The Economic and Social Council may make suitable arrangements for consultation with nongovernmental organizations which are concerned with matters within its competence. Such arrangements may be made with international organizations and, where appropriate, with national organizations after consultation with the Member of the United Nations concerned.

Article 72

1. The Economic and Social Council shall adopt its own rules of procedure, including the method of selecting its President.

2. The Economic and Social Council shall meet as required in accordance with its rules, which shall include provision for the convening of meetings on the request of a majority of its members.

CHAPTER XI
DECLARATION REGARDING NON-SELF-GOVERNING TERRITORIES

Article 73

Members of the United Nations which have or assume responsibilities for the administration of territories whose peoples have not yet attained a full measure of self-government recognize the principle that the interests of the inhabitants of these territories are paramount, and accept as a sacred trust the obligation to promote to the utmost, within the system of international peace and security established by the present Charter, the well-being of the inhabitants of these territories, and, to this end:

a. to ensure, with due respect for the culture of the peoples concerned, their political, economic, social, and educational advancement, their just treatment, and their protection against abuses;

b. to develop self-government, to take due account of the political aspirations of the peoples, and to assist them in the progressive development of their free political institutions, according to the particular circumstances of each territory and its peoples and their varying stages of advancement;

c. to further international peace and security;

d. to promote constructive measures of development, to encourage research, and to co-operate with one another and, when and where appropriate, with specialized international bodies with a view to the practical achievement of the social, economic, and scientific purposes set forth in this Article; and

e. to transmit regularly to the Secretary-General for information purposes, subject to such limitation as security and constitutional considerations may require, statistical and other information of a technical nature relating to economic, social, and educational conditions in the territories for which they are respectively responsible other than those territories to which Chapters XII and XIII apply.

Article 74

Members of the United Nations also agree that their policy in respect of the territories to which this Chapter applies, no less than in respect of their metropolitan areas, must be based on the general principle of good-neighborliness, due account being taken of the interests and well-being of the rest of the world, in social, economic, and commercial matters.

CHAPTER XII
INTERNATIONAL TRUSTEESHIP SYSTEM

Article 75

The United Nations shall establish under its authority an international trusteeship system for the administration and supervision of such territories as may be placed thereunder by subsequent individual agreements. These territories are hereinafter referred to as trust territories.

Article 76

The basic objectives of the trusteeship system,

in accordance with the Purposes of the United Nations laid down in Article 1 of the present Charter, shall be:

a. to further international peace and security;

b. to promote the political, economic, social, and educational advancement of the inhabitants of the trust territories, and their progressive development towards self-government or independence as may be appropriate to the particular circumstances of each territory and its peoples and the freely expressed wishes of the peoples concerned, and as may be provided by the terms of each trusteeship agreement;

c. to encourage respect for human rights and for fundamental freedoms for all without distinction as to race, sex, language, or religion, and to encourage recognition of the interdependence of the peoples of the world; and

d. to ensure equal treatment in social, economic, and commercial matters for all Members of the United Nations and their nationals, and also equal treatment for the latter in the administration of justice, without prejudice to the attainment of the foregoing objectives and subject to the provisions of Article 80.

Article 77

1. The trusteeship system shall apply to such territories in the following categories as may be placed thereunder by means of trusteeship agreements:

a. territories now held under mandate;

b. territories which may be detached from enemy states as a result of the Second World War; and

c. territories voluntarily placed under the system by states responsible for their administration.

2. It will be a matter for subsequent agreement as to which territories in the foregoing categories will be brought under the trusteeship system and upon what terms.

Article 78

The trusteeship system shall not apply to territories which have become Members of the United Nations, relationship among which shall be based on respect for the principle of sovereign equality.

Article 79

The terms of trusteeship for each territory to be placed under the trusteeship system, including any alteration or amendment, shall be agreed upon by the states directly concerned, including the mandatory power in the case of territories held under mandate by a Member of the United Nations, and shall be approved as provided for in Articles 83 and 85.

Article 80

1. Except as may be agreed upon in individual trusteeship agreements, made under Articles 77, 79, and 81, placing each territory under the trusteeship system, and until such agreements have been concluded, nothing in this Chapter shall be construed in or of itself to alter in any manner the rights whatsoever of any states or any peoples or the terms of existing international instruments to which Members of the United Nations may respectively be parties.

2. Paragraph 1 of this Article shall not be interpreted as giving grounds for delay or postponement of the negotiation and conclusion of agreements for placing mandated and other territories under the trusteeship system as provided for in Article 77.

Article 81

The trusteeship agreement shall in each case include the terms under which the trust territory will be administered and designate the authority which will exercise the administration of the trust territory. Such authority, hereinafter called the administering authority, may be one or more states or the Organization itself.

Article 82

There may be designated, in any trusteeship agreement, a strategic area or areas which may include part or all of the trust territory to which the agreement applies, without prejudice to any special agreement or agreements made under Article 43.

Article 83

1. All functions of the United Nations relating to strategic areas, including the approval of the terms of the trusteeship agreements and of their alteration or amendment, shall be exercised by the Security Council.

2. The basic objectives set forth in Article 76 shall be applicable to the people of each strategic area.

3. The Security Council shall, subject to the provisions of the trusteeship agreements and without prejudice to security considerations, avail itself of the assistance of the Trusteeship Council to perform those functions of the United Nations under the trusteeship system relating to political, economic, social, and educational matters in the strategic areas.

Article 84

It shall be the duty of the administering authority to ensure that the trust territory shall play its part in the maintenance of international peace and security. To this end the administering authority may make use of volunteer forces, facilities, and assistance from the trust territory in carrying out the obligations towards the Security Council undertaken in this regard by the administering authority, as well as for local defense and the maintenance of law and order within the trust territory.

Article 85

1. The functions of the United Nations with regard to trusteeship agreements for all areas not designated as strategic, including the approval of the terms of the trusteeship agreements and of their alteration or amendment, shall be exercised by the General Assembly.

2. The Trusteeship Council, operating under the authority of the General Assembly, shall assist the General Assembly in carrying out these functions.

CHAPTER XIII
THE TRUSTEESHIP COUNCIL

Composition

Article 86

1. The Trusteeship Council shall consist of the following Members of the United Nations:

a. those Members administering trust territories;

b. such of those Members mentioned by name in Article 23 as are not administering trust territories; and

c. as many other Members elected for three-year terms by the General Assembly as may be necessary to ensure that the total number of members of the Trusteeship Council is equally divided between those Members of the United Nations which administer trust territories and those which do not.

2. Each member of the Trusteeship Council shall designate one specially qualified person to represent it therein.

Functions and Powers

Article 87

The General Assembly and, under its authority, the Trusteeship Council, in carrying out their functions, may:

a. consider reports submitted by the administering authority;

b. accept petitions and examine them in consultation with the administering authority;

c. provide for periodic visits to the respective trust territories at times agreed upon with the administering authority; and

d. take these and other actions in conformity with the terms of the trusteeship agreements.

Article 88

The Trusteeship Council shall formulate a questionnaire on the political, economic, social, and educational advancement of the inhabitants of each trust territory, and the administering authority for each trust territory within the competence of the General Assembly shall make an annual report to the General Assembly upon the basis of such questionnaire.

Voting

Article 89

1. Each member of the Trusteeship Council shall have one vote.

2. Decisions of the Trusteeship Council shall be made by a majority of the members present and voting.

Procedure

Article 90

1. The Trusteeship Council shall adopt its own rules of procedure, including the method of selecting its President.

2. The Trusteeship Council shall meet as required in accordance with its rules, which shall include provision for the convening of meetings on the request of a majority of its members.

Article 91

The Trusteeship Council shall, when appropriate, avail itself of the assistance of the Economic and Social Council and of the specialized agencies in regard to matters with which they are respectively concerned.

CHAPTER XIV

THE INTERNATIONAL COURT OF JUSTICE

Article 92

The International Court of Justice shall be the principal judicial organ of the United Nations. It shall function in accordance with the annexed Statute, which is based upon the Statute of the Permanent Court of International Justice and forms an integral part of the present Charter.

Article 93

1. All Members of the United Nations are *ipso facto* parties to the Statute of the International Court of Justice.

2. A state which is not a Member of the United Nations may become a party to the Statute of the International Court of Justice on conditions to be determined in each case by the General Assembly upon the recommendation of the Security Council.

Article 94

1. Each Member of the United Nations undertakes to comply with the decision of the International Court of Justice in any case to which it is a party.

2. If any party to a case fails to perform the obligations incumbent upon it under a judgment rendered by the Court, the other party may have recourse to the Security Council, which may, if it deems necessary, make recommendations or decide upon measures to be taken to give effect to the judgment.

Article 95

Nothing in the present Charter shall prevent Members of the United Nations from entrusting the solution of their differences to other tribunals by virtue of agreements already in existence or which may be concluded in the future.

Article 96

1. The General Assembly or the Security Council may request the International Court of Justice to give an advisory opinion on any legal question.

2. Other organs of the United Nations and specialized agencies, which may at any time be so authorized by the General Assembly, may also request advisory opinions of the Court on legal questions arising within the scope of their activities.

CHAPTER XV

THE SECRETARIAT

Article 97

The Secretariat shall comprise a Secretary-General and such staff as the Organization may require. The Secretary-General shall be appointed by the General Assembly upon the recommendation of the Security Council. He shall be the chief administrative officer of the Organization.

Article 98

The Secretary-General shall act in that capacity in all meetings of the General Assembly, of the Security Council, of the Economic and Social Council, and of the Trusteeship Council, and shall perform such other functions as are entrusted to him by these organs. The Secretary-General shall make an annual report to the General Assembly on the work of the Organization.

Article 99

The Secretary-General may bring to the attention of the Security Council any matter which in his opinion may threaten the maintenance of international peace and security.

Article 100

1. In the performance of their duties the Secre-tary-General and the staff shall not seek or receive instructions from any government or from any other authority external to the Organization. They shall refrain from any action which might reflect on their position as international officials responsible only to the Organization.

2. Each Member of the United Nations undertakes to respect the exclusively international character of the responsibilities of the Secretary-General and the staff and not to seek to influence them in the discharge of their responsibilities.

Article 101

1. The staff shall be appointed by the Secretary-General under regulations established by the General Assembly.

2. Appropriate staffs shall be permanently assigned to the Economic and Social Council, the Trusteeship Council, and, as required, to other organs of the United Nations. These staffs shall form a part of the Secretariat.

3. The paramount consideration in the employment of the staff and in the determination of the conditions of service shall be the necessity of securing the highest standards of efficiency, competence, and integrity. Due regard shall be paid to the importance of recruiting the staff on as wide a geographical basis as possible.

CHAPTER XVI

MISCELLANEOUS PROVISIONS

Article 102

1. Every treaty and every international agreement entered into by any Member of the United Nations after the present Charter comes into force shall as soon as possible be registered with the Secretariat and published by it.

2. No party to any such treaty or international agreement which has not been registered in accordance with the provisions of paragraph 1 of

this Article may invoke that treaty or agreement before any organ of the United Nations.

Article 103

In the event of a conflict between the obligations of the Members of the United Nations under the present Charter and their obligations under any other international agreement, their obligations under the present Charter shall prevail.

Article 104

The Organization shall enjoy in the territory of each of its Members such legal capacity as may be necessary for the exercise of its functions and the fulfillment of its purposes.

Article 105

1. The Organization shall enjoy in the territory of each of its Members such privileges and immunities as are necessary for the fulfillment of its purposes.

2. Representatives of the Members of the United Nations and officials of the Organization shall similarly enjoy such privileges and immunities as are necessary for the independent exercise of their functions in connection with the Organization.

3. The General Assembly may make recommendations with a view to determining the details of the application of paragraphs 1 and 2 of this Article or may propose conventions to the Members of the United Nations for this purpose.

CHAPTER XVII
TRANSITIONAL SECURITY ARRANGEMENTS

Article 106

Pending the coming into force of such special agreements referred to in Article 43 as in the opinion of the Security Council enable it to begin the exercise of its responsibilities under Article 42, the parties to the Four-Nation Declaration, signed at Moscow, October 30, 1943, and France, shall, in accordance with the provisions of paragraph 5 of that Declaration, consult with one another and as occasion requires with other Members of the United Nations with a view to such joint action on behalf of the Organization as may be necessary for the purpose of maintaining international peace and security.

Article 107

Nothing in the present Charter shall invalidate or preclude action, in relation to any state which during the Second World War has been an enemy of any signatory to the present Charter, taken or authorized as a result of that war by the Governments having responsibility for such action.

CHAPTER XVIII
AMENDMENTS

Article 108

Amendments to the present Charter shall come into force for all Members of the United Nations when they have been adopted by a vote of two thirds of the members of the General Assembly and ratified in accordance with their respective constitutional processes by two thirds of the Members of the United Nations, including all the permanent members of the Security Council.

Article 109

1. A General Conference of the Members of the United Nations for the purpose of reviewing the present Charter may be held at a date and place to be fixed by a two-thirds vote of the members of the General Assembly and by a vote of any seven members of the Security Council. Each Member of the United Nations shall have one vote in the conference.

2. Any alteration of the present Charter recommended by a two-thirds vote of the conference shall take effect when ratified in accordance with their respective constitutional processes by two thirds of the Members of the United Nations including all the permanent members of the Security Council.

3. If such a conference has not been held before the tenth annual session of the General Assembly following the coming into force of the present Charter, the proposal to call such a conference shall be placed on the agenda of that session of the General Assembly, and the conference shall be held if so decided by a majority vote of the members of the General Assembly and by a vote of any seven members of the Security Council.

CHAPTER XIX
RATIFICATION AND SIGNATURE

Article 110

1. The present Charter shall be ratified by the signatory states in accordance with their respective constitutional processes.

2. The ratifications shall be deposited with the Government of the United States of America, which shall notify all the signatory states of each deposit as well as the Secretary-General of the Organization when he has been appointed.

3. The present Charter shall come into force upon the deposit of ratifications by the Republic of China, France, the Union of Soviet Socialist Republics, the United Kingdom of Great Britain and Northern Ireland, and the United States of America, and by a majority of the other signatory states. A protocol of the ratifications deposited shall thereupon be drawn up by the Government of the United States of America which shall communicate copies thereof to all the signatory states.

4. The states signatory to the present Charter which ratify it after it has come into force will become original Members of the United Nations on the date of the deposit of their respective ratifications.

Article 111

The present Charter, of which the Chinese, French, Russian, English, and Spanish texts are equally authentic, shall remain deposited in the archives of the Government of the United States of America. Duly certified copies thereof shall be transmitted by that Government to the Governments of the other signatory states.

IN FAITH WHEREOF the representatives of the Governments of the United Nations have signed the present Charter.

DONE at the city of San Francisco the twenty-sixth day of June, one thousand nine hundred and forty-five.

APPENDIX B

Summary Information on Specialized Agencies

(As of Dec. 31, 1956)

Name of Agency and Location of Headquarters	Major Functions	Net Budget for 1957 (In thousands)	Name of Chief Officer	Date of Establishment[b]	Entry into Force of Agreement with United Nations
International Labour Organisation (ILO) Geneva, Switzerland	Brings together government, labor, management to consider industrial, manpower and related problems; establishes labor standards by international conventions; provides technical assistance for improvement of labor conditions and living standards and promotion of economic and social stability.	$ 7,618	David A. Morse (United States)	Apr. 11, 1919	Dec. 14, 1946
Food and Agriculture Organization of the United Nations (FAO) Rome, Italy	Seeks to increase production from farms, forests, and fisheries, and to improve distribution; provides expert assistance to governments in agricultural problems; works to improve nutrition.	$ 6,800	B. R. Sen (India)	Oct. 16, 1945	Dec. 14, 1946
United Nations Educational, Scientific and Cultural Organization (UNESCO) Paris, France	Seeks to broaden base of education throughout the world, to bring benefits of science to all countries, and to encourage cultural interchange in order to increase mutual understanding.	$10,796 (for 1956)	Luther H. Evans (United States)	Nov. 4, 1946	Dec. 14, 1946
International Civil Aviation Organization (ICAO) Montreal, Canada	Encourages use of safety measures, uniform regulations for operation, simpler procedures at borders; promotes use of new technical methods and equipment.	$ 3,568 (Canadian)	Carl Ljungberg (Sweden)	Apr. 4, 1947	Apr. 4, 1947

556

Organization	Function	Budget (thousands)	Director (nationality)	Established	Effective
International Bank for Reconstruction and Development (IBRD) Washington, D.C.	Makes loans for productive projects, furnishes technical advice, and promotes private foreign investment.	$ 7,615 (for 1955–56 fiscal year) met from income	Eugene R. Black (United States)	Dec. 27, 1945	Nov. 15, 1947
International Monetary Fund (IMF) Washington, D.C.	Promotes exchange stability, maintenance of orderly exchange arrangements among members, and international monetary co-operation; sells currency to members in temporary balance-of-payments difficulties and advises governments on financial problems.	$ 5,342 (for 1955–56 fiscal year) met from earnings and capital	Per Jacobsson (Sweden)	Dec. 27, 1945	Nov. 15, 1947
World Health Organization (WHO) Geneva, Switzerland	Acts as clearinghouse for medical and scientific information; sets international standards for drugs and vaccines and administers international sanitary regulations; helps, on government request, to fight disease and improve health services.	$10,700	M. G. Candau (Brazil)	Apr. 7, 1948	Apr. 7, 1948 (Approved by General Assembly Nov. 15, 1947)
Universal Postal Union (UPU) Berne, Switzerland	Unites members for reciprocal exchange of correspondence.	$ 457 (for 1956)	Fritz Hess (Switzerland)	1874	Nov. 15, 1947
International Telecommunication Union (ITU) Geneva, Switzerland	Promotes international co-operation for improvement and rational use of telecommunications of all kinds.	$ 1,498	Marco Aurelio Andrada (Argentina)	1865	Nov. 15, 1947
World Meteorological Organization (WMO) Geneva, Switzerland	Promotes international co-operation in field of meteorology, especially in establishment of world-wide networks of meteorological stations and rapid exchange of weather data.	$ 425	D. A. Davies (United Kingdom)	Mar. 23, 1950	Dec. 20, 1951

[a] Source: U.N. Department of Public Information. Excluded are the International Refugee Organization, a temporary specialized agency established in 1946 and terminated in 1952; the Intergovernmental Maritime Consultative Organization, which will come into being on ratification of its convention by four additional states; and the International Atomic Energy Agency, the statute of which was opened for ratification on October 26, 1956.

[b] Acting through preparatory commissions or similar organs, FAO, UNESCO, ICAO, and WHO actually began functioning before their formal establishment. The Universal Postal Union was known until 1878 as the General Postal Union. The International Telecommunication Union was established as the International Telegraph Union and adopted its present title in 1932. A forerunner of the World Meteorological Organization was established in 1879 by agreement among meteorological officials of states. The intergovernmental agreement on which the present organization rests entered into force March 23, 1950.

APPENDIX C
Membership of United Nations and Specialized Agencies[a]
(As of Jan. 9, 1957)

Country or Territory	United Nations	Specialized Agencies									
		ILO	FAO	UNESCO[b]	ICAO	IBRD	IMF	WHO[c]	UPU[d]	ITU[e]	WMO[f]
Afghanistan	X	X	X	X	X	X	X	X	X	X	X
Albania	X	X	—	—	—	—	—	g	X	X	—
Argentina	X	X	X	X	X	X	X	X	X	X	X
Australia	X	X	X	X	X	X	X	X	X	X	X
Austria	X	X	X	X	X	X	X	X	X	X	X
Belgium	X	X	X	X	X	X	X	X	X	X	X
Bolivia	X	X	X	X	X	X	X	X	X	X	X
Brazil	X	X	X	X	X	X	X	X	X	X	X
Bulgaria	X	X	—	X	—	—	—	g	X	X	X
Burma	X	X	X	X	X	X	X	X	X	X	X
Byelorussian S.S.R.	X	X	—	X	—	—	—	g	X	X	X
Cambodia	X	—	X	X	X	—	—	X	X	X	X
Canada	X	X	X	X	X	X	X	X	X	X	X
Ceylon	X	X	X	X	X	X	X	X	X	X	X
Chile	X	X	X	X	X	X	X	X	X	X	—
China	X	X	—	X	X	X	X	X	X	X	X
Colombia	X	X	X	X	X	X	X	—	X	X	—
Costa Rica	X	X	X	X	—	X	X	X	X	X	—
Cuba	X	X	X	X	X	X	X	X	X	X	X
Czechoslovakia	X	X	—	X	X	—	—	g	X	X	X
Denmark	X	X	X	X	X	X	X	X	X	X	X
Dominican Republic	X	X	X	X	X	X	X	X	X	X	X
Ecuador	X	X	X	X	X	X	X	X	X	X	X
Egypt	X	X	X	X	X	X	X	X	X	X	X
El Salvador	X	X	X	X	X	X	X	X	X	X	X
Ethiopia	X	X	X	X	X	X	X	X	X	X	X
Finland	X	X	X	X	X	X	X	X	X	X	X
France	X	X	X	X	X	X	X	X	X	X	X
Germany, Federal Republic of	—	X	X	X	X	X	X	X	X	X	X
Greece	X	X	X	X	X	X	X	X	X	X	X
Guatemala	X	X	X	X	X	X	X	X	X	X	X
Haiti	X	X	X	X	X	X	X	X	X	X	X
Honduras	X	X	X	X	X	X	X	X	X	X	X
Hungary	X	X	—	X	—	—	—	g	X	X	X
Iceland	X	X	X	—	X	X	X	X	X	X	X
India	X	X	X	X	X	X	X	X	X	X	X
Indonesia	X	X	X	X	X	X	X	X	X	X	X
Iran	X	X	X	X	X	X	X	X	X	X	—
Iraq	X	X	X	—	X	X	X	X	X	X	X
Ireland	X	X	X	—	X	—	—	X	X	X	X
Israel	X	X	X	X	X	X	X	X	X	X	X
Italy	X	X	X	X	X	X	X	X	X	X	X
Japan	X	X	X	X	X	X	X	X	X	X	X
Jordan	X	X	X	X	X	X	X	X	X	X	X
Korea, Republic of	—	—	X	X	X	X	X	X	X	X	X
Laos	X	—	X	X	X	—	—	X	X	X	X
Lebanon	X	X	X	X	X	X	X	X	X	X	X
Liberia	X	X	X	X	X	—	—	X	X	X	—
Libya	X	X	X	X	X	—	—	X	X	X	X
Luxembourg	X	X	X	X	X	X	X	X	X	X	X
Mexico	X	X	X	X	X	X	X	X	X	X	X
Monaco	—	—	—	X	—	—	—	X	X	X	—
Morocco	X	X	X	X	X	—	—	X	X	e	f
Nepal	X	—	X	X	—	—	—	X	—	—	—

Country or Territory	United Nations	Specialized Agencies										
		ILO	FAO	UNESCO[b]	ICAO	IBRD	IMF	WHO[c]	UPU[d]	ITU[e]	WMO[f]
Netherlands	X	X	X	X	X	X	X	X	X	X	X[e]	X
New Zealand	X	X	X	X	X	—	—	X	X	X	X	X
Nicaragua	X	—	X	X	X	X	X	X	X	X	X	—
Norway	X	X	X	X	X	X	X	X	X	X	X	X
Pakistan	X	X	X	X	X	X	X	X	X	X	X	X
Panama	X	X	X	X	—	X	X	X	X	X	X	—
Paraguay	X	X	X	X	X	X	X	X	X	X	X	X
Peru	X	X	X	X	X	X	X	X	X	X	X	X
Philippines	X	X	X	X	X	X	X	X	g	X	X	X
Poland	X	X	—	X	X	—	—	g	X	X	X	
Portugal	X	X	X	—	X	—	—	X	X	X	X	
Rumania	X	X	—	X	—	—	—	g	X	X	X	
San Marino	—	—	—	—	—	—	—	—	X	—	—	
Saudi Arabia	X	—	X	X	—	—	—	X	X	X	—	
Spain	X	X	X	X	X	—	—	X	X	X	X	
Sudan	X	X	X	X	X	—	—	X	X	X	f	
Sweden	X	X	X	X	X	X	X	X	X	X	X	
Switzerland	—	X	X	X	X	—	—	X	X	X	X	
Syria	X	X	X	X	X	X	X	X	X	X	X	
Thailand	X	X	X	X	X	X	X	X	X	X	X	
Tunisia	X	X	X	X	—	—	—	X	X	e	f	
Turkey	X	X	X	X	X	X	X	X	X	X	X	
Ukrainian S.S.R.	X	X	—	X	—	—	—	g	X	X	X	
Union of South Africa	X	X	X	X	X	X	X	X	X	X	X[e]	X
Union of Soviet Socialist Republics	X	X	—	X	—	—	—	g	X	X	X	
United Kingdom	X	X	X	X	X	X	X	X	X	X	X	
United States	X	X	X	X	X	X	X	X	X	X	X	
Uruguay	X	X	X	X	X	X	X	X	X	X	X	
Vatican City	—	—	—	—	—	—	—	—	X	X	—	
Venezuela	X	X	X	X	X	X	X	X	X	X	X	
Vietnam	—	X	X	X	X	X	X	X	X	X	X	
Yemen	X	—	X	—	—	—	—	X	X	X	—	
Yugoslavia	X	X	X	X	—	X	X	X	X	X	X	
Total Members	80	77	74	80	70	60	60	84	96	91	95	

APPENDIX D

Membership of Regional Economic Commissions
(As of Dec. 31, 1956)[a]

ECONOMIC COMMISSION FOR EUROPE (ECE)[b]

Albania[c]
Austria[c]
Belgium
Bulgaria[c]
Byelorussian Soviet Socialist Republic
Czechoslovakia
Denmark
Finland[c]
France
Germany, Federal Republic of[d]
Greece
Hungary[c]
Iceland
Ireland[c]

Italy[c]
Luxembourg
Netherlands
Norway
Poland
Portugal[c]
Rumania[c]
Soviet Union
Spain[c]
Sweden
Turkey
Ukrainian Soviet Socialist Republic
United Kingdom
United States
Yugoslavia

ECONOMIC COMMISSION FOR ASIA AND THE FAR EAST (ECAFE)

Afghanistan
Australia
Burma (Apr. 19, 1948)[e]
Cambodia (Aug. 20, 1954)[f]
Ceylon (Dec. 10, 1954)[f]
China
France
India
Indonesia (Sept. 28, 1950)[e]
Japan (June 24, 1954)[f]
Republic of Korea (Oct. 20, 1954)[f]

Laos (Feb. 16, 1955)[f]
Nepal (June 6, 1955)[f]
Netherlands
New Zealand
Pakistan
Philippines
Soviet Union
Thailand
United Kingdom
United States
Vietnam (Aug. 23, 1954)

ECONOMIC COMMISSION FOR LATIN AMERICA (ECLA)[g]

Argentina
Bolivia
Brazil
Chile
Colombia
Costa Rica
Cuba
Dominican Republic
Ecuador
El Salvador
France
Guatemala

Haiti
Honduras
Mexico
Netherlands
Nicaragua
Panama
Paraguay
Peru
United Kingdom
United States
Uruguay
Venezuela